'A clear and articulate road trip through forensic psychology with a stop or tw some common myths.'

Carla Chiver

'A fresh and unique pedagogical take on forensic psychology. This textbook offers a nuanced deep-dive into the most central themes of the field. Combining the latest research with the critical questions students and practitioners wrestle with, it makes for a truly engaging reading and learning experience!'

Tom Pakkanen, Åbo Akademi University, Finland

'An up-to-date, comprehensive and clear introduction to all the key areas in forensic psychology. The use of case studies and discussion questions encourage critical thinking and brings home the fact that our science has real world impact.'

Steven Watson, University of Twente, The Netherlands

'This is a great book which covers many important forensic issues.'

Paul Valliant, Laurentian University, Canada

FORENSIC PSYCHOLOGY

FACT AND FICTION

THOMAS DAVIS

macmillan international
HIGHER EDUCATION

RED GLOBE PRESS

First published 2021 by
RED GLOBE PRESS

Red Globe Press in the UK is an imprint of Macmillan Education Limited, registered in England, company number 01755588, of 4 Crinan Street, London, N1 9XW.

Red Globe Press® is a registered trademark in the United States, the United Kingdom, Europe and other countries.

ISBN 978-1-352-01121-0 paperback

This book is printed on paper suitable for recycling and made from fully managed and sustained forest sources. Logging, pulping and manufacturing processes are expected to conform to the environmental regulations of the country of origin.

A catalogue record for this book is available from the British Library.

A catalog record for this book is available from the Library of Congress.

Publisher: Luke Block

Associate Development Editor: Sophiya Ali

Cover Designer: Laura de Grasse

Production Manager: Georgia Park

Marketing Manager: Helen Jackson

BRIEF CONTENTS

CONTENTS

PART IV: APPLYING PSYCHOLOGY TO FORENSIC TECHNIQUES

LIST OF FIGURES

LIST OF TABLES

LIST OF FEATURES

CASE STUDIES

GLOBAL PERSPECTIVES

APPLY IT

ABOUT THE AUTHOR

Thomas Davis PhD is a Professor of Psychology and the Psychology Program Chair at Nichols College, Dudley, Massachusetts. He has over two decades of teaching experience in forensic psychology. Originally specialising in cognitive neuroscience, he has cultivated interests in the application of psychology to enhance human memory, the effects of video games on social and intellectual development and all things related to biological psychology. Recipient of the Stansky Distinguished Professor Award, his primary focus is teaching and learning *from* his students. He lives in Connecticut with his wife where they enjoy exploring the outdoors together.

TOUR OF THE BOOK

LEARNING OUTCOMES

Structure your learning by focusing on the key points of understanding for each chapter.

FACT VERSUS FICTION

The chapters include commonly held fictional beliefs versus the myth-busting facts.

FICTION: Victims and offenders have unpredictable motivations that prevent predictions of risk.

Versus

FACT: Like offenders, victims have similar motivations that offer predictions of risk.

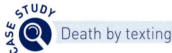

CASE STUDY — Death by texting

Conrad Roy was only 18 years old when he died by suicide on 13 July 2014. Conrad had previously tried to kill himself in October 2012 after his parents divorced. But things seemed to be improving as Conrad met

Discussion Questions:

1. How much blame for Conrad Roy's death does Mic the offender, the victim or something in between?
2. Do you think that the nature of their mainly digital blame?

CASE STUDIES

Real-world examples that offer an accessible and interesting introduction to the chapter material and show application in context.

DISCUSSION QUESTIONS

Answer the case study questions to build your critical thinking skills.

Blood feuds and blood marriage in South Sudan

In the state of Eastern Equatoria in South Sudan, the solution to a blood fe
marriage. Without prisons, this tradition for resolving disputes and solving
practised today. This was the case for eight-year-old Atia Odongi, whose b
during a cattle dispute. As compensation, Atia was given to the man's famil
to a son in her new family when she turned nine, and then given to a young
man died. Often, the new family exploits the girls given in blood marriage. .

GLOBAL PERSPECTIVES

Focus on the global application of forensic psychology through examples of real-world events and people from a range of diverse countries and cultures.

APPLY IT

This interactive feature offers brief applied experiments, self-assessments and activities you can do to personalise the information.

Are you cyberstalking?   'Yes' or 'no'

1 Checked my partner's email account to see who they were talking to or emailing without my partner's knowledge.

2 Kept tabs on the whereabouts of my partner using social media.

3 Checked my partner's phone to see who they were talking to or texting without my partner's permission.

CRITICAL THINKING AND APPLICATION QUESTIONS

1   Describe how forensic victimology differs from other types of victimology.

2   Describe four ways that forensic victimologists serve investigations and court proceedings.

3   How do the factors of the seven-factor model of victim characteristics relate to crimes of interpersonal violence?

CRITICAL THINKING AND APPLICATION QUESTIONS

Questions that allow you to think about the implications of the material you have just read.

KEY TERMS

Definitions of key terminology are placed in the margins for easy reference.

General victimology
– The study of all victims, not just victims of crime.

CHAPTER REVIEW

Forensic victimisation is an essential comp
Learning about the role of the victim in re
interactions and risk assessment. It is impor
victimised twice by being held responsible
for the victims of abuse via social media. T
suffering. Yet, the psychological rules that g

CHAPTER REVIEW

Consolidates the chapter material and serves as a handy revision tool.

NAMES TO KNOW

Explore this further reading list at the end of each chapter. Know the key contributors in the field and explore a range of books, articles and videos to deepen your learning.

NAMES TO KNOW

Wayne Petherick
Investigates stalking and is developing a response–o
the response style of victims of stalking and how
harassment.

• Petherick, W., Turvey, B. E. and Ferguson, C. E.
Academic Press.

• Petherick, W. and Ferguson, C. (2014) Forensic

DIGITAL RESOURCES

 Go online to the companion website for this book to access a suite of teaching and learning materials: **www.macmillanihe.com/Davis-Forensic-Psych**

Accompanying this book is a comprehensive suite of supportive resources to help both students and instructors get the most out of their learning and teaching.

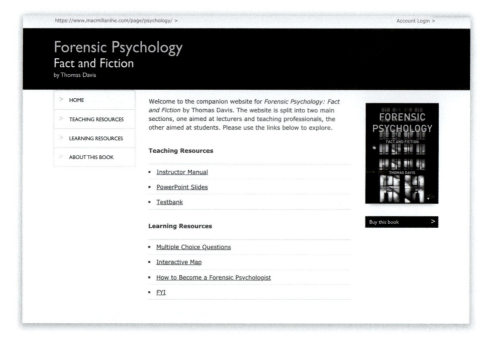

Resources to help instructors teach with the book include:

- **Instructor manual:** A useful guide on how to strategically plan lessons and advice for the novice to the advanced instructor. This manual also includes a range of activities and resources for instructors to use in class.
- **Lecture slides:** Detailed PowerPoint slides that map on to each chapter in the book.
- **Lecturer test bank:** Contains over 300 multiple-choice questions and essay questions targeting key ideas in the book. Instructors can select those relevant for their course for use in formative or summative assessments.

Students can benefit from the following resources:

- **Student test bank:** An interactive bank of 260 multiple-choice questions to check your knowledge and understanding of each chapter.
- **Spotlight map:** An interactive 3D map that allows you to compare key information and statistics on crime around the world.
- **How to become a forensic psychologist:** Explore the pathways to becoming a forensic psychologist in different territories across the globe.
- **FYI:** Interesting material that answers frequently asked questions from students related to the chapter material.

PREFACE

Sic parvis magna, Latin for 'greatness from small beginnings', was the motto of renowned explorer Sir Francis Drake (1540–96). Like Drake's motto, the humble origins of this textbook came from a small beginning – the simple search for the truth.

The truth matters. Psychology is built on the principles of the scientific method and sceptical thinking. As a psychology professor, I care about the truth, because rational behaviour begins with knowing the truth. We sometimes make decisions based on things we want to believe are true rather than considering the real state of the world. When the truth is buried under a mountain of misrepresentations, we cannot make wise decisions. This is because pseudoscience and superstition prevent us from seeing the world as it really is. We believe in myths because they provide easy answers, defy analysis and give us a false sense of emotional security. However satisfying and reassuring our false beliefs are, it is better to see the world as it really is. For example, believing that punishment is the most effective means to control behaviour has led to increased violence and crime. Pressuring people to tell the truth has sometimes led to false confessions. Discovering that there is no ultimate truth machine that reveals lies offers new opportunities to try more effective methods of finding the truth.

There are three reasons why we are fascinated with forensic psychology. First, crime can affect any of us, regardless of age, gender, ethnicity or social status. It seems to happen randomly, and when it does, it can devastate people's lives. Second, the inside world of crime – the work of legal counsel, court proceedings and police investigations – is rarely experienced by the public. But it is the third reason that drives our obsession with understanding the darkest of human behaviours. The study of forensic psychology allows us to explore our darkest nature from a safe distance. When you embark on a journey of discovery, you do not know where it is going to take you, but it will always take you somewhere unexpected.

TO THE STUDENT

The study of forensic psychology offers fascinating insights into the origins and motives of criminal behaviours and the practical applications of psychological principles. Perhaps you want to be a forensic psychologist, or maybe you are just curious about how people behave in criminal and legal settings, and why they behave in these ways. Either way, *Forensic Psychology: Fact and Fiction* is designed to meet your need for information. It provides a comprehensive overview of forensic psychology, bridges the gap between research and application, and explores the 'mystique' that surrounds the topics of the field. Through a focus on global research, examples and real-life cases studies, you will learn about fascinating topics such as the reliability of eyewitness testimony, indicators of deception and methods of lie detection, the willingness of innocent people to confess to crimes, and our ability to profile and capture offenders.

The purpose of this textbook is to dispel the myths surrounding the practice of forensic psychology, combining both psychological and legal perspectives. Although psychology and law are two different fields, they are united by their focus on human behaviour. Psychology seeks to understand and explain human behaviour, while law seeks to regulate human behaviour.

How to use this book

Reading your textbook with no educational destination in mind (other than completing the next day's assignment on time) is like driving without knowing the route to your destination. You may arrive at your destination, but you waste a lot of valuable time driving aimlessly. To get the most out of your experience, prepare and plan for your journey.

My goal is to provide you with the most current and relevant knowledge and information in the field of forensic psychology. However, I want to present this knowledge in a way that you find useful so you can easily apply it to your daily personal and professional lives. The best way to accomplish this is by sharpening your critical thinking ability, which this book will help you achieve. This will serve you well as you explore research in forensic psychology.

Before you read a chapter, try to understand where it fits into your overall journey. As you read, ask yourself these questions:

- How is this material related to my future goals and ambitions?
- What experiences have I had that are like what I am reading?
- What other outcomes might have happened?
- Are there any fallacies in the reasoning?

How this book is organised

This textbook is divided into four parts:

- Part I: What is Forensic Psychology?
- Part II: Getting Accurate Information
- Part III: Getting Truthful Information
- Part IV: Applying Psychology to Forensic Techniques

Part I: What is Forensic Psychology? is where you prepare for your journey. Chapter 1 introduces you to the captivating field of forensic psychology, its history and its contemporary directions.

The next stop on your journey is Part II: Getting Accurate Information. Forensic psychologists must make sure their information is correct, both factually and legally. Therefore, the four chapters in this section focus on obtaining information from various individuals and situations, and the conditions that create effective interviews. This material will help you understand the challenging process of gathering information in different contexts. You must also consider the unique situations and motivations of suspects.

For this reason, Part III: Getting Truthful Information examines the challenges forensic psychologists face when obtaining valid information. The three chapters in this section will help you understand the ways forensic psychologists overcome deception, develop offender profiles and determine whether some people have the mental capacity to be criminally responsible.

The last stop on your journey is Part IV: Applying Psychology to Forensic Techniques. Here the research-to-applications orientation of the text is the focus. The five chapters in this section explore the broad areas of forensic psychological application ranging from prisons, courtrooms and police training to the broader fields of violence and victimology. This last stop enables you to see the psychology behind the forensic fields of application. In this way, you can see the career opportunities available in this discipline.

TO THE INSTRUCTOR

This textbook is built on a proven foundation of learning theories with applied pedagogical techniques that appeal to today's student. It is unique in both its critical approach to the material (fact versus fiction) and its applied psychological perspectives. Finally, it is classroom tested and student friendly because it is written from the perspective of an instructor rather than a researcher or legal practitioner. To assist you, this textbook has a range of carefully crafted pedagogical features to help your students identify and retain key information.

Pedagogical approaches

All instructors appreciate that the connection between teaching and learning is a deceptively complex process. However, having well-planned pedagogy can improve the quality of your teaching and the way students learn, helping them gain a deeper grasp of fundamental material.

Students often begin their first course in forensic psychology overconfidently, believing they already understand all there is to know about the intersection of psychology and law. They are frequently surprised, and sometimes disappointed, to find that the reality of forensic science is not what they thought it was. Managing their experience is both a challenge and an opportunity. As instructors, we must challenge these mistaken ideas with knowledge and patience as we communicate our excitement about this fascinating discipline.

Effective instructors not only help students understand and apply forensic psychology's principles, concepts and critical thinking skills but they also pursue the goal of awakening a sense of wonder about the perplexing questions of human behaviour. Encouraging active learning and student engagement accomplishes that goal. This textbook features a range of pedagogical features to encourage interactive learning. For example, there is a set of targeted discussion questions related to every case study so you can encourage class discussion with students and get them thinking critically.

While motivating students can be a difficult task, the rewards are worth the investment. Motivated students are more excited to learn and participate. Simply put, teaching a class full of motivated students is enjoyable for teacher and student alike. Some students are self-motivated, with a natural love of learning. But even with the students who do not have this natural drive, a great teacher can make learning fun and inspire them to reach their full potential.

Critical thinking and applications

Study in every discipline offers an opportunity to develop critical thinking skills. Each discipline tends to define what it means to think critically in its own way. Even within the disciplines of psychology and law, there is no single definition of critical thinking. This richness of definition can be a source of confusion to any new student trying to become a better critical thinker. Critical thinking activities that encourage discovery are more likely to lead to meaningful learning than dutiful reading and memorisation. Reflective reading and application take effort, but are more likely to have enduring effects on knowledge and thinking skills. Although instructors who invest class time in active learning and critical thinking are bound to cover less content than those who practise more content-oriented methods, the compromise is worth it. Students who practise critical thinking emerge with a better orientation to the discipline and a better foundation for using psychology in their lives.

Like all sciences, psychology attempts to explain how things work. The science of psychology investigates how human beings and other organisms behave, think and feel. Although the focus of studies in forensic psychology may be as diverse as offender motivations for deception, brain trauma and violence, and the cognitive abilities of children, learning about each involves the same type of critical thinking skills that promote the basic goals of psychology: describing, explaining, predicting and controlling behaviour.

Several features in this textbook aid critical thinking and application. Every chapter begins with an introduction focusing on the chapter's important psychological issues This is followed by student-centred **Learning objectives** and the specific **Fact versus fiction** addressed in each chapter section. To help students connect forensic concepts to their own unique perspectives, each chapter has an **Apply it** exercise. Finally, each chapter has **Critical thinking and application questions** that emphasise Bloom's taxonomy of higher-order skills, including evaluating and creating new connections between concepts.

The fact versus fiction approach

Seeking (and finding) the truth is a powerful motivator for students. Along the way, reinforcing open-mindedness with a healthy dose of empirical support rewards this pursuit. The challenge is presenting information in a way that does not blame the student for their misconceptions, but rewards them for their critical thinking and scepticism.

Forensic psychology is an exciting field, but it is plagued by false information from many sources, including the entertainment media. Each chapter presents facts and fictions as the core of the story of forensic psychology. This offers students an appealing way to cultivate their scepticism and critical thinking abilities. As authentic cases of cyberstalking, false confessions and victim blaming show, the truth is far more interesting than fiction, and, ultimately, empirically based solutions are more valuable than sensational true crime narratives.

Real-world examples

We have seen the phrase 'based on a true story' before, but it warns the reader to prepare themselves because what they're about to read really happened; real lives were affected and there were consequences. Knowing that a story is real amplifies its impact and increases its memorability. In the same way, every example presented in the textbook is a true story. Some stories are presented as **Case studies** with controversial discussion questions, while others are presented as **Global perspectives** to showcase the global nature of forensic psychology. These true stories provide students with a richer appreciation of the ubiquitous nature of forensic psychology in their jurisdictions. Finally, other real-life examples are woven into the chapter narrative to explain complex concepts like slip-and-capture errors, confirmation bias and establishing legal responsibility.

Content support

Learning works best when supported by a scaffold. In the same way that a scaffold is a temporary structure supporting a building under construction, the information is presented in a similar way to support student learning. For example, each chapter features **key terms** that are defined in the margins for ease of access. Each chapter is divided into four sections with a corresponding fact versus fiction, an interim summary and critical thinking and application questions. Finally, researchers who have made significant contributions to the chapter material are presented as **Names to know** at the end of each chapter. This allows the reader to follow the main researchers in their disciplines.

Online **test banks** for both lecturers and students include multiple-choice and essay questions (with suggested correct responses), targeting key ideas in the textbook. Finally, an **instructor manual** is available for each chapter, providing detailed teaching strategies and resources. The instructor's manual is written with the novice instructor in mind but also contains materials and resources for the experienced instructor. Examples include ways to conduct more effective discussions, tips for online teaching, and activities to help students apply what they are learning in a more personal way. **PowerPoint** slides also accompany each chapter. These slides are presented in a comprehensive outline format.

Why is a new approach to forensic psychology needed?

This textbook's approach is unique in several ways. First, it focuses on the fictions too often portrayed as fact by the entertainment media. Second, it portrays the global nature of forensic psychology. All countries have crime and its effects are similar across jurisdictions. Third, every example is true. There are no made-up stories to illustrate forensic concepts. Fourth, extensive current research supports the content.

AUTHOR'S ACKNOWLEDGEMENTS

I would like to thank everyone at Red Globe Press, especially Luke Block and Sophiya Ali for their enduring support, patience and expert guidance. A hearty thanks to all my students, past and present, who have taught me so much. My most special thanks belong to my loving wife, who is my best friend and patient editor.

PART I

WHAT IS FORENSIC PSYCHOLOGY?

1 WHAT IS FORENSIC PSYCHOLOGY?

Chapter Introduction

Forensic psychologists apply knowledge of the mind and human behaviour to the criminal justice system. Their goal is to reveal the mysteries that drive criminal behaviour and to improve the lives of those affected by crime. Forensic psychology offers insights into the origins of criminal behaviours by drawing on a century of psychological research. If your knowledge about this field is from entertainment media, then plan to have your expectations challenged. The truth is there's more than profiling serial killers and investigating crime scenes. In reality, forensic psychology is more complex and fascinating. Successfully navigating this complex field of study requires sharp critical thinking skills and a sceptical mind. While all forensic psychologists work in the intersection of psychology and law, their daily roles differ significantly.

Learning Outcomes

What is forensic psychology?
- Compare the goals of forensic psychology with other closely related fields.

The roots of forensic psychology
- Describe how forensic psychology fits into the larger field of psychology.

Thinking like a scientist
- Explain how the scientific method is used to make better decisions.

Roles and responsibilities of a forensic psychologist
- Describe the skills and areas of application of forensic psychologists.

WHAT IS FORENSIC PSYCHOLOGY?

FICTION: Forensic psychology is the practice of offender profiling.	*Versus*	**FACT:** Forensic psychology involves evaluations of mental competency, ability to stand trial, working with witnesses, designing interventions to reduce offender recidivism and ways to help victims of violent crime.

Why do we need forensic psychology?

- *Australia, 2018:* The rape and murder of 22-year-old Melbourne comedian Eurydice Dixon by James Todd shocked Australia. Todd had stalked Dixon for more than 2.5 miles as she walked home before murdering her. This case sparked rage over victim blaming and women's lack of safety in public spaces (Cooper, 2018).

- *Canada, 1987:* Kenneth Parks drove 14 miles to his in-laws' house and let himself in. He beat his mother-in-law with a tyre iron and stabbed her repeatedly with a kitchen knife. Although his mother-in-law died, Parks was cleared of all charges. The verdict was that he had no motive and was found to have been sleepwalking during the entire attack (Harvey, 2018).

- *United States, 1932:* Aviator Charles Lindbergh's 20-month-old son was kidnapped from his cot and later found murdered. The nation was fascinated by the crime and the two years of police work that followed. Bruno Richard Hauptmann, a German carpenter, was eventually convicted and executed for the crime. He never confessed. But, before the trial was over, more than 200 other people did (Herbert, 2009).

- *United Kingdom, 2001:* An innocent suspect (Barry George) was convicted of murdering Jill Dando after witnesses discussed the case with each other and changed their minds based on the information that only one witness presented. After the discussion, an eyewitness went from being 'uncertain' to 'ninety-five per cent sure' that George was the correct suspect (Sturke, 2009).

These four stories reveal the global nature and scope of forensic psychology. Forensic psychology studies a range of behaviours from blaming the victims of violent crimes, sleepwalking homicide and voluntary false confessions, to the uncertainty of eyewitness memories. Yet, for all its mainstream popularity, forensic psychology remains a puzzling mix of fact and fiction.

Why are we fascinated with crime and criminal behaviour? Are we, as Sigmund Freud believed, repressing evil passions deep within our subconscious? A more likely explanation is that criminal behaviour both frightens and fascinates us, making us curious about the origins of these behaviours. We enjoy watching legal dramas because they play upon the clash between good versus evil; and critical pieces of evidence appear at the last minute and clever lawyers always prevail and save the day for their clients (typically in under an hour). In the same way, the entertainment media portrays crime-related jobs as adrenaline-fuelled careers. The media's portrayal of forensic psychology shows the public's genuine concern and naive fascination with the criminal justice system, often exaggerating the frequency of some aspects of the field, such as serial killers or criminal profiling, while ignoring its true scientific base (Grogan and Woody, 2016; Ramos, Ferguson and Frailing, 2016; Wheeler et al., 2018). Despite the convoluted and often outright mistaken portrayals of forensic psychology in the media, its presence has raised awareness and inspired interest in the field (Loh, 1981).

Defining forensic psychology

Forensic psychology applies the production and application of psychological knowledge to criminal justice systems (Weiner and Hess, 2006). It includes activities as varied as courtroom testimony, child custody evaluations, law enforcement candidate screenings, treatment of offenders in correctional facilities, and research in the area of offender behaviour. Psychologists interested in this line of applied practice work in prisons, rehabilitation centres, police departments, law firms, schools, government agencies or in private practice, to name a few (Freedheim, 2003).

Forensic psychology supplies important missing elements when solving a criminal case. Professionals in this field are often able to help narrow the suspect list or provide a motive for a crime. In some cases, the expert testimony of a forensic psychologist might be the last piece of the puzzle when trying to convict a suspect. Forensic psychology is also an important part of crime prevention. Professionals in this field might be called upon to design rehabilitation programmes for offenders to help them become law-abiding citizens. Research on offender and victim risk can also identify situations and people who have the potential to commit crimes (DeMatteo, Fairfax-Columbo and Desai, 2019).

> **Forensic psychology** – *A field of psychology that applies the production and application of psychological knowledge to criminal justice systems.*

Test yourself: the facts and fictions of forensic psychology	True or false?
1. All imprisoned offenders suffer from mental illness	
2. Eyewitnesses are the most reliable source of case-related information	
3. Forensic psychology is the same as forensic science	
4. Lie detectors used by trained technicians can detect lies	
5. Human memory works like a video camera	
6. Mentally ill suspects should be treated the same as those who are not mentally ill	
7. Most jurors follow the judge's instructions	
8. A person cannot have a memory of something that never happened	
9. People only confess when they have actually committed the crime they are being charged with	
10. The key component of forensic psychology is criminal profiling	
11. Long jail terms are the best way to prevent future crimes	
12. Unlike the rest of us, police can tell when a suspect is lying	
13. Victims of violent crime are never blamed for the crimes they suffer from	

Note: The answer to all these questions is 'false'.

Forensic psychology is often confused with criminology, crime scene investigation and forensic science. These three areas investigate behaviour from different perspectives but have similar goals when dealing with crime and the criminal justice system. Forensic psychology investigates areas of crime, criminal behaviour and criminality by applying a behavioural approach, which perceives offenders as having a behavioural problem deriving from deviant ways of thinking and perceiving the world. The forensic psychologist examines these thoughts, perceptions and behaviours using a variety of clinical assessments, and then uses the results of these assessments to identify areas that can be affected by appropriate treatment intervention. A forensic psychologist is not a criminologist, a crime scene investigator or a forensic scientist. Despite a common focus on crime, these three disciplines' perspectives are fundamentally different. To distinguish forensic psychology from these disciplines, it is important to understand the differences.

Criminology

Unlike forensic psychologists, criminologists are not involved in assessing the mental competency of an offender, nor do they provide therapy and other treatment interventions. Rather, criminologists are more likely to be involved with providing advice about complicated types of crime, such as fraud or corporate crime and drug cartels. Criminology is a branch of sociology and studies criminal behaviour at the micro and macro levels, that is, individual and social. Using scientific methods and tools, criminologists study the crime, the behaviour of the criminal as well as the victims of the crime. The purpose of criminology is to understand why crimes take place, the impacts they have and leave behind, and how to prevent those crimes from happening again in the future. Criminologists use statistics, empirical evidence, past research and quantitative methods to study crime. They are dedicated to studying the causes of crime and its social impact.

Crime scene investigation

Crime scene investigators or scenes of crime officers work on their own gathering physical crime scene evidence that is packaged and given to the forensic scientist to examine in a forensic laboratory. These roles are very different from forensic psychologists. They are skilled in photography and using video-recording equipment to record evidence at the crime scene and on the victim. They are skilled at recovering and storing evidence, such as fingerprints and DNA, without causing contamination. They look for other relevant information, which could be physical evidence of the crime event, and help establish the motives of the criminal and other details of how the act was committed, such as tyre tracks, footprints or broken glass, to establish means of entry and escape from the crime scene.

Forensic science

Unlike forensic psychology, which focuses on behavioural models of criminal behaviour, forensic science focuses on knowledge of scientific methods derived from biology, chemistry, medicine and even physics. While the CSI provides the physical evidence, the forensic scientist investigates the significance of the physical evidence using a variety of laboratory-based methods. They apply tests that include the examination of hair and fibres, insect infestations, DNA profiling and bodily fluids. They may perform chemical tests examining paint and glass, shoeprint impressions, facial reconstructions and anthropological reconstructions, that is, piecing bone fragments together to reconstruct the victim's skeleton.

The origins of forensic psychology

Centuries before psychology appeared on the scene, philosophers struggled to understand antisocial and evil behaviours, while legal scholars wrestled with issues of criminal law and punishment. It was not until the early decades of the twentieth century that this new discipline of psychology was introduced into the legal system. The effort was led by pioneering psychologists with unique perspectives in the laboratory and the courtroom.

Sigmund Freud (1973) ventured into the intersection of psychology and the law by comparing the establishment of the facts in a criminal proceeding via psychological research techniques to uncovering repressed memories in psychoanalysis via free association. In his discussion of psychiatric involvement in the establishment of facts in legal proceedings, he anticipated many of today's controversies, such as the use of the lie detector, hypnosis, sodium amytal interviews, and psychological testimony on the issue of the credibility and reliability of testimony (Goldstein, 1983). Freud's enthusiastic predictions reflected optimism that the law would embrace psychological principles and methods. This connection did not take place for several more decades with the creation of the first psychological laboratory.

Psychology in the laboratory

The seeds of forensic psychology were planted in 1879, when Wilhelm Wundt established the first experimental laboratory in Germany. Wundt's research was important because it separated psychology from philosophy by analysing the mind in a more structured way. Wundt championed and refined the experimental method within psychology. His rigorous methods provided the framework for applied psychological investigations, including legal issues. However, Wundt was cautious of applying psychology until enough research had been conducted. He warned his students against the premature use of partial information as irresponsible and dangerous. Wundt described psychology as a science apart from philosophy and biology and was the first person to ever call themselves a psychologist.

Another key figure in the history of forensic psychology was one of Wundt's students, Hugo Münsterberg. Münsterberg set up his own psychological laboratory at Harvard University with the goal of introducing applied psychology to the courtroom (Spillman and Spillman, 1993). Münsterberg wrote about many areas of psychology, often taking a controversial stance (Hale, 1980). For example, when commenting on Freud's conception of the unconscious mind, Münsterberg (1909, p. 125) said: 'The story of the subconscious mind can be told in three words: there is none.' He laid the foundation for forensic psychology with the publication of his landmark text *On the Witness Stand: Essays on Psychology and Crime* (Münsterberg, 1908), which stated that psychology could improve the understanding of courtroom issues and procedures. Relying in part on his own experience as an expert witness, Münsterberg considered such topics as memories of witnesses, crime detection, false confessions, hypnosis and crime prevention. He was astonished 'that the work of justice is ever carried out in the courts without ever consulting the psychologist' (1909, p. 194). It was his investigations of perception and memory research that firmly established him as the founder of forensic psychology, supplying key insights into the reliability of witness testimony. Unfortunately, Münsterberg's claims for the practical benefits of psychology in the courtroom were ridiculed by the legal profession (Wells, Memon and Penrod, 2006). Yet his text was prophetic, predicting important research gains in the study of eyewitness memory and in obtaining valid confessional evidence.

Psychology in the courtroom

As predicted by Freud, psychologists began testifying in court as expert witnesses. For example, in 1896, Albert von Schrenck-Notzing provided an opinion testimony in the trial of a man accused of murdering three women. The murders had received widespread and sensational press coverage in the months prior to the trial, and Schrenck-Notzing (1897) believed that this pretrial publicity, through a process of suggestion, clouded witnesses' memories because they were unable to separate their own original accounts from the press reports. He confirmed his opinion with psychological research (Hale, 1980).

James McKeen Cattell examined the psychology of courtroom testimony in 1895. Cattell (1895) posed a series of questions to his university students, asking them to provide a response and rate their degree of confidence in their answer. In his informal study, he asked 56 college students a series of questions. The four questions were: Do chestnut or oak trees lose their leaves earlier in autumn? Do horses in the field stand with head or tail to the wind? In which direction do the seeds of an apple point? What was the weather one week ago today? Most importantly, he asked students to rate their confidence in their answers. His findings revealed that confidence did not equal correctness. Some students were confident regardless of whether their answers were correct, while others were always insecure, even when they provided the right answer. He found a surprising degree of inaccuracy with eyewitnesses being unsure of themselves and raised issues about the validity of their usefulness in court.

Psychologist William Stern also studied witnesses' ability to recall information by staging a fake argument in a law class, which finished with one of the students drawing a handgun. At that point, the professor intervened and stopped the fight. Then students were asked to provide written and oral reports of what happened. Findings revealed that each student made anywhere from 4 to 12 errors. The inaccuracies peaked with the second half of the dispute, when tension was highest. Stern concluded that emotions reduced the accuracy of recall. Further research revealed that suggestive questions could compromise the accuracy of eyewitness reports; there are significant differences between adult and child witnesses; the events that occur between the original event and its recall can dramatically affect memory; and suspect line-ups are not helpful unless they are matched for age and appearance (Benjamin and Baker, 2004).

IN SUMMARY

Forensic psychology is the intersection of psychology and law and is different from criminology, crime scene investigation and forensic science. The history of forensic psychology is marked by many important milestones, both in the research laboratory and in the courtroom.

 ## CRITICAL THINKING AND APPLICATION QUESTIONS

1   Review the description of forensic psychology, then find three examples of forensic psychology as portrayed in the media (films, television, books) and evaluate their accuracy.

2   Most forensic psychologists have no formal training in law. Do you think this is appropriate, given the extent to which many of these psychologists are involved in the judicial system?

3   Imagine that you are invited to testify as an expert witness. You are supposed to act as an educator to the judge and jury, not as an advocate for the defence or the prosecution. To what extent do you think you could do this and why?

THE ROOTS OF FORENSIC PSYCHOLOGY

FICTION: Forensic psychology is a unique and independent field of psychology.

Versus

FACT: Forensic psychology combines several psychological perspectives.

Psychology is the scientific study of the mind and behaviour. It embraces all aspects of the human experience, from the functions of the brain, the social dynamics of groups, and the developing child to caring for the aged (APA, 2013a). The word 'psychology' is derived from the Greek word *psyche*, meaning 'life' or 'breath' (Cherry and Mattiuzzi, 2010). It is a multifaceted discipline that examines mental and behavioural processes from many perspectives.

Psychology
– The scientific study of the mind and behaviour.

Psychological perspectives

There are universal psychological principles that act as unseen forces shaping our minds and behaviours. Some of these forces are conscious, while others exist deeper, influencing our behaviour in mysterious ways. These principles form the roots of forensic psychology and are reflected in unique psychological perspectives (Table 1.1). Each perspective makes unique assumptions about human behaviour from its origins and motivations to intervention strategies for change. No single perspective has explanatory powers over others and the different perspectives reflect the complexity and richness of human behaviour (Hearnshaw, 2020; Wertheimer, 2012). For example, some psychologists might attribute a certain behaviour to biological factors (genetics), while another psychologist might consider early childhood experiences to be a more likely explanation. The common theme that these perspectives share is their focus on explaining behaviour (Lowry, 2017).

Table 1.1: Psychological perspectives

Psychological perspectives	Description and application
Behavioural psychology	Investigates how environmental factors (stimuli) affect observable behaviour (the response) *Application:* Effects of token reinforcement in prison (Milan, Throckmorton, McKee and Wood, 1979)
Clinical psychology	Specialises in the assessment of mental health issues, competency and makes predictions of future criminal or dangerous behaviour *Application:* How solitary confinement affects post-traumatic stress disorder (PTSD) (Piper and Berle, 2019)
Cognitive psychology	Investigates internal mental processes, such as perception, problem solving, memory, decision making and artificial intelligence *Application:* The accuracy of eyewitness memories (Shapira and Pansky, 2019)
Developmental psychology	Studies the psychological changes that a person experiences over the lifespan *Application:* The inability of emerging adults to understand the consequences of their actions (Smith, Fritz and Daskaluk, 2018)

(continued)

Evolutionary psychology	Examines how human behaviours and psychological adaptation have been affected by natural selection *Application:* Sex differences in cyberaggression strategies (Wyckoff, Buss and Markman, 2019)
Neuropsychology	Examines the structure and function of the brain in relation to behaviours and psychological processes *Application:* The role of neurotransmitters in violence and aggression (Miczek et al., 2017)
Social psychology	Examines social influences on human behaviour by explaining how feelings, behaviour and thoughts are influenced by the actual, imagined or implied presence of other people *Application:* How juries make attributions of guilt or innocence (Peter-Hagene, Salerno and Phalen, 2019)
Sociocultural psychology	Understanding a person's behaviour requires knowing about the cultural context in which the behaviour occurs. Culture is the shared knowledge, practices and attitudes of groups of people and can include language, customs and beliefs about what behaviour is appropriate and inappropriate *Application:* Honour-related violence (Ermers, 2018)

The influence of psychological perspectives on forensic psychology is a constantly evolving process. The specialty of artificial intelligence (AI) is a new weapon in the fight against crime.

Global Perspectives

Unleashing machine learning on crime scene evidence

Dr. Eduardo Fidalgo and his research team from the University of León in Spain are applying cognitive psychology to crime scene evidence. They are creating an evidence recognition tool using machine learning to identify objects in police photographs and search for links with other crimes. Machine learning is an AI application that provides systems with the ability to automatically learn and improve from experience. Traditionally, crime scene photographs capture information that police use to link the crime scene to suspects. Sifting through the vast amount of information is a challenging task for humans, but not for computers. Fidalgo and his team are using these images to train computers to spot clues in crime scene photographs (Saikia, Fidalgo, Alegre and Fernández-Robles, 2017). AI tools developed by cognitive psychologists speed up data analysis and make criminal investigations and crime scene linkage more effective.

Applying psychological perspectives

The different perspectives in psychology illustrate the ability of each approach to describe the rich texture of human behaviours. In this section we will discover how the same behaviour can be explained using different perspectives.

Evie Amati attacked three strangers with an axe at a convenience store in Sydney, Australia in the early hours of 7 January 2017. Her trial focused on whether she was mentally ill during the attack. But it was the graphic CCTV footage of the attack that made headlines. Amati could be seen entering the convenience store with an axe, before delivering one blow to customer Ben Rimmer's face, and a second that shattered the base of the skull of another customer, Sharon Hacker. Hacker was saved from a more severe injury by her thick dreadlocks. Amati pleaded not guilty to the charge of attempted murder because of mental illness. Her legal counsel told the court there was no doubt Amati's body carried out the axe attack, but that she had been possessed by voices in her head, telling her to 'kill, kill' (Makkar, 2019). However, several issues complicated the case. There were issues of gender dysphoria (the distress a person feels due to a mismatch between their gender identity and their sex assigned at birth), the discrimination faced by transgender people, mental health and psychosis. Amati also had a complex combination of seven different substances in her blood at the time of the attack, including alcohol, cannabis, amphetamines, antidepressants and hormone medication. Prosecutors argued that Amati was angry and upset after she felt a date had rejected her because she is transgender. Because she was uninhibited by illegal drugs and alcohol, she conducted the attack to reward her homicidal fantasies. But the defence testified that Amati was in a drug-induced psychosis at the time of the attack, which arose from a major depressive disorder caused by the medication she was taking (Sutton, 2019).

Interpreting the psychological motivations for Amati's actions begins with neuroscience and the role of substances that altered her brain's prefrontal cortex's inability to inhibit her behaviour. A clinical perspective would focus on the voices in her head as indicative of symptoms of schizophrenia (a breakdown in the relation between thought, emotion and behaviour, leading to faulty perception, inappropriate actions and feelings, and withdrawal from reality). A sociocultural perspective would focus on her rage from social rejection because of her gender status. A cognitive explanation would review the altered perceptions of impulse control due to feelings of anger and rage. Finally, a behavioural explanation might focus on Amati's earlier history of reward for aggressive behaviours.

CASE STUDY

Andrea Yates and the insanity defence

On 20 June 2001, Andrea Yates drowned her five children in the bath at their home in Clear Lake, USA. It was unbelievable, but was it understandable?

According to Yates's 90-minute confession, she first drowned two-year-old Luke, followed by Paul (three) and John (five). She carried each child's body to the master bedroom, placed it on the bed and covered it with a sheet. As she was drowning six-month-old Mary, Noah (seven) confronted her: 'What's wrong with Mary?' he asked and then, realising what was happening, fled. She chased Noah

Andrea Yates stands with her lawyer George Parnham at her retrial in 2006, pleading 'not guilty' due to insanity

Source: Pool/Getty Images News/Getty Images

through the house, dragged him to the bath and drowned him alongside his sister. There is no evidence that any of the children were drugged (O'Malley, 2004; Easton, 2002).

Next, Andrea telephoned the police, saying cryptically, 'It's time.' Then she called her husband, Russell Yates, and told him 'You'd better come home.' 'Is anyone hurt?' he asked, alarmed by her tone of voice. 'Yes,' she said. 'The children. All of them.' Then she tried to slit her throat. Russell found her in the bathroom and stopped her. She had been taking an antidepressant called Sertraline and had flushed the drug down the toilet (Barnett, 2005; Resnick, 2007).

Her attorneys said the murders were brought on by psychotic delusions, worsened by repeated episodes of postpartum depression. Her husband said the two of them had always planned on having a big family but demons took hold of his wife (O'Malley, 2004; Denno, 2003).

During the trial, psychiatrist Park Dietz, the prosecution's expert witness, testified that Yates got the idea to drown her children from an episode of the US television show *Law & Order*. However, there was no such episode (Park, 2008). Yates was convicted of capital murder for killing her four sons and baby daughter. She was sentenced to life in prison, but her conviction was overturned on appeal. She was found not guilty in 2006 by reason of insanity and was sent to a mental hospital in Texas (Galanti, 2002).

Discussion Questions:

1   Was Yates responsible for her actions? What evidence supports your answer?

2   Which psychological perspective would include Andrea Yates's experiencing psychotic delusions?

3   Which psychological perspective (Table 1.1) would include Andrea Yates's postpartum depression?

IN SUMMARY

Psychology is the study of the mind and behaviour. Psychology consists of many perspectives that make unique assumptions about human behaviour from its origins, and motivations to strategies for change.

 ## CRITICAL THINKING AND APPLICATION QUESTIONS

1   In what ways might a *behavioural psychologist* disagree with a *cognitive psychologist* about the cause of aggression?

2   In what ways might a *social psychologist* disagree with an *evolutionary psychologist* about the cause of aggression?

3   In what ways might a *neuropsychologist* and a *sociocultural psychologist* disagree about the cause of aggression?

THINKING LIKE A SCIENTIST

FICTION: Sceptics are cynical people.

Versus

FACT: Scepticism is about open-mindedness and is a skill that helps people make better decisions.

Heaven's Gate: the power of cults over rational thinking

Police entered a mansion in Rancho Santa Fe, an exclusive suburb of San Diego, USA, and discovered 39 victims of a mass suicide. The deceased women and men of varying ages were all found lying peacefully in matching dark clothes and Nike sneakers and displayed no signs of blood or trauma. They were members of the Heaven's Gate religious cult, whose leaders preached that suicide would allow them to leave their bodily 'containers' (Davis, 2016). After the 1995 discovery of the Hale-Bopp comet, the Heaven's Gate members believed that an alien spacecraft was on its way to earth, hidden from human detection behind the comet. In late March 1997, as the comet reached its closest distance to earth, the members consumed a lethal mixture of hydrocodone, phenobarbital and vodka and then lay down to die, hoping to leave their bodily vessels, enter the alien spacecraft, and pass through Heaven's Gate into a higher existence (Chryssides, 2016).

Discussion Questions:

1   How do cults persuade people to believe their bizarre doctrines?

2   Why do you think the Heaven's Gate cult members wore identical clothing?

3   In what ways are cults and terrorist organisations similar?

Why aren't cult members sceptical about the bizarre claims their cults make? The answer lies in the use of behaviour modification. Members can be taught techniques such as thought stopping, where they are encouraged to stop doubts from entering their consciousness, often with a key phrase they repeat; thus they do not consider the claims rationally. Cults isolate the subject from outside influences via phobia indoctrination, where they play on a person's irrational fears, with threats such as the person will develop cancer or go insane if they ever leave or question the group (Hassan, 2000). Without the ability to apply scientific reasoning skills, we become vulnerable to losing our autonomy. As the French writer Voltaire stated: 'Those who can make you believe absurdities can make you commit atrocities.'

The need for scientific reasoning

Why do people join cults? It is not because they lack the intelligence to see reality, rather they turn off that part of their sceptical mind. A common explanation for why people do strange things is that they are 'crazy' or have something wrong with them. In this section, we will investigate different classes of explanation for why people do and believe 'crazy' things.

The consequences of faulty reasoning in forensic psychology (and for all of us) can have dangerous and misleading results when deciding which research to rely on. Making decisions on anecdotal evidence or unsupported sources is risky. This can cause people to avoid potentially lifesaving treatments, while choosing risky choices that could lead to injury or worse. Furthermore, incorrect knowledge leads to confusion about scientific facts, causing doubt and further questions, such as false beliefs about vaccinations. Unfortunately, once false information is released, it often spreads quickly, causing more misunderstandings (Pratkanis, 2020).

Developing a strategy for discerning fact from fiction is an essential skill, because scientific reasoning makes us face the possibility that we can be wrong, and we are deceiving ourselves. As Tavris and Aronson (2007, p. 108) explain, 'science is a form of arrogance control'.

Characteristics of scientific thinking

Applying a set of rules or guidelines for making judgements about our world can help us avoid the natural flaws in our thinking (Fleer, 2019). Forensic psychologists use both creative and critical thinking to refine and test their theories of human behaviour (Griffiths and Rachlew, 2018).

Scepticism

Oscar Hartzell claimed to be the sole heir to the Drake fortune, a multi-billion-dollar trust fund left by the legendary explorer Sir Francis Drake. Unfortunately, the British government refused to release those funds without a legal fight. Hartzell invited investors to help pay for the legal fees and in return they would share in the fortune after victory in court (Rayner, 2003). You have probably guessed that this was a scam, but in the 1920s thousands of people believed the story and contributed their hard-earned money. Why did they do this? The simple reason is that they were not sceptical. 'Sceptic' is derived from a Greek word meaning 'questioning' or 'thoughtful' (Ross, 1996). Sceptical thinking can be seen as a continuum (Figure 1.1).

Figure 1.1: Scepticism as a continuum

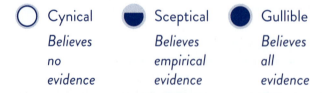

At one end of the continuum is gullibility, believing all evidence without question, and at the other is cynicism, believing no evidence and staying closed-minded. The sceptical thinker falls between the two, by weighing the evidence before making a decision. Scepticism allows someone to accept as fact that which has been proved beyond a reasonable doubt (Perlman, 2018). As an added benefit, if we continue to question our knowledge, our knowledge grows.

Open-mindedness

The key to being open-minded is to balance gullibility and cynicism. Forensic psychologists must be willing to pursue unpopular or controversial ideas because this helps understand the true nature of our world (Wojcieszak, Winter and Yu, 2020). For example, studying the behavioural patterns of the victims of violent crime was viewed in the 1970s as blaming the victims for being victims. However, studying the patterns of interactions between the offender and the victim revealed patterns of behaviours that are used to assess risk for victims of crimes from fraud (Choi, Lee and Chun, 2017), bullying (Santoyo and Mendoza, 2018) and cyberstalking (Reyns, 2019).

Objectivity

When evaluating research, we must be careful that our personal biases, feelings, beliefs and prejudices do not cloud our view of empirical evidence. Objectivity is particularly challenging for psychologists because we often study phenomenon from our own direct experience. This can make being objective difficult. But in the battle between objective data and personal opinion, the data always wins.

The challenge for objectivity is being aware of the flaws in our own thinking. We often rely on mental shortcuts called **heuristics** (Table 1.2). Derived from a Greek word meaning 'to discover', heuristic describes a rule or a method that comes from experience and helps you think through things, like the process of elimination, or the process of trial and error (Reimer and Rieskamp, 2007). These help us when we do not have the time to work through a decision.

Heuristics – *Mental shortcuts that evolve from experience.*

Table 1.2: Examples of common heuristics

Heuristic	Description and example
Availability	We judge the likelihood of a situation occurring based on how easily we can think of a similar situation *Example:* Juror decision making (Platania and Crawford, 2012)
Belief perseverance	Maintaining a belief despite contradictory information *Example:* Criminal investigative failures (Rossmo, 2006a)
Confirmation bias	When we only look for the evidence that confirms what we already believe, thereby strengthening the original belief *Example:* Cognitive bias in forensic mental health assessment (Zapf, Kukucka, Kassin and Dror, 2018)
Focusing effect	A bias in which we emphasise some pieces of information while undervaluing other pieces *Example:* Hazard perception during police pursuits (Crundall, Chapman, Phelps and Underwood, 2003)
Hindsight bias	A sense that we knew it all along after learning the actual outcome *Example:* Identifying sexual grooming behaviours of child molesters (Winters and Jeglic, 2016)
Stereotypes	When people form opinions or make judgements about things they have never seen or experienced *Example:* Perceptions of older adult jurors: the influence of ageing stereotypes (O'Connor and Evans, 2020)

Why do we believe in 'lunacy'?

An example of how heuristics can create flawed thinking is the lunar effect, sometimes called the 'Transylvania effect' (Qazi, Philip, Manikandan and Cornford, 2007). As the full moon casts its silver gleam, people on earth go mad. It is a story – anecdotal evidence that gets repeated about classrooms of students misbehaving, hospitals seeing rising intakes of mental illness, violent crime victims and people getting hurt in freak accidents. Lieber and Agel (1978) theorised that just as the moon controls the tides, its gravitational pull affects the fluid balance in human brains. One survey revealed that 45 per cent of college students believe moonstruck humans are prone to unusual behaviours (Quincey, 1995). In 2007, several police departments in the UK increased the number of officers on night duty when there was a full moon to cope with presumed higher crime rates (Arkowitz and Lilienfeld, 2009). But there is a problem with all these theories: they are not true.

Fortunately, we can test the question, 'is there a correlation between some kind of event and the lunar cycle?' scientifically. There have been hundreds of studies of human behaviour during the full moon involving accident and emergency visits (Thompson and Adams, 1996; Rotton and Kelly, 1985), births (Bauer, Bender, Heining and Schmidt, 2013), suicides (Chaudhari et al., 2018), crime (Kelly, Rotton and Culver, 1985), absenteeism (Sands and Miller, 1991) and crisis centre calls (Gorvin and Roberts, 1994). The conclusion is that there is no lunar effect.

Why does belief in the lunar effect remain? The answer is a combination of three heuristics: availability, confirmation bias and belief perseverance:

1   The *availability heuristic* causes better recall for events that happened during a full moon because full moonlit nights are distinctive and more easily recalled.

2   *Confirmation bias* causes us to notice, accept and remember information that confirms our belief in the lunar effect, while ignoring, forgetting or explaining away contradictory information.

3   *Belief perseverance* occurs when, even after being presented with overwhelming evidence that there is no lunar effect, some people continue to believe it, because their personal experience influenced them more than impersonal data (Boudry and Braeckman, 2012).

The essence of critical thinking is setting aside personal anecdotes, experiences and beliefs, and embracing rigorous data and analysis.

Empiricism

Empirical reasoning is an important quality that differentiates science from other disciplines like philosophy and theology. The skill of empirically investigating possible answers to important forensic questions is critically important for understanding forensic research. However, just like everyone else, forensic psychologists have their own opinions about the nature of reality. The difference is being willing to test ideas and admit when they are unsupported; purposely evaluating the truthfulness of our assumptions even if it means that our ideas were wrong.

Suppose you are sceptical about the jury use of heuristics when deciding on the guilt or innocence of a suspect. You would want to evaluate this possibility using **empirical evidence**, which is based on the systematic use of observation and measurement, as opposed to using **anecdotal evidence**, which is based on non-systematic methods, such as examining personal experiences and opinions (word of mouth) rather than facts. The difference is illustrated in the field of clinical psychology in the classic study by Meehl (1954). Meehl compared the accuracy of a clinician's professional judgement with judgements based on an empirically derived algorithm (a step-by-step method of solving a problem). Meehl's analysis revealed that the algorithm provided more reliable diagnoses than clinical judgements. For example, the algorithm would always reach the same conclusion when presented with the same facts, while clinicians would vary in their

Empirical evidence
– Evidence based on the systematic use of observation and measurement.

Anecdotal evidence
– Evidence based on non-systematic methods such as examining personal experiences and opinions rather than facts.

judgements despite using the same data. According to Grove and colleagues (2000), studies comparing mechanical and clinical judgements showed that mechanical diagnoses produced higher quality diagnoses.

Apophenia

Humans are pattern-seeking creatures and we see relationships and mistake them for causes. **Apophenia** is perceiving connections and meaningfulness in unrelated things and is a normal human experience (Steyerl, 2016). It is not usually pathological but can become so in schizophrenia, when pattern recognition and interpretation run wild (Fyfe, Williams, Mason and Pickup, 2008; Bering, 2019). Enders and Smallpage (2019) described this as a form of 'patternicity'. Our brains are pattern detection machines evolved to uncover meaningful relationships and make predictions about survival and reproduction. Examples of apophenia, or patternicity, are everywhere. Many people perceive faces in random places – clouds, patterns of dirt left on cars, or on the moon (Hobbs, 2019).

Sometimes, our patternicity skills have unintentional consequences. For example, the symptoms of autism spectrum disorder (ASD) often appear in children during the time when they receive their vaccination (Wu et al., 2020). Therefore, despite a lack of evidence showing a causal connection, some parents do not vaccinate their children, believing that vaccinations *cause* ASD (Gray, 1995; Bennett, Webster, Goodall and Rowland, 2018; DeStefano and Shimabukuro, 2019; Davidson, 2017).

Thinking scientifically requires understanding the phrase *correlation does not imply causation*. **Correlation** is a statistical technique that tells us how strongly a pair of variables are linearly related and change together. It does not tell us the why and how behind the relationship but only that a relationship exists. **Causation** goes a step further than correlation, stating that any change in the value of one variable will cause a change in the value of another variable. Most correlations are coincidences and because it seems like one factor is influencing the other, it does not mean that it does. In some cases, there are hidden factors that are related on some level. For example, the crime rate in Japan is decreasing (Ellis and Hamai, 2017) and there is a correlation between the decrease in crime and the increase in the size of the police force. Perhaps a hidden factor explaining the correlation is Japan's use of the death penalty (Muramatsu, Johnson and Yano, 2018), its ageing population (Kavedžija, 2016) or its strict gun control laws (Young, 2019; Sakurai, 2019). All these factors are correlated, but decreasing crime is not *caused* by any one of these factors.

Becoming better consumers of research

Thinking scientifically has another benefit: it can help make us better consumers of research. We are presented with information and statistics portrayed as 'facts' despite their having little, if any, supporting scientific evidence. For example, using graphology (the study of handwriting) (Thorpe, 2018), forensic podiatry (the study of footprints, gait and other foot-related evidence) (Nirenberg, 2016) and hair analysis (analysing hair to find out about the person it came from) (Cuypers and Flanagan, 2018) are all examples of **pseudoscience** – claims or beliefs that are misrepresented as being derived from the use of the scientific method. One of the problems with pseudoscience is that it appears credible by closely mimicking the surface appearance of science (Hansson, 2013). It is not that we should dismiss pseudoscience as useless, uninteresting or false, it is just not science. Scientific methods build reliable knowledge and avoid creating false beliefs.

Apophenia
– Perceiving connections and meaningfulness in unrelated things, that is, patternicity.

Correlation
– A statistical technique that tells us how strongly a pair of variables are linearly related and change together.

Causation
– When changes in the value of one variable cause changes in the value of another variable.

Pseudoscience
– Claims or beliefs that are misrepresented as being derived from the use of the scientific method.

People are more likely to accept such claims because they are often accompanied by numerical support, and use specialised jargon. Bold statements in multisyllabic scientific jargon give the false impression that they are supported by laboratory research and hard facts. An example is the 'Dunning–Kruger effect', which means the less you know, the more likely you are to perceive yourself as an expert (Kumar, 2019). Another ploy is showing individuals associated with important sounding institutions or organisations. Once we learn to carefully evaluate evidence, rather than relying on a claim's believability or promoter, we become less vulnerable to being taken advantage of by pseudoscientific claims. Ultimately, this will help us make better decisions.

Good consumers of research evaluate information critically (Can and Saribas, 2019). First, consider the source of the information. Is the source impartial? Or are they sponsored by the product they promote? Next, consider the goal. Would their claim help them advance a certain agenda or promote a particular viewpoint? Finally, examine the information. What is the nature of the data? Is it from an experiment or a collection of testimonials and anecdotes? Even if it seems to be a research experiment, examine the data for quality. How many participants were included, what was the comparison group, and were the variables operationally defined, that is, defining a variable in terms of the way it is measured? Are the claims testable? Can their claims be disproven? Finally, remember that sceptics are open-minded and neither gullible nor cynical.

IN SUMMARY

Knowing more about research paired with scientific scepticism helps evaluate the validity of research claims and allows people to become better consumers of research information. The skill of applying scientific methodology builds upon reliable knowledge and avoids false beliefs.

 ## CRITICAL THINKING AND APPLICATION QUESTIONS

1   Watch a selection of adverts. Record how many make scientific claims as part of their persuasive appeal. For each advert, determine if the claim is based on pseudoscience or science.

2   The phrase 'correlation does not imply causation' is often used. But where does it apply in your life? Describe a unique example from your own experience that demonstrates this concept.

3   Does psychic ability exist? Design a detailed experiment that would scientifically test for psychic ability. To get started, research the use of 'Zener cards'.

ROLES AND RESPONSIBILITIES OF A FORENSIC PSYCHOLOGIST

FICTION: Forensic psychologists work only in courtrooms.

Versus

FACT: Forensic psychologists work in a variety of environments: courtrooms, prisons, schools, private practice.

The roles of the forensic psychologist

The purpose of this section is to show the varied and broad scope of a career in forensic psychology. What is common across the various careers is the intersection of psychology and the law, the differences are the roles they perform. These roles may be clinical, experimental, actuarial or advisory (Gudjonsson and Haward, 2016). However, these roles are not mutually exclusive, and one individual can perform more than one role. Some of the best-known forensic psychologists are both clinicians and experimenters, while others are actuarial specialists and advisers.

Clinical role

Clinically oriented forensic psychologists assess individuals to provide a clinical judgement. Clinical psychology focuses on the assessment of personality and the treatment of mental illness. The clinically oriented forensic psychologist can use interviews, assessment tools or psychometric tests (special questionnaires, MMPI-2-RF) to aid in their assessment across many venues (Logan, 2018). They can inform the police, the courts, and the prison and probation services. These assessments provide information about the psychological functioning of an individual and affect how the criminal justice system processes the individual (Place and Meloy, 2018).

Comparing clinical and forensic evaluation

The ethical responsibilities are different between a forensic psychologist's interactions with a client in a forensic setting and a clinical psychologist's interactions with a client in a clinical setting. The forensic evaluation attempts to obtain reliable and accurate information, while the clinical evaluation attempts to provide therapy via the treatment of symptoms such as depression and anxiety (Perona, Bottoms and Sorenson, 2005). The focus of the interview is also different. While the forensic psychologist is trying to determine the accuracy of the client's recall of events, the clinical psychologist is concerned with the client's attributions and perceptions of these events (Goodman and Melinder, 2010). Each perspective approaches the interview in a different way. The forensic approach is objective and neutral to avoid biases, while the clinical approach is empathic, to help form a therapeutic alliance (Vera et al., 2019). Finally, the interview styles for the forensic approach are formal with restricted confidentiality and are recorded, and the clinical approaches are more variable, with traditional confidentiality and the sessions are not recorded (Sternberg et al., 2001).

Fitness to stand trial assessments

A clinically oriented forensic psychologist may be asked to determine whether an individual is fit to stand trial or whether they have a mental illness, which means that they would be unable to understand the proceedings. Assessing mental competency examines specific mental health aspects of clinical practice within the legal context. Courts use forensic psychologists as experts to assist in making legal decisions, but the focus is on addressing the legal question before the court, not in answering a psychological question (Blake, Ogloff and Chen, 2019). Although sanity and competency both focus on the mental health aspects of the law, these concepts are often confused. Sanity focuses on a person's mental state at the time of a crime, and competency focuses on a person's mental state at the present moment (Kois, Chauhan and Warren, 2019).

Risk assessment

Another essential role for forensic psychologists is risk assessment, sometimes referred to as 'violence prediction', because the primary focus is predicting whether a person will become violent. However, risk assessment is not simply about making a choice about whether an individual is going to become violent or not, but also identifying the factors that are likely to increase and decrease the risk for violence, the immediacy of the violence, the severity of any possible violence, and the ways in which the violence can be managed (Garrett and Monahan, 2019; Olver and Wong, 2019).

Victimology and victim services

When we speak of 'crime victims', we are referring to individuals who have been physically and/or emotionally harmed by crimes against themselves or their property. The forensic psychologist assesses and treats the victim of sexual assault, intimate partner violence, child abuse, attempted murder or robbery. They conduct psychological assessments for personal injury matters having to do with auto accidents, product liability, sexual harassment and discrimination, and medical negligence or workers' compensation (Ofori-Dua, Onzaberigu and Nimako, 2019; Singh and Maria, 2019). Another important part of their job is to educate and train victim service providers about psychological reactions to criminal victimisation, such as PTSD (Youstin and Siddique, 2019).

Sexual offenders

Forensic psychologists work increasingly with sexual offenders. The focus is on risk assessment and reducing sexual violence. A sexual offender is an individual who has committed a sexual act that involves the use of force or a threat against a nonconsenting person (Harper, Hogue and Bartels, 2017). Sexual offences can include a wide range of sexual acts against a wide range of victims. Once an allegation is made, the role of a forensic psychologist in a sexual assault case varies depending on what is needed or requested of them and who is making the request. A forensic psychologist can be hired to evaluate the alleged victim or the alleged perpetrator. Some areas of the evaluation can include assessment of personality style, emotional reactions, malingering and intellectual ability (Hanson et al., 2017; Olver, Coupland and Kurtenbach, 2018). A forensic psychologist could be hired as a therapist to address the emotional reaction of being accused or being a victim. If a case goes to trial, a forensic psychologist could serve as a jury consultant to assist in acquiring an unbiased jury. A forensic psychologist could be hired as a fact witness. The fact witness is considered an expert by the court in the area that needs to be explored and capable of answering important questions.

Child custody evaluations

When separated or divorcing parents fight over custody of their child, the court system may be called to resolve the dispute (Goldstein, 2016). Forensic psychologists follow a set of guidelines to evaluate both parental fitness and the best interest of the child. They include interviews to evaluate social history and mental status of parents and child, standardised testing of both parents and child, and behavioural observations often conducted in the home of both parents and child (Drozd, Saini and Vellucci-Cook, 2019). A forensic psychologist may use outside sources, such as interviews with a child's teacher, doctor or others who have had interactions with the family. Similarly, documents such as medical records, criminal histories and school records may be used (Quinnell and Bow, 2001). These evaluations are always nonconfidential, and the findings are reported to the court. Thus, child custody evaluators must be comfortable making specific recommendations to both the families and the court, according to the findings of the evaluation (Valerio and Beck, 2017). Although child custody evaluations can be emotionally taxing, time-consuming and ethically challenging, the role of a forensic psychologist in this specialised area is important to the families, the courts and the children in need of help (Yee, 2019).

Criminal profiling

One of biggest misconceptions about forensic psychology is the high frequency of criminal profiling. Torres, Boccaccini and Miller (2006) surveyed forensic psychologists and found that less than 10 per cent had ever engaged in crime scene investigation or criminal profiling. Fewer than 25 per cent believed that profiling was scientifically reliable or valid. Although psychologists might interview serial killers as research or preparation for the court, they are not investigators, and most are not behavioural profilers. Most law enforcement agencies do not regularly use criminal profiling methods. When they do, they typically employ profilers with extensive backgrounds in law enforcement rather than in psychology (Fox and Farrington, 2018).

Experimental role

The use of psychological assistance is not limited to clinical analysis or testifying in court, it may involve the forensic psychologists performing research to inform a case.

Scientific jury selection

Social and experimentally oriented forensic psychologists often help attorneys select juries or conduct focus groups to identify the most convincing arguments. Working from the assumption that a knowledge of juror demographics, attitudes and broad personality characteristics can predict juror verdict decisions, psychologists try to assist justice systems in their selection of jurors. This process involves identifying what views are likely to be held by the individuals serving on a jury and eliminating those people thought to be opposed to the evidence in the case. In theory, these jury selection procedures remove biased jurors, who are considered incapable of making fair and impartial decisions, from criminal trials (Oostinga and Willmott, 2017). However, in practice, trial consultants typically advise defence lawyers which jurors are most likely to favour their explanation of the evidence (Lieberman and Olson, 2009). This has led many to question the ethics behind scientific jury selection, particularly when considering that the high cost of trial consultancy often means only the wealthiest defendants can afford to make use of their services.

Eyewitness research

Research-oriented forensic psychologists develop guidance on how to interview witnesses and suspects, for example interviews with vulnerable witnesses (young, elderly, learning impaired) (Wixted, Mickes and Fisher, 2018). This research can be used to inform the police on how best to retrieve the information they require from such witnesses without causing them too much stress, while ensuring that the information retrieved is accurate (Fisher and Schreiber, 2017).

Detecting deception

Research performed by forensic psychologists investigating the detection of deception has useful applications for the police when interviewing witnesses and suspects. Forensic psychologists have found that the strategic use of evidence consistently shows increases in deception detection accuracy rates above chance levels (Granhag and Hartwig, 2015). Researchers have discovered that another way to make lying more difficult is to increase interviewees' cognitive load by asking them to tell their stories in reverse order. Truth tellers can rely on their memories to tell their story backwards, often adding more details, but liars tend to struggle (Jian et al., 2019; Bird, Gretton, Cockerell and Heathcote, 2019). Research shows that liars also often provide fewer details about time, location and information they heard (Granhag and Vrij, 2017; Hudson, Vrij, Akehurst and Hope, 2019).

Actuarial role

Actuarial-focused forensic psychologists make extensive use of statistics to understand a case. One example of how a forensic psychologist may act in an actuarial role is reporting about event probabilities (Lynch, 2019). For example, a court may want to know the likelihood of an offender reoffending before the sentence is decided. In these situations, a forensic psychologist informs the presentencing report to the court.

Offender assessment

Forensic psychologists are involved in the assessment, rehabilitation and management of offenders, either in the community or when held in incarceration. This role involves working with offenders to reduce their chances of reoffending in the future or addressing the psychological needs of offenders. These psychological needs may be the result of the crime they committed (the development of PTSD) or their prison environment (developing depression due to being away from their family) (Newsome and Cullen, 2017), or suicidal intentions from prolonged solitary confinement (Bonta and Wormith, 2018).

A main task of the forensic psychologist is the assessment of offender risk of reoffending, their risk of harm (to others as well as themselves) and their needs (accommodation, finances and mental health). These assessments can be used to manage offenders' unique risks and needs. The forensic psychologist uses this information to plan rehabilitation activities that offenders carry out during their sentence. This could include basic skills courses (see Global Perspectives box below), treatment programmes for drug misuse, for example, or individual sessions for specific issues, such as anger management and impulse control (Haas and Smith, 2019; Farringer, Duriez, Manchak and Sullivan, 2019).

Global Perspectives

Paws for Progress: prison-based animal programmes in the UK

Paws for Progress is a non-profit organisation dedicated to enhancing the wellbeing of people and animals. The founding programme is based at HMYOI Polmont, Scotland's national holding facility for male offenders aged 18–21 years; it has since expanded beyond this facility. In this innovative model, men are taught how to train and rehabilitate rescue dogs for rehoming. Working under the guidance of the Paws for Progress training instructor and course instructor, participants learn to work as a team and use positive reinforcement methods, such as

An inmate with his dog during a prison-based training and rehabilitation programme using rescue dogs for rehoming

Source: Oliver Bunic/AFP/Getty Images

clicker training, to help the dogs. The service is carefully designed so that it is beneficial for the dogs involved, helping them to find new homes, as well as providing valuable dog care education for the men. Mercer, Gibson and Clayton (2015) found a significant effect on the participants, citing four areas of improvement: increasing responsibility; building trust; enhancing communication; and impacting on mood and behaviour.

Crime analysis

Forensic psychologists are employed by the police or policing agencies (in the UK, the National Crime Agency) to analyse crime data to aid police investigations (Piza, Welsh, Farrington and Thomas, 2019). One common role of crime analysis is **crime linkage** (Davies and Woodhams, 2019). This process involves connecting crimes based on similarities in the behaviours of the offenders as reported by the victim or as inferred from the crime scene. The police use this information to investigate the potential that the same offender committed multiple crimes. This allows efficient use of the resources by avoiding duplication of work (Kumar and Nagpal, 2019).

Crime linkage – *Linking crimes based on the similarities in the behaviours of the offenders or as inferred from the crime scene.*

Advisory role

This role involves the use of the psychologist's expertise to advise the police, courts or prison and probation services.

Police psychology

Forensic psychologists advise police about how to proceed with an investigation, for example by providing advice about the most effective way to interview a particular suspect. Alternatively, legal counsel may request advice on how to cross-examine a vulnerable witness. Another area of input is police officer recruitment using psychometric tests that measure psychological characteristics important to performing police duties. Another area of application is the control of stress. The stress faced by police officers is more intense than other types of employment (Liakopoulou et al., 2020), and there is a greater need for stress management measures. Psychologists advise police what mechanisms would be beneficial, such as peer support (Bonkiewicz, 2019), but they also provide professional services to police officers who require more intensive stress management, such as rational emotive health coaching (Onyishi, Ede, Ossai and Ugwuanyi, 2020).

Expert witness

Sometimes, court cases involve complex issues that are deemed to be beyond the knowledge of the average layperson serving on a jury. In these situations, the court uses an expert witness who has experience relating to the issue in question. Under some circumstances, expert witnesses can provide their opinion, rather than the facts, on the issue being discussed (Marion, Kaplan and Cutler, 2019). The way the expert witnesses are called to the court depends on the jurisdiction. For example, in some European countries, an expert witness is called by the court itself to provide information when it is needed. However, in the UK, Canada and the USA, the expert is instructed by either the defence or prosecution to provide support for their version of events (Horton and Soper, 2019; Hackman, Raitt and Black, 2019).

IN SUMMARY

A career as a forensic psychologist can follow many paths. These include clinically oriented roles of assessing fitness to stand trial, risk of violence assessments, collaborating with victims of crime, sexual offenders, and child custody evaluations. Experimental roles include scientific jury selection, research investigating eyewitness memory and deception. Actuarial roles include offender assessment and crime analysis investigations. Finally, the advisory role includes applying expertise to the police and as expert witnesses for the courts. All of these roles are varied and challenging.

 CRITICAL THINKING AND APPLICATION QUESTIONS

1   You are a forensic psychologist assigned to interview a child who may have suffered sexual abuse. Describe how the interview would be different if the interview was for the courts (a forensic interview) or for therapy.

2   Why is scientific jury selection considered controversial? Research this topic to find out if it is effective.

3   What roles played by forensic psychologists were not reviewed in this section? Research careers in forensic psychology to find out.

CHAPTER REVIEW

In this chapter we constructed a foundation for understanding, investigating and exploring the intersection of psychology and law known as 'forensic psychology'. As we examine the layers of fact and fiction behind offender behaviours, we expose the psychological roots of this field. Applying the varied psychological perspectives is a useful way to discover alternative explanations of the motivations of offenders. As you will discover, a sceptical mind will serve you well as we investigate the many facts and fictions surrounding this field. Our exploration of the diverse roles forensic psychologists perform will be useful as we apply the four perspectives throughout this textbook.

NAMES TO KNOW

Michael Shermer

An American science writer, historian of science, founder of The Skeptics Society, and editor-in-chief of its magazine *Skeptic*, which is largely devoted to investigating pseudoscientific and supernatural claims.

- Shermer, M. (2020) Why people believe conspiracy theories. *Skeptic*, 25(1), 12–18.

- Shermer, M. (2018) Reason (and science) for hope: A review of *Enlightenment Now: The Case for Reason, Science, Humanism, and Progress* by Steven Pinker. *Skeptic*, 23(2), 58–60.

Corine de Ruiter

A consultant for criminal justice agencies and a licensed clinical psychologist in The Netherlands. Her research includes a focus on the relationship between violence and mental disorders, as well as the risk for future violence.

- De Ruiter, C. and Kaser-Boyd, N. (2015) *Forensic Psychological Assessment in Practice: Case Studies.* Routledge.
- Chakhssi, F., Bernstein, D. and de Ruiter, C. (2014) Early maladaptive schemas in relation to facets of psychopathy and institutional violence in offenders with personality disorders. *Legal and Criminological Psychology*, 19, 356–72.

Patricia Zapf

Investigates the assessment of criminal competencies. Her manual, *Suicide Assessment Manual for Inmates*, is internationally recognised within the prison system and forensic psychology field.

- Zapf, P. A. (2006) *Suicide Assessment Manual for Inmates (SAMI).* Mental Health, Law, and Policy Institute, Simon Fraser University.
- Cutler, B. and Zapf, P. A. (2014) *APA Handbook of Forensic Psychology.* APA.

PART II

GETTING ACCURATE INFORMATION

2 TECHNIQUES FOR INTERVIEWING EYEWITNESSES

Chapter Introduction

Without physical evidence, we must rely on the accuracy of eyewitnesses. Yet once we understand the fragile nature of memory, we begin to doubt the reality of our own memories. Eyewitnesses' memories are easily distorted but they can be preserved through the application of psychologically based interview tactics. But how can you help an eyewitness identify the correct offender? This task requires an exploration of the ways to conduct and design unbiased recognition tests.

Learning Outcomes

Why are eyewitness reports so persuasive?

- Explain how memories are formed and distorted.

Interviewing witnesses (information generation)

- Describe ways to enhance the retrieval of memories during eyewitness interviews using the cognitive interview technique.

Is the live line-up dead? Improving eyewitness identification procedures

- Demonstrate how to achieve unbiased recognition information from an eyewitness.

The role of the forensic psychologist

- Describe how a forensic psychologist applies psychological concepts to create valid and reliable methods.

WHY ARE EYEWITNESS REPORTS SO PERSUASIVE?

....

FICTION: Eyewitness memories are accurate.

Versus

FACT: Eyewitness memories are continually rewritten based on expectations, biases and preconceptions.

....

Juries consider eyewitness accounts the *second* most persuasive piece of evidence to prove guilt (Semmler, Brewer and Douglass, 2011). What is more persuasive than an eyewitness? A signed confession (Shifton, 2019). Eyewitness evidence is powerful because lawyers, judges, juries and the public believe that the way we remember an event must be the way it happened.

Besides the moral injustice of false convictions, inaccurate eyewitnesses can mislead the initial stages of police investigations. Inaccurate eyewitness information wastes valuable time following false leads, for example interviewing witnesses and researching criminal histories, while building a case against an innocent person. Meanwhile, because of this inaccurate information, the real offender remains free to commit more crimes.

CASE STUDY

A case of eyewitness misidentification

In the provocatively titled book *Picking Cotton* (Thompson-Cannino, Cotton and Torneo, 2009), exoneree Ronald Cotton and abuse victim Jennifer Thompson-Cannino tell an emotional story of misidentification and wrongful conviction in North Carolina, USA. In 1984, a black man broke into her apartment while she was asleep and raped Jennifer, a white college student, at knifepoint. During the assault, she had the presence of mind to study her attacker and try to memorise his appearance. She offered to make her attacker a drink and escaped. Three days later, at the police department, she helped create a composite sketch, and Ronald was arrested shortly afterwards. The police were interested because in two separate incidents in July 1984, an assailant broke into an apartment, cut phone wires, sexually assaulted a woman, and searched through her belongings, taking money and other items.

Even though Jennifer was unsure that Ronald was her rapist, she spent much more than the normal amount of time studying the photo array and eventually selected the photo of Ronald. After her choice, the investigators told Jennifer that she'd done a 'great' job. Later, she viewed a physical line-up in which the only member who had also been in the previously presented photo array was Ronald. After identifying him a second time, the detective told her: 'We thought that might be the guy. It's the same person you picked from the photos.' Ronald, who had a weak alibi and a minor criminal record, was tried, convicted and sentenced to life plus 54 years for first-degree rape, first-degree sexual offence and first-degree breaking and entering.

During his time in prison, Ronald was a model prisoner who continued to profess his innocence. One day he spotted a fellow prisoner, who bore a strong resemblance to him. His name was Bobby Leon Poole. Ronald intuitively knew that Bobby was the rapist for whom he was doing time. As further evidence, he later got a tip from a fellow inmate that Poole had bragged about raping two white women. Bobby denied the statement and the alleged confession did not sway the prosecutor or judge.

Then, the Innocence Project – a global organisation whose mission is to exonerate the wrongfully convicted – arrived to re-examine the evidence. Ronald Cotton spent 10.5 years in prison before a DNA test cleared him of rape and identified the real rapist (Jones, 2013).

The police told Jennifer that DNA testing had proven Ronald innocent and implicated the real perpetrator, Bobby Leon Poole. She was shocked and overcome with feelings of guilt, but soon came to realise that eyewitness misidentifications are not rare. Surprisingly, she did not recognise Bobby during his trial. In 1995, Ronald was exonerated and released. He forgave Jennifer and they became good friends and now travel the world together to educate the public about wrongful convictions and reforms – especially in relation to eyewitness identification procedures.

Discussion Questions:

1   Why should the amount of time it took Jennifer to recognise Ronald Cotton's photo from the photo array indicate a problem with her memory?

2   How was Jennifer's level of confidence in her mistaken identification manipulated by the detectives?

3   If not from the original traumatic event, where did Jennifer's memory of Ronald Cotton originate?

How memories are made

Is seeing believing? According to statistics published by the Innocence Project (2020), eyewitness misidentifications have contributed to 69 per cent of the more than 367 wrongful convictions in the USA overturned by post-conviction DNA evidence (Figure 2.1). The real offenders were convicted of 152 additional violent crimes, including 82 sexual assaults, 35 murders and 35 other violent crimes, while the innocent sat behind bars for their earlier offences.

Figure 2.1: Eyewitness misidentifications as the leading cause of wrongful convictions compared to other causes*

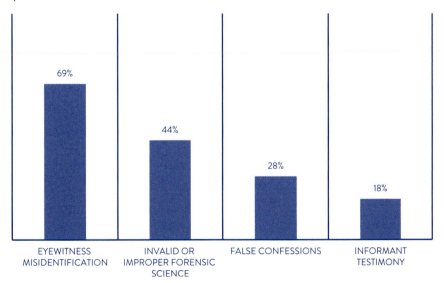

*Based on 367 DNA exonerations
Source: Innocence Project (2020) *DNA Exonerations in the United States.* Retrieved from www.innocenceproject.org/dna-exonerations-in-the-united-states/.

Our sense of identity comes from the memories of our past. These kinds of memories are known as **episodic memories**, our memories of specific, personally experienced events, such as graduations or birthdays (Tulving, 1984). These are the types of memories that the criminal justice system collects from eyewitnesses and their courtroom testimony. These are also the most fragile and easily altered memories.

People talk about memory as if it were something they have, like large feet or red hair. But memory is not something you can see like a part of your body; it is an idea that refers to a process of remembering. To understand how memories form, consider when your memory fails. Have you ever forgotten your phone, a name, or an assignment? If so, then your memory failed at one or more of the three stages of the memory process – encoding, storage and retrieval (see Figure 2.2).

Figure 2.2: Three stages of memory formation

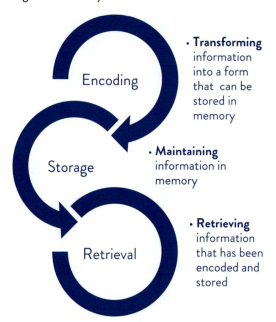

The first stage, *encoding*, is the transformation of information into a form that can be stored. For example, if you see a bank robbery, you try to form a visual image of the scene. The second stage, *storage*, involves maintaining the information in your working memory by rehearsing the information or connecting it to other information (Engle, 2010). The final stage is *retrieval*, when the information is pulled from storage. This three-stage process can fail when memories are neither encoded, rehearsed, nor recalled.

Memory storage relies on our ability to encode and retrieve information. When we store facts and experiences, we weave them into the complex tapestry of ideas that expand the depth of our memories. However, the journey from perceptual encoding to retrieval forms an information bottleneck. This happens because our storage process, also known as 'consolidation', is much slower than our perceptual experience of the world. This slow transfer of information from perceptual encoding to memory storage is like trying to fill a bath with a thimble (Carr, 2010).

It was once believed that each neuron stored a single memory (Barlow, 1972). Our brains held a 'grandmother cell', a theoretical neuron that responds only to a single complex, specific and meaningful stimulus, such as the image of one's grandmother (Gross, 2002). Karl Lashley searched for this unique physical trace of memory, called the **engram**. Lashley attempted to discover the specific location of the learning centre of the brain by systematically disconnecting different regions of a rat's cerebral cortex (Dewsbury, 2002). To his surprise, all the rats showed some degree of impaired learning, but none were seriously impaired. Although Lashley never found the engram, he did discover something more profound. Memories are distributed throughout the brain. They connect brain locations for emotion, vision, hearing, language and other mental processes. This finding means that memories are changes in the patterns of connections between neurons.

> **Engram** – *The physical trace of a memory in the brain.*

The billions of neurons in our brain work like an orchestra creating a symphony of thoughts (Glick, 2011). Far from existing as a single note or neuron, our memories are stored in a vast web of neural networks (Ferbinteanu, 2019). As neurons are activated together, they form a web of connections between people, things and emotions (Greene, 2010). In this way, storage means that a single memory cue can reactivate a network of neurons, allowing you to relive the experience.

How does a single cue trigger memories? The answer lies in the **spreading activation model of semantic memory** (Collins and Loftus, 1975). This model assumes that information is organised on the basis of relatedness. Memories are like nodes; those that are activated together form stronger connections and make it easier to activate each other. In a network of memories represented by nodes, the shorter the links, the faster our brains make connections between the nodes. Also, the longer a concept is retrieved, the greater the spread of activation among the nodes of our memories (Anderson, 1983). In this way, memory cues can trigger further memories along our networks of information. As shown in Figure 2.3, trying to activate the forgotten first name 'Harry' activates multiple nodes. Some of these connections are stronger than others, as shown by thicker lines.

> **Spreading activation model of semantic memory** – *Networks of associated ideas are linked together and spread from one node to another.*

Figure 2.3: Spreading activation model of neural network

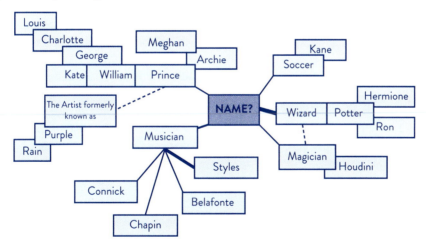

The reconstructive nature of memory

Because we use the past to decode the present, even the subtle differences in the wording of a question can alter our recollections (Schacter, 2012). Unlike a jigsaw puzzle, the pieces of our memories are not always reassembled precisely, as was shown by Loftus and Palmer (1974). They showed participants a video of a car accident. Half the subjects were asked to estimate how fast the cars were going when they 'smashed' into each other, while the other half were asked how fast the cars were going when they 'hit' each other. The subjects who heard 'smashed' reported significantly higher speed estimates than those who heard 'hit'. Unexpectedly, many subjects who heard 'smashed' also reported seeing broken glass and other artefacts of a severe collision that never existed as they reassembled their memories of the video.

Strange as it may seem, with all this reconstruction, there is no such thing as a 'real' memory. Every time you recall a memory from the past, it changes slightly. The fish you caught becomes larger, the party wilder, the concert more amazing. This is because all our memories are reconstructed, with bits and pieces of similar past experiences used to fill in the missing gaps of knowledge (Domingo, Treder, Kerrén and Wimber, 2019).

Our memory of an event changes because of pre-event information (what we knew before) and post-event information (what we knew after). Decades ago, Bartlett (1932) demonstrated this effect with the game called 'telephone'. In this game, each person tells the same story one after the other and the changes are reported at the end. In Bartlett's controlled version of this game, the information contained in the story increasingly conforms to what we expect to happen. The reason is that when we are unsure of information, we fill in the gaps with a mental shortcut known as a **cognitive schema** (Flavell, 1996). A schema is a cognitive framework or concept that helps organise and interpret information (Rumelhart, 1980). However, these mental frameworks also cause us to exclude new information and focus only on information that matches our pre-existing schema. Schemas make it difficult to remember new information that does not conform to our established ideas about the world. The consequence of this is that what we already know affects what we remember and information after the event changes the original memory trace to fit our schema.

> **Cognitive schemas**
> – Patterns of thought that organise information.

IN SUMMARY

An eyewitness's memory is not a permanent record, because our episodic memories are continually reconstructed every time they are retrieved. Consequently, eyewitness memories are fragile and susceptible to alterations based on our expectations, biases and preconceptions.

CRITICAL THINKING AND APPLICATION QUESTIONS

1   Your childhood friend discovered that a long-cherished memory of saving a drowning camper during summer camp happened to her sister and not her. She cannot understand how this could have happened. They both attended the same camp for over a decade and shared these memories every holiday. Explain how this could have happened.

2   Imagine you are the leader of a jury that has listened to a confident eyewitness. The other members of the jury are about to decide the case based only on the eyewitness information. Explain to them why eyewitness memories may not be as dependable as they believe them to be.

3   Describe a detailed example when your memory about a past event was proven wrong. How did your cognitive schema of the event alter your memory?

INTERVIEWING EYEWITNESSES (INFORMATION GENERATION)

FICTION: The standard police interview is the best way to retrieve information from an eyewitness.	*Versus*	**FACT:** Alternative methods like the cognitive interview are more effective than the standard interview.

The standard interview

Obtaining complete and accurate information from a witness is critical in an investigation. Yet, accurate recall is difficult to attain (Innocence Project, 2018; Goodman, Aman and Hirschman, 1987). Part of the difficulty is that the standard interview generally relies on closed-ended questions. Another difficulty is that the standard interview has three competing goals. Police are trying to:

1   discover if a crime has been committed

2   find evidence to identify the individual responsible

3   determine whether the witness is telling the truth (Brewer, Weber and Guerin, 2019; Kebbell and Wagstaff, 1997).

Additional challenges include performing the standard interview under noisy, confusing and disorienting conditions with pressure to quickly locate eyewitnesses. As if this were not enough, police job performance is measured by how quickly reports are filed (Tang and Hammontree, 1992). This pressure is common and frequently reported in German (Berresheim and Weber, 2003), Canadian (Snook and Keating, 2010) and US police departments (Schreiber and Fisher, 2005).

Problems with the standard interview

Overuse of closed-ended questions

Asking closed-ended questions, such as 'Was she wearing a cap or a hood?', prevents the witness from revealing spontaneous information (Wise and Safer, 2012). This question format also encourages guessing on the part of the witness, unless the witness is told that they should not respond unless they are sure, which is rarely done (Krauss et al., 2017). Closed-ended questions are frequently used during semi-structured interviews (Adams, 2015) and examples are presented in Table 2.1.

Table 2.1: Classifications of closed-ended questions used during interviews

Type of question	Description	Example
Clarification	Interviewer checks for accuracy and provides feedback indicating which information is known and understood (Stoyanchev, Liu and Hirschberg, 2012)	Interviewee: 'I left work and drove home and was there until I left for work again in the morning.' Interviewer: 'So you never left your house all night?'

(continued)

Forced choice	Questions that offer the interviewee a limited number of possible responses, (yes or no), none of which may be the interviewee's preferred answer (Peterson and Grant, 2001)	'Do you know why I stopped you?' 'Did he have a gun?' 'Was the suspect short or tall?' 'Did you go home after work?'
Leading	The answer is embedded in the question, suggesting the correct response desired by the interviewer (Weinberg, Wadsworth and Baron, 1983)	'You needed the money, right?' 'You didn't see the stop sign, did you?' 'You never came home that night, right?'
Multiple questions	The interviewer asking several questions at once, without giving the interviewee a chance to respond after each question (Griffiths and Milne, 2006)	'Did you go directly home after work … or stop somewhere along the way … When did you arrive home?'
Opinion/ statement	An interviewer supplies their own opinion and expects the interviewee to answer (Snook and Keating, 2011)	'I think you stole the money on your way home from work.'

Snook, Luther and Milne (2012) investigated the everyday questioning practices of Canadian police. Eighty transcripts of police interviews showed that less than 1 per cent of the questions asked in an interview were open-ended, while closed-ended questions comprised 35 per cent of the questions.

Frequent interruptions

In their haste to collect evidence, police often interrupt the eyewitnesses' narrative of the crime. This not only interrupts the chronological sequence of their memory but prevents witnesses from volunteering information (Fisher, Geiselman and Amador, 1989). Good interview practices allow the witness time to fully disclose relevant details of the crime (Judges, 2000) by waiting before asking the next question to make sure the witness has completed their response (Wise, Dauphinais and Safer, 2007).

Repeating questions and using leading questions

Another ineffective interview practice is asking the same question several times during the same interview (Fisher, 1995). Repeating the same question creates two problems. First, if the witness did not respond to the question the first time, repeated questioning creates a **demand characteristic** – an implicit appeal for the witness to respond in a certain way – even if the witness is not confident in their response (Gudjonsson, 2010). Second, if the witness did indeed provide an answer the first time the question was asked, the repetition implies that the answer was not satisfactory, creating pressure to respond differently (Fisher, 1995). According to Bruck, Ceci, Francoeur and Barr (1995), the repeated misinformation becomes a part of their memory of the event – they use the interviewer's words in their inaccurate statements.

Demand characteristics – *Subtle cues that communicate the interviewer's expectations.*

Egocentric questioning strategies

Like everyone, police rely on schemas to reduce their cognitive load. To combat this, police should ask questions that are compatible with the witness's current thoughts and narrative of the crime. For example, if the witness is thinking or talking about the perpetrator's face, the questions should be about the face and not about other aspects of the incident (Technical Working Group on Eyewitness Evidence, 2003).

Contaminating the eyewitness memory of crimes

Presenting the witness with information from sources other than their memory of the crime, such as media, police and other eyewitnesses, contaminates the original memory (Fisher, 1995). This is known as the **unconscious transference effect**, where information is encoded without remembering its source (Hinz and Pezdek, 2001; Ross, Ceci, Dunning, Toglia, 1994). This makes post-event information seem like part of their original memory (Loftus, 2003). This effect happens most often when the source of the information is highly credible, there is some uncertainty about the event, and when the information is about minor details (Judges, 2000).

In conclusion, the problems with the standard interview are that these practices reward witnesses who withhold information, do not provide any unsolicited information, give abbreviated answers, and volunteer answers to questions they are unsure about. These practices also disrupt the natural process of memory search, making memory retrieval inefficient. A more efficient solution is the cognitive interview approach.

The cognitive interview

The **cognitive interview** is a procedure that enhances the memory recall of eyewitnesses without contaminating their memory (Fisher, Milne and Bull, 2011). An advantage of the cognitive interview is the application of three overlying categories of interview techniques – social dynamics, communication and cognitive processes (Figure 2.4) – into several specific applications (Eisenberg, 2019).

Unconscious transference effect – *When an eyewitness to a crime misidentifies a familiar but innocent person from a police line-up.*

Cognitive interview – *Interview process to enhance retrieval of information from the perspective of eyewitnesses' memory.*

Figure 2.4: Categories of cognitive interview techniques

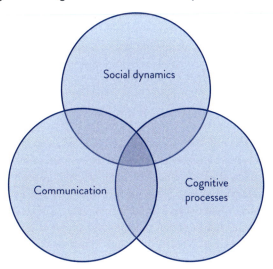

The origin of the cognitive interview began when Ronald Fisher's friends kept forgetting things in his apartment. Asking questions to trigger their memories helped them find their lost items. Realising that he was applying the same theories of memory he was teaching, he contacted a colleague, Ed Geiselman, and asked him who could use this skill of helping someone to remember details? Geiselman's first response was the police since they solve crimes by getting witnesses to remember details about an incident or series of incidents. They worked with the behavioural sciences unit of the Los Angeles Police Department and inquired about the kind of police training provided when interviewing cooperative witnesses. While they did supply formal training about interrogating suspects, they were surprised to find that the police department offered little training interviewing cooperative witnesses (Geiselman et al., 1984).

The psychology behind the cognitive interview

The cognitive interview approach treats memories like trace evidence found at a crime scene and applies three theoretical perspectives: encoding specificity theory, multiple trace theory and schema theory.

Encoding specificity

Encoding specificity – Memory is better when conditions during retrieval match those when the memory was stored.

Tulving (1982, 1983) suggested that the most effective retrieval cues are those that give the most overlap between the stored information and the retrieval cue. An effective way to enhance recall is to reconstruct the original context of the memory (Wheeler and Gabbert, 2017; Flexser and Tulving, 1978). Matching subjective perceptions (thoughts, emotions) during the time of encoding is known as **encoding specificity**. When we encode a memory, we not only record the visual and other sensory data, we also store our emotional state (Mackmen, Clark and McManus, 2000). Our present mood affects the memories that are most easily available to us, so that when we are happy we recall happy memories and vice versa (Thorley, Dewhurst, Abel and Knott, 2016).

Multiple-trace theory

Multiple trace theory – Every memory has many unique components that can be activated with the proper cue.

Another theory behind the cognitive interview is **multiple trace theory**. Because our memories are composed of a network of associations, there are many paths to reach a single memory (Tulving, 1984). This concept is demonstrated by the **tip-of-the-tongue phenomenon**, where a memory feels easily available and yet cannot be retrieved. To recall the name of a friend from school, you might try to activate other traces of memory like where they sat in the classroom, what sports they played, or their nickname (Schacter, 1999).

Schema theory

Tip-of-the-tongue phenomenon – Failure to recall a specific word or term with awareness that they know the word or term.

Familiar events form schemas, and our schemas guide our encoding of events (Schank and Abelson, 1977). A witness's earlier experiences allow them to fill the empty categories with information that fits their schema. For example, the question 'What did you eat this morning?' activates the schema for breakfast food and the categories of breakfast food. You might respond, 'I had bacon and something else ... oh yeah ... eggs.' The empty category of eggs becomes much easier to complete under the context of a breakfast schema than a dinner schema. When a memory is retrieved, our schemas provide an organised information system to search. The typical interview sequence follows seven phases (Figure 2.5).

Figure 2.5: Seven phases of the cognitive interview

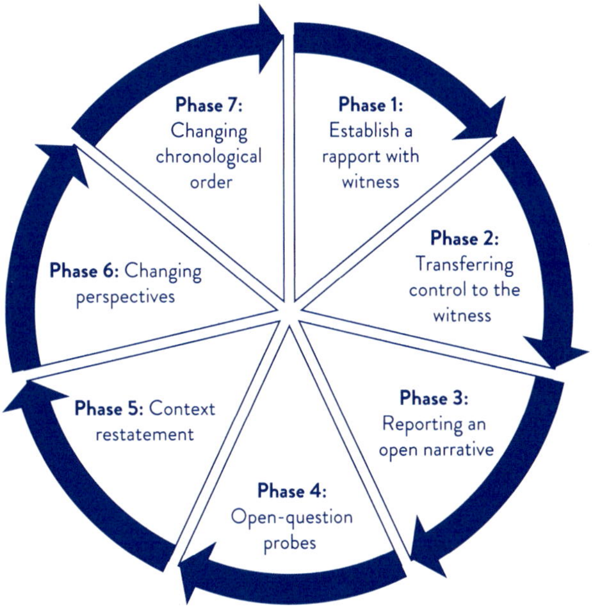

The seven phases of the cognitive interview

Phase 1: Establish a rapport with the witness

Rapport building is one of the most important interviewing techniques applied in police interviews. Expert police interviewers assert that rapport building is a best practice (Russano, Narchet, Kleinman and Meissner, 2014). Rapport-building techniques can be used to secure cooperation from interviewees, gather as much reliable information as possible, and create a positive interpersonal interaction (Dhami, Goodman-Delahunty and Desai, 2017).

Police need to develop rapport and empathy to improve eyewitness cooperation when revealing information. Empathy is expressing an understanding of another person's thoughts, feelings and condition (Gerace, Day, Casey and Mohr, 2017). Rapport is enhanced by empathising with the witness's situation, avoiding judgmental comments and establishing common ground. Even a simple question like 'How are you doing?' builds rapport and can reveal a physical or mental condition, such as intoxication, confusion, anxiety, that impairs a witness's ability to recall or report information (Technical Working Group on Eyewitness Evidence, 2003). Good rapport is genuinely responding to the witness's earlier answers and concerns while avoiding memorised questions that sound artificial, for example 'Is there anything you can tell me that would further assist this investigation?'

Phase 2: Transferring control to the witness

The cognitive interview is 'witness centred' not 'interviewer centred'. Typically, the witness sits passively while waiting for the interviewer to ask questions (Fisher, Geiselman and Raymond, 1987). To transfer control, the interviewer uses open-ended questions without interruption and specifically tells the witness that they should do most of the talking. For example, rather than saying, 'Please tell me all you remember about the robbery', the question should be: 'Please tell me about the robbery and any details, no matter how insignificant they might seem to you, since you might have seen something no other witness saw.'

Phase 3: Reporting an open narrative

Witnesses should be encouraged to report what they remember completely without filtering anything they consider to be irrelevant or which they have only partial recall (Fisher and Geiselman, 1992). At this stage of the interview, the instruction to search their memories for details can lead to the recall of additional relevant information, such as 'Picture the robbery again, and report any detail, no matter how trivial it might seem' (Geiselman and Fisher, 1988). This open narrative approach often yields new information and eyewitnesses who report more details are perceived as more credible witnesses in the courtroom (Bell and Loftus, 1980).

Phase 4: Open-question probes

Open-ended questions, such as 'Tell me, in your own words, what happened', invite elaboration (Stolzenberg, McWilliams and Lyon, 2017). Consequently, the interviewer is less likely to lead the witness when framing questions in an open manner (Newlin, Webber, Morris and Howarth, 2015).

Phase 5: Context restatement

The witness is encouraged to mentally reconstruct the scene of the crime. Contextual restatement includes emotional components, 'What were you feeling during the robbery?', perceptual components, 'Try to remember the crime scene, picture the room, what sounds, or smells did you perceive?', and sequencing of the memory traces, 'What were you first doing at the time?', thereby capturing any stray traces of the original memory (Campos and Alonso-Quecuty, 1999).

APPLY IT

How to use context restatement to enhance your memory

Try to answer the question: 'How many windows are there in your home?'

Now use context restatement to answer the same question:

'Try to visualise the place where you live and think about how many windows there are in that place. Picture in your mind's eye yourself facing your home. Count every window you see from left to right, try to include every window no matter how small. Then mentally walk to the left side of your home and count each window. When you have finished, walk to the back, and count each window from left to right. Finally, mentally walk to the last side of your home and count each window you can remember.'

Most people find that context restatement significantly enhanced their ability to accurately count all the windows in their home. Did you find that your recall was significantly better?

Phase 6: Changing perspectives

The witness is encouraged to imagine themselves in the body of the victim or another witness and report what they would have seen. Reporting the incident from a different perspective increases the amount of detail by reducing the impact of cognitive schemas (prior knowledge and expectations) that limit memory search.

Phase 7: Changing chronological order

Normally, telling a coherent story requires starting at the beginning, but with this method, the witness is encouraged to recall from a variety of points – from the end, the middle, or even the most memorable event. The purpose is to capture more detail because changing the sequence takes the subject out of the confines of their expected schemas and activates more elusive memory traces (Memon et al., 1997).

Is the cognitive interview effective?

In the first study of its kind, Satin and Fisher (2019) showed that the cognitive interview is effective for both eyewitness descriptions and enhancing photo identification accuracy. Their study examined the effectiveness of the cognitive interview approach in two critical areas: whether it improves witness descriptions of a perpetrator's appearance and whether these descriptions help investigators to find the perpetrator. First, college students saw a simulated robbery and were interviewed using either the cognitive or standard interview to elicit a description of the robber. They found that the cognitive interview produced nearly three times as many descriptors, and at comparable levels of accuracy. Next, 387 college students and 71 police used these descriptions to find the perpetrator among a group of suspect photographs. The descriptors from the cognitive interview increased the rate of finding the perpetrator by 30 per cent for both student and police investigators.

Fisher, Geiselman and Amador (1989) ran the first field study of the cognitive interview with the help of police detectives in Miami, Florida. A **field study** refers to research that is undertaken in the real world, where the confines of a laboratory setting are abandoned in favour of a natural setting (Pontis, 2018). The study began with a pretraining phase where sample interviews were collected from the detectives using their regular interview procedures. Then, half were given a four-hour training session in all the components of the cognitive interview. Before using the cognitive interview with actual witnesses, the detectives received feedback from a practice interview. To measure the effectiveness of training, they compared the number of facts obtained by comparing each officer's technique before and after training, and with the number of correct facts elicited by trained police compared with the untrained police. The cognitive interview was superior in both comparisons.

> **Field study** – Research where the confines of a laboratory setting are abandoned in favour of a natural setting.

Criticisms of the cognitive interview

The main area of concern is that along with generating more information, the cognitive interview also generates more errors. A solution was discovered by Memon, Meissner and Fraser (2010). Simply advising witnesses to use 'I don't know' answers and asking them not to guess significantly reduced errors. Another concern is the challenge of applying the change perspective and reverse chronological order procedures. These two approaches require a lot of time and produce little additional useful information (Dando, Ormero, Wilcock and Milne, 2011), are difficult to learn and use (Paulo, Albuquerque, Vitorino and Bull, 2017) and may increase omissions (Fisher, Milne and Bull, 2011). Also, evidence obtained by asking subjects to imagine another perspective is viewed as speculation and subjective and therefore difficult to use in legal proceedings (Memon and Köhnken, 1992). Finally, using all the components of the cognitive interview in the field is limited by time constraints (Dando, Wilcock and Milne, 2008).

IN SUMMARY

Increasing recall is crucial for investigative interviews. Methods such as the cognitive interview are more effective in retrieving accurate memories from eyewitnesses than the standard police interview.

 CRITICAL THINKING AND APPLICATION QUESTIONS

1   Imagine that you are an experienced police detective and must teach another detective how to conduct a cognitive interview with an eyewitness of a bank robbery. Outline your interview questions (pay close attention to the specific components of the cognitive interview).

2   Compare the differences in goals between the standard interview and the cognitive interview.

3   Which components of the cognitive interview lend themselves to field applications? Specifically, what are some of the obstacles preventing the application of cognitive interview components in the field as opposed to a controlled laboratory experiment?

IS THE LIVE LINE-UP DEAD? IMPROVING EYEWITNESS IDENTIFICATION PROCEDURES

FICTION: The traditional live line-up is an extensively used and effective method of identification.   *Versus*   **FACT:** The live line-up is flawed, and alternative methods are more effective and used more often.

Typical identification procedures

Imagine you are in a bank when you hear a loud alarm and a gunshot; you find yourself facing an escaping bank robber. Later, the police request that you attend an identity parade. You logically assume that the police think they have apprehended the offender. Will your assumption that they have the offender in custody make you more likely to identify an innocent person? According to research, the answer is 'yes' (Malpass and Devine, 1984).

Identifying a suspect seems like an easy task, but it is deceptively challenging. In fact, a good identity parade is like a good experiment (Wells and Luus, 1990). For example, both include:

- a control group – a line-up with a mock witness in order to test the fairness of the line-up

- an experimenter who is unaware of the hypothesis

- an investigator who does not know who the suspect is

- questions that are phrased in a way that they do not demand a particular answer

- the procedure does not imply that the suspect is in the line-up.

There are different approaches to identifying the offender from potential suspects (Table 2.2). The use of each approach depends on the circumstances of the crime. Each approach has potential biases of which the administrator should be aware.

Table 2.2: Types of eyewitness identification procedures

Type	Presentation description	Types of bias
Line-up or identification parade	Presentation of a group of persons including one suspected of having committed a crime assembled for the purpose of discovering whether a witness can identify the suspect from the foils	• *Instruction bias:* Did they suggest to the witness that the perpetrator was definitely in the line-up/ identity parade? • *Simultaneous versus sequential processing:* Witnesses can make simultaneous comparisons among potential suspects, but are unable to use this strategy with sequential presentation
Show up	A witness is shown one person (the suspect) and asked whether that person is the perpetrator	• *Suggestive influences:* Because there is only one person presented to the witness, it is obvious who the suspect is. The manner in which the suspect is presented (seeing the suspect in handcuffs or in the back of a police car) may be suggestive of the suspect's guilt
Photo line-up or photo array	Presentation of photographs to a witness of a crime to discover or confirm the identity of a criminal suspect	• *Verbal overshadowing:* The tendency of verbalisation to impair the recall of visual memories, resulting in unreliable eyewitness accounts • *Image consistency:* Ensuring that all photographs have similar backgrounds, lighting and distance from the camera to the suspect
Confirmatory photograph	Presenting a single photograph (often from social media sources) to a witness to confirm the identity of a suspect	• *Unconscious transference:* If the witness has seen the suspect's image somewhere other than when committing the crime, it is possible that they are transferring that memory into their memory of who committed the crime (source confusion)

PART II

System
variables
– Variables
affecting the
accuracy of
eyewitness
identifications,
under control
of the criminal
justice system.

Estimator
variables
– Variables
that affect
the accuracy
of eyewitness
identifications,
but cannot be
controlled by
the criminal
justice system.

System and estimator variables

Both eyewitness testimony and suspect identification decisions are affected by two kinds of variables: system variables and estimator variables (Wells, 1978). **System variables** are factors that are under the control of the police conducting the investigation. **Estimator variables** are factors associated with the witnesses and their view of the crime, which are not under the control of the police or the judicial system. Distinguishing between estimator and system variables is crucial, because controlling estimator variables increases our chances of identifying accurate and inaccurate witnesses, while controlling system variables helps prevent mistaken identifications (Wells and Olson, 2003).

Source: Vintage Images/Getty Images

System and estimator variables affect eyewitness identification accuracy during police line-ups

Table 2.3: Examples of system and estimator variables

System variables	Estimator variables
Pre-line-up instructions	Effect of post-event information on witness confidence
Line-up construction	Disguise
Foil bias	Gender differences
Clothing	Age
Presentation method	Intellectual challenges
Investigator bias and the double-blind procedure	Racial differences
	Alcohol intoxication and other drugs
	The effect of stress
	Weapon focus

System variables

System variables are characteristics of a line-up (recognition test) that are related to the retrieval stage of memory (Kurosawa, 1996; Wells, 1978).

Pre-line-up instructions

Can what you are told by the police *after* a crime distort your memory? Malpass and Devine (1981, p. 484) showed this effect when they had their subjects identify the culprit they had previously seen in their lecture hall during a staged act of vandalism. Half the subjects were presented with a line-up where the vandal was among the choices, while the other half were presented with a 'vandal-absent' line-up. Under these two conditions, half the witnesses were given biased instructions: 'We believe that the person ... is present in the lineup ... which of these is the person you saw?' The other half were given unbiased instructions: 'The person ... may be ... in the lineup. It is also possible that he is not in the lineup.' The results showed that instructions significantly influenced eyewitness performance.

Results showed that the type of instructions did not affect identification accuracy under the vandal-present condition with and without biased instructions. However, the instructions did have a significant effect in the 'vandal-absent' condition. Table 2.4 shows that under the biased instruction condition, 78 per cent of the subjects identified an innocent person! Why did this happen? The subjects in the biased condition (like subjects in a police station) expect the culprit to be present in the line-up. They feel the pressure to choose somebody (anybody) who resembles the reconstructed memory of the offender the most.

Table 2.4: Line-up instruction bias results from Malpass and Devine (1981)

		Vandal present	**Vandal absent**
Instructions	Biased	75 per cent correct identification	**78 per cent wrong identifications**
	Unbiased	83 per cent correct identifications	33 per cent wrong identifications

Source: Malpass, R. S. and Devine, P. G. (1981) Eyewitness identification: Lineup instructions and the absence of the offender, *Journal of Applied Psychology*, 66(4), 482–9. American Psychological Association. Adapted with permission.

Obviously, this technique does not eliminate the possibility that some witnesses still feel pressure to choose someone. To counter this, the witness should be told that the offender may or may not be in the line-up and that not making a choice still supplies useful information. Specifically, answers such as 'I don't recognise anyone' are acceptable (Steblay, 2018). As an additional safeguard, Wells, Seelau, Ryan and Luus (1994) suggest beginning the identification line-up with a target-absent condition or a blank line-up – a line-up that only has known innocent participants with no suspect. However, it will eventually become common knowledge that police begin with a target-absent condition. In general, police prefer not to use the blank line-up method because it 'tricks' the eyewitness and lowers eyewitnesses' trust in the police (Wells and Olson, 2003).

Line-up construction and fairness

A fair recognition test is one in which the suspect does not stand out from the other known innocent people in the line-up due to the design of the recognition test. One of the most infamous examples involved a suspect described as a 'black man', who was part of a six-person line-up containing one black suspect and five white **foils** – also known as line-up fillers (Ellison and Buckhout, 1981). The police offered as their excuse for having a single

Foils – *Also known as line-up fillers (an innocent person in a police line-up), they test an eyewitness's recognition memory.*

black suspect among five white foils that there were few black people in their city, so the line-up was representative of the population and there were no similar foils readily available.

Foil bias

When constructing the line-up, which foils do you need to select; people who look like the suspect or people who match the description given by the witness? In a fair line-up, attempts should be made to include foils in the line-up who are similar to the suspect's general physical characteristics as stated in the verbal description given by the witness (Penrod and Bornstein, 2007). But what if the witness describes an offender with a scar on his/her right cheek and the suspect is the only person in the line-up with a scar on the right cheek? Lindsay and Wells (1980) recommend concealing unique features such as tattoos or scars rather than duplicate it on all suspects. However, more recent research finds that duplicating the same feature across the foils results in the same identification accuracy as concealment (Colloff, Wade and Strange, 2016). The important point to remember is that when the suspect stands out in the line-up relative to the other line-up members, uncertain eyewitnesses may be cued to identify the suspect based only on distinctiveness rather than a true match between their memory of the culprit and that line-up member.

Another question is how many foils do you need to select? If witnesses are induced to make line-up identification, a fair line-up will expose the innocent suspect to an identification risk of one divided by the number of persons in the line-up. A line-up in which only two members (the defendant and one other) fit the witness description of the offender increases the identification risk to 50 per cent. Most researchers recommend a line-up of six (one suspect and five foils) to reduce the probability of randomly selecting the suspect to 16 per cent (Wells et al., 1994).

How do you know if a line-up is fair? One technique is to conduct the line-up with a mock witness (people who have not seen any of the line-up members before). In a fair line-up, each of the line-up members should be chosen as the perpetrator at the level of chance. Specifically, in a six-person line-up, each of the members should be chosen no more than 16.7 per cent of the time (1/6).

Clothing

There are two options. The first option is to dress the suspects to match the offender at the scene of the crime (Freire et al., 2004). A second option is to dress the suspects in different clothes from those worn by the offender at the scene of the crime. This second option offers the opportunity to conduct a second test (separate from the line-up) where the witness can identify the clothing worn by the perpetrator (Yarmey, Yarmey and Yarmey, 1996).

Global Perspectives

Virtual identification parades in the UK

Identity parades in the UK have been replaced with a high-tech alternative called VIPER (Video Identification Parade Electronic Recording), which is a digital system for conducting identity parades. Rather than recruit a group of volunteers who resemble a suspect, police can retrieve a choice of prerecorded video recordings of people unrelated to the case. Anyone can volunteer to be part of the database, as long as they don't have facial tattoos or many piercings. Police create a virtual parade, using clips taken from this library, and a witness is then shown these, along with recordings of the current suspect. VIPER was developed by West Yorkshire Police and is now widely used in the UK (Pike et al., 2000). Research shows that correct identification rates of adult mock witnesses do not differ when VIPER line-ups are compared to static photographs (Darling, Valentine and Memon, 2008). Using data supplied by the National VIPER Bureau, researchers reported that VIPER parades produced a slightly higher rate of suspect identifications than live parades – 39 per cent as compared to 35 per cent (Pike, Brace and Kynan, 2002).

Presentation method

There is disagreement about whether simultaneous presentation (all suspects at once) or sequential presentation (suspects shown one at a time) lead to better eyewitness performance. This is a critical issue for the criminal justice system. On one hand, witnesses given a sequential line-up are less likely to identify an innocent suspect; on the other hand, it is less likely that a guilty suspect would be identified.

Sequential presentation

Early research on line-up formats indicated that sequential line-ups provide better witness discrimination than simultaneous line-ups (Lindsay and Wells, 1985; Steblay, Dysart, Fulero and Lindsay, 2001). Better discrimination means that witnesses were less likely to identify a known innocent foil as the suspect. Wells (1984) explains this effect as due to the **absolute-relative judgement theory**, where sequential line-ups provide better witness discrimination because the format encourages witnesses to make a specific judgement against their own memory of the suspect. The witness must decide if the current suspect is the offender before moving to the next suspect without knowing what the next face will look like.

When evaluating faces in a sequential line-up, eyewitnesses may be more conservative during the early part of the line-up compared to later. This position bias happens because witnesses are more concerned with making a misidentification early in the line-up, encouraging conservative judgements, but towards the end of the line-up, witnesses worry that they will make no identification and switch to more liberal judgements (Carlson, Gronlund and Clark, 2008). Position effects are concerning because they suggest that a suspect's order in the line-up affects their chances of being picked, rather than if they are guilty. Although not every study has found a position bias (Carlson and Carlson, 2014), position bias can appear in simultaneous line-ups, with identifications influenced by whether the suspect is in the centre, beginning or end of the presentation (Wells, Steblay and Dysart, 2015).

The differences between the presentation methods seems to disappear under high stakes conditions, as shown by Amendola and Wixted (2015) when using real-world cases in police departments that randomly assigned cases to either a simultaneous or a sequential line-up. They found that witnesses viewing a simultaneous line-up were just as conservative as witnesses viewing a sequential line-up. Given the high stakes decision making of witness identification, witnesses in real-world cases are more conservative than laboratory participant witnesses regardless of line-up format.

Simultaneous presentation

Simultaneous line-ups promote relative judgements, by viewing all suspects together, witnesses estimate which one is closest to their memory. Some researchers have found a slight advantage for simultaneous line-ups (Carlson and Carlson, 2014). This simultaneous advantage is explained by **diagnostic feature detection theory**. This theory states that simultaneous line-ups lead to better discriminability because viewing all line-up suspects (suspect and known innocent foils) together allows witnesses to compare and contrast specific features in each face (Wixted and Mickes, 2014). It may not be surprising then that, in addition to a lower rate of false identifications (picking a known innocent foil), there are more correct identifications from simultaneous line-ups than from sequential line-ups (Moreland and Clark, 2020). The fewer overall identifications made from sequential line-ups suggests that this format promotes more conservative responding in witnesses than simultaneous line-ups (Palmer and Brewer, 2012).

Absolute-relative judgement theory – A strategy found in sequential line-ups when witnesses compare faces from memory rather than to each other.

Diagnostic feature detection theory – Simultaneous line-ups lead to better discriminability because viewing all line-up suspects together allows witnesses to compare specific features in each face.

PART II

There is still debate as to whether simultaneous or sequential line-ups produce better witness identifications. There is no overwhelming evidence for either side. In fact, there is mixed evidence for many of the findings, with some researchers finding an effect and others not detecting the same effect. Ongoing obstacles for researchers in this area include different findings between laboratory studies and real-world cases.

Investigator bias

Double-blind procedure – *Neither the eyewitness nor the line-up administrator knows the identity of the suspect.*

Human decision makers are biased. Typically, the person who administers a line-up is the case detective who knows the identity of the suspect and the foils. To avoid bias, it is important to keep the investigator unaware of the identity of the suspect when they interact with witnesses preventing them from unintentionally communicating their knowledge about which line-up member is the suspect and which members are only foils. This requires double-blind testing, which is well established in the behavioural sciences (Rosenthal, 1976) but is generally unused in criminal investigation procedures. In the **double-blind procedure**, neither the line-up administrators nor the eyewitnesses are made aware of the suspect's identity, thus reducing the potential influence of verbal and nonverbal bias (Douglass and Smalarz, 2019).

Estimator variables

Knowledge of estimator variables allows us to judge whether an eyewitness is likely to be accurate in their identification based on the circumstances of their view of the suspect.

Effect of post-event information on witness confidence

Juries often rely on witness confidence to infer witness accuracy (Wixted et al., 2015). However, the relationship between eyewitness confidence and accuracy is inconsistent (Gustafsson, Lindholm and Jönsson, 2019). Accurate witnesses are as confident as inaccurate witnesses (Brewer, 2006). Witness confidence is influenced by information that the witness receives after the identification line-up; for example, when a witness receives feedback that they identified the same suspect the police did, or that another witness chose the same suspect. Post-event information feedback can make confident witnesses overconfident and it alters other memories related to the crime. Overconfident witnesses tend to overstate the amount of time seeing the suspect, or state that they were closer than they were (Wells and Bradfield, 1998). Unfortunately, post-event confirmation is difficult to prevent because by the time a witness gives evidence in court, they have already received confirming feedback. Witnesses are not asked to attend court if they identified the 'wrong' person (Semmler, Brewer and Wells, 2004).

Because recognition is faster than recall, accurate eyewitness identifications are made significantly faster than inaccurate ones (Ackerman and Koriat, 2011) and witnesses are more accurate when they do not have to be precise. Researchers applied a radical alternative to the traditional line-up (Brewer, Weber, Wootton and Lindsay, 2012). Based on the premise that stronger memory traces are easier to activate than weaker traces, witnesses had a response deadline of only two seconds. Then, instead of only asking for an identification of the correct suspect, the researchers asked the witness to rate how confident they were about their choice. Their experiment used a series of short films of crimes ranging from shoplifting to car theft. Participants examined 12 portraits, only one of which was the actual suspect. Surprisingly, a two-second response deadline increases eyewitness accuracy performance by 25 per cent and when quizzed one week later, those forced to choose quickly were significantly more accurate.

Disguise

How well do people identify faces, even under optimal conditions? Disguise prevents encoding, and identification and identification accuracy generally decreased with the degree of disguise (Mansour et al., 2012). Kemp, Towell and Pike (1997) examined the effectiveness of placing the owner's photograph in a credit card as a means of preventing fraud. In a field study using experienced supermarket checkout operators, staff showed poor accuracy in discriminating identity. Overall, they incorrectly accepted 50 per cent of fraudulent cards containing photographs that did not match the holder.

Gender differences

Common stereotypes suggest that women make more accurate eyewitnesses than men. This misconception is based on studies showing better perceptual abilities in colour vision (Bowmaker, 1998), smell (Dalton, Doolittle and Breslin, 2002) and visual information processing (Murray et al., 2018). Do these enhanced perceptual abilities increase the accuracy of eyewitness identification? Shapiro and Penrod (1986) found that while women seem more accurate than men, they made more identification attempts and, as a result, more mistaken identifications than men, thus cancelling any advantage. Overall, neither gender shows a consistent advantage identifying perpetrators (Geiselman et al., 1984).

Age

Under certain circumstances, children make better eyewitnesses than adults. Researchers showed children and adults videos of a typical bank robbery that did not include a gun (Otgaar, Howe, Merckelbach and Muris, 2018). The adults were more likely than children to agree that they had seen the gun that was not there. In this situation, the lack of detailed cognitive schemas created more accurate memories in children. Laboratory studies show that older subjects make fewer correct responses in tests of face recognition, especially after 50 years of age (O'Rourke, Penrod, Cutler and Stuve, 1989). Police tend to consider witnesses over the age of 60 less dependable and thorough (Allison, Wright and Holliday, 2010). Compounding this effect, potential jurors also believe that older witnesses are less competent. Evidence of age stereotyping is presented by Kwong See, Hoffman and Wood (2001), who found that participants judged a younger (age 28) female witness as more accurate and competent than an older (age 82) female witness, although they did consider the older female to be more honest.

Intellectual challenges

The criminal justice system generally believes people with intellectual challenges have inferior memory and therefore produce less effective testimony (Kebbell and Wagstaff, 1999). To investigate this stereotype, Ternes and Yuille (2008) examined the performance of witnesses with and without intellectual challenges. In a clever twist, participants had to identify a photographer who had taken their picture one to two weeks earlier. Findings showed no difference in accuracy between the two groups. Although fewer details were given by those in the intellectually challenged group, these details were still accurate.

Question format can negatively affect witnesses with cognitive impairment. For example, such witnesses often display an **acquiescence bias** – they are more likely to answer 'yes' to questions of which they are unsure. This produces unreliable and contradictory statements, especially during cross-examination. The solution is to use open-ended questions that encourage free recall, such as 'Tell me what you saw yesterday morning' (Kebbell and Hatton, 1999).

Acquiescence bias – *The tendency for respondents to agree with statements regardless of their content.*

Racial differences

The **cross-race effect** is the tendency for eyewitnesses to be better at recognising faces of people who are of the same race as them than those who are of a different race to them (Wilson, Hugenberg and Bernstein, 2013). Sadozai, Kempen, Tredoux and Robbins (2019) explain that the bias is due to the depth of cross-racial friendships rather than the number of friends of different races. In this context, depth of friendship includes more than just the number of shared activities, it includes the depth of self-disclosure, emotional expressiveness and connectedness (Plummer, Stone, Powell and Allison, 2016).

Alcohol intoxication

Alcohol intoxication reduces memory and increases suggestibility during questioning (Oorsouw, Broers and Sauerland, 2019). Memory impairment is due to less rehearsal, poor attention and poor visual information processing. This leads to poor encoding (Saults, Cowan, Sher and Moreno, 2007) and impairs retrieval and storage (Dudai, 2004; Lee, Roh and Kim, 2009) by disrupting the consolidation of memories (Karlén, 2017). Curiously, alcohol consumption *during* encoding and retrieval does not impair face identification during recognition (Altman et al., 2018).

The effect of stress

The effects of stress on memory can be viewed through the **cue utilisation hypothesis** – as arousal increases, attention narrows, blocking the encoding of information (Easterbrook, 1959). However, the relationship between stress and eyewitness memory is more complex, and stressful situations do not always impair memory; in fact, they may even enhance it (Cahill and Alkireb, 2003). Evidence for stress enhancing memory is supported by **flashbulb memories** – extremely vivid memories of an emotional event (Maswood, Rasmussen and Rajaram, 2018). The intensity of an experience enhances the memory by entangling emotional and factual components and increasing the amount of memory cues connected with the event. There are three circumstances likely to create a vivid flashbulb memory (Conway, 1995):

1   the memory trace is important to the individual

2   it is a surprising event

3   it has an emotional effect on the individual.

Weapon focus

Another estimator variable is the **weapon focus effect**. When a weapon is produced, subjects focus on the weapon rather than other features of the incident (Kebbell and Wagstaff, 1999). This produces poorer recall of the weapon holder's face, lower line-up accuracy, and lower ability to describe the features of the perpetrator (Steblay, 1997). An explanation is that eyewitnesses give more accurate descriptions of unusual threatening objects when compared with descriptions of novel but nonthreatening objects (Mansour, Hamilton and Gibson, 2018). Remarkably, bank tellers (Fashing, Ask and Granhag, 2004) and the police (Hulse and Memnon, 2006) seem immune to its effects. In fact, it had been shown that educating people about the weapon focus effect can neutralise it, increasing concentration on the peripheral details of the perpetrator's appearance (Pickel, Ross and Ruelove, 2006).

Examples of flawed procedures in the Steve Titus case

CASE STUDY

It was dusk on an October night in 1980 when a young female hitchhiker was picked up on Pacific Highway South, 10 miles outside Seattle, Washington, by a man with a beard and a three-piece suit. Instead of driving her to Tacoma, the man turned onto an isolated dirt road, raped her, and left her by the side of the road. Steve Titus was stopped for questioning by police because his car's licence plate and description were both generally like those given by the rape victim. He willingly cooperated with the police when they asked him if they could take his photograph. The victim was shown Steve's two photographs (a profile and full-face shot) with photos of five other men who resembled Steve. However, Steve's photos were smaller than the others and were not separated by a black line as the other photos were. Police instructed the victim: 'Tell me which one raped you.' After studying the photos for five minutes, the victim finally pointed to one of Steve's photos and said, 'This one is the closest' (Olsen, 1991, p. 169). On this basis, the victim identified Steve as her rapist and, mostly because of her testimony, Steve was found guilty.

But a few months after Steve's conviction, an investigative report with the *Seattle Times* led police to question the verdict. Small but significant details did not make sense. For example, the victim reported that the car had velvet seats and Steve's were vinyl. The rapist was wearing a three-piece suit, and Steve did not own any kind of suit (Olsen, 1991). New evidence suggested it was Edward Lee King (Olsen used the pseudonym Mac Smith in his book), who later confessed to the rape. He was believed to have committed more than 50 rapes, including this one. When the victim saw the photograph of the new suspect, she realised that he was her rapist and broke down in tears (Wise, Dauphinais and Safer, 2007).

Although Steve Titus was released, his life was in shambles: he spent all his savings on his defence, lost his job and good reputation, and his fiancée left him. Steve spent the next four years in a struggle to sue the authorities. Eleven days before the case was to come to trial, Steve died of a heart attack. Ten months later, his estate was awarded a settlement of $2.8 million.

Discussion Questions:

1   Does this case reflect problems with system or estimator variables?

2   Based on what we know about human memory and recognition, what mistakes can you identify in the *presentation* of the photos?

3   When the photo of Steve Titus was chosen, the witness said: 'This one is the closest.' Based on what we know about human memory and recognition, what mistakes can you identify in the *selection* of the photo?

IN SUMMARY

The traditional live line-up is expensive and time-consuming and is rarely used. Alternative methods like the photo array are used more often. With proper design and taking into account system and estimator variables, line-ups can produce accurate identifications.

CRITICAL THINKING AND APPLICATION QUESTIONS

1   What practical advice would you offer police about the fair and effective conduct of line-ups?

2   How can you apply the double-blind approach used in psychological experiments to suspect line-ups and the review of photo arrays?

3   What evidence supports and undermines the influence of the weapon focus effect?

THE ROLE OF THE FORENSIC PSYCHOLOGIST

FICTION: Forensic psychology cannot improve on the traditional methods of collection and preservation of memories.

Versus

FACT: The application of psychological concepts offers more valid and reliable methods to collect and preserve memories.

We end this chapter reviewing three essential roles forensic psychologists play to ensure accurate identifications. First, applying psychological safeguards to ensure effective data collection through standardised methods for identification procedures. Second, applying the same techniques already used to preserve physical evidence to preserve memories. Third, increasing education to address the fiction that the live line-up is superior to other methods of identification.

First, psychological safeguards need to apply the same approaches to designing line-ups and ensuring that the identification of a suspect is the product of the eyewitness's memory and not the identification procedure. These safeguards include:

- eliminating the presence of demand characteristics by reducing pressure on the eyewitness to make a choice

- avoiding subtle confirmatory biases by asking questions about the suspect and not asking the same questions about the foils

- leaking the hypothesis and making it obvious to the eyewitness which person in the line-up is the suspect

- making judgements from small sample sizes based on only one eyewitness

- using a control group. For example, police can investigate if people who did not see the crime, but have only the eyewitness description of the perpetrator, can still identify the suspect.

Second, the forensic psychologist's most significant role is the process of collecting and preserving eyewitness memory. Specifically, eyewitness evidence should be treated like trace evidence collected at the crime scene (DNA, fingerprints, bullet ballistics). Like trace evidence, memories have a physiological basis in the patterns of biochemical changes in the brain. Additionally, eyewitness evidence, like other types of trace evidence, depends on the use of proper procedures in collection and preservation. Proper procedures prevent contamination of physical evidence in the same way that post-event information contaminates or distorts memories. When post-event information alters a memory, the original memories are lost.

Global Perspectives

The unbiased nature of DNA evidence

Australia has its share of innocent people who were falsely convicted. Among the most high-profile cases are:

- Lindy Chamberlain, who was wrongfully convicted of murdering baby Azaria

- Andrew Mallard, who was wrongfully convicted of murder

- Pamela Lawrence, who served 12 years in jail

- Alexander McLeod-Lindsay, who served a 9-year jail term for the attempted murder of his wife before he was eventually exonerated

- Roseanne Beckett, who served 10 years for planning to kill her husband but was exonerated, and awarded $4 million in damages (Koubaridis, 2016).

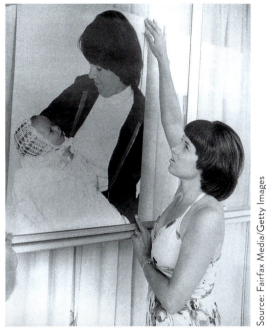

Source: Fairfax Media/Getty Images

Lindy Chamberlain with a photo of herself and Azaria, her missing nine-month-old baby daughter, following the first inquest that concluded a dingo took her baby from a bassinet inside a family tent

Innocence Projects were inspired by DNA testing methods in the early 1990s to prove claims of innocence (for more information on worldwide Innocence Projects, go to www.innocenceproject.org.) Their mission is to free innocent people and to reform systems responsible for their unjust imprisonment. Griffith University in South East Queensland established its own Innocence Project in 2001 and employs students to examine cases without charge, supervised by lawyers and academics. It discovered that DNA testing is unbiased, sometimes supporting the defence and sometimes the prosecution.

In 1991, Shane Sebastian Davis was incarcerated for nearly two decades for a murder he claimed he didn't commit. Davis was convicted of killing a 19-year-old South African woman named Michelle Cohn who was on holiday on Australia's Gold Coast with her family. The Griffith University Innocence Project convinced the state to retest the DNA evidence using more accurate technology. In 2010, retesting confirmed with even *greater* accuracy that the original DNA evidence was correct, and Davis was, in fact, guilty (Taylor, 2010).

Third, research evidence points to the demise of the live line-up (identification parade) as an effective identification tool. For all its flaws, there is still a stubborn belief in the power of a live line-up over other methods. Fitzgerald, Price and Valentine (2018) investigated this widely held belief known as the **line-up superiority hypothesis** – the belief that the live presentation of line-up members produces the best eyewitness identification outcomes. The consequence of this belief is that it makes eyewitnesses more conservative in their identifications from a live line-up compared with a photo or video identification (Dent and Stevenson, 1979). Price and colleagues (2018) suggest that this is based on an intuitive belief that the realism offered by a live line-up offers more behavioural and physical cues. While there is some support that extra physical cues

Line-up superiority hypothesis – *The belief that live presentation of line-up members yields the best eyewitness identification outcomes.*

improve the ability to match images (Rice et al., 2013), the connection has not been made with eyewitness identification accuracy.

Finally, Wells, Memon and Penrod (2006) question whether the existence of the live line-up technique has stifled progress in eyewitness identification. Without the traditional line-up, new empirical identification methods may have been established. For example, measures based on brain activity (Xue, Chen, Lu and Dong, 2010), automated measures of gait analysis (Seckiner et al., 2019) and micro-expressions (Matsumoto and Hwang, 2018).

IN SUMMARY

The application of psychological concepts offers more valid and reliable ways to ensure standardised methods for identification procedures and the preservation of memories.

 CRITICAL THINKING AND APPLICATION QUESTIONS

1   Review three roles the forensic psychologist plays to ensure accurate identifications. Find a peer-reviewed research article related to one of these three roles. Include the source of the research, the hypothesis and at least one major finding.

2   In what ways should memories be treated like trace evidence found at a crime scene?

3   Despite the challenges and availability of better methods, why do you think the belief in the superiority of the live identification procedure exists?

CHAPTER REVIEW

We began by investigating the myth that memory is a recording that can be accurately replayed when needed. The truth is that memories are continually rewritten with information from before and after the event, and altered based on our expectations, biases and preconceptions. Once the process of memory is understood, the advantages of the cognitive interview over the standard interview technique are obvious. We can obtain more accurate and useful information from eyewitnesses by applying the cognitive interview than the standard interview. Finally, despite the belief in the superiority of live identification procedures, this approach is not as effective, fair, or accurate as other methods like photo and video presentations. In conclusion, unless we are relentlessly sceptical of the past, we will continue to confuse fact with fiction while innocent victims are punished.

NAMES TO KNOW

Elizabeth Loftus
A leading researcher in the *unreliability* of eyewitness testimony. Her innovative studies show how leading questions could influence eyewitness reports and demonstrate the misinformation effect.

- Loftus, E. F. (2018) Eyewitness science and the legal system. *Annual Review of Law and Science*, 14, 1–10.

- Loftus, E. F. and Palmer, J. C. (1974) Reconstruction of automobile destruction: An example of the interaction between language and memory. *Journal of Verbal Learning and Verbal Behavior*, 13(5), 585–9.

Becky Milne

A chartered forensic psychologist and scientist. The main focus of her work is the examination of police interviewing and investigation.

- Ryan, N., Westera, N., Kebbell, M. R., Milne, B. and Mark, H. (2019) Where is the body? Investigative interviewing strategies in missing body homicide cases. *Investigative Interviewing: Research and Practice*, 10(1), 61–77.

- Ryan, N., Westera, N., Kebbell, M., Milne, B. and Mark, H. (2020) To know where the bodies are buried: The use of the cognitive interview in an environmental scale spatial memory retrieval task. *Applied Cognitive Psychology*, https://doi.org/10.1002/acp.3640.

Amina Memon

Investigates real-world cognitive techniques in police investigations by applying social psychological approaches to understanding memory, decision making, detection of deception and credibility assessment.

- Memon, A., Andrews, B. and Davies, G. (2014) Memory: Sifting the evidence. *The Psychologist*, 27(9), 636.

- Theunissen, T., Meyer, T., Memon, A. and Weinsheimer, C. (2017) Adult eyewitness memory for single versus repeated traumatic events. *Applied Cognitive Psychology*, 31(2), 164–74.

PART II

3

TECHNIQUES FOR INTERVIEWING CHILDREN

Chapter Introduction

Interviewing children about physical and sexual abuse is the most critical step in a child sexual abuse evaluation. Unfortunately, it can also be the most difficult and frustrating part of an investigation. It is possible to obtain valuable information from children, but doing so requires careful investigative procedures, as well as a realistic awareness of their abilities. In this chapter, you will discover that children's cognitive abilities are both similar and different to adults in important ways. Regrettably, the lessons learned from psychological research have been inconsistently applied to protect children from further psychological trauma. Because of this, courts have considered children unreliable and their testimony inadmissible, allowing their victimisers to go unpunished.

Learning Outcomes

Are children good witnesses?

- Be able to justify children's capacity to provide valid and reliable information under the right circumstances.

Best practices when interviewing children

- Explain what interview procedures should be avoided with children to collect accurate and reliable information.

How to conduct a forensic interview

- Demonstrate the best practices for interviewing children using the revised National Institute of Child Health and Human Development (NICHD) interview protocol.

Managing the challenges of compassion fatigue

- Describe the characteristics and ways to prevent compassion fatigue.

ARE CHILDREN GOOD WITNESSES?

FICTION: Children are second-class witnesses compared with adults.

Versus

FACT: If interviewed properly, children are equal and sometimes better witnesses than adults.

When interviewing children, forensic psychologists are challenged to identify anything that prevents comprehension, recall and reporting of past events (Azzopardia et al., 2019). For example, did the child have a reason to withhold, fabricate or falsify information? Can a child understand the events they observed? However, sometimes it is not the children but rather the adults that are the root of the problem, as illustrated by the case of the McMartin preschool.

CASE STUDY — The McMartin preschool

Source: Ken Lubas/Los Angeles Times/Getty Images

It started with a phone call to the local police by Judy Johnson, the mother of a two-and-a-half-year-old boy who attended McMartin preschool in California, USA. Johnson claimed that a school aide, Ray Buckey, the 25-year-old son of the owner of the preschool, had molested her son. Despite the fact that the boy was unable to identify Ray from photos and medical investigations showed no signs of sexual abuse, the police conducted searches of Ray's home, confiscating 'evidence', such as a rubber duck, graduation robe, Teddy bear, *Playboy* magazines, and arrested Ray (Leroy and Haddad, 2018).

Raymond McMartin and his mother Peggy Buckey on trial in the McMartin preschool child molestation case

Afterwards, 200 parents received a letter from the chief of police informing them that Ray, an employee of their child's preschool, had been arrested for child molestation. The letter asked parents to 'question your child to see if he or she has been a witness to any crime or if he or she has been a victim'. After providing a list of possible criminal acts, the letter stated that 'any information from your child regarding having ever observed Ray leave a classroom alone with a child during nap period, or if they have ever observed Ray tie up a child, is important'. Judy Johnson's reports of misbehaviour at the McMartin preschool became increasingly bizarre. She claimed that Peggy Buckey, Ray's mother, was involved in satanic practices: she was said to have taken Johnson's son to a church, where the boy was made to watch a baby being beheaded, and then was forced to drink the blood. She insisted that Ray had sodomised her son while his head was in the toilet and had taken him to a car wash and locked him in the trunk. Johnson told police that Ray pranced around the preschool in a cape and a Santa Claus costume, and that other teachers at the school chopped up rabbits and placed 'some sort of star' on her son's bottom (Butler, Fukurai, Dimitrius and Krooth, 2001).

Eventually, prosecutors recognised Judy's bizarre allegations as the delusions of a paranoid schizophrenic, whose dark visions infested the attitudes of the community (Leroy and Haddad,

2018). It was too late to stop the accusations. The letter from the police led to demands from parents for a full-scale investigation of the McMartin preschool. Giving in to this pressure, the District Attorney's office handed the investigation to Kee MacFarlane, a consultant for the Children's Institute International (CII), an agency for the treatment of abused children. Parents were encouraged to send their children to the CII for two-hour interviews. Ultimately, 400 children were interrogated, often using leading questions and offers of rewards to report abuse. At first, children denied seeing any evidence of abuse, but eventually many told the stories that they wanted to hear. The stories became more bizarre. In addition to sexual abuse, the children had been taken on plane rides and forced to drink blood and watch animal mutilations. By March 1984, 384 former McMartin students had been identified as sexually abused (Nathan and Snedecker, 1995).

This was one of the first multi-victim, multi-offender child abuse cases – an investigation that lasted six years with no convictions (Butler, Fukurai, Dimitrius and Krooth, 2001).

Discussion Questions:

1   How did the content of the letter alter the way parents interviewed their children?

2   What physical evidence was produced to verify the claims of molestation?

3   Why does having multiple victims seem to increase the perception of guilt? (Remember, no convictions were obtained.)

What does it mean to be a vulnerable witness?

A witness can be vulnerable due to their age, incapacity or circumstances (Cooper and Mattison, 2017). While physical vulnerability is easier to define, psychological vulnerabilities are best thought of as *potential* risk factors. These risk factors place children at a disadvantage in terms of coping with the demands of an interview and providing detailed, accurate and clear answers to questions (Gudjonsson, 2010). In fact, until the 1980s, children were considered inferior to adults and labelled 'second-class witnesses' (Westcott, 2006).

Exposure to adverse childhood experiences

A predictor of physical and psychological vulnerability is exposure to adverse childhood experiences (ACEs). An **adverse childhood experiences (ACE) score** is the frequency of abuse, neglect and other adverse experiences during childhood.

The Adverse Childhood Experiences (ACE) Study is one of the largest investigations ever conducted to assess associations between childhood exposure to traumatic stressors and health and wellbeing in adulthood. The study surveyed 217,337 adult health maintenance organisation members who responded to a questionnaire about adverse childhood experiences, including childhood abuse, neglect and family dysfunction (ACE Study, 2018). The ACE Study revealed that higher scores are strongly related to adult health problems (Larkin, Shields and Anda, 2012). Health problems related to higher ACE scores include greater rates of depression, suicide attempts, alcoholism, drug abuse, sexual promiscuity, domestic violence, cigarette smoking, obesity, physical inactivity and sexually transmitted diseases. In addition, the more adverse childhood experiences reported, the more likely a person was to develop heart disease, cancer, stroke, diabetes, skeletal fractures and liver disease (Gilbert et al. 2019; Ports et al. 2019; Felitti et al., 1998).

However, there is a positive side to this study. Exposure to adverse childhood experiences does *not* guarantee poor health across generations (Bethell, Newacheck, Hawes and Halfon, 2014). The reason for this optimism is that the ACE scores do not

Adverse childhood experiences (ACE) score – *The frequency of distinct types of abuse, neglect and other adverse experiences during childhood.*

count the frequency of positive experiences, such as sensitive and supportive relationships, during infancy and early childhood, which can help build resilience and protect a child from the effects of trauma (Merrick and Guinn, 2018).

The ACE Pyramid (see Figure 3.1) is the conceptual framework for the ACE Study. The pyramid represents missing information connecting adverse childhood experiences with risk factors that lead to physical and psychological health consequences higher up the pyramid, that is, later in life (CDC, 2012).

Figure 3.1: The ACE Pyramid: mechanisms by which adverse childhood experiences influence health and wellbeing throughout the lifespan

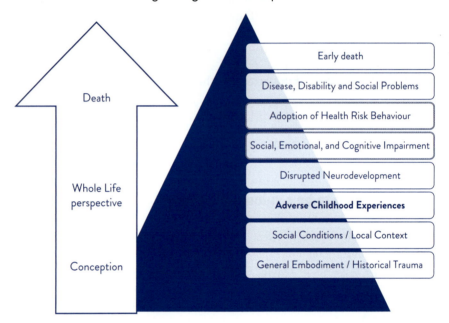

Source: ACE Study, CDC-Kaiser, 2018. ACE Pyramid developed by the Centers for Disease Control and Prevention. Reproduction does not constitute its endorsement or recommendation by the US Government, Department of Health and Human Services, or Centers for Disease Control and Prevention.

How is a child determined 'competent' and 'credible' to stand trial?

Competency – *The ability to deliver reliable testimony.*

The **competency** of any witness is their ability to deliver reliable testimony, while the **credibility** of a witness is the degree to which a judge or jury believes that the witness can deliver honest and accurate testimony. In many judicial systems, determining if a witness is competent is often left to the judge (Evans and Lyon, 2012), who usually relies on four characteristics to assess witness credibility:

1   *Honesty*: Is the child able to give accurate evidence?

2   *Memory*: Is the child's memory accurate and complete?

3   *Suggestibility*: Do they show distorted memories after questioning?

4   *Communication ability*: Can they communicate adequately?

Credibility – *The degree to which a judge or jury believes that the witness can deliver honest and accurate testimony.*

Together, these form an assessment of how well the witness understands the questions and can communicate about the issue in question (Bala, Ramakrishnan, Lindsay and Lee, 2005; Lyon and Saywitz, 1999).

Are children good observers?

Children's *recognition memory*, that is, the ability to recognise previously encountered events, objects or people, becomes more dependable and accurate with age (Riggins and Rollins, 2015). For example, recognition memory is evident in children less than a year old, and by the time a child is five years old, they demonstrate adult-level recognition memory performance (Karably and Zabrucky, 2009). For simple recognition memory, children outperform adults. When identifying pictures of animals seen previously, children displayed accurate recognition rates of 31 per cent, while adults scored only 7 per cent (Sloutsky and Fisher, 2004). The surprising explanation is that, unlike children, adult recognition recall is slowed by filtering their perceptions through their vast networks of memory (Sloutsky and Fisher, 2004). Therefore, for simple events that do not require earlier experience to understand, children have an advantage (Perlmutter and Myers, 1976). However, without previous experience, children have greater difficulty understanding more complicated behaviours, such as drug use, deception and sexual issues. The lack of experience makes them more susceptible to the misleading effects of leading questions (Goodman and Melinder, 2010).

Sadly, children's ability to *identify* a perpetrator is not the crucial issue, because 80 per cent of the people responsible for child maltreatment are the children's own parents (Kolk, 2005). So, if recognition memory is not a problem for collecting forensically relevant information from children, what is? The answer lies in the developing brain's ability to accurately reconstruct the past. While children are more observant than adults, their accuracy decreases when asked to recall autobiographical information (i.e., episodic memory; see Chapter 2).

The origins of the myth that children make poor witnesses

Sigmund Freud's belief that children confuse memories of fantasy with memories of reality is the origin of doubts about children's testimony (Alison, Kebbell and Lewis, 2006). Early in Freud's career, his adult clients described traumatic sexual experiences from their early childhood. Freud reported that many young girls were sexually abused by adults (most often their fathers). Freud initially believed these reports of abuse and thought that he had uncovered the origins of neurosis – a coping strategy caused by unsuccessfully repressed emotions from past experiences. Unfortunately, Freud changed his mind and decided that his patients' reports were only repressed memories of childhood fantasies, rather than real memories of childhood experiences (Boag, 2006; Masson, 1984). Although we may never know the reason why Freud changed his mind, Goldberg (2010) offers several explanations, from Freud's own molestation as an infant by his nursemaid, the poor reception of his paper on the sexual origins of hysteria in 1896, to the prevalence of infantile sexual molestation at that time (Gay, 2006). Decades after Freud cast doubt on children's testimony, questions about the ability of children to provide legally accurate testimony are still widespread.

However, juror belief in the credibility of children's testimony is tenuous. Whether jurors believe a child depends on many factors. These include how the child was interviewed before appearing in court, the child's motives to lie or tell the truth, the child's demeanour, and the nature of the child's testimony (Bala, Ramakrishnan, Lindsay and Lee, 2005).

Childhood memory and amnesia

The alleged gap between the reliability of memory between children and adults appears exaggerated (Saywitz, Lyon and Goodwin, 2017; Spencer and Flin, 1990). Adult memories are as fragile and susceptible to the distorting influences of suggestion and misinformation as children's (Otgaar, Howe, Muris and Merckelbach, 2019). Research on child development shows that by the time a child is four years old, they have the moral, cognitive and linguistic capacity to be a credible witness (Piaget, 1964).

With careful prompting, children as young as two years old can answer questions about recent events (Morrison and Conway, 2010). Over the next four or five years, children's recall improves, and they can describe important events in their lives. By the age of seven or eight, most children have well-developed episodic memories (van Abbema and Bauer, 2005). However, when questioned about earlier memories, children and adults seldom recall accurate memories of events that happened earlier than age three or four, and these early memories become harder to access as they age (Bauer and Larkina, 2014; Madsen and Kim, 2016).

An explanation of **childhood amnesia** – people's inability to remember anything that happened to them prior to three or four years of age – lies in the critical periods of brain development around age four. If we think of memory as a set of dynamic processes, then our ability to form lasting memories happens during the critical periods of interaction between developing brain structures (Craik, 2020). Specifically, long-term lasting memories require the interaction of two essential structures in our memory system, the **hippocampus** (responsible for consolidating memories) and the **amygdala** (responsible for giving memories their emotional significance) (Alberini and Travaglia, 2017; Manns et al., 2003). As these structures mature, the ability to retain personally experienced information (i.e., episodic memories) strengthens (Wang et al., 2019).

Childhood amnesia –
The inability of adults to remember episodic experiences that occurred prior to age three.

Hippocampus –
A brain structure responsible for consolidating memories.

Amygdala –
An almond-shaped brain structure responsible for the response to and memory of emotions, especially fear.

When do our earliest memories begin?

There is something strangely consistent about our earliest childhood memories. To find out, ask three people to describe their earliest childhood memories. When finished, ask them to estimate how old they were. You should see two patterns. First, the most frequently reported age is between three and four years and, second, the memories involve feeling strong emotions, such as happiness, pain, anger, frustration.

This is because the brain structures responsible for the storage of long-term memories, like our hippocampus, do not mature until around ages three or four years and emotional memories activate a nearby structure called the amygdala. Your amygdale (there are two, one in each hemisphere) handle adding emotional flavour to your memories. If you think about it, without emotion, the memory of your grandmother would be equal to where you parked your car. Therefore, when someone claims to remember their time in the womb or birth experience, or any memories younger than age three, you should be sceptical about the real source of those memories.

Discovering the causes of childhood amnesia is ethically challenging, because we cannot intentionally expose children to traumatic events. Thus, we do *not* know if traumatic memories are inaccessible because they are encoded and stored differently from memories of non-traumatic events (Pezdek and Lam, 2007). What we *do* know is that most people who are victims of childhood sexual abuse remember all or part of what happened to them (Howe, 2019; Goodman et al., 2003).

When do we learn to lie?

Although children as young as two years old have the ability to lie, they do not understand the motivations for lying (Ekman, [1985]2009). Children's ability to lie matures with age. For example, children around the age of two begin by telling *primary lies*, that is, lies intended to conceal wrongdoings – 'I did not take the biscuit.' But they do not take the mental state of the listener into consideration. Around the age of four, children learn to tell *secondary lies*, that is, more believable lies matching the listener's mental development – 'I didn't take the biscuit, the dog ate it.' By age eight, children learn to tell *tertiary lies*, that is, lies that are more consistent with known facts and follow-up statements – 'I didn't take the biscuit, look at my hands, there's no chocolate on them' (Talwar, Gordon and Kang, 2007).

The ability to accurately recall events matures during childhood, as does the ability to distinguish experiences and thoughts as your own or someone else's. This ability is known as the **theory of mind** (Korkmaz, 2011) and it explains when children master the ability to keep secrets and lie (Gordon, Lyon and Lee, 2014). Evidence of an emerging theory of mind typically appears around age four (Korkmaz, 2011). Lying relies on the theory of mind, because successful liars must understand both their mental state and their listener's. Finally, the development of humour depends on a child's developing theory of mind because both are complex, higher-order cognitive processes that rely on an understanding of the beliefs and motivations of others (Aykan and Nalçacı, 2018).

> **Theory of mind** – *Understanding the mental states of others and recognising that those mental states differ from our own.*

PART II

IN SUMMARY

Beliefs that children have limited ability to observe, recall and report memories is a myth. Children do make good witnesses if they are interviewed in a developmentally appropriate manner.

 CRITICAL THINKING AND APPLICATION QUESTIONS

1   Historically, children were considered 'second-class witnesses'. What are the biases against using children as eyewitnesses?

2   Your roommate describes their earliest memory as being in the womb and hearing their mother's heartbeat. Explain why this is not possible by describing when our memory processing abilities develop. Can you offer an alternative explanation of this memory?

3   Present a unique example that shows how a child's *lack* of a theory of mind affects their ability to understand deception or humour.

BEST PRACTICES WHEN INTERVIEWING CHILDREN

FICTION: Child interviews must use specific focused questions because abused children do not disclose their abuse.

Versus

FACT: Using specific focused questions is a problem because children are more vulnerable to suggestive questioning formats.

Interviewing children is a strategic challenge, because the interviewer must collect complete, truthful and forensically accurate information while deciding how much information to present (Teoh and Lamb, 2013; APSAC, 2012). Also, interviewers must be aware of their own pre-existing beliefs that can bias their information-gathering strategies (Orbach and Pipe, 2011).

The Sam Stone study: suggestive questioning and stereotypes

How much can improper interview strategies distort a child's memory? Leichtman and Ceci (1995) asked this question in their classic experiment that began with the classroom visit of a stranger named Sam Stone. Sam's visit was always the same. First, he entered the classroom and said 'hello' to a teacher sitting among the children during a storytelling session, and he was introduced by the teacher. Next, he commented on the story the teacher was reading, by saying 'I know that story; it's one of my favourites!' and strolled around the perimeter of the classroom. Finally, he left, waving goodbye to the children (Leichtman and Ceci, 1995, p. 1).

The children were exposed to three conditions: stereotypes, suggestion, and a combination of both. In the stereotype group, the teacher read stories about Sam's clumsy nature before his visit. In the suggestion group, the children were not given any stereotype information about Sam's clumsy nature, but were interviewed with suggestive questions that implied Sam had ripped a book and stained a teddy bear. In the stereotype *and* suggestion group, the children were read the stereotyping stories and interviewed with suggestive questions.

After five weeks, all the children were asked a free recall question: 'Remember the day Sam Stone visited your school? Well, I wasn't there that day, and I'd like you to tell me everything that happened when he visited.' This was followed by specific but neutral probing questions regarding whether Sam had damaged the book or the teddy bear: 'Did you hear about the book or teddy bear and see Sam do something to them during his visit?' Additionally, for only those children whose answers to the questions indicated that they actually saw Sam commit the non-events, gentle challenge questions were posed, to attempt to gauge the strength of their statements: 'You didn't really see him do this, did you?'

In an ingenious conclusion, the authors showed a video of the children describing Sam's actions to various groups of child protection professionals. Their intention was to see if they could distinguish between the accurate and inaccurate accounts based only on the children's statements. They could not. In fact, the professionals rated the children who gave the accurate responses of the events as the least credible, and the children who gave the inaccurate responses as the most credible!

Discussion Questions:

1   Do you believe that this was a realistic experiment? Specifically, in what ways was the experiment similar to what might happen during courtroom testimony?

2   Does research support or refute the idea that a comparable experiment redesigned to use adults would reveal similar findings?

3   If you were allowed to interview the children, what strategies would you use to find out which were telling the truth, and which were relying on false memories?

The role of the interviewer

Children can be vital sources of information during criminal investigations and court proceedings. The best hope for truthful testimony is competent pretrial interviewing combined with a legal system that prepares children for the courtroom experience, supports them through the process and allows a reasonable amount of cross-examination. Whenever children are involved in the fact-finding process associated with legal proceedings, the question of their fitness as a witness is the prime consideration. The issues of competency and reliability have traditionally been defined in terms of the characteristics of the witness (e.g., age, IQ), but with children, the way questions are asked has a stronger influence on the accuracy of their answers than does any characteristic of the child (Klemfuss and Ceci, 2012).

Poorly constructed interviews can have terrible consequences: from memory contamination and distortion to false convictions or even releasing abusers to harm other children. With these consequences in mind, we will review six questionable interview strategies (Figure 3.2).

Figure 3.2: Six questionable strategies when interviewing children

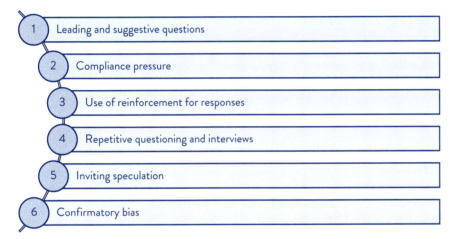

1. Leading and suggestive questions
2. Compliance pressure
3. Use of reinforcement for responses
4. Repetitive questioning and interviews
5. Inviting speculation
6. Confirmatory bias

Leading and suggestive questions

A challenge when interviewing children who are reluctant to respond is to avoid **leading questions** – questions that assume a specific answer. For the interviewer, the dilemma is that without using this strategy, the child might be reluctant to respond. Yet, the nature of the question might cause the child to answer in the suggested way, even when the answer does not reflect the child's factual beliefs. More than simply asking the child a set of leading questions, **suggestive questioning** is more manipulative and subtle. Garvin, Wood, Malpass and Shaw (1998) explain that suggestive questions introduce new information into an interview when the child has not already provided that information.

Another suggestive questioning strategy is using manufactured experiences; the use of figure drawing, anatomically correct dolls and visualisation procedures. Using manufactured experiences is a controversial topic in the field of forensic interviewing (Earhart, La Rooy and Lamb, 2016; Wolfman, Brown and Jose, 2018). While some researchers recommend the use of anatomically correct dolls with nonverbal children who can communicate by pointing (Collings, 2017), others have recommended caution or limiting the use of media (Lyon, 2015), some recommend ending the use of these tools (Poole and Dickinson, 2011)

Leading questions – *Questions that assume a specific answer.*

Suggestive questioning – *Introducing new information into an interview when the child has not already provided that information.*

and yet others have said that the use of dolls or diagrams is similar to 'ancient divination techniques' (Poole and Bruck, 2012).

Any critique of anatomical dolls, the most controversial of the manufactured experiences, must consider the specific function the dolls serve in the evaluation. Specific uses of anatomical dolls include sexual abuse evaluations, comforter, icebreaker, anatomical model, demonstration aid, memory stimulus, diagnostic screen and diagnostic test (Everson and Boat, 1994). Importantly, the use of dolls to diagnose sexual abuse (diagnostic test use) is *not* endorsed by *any* guidelines and is open to significant criticism (Wolfman, Brown and Jose, 2018).

The critical problem with these techniques is the introduction of a significant amount of new experiences that must be incorporated into the child's memory and later distinguished by the child from the memory of actual events (Lamb et al., 2018; Blizard and Shaw, 2019).

Compliance pressure

Compliance pressure was initially demonstrated in Solomon Asch's classic experiment (Asch, 1955). Asch asked groups of students to take part in a 'vision test' examining different length lines. The unique part of Asch's experiment was that all but one of the participants were **confederates** – persons who are accomplices helping the experimenter. The study was really about how often the remaining students would conform their behaviour to match the confederates' strange behaviour. To create the pressure to conform, the real subject and the confederates were asked a variety of questions about the lines – which line is longer than the other, which lines are the same length. The group was told to report their answers to each question aloud. The confederates always provided their answers before the study participant, and always gave the same answer as each other. The confederates answered a few questions correctly but eventually began confidently giving incorrect responses. Before the experiment, Asch assumed that most people would not conform to something so obviously wrong; however, when surrounded by individuals all voicing an incorrect answer, 75 per cent of the participants complied and gave an incorrect answer to at least one question. These strategies create enormous conformity pressure (Candel, Merckelbach, Loyen and Reyskens, 2005).

Given the power of conformity, it is not surprising that the statements of other witnesses affect witness memory (Shaw, Garvin and Wood, 1997). This effect is exploited when the interviewer tells the child that they have already obtained information from another child about the topic. For example, 'Every single kid in a class picture had already talked to her about a whole bunch of yucky secrets from the school' (Garvin et al., 1998, p. 348).

> **Confederate** – A person who is an accomplice helping the experimenter.

Use of reinforcement for responses

Reinforcement is any consequence that causes the preceding behaviour to increase (Skinner, 1938). Radical behaviourist B. F. Skinner believed that a behaviour (i.e., an operant) is shaped by its consequences. Positive consequences (reinforcement) shape our behaviour as much as negative consequences (punishment) (Skinner, 1971). In the context of interviewing children, strategically presenting or removing rewards and punishments manipulates the child's responses. The effects of four types of operant reinforcement strategies are shown in Table 3.1. It is important to remember that children are more vulnerable than adults to suggestive influences of reinforcement (Friedman and Ceci, 2000) and these manipulative interview strategies should *never* be applied during an interview.

Table 3.1: Four improper operant reinforcement strategies

During the interview ...	Something the child *likes*	Something the child *dislikes*
Stimulus is *presented*	**1 Positive reinforcement** 'If you tell me more about "X", I will share this biscuit with you.'	**2 Positive punishment** 'If you don't talk about "X", I'll be very disappointed in you.'
Stimulus is *removed*	**3 Negative punishment** 'I'll return your favourite toy once you finish talking about "X".'	**4 Negative reinforcement** 'If you just tell me what I want to know, this interview is over, and you can go home.'

Note: In this context, the terms 'positive' and 'negative' mean that the stimuli are either present or not. 'Positive' and 'negative' are not the equivalent of 'good' and 'bad'.

As shown in Table 3.1, subtle social reinforcement strategies in the form of approval and disapproval can lead children to make false statements. Expanding on this approach, Billings et al. (2007) examined how social reinforcement induces children to make false statements using only mild forms of social reinforcement, such as praise and encouragement. They presented children with a staged crime, the theft of a highly attractive toy from their school, and interviewed them about its disappearance. The questions were designed to bring about three increasing levels of self-incriminating false statements: admitting guilty knowledge of the theft, admitting having seen the fictitious theft, and admitting having taken part in the fictitious theft. As predicted, children who received social reinforcement were more likely to make self-incriminating admissions than children in the control condition. They found that not only did reinforcement by the interviewers quickly persuade children to make self-incriminating false admissions about the apparent theft, but the self-incriminating admissions were more frequent among younger children.

Repetitive questioning and interviews

Imagine being interviewed, and the interviewer keeps asking the same question. Would you change your answer? While most adults would respond 'no', the answer is different for children. Garvin, Wood, Malpass and Shaw (1998) described this tactic as the **ask-and-answer procedure**. Surprisingly, research reveals that children will change their answers to repeatedly presented forced choice questions; for example, 'Did he touch you?' Siegal, Waters and Dinwiddy (1988) explain that, unlike adults, children assume that their first answer was wrong, and they change it to please the interviewer. As a result, children are more susceptible to social pressure and as question repetition increases, so does the frequency of the child's self-contradictions. This pattern of responding is known as an acquiescence error, and unlike false memories, acquiescence errors do not necessarily imply changes in memory (Andrews, Lamb and Lyon, 2015).

Another consequence of acquiescence errors is that changing their answers when asked the same question lowers children's credibility in the view of judges and juries (Voogt, Klettke, Crossman, 2016). Despite the evidence that consistency and accuracy are weakly related (Fisher, Brewer and Mitchell, 2009), the perceived credibility of children's testimony is influenced by consistency in responses to repeated questions (Memon and Vartoukian, 1996). Most importantly, it has been assumed that answers to repeated questions will be less accurate than original answers because witnesses react to the social pressure of repeated questions by offering speculative responses, such as 'I might have seen him in my bedroom' (Moston, 1990).

Positive reinforcement – Giving something good or desirable to increase the occurrence of a particular behaviour.

Positive punishment – Giving something bad or undesirable to reduce the occurrence of a particular behaviour.

Negative punishment – Taking something good or desirable away to reduce the occurrence of a particular behaviour.

Negative reinforcement – Taking something bad or undesirable away to increase the occurrence of a particular behaviour.

Ask-and-answer procedure – A series of quick closed-ended questions.

Not only the repetition of questions, but also the repetition of interview sessions can potentially create inaccurate statements (Newlin et al., 2015). Despite the preference for a single forensic interview, repeated interviews are the norm rather than the exception. Children are often questioned many times by parents, relatives and social workers. Additionally, in many jurisdictions, such as the UK, Australia and the USA, informal interviews often precede the formal interview (La Rooy, Lamb and Pipe, 2009). Additional interviews may also be needed when abuse is not disclosed in the first interview but there is good reason to suspect that it occurred (McElvaney, 2015). Interviewers can build trust across multiple interviews when victims are reluctant to reveal information, when they have been threatened, or told to keep the abuse a secret (Gagnier and Collin-Vézina, 2016).

When a child's testimony is vital for an investigation, a well-conducted supplementary interview may be an effective way of gaining further investigative leads. Duron and Cheung (2016) suggest that repeated interviews can improve children's memory performance by helping recall and reducing forgetting. This effect is present when children are interviewed in a way that is consistent with best practice and are not influenced suggestively outside the interview context. But, when children are suggestively questioned about false events, adverse effects of repeated interviews emerge (La Rooy, Heydon, Korkman and Myklebust, 2016).

To avoid the negative effects of repetitive interviews, Duron and Remko (2015) recommend clearly defining the circumstances that demand more than one interview, weighing the need for more information, including the disclosure of abuse, with the potential of increased contradictory statements (Block et al., 2013). Frequently, the added interview is not worth the risk of the child experiencing added trauma when providing multiple accounts of the abuse (Faller, Cordisco-Steele and Nelson-Gardell, 2010). However, the risk may not be as great as imagined. Research found that when second sexual abuse interviews of children were conducted as well as initial interviews, the children provided new details with few contradictions (Waterhouse et al., 2016).

Inviting speculation

Asking a child to 'pretend' or 'imagine' events is sometimes used when children have not provided answers on their own, either because of social or emotional barriers or because there is no memory of the event (Schreiber and Parker, 2004). This happens when an interviewer encourages a child to imagine different scenarios – 'What do you think it would feel like if he did that to you?' (Bjorklund, 2000). Unfortunately, these speculative responses are often misinterpreted by children as actual memories and this confusion decreases memory accuracy (Schreiber and Parker, 2004).

Confirmatory bias

Interviewers tend to accept information that confirms their existing beliefs while rejecting information that disagrees with those beliefs. This is the confirmatory bias, and it has harmful effects on child witnesses. Specifically, pre-established beliefs about the accuracy and credibility of the child may make the interviewer unintentionally focus on some statements and ignore others that do not fit the interviewer's beliefs (APA, 2018).

Bruck, Ceci, Melnyk and Finkelberg (1999) discovered that interviewer bias develops quickly in an interview situation and contaminates both the accuracy of the child and interviewer. In a clever experiment, Bruck et al. (1999) examined the effects of confirmatory bias on trained interviewers experienced with interviewing children. The experiment began with a staged surprise birthday party for a research assistant. Preschool children surprised a research assistant for her birthday, played games, ate cake and watched magic tricks.

Another group of children were told it was the research assistant's birthday, but instead of attending the party, they only coloured a picture with the research assistant. Several weeks later, trained interviewers were not told about the two events but were asked only to discover what happened from each child. Each interviewer interviewed four children, where the first three children attended the birthday party, and the fourth child attended only the colouring event.

Bruck et al. (1999) found that the children who were interviewed last (all of whom only attended the colouring event) produced twice as many errors as the children who actually attended the birthday party; 60 per cent of the children who only coloured made false claims that involved attending a birthday party. This result suggests that the interviewers had formed a biased belief that all the children had attended a birthday party. By the time they interviewed the fourth child in their group, they structured their interviews in such a way as to produce claims consistent with their expectation. Thus, if interviewers have the belief that all the children they interview have experienced a certain event, then it is likely that many of the children will come to make similar claims even though they were non-participants (or non-victims). Interestingly, even when the child who only coloured correctly denied attending a birthday party, 84 per cent of their interviewers reported later that all the children told them they had attended a birthday party. This data suggests that regardless of what children actually say, confirmatory bias leads interviewers to inaccurately report the child's claims in order to make them consistent with their own hypotheses.

To counteract the confirmation bias, interviewers questioning a child about an event should explore alternative hypotheses about what may have happened (Otgaar et al., 2017). For example, if the interviewer believes a parent abused the child, the interviewer should also ask questions that allow the child to disclose information that could suggest the parent is innocent, such as asking about whether a neighbour or babysitter abused them. Evaluating alternative hypotheses is important because there are many situations in which a child's statements may be misunderstood, even in the absence of suggestive questioning (Newlin et al., 2015).

IN SUMMARY

Interviewing children is a strategic challenge, where interviewers avoid suggestive questions that require speculation, confirmation by others, and how feedback and reinforcement is given in terms of confirmation bias. In many ways, the same rules of interviewing apply to both children and adults.

CRITICAL THINKING AND APPLICATION QUESTIONS

1   Redesign Leichtman and Ceci's Sam Stone experiment examining suggestive questioning and stereotyping for adults. What changes would you make in the design of the experiment? Do you believe you would find the same results regarding stereotype induction and suggestion?

2   The local police have asked you to explain why their current use of operant reinforcement strategies will increase false statements from children. With unique examples, explain why children are susceptible to each of the four operant conditioning strategies (Table 3.1).

3   From your perspective, rank the six most frequent mistakes to avoid during an interview from the easiest to the most challenging (Figure 3.2). Then find a research article that explores this challenge.

HOW TO CONDUCT A FORENSIC INTERVIEW

FICTION: The forensic interview is like a conversation between a parent and child.	*Versus*	**FACT:** Forensic interviews are developmentally sensitive and rely on specialised interview procedures to enhance comprehension, recall and reporting of past events.

Origins of the forensic interview

> **Forensic interview** – *A structured conversation to elicit detailed information about event(s) a child may have experienced or witnessed.*

A **forensic interview** is a legally sound and developmentally proper method of gathering factual information. The following approach is grounded in the revised National Institute of Child Health and Human Development (NICHD) Protocol, which is an internationally used protocol (Canada, Finland, Israel, Japan, Korea, Norway, Portugal, Scotland and the USA) for the investigative interviewing of children, developed in the USA at the National Institute of Child Health and Human Development (NICHD) (La Rooy et al., 2015).

This approach is based on research into children's development of cognitive and communicative abilities and questioning techniques that enhance children's ability to provide accurate information about their past experiences (La Rooy et al., 2015). The forensic interview model emphasises flexible thinking and decision-making approaches throughout the interview, as opposed to a scripted format. Many parties use the results of forensic interviews, including law enforcement, victim advocates, child protection investigators, medical and mental health practitioners (Jones, Cross, Walsh and Simone, 2005).

 Global Perspectives

Iceland's novel approach for interviewing children

The concept of 'Barnahus' translates as 'children's house' in English and originates in Iceland. This approach builds on the understanding that child abuse is a complex phenomenon, demanding highly specialised expertise and coordinated services. Another core element of the Barnahus idea is that it is supposed to be a safe place for disclosing abuse, often interpreted as a child-friendly, child-centred and supportive setting, as well as a place that is safe from persons suspected of abuse. This is intended to provide the best possible circumstances for children to disclose abuse and to feel safe, thereby avoiding further victimisation. The Barnahus model seeks to reduce some of the trauma experienced by victims of child sexual abuse by making the approach child focused, emphasising the importance of a safe and supportive environment in which to be seen by specialists, give evidence and receive support. For example, within the models used in Iceland, children are interviewed and examined within a week of the abuse allegation being made. These interviews are conducted and recorded in a single location with specially trained officers and medical professionals, and they are then used in court as evidence, avoiding the victim having to revisit court in order to give evidence or testify (Søbjerg and Thams, 2016). Evaluations of this model of intervention have found significantly better outcomes for child victims and their families because of the multidisciplinary and multi-agency approach. An adapted model for adult victims could also be a possibility in the future (Qasir et al., 2018).

Application of the NICHD Protocol

Here, we outline the application of the NICHD Protocol. This four-part approach (see Figure 3.3) is an evidence-based solution to improve interviewing standards. The NICHD Protocol was developed in the mid-1990s to address shortcomings in the quality of interviews. It was created with input from a wide range of professionals, including lawyers, developmental, clinical and forensic psychologists, police officers and social workers, and has been the focus of intensive forensic evaluation and research (Bull, 2010; Saywitz, Lyon and Goodman, 2011) and is now widely used internationally.

Figure 3.3: Phases of the NICHD Protocol

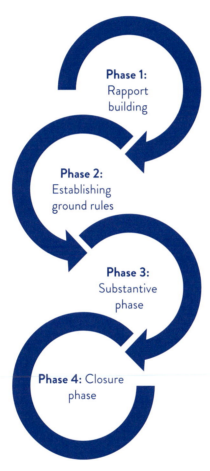

Phase 1: Rapport building

The first phase creates a relaxed and supportive environment for children (Lewy, Cyr and Dion, 2015). It has three parts. First, it lays the foundation for a valid interview by rehearsing and rewarding the expected levels of responses to open-ended questions. Second, it creates a sense of understanding and trust between the interviewer and the child. Third, the interviewer measures the child's linguistic patterns and willingness to take part in the interview (Hershkowitz, Lamb, Katz and Malloy, 2015).

The challenge is to provide support without suggestion. Ideally, rapport building will decrease anxiety and distress, empower children and increase their level of engagement.

Most importantly, the increased rapport will encourage children who have been abused to talk about their experiences (Siegman and Reynolds, 1983). As evidence of the powerful effects of rapport building, Hershkowitz (2009) discovered that interviewer support increases the production of forensically relevant details. Interviewer support was achieved by addressing the children by name and encouraging children's efforts, but not their topics, in a non-suggestive manner. The effectiveness of supportive interviewer behaviour depends on many factors, including individual differences in children's ages and verbal ability (Hershkowitz, 2009), as well as attachment styles, or working memory capacity (Davis and Bottoms, 2002). Most research finds that there is no evidence that interviewer supportiveness can be harmful to accuracy, unless it is associated with suggestiveness (Bottoms, Quas and Davis, 2007).

During the rapport-building phase, it is important to establish the ground rules for telling truths versus telling lies. Lyon and Evans (2014) offer one approach; simply ask the child to promise to tell the truth before the substantive phase of the interview (phase 3). Additionally, documenting a developmentally appropriate oath to tell the truth before the substantive phase increases the perception that the child is a competent witness and that the recorded interview will be admitted into evidence (Russell, 2006).

The practice interview teaches children how to give detailed responses to open-ended questions (Brubacher, Roberts and Powell, 2011). To accomplish this, Hershkowitz et al. (2015) recommend that the interviewer select a neutral topic from the child's response to an earlier question, like 'What do you like to do for fun?' Then the interviewer should tell the child to describe that topic in detail. Meanwhile, during this free narrative, the interviewer supports this process with open-ended questions using the child's own words as prompts for greater elaboration. For example, 'That's interesting, please tell me more about "X".' This clarification allows the child to practise providing forensically detailed descriptions about a neutral event.

Phase 2: Establishing ground rules

The second phase begins with an age- and context-appropriate review of instructions. Dickinson, Brubacher and Poole (2015) encourage setting up ground rules because they are easy to comprehend and take little time to deliver (typically two to four minutes) and, most importantly, are associated with improved accuracy in previous research. The number and type of instructions depend on the age of the child. For example, children under six who have not developed a theory of mind might be reminded that the interviewer was not there and does not know what happened, thus countering the child's misunderstanding that thoughts in their head are freely available to everyone (i.e., theory of mind).

Reviewing and rehearsing interview instructions during the rapport-building phase creates an expectation that the child's role is to give accurate and complete information (APSAC, 2012). For example, telling the child 'It's okay to say, "I don't understand" or "I don't know" or "If I make a mistake, please correct me"' should reduce acquiescence responses from the child. In the same way, telling the child to only talk about what really happened focuses them on maintaining accurate responses.

Phase 2 ends with a practice interview to confirm that the child can provide forensically relevant details. The interviewer practises and reviews each guideline until the child shows spontaneous use of these skills. Practice includes asking the child a question to which the child would not know the answer to verify that the child will respond 'I don't know' (Anderson, 2013). For example, the interviewer might say 'So, if I ask you, "What is my dog's name?", what would you say?' The interviewer should reinforce the correct response with, 'thank you for saying you didn't know or understand my question' (Saywitz, Lyon and Goodman, 2011).

The practice interview continues moving from open-ended to focused questions. For example, the interviewer might ask 'I want to know more about what you like to do,' or 'Earlier you mentioned [activity or event], tell me everything about that,' to 'Tell me everything that happened on [the event].' When the interviewer believes that the child responds appropriately, the next phase begins.

Phase 3: Substantive phase

This phase collects information about the event under investigation. The questioning approach is like a funnel (Figure 3.4), starting with a free narrative description of events, followed by strategies like open-ended questions and clarification approaches and ending with closed-ended questions to evaluate alternative hypotheses. This funnel approach supports the child's narrative stream and reduces interviewer bias (Harris, 2010). It is important to emphasise that there are no standard questions for every interview, only a general approach (APSAC, 2012).

Figure 3.4: The NICHD Protocol funnel approach

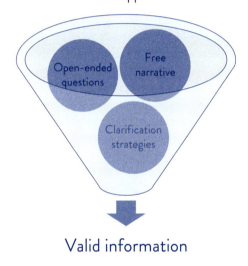

Valid information

To avoid introducing suggestive questions by introducing information the child has not already mentioned, the child should raise the reason for the interview. Therefore, before the free narrative questions begin, the child is asked 'Do you know why you are here today?' In this way, the interviewer offers a series of open and non-leading prompts to name the target event(s) under investigation. If the child does not respond to the opening question, the interviewer offers carefully worded and increasingly focused prompts, such as 'Your mother said something happened to you recently, would you like to tell me about it?' to more focused 'You told your teacher that "X" touched you in a way that made you feel bad, would you please tell me about that.'

Once the child responds with a statement, the free recall phase begins with the interviewer's request to 'Tell me everything about "X".' Only after exhausting the information from free recall should interviewers use open-ended questions supported with focused recall questions that include details previously mentioned by the child (APSAC, 2012).

Because children often experience multiple incidents of abuse, the interviewer should ask the child to indicate whether the incident occurred 'one time' or 'more than one time' and then ask for incident-specific information using follow-up questions, such as 'Then what happened?', and cued questions, such as 'You said a [person/object/action]. Tell me everything about that', referring to details mentioned by the child to produce clean free recall accounts of the alleged incident/s (Lamb et al., 2007a, pp. 1204–5). At this point, it is appropriate to follow up with 'wh' prompt questions, such as what, why, who, when, where, so as to elicit exact details the child has already disclosed (Ahern, Andrews, Stolzenberg and Lyon, 2015). These 'wh' types of questions should be used instead of 'yes-no' or multiple-choice questions; for example, 'Did "X" touch you?' becomes '*What* did "X" do with their hands?', which may be followed by '*Where* did "X" touch you?'

Interviewers are cautioned to avoid or delay the use of any recognition props (dolls, figure drawings) and closed-ended questions (those that present response options) for as long as possible (Lamb et al., 2007a). However, using external aids (dolls, drawings) is recommended when there is reason to believe that the child has been abused and the risk of continued abuse is greater than the risk of continuing with the interview if no abuse has occurred (Lamb et al., 2007b).

After tracing the paths of the child's memories using free narrative and open-ended questions, context-appropriate questions are used to explore other alternative explanations for the child's statements. This allows the child to explain contradictory information, especially if it provides forensically relevant details, such as the subject's identity or the specific act of abuse. Examples of context-specific, non-leading questions include 'You said "X" got into bed with you. Tell me everything that happened when "X" got into bed with you.' Furthermore, the circumstances concerning the target event may need further exploration, for example when distinguishing abuse from caring activities: 'Earlier you mentioned that your mother "hit you with this long thing". Tell me about that thing.' Finally, questions about the sources of the child's information may reveal possible contamination or coaching; for example, 'Now I want to understand how other people found out about [the last incident]' or 'Who was the first person besides you and [the perpetrator] to find out about [alleged abuse as described by the child]?'

Phase 4: Closure phase

These are emotionally challenging conversations for a child, and the goal of this final phase is to provide a respectful end. This phase focuses on the socioemotional needs of a child, transitioning to neutral topics, allowing for questions about the interview and the opportunity to discuss future safety. Various strategies include asking if there is something else the interviewer needs to know, if there is something else the child wants to tell or ask the interviewer. Finally, introducing a neutral topic like 'What will you do after this interview today?' prepares the child to end the interview. Lamb et al. (2007a) recommend thanking the child for their effort rather than the specific content they supplied.

Testing the effectiveness of the NICHD Protocol

While learning to use the NICHD Protocol requires extensive and continuous training to maintain the high quality of interviewing, research shows the investment in training is worth the effort (Orbach et al., 2000). Across studies, protocol interviewers used more open-ended prompts than non-protocol interviewers. More details were obtained using open-ended invitations and fewer were obtained using focused questions in protocol interviews than in non-protocol interviews. In addition, these NICHD interviewers needed fewer questions to get relevant information. Finally, controlled studies have repeatedly shown that the quality of interviewing reliably improves when interviewers employ the NICHD Protocol. No other technique has been proven to be equally effective (Lamb et al., 2007a).

Remaining controversies and challenges

Forensic interviewing to determine the likelihood of child sexual abuse is a dynamic and evolving area of practice. Research is driven by the concern that forensic interview practices might elicit false reports of sexual abuse and thereby jeopardise the lives of innocent adults. What is also concerning is that children three years of age and younger cannot be reliably interviewed with current forensic interview structures (Faller and Hewitt, 2007).

Although forensic interviewing shows interviewers how to build rapport with alleged victims, it does not address motivational factors that make some children reluctant to disclose abuse (Pipe, Lamb, Orbach and Cederborg, 2007). Nondisclosure is important because more than a third of suspected victims do not report abuse during interviews (Lippert, Cross, Jones and Walsh, 2009), even when there is unambiguous evidence that they were abused (Hershkowitz, Horowitz and Lamb, 2005).

Areas of future application include the following challenges offered by Faller (2015), collected by examining 40 years of progress interviewing children:

1   Whether an interview structure should be flexible, semi-structured, or scripted

2   If ground rules should be introduced

3   Whether children need to complete the truth/lie exercise

4   What the most appropriate types of questions are

5   Whether media should be employed in forensic interviews

6   Whether children should be allowed more than one interview.

IN SUMMARY

Conducting an effective forensic interview relies on developmentally sensitive and specialised interview procedures found in the NICHD Protocol to enhance comprehension, recall and reporting of past events.

 ## CRITICAL THINKING AND APPLICATION QUESTIONS

1   Imagine that you are the mentor for someone about to conduct their first forensic interview with a child. Your mentee asks you: 'How do I balance the need for forensically relevant information with the welfare of the child?' What is your response?

2   In the revised NICHD forensic interview, the discussion of ground rules was moved before the rapport-building phase. Why do you think this change was made?

3   Review the list of six challenges for the forensic interview outlined by Faller (2015), select one and outline an experiment to investigate the challenge.

MANAGING THE CHALLENGES OF COMPASSION FATIGUE

....

FICTION: Working with children in a forensic setting is no different than working with adults.

Versus

FACT: Working with children in a forensic setting presents significant potential for developing compassion fatigue.

....

The foundation of moral forensic practice is built on helping victims of child sexual abuse by maintaining a code of ethical practice protecting children. Forensic psychologists investigating a child's allegations will not be able to apply their methods effectively unless they understand the child's developmental stage and the functions of the basic cognitive mechanisms (attention, perception, memory). Forensic psychologists also need to cultivate the skills of rapport building and communication through empathy, patience, sensitivity and warmth. These qualities play a vital role in obtaining credible testimony and, at the same time, protect the child from the risk of further victimisation (Themeli and Panagiotaki, 2014).

A forensic psychologist plays four distinct roles in response to claims of child abuse. These roles include evaluating the child, assessing their competency to testify, preparing the child to testify, and testifying as an expert witness. For example, judges and attorneys who question children in court are often apprehensive about the competency and credibility of young witnesses. Forensic psychologists explain how children can be manipulated by improper interview methods, how to prepare a child for court, how to question children, and how to determine if special courtroom procedures are needed (Gianvanni and Sharman, 2015).

Should children's testimony be treated as equivalent to an adult's testimony?

Source: Mark McMahon/Corbis Historical/Getty Images

Balancing forensic and therapeutic perspectives

Forensic psychologists must find a balance between their different roles during forensic evaluation and clinical evaluation of child sexual abuse (Poole and Lamb, 1998; Raskin and Esplin, 1991). The forensic role refers to the specific procedures of the criminal justice system. Forensic evaluation involves investigating facts, establishing what happened and how it happened, using structured interview protocols and focusing on the actual events that took place and not on their psychological impact on the child (Sattler, 1998). The clinical role refers to mental health and therapeutic intervention (Faller, 2007). Therapeutic evaluation involves clinical assessment and therapeutic intervention, using the techniques beyond the structured interview; a more flexible approach allows an actively supportive approach towards the child.

Psychological risks of compassion fatigue and secondary traumatisation

Cultivating a keen sense of intrapersonal insight is vital to meet the challenges of working with traumatised children. Forensic interviewers of child sexual abuse suffer increased potential for **secondary trauma** – indirect exposure to a trauma through a first-hand account or narrative of a traumatic event (Azar, 2000). Secondary trauma involves the transfer and acquisition of negative emotions and dysfunctional cognitive states due to prolonged and extended contact with people who have been traumatised (Motta, 2020).

The characteristics of secondary traumatic stress are similar to post-traumatic stress disorder (PTSD), including symptoms of hyperarousal, avoidance and intrusive thoughts or memories relating to the trauma of another (Bride, 2004). The diagnostic criteria for PTSD acknowledge the potentially traumatising effect of 'repeated or extreme exposure to details of the traumatic events' (APA, 2013, p. 271).

Over time, the cumulative exposure to child sexual abuse can result in internalising the traumatic experiences, leading to **compassion fatigue**, a combination of secondary traumatic stress and burnout (Stamm, 2010). **Burnout** describes the physical and emotional exhaustion that people can experience when they have low job satisfaction, feel powerless and overwhelmed (Russo et al., 2020). However, burnout does not include a decline in the ability to feel compassion for others. Compassion fatigue and secondary trauma are more complicated than just being tired and overworked and are often caused by a conflict between our deepest values and the work we are required to do, a phenomenon known as **moral distress** (Campbell, Ulrich and Grady, 2018; Jameton, 1993).

Negative effects on forensic interviews

Maintaining empathy with the traumatised child during interviews is challenging. Secondary traumatisation can lead to the need to withdraw and disengage from the child or respond inappropriately or disproportionately physically and psychologically. Over time, the forensic psychologist's worldview changes and they may identify so closely with the traumatised child that they cannot conduct effective forensic interviews (Perron and Hiltz, 2006).

Secondary trauma – *Indirect exposure to a trauma through a first-hand account or narrative of a traumatic event.*

Compassion fatigue – *The emotional residue or strain of exposure from working with those suffering from the consequences of traumatic events.*

Burnout – *The physical and emotional exhaustion associated with increased workload and institutional stress.*

Moral distress – *A conflict between our deepest values and the work we are required to do.*

Silencing response – *A process of psychological withdrawal where children are unintentionally silenced because the information shared is too distressing.*

A consequence is the **silencing response**, a process of psychological withdrawal where children are unintentionally silenced because the information they are sharing is too distressing to accept (Sinclair et al., 2017). Some examples of the silencing response are changing the subject, avoiding the topic, boredom, feeling angry with the child, using humour to change or minimise the subject, faking interest, not believing children and not being able to pay attention (Baranowsky, 2002). This response is maintained through negative reinforcement. There is a short-term relief of discomfort through avoidance and this brief rewarding feeling of relief increases the use of this response strategy (Kim and Lee, 2014).

Managing compassion fatigue and secondary traumatisation

Turgoose and Maddox (2017) identified the main predictors of compassion fatigue, including the professionals' own trauma history and a high degree of empathy. Surprisingly, compassion fatigue is *not* associated with caseload (the *number* of forensic interviews conducted) or length of employment but it *is* associated with insufficient training, identification with the victims, insufficient support in the workplace, and insufficient social and familial support (Perron and Hiltz, 2006).

The key components of secondary trauma prevention are found in professional and personal coping strategies (Herman, 1992; Dagan, Ben-Porat and Itzhaky, 2016). Specifically, four strategies are important for the prevention of secondary traumatisation in mental health care providers (Bonach and Heckert, 2012; Pearlman and Saakvitne, 1995):

1   *Professional strategies*, such as balancing caseloads and available supervision.

2   *Organisational strategies*, such as enough release time and safe physical space.

3   *Personal strategies*, such as respecting one's own limits and maintaining time for self-care activities.

4   *General coping strategies*, such as self-nurturing and seeking connection.

IN SUMMARY

Professionals who work in mental health settings are at risk of developing compassion fatigue via secondary traumatisation. There are effective coping skills that involve professional, organisational and personal strategies.

 ## CRITICAL THINKING AND APPLICATION QUESTIONS

1   What other occupations suffer from secondary trauma? Are the psychological effects similar to people who work with child sexual abuse?

2   A psychologist recently interviewed a large number of children traumatised by the experience of a horrific school shooting and the psychologist seems to be suffering from burnout and compassion fatigue. Design a plan to cope with these feelings. Your plan should include short-, medium- and long-term goals.

3   Create an infographic (a visual image such as a chart or diagram used to represent information) for people unfamiliar with the best practices for interviewing children.

CHAPTER REVIEW

The field of forensic child interviewing has evolved. Gone are the days when child witnesses were treated with greater distrust than adult witnesses. Forensic psychologists have worked hard to dispel the myths that children do not have the same observational abilities as adults and that children have difficulty in distinguishing reality from fantasy as well as truths from lies. In response to these assumptions, we have developed developmentally sensitive questioning techniques, identified sources of suggestion, and established structured interview protocols. Under the right interview methods, children's eyewitness skills are equal to that of an adult. Yet, it is too easy to form simplistic views of children's capabilities, views that may harm children in actual cases and that also may harm innocent people falsely accused of crimes against children. We must guard against overly optimistic or pessimistic views of children's abilities. We must also be careful that our science does not deceive us, but instead supplies a complete and accurate account of children's abilities as witnesses. Most importantly, we must keep in mind that our ultimate goal is to reduce secondary traumatisation and long-term consequences for children providing testimony about violence they have experienced or witnessed.

NAMES TO KNOW

Michael E. Lamb

Research focuses on forensic interviewing and the factors affecting children's adjustment. Lamb and his colleagues have shown how developmentally sensitive interviewing improves the amount and quality of information obtained from young victims, witnesses and offenders in investigative settings.

- Hershkowitz, I., Lamb, M. E. and Katz, C. (2014) Allegation rates in forensic child abuse investigations: Comparing the revised and standard NICHD protocols. *Psychology, Public Policy, and Law*, 20(3), 336–44.

- Spencer, J. R. and Lamb, M. E. (eds) (2012) *Children and Cross-examination: Time to Change the Rules?* Bloomsbury.

Stephen Ceci

Examines the connections between children and the law – suggestibility, competence to testify, deception, coerced confessions.

- Ceci, S. J. and Bruck, M. (1995) *Jeopardy in the Courtroom: The Scientific Analysis of Children's Testimony*. APA. (Winner of the William James Book Award by APA)

- Ceci, S. J., Leichtman, M. and Putnick, M. (eds) (1992) *Cognitive and Social Factors in Deception Among Preschoolers*. Erlbaum.

Thomas D. Lyon

Research interests include child abuse and neglect, child witnesses, and domestic violence.

- O'Connor, A. M., Lyon, T. D. and Evans, A. D. (2019) Younger and older adults' lie-detection and credibility judgments of children's coached reports. *Psychology, Crime & Law*, 25(9), 925–44.

- Stolzenberg, S. N., McWilliams, K. and Lyon, T. D. (2017) Ask versus tell: Potential confusion when child witnesses are questioned about conversations. *Journal of Experimental Psychology: Applied*, 23(4), 447–59.

PART II

4 TECHNIQUES FOR INTERVIEWING VULNERABLE PEOPLE

Chapter Introduction

Vulnerable people can provide valuable information and assistance. This chapter explores the complex nature of vulnerability and shows what can be done to assist police and prosecutors, while supporting vulnerable victims, witnesses and suspects. We examine the evidence that there are hidden populations of vulnerable people who are a valuable source of information if treated appropriately. Our exploration begins with a survey of the categories of vulnerability and the consequences of improper interview methods. Sometimes, vulnerable people are seen as a credibility risk for an investigation and are not interviewed. This assumption questions their testimonial reliability during interviews and when testifying. Next, we examine the myth that people with intellectual and social communication challenges cannot provide useful information. Finally, we survey the best interview practices for forensic psychologists in terms of their present and future roles in this area, because how we treat vulnerable people reflects a civilised society.

Learning Outcomes

Recognising vulnerable people
- Clearly explain why identifying vulnerable people is important for the criminal justice system.

People with cognitive impairments
- Describe the most effective interview strategies when working with people with cognitive impairments.

People with social communication impairments
- Describe the most effective interview strategies when working with people with social communication impairments.

The roles of the forensic psychologist
- Compare the distinct roles played by forensic psychologists when dealing with vulnerable witnesses, victims or suspects.

RECOGNISING VULNERABLE PEOPLE

FICTION: Vulnerable witnesses lack the ability to provide accurate and reliable information.	*Versus*	**FACT:** Early identification of relevant vulnerabilities and proper strategies during the interview process helps ensure accurate and reliable information.

- Martha Al-Bishara, an 87-year-old woman from Georgia, USA, was using a knife to cut dandelions in the woods near her rural home. Police officers who were called to the scene repeatedly asked Martha to drop the knife. The officers reported that 'her demeanor was calm, even when we had our guns out'. Officers even made hand gestures to pantomime dropping a knife, but she still did not comply. At that point, Martha began to walk towards the police and did not react when one of the officers turned on his Taser. When Martha was 4.5 meters (five yards) away, still holding the knife in her hand, the officer fired his Taser, striking her in the chest (Allen, 2018).

- Peter Russell, a 59-year-old man from Lincolnshire, UK, was stunned by a Taser several times. Mrs Russell said her husband became agitated when police came to assist doctors with his transfer to hospital. She explained that he was petrified and scared of going to the hospital. Peter ripped out the barbed darts embedded in his skin while officers restrained him until three more officers arrived (*Metro News*, 2012).

- Iole Pasquale, an 80-year-old woman from Ontario, Canada, was walking along a deserted road at 3 am carrying a bread knife at her side. Police told Iole, whose first language is Italian, to drop the knife. She responded in a manner that was neither threatening nor assaultive, saying 'the knife is not for you'. The police Tasered her. She fell and fractured her right hip (Kane and Pagliaro, 2013; Martin, 2013).

One theme connects these three stories about Martha, Peter and Iole. They are all vulnerable people diagnosed with Alzheimer's disease. These tragic stories highlight the importance of recognising and adapting our responses to the unique needs and characteristics of vulnerable people.

Defining vulnerability

How we treat the vulnerable among us is crucial for the fair administration of justice and requires skill, experience, education and understanding. Proper treatment includes effective assessment and management of vulnerable witnesses, victims and suspects. Effective vulnerability assessment prevents unintended health and criminal justice consequences and manages harmful outcomes in cases where prevention is not possible. However, there is no globally accepted definition of 'vulnerable' regarding witnesses, victims or suspects (Enang et al., 2019; Bull, 2011).

Anyone can be considered vulnerable if we use a broad enough definition. For example, Larkin (2009) defines vulnerability as a state or condition where a person is in danger, threatened, experiencing health challenges, or requiring support. While this definition emphasises that vulnerability is not a stable characteristic over situations and a person's lifetime, it is vague about the specific intervention strategies for law enforcement. Defining vulnerability also depends on the *context*. For example, cases categorised as domestic abuse, or hate crimes, do not make the victims of such crimes vulnerable. Likewise, an older or cognitively impaired person may not be vulnerable, but when they are required to give evidence in court with the defendant present, they may become vulnerable.

Our language reflects our respect for individuals of any population group or designation. Historically, terms that were once widely used have been replaced by other, more appropriate words. For example, the term 'mental retardation' was once a common description and is now judged to be hurtful to individuals who have low intelligence. In its place, the terms 'intellectual impairment' or 'an individual with an intellectual impairment' are used (APA, 2013a). We now use a 'person-first' model when referring to individuals. For example, instead of the 'wheelchair person', the 'person who uses a wheelchair'. The concept of *having* a disability rather than *being* disabled allows recognition of other aspects of an individual's life (grandmother, father, professional experiences).

In addition, the Australian Psychological Society's Ethical guidelines on reporting abuse and neglect, and criminal activity (APS, n.d.) includes a section specifically related to reporting the abuse of people from 'vulnerable groups other than children', which includes older adults in aged care facilities, people with an intellectual disability, those covered by guardianship acts, and those covered by mental health acts.

Vulnerability can be a temporary state. Understanding your rights when arrested is important, but what if your brain was in a temporary state of shock? In a provocative experiment, Kane and White (2015) found that Taser exposure led to significant and substantial reductions in short-term auditory recall and comprehension. These effects lasted up to one hour for most subjects, all of whom returned to normal cognitive functioning within the hour. The consequence is that tasering affects the ability of a person to understand the consequences of making self-incriminating statements. The effects may be even worse in a real-world situation, because these experiment participants were students accustomed to taking tests, who were sober and drug free when tasered. The researchers predict that the reduction in cognitive ability would be greater in a sample that might be intoxicated or mentally ill when tasered. Based on this study, they recommend that police wait an hour after Taser deployment before engaging suspects in custodial interrogations.

It is important to stress the distinction between being vulnerable and being unreliable. With the necessary support, most people who are vulnerable can give reliable evidence. Additionally, being vulnerable is different from being incompetent to give evidence (Ewin, 2015). Adjustments can be made to remove a vulnerable person's barriers to effectively participate in the criminal justice system.

A more precise approach involves recognising psychological vulnerability as a potential risk factor. In this approach, psychological vulnerabilities are best understood as potential 'risk factors' rather than conclusive signs of unreliability. Therefore, the greater the communication and social barriers, the more vulnerable the interviewee is to providing information that is misleading, unreliable and self-incriminating (Powell, 2002). The advantage of this approach is that it offers a personalised definition of vulnerability (Whitelock, 2009).

Comprehensive definitions of vulnerability should include a weakness to suggestibility. The UK Police and Criminal Evidence Act 1984 (PACE) Code C definition of vulnerability is a comprehensive approach that defines vulnerability as any person with a mental health condition or mental disorder that causes them to have difficulty understanding or communicating about any of the procedures and processes connected with: 'their arrest and detention; or ... their voluntary attendance at a police station ... for the purpose of a voluntary interview' (Home Office, 2019, p. 9, para. 1.13(d)). Included in this definition is the subject's ability to understand the significance of what they are being told in terms of comprehending questions and the significance of their replies. This approach includes those who are vulnerable to suggestion either by:

> providing unreliable, misleading or incriminating information without knowing or wishing to do so; accepting or acting on suggestions from others without consciously knowing or wishing to do so; or readily agreeing to suggestions or proposals without any protest or question. (Home Office, 2019, p. 9, para. 1.13(d))

Why is it important for police to recognise vulnerable persons?

In the USA, people with impairments are the single largest minority group, according to the American Community Survey. This annual government survey, which helps local officials, community leaders and businesses understand the changes taking place in their communities, estimated that the overall rate of people with impairments in the US population in 2016 was 12.8 per cent (Kraus, Lauer, Coleman and Houtenville, 2018). Police who have the training to work with this population have a significant advantage over police who do not. The more educated the officer is about the characteristics of cognitive and communication impairments, the more likely it is that safe and positive outcomes will occur between law enforcement and people with these challenges.

Sometimes, vulnerable people are seen as a credibility risk for an investigation and are not interviewed. This happens because traditional investigative methods are standardised. For example, treating each new crime victim equally and taking the same steps, such as investigating the scene, interviewing all the victims and witnesses, documenting the findings, and planning the next steps. However, if the police do not interview the crime witness or victim who has an impairment, this will weaken the case. Furthermore, improper interviewing of persons with impairments, involving witnesses and victims of crime, rarely move forward for prosecution. In other words, when an interview has not occurred or has not followed the steps of a traditional interview, it is difficult to defend the interview content and procedures.

The identification of psychological vulnerabilities is critical before a police interview. The interview can place witnesses, victims and suspects at a disadvantage in many ways. These include being able to cope with the demand characteristics of the interview, making informed decisions that indicate an understanding of the consequences of their answers and statements to the police, to providing the police with relevant, detailed and accurate answers to questions. Police interviews can have potentially damaging consequences, not just for the wrongfully convicted, but also on occasions preventing the apprehension of the real offender who may continue to commit serious crimes (Kassin et al., 2010a).

In most cases, vulnerabilities are not identified, and even if identified, this information is not always acted on in terms of providing support. This problem needs a solution. Reliable screening methods for everyone need to be developed and applied (Gudjonsson, 2010).

Legal competency – The mental ability of an individual to understand and participate in legal proceedings.

Legal competency to take part in the criminal process

Assessment of competence to stand trial is the most common forensic evaluation performed in US cases (Hoge, 2016). **Legal competency** states that individuals should be able to understand the charges against them, appreciate the nature and range of penalties, and communicate with their attorney (Gudjonsson and Grisso, 2008). The legal principle of proving a person's competence to stand trial evolved from English common law (Glazebrook, 1972). In the beginning, the focus was on the ritual of pleading before the court as guilty or innocent before the trial could continue (Grisso, 2003).

One reason it is important to identify vulnerable witnesses, victims and suspects is to confirm that they can achieve legal competencies. Legal competencies include the ability to stand trial and plead their case, to waive their legal rights during interrogation, and the ability to give accurate evidence (Gudjonsson and Grisso, 2008; Grisso, 2003). The legal system recognises that vulnerable individuals may not have the ability to make informed decisions in their lives. Therefore, legal practice relies on forensic psychologists to aid the courts in their review of mental capacities related to the challenges of establishing competence.

Global Perspectives

The importance of culturally sensitive interview strategies

Australia has a population of Indigenous peoples with a unique set of possible vulnerable characteristics (Cooke, 2004). Awareness of these characteristics is important because they can affect reliable and accurate communication within the criminal justice system.

These unique Australian populations display exceptional cognitive skills, including language differences that alter the expression of distance

Source: Mansell/The LIFE Picture Collection/Getty Images

Torres Strait Islanders have exceptional cognitive skills and language differences that require culturally sensitive interview strategies

and time (ALRC, 1986). For example, the language of the Australian Aboriginal community of Pormpuraaw does not use relative spatial terms like left and right, instead, they rely on absolute direction terms – north, south, east and west. Thus: 'Please move your plate a little bit to the south-southwest.' To communicate clearly, members of these communities must be aware of their direction. As Boroditsky and Gaby (2010) explain, to say 'hello', one says, 'Where are you going?' and an appropriate response would be 'a long way to the north-northwest'. So, if you do not know your exact directions, you cannot get past 'hello'. Good interviewers need to consider both context *and* culture.

IN SUMMARY

Early identification of vulnerable people and the use of proper strategies during the interview process helps ensure accurate and reliable information.

CRITICAL THINKING AND APPLICATION QUESTIONS

1   Discuss the differences between 'having' a condition and 'being' a condition. In your discussion, apply examples of the objectification of a person, that is, the action of degrading someone to the status of a mere object.

2   What is the range of consequences for an unidentified vulnerable person in the criminal justice system?

3   Under what circumstances would individuals belonging to migrant populations fit our definitions of vulnerability?

PERSONS WITH COGNITIVE IMPAIRMENTS

FICTION: People with intellectual impairments do not make convincing and credible witnesses.

Versus

FACT: Cognitive impairment is unrelated to the reliability of memory or the ability to distinguish the truth from a lie.

CASE STUDY

Low intelligence and vulnerability

Johnny Lee Wilson, of Aurora, Missouri, was arrested for the murder of 79-year-old Pauline Martz. Pauline Martz had been beaten and burned alive when the killer set her home ablaze. Acting on an eyewitness tip, police were led to Johnny Lee Wilson. After being interrogated for four hours, he confessed to the crime. However, Johnny Lee suffered from mild cognitive impairment and had an IQ of only 76 (Pokin, 2017). He was threatened and intimidated by police during his interrogation and led to believe he would be allowed to go home if he confessed. The details about the murder were revealed to him during questioning and he seemed unaware of what he was doing when entering his plea in court. Johnny Lee also had an alibi for the time the murder took place and the eyewitness who implicated him was another man with a mental impairment who later admitted to lying. However, as a result of his guilty plea, Johnny Lee did not receive a trial by a jury, and was sentenced to life imprisonment without the possibility of parole in 1987. A convicted murderer named Chris Brownfield eventually came forward and confessed that he and an accomplice had killed Pauline during a robbery. In 1995, Johnny Lee was finally granted a pardon and released after serving nine years (Devaney, 1996).

Discussion Questions:

1   How did Johnny Lee Wilson's low IQ affect his false confession? For example, was he more trustful of authority figures? Was his ability to understand the legal process affected?

2   If you were hired as an advocate for Johnny Lee Wilson knowing his vulnerabilities, what would you have advised him and the investigators to do differently?

Cognitive impairment – *When a person has trouble remembering, learning new things, concentrating, or making decisions that affect their everyday life.*

The purpose of this section is to review the characteristics of people diagnosed with conditions that impair cognition. **Cognitive impairment** refers to when a person has trouble remembering, learning new things, concentrating, or making decisions that affect their everyday life. Cognitive impairment can range from mild to severe, affect people of all ages and is not caused by any one disease or condition. For example, while Alzheimer's disease and other conditions such as stroke and traumatic brain injury can cause cognitive impairment, other impairments are treatable and acute. These include medication side effects, vitamin B12 deficiency and depression (Shenkin, Russ, Ryan and MacLullich, 2013).

It is important to emphasise that cognitive impairment and mental illness are *not* the same concept and require different responses. Many people who have cognitive impairments have excellent recall of traumatic or extraordinary events in their lives. However, research has consistently shown that cognitive impairments are associated with increased suggestibility (Clare and Gudjonsson, 1993).

People with cognitive impairments may not look or act 'impaired', and it is the obscured nature of many impairments that decreases proper responses. Specifically, people with cognitive impairments require a different response from officers, different strategies for communication and different resources/support (Christiansen, 2017). When working with a person with a cognitive impairment, police must establish the person's level of functioning and the required form of communication, such as sign language or pictograms (Bellamy et al., 2019).

Older adults as witnesses

Criminal justice investigators and jurors tend to stereotype older witnesses as incompetent, often associating old age with failing memory (Aizpurua, Garcia-Bajos and Migueles, 2011). Researchers examined this ageist stereotype when they showed university students a slide show of a man shoplifting in a bookshop and told participants they would be completing a memory test (Kwong See, Hoffman and Wood, 2001). After a delay, all students read a 575-word eyewitness account of the crime. Although the narrative was exactly the same, participants were told they were reading a narrative from the memory of either a 28-year-old female or an 82-year-old female with a photograph included. Participants rated their witness on characteristics such as competence, accuracy, memory, honesty and sincerity. As a subtle ploy, the story included misinformation on four details seen in the slide show. For example, the shoplifter took a green notebook, but the witnesses' narrative reported that it was red. By comparing memory for the four misleading items in the narrative, the researchers could check whether the participants were in fact being misled by the eyewitness accounts – an indirect way of testing if the witness was being believed. They found that the 82-year-old witness was believed less than the 28-year-old who was believed to be more competent. In the case of older witnesses, juries believe them to be more honest, but less accurate (Yarmey, 1984). This data suggests that negative beliefs associating incompetence with old age may compromise the believability of older eyewitnesses.

Despite negative stereotypes, with the correct methods older witnesses can provide accurate testimony. However, they are particularly vulnerable to leading questions and misinformation – information presented after the witnessed event (Pica and Pozzulo, 2018; Henkel, 2013). Therefore, like any witness, it is important to interview them as soon as possible after an incident using a structured interview and an open-ended questioning strategy to reduce suggestibility influences from the interviewer (Sternberg, Lamb and Esplin, 2002).

Exploitation of people with dementia

The older person's potential vulnerabilities are often exploited when they are the victim of a crime. Research about the abuse of older people is 20 years behind the fields of child abuse and domestic violence (NCEA, 2019). This category of abuse includes vulnerable older people with various mental, physical, and social vulnerabilities (Cooper and Livingston, 2016). Our focus is on **dementia**, a decline in intellectual ability, including significant impairment of memory and other cognitive functions; it can be caused by many factors unrelated to advanced age (Qiu et al., 2013).

A victim's ability to accurately remember the events of a crime is the key to successful prosecution. In the case of mistreatment of older people, the victims and offenders are often the only eyewitnesses. This is also the case with the financial exploitation of older individuals. Even with adequate documentation of the financial crime, the alleged offender can argue that the money was not stolen, but freely given, when the alleged victim cannot reliably state that no such permission was granted (Weissberger et al., 2019). In these cases,

Dementia –
A decline in intellectual ability, including significant impairment of memory and other cognitive functions.

the focus and sole source of evidence of the investigation is the victim. Unfortunately, if the victim is diagnosed with dementia, the criminal justice system may falsely assume that the case cannot be pursued (Woods and Pratt, 2005). If a witness can understand their obligation to tell the truth and give clear, consistent, accurate accounts, then people with mild or moderate dementia should be considered and evaluated for their ability to serve as witnesses to criminal events (Jones and Elliot, 2005). However, the ability to cope with the stress of cross-examination and the risk of further cognitive deterioration needs to be managed with modifications similar to those already in place for child witnesses, such as multidisciplinary teams and speedy trials (American Bar Association, 2002).

Recognising the symptoms of Alzheimer's

Worldwide estimates of dementia in 2015 were 47 million and by 2050 projections are that 135 million people will have some form of dementia (Cooke, Day and Mulcahy, 2019). A specific form of dementia is Alzheimer's disease. Alzheimer's typically progresses slowly through three general stages (Figure 4.1) — mild (early stage), moderate (middle stage) and severe (late stage). Since Alzheimer's affects people in different ways, the timing and severity of dementia symptoms vary, as each person progresses differently through the stages of Alzheimer's (www.alz.org).

Figure 4.1: Stages of Alzheimer's

Mild (early stage)

- Problems coming up with the right word or name
- Trouble remembering names when introduced to new people
- Challenges performing tasks in social or work settings
- Forgetting material that one has just read
- Losing or misplacing a valuable object
- Increasing trouble with planning or organising

Moderate (middle stage)

- Forgetfulness of events or about one's own personal history
- Being unable to recall their own address
- Confusion about where they are or what day it is
- Changes in sleep patterns, such as sleeping during the day and becoming restless at night
- An increased risk of wandering and becoming lost
- Personality and behavioural changes, including suspiciousness and delusions or compulsive, repetitive behaviours

Severe (late stage)

- Need round-the-clock assistance with daily activities and personal care
- Lose awareness of recent experiences as well as of their surroundings
- Experience changes in physical abilities, including the ability to walk, sit, and, eventually, swallow
- Have increasing difficulty communicating
- Become vulnerable to infections, especially pneumonia

Source: The Alzheimer's Association 2018. Reproduced with permission.

Types of memory loss associated with Alzheimer's

Alzheimer's is not a normal part of ageing. Approximately 200,000 Americans under the age of 65 have younger-onset Alzheimer's, also known as early-onset Alzheimer's. For those diagnosed with Alzheimer's, the earliest symptoms are disruptions of episodic memory; for example, not remembering recent conversations or an address after five minutes. As the disease progresses, there are further declines in semantic memory, that is, memory involving the ability to recall words, concepts or numbers, which is essential for the use and understanding of language.

Although verbal information is forgotten after a few minutes, procedural memory – skill memories – survives. These are the memory processes that survive the longest in Alzheimer's. For example, the frequently practised skill of making tea (Rusted and

Sheppard, 2002), or playing the piano (National Institute on Aging, 2019). But by the late stages of this disease, memory fails completely, and other cognitive systems follow. The later stages may include personality changes, loss of judgement, disorientation, confusion, loss of speech and eventually the inability to perform daily activities, such as eating, dressing and bathing (Alzheimer's Association, 2019).

Types of memory loss associated with Down syndrome

Older people with Down syndrome often suffer from a similar form of Alzheimer's and can also be considered vulnerable. Down syndrome is the most frequent chromosomal cause of mild to moderate intellectual impairment, occurring in all ethnic and economic groups (NIH, 2019). As they age, those affected by Down syndrome have an increased risk of developing a type of dementia that is very similar to Alzheimer's (Beacher et al., 2009). Virtually all individuals with Down syndrome have brain damage characteristic of Alzheimer's by age 40 (Schupf et al., 1998). Diagnosing dementia in a person with Down syndrome is hard because of the difficulty in assessing changes in thinking skills in those with cognitive impairments. The challenge for interviewing is that most adults with Down syndrome will not self-report concerns about memory (NIH, 2019).

Interviewing strategies for people with cognitive impairment

On initial contact with someone diagnosed with a cognitive impairment, whether witness, victim or suspect, the following are appropriate strategies. Avoid giving the impression of anger by speaking slowly and in a non-threatening, low-pitched voice, and communicate clearly by using short, simple words. For example, ask one question at a time and allow time for response. If necessary, repeat your question using the exact wording. People with these kinds of dementia may only grasp a part of the question at a time. If possible, avoid physical restraints, because confinement may trigger agitation, which may increase confusion and disorientation (Alzheimer's Association, 2006).

The interviewer should test the subject's memory by asking corroborative questions during the interview. These questions measure the subject's accuracy for long-term memory recall by requesting information that can be independently verified. For example, when discussing a burglary that occurred 20 years ago, the subject may be asked their home address, where they were employed and who their supervisor was. This quick test will provide insight into the integrity of the subject's memory. Next, allow the subject time to recall the information (Kipps and Hodges, 2005).

Effective strategies include prompting the person by asking open-ended questions, such as 'Tell me everything you remember about what happened yesterday morning when you entered the bank and saw the robbery', and allowing enough time for their response. Gradually move on to more complex questions, such as 'How did they get the money from the teller?', and follow up with related questions to keep the conversation going: 'Can you describe each of the masked people.' If the interviewee shows confusion or frustration with the question, change the subject, because the question can be rephrased and asked again at another time (Mitchell et al., 2014). For the subject, remembering recently learned information is especially difficult. Interviewers are likely to encounter confusion about places or times (which may be mild at first), an inability to name everyday objects (anomia) and difficulty organising thoughts, calculations and repeating stories (Khachiyants, Trinkle, Son and Kim, 2011).

Another strategy relates to the timing of the interview. Specifically, schedule the interview early in the day. In the mid to late stages of Alzheimer's, confusion and agitation are worse in the late afternoon and evening, a symptom described as **sundowning**.

Sundowning – *Symptoms of confusion and agitation that worsen in the late afternoon and evening and improve earlier in the day.*

These behaviours can include confusion, disorientation, anxiety, agitation, aggression, pacing, wandering, and resistance to redirection (Khachiyants, Trinkle, Son and Kim, 2011). Frequently, it is these sundowning behaviours that are a common cause of institutionalisation of patients suffering from dementia (Hess, 1994).

When reminiscing, some decades dominate

Conduct the following experiment:

Select someone aged 50 years or older. Ask them the following question: 'Imagine you are stranded on a desert island and can bring eight music recordings to keep you company, what would you bring?' (This question is derived from the BBC Radio 4 show *Desert Island Discs*.) Record the details of the songs and their explanations. Then research when the eight songs were released. Did you find that most of the songs and their accompanying memories were from their adolescence and early adulthood?

Reminiscence bump – *The tendency for older adults to have increased recollection for events that occurred during their adolescence and early adulthood.*

As people reminisce about their lives, researchers have found that they tend to remember more events that occurred during their adolescence and early adulthood. This is known as the **reminiscence bump**. One theory that explains this effect is that the events from this decade are when people are most preoccupied with forming an identity, which keeps evolving as people grow older (Jansari and Parkin, 1996).

The idea began with Martin and Smyer (1990). These researchers interviewed middle-aged and older adults to reflect on their lives. Surprisingly, the participants tended to remember events from their twenties and early thirties as most significant. Their explanation is that these were the years when they made the friends they would keep for the rest of their lives, met the people they would marry, and started their career. A biological explanation is that the reminiscence bump occurs because memory storage in autobiographical memory is not constant over time. Rather, memory storage increases during times of changes in the self and in life goals, such as the changes in identity that occur during adolescence (Janssen, Kristo, Rouw and Murre, 2015). The tragedy is that in many persons with dementia, these long-term memories disappear.

IN SUMMARY

If proper strategies are used, cognitive impairment is unrelated to the reliability of memory or to the ability to distinguish the truth from a lie.

 ## CRITICAL THINKING AND APPLICATION QUESTIONS

1   Why are people with cognitive impairments considered vulnerable? Please include examples of two forms of cognitive impairment.

2   What are the unique challenges for police when interviewing a person diagnosed with Alzheimer's?

3   How does asking open-ended questions, rather than closed-ended questions, help recall and reduce interviewer bias?

PEOPLE WITH SOCIAL COMMUNICATION IMPAIRMENTS

FICTION: People with communication difficulties are intellectually impaired and their information cannot be used in a court of law.	*Versus*	FACT: People diagnosed with conditions that impair their social communication ability can still provide forensically relevant testimony.

The purpose of this section is to review the characteristics of people diagnosed with conditions that impair their social communication ability, such as expressive aphasia and autism spectrum disorder.

A **social communication impairment** refers to the impairment of a person's ability to convey information and ideas. Speech production problems do not signal an intellectual impairment; they may indicate that the individual has a disability such as cerebral palsy, or has experienced a stroke, and the mechanisms of speech production are impaired, for example coordination of the mouth, lips, tongue and breathing to produce voice. Yet, in most cases, intellectual ability is intact. For example, the late Stephen Hawking, a brilliant astrophysicist who was diagnosed with amyotrophic lateral sclerosis (a type of motor neurone disease), used computerised voice technology to speak. His impairment affected only his verbal responding, not his cognitive functioning (Dobson, 2002).

Social communication impairment – *A disorder characterised by difficulties with the use of verbal and nonverbal language for social purposes.*

CASE STUDY

Overcoming communication impairment

Kara Hoyte was an aspiring 19-year-old model from Norbury, a district in southwest London, when Mario Celaire viciously attacked her in February 2007. Her story began when Kara returned to her flat after work around 11 pm, and her boyfriend Junior Clarke phoned to say he would be over in 20 minutes. When her door buzzer sounded, she thought it was Junior, but instead it was Mario Celaire, her first boyfriend, whom she previously dated when she was 15. Kara had ended their relationship years ago, but Mario refused to accept it, repeatedly calling and asking her out. Now he stood in her flat demanding she join him for a night on the town. Kara declined, turning her back on him as he left. But as she turned her back, he suddenly grabbed a hammer she kept by the door and struck her repeatedly on the head. Medical reports would show that as she lay there, he continued to beat her head with such viciousness that her skull split open and bits of bone became embedded in her brain (Cohen, 2009).

Kara woke up in the hospital intensive care unit after a three-day coma. She had lost the ability to speak and was suffering from a disorder known as **expressive aphasia**, which affects the ability to produce language, although comprehension remains intact (Vignolo, 1964). Incredibly, she saw the man who tried to murder her entering her intensive care unit. Without the ability to speak, she was helpless to respond. Her family greeted Mario, assuming he was there only out of concern for Kara's recovery. Kara could only turn away in pain and fear.

Later, her mother sensed her anxiety and had the idea of writing down questions with 'yes' or 'no' answers. Although partially paralysed, Kara could still point. 'Do you know who attacked you?' she asked. Kara pointed to 'yes'. Kara's mother then listed every person Kara knew, but Kara kept indicating 'no' until she wrote 'Mario Celaire', a man the family least suspected. At that point, Kara started frantically hitting 'yes' on the board (Hines, 2009).

Expressive aphasia – *The inability to produce language while language comprehension remains intact.*

With the help of forensic experts and a registered intermediary (see below), Kara met the legal requirements for competency and was able to give an account of the attack using writing, drawing and gestures (Adams, 2009). In a surprising turn of events, nine months after the attack, Kara recovered enough of her voice to tell detectives the rest of the story. Mario Celaire, she said, admitted to 'mistakenly' killing his previous girlfriend, Cassandra McDermott, in 2001. Although he had been acquitted of her murder in 2002, Kara's new information and testimony led to Mario Celaire being imprisoned for life in 2009 (Gudjonsson, 2010).

Discussion Questions:

1   Why do you think juries tend to doubt the ability of people with a communication impairment?

2   Besides using a white board to elicit responses to the closed-ended questions, can you think of an effective way to use less leading and more open-ended questions with Kara?

Identifying the signs and symptoms of autism spectrum disorder (ASD)

'If you've met *one* person with autism, you've met *one* person with autism' is a now-famous quote from Stephen Shore, co-author of *Understanding Autism for Dummies* (Shore and Rastelli, 2006). Despite some common traits within the autistic community, Stephen Shore's quote illustrates the necessity of considering each interviewee as an individual. Furthermore, using appropriate interviewing techniques gives each unique interviewee an effective voice in the criminal justice system.

> **Autism spectrum disorder (ASD)**
> – Impairments in social communication and interaction and difficulties in verbal and nonverbal communication.

Individuals diagnosed with **autism spectrum disorder (ASD)** face challenges in social communication and interaction and difficulties in verbal and nonverbal communication (APA, 2019). The symptoms can range from mild to severe and the severity of symptoms are different in each person. Because of this, ASD is often referred to as a 'hidden' condition because there are no obvious indicators of impairment (Maras et al., 2018).

Interacting with police can be a difficult experience for anyone, let alone a person with ASD. Certain characteristics associated with ASD can negatively (and sometimes positively) impact police investigations (Young and Brewer, 2019). The challenge is to effectively manage the interview in a way that does not place vulnerable people at an unfair disadvantage by not adapting best interview practices.

A challenge when interviewing individuals with ASD is overcoming social interaction and communication difficulties; for example, supporting a shared conversation during the interview involves understanding and responding to social cues, such as eye contact and facial expressions. Normally, these conversational behaviours develop as individuals refine their theory of mind (Loth et al., 2018). However, without a well-developed theory of mind, those with ASD may suffer from what is known as 'mind blindness' (Frith, 2001) and have difficulty decoding the meaning of the social language skills used in our daily interactions. The social components of language include what we say, how we say it, our nonverbal communication such as voice intonation, facial expressions, body language, personal space distances, and how appropriate our interactions are in a given situation (Smukler, 2005).

The experience of mind blindness is also felt by the interviewer. Research by Edey et al. (2016) suggests that we are better at interpreting the movements of others who move like us, and individuals with ASD move differently than others; for example, greater frequency of arm movements that are jerkier, with greater acceleration and speed (Cook, Blakemore and Press, 2013). This finding raises the possibility that those interviewing people with ASD have difficulty interpreting the actions of individuals with autism, in the same way that those with autism have problems interpreting and predicting typical movements (Aransih and Edison, 2019; von der Lühe et al., 2016; Cook, 2016). Therefore, 'social impairments' displayed by individuals with ASD may represent a failure by interviewers to infer the correct mental states from the movements of those with ASD. In the same way that seeing a smile triggers the attribution of happiness, perception of fast and accelerated movements may trigger the attribution of anger (Atkinson, Tunstall and Dittrich, 2007).

The interaction difficulties between interviewers and individuals with ASD is shared by both parties; typical individuals may make less accurate mental state attributions about individuals with autism (demonstrate 'mind blindness') in the same way that individuals with autism appear to display mind blindness towards typical individuals.

A second challenge includes the restricted and repetitive patterns of behaviours, interests or activities, and a need for a predictable routine or structure (Meier et al., 2015). A third challenge includes experiencing the sensory aspects of the world in an unusual or extreme way, such as indifference to pain/temperature, excessive smelling/touching of objects, fascination with lights and movement, and being overwhelmed with loud noises (Myles et al., 2004).

Inconsistency of findings has always been a problem for autism research. This variability is primarily due to developmental differences and differences in social cognitive level. However, the findings that have been replicated across studies show that people with ASD display similar characteristics of observation and memory functioning (Williams, Goldstein, Minshew, 2006). In the context of the forensic interview, people with ASD make keen observers. People with ASD show unusually broad attentional focus and sharp perceptions during visual search, visual discrimination and embedded figure detection (Samson, Mottron, Soulières and Zeffiro, 2012), as well as resistance to **change blindness** – noticing details typically ignored by most persons (Smith and Milne, 2009). Besides perceptual advantages, memory advantages are also present, such as superior semantic memory recall (Brezis, 2015), cued recall and recognition (Gaigg and Bowler, 2008).

Most deficits in people with ASD are related to impaired executive functioning (Happé, Booth, Charlton and Hughes, 2006). Executive functions support the cognitive skills of mentally playing with ideas; taking the time to think before acting; meeting novel, unanticipated challenges; resisting temptations; and staying focused (Diamond, 2013). **Executive dysfunction** refers to disruption to the efficacy of executive functions (Pennington et al., 1997).

The impairment of executive functioning skills results in difficulty understanding the perspective of others (Baron-Cohen, 1989), difficulty with planning, and inhibition (Hill, 2004). Additional memory impairments include difficulty recalling the origin of a memory (Hala, Rasmussen and Henderson, 2005; Bowler, Gardiner and Berthollier, 2008), difficulty in spontaneously using organisational strategies to aid recall (Bebko, Rhee, McMorris and Ncube, 2015), and difficulty in the recall of personally experienced events – episodic memory (Crane, Goddard and Pring, 2013). These episodic memory difficulties are related to theory of mind impairments in those with ASD (Adler, Nadler, Eviatar and Shamay-Tsoory, 2010; Baron-Cohen, 1989).

Change blindness – *When a change in a visual stimulus is introduced and the observer does not notice it.*

Executive dysfunction – *Disruption to the efficacy of executive functions, the cognitive processes that regulate, control and manage thoughts and actions.*

Interviewing strategies for people with social communication challenges

Preplanning stages of the interview

Preplanning strategies are essential to accommodate the needs of people diagnosed with ASD, for example, finding out about the person's specific needs. Thus procedures should be outlined in advance and communicated before the interview. Typically, this should match their unique communication needs, clearly outlining procedures and explaining what will happen during the interview using unambiguous language and, in some circumstances, pictures (Teachman and Gibson, 2018).

It is important to prepare an interview environment that considers sensory needs. Individuals with autism may find it difficult to process everyday sensory information, such as sights and smells. Murrie, Warren, Kristiansson and Dietz (2002) recommend interviewing the person in a familiar location to avoid this distraction. Minimally, consider reducing the intensity of illumination and mechanical noises such as ventilation sounds. A final consideration is allowing the person to hold or play with a familiar object or 'fiddle toy' (stress ball, therapy cubes, sensory bracelets), since this may improve concentration (National Autism Resources, 2019).

Routines bring comfort and new situations can create stress and overstimulation. Stressful triggers include the presence of a new situation, unknown people, noises, or unanticipated surprises. The behavioural coping responses to overstimulation can range from **stimming**, 'self-stimulating' behaviours that are calming, repetitive and ritualistic and can involve any of the senses (Cheol-Hong, 2017), to more intense expressions, including inappropriate verbal statements, or other actions that may be mistakenly viewed as an indication of hostility, criminal intent, alcohol or drug intoxication. Fortunately, there are distress indicators, sometimes referred to as the **rumble stage** (Church, Alisanski and Amanullah, 2000). During this stage, behaviours include pacing, rocking, or seeking reassurance by repetitive questioning and anger rumination (Patel, Day, Jones and Mazefsky, 2017). To prevent this, lessening sensory stimulation, taking more frequent breaks or redirecting attention speeds recovery (Barry-Walsh and Mullen, 2004).

Appropriate interview structure (question type and sequencing)

Creating a situation for individuals with ASD that accentuates their strengths and not their weaknesses is the goal (Desaunay et al., 2020). Beginning the interview with standard, open narrative questions is not an effective strategy with those diagnosed with ASD. Part of the reason is that free recall supplies less support for retrieval (Bowler, Gaigg and Gardiner, 2015). When provided with more structure, that is, when asked to choose between information they were and were not previously exposed to, they correctly chose the information they had seen before (Gaigg, Gardiner and Bowler, 2008). Based on this finding, interviewers should try to provide maximum task support by testing their memory under conditions that present the context of the original event, a concept known as the **task support hypothesis**. Interview support must be very close to the original, remembered event. Using vague, general, non-specific instructions is detrimental to people with ASD.

Although a free recall task strategy permits uninterrupted recall from the interviewer, recalling even trivial events, when used with a person diagnosed with ASD, it may lead to overloading, especially when requested to supply contextual details about the event, such as 'What model car did he drive, what colour was it?' The best practice is the use of a simple

---

Stimming – A behavioural coping response involving repetitive and calming behaviours that can involve any of the senses.

Rumble stage – The initial signs of distress displayed in ASD before expressing intense behaviours from stimulus overload.

Task support hypothesis – The idea that situations can be created for individuals with autism that capitalise on their areas of strength – in the case of memory, creating situations that increase their ability to remember.

structured interview (Koegel, Bradshaw, Ashbaugh and Koegel, 2014) or drawing activity plans, (Peters, Forlin, McInerney and Maclean, 2013), rather than the more complicated cognitive interview technique reviewed in Chapter 2 (Geiselman, Fisher, MacKinnon and Holland, 1985). Extended interview time is needed, because the subject may react slowly to questions, a behaviour known as **delayed response latency**. This behaviour should not be confused with stubbornness. It may take several uninterrupted seconds for the subject to understand and respond (Lamella and Tincani, 2012). Finally, to minimise stress, the interview should be as short as possible (10–15 minutes), with a countdown timer to show how much time until the next break. If the interview scenario is too difficult to manage, research shows that email interviewing is effective for some people with ASD (Benford and Standen, 2010).

Other strategies include focusing on remembering intricate details and having to recall them sequentially, rather than jump to what the interviewer believes are the vital facts. Therefore, the interview requires more supportive behaviours and time to recall *relevant* details (Sarrett, 2017). In the same manner, asking questions with 'open' and 'unsupported' cues is not effective, because this approach requires inferring what information the interviewer wants and risks receiving irrelevant information. For example, the question 'Start at the beginning, and tell me what happened?' may receive the response 'I was born.' As an alternative, asking a precise, single clear question, such as 'When you exited the city bus at noon yesterday, what did you see across the street?', will more likely elicit the information the interviewer is looking for. Clear questions are important because the person with ASD may have an alternative understanding of the world. According to Hamilton (2006), although intelligent, they may not understand everyday terminology. In fact, they may interpret what you say literally. For example, you may want them to wait in the next room, so you ask them to 'step outside'. They may respond by walking out to the car park. Asked to take a seat, and they may pick up a chair.

> **Delayed response latency** – *An increased length of time between the last word of the interviewer's question and the first word of the subject's response.*

PART II

The Vulnerable Person Registry: Canada's answer to helping vulnerable persons

> There was one particular young adult with autism we had dealt with before, who loved to play with toy guns and point them at people. He had a complete infatuation with cops, always wanting to check out their guns and things like that. He would stand on Yonge Street and point his toy gun at passing cars. Fortunately, he was on the registry, so we knew what we were dealing with. (O'Malley, 2017, para. 19)

This description from Sgt Palmer illustrates the advantages of Ontario's Vulnerable Person Registry. This registry allows improved police response to vulnerable persons who may require emergency aid due to their condition. It speeds up finding and helping vulnerable residents by making important personal information readily available to responding officers. In the event a vulnerable person requires police aid, their physical description, medical history, areas they frequent, triggers and de-escalation techniques are available to emergency responders. Speaking with uniformed police officers can be a challenging, stressful experience. But often, when officers meet a vulnerable person, there are important things they need to know to ensure everyone's safety. The benefits of approaches like this are safer communities, officer safety and reduction of strain on department resources (IACP's Alzheimer's Initiatives, 2019).

Helping persons with ASD via registered intermediaries

Appointing a communications specialist known as a **registered intermediary** helps police officers obtain the best evidence from vulnerable victims and witnesses (O'Mahony, 2010). The purpose of the intermediary is to ease the questioning of vulnerable witnesses, but there are clear differences in the application of their role. Intermediaries come from a wide variety of professional backgrounds, including speech and language therapy, psychology, and social work (Cooper and Mattison, 2017).

The Witness Intermediary Scheme (WIS) was rolled out across England and Wales in 2008, and schemes based on the English model were introduced in Northern Ireland in 2013 and in New South Wales, Australia in 2016. Across all three jurisdictions, the purpose of the registered intermediary is to help communication with, and specifically the questioning of, vulnerable people. Despite having a shared purpose and origin, there are marked yet unexplored differences in the ways these witness intermediary schemes operate (Agneswaran, 2018).

Registered intermediaries are specialists who help vulnerable victims, witnesses, suspects and defendants with significant communication deficits to communicate their answers more effectively during a police interview and when giving evidence at trial. The registered intermediary role is also impartial, as intermediaries are responsible directly to the court. Their role includes advising criminal justice system professionals (legal advocates and lawyers) on how best to frame questions. However, providing this service depends on the victim, witness or suspect disclosing their diagnosis, or, alternatively, the police recognising vulnerability (Plotnikoff and Woolfson, 2015).

In England and Wales, intermediaries can be seen over the live link sitting next to the vulnerable witness while they are being cross-examined or sitting/standing next to the witness when they are being cross-examined in the courtroom. They are also allowed to intervene during questioning (at the judge's discretion), if their communication recommendations for the vulnerable person are not adhered to (Ministry of Justice, 2015).

It is worth noting that there is concern among police as to whether registered intermediaries always fully understand their role and whether they might be detrimental to an interview, for example by intervening inappropriately or even offering the suspect an alibi during interview (Collins, Harker and Antonopoulos, 2016). Because of the possible intrusiveness of the presence of the intermediary in court, it is important to consider the effect this has on jury perceptions of the vulnerable person the intermediary is assisting. Nevertheless, the presence of a registered intermediary has beneficial effects for vulnerable adult suspects, such as decreasing interrogative pressure in interviews, and encouraging the presence and better ASD informed involvement of legal representation (Mattison, Dando and Ormerod, 2015).

> **Registered intermediary**
> – Specialists who help vulnerable people communicate more effectively during a police interview and when giving evidence at trial.

IN SUMMARY

People diagnosed with conditions that impair their social communication ability, such as expressive aphasia or autism spectrum disorder, can provide forensically valid information. Forensic psychologists are obliged to identify and accommodate vulnerable individuals through proper interview strategies and the use of registered intermediaries.

 ## CRITICAL THINKING AND APPLICATION QUESTIONS

1   It is important to give the person with ASD appropriately detailed information so they know what will happen, and what to expect during a witness interview. Create a visual timetable to support a person's understanding and expectations. This should include pictures and clearly show the order in which things will happen.

2   Many interviewers follow the advice offered by the acronym CREDO (compassion, respect, empathy, dignity and openness) regarding the interviewees' needs. Explain how you would support the CREDO approach when interviewing a 60-year-old woman with ASD who was robbed. Her apartment was ransacked, and she was roughly treated and tied to a chair for four hours before the police arrived.

3   Law enforcement agencies are working to increase knowledge and awareness of people with impaired communication. Imagine you are a paid consultant giving a speech to a police organisation. Outline what to do and what not to do when confronting a person who may be diagnosed with ASD.

PART II

THE ROLES OF THE FORENSIC PSYCHOLOGIST

....

FICTION: Interviewing vulnerable persons is a waste of valuable resources because it does not collect forensically useful information.

Versus

FACT: Forensic psychology offers ways to obtain accurate, reliable and forensically relevant information from vulnerable persons.

....

So far, this chapter has explored the nature of vulnerability and identified what can assist police and prosecutors, assessing vulnerability in different contexts and provide the support that vulnerable witnesses, victims and suspects require. Forensic psychologists need to lead the charge for more empirical research, including real-world non-laboratory studies to identify optimal techniques for obtaining best evidence from individuals previously ignored because of their vulnerable status.

The nature of vulnerability, in the context of a case progressing through the criminal justice system, is not clearly understood by police and prosecutors. Therefore, opportunities are available for forensic psychologists to persuade lawyers, investigators and judges that they need a better understanding of the psychological factors that affect the reliability of vulnerable witness testimony and the weight it should be given. The forensic psychologist often plays the role of witness consultant, providing valuable input as a participant in witness development teams. Forensic psychologists assist the court by preparing psychologically vulnerable clients to tell their stories effectively during trial.

The importance of adequate police training in the identification of vulnerable witnesses cannot be overstated. Future research should examine police effectiveness in identifying vulnerabilities, as well as ensuring that appropriate training and procedures are in place to respond to witnesses' special needs (Smith and Tilney, 2007).

It is important to remember that the police are not required to be experts on cognitive and social communication disorders, but they should be sufficiently trained to detect possible signs of vulnerability and be able to respond appropriately. Fortunately, there has been an increase in the number of locations that combine the perspectives of individual police services and mental health practitioners (in some cases even including those who are diagnosed with the disorder themselves). The two agencies must work together, in partnership, to achieve their common goal, namely to ensure that the guilty are convicted and the innocent are protected.

IN SUMMARY

Forensic psychology offers ways to obtain accurate, reliable and forensically relevant information from vulnerable persons. More empirical research is needed to identify the best practices for individuals previously ignored because of their vulnerable status.

 CRITICAL THINKING AND APPLICATION QUESTIONS

1   Outline the elements of a training programme to assist the police in identifying people with vulnerabilities. Begin by explaining why training is important and focus on the key symptoms essential for identification that the police may not be aware of.

2   Now that you have learned about people with communication challenges, how accurately are they depicted in the entertainment media? Try to find an example of a vulnerable person and evaluate the accuracy of their portrayal.

3   Search for information online about your local jurisdiction. What information is available about how they identify and accommodate vulnerable people? How accurate or detailed is it?

CHAPTER REVIEW

Our exploration concludes by recognising that there are individuals who are labelled as 'vulnerable' by the criminal justice system. This label is not meant to discriminate against or stereotype people by treating them as one group, rather, the label 'vulnerable' in this context helps identify and provide fair treatment for witnesses, victims and suspects. This is important, because although they have the capability to supply dependable and forensically useful information, if they are not identified or managed properly, their information is ignored or sometimes rendered invalid. Finally, with the proper procedures, those diagnosed with intellectual and social communication challenges can supply forensically relevant, accurate and valuable information for the criminal justice system.

NAMES TO KNOW

Gisli Gudjonsson

An internationally recognised researcher into the measurement and application of interrogative suggestibility, psychological vulnerabilities and false confessions.

- Gudjonsson, G. (2017) Memory distrust syndrome, confabulation, and false confession. *Cortex*, 87, 156–65.

- Gudjonsson, G. (2018) *The Psychology of False Confessions: Forty Years of Science and Practice*. Wiley.

Kelly Richards

Investigates young people with cognitive disabilities and their contact with the police and youth justice, and reintegrating child sex offenders via circles of support and accountability.

- Richards, K. and Kathy, E. (2019) Young people with cognitive impairments and overrepresentation in the criminal justice system: Service provider perspectives on policing. *Police Practice and Research*, 20(2), 156–71.

- Richards, K. (2019) Sympathy for the devil? Child sexual abuse, public opinion and the cycle-of-abuse theory. In K. Gleeson and C. Lumby (eds) *Age of Consent* (pp. 87–101). University of Western Australia Press.

Uta Frith

Best known for her research on autism spectrum disorders. She was one of the initiators of the study of Asperger's syndrome and her work on theory of mind in autism proposes that people with autism have specific difficulties understanding other people's beliefs and desires.

- Frith, U. (2003) *Autism: Explaining the Enigma* (2nd edn). Wiley-Blackwell.

- Frith, U. (2013) Autism and dyslexia: A glance over 25 years of research. *Perspectives in Psychological Science*, 8(6), 670–2.

PART II

5 INTERVIEWING SUSPECTS: FROM INTERROGATION TO INVESTIGATION

Chapter Introduction

A confession is the most powerful influence on a jury's judgement of guilt, which makes investigative interviewing an important skill for police work. This chapter explores how subtle forms of psychological manipulation can undermine the integrity of confession evidence. Our investigation explores the range of reasons suspects give false confessions. We also investigate the unfortunate consequences of interrogation tactics that yield false confessions. We conclude by examining the power of confessions to overrule innocence and evidence.

Learning Outcomes

A brief history of getting information from uncooperative suspects

- Describe the historical trends for the shift from interrogation to investigation.

Adversarial versus inquisitorial interviewing

- Describe the differences between the two main approaches for investigative interviewing.

False confessions and the paradox of innocence

- Be able to explain how and why an innocent person can be convinced they committed a crime.

Why confessions overrule innocence and evidence

- Describe the ways that being innocent can put potential suspects at a disadvantage during an interrogation.

A BRIEF HISTORY OF GETTING INFORMATION FROM UNCOOPERATIVE SUSPECTS

FICTION: The purpose of interrogation is to obtain a confession by any means necessary.	*Versus*	**FACT:** It can be psychologically harmful and ineffective if confrontational and aggressive approaches are used to obtain a confession.

CASE STUDY

The 'Norfolk Four'

Derek Tice, Danial Williams, Joseph Dick and Eric Wilson, collectively known as the 'Norfolk Four', were wrongfully convicted of rape and murder based on false confessions. Each person experienced high-pressure interrogation tactics, including threats of the death penalty and questionable use of lie detector tests, even though the details of their confessions did not match the crime scene, the other confessions, or the confession of the real killer.

Their story began on 8 July 1997, in Norfolk, Virginia, when not one but four innocent men separately confessed to a horrific crime that none of them committed. Nineteen-year-old US Navy sailor Billy Bosko returned home after being at sea to find his wife Michelle Bosko lying dead on the floor of their bedroom, raped and stabbed. He ran across the hallway to his neighbour Danial Williams to ask him to call for help. That fateful phone call began the nightmare for Danial Williams, as the police focused on Williams as a suspect, even though he had an alibi. Williams' wife remembered waking up in the middle of the night with him next to her as she heard loud male and female voices in Michelle Bosko's flat. Unfortunately, the police ignored that alibi and the DNA evidence proving Williams' innocence (Williams' wife died four months later from ovarian cancer without ever being questioned). The police already believed that Williams was guilty, now all they needed was a confession.

Although he passed a polygraph (lie detector) test, the police told Williams that he had failed it. Williams decided that he was never going to escape the interrogation unless he confessed to a crime he did not commit. After 11 hours of interrogation without food or sleep, Williams signed his confession, saying he beat her with a shoe (Berlow, 2007). The same day, autopsy results indicate she was stabbed and strangled – not beaten, as Williams had confessed. Williams then signed another confession, saying he stabbed Michelle Bosko. He was arrested and charged with capital murder and rape.

When the DNA evidence cleared him, the police decided that he must have had a partner and started questioning Joe Dick, Williams' former roommate. Dick, with a low IQ and suggestible personality, was easily persuaded by the police that he committed the crime with Williams, and he confessed as well (Dick also had an alibi the police never verified). After many hours, he began naming any men he knew as his accomplices until a total of seven men were charged with the crime. Even when the real killer, Omar Ballard, confessed to the crime and was convicted via his DNA, the police were still convinced that the eight men conspired together. Ballard has admitted repeatedly, and confirms in sworn testimony to a Virginia court, that he committed this crime alone.

The physical evidence conclusively proves that Ballard – and only Ballard – was the source of semen and blood recovered from the crime scene. There was no DNA or other physical evidence linking the four sailors or anyone other than Ballard to this crime. It so happened that on that day – at the very same hour while Danial Williams was being interrogated – the police were obtaining an arrest warrant for Omar Ballard for an assault two weeks earlier in the same apartment complex. No one made the connection (Jackman, 2017). Nevertheless, four innocent men were convicted based on false confessions extracted by a detective who has a documented history of eliciting false confessions (Wells and Leo, 2008).

Discussion Questions:

1   In most countries, jurors may not find a person guilty if there is more than a 'reasonable doubt' of their guilt. What does that mean? Based on the evidence described, do you think a jury could have had reasonable doubts about the Norfolk Four's innocence or guilt?

2   Before questioning by police, suspects must be told their legal rights, which typically include the right to remain silent and to speak to legal counsel. Why might these men have waived their rights? How might their story have been different if they had insisted on exercising these rights?

3   Eventually, these men were found (or pleaded guilty) to the crime in court, even though there was no evidence linking them to the crime. In what ways were the following parties responsible for the outcome: the four men themselves; the police; the lawyers; and, in the case of a court trial, the jury?

The power of confession evidence

A **confession** is a detailed statement that admits all the facts necessary for the conviction of a crime (Kassin, 2008a). Confessions are so persuasive that their introduction makes the other aspects of a trial unnecessary (McCormick, 1972). In fact, confessions are the most incriminating form of evidence, followed by eyewitness and character testimony (Kassin and Neumann, 1997).

> **Confession** – A detailed statement that admits all the facts necessary for the conviction of a crime.

Frequently considered the most undeniable proof of guilt, a confession relieves doubts in the minds of judges and jurors more than any other evidence (Wrightsman, Nietzel and Fortune, 1994). In fact, a truthful confession is unbelievably valuable for police. It makes it easier to recover goods, leads to compensation and satisfaction for the victims, and often results in a conviction during trial (Kassin et al., 2010b). Under these circumstances, the interrogator has no need to consider the suspect's credibility any further, case closed.

Successful interrogators have three goals to achieve:

1   Overcome the subject's reluctance to talk and promote cooperation and engagement instead.

2   Use techniques that help the retrieval of accurate and complete information while avoiding those that corrupt or distort accurate recall.

3   Because the subject may deliberately conceal or fabricate information, the interrogator must weigh the likelihood that the information is truthful (Evans et al., 2010).

Why are juries persuaded by confession evidence?

The myth that innocent people do not confess biases even the most educated jury. Therefore, inadmissible evidence like coerced confessions are typically excluded from trial records, because even retracted false confessions influence juries. Thus, past convictions were automatically reversed whenever a court found that a coerced confession was mistakenly presented as evidence (Kassin and Neumann, 1997).

**Fundamental
attribution
error** –
*Attributing
other people's
behaviour
to internal
causes, while
underestimating
the importance
of external
causes.*

Why confessions exert such a powerful influence over juries is explained by the **fundamental attribution error** – the tendency to attribute other people's behaviour to internal causes, while underestimating the importance of external, situational factors (Ross, Amabile and Steinmetz, 1977). In the context of jury decisions of guilt, the jury believes the cause of a confession is because of being guilty (an internal cause, a character flaw), while overlooking the possible use of coercive tactics during interrogation (situational factors, sleep deprivation). The fundamental attribution error explains how confession evidence influences jurors, even when the confession is unreliable (Gilbert and Malone, 1995). Unfortunately, once a suspect makes a confession, even if the confession is later ruled inadmissible by the court, juries often hold on to newly formed beliefs even after they have been discredited (Anderson, Lepper and Ross, 1980), or they were instructed to ignore them by a judge (Kassin and Sukel, 1997). In other words, *what* you say is more influential than *why* you say it (Wrightsman, 2013).

Leo (2008) offers three reasons why jurors find false confessions difficult to understand in the absence of a mental vulnerability or physical intimidation. First, although few jurors understand the degree to which police interrogation is a manipulative form of persuasion, many acknowledge they know less than they should when asked to consider interrogation and confession evidence (Henkel, Coffman and Dailey, 2008). Second, a strange form of egocentric belief surrounds most jurors regarding false confessions. Specifically, jurors find it hard to believe that suspects would go against their own self-interest by confessing to something they did not do (Leo and Liu, 2009). Third, because those same jurors believe they would never falsely confess, they apply the same logic to explain the behaviour of others. Research by Leo (2008) supports these three perspectives, finding that college students and potential jurors believe that false confessions are more likely for others (87 per cent) than for themselves (32 per cent).

The origins of psychological interrogation

Before the 1930s, physical abuse during police interrogations was just another tool in their inventory. Physical abuse was a legal method of getting a confession, including deprivation of food and water, bright lights, physical discomfort and long isolation, beating with rubber hoses and other instruments that don't leave marks (Layton, 2006).

American police routinely used coercive interrogation practices until the late 1930s. In 1937, the US Supreme Court ruled that confessions obtained by force cannot be used as evidence at trial. In the case of *Brown* v. *Mississippi* (297 U.S. 278, 1936), the Supreme Court denied a 'voluntary' confession that was obtained after police repeatedly suspended a suspect from a tree and whipped him. The result was that, by the 1950s, confessions were considered involuntary not only if police physically beat suspects, but also if they held suspects in custody for an unnecessarily extended period, deprived the suspect of sleep, food, water or bathroom facilities, promised some benefit if the suspect confessed, or threatened some harm if the suspect did not confess (McMillen, 1990).

Third degree
– *The first
degree is
arrest, the
second is
transportation
to jail and the
third degree is
interrogation
with physical
pain.*

The movement away from physical methods is reflected in early police interrogation training manuals. The first manual was W. R. Kidd's 200-page pocket-sized book *Police Interrogation*, which emphasised the importance of shifting to psychological interrogation methods. Kidd's manual condemned the traditional physical practices as 'not only vicious, but useless' (Kidd, 1940, p. 46). The manual further explains why the **third degree** should never be used. First, this harsh approach produced false confessions that are inadmissible in court, thus breaking public confidence in the police. Second, while physical force is no longer the common tool of the police interrogator, a new, psychologically oriented coercion appeared. This form of psychologically oriented coercion is more sinister because it is often unrecognised. The movement against forced confessions was not moral, but practical. To prosecute a suspect, the courts cited the unreliability of the confession's contents when induced by a promise of benefit or a threat of harm (Wigmore, 1966).

If police obtain information through any of these illegal means, the information cannot be used by the prosecutor at trial. This is known as **the fruit of the poisonous tree** metaphor (Dressler, 2002). This legal metaphor states that if the source of the evidence (the 'tree') is tainted, then everything gained from it (the 'fruit') is also tainted (Pitler, 1968). The reason is that confessions obtained using torture are considered subjective evidence, because torture may lead to the suspect confessing anything. Even without torture, the mere existence of false confessions proves that confessions do not provide enough proof of guilt.

Can torture produce forensically useful information?

The deliberate infliction of physical and mental suffering is best used for spreading fear, terror, or seeking vengeance and punishment, not extracting information (O'Mara, 2016). But our cultural imagination is driven by the entertainment media showing the successful use of torture during interrogation, creating the myth that torture is a necessary evil (Gearty, 2007).

If the goal of torture is to extract actionable information, it is important to distinguish between terroristic torture and interrogational torture. While **terroristic torture** is torture used as a warning, **interrogational torture** is torture used for extracting information. It is also important to distinguish between forward-looking and backward-looking torture (Shue, 1978). Backward-looking torture extracts information about past terror actions, and forward-looking torture extracts information about future terrorist plots (Bufacchi and Arrigo, 2006). Our exploration of torture focuses on forward-looking interrogational torture.

Our beliefs about interrogation come from what we see portrayed in the entertainment media, not from experience. We see torture portrayed as effective. This is the case in the film *Zero Dark Thirty* (Boal, Ellison and Bigelow, 2012). *Zero Dark Thirty* implied that the use of torture on al-Qaeda-affiliated detainees led to the discovery and eventual death of Osama bin Laden (founder of al-Qaeda). The film claimed it was based on first-hand accounts of actual events. The problem is that the film misrepresented the controversial interrogation techniques now widely condemned as torture. In the film, Central Intelligence Agency (CIA) operatives use enhanced interrogation techniques on detainees to find bin Laden's courier, known as Abu Ahmed al-Kuwaiti. After which, a detainee (a CIA operative named Maya) tells the protagonist that he will provide information because he has no desire to be tortured again. Ultimately, Maya reveals that 20 sources have helped to identify al-Kuwaiti and his relationship to bin Laden.

Unlike the film, according to a US Senate report (SSCI, 2014), the key information about al-Kuwaiti was not obtained using enhanced interrogation techniques. Instead, it came from an al-Qaeda operative named Hassan Ghul, who, without any enhanced interrogation techniques, freely provided his captors with information (Temple-Raston, 2014). Ghul told the CIA that al-Kuwaiti was bin Laden's 'closest assistant' and even said he believed bin Laden was living in a house in Pakistan. It was only after Ghul offered this information that the CIA decided to press him further. He was transferred to an undisclosed 'black site' prison, where he was placed in a 'hanging' stress position and kept awake for 59 hours straight. He began hallucinating and gave no actionable threat information (Dockterman, 2014). The problem is that *Zero Dark Thirty*'s torture scenes create the false impression that these interrogations provided early clues about the identity of Osama bin Laden's courier, who would ultimately lead the CIA to Osama bin Laden (Taddonio, 2015).

The fruit of the poisonous tree – *A legal metaphor stating that evidence obtained as the result of a coerced statement is inadmissible.*

Terroristic torture – *Torture used as a warning by sending a message to people.*

Interrogational torture – *Torture for the purpose of extracting information.*

PART II

In fact, the US Senate Select Committee on Intelligence Report (SSCI, 2014) stands in stark contrast to this belief. The report reveals that much of the information gathered in the enhanced interrogations was inaccurate and that torture often led to fabricated confessions and information divulged solely to appease interrogators and prevent further torture.

The ticking bomb scenario

Ticking bomb scenario – *A hypothetical reason to justify the use of torture.*

We ban torture because it is cruel and inhumane, but there is one exception to the taboo of torture, the hypothetical **ticking bomb scenario** (Spino and Cummins, 2014). Imagine that a captured terrorist has hidden a bomb in the heart of a nearby city. Rather than hide his guilt, he brags about the imminent explosion and the catastrophic amount of human suffering it will cause. Fortunately, there is still time to prevent this catastrophe and it appears that torture is the only choice to quickly extract the information about the bomb's location.

This scenario suggests that using torture to prevent greater killing is sometimes permissible, akin to the idea of fighting fire with fire (O'Mara, 2018). Bufacchi and Arrigo (2006) describe the three common elements of this scenario:

1   The lives of many citizens are in danger.

2   The catastrophe is imminent and there is little time to act.

3   We have captured the person with the information that prevents the catastrophe from happening.

While justifications for torture thrive in fantasy (Shue, 2006), once the fantasy of imagination takes hold, scepticism and rational thought leave. The flaw with the ticking bomb scenario is the assumption that torture is the only way of extracting information from the terrorist. Unfortunately, despite the hypothetical nature and circular reasoning, this argument is still considered by legal theorists and criminal justice enforcement as a rational justification for torture (Dershowitz, 2006).

Global Perspectives

Perceptions on the use of torture

Figure 5.1: Can a captured enemy combatant be tortured to obtain important military information?

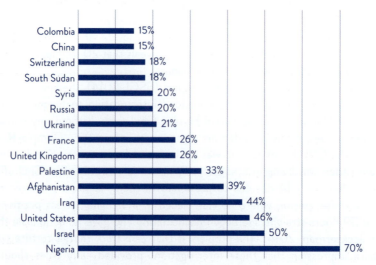

*Number responding 'Yes' (N = 17,762)
Source: Data from WIN/Gallup International (2016) *People on War – 2016 Survey*. ICRC.

The 2016 *People on War* survey is based on a global survey carried out from June to September by WIN/Gallup International and its local partners, and reflects the opinions of 17,762 people in 16 countries. Although two-thirds of respondents consider torture to be wrong, torturing a captured enemy combatant to obtain important military information is viewed as an acceptable act by slightly more than a third. This proportion has significantly increased since 1999. Most of these people stated that their opinion did not change after they learned that torture is considered illegal according to the UN Convention against Torture, whether because they think torture is sometimes justified or because they think it is inherent to wars. A higher proportion of people living in countries affected by armed conflict, such as Israel and Nigeria, responded that torture is wrong. More people living in the P5 (permanent members of the United Nations Security Council) countries – China, France, Russia, the UK and the USA – and Switzerland tend to acknowledge the physical and psychological effects of torture than people living in countries affected by armed conflict.

The ineffectiveness of enhanced interrogation techniques

Enhanced interrogation techniques, such as prolonged sleep deprivation and intense pain, destroy the very memories they are supposed to recover. Interrogation's goal is to access the information in long-term memory, revealing personally experienced events and intentions for future actions (O'Mara, 2009). Unlike the entertainment media portrayals of torture, evidence shows that repeated and extreme pain and stress impair memory functioning. In fact, the ideal conditions for encoding, storage and retrieval of memories are time, cooperation and low stress, the three important components missing from the ticking bomb scenario.

There are three main reasons why enhanced interrogation techniques are ineffective:

1   Torture does not persuade people to make a reasoned decision to cooperate, but produces panic, dissociation, unconsciousness and long-term neurological damage (O'Mara, 2016).

2   If the goal is for the subject to provide accurate and detailed recall, extreme pain, cold, sleep deprivation and fear of torture itself all damage memory, mood and cognition (Danzig, 2012).

3   People experiencing torture speak less and produce less information to verify (Vrij et al., 2017).

A closer examination of sleep deprivation, pain and drowning confirms their futility for memory retrieval. One of the first symptoms of sleep deprivation is disordered thoughts and bursts of irrationality. Beyond 24 hours of sleep deprivation, people show severe declines in memory retrieval and coherent speech (Longordo, Kopp and Lüthi, 2009). Eventually, sleep deprivation causes hallucinations and a break with reality. Even if the person knew the vital piece of information (the location of a ticking bomb), sleep deprivation makes it unlikely they could accurately and meaningfully communicate that information (Max, 2007).

Studies of people in severe chronic pain show that pain damages memory by shrinking the hippocampus, a structure required for memory consolidation (Sutherland, 2012). The process of suffocation by water is known as *waterboarding*. The individual is strapped to a tilted board, with legs above their head and a cloth over their face, covering their nose and mouth. Water is continuously poured over the cloth to prevent breathing, simulating drowning, and causing a panic response. Repeating the process for about 40 seconds creates a **fight-or-flight response** equal to experiencing the trauma of a near-death experience (Jones, 2010). The lack of oxygen draws activity away from brain regions

Fight-or-flight response – *A physiological reaction that prepares our bodies to stay and fight or to flee when threatened.*

associated with higher cognitive function and memory in favour of brainstem regions concerned with reflexive responses supporting immediate survival (O'Mara, 2018). Thus, waterboarding for memory retrieval is ineffective.

Finally, the analysis of millions of internal CIA documents related to the torture of terrorism suspects concluded that the enhanced interrogation techniques are an ineffective way of acquiring intelligence or gaining cooperation from detainees. The report adds that many CIA detainees fabricated information, resulting in faulty intelligence (SSCI, 2014).

If enhanced interrogation methods involving extreme stress do not reveal information stored in memory, then what does? Surveys of interrogators revealed that rapport and relationship-building techniques are employed most often and are perceived as the most effective methods, particularly in comparison with confrontational techniques (Redlich, Kelly and Miller, 2014). Research reveals that detainees are more likely to reveal meaningful information earlier in the interview and their disclosures were more complete in response to non-coercive strategies, especially rapport building (Goodman-Delahunty, Martschuk and Dhami, 2014).

IN SUMMARY

Historically, the purpose of interrogation was to obtain a confession by any means necessary. However, these confrontational and aggressive approaches were physically and psychologically harmful and ineffective.

 ### CRITICAL THINKING AND APPLICATION QUESTIONS

1   Create a unique example that illustrates the 'fruit of the poisonous tree' metaphor from your own experience.

2   Imagine if the use of torture had supplied direct information leading to Osama bin Laden's death, as the film *Zero Dark Thirty* tried to show. Would a government be less morally guilty for the acute suffering it inflicted on unarmed and defenceless people if innocent lives had been saved as a result?

3   Find an example of the 'ticking time bomb' scenario in a search of entertainment media. Which of the three common elements described by Bufacchi and Arrigo (2006) were used to justify this scenario?

ADVERSARIAL VERSUS INQUISITORIAL APPROACHES

FICTION: Suspects respond best to an adversarial approach.   *Versus*   **FACT:** Suspects respond best to inquisitorial approaches.

Deception in the interrogation room

Making false accusations, shouting, invading someone's space, pretending to have evidence, telling a suspect they failed a polygraph are all legal tactics in the USA. Although prohibited from using physical force, police can use a variety of powerful psychological strategies to extract confessions, including the use of deception during interrogation (Najdowski and

Bonventre, 2014). Police have been allowed to falsely claim that a suspect's accomplice confessed when, in fact, he had not (*Frazier* v. *Cupp*, 394 U.S. 731, 1969), to falsely state finding a suspect's fingerprints at a crime scene when there were none (*Oregon* v. *Mathiason*, 429 U.S. 492, 1977), and to lie about possessing incriminating DNA evidence and satellite photography showing the suspect's car at a crime scene (*State* v. *Nightingale*, 58 A. 3d 1057, 2012). Yet threats and promises are not allowed. It is feared that threats and promises will coerce suspects to give involuntary or unreliable confessions.

How does an interrogation differ from an interview?

Most interrogation manuals suggest beginning with an interview before the actual interrogation, but how do these two techniques differ?

Table 5.1: Differences between interviews and interrogations

	Interview	Interrogation
Focus	Informal format, no accusations	Formal format, accusatory
Purpose	Gather information	Learn the truth
When	Conducted early during an investigation	Conducted only when the investigator is certain of the suspect's guilt
Where	Conducted in a variety of environments	Conducted in a controlled environment
Format	Informal; flexible and free-flowing interactions	Formal; structured and rehearsed interactions
Who speaks	Suspect 80 per cent, interviewer 20 per cent	Suspect 20 per cent, interviewer 80 per cent

Rights against self-incrimination

Legally, we all have rights even if we are unaware and need reminding of them. Among these rights is the right not to incriminate yourself. These rights are found globally. For example, in Australia, suspects have the right to refuse to answer questions posed to them by police before trial and to refuse to give evidence at trial (Australian Law Reform Commission, 2015). In Canada, even the right to silence is protected under Section 7 and Section 11(c) of the Canadian Charter of Rights and Freedoms. The accused may not be compelled as a witness against himself in criminal proceedings, and therefore only voluntary statements made to police are admissible as evidence.

Clear knowledge of your legal rights is explicitly stated in the European Union. European law includes five innovations (European Commission, 2011):

1   Suspects will be informed of their rights following the arrest.

2   They will be given a 'letter of rights' spelling out their rights in writing.

3   The letter of rights will be easy to understand, without legal jargon.

4   It will be made available in a language the suspect understands.

5   It will contain practical details about the person's rights.

In the USA, the case of *Miranda* v. *Arizona* (384 U.S. 436, 1966) addressed the need for individuals in police custody to understand their constitutional rights before being questioned by police. When the case of *Miranda* v. *Arizona* reached the US Supreme Court in 1966, coercive police interrogation met its final review. Ernesto Miranda confessed to rape and kidnapping after two hours of interrogation, and the appeal to the US Supreme Court alleged that Miranda was not aware of his right to remain silent under the US Fifth Amendment of the Constitution or his right to receive legal counsel under the US Sixth Amendment of the Constitution. The Supreme Court's decision established what are now known as 'Miranda Rights' to safeguard against a suspect falling into an involuntary confession because they think they have no choice but to speak. Police must clearly tell any suspect of their right to silence and counsel before beginning an interrogation or any other attempt to gain a statement from a suspect. The Miranda decision tries to eliminate suspect ignorance as a contributing factor to involuntary confessions. The Miranda Warning is as follows:

> You have the right to remain silent. Anything you say can, and will, be used against you in a court of law. You have the right to an attorney. If you cannot afford one, one will be appointed to you.

CASE STUDY   Legal trickery: calling 'Mr Big'

A 'Mr Big' tactic is a controversial undercover operation developed in Canada during the 1990s. Although banned in other countries such as the USA and Britain, the practice is still used in Canada and Australia (Connors, Patry and Smith, 2019).

Through a series of seemingly chance encounters, the officers befriend their target, and over a period of weeks or months, the officers gain the suspect's trust. The ploy begins when the police operative befriends the suspect. The police operative may 'meet' the suspect while in custody or at a place of employment (Sands, 2005). The operative then spends time establishing a friendship with the suspect, buying meals and gifts, going out to bars and nightclubs, and spending money. Eventually, the undercover officer introduces the suspect into a criminal gang (created by police) where they complete simple tasks – counting money, acting as a lookout – for large sums of money (up to several thousand dollars per week). Later, the undercover officer informs the suspect that they have been selected for promotion within the organisation, but a condition of that promotion is a meeting with 'Mr Big'.

At this stage, the suspect is informed that to be accepted into the organisation, they must confess to a crime. The confession provides the organisation with information to use against the suspect if necessary. In addition, suspects are sometimes told that the confession will allow the organisation to use its contacts to 'get rid of' any evidence against the suspect. Thus, police will not find out about the criminal gang's activities while in the pursuit of the suspect. Sometimes, 'Mr Big' will tell the suspect that the organisation has a person who is willing (either for money or for other considerations) to confess to the crime (Sands, 2005). However, the suspect must provide a detailed confession to the crime in question (the one under police investigation) in order to secure their promotion. This confession is required orally and usually in writing and is covertly videotaped by police (Smith, Stinson and Patry, 2009).

Discussion Questions:

1   The 'Mr Big' tactic is often criticised. In the interests of serving the public while obtaining justice, what are the critical flaws associated with this approach? Critically reflect on its use, focusing on the parts of this approach you believe are ethically questionable.

2   Keenan and Brockman (2011) examined 81 'Mr Big' tactics and reported that in 75 per cent of them, police were able to either clear the suspect or charge them with the crime, while the remaining 25 per cent are still unresolved. In the cases where the suspects were prosecuted, 95 per cent resulted in a conviction. Based on these results, do you believe that the success of this approach justifies the risks of coercion and false confessions?

3   While the criminal justice system has its failings, public confidence in the legitimacy of the system is essential for its operation. By continuing to use the 'Mr Big' tactic, do police investigators risk losing public and community confidence in their methods?

The Reid technique: an adversarial approach

In the Reid technique, interrogation is an accusatory process, in which the investigator tells the suspect that the results of the investigation clearly indicate that they did commit the crime in question. The Reid technique user's goal is to make the suspect gradually more comfortable with telling the truth. The Reid method is an adversarial system of interviewing and interrogation widely used by police departments in the USA and Canada (Meissner, Surmon-Böhr, Oleszkiewicz and Alison, 2017).

Critics of the Reid approach question whether these adversarial approaches are too confession focused rather than information focused (Kozinski, 2018). The more aggressive nature may be why this system has been found to produce false confessions, especially in juveniles (Spierer, 2017). Another concern regarding the Reid technique is the lengthy, stressful interrogation methods used. Ultimately, the best use of this technique may be to educate police about the risk and reality of false confessions.

The nine steps of the Reid technique

This is a nine-step interrogation process, during which the suspect's resistance to confess is progressively broken down.

Step 1: Direct positive confrontation

The goal of this step is to convince the suspect that the investigation clearly shows that they are responsible for committing the crime. However, to persuade a guilty suspect to tell the truth, the interrogator often exaggerates their evidence and their confidence in the suspect's guilt. From a legal perspective, the earlier false statements only represent the investigator's *beliefs*, and the distinction between an investigator stating a *false belief*, which is generally acceptable, and making a *false statement*, which could risk the admissibility of a confession, is vague.

Step 2: Theme development

In this stage, a potential story and motives for the suspect are told or implied. If interrogators believe that the suspect is emotional, they try to build a rapport with them by offering them a moral excuse for having committed the offence. Kassin and McNall (1991) described this approach as the **minimisation approach** – a police interrogator lulls the suspect into a false sense of security by offering sympathy. This is done by telling them that anyone else in the same situation would have acted the same way, thus minimising

Minimisation approach – *Interrogation in which an interrogator tries to alleviate a suspect's anxiety associated with confessing to a crime.*

the moral seriousness of their behaviour, while offering a morally acceptable alternative motivation, such as blaming others. Besides providing a way out of the interrogation, another goal of minimisation is to reduce the perceived consequences of telling the truth (Luke and Alceste, 2019).

Step 3: Handling denials

The goal of this step is to stop the subject from repeating their denial of guilt and repeating their story of the incident. Inbau, Reid and Buckley (1986) explain that the more the suspect repeats the lie, the greater the challenge the interrogator has persuading them to tell the truth. This idea is based on the belief that guilty suspects will change their stories by supplying reasons why the accusation is wrong, such as 'I couldn't have driven the getaway car, because I was at work.'

Step 4: Overcoming objections

The purpose of this step is to make the suspect feel that their objections will have no effect. To keep the suspect from rehearsing their objections, Inbau, Reid and Buckley (1986, p. 158) recommend keeping control over the interrogation by showing sympathetic understanding and returning to the conversation theme: 'That may be true, but the important thing is …', for example.

Step 5: Maintaining the suspect's attention

If the suspect's attention begins to wander, the interrogator must regain control. The techniques offered include moving physically closer to the suspect, leaning towards them, touching them (gently), and saying their first name while maintaining eye contact (Sokara et al., 2009).

Step 6: Handling suspect's passive mood

The purpose of this step is to make the suspect feel remorseful. Waiting until the suspect shows signs of attentiveness, the interrogator reviews the possible reasons the suspect committed the crime and sympathetically urges the suspect to tell the truth. The interrogator also reviews the negative consequences of the crime on its victims (Woody, 2019).

Step 7: Presenting an alternative question

The purpose of this step is to present the suspect with two likely scenarios that lead to an admission of guilt (Woody, 2019). At this point, the suspect is offered the chance to give an explanation (or at least an excuse) for the crime. For example, 'Was this your own idea, or did someone talk you into it?'

Step 8: Having suspect orally relate various details of the offence

Once the suspect selects an alternative from the previous step, a detailed confession is cultivated. The interrogators need a confession that reveals the circumstances, motive and details of the crime. Inbau, Reid and Buckley (1986) recommended that the interrogators use clear, brief, emotionally free questions that can be answered with a single word.

Step 9: Converting an oral confession into a written confession

Confessions must be written and signed. This counters later denials of an oral confession (Inbau, Reid and Buckley, 1986).

Does the Reid technique increase false confessions?

The nine-step approach is not about telling the truth as much as changing the suspect's attitude about the consequences of a confession (Petty, Wegener, Leandre and Fabrigar, 1997). For example, suspects often deny accusations because denials have only positive consequences, while a confession leads to a conviction (a negative consequence). Therefore, while police cannot eliminate the consequences of confessing, they can give the impression that a denial will also lead to a conviction. Unfortunately, by using this technique, the motivation to confess increases in both guilty *and* innocent suspects!

The next stage in the evolution of interrogations: the PEACE model

In 1990, after a rash of false confessions in the UK, the government appointed a commission of detectives, academics and legal experts to develop an interview method that would reflect then-current psychological research. After two years' work, the commission unveiled its technique, called PEACE, an acronym for Preparation and planning, Engage and explain, Account (clarify and challenge), Closure, Evaluate (Figure 5.2). It was conceived as a way to reduce the proliferation of false confessions that were resulting from an accusatory style of interviewing.

The **PEACE model of interviewing** moves away from the adversarial and confrontational style of investigation to inquisitorial and investigative interviewing. The goal of the PEACE procedure is to obtain accurate and reliable evidence and to discover the truth in a crime investigation.

> **PEACE model of interviewing** – *This model uses a conversational, non-confrontational approach to getting information from an investigation interview subject.*

Figure 5.2: Steps in the PEACE procedure

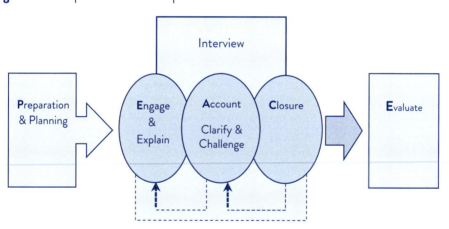

Planning and preparation

Planning and preparation include reading the case file, preparing the mechanics of the interview, and understanding the facts of the case. Specifically, the interviewers create a script outlining their approach and agree on the explicit goals and purpose of the interview (Walsh and Milne, 2008).

Engage and explain

Engage and explain are the early phases within the actual interview. At this stage, the interviewers tell the suspect about the charges brought against them, their rights and what procedure the interview will follow. During this stage, interviewers build rapport, engage the suspect and encourage them to give their point of view about important events. The explanation is next, where the interviewer outlines the reasons for the interview and the roles each person will play; for example, 'as the interviewer, I am trying to find out the truth and will ask you for your account of what happened' (MacDonald, Snook and Milne, 2017).

Account (clarify and challenge)

The third phase, *account*, is the heart of the interview. Unlike the Reid approach, investigators are not allowed to deceive suspects and the interviewer's aim is to *clarify* the suspect's account. For example, if the suspect said they were driving a red car, the interviewer would ask for more details of the car – the interior colour, the year and so on. Suspects are encouraged to speak freely and provide a complete account of their involvement with the crime, while closed-ended questions are kept to a minimum (Bull and Milne, 2004; Shepherd, Mortimer, Turner and Watson, 1999). The advantage of this is that the more detail the interviewers collect, the more information there is to test the suspect's account against the witness's account and other evidence. Interviewers are tasked with finding out as much information as possible that can be verified from other sources. During the *challenge* phase, investigators challenge the suspect's account in a calm controlled manner without anger or threat, because anger, threats and coercion raise the risk of suggestibility. Interviewers present inconsistencies and inaccuracies provided by the witnesses and other sources in a matter-of-fact way (Walsh and Milne, 2008). The advantage of coming to this stage at the end of the interview, rather than the beginning, is that there is less chance that the interview process will create uncertainty in the suspect about their account and, with it, increased suggestibility and confabulation – the spontaneous recall of events that did not happen (Clarke and Milne, 2017).

Closure

Once the suspect has completed their narrative, the investigator provides the opportunity to correct any discrepancies. Baldwin (1993) outlines important goals for this phase. Specifically, by the end of the interview, everyone should understand what has happened and what will happen in the future. Furthermore, closure should give the suspect the chance to ask any questions and end the interview in a positive mood. A positive conclusion will prepare the way for more interviews if needed.

Evaluate

The final phase requires interviewers to evaluate the facts obtained during the interview and decide whether the goals of the interview were achieved. Evaluation can also help interviewers improve their interviewing skills, because a critical element of the evaluation phase is to reflect on the interview and evaluate how it could have been improved.

Is the PEACE procedure effective?

The goal of the PEACE procedure is to obtain accurate and reliable evidence and to discover the truth in a crime investigation. This model emphasises ethical principles, distinguishing it from other coercive and persuasive approaches described earlier in this chapter. Yet the question remains, is the increased effort worth the cost? Holmberg and Christiansen (2002) found that the reported experiences of convicted sexual offenders and murderers support this approach. The interviewers were perceived as engaging, positive, empathic, accommodating and cooperative, which reflect the goals of this approach. Most importantly, the experience of a humanitarian interview was positively related to the offender's admission of crime (Holmberg and Christiansen, 2002). Similarly, researchers found that the PEACE procedure increased the chances of obtaining authentic confessions because the interviewers are open-minded, act according to ethical principles and show humanity (Kebbell, Hurren and Mazerolle, 2006).

Military use of rapport and persuasion strategies

The intelligence community has learned that the best way to persuade a suspect to talk is to begin with a foundation of rapport (Meissner, Surmon-Böhr, Oleszkiewicz and Alison, 2017). However, building rapport is difficult because the techniques used are often very subtle. For example, rapport is enhanced by mimicking and anticipating the nonverbal behaviour of the suspect, such as sitting down or leaning forward (Genschow, Klomfar, d'Haene and Brass, 2018).

Global Perspectives

Germany's master interrogator

The power of rapport building is demonstrated by the story of Hanns-Joachim Scharff, a German Luftwaffe interrogator, during the Second World War. Scharff was known for never using physical means to obtain information. Instead, Scharff used a secret weapon – kindness. For example, Scharff would take his prisoners on strolls through the nearby woods, first having them swear that they would not try to escape during their walk. Rather than use these nature walks as a time to directly ask his prisoners obvious military-related questions, he relied on the prisoner's desire to speak to anyone outside isolated captivity about informal, generalised topics (Toliver, 1997).

The Scharff technique works by collecting information from people who are motivated to reveal some but not all information. By using a combination of perspective taking (considering the world from another individual's viewpoint) and empathy (the ability to connect emotionally with another individual), prisoners often volunteered information without realising it (Granhag, Montecinos and Oleszkiewicz, 2015).

The typical conversation began by asking a prisoner a question Scharff already knew the answer to, informing the prisoner that he already knew everything about him, but his superiors had given instructions that the prisoner himself had to say it. Scharff continued asking questions that he would then supply the answers to, each time hoping to convince his captive that there was nothing he did not already know. When he eventually got to the piece of information he did *not* have, prisoners would often give the answer, assuming Scharff already knew it (Oleszkiewicz, Granhag and Montecinos, 2014).

Here is how Scharff applied his ingenious technique for finding out about US tracer bullet colours. Tracers are ammunition that illuminate the flight of the bullet so that the pilot can see where the bullets are hitting (Granhag, Kleinman and Oleszkiewicz, 2016). In a friendly conversation, without asking for any information, Scharff said to one American pilot he knew that America must have a chemical shortage because American tracer bullets were leaving white rather than red smoke. The pilot responded by correcting him with the information the German commanders wanted. There was no chemical shortage, because white smoke signals to pilots that they would soon be out of ammunition. Of the 500 pilots Scharff interviewed, he failed to get the information he desired out of just 20.

Strategies of rapport building

There is little evidence that harsh adversarial interrogations work – unless your goal is to obtain a high rate of false confessions. And the belief that liars reveal themselves when under extreme emotional stress also lacks support (Delahunty, Martschuk and Dhami, 2014). While persuading a suspect to cooperate is a challenging task, interviewers who build rapport via social influence tactics are more successful (Delahunty, Martschuk and Dhami, 2014). When prisoners are undecided about confessing or had previously decided to deny the allegations, the relationship-focused approach produced more confessions, revealing previously undisclosed information (Wachi et al., 2015).

Rapport-building and self-disclosure strategies work together to increase cooperation (Stokoe, 2009). Studies on self-disclosure show that people like and respond better to those who disclose information to them (Luke, Dawson, Hartwig and Granhag, 2014). For example, Hackel (2014) describes an incident during a US Army interrogator's interview with an Iraqi insurgent when the insurgent disclosed that he had watched the US TV series *24* on illegal DVDs and was a fan of the main character Jack Bauer. The interviewer made a connection that resulted in the insurgent recanting previous false information and giving accurate information. The increased rapport reduced his defences and led to actionable intelligence and the capture of other higher individuals in the organisation.

Experienced interviewers also use reciprocity (McCauley, 2007). When a small favour is given without asking for something in return, the favour creates a relationship and engages the **norm of reciprocity** – feeling an obligation to return the favour. Reciprocity offers three tactical applications (Perugini, Gallucci, Presaghi and Ercolani, 2002): an instrumental tactic (giving water or food), an identity tactic (showing respect or honour), and a rapport-based tactic (showing empathy).

Another strategy is to use the power of commitment and consistency to create **cognitive dissonance**. This is when we try to maintain consistency between our beliefs and behaviours, and inconsistency creates anxiety (Festinger, 1957). To be consistent, people commit to requests that align with their existing beliefs and their previous behaviour. An example is the **foot-in-the-door technique**, where agreeing to a small request increases the chance of agreeing to a second, larger request. The foot-in-the-door tactic works because of the principle of consistency (Freedman and Fraser, 1966). After agreeing to the small request, people find it easier to agree to a bigger one to maintain the impression of being a consistent person. This is a common tactic used to recruit members to terroristic and cult-like organisations. The individual makes a small commitment (reads a pamphlet), which is followed by a request for a greater commitment (attend a meeting). In this way, a series of small behaviours increases commitment and the person explains their previous actions by reframing them as evidence of their belief in the organisation (Aronoff, Lynn and Malinoski, 2000).

Norm of reciprocity – *Social rule when people feel an obligation to return a favour.*

Cognitive dissonance – *An anxiety-producing situation where our attitudes, beliefs and behaviours are inconsistent, requiring a change to restore consistency.*

Foot-in-the-door technique – *After agreeing to a small request, people find it easier to agree to a bigger one.*

IN SUMMARY

Suspects respond better to inquisitorial approaches and provide accurate evidence without the use of coercive tactics rather than intimidating suspects into making false confessions.

CRITICAL THINKING AND APPLICATION QUESTIONS

1   In some countries, when interrogating a suspect, police can use trickery – they can mislead suspects about what they know and what evidence they have. What are the consequences (if any) of excluding deception and misrepresentation from the interrogation room?

2   Imagine you are a legal consultant and you have been asked to explain to a jury the difference between interview practices that are unduly coercive and those that are not. What guidelines would you recommend the jury follow to distinguish when a person is being coerced and being persuaded?

3   Explain how each of the compliance techniques – self-disclosure, norm of reciprocity and foot-in-the-door – function during an investigative interview. As opposed to torture, why are social influence tactics like this often described as 'compliance without pressure'?

FALSE CONFESSIONS AND THE PARADOX OF INNOCENCE

FICTION: Innocent people do not confess to crimes they did not commit.	*Versus*	**FACT:** Innocent people do confess to crimes they did not commit, sometimes even creating false memories of their participation in the crime.

• Darryl Beamish, of Perth, Australia, was a deaf teenager when he was charged with the 1959 axe murder of 22-year-old socialite Jillian Brewer. Beamish was sentenced to death by hanging, based on his police pressured false confession. Years later, in 1963, serial killer Eric Edgar Cooke supplied a detailed confession to the murder. Beamish's death sentence was changed to life but he was not released until 1977, after 15 years' imprisonment (Blackburn, 2002).

• Romeo Phillion, from Ottawa, Canada, spent three decades in prison for a murder that he did not commit. In trouble with the law on an unrelated matter, Phillion had confessed to murdering Leopold Roy, a firefighter from Ottawa. Although his confession was given freely, Phillion retracted it to another police officer on the same night — and repeatedly thereafter. Unfortunately, because of his confession and faulty eyewitness testimony, he was found guilty by a jury. Thirty-one years later, a police investigation report surfaced that proved Phillion was in another town at the time of Roy's murder and he was released. It is now believed that Phillion suffered from antisocial personality disorder and had a desire for notoriety. Had police recognised Phillion's personality disorder and offered mental health services, his false confession may have been prevented (Bodine, 2014).

Source: Tory Zimmerman/Toronto Star/Getty Images

Romeo Phillion is finally released after serving more than 30 years after his false confession for murder

- Jerry Hobbs, from Illinois, USA confessed to raping and murdering his eight-year-old daughter and her nine-year-old friend in 2005. Because he was searching for his daughter all night before his arrest, Hobbs had not slept for 24 hours. After his arrest, he was interrogated for 20 continuous hours, and, after nearly two days with no sleep, he confessed. After five years in jail, Hobbs was exonerated when DNA evidence from semen in his daughter's body matched that of Jorge Torrez, a convicted killer who had lived in the Zion Park area where the murders took place (Newton, 2015).

The psychology of false confessions

Confessions are proven false in many ways; for example, when it is discovered that the confessed crime was never committed, when evidence shows that it was impossible for the confessor to have committed the crime, when the real perpetrator is caught, or via DNA or other trace evidence (Kassin, 2008b).

Despite the belief that people do not confess to crimes they did not commit, many people have been convicted, prosecuted and imprisoned because of false confessions. Surprisingly, it is not a new phenomenon. As early as 1908, Hugo Münsterberg wrote about false confessions and described it as a normal reaction to the emotional shock of arrest and interrogation (Münsterberg, 1908).

There are legal but deceptive interrogation tactics that increase the risk that innocent people will confess to crimes they did not commit. Self-incriminating statements often result from a mental cost–benefit analysis, and a false confession becomes an escape from the interrogation. This thinking is clear post-confession, when subjects say, 'I just wanted to go home' (Kassin et al., 2010b). Unfortunately, judges and juries are unable to distinguish whether the suspect made self-incriminating statements, whether these statements were voluntary or coerced, or whether the suspect was of sound mind during the interrogation.

In the USA, over thirty years of DNA exonerations indicate that 28 per cent of the over 367 wrongful convictions overturned by DNA evidence involved some form of false confession. Specifically, 49 per cent were 21 years old or younger, 33 per cent were 18 years old or older and 10 per cent of the false confessors had mental health or mental capacity issues (Innocence Project, 2020).

Although it is difficult to understand why a person would confess to a crime they did not commit, there are common causes. One cause is the compromised reasoning ability of the suspect, due to exhaustion, stress, hunger, substance use and, in some cases, cognitive impairments (Kassin, 2008b). Other causes include real or perceived intimidation of the suspect by law enforcement (Baldwin, 1993), the use of force by law enforcement during the interrogation, or the perceived threat of force (Skolnick and Fyfe, 1993). The use of devious interrogation techniques, such as lying about the presence of incriminating evidence (Gohara, 2006), and fear, on the part of the suspect, that failure to confess will yield a harsher punishment (Kassin and Gudjonsson, 2004) also cause suspects to confess.

APPLY IT

How to implant a false memory of a crime

Read this list:

> Steal, Robber, Jail, Villain, Bandit, Criminal, Rob, Police, Money, Bad, Burglar, Crook, Crime, Gun, Bank

Count to 30. Now, recall the words in the list. Did you remember the word 'thief'? If so, you are the victim of an implanted **false memory**. Read the list again to prove to yourself that the word 'thief' is not there.

You have just experienced the *DRM task* (named after its authors, Deese, Roediger and McDermott). The words in the list are all semantically related, that is, from the same category. Most people remember the related but missing word ('thief'), known as a 'lure', as often as the other words (Roediger and McDermott, 1995). What is interesting is that people report that they are sure that they remember hearing the missing word, which is a false memory for an event that never occurred (Perdilla-Delgado and Payne, 2017).

Why does this happen? The false memory is the result of a **source monitoring error**. Simply, we remember thinking about the missing word while reading the list, and then mistake the source of the memory as the list rather than our own thoughts (Johnson, Hashtroudi and Lindsay, 1993). Source monitoring errors are often the reason someone has a 'memory' for a crime they did not commit.

False memory – The memory for an event that never occurred.

Source monitoring error – A type of memory error where a specific remembered experience is incorrectly thought to be the source of the memory.

Why do innocent people confess?

Clearly, knowing that they are innocent should make it *less* likely that an innocent person will confess. However, suspects are told (sometime falsely) that there is additional information that will prove their guilt. Astonishingly, the innocent person is *more* likely to confess, because believing that proof of their innocence is imminent makes it easier to confess. Additionally, making a false confession offers the immediate reward of ending the interrogation (Kassin, 2017).

This counterintuitive behaviour of innocent suspects is described as the **paradox of innocence** – when an innocent person is more likely to confess to committing a crime than a guilty suspect (Soree, 2005). How is this paradox explained? One explanation is the belief in the just-world hypothesis, which is the idea that people have a need to believe that their environment is a just and orderly place where people usually get what they deserve (Lerner and Miller, 1978). From the perspective of the innocent suspect, they believe that since there was no wrong behaviour, there will be no consequences (Grinnell, 2018).

Paradox of innocence – When an innocent person is more likely to confess to committing a crime than a guilty suspect.

Illusion of transparency
– A tendency for people to overestimate the degree to which their personal mental state is known by others.

Sometimes, knowing you are innocent can work against you because of the **illusion of transparency** – a tendency for people to overestimate the degree to which their personal mental state is known by others (Gilovich, Savitsky and Husted, 1998). People believe that when they tell the truth, others will believe them, and that when they lie, others will figure that out too. This belief comforts the person who did nothing wrong and explains why the innocent suspect waives their rights to legal counsel or silence, believing that, in the end, they will be found innocent because it is plainly obvious (to them).

Laboratory evidence

Kassin and Kiechel (1996) devised a clever experiment to induce false confessions. In their experiment, two students sat at a table with a computer. A confederate (an accomplice of the experimenter) playing the role of a student read individual letters from a chart for the subject to type. Before beginning, the experimenter warned the students not to hit the Alt key, because this causes the computer to crash and the data would be lost. In fact, the computer was always programmed to crash exactly 60 seconds into the experiment. When this happened, the experimenter asked each participant if they had pressed the Alt key, acted as if he was upset when it was 'discovered' that the data had disappeared, and requested that the participant sign a confession.

The first time Kassin and Kiechel (1996) tried the experiment, half of the innocent participants were so intimidated by the accusatory question that they signed the confession. When the experimenter added false incrimination – instructing the confederate to say that he had seen the subject hit the Alt key – the rate of false confession nearly doubled to 94 per cent. When another confederate, posing as a fellow student, asked what had happened, the subjects blamed themselves, responding 'I hit the wrong button', rather than 'They said I hit the wrong button.' Some participants even confabulated details, explaining how they hit the Alt key with the side of their hand. This suggests that not only had they internalised their guilt; they had created a believable story to explain it. As more evidence of internalised guilt, during the debriefing when students were told the experiment was a hoax, they sometimes replied, 'You're just trying to make me feel better' (Perillo and Kassin, 2011).

While provocative, these kinds of experiments are criticised for not being realistic. Critics cite that the 'crime' was an accident and, unlike a real crime, it was a low-stakes situation with no real-world consequences. To address these concerns, researchers created 'the cheating paradigm' (Russano, Meissner, Narchet and Kassin, 2005). Students were asked to solve various logic problems, some with a partner and others individually. A few students – confederates of the researchers – were told to pretend to be emotionally upset while working alone. Inevitably, some students helped their upset partners during the individual section of the experiment, in other words, they cheated. An advantage of this scenario is that it produces guilty and innocent subjects because not all the students helped the upset confederate. Also, unlike hitting the Alt key, this behaviour was intentional, not accidental, and the confession had important consequences, because cheating violated the university's academic code. Russano and her colleagues (2005) used this realistic scenario to evaluate the minimisation tactics associated with the Reid technique. Using minimisation proved especially effective to elicit confessions from innocent and guilty subjects alike; this occurred when the experimenters told students, 'You probably didn't realise what a big deal this was' (p. 483). This raised the confession rate among guilty parties by 35 per cent, but the confession rate among innocent participants tripled! The conclusion is that Reid tactics like minimisation are extremely effective in producing confessions but not particularly good at separating the true ones from the false ones.

Types of false confessions

Analysis of the variety of false confessions observed in the real world led Kassin and Wrightsman (1985) to define three types of false confessions: coerced-compliant, voluntary false, and coerced-internalised (Table 5.2).

Table 5.2: Three categories of false confessions

Type of false confession	Description
Coerced-compliant	When innocent people confess to avoid harsh interrogation, or they believe that the consequences of a confession are less than denial *Most frequent*
Voluntary false	False confessions that are made freely, without any prompting or coercion by the police, for a crime when the person is innocent *Rare*
Coerced-internalised	When innocent people genuinely believe that they have committed the crime, because of highly suggestive interrogation techniques *Most rare*

Coerced-compliant false confessions

Coerced-compliant false confessions result from the cost–benefit pressure of the interrogation process. This occurs when the suspect knows that they are innocent but perceives that the short-term benefits of confession, such as being left alone, fed, or released, outweigh the long-term costs, for example, a loss of reputation, conviction and incarceration. Specifically, the suspect falsely confesses to escape the pressure of the interrogation, or because they believe (or have been led to believe) that they will be allowed to go home, to sleep or eat, to call their family, or that the charges against them will be dropped. This effect was documented as early as the Salem witch trials of 1692–93, in which several women 'confessed' to witchcraft (Karlsen, 1989). A more recent demonstration is the Central Park jogger case, in which five teenage boys (aged 14–16) confessed to attacking a 28-year-old woman in New York City in 1989. She survived her horrific injuries, having been in a coma for 12 days, but has no memory of the assault (Meili, 2003). The interrogation of the five boys lasted between 14 and 30 hours. Based only on these confessions, all were ultimately tried, convicted and sentenced to prison. Four of the confessions were videotaped and presented at trial. The suspects later claimed that they had given the investigators what they wanted to hear and that they were led to believe that they would be sent home afterwards. Thirteen years later, Matias Reyes confessed, and DNA testing exonerated the five boys and led to Reyes' conviction (Kassin, 2008b).

Coerced-compliant false confession – When an innocent person believes that the immediate benefits of confession outweigh the long-term costs.

PART II

Source: NY Daily News Archive/Getty Images

Matias Reyes was eventually identified as the real offender in the Central Park jogger case

Voluntary false confessions

A **voluntary false confession** is one in which a person falsely confesses to a crime without any pressure or coercion. Typically, people arrive voluntarily at the police station, and confess to having committed a crime they have heard about in the news or seen on television. One example of a voluntary false confession was that of John Mark Karr, who confessed to the murder of six-year-old child beauty queen, JonBenét Ramsey, in 2006. Karr was obsessed with the Ramsey murder and eventually made statements implicating his involvement in her death. Ultimately, DNA evidence from the Ramsey murder did not match Karr's samples and testimony from relatives indicated that he was elsewhere when the incident occurred (Kassin, 2008b).

Gudjonsson (2003) describes six reasons why someone might provide a voluntary false confession:

1   People may make false confessions due to a dark desire for notoriety, even if it means imprisonment. For example, researchers reviewed a case of a man who confessed to murder to impress his girlfriend (Huff, Rattner, Sagarin and MacNamara, 1986).

2   Some confess to relieve a sense of guilt. Gudjonsson (2003) relates the case of a man who, while suffering from depression due to a disturbed childhood, confessed to murders that had taken place in a part of the country where he had been once.

3   People are unable to distinguish reality from fantasy.

4   Research shows that the desire to protect someone else is likely to be the most common motivation behind a voluntary false confession (Sigurdsson and Gudjonsson, 1996).

5   People may give a false confession because they see no way to prove their innocence, for example after failing a polygraph or after some psychological expert labels them guilty, and so they confess to reduce their punishment.

6   Suspects may confess to hide other non-criminal facts; for example, the case of a woman who falsely confessed to a murder to hide the fact that she was cheating on her husband at the time of the murder (Huff et al., 1986).

Coerced-internalised false confessions

The final type is the **coerced-internalised false confession**. This is the most unusual and rare confession when a person falsely confesses to a crime believing that they are responsible for the criminal act (Henkel and Coffman, 2004). These confessions can result from interrogation tactics that manipulate or distort the memory of the individual, causing them to develop false memories of their involvement in the crime (Loftus, 1997).

Inducing participants to create false memories is a common research approach, and researchers have used the following scenarios: false stories of committing a crime (Shaw and Porter, 2015), getting lost in a shopping mall (Loftus, 1997), being involved in an accident at a family wedding (Hyman, Husband and Billings, 1995), having tea with Prince Charles (Strange, Sutherland and Garry, 2006), being attacked by a vicious animal (Porter, Yuille and Lehman, 1999), and cheating on a test (Russano et al., 2005). Participants in these studies construct a new memory using real autobiographical memory fragments with false external sources (Conway, 2002). These memories feel real because of their emotional content (Laney and Loftus, 2008) and the areas of brain activation are indistinguishable from authentic memories (Stark, Okado and Loftus, 2010).

Situations that cause false memories include presenting false evidence, leading the suspect to assume they repressed or forgot the event, coercing the suspect make a partial admission of guilt, and rehearsing speculative details of their involvement in the case (Kassin, 2012). For example, presenting false evidence convinced 17-year-old Marty Tankleff, from Long Island, New York, that he murdered his parents despite a complete lack of evidence. Tankleff's wealthy parents, Seymour and Arlene Tankleff, were found bludgeoned and stabbed in the family's home on 7 September 1988. Tankleff denied the allegation for hours. Then his interrogator lied, telling him that his hair was found on his mother, and forensic testing indicated that he had showered, washing off his mother's blood. They also said that his hospitalised father had emerged from his coma to identify Marty as his attacker (in fact, his father never regained consciousness) (Firstman and Salpeter, 2008). Tankleff confessed, but shortly thereafter retracted his confession. Even though he retracted his confession, Tankleff was convicted and spent 18 years in prison. Tankleff claimed that his father's business partner, Jerry Steuerman, was behind the killings. Steuerman, who denied any role in the couple's murders, invoked his right against self-incrimination when Tankleff's lawyers wanted to question him (Lam, 2017). However, on December 18, 2007, the Appellate Division of the New York Supreme Court in Brooklyn unanimously overturned the convictions and released Tankleff. The court ruled that if a jury heard all the new evidence, it would probably acquit Tankleff (Firstman and Salpeter, 2008).

False confessions and mandatory recording of interrogations

Electronic recording of interrogations is the single best reform available to reduce false confessions (Sullivan, 2005). The benefits of complete audio or video recording of custodial interviews have become increasingly obvious for both sides of the law. For suspects, recordings expose abusive tactics and falsehoods about confessions. For law enforcement, recordings keep them from defending unjust charges of using overly coercive methods or misstating what happened (Linkins, 2007). Furthermore, legal counsel no longer engages in courtroom disputes as to what took place because there is a clear and conclusive record of the interrogation. The interviews may contain statements favourable to the defence,

Coerced-internalised false confession – *When an innocent person falsely confesses to a crime truly believing that they are responsible for the criminal act.*

PART II

or admissions that strengthen the prosecution's case, but in either event, judges do not have to compare conflicting versions of what happened. Unlike the traditional interview, in which the police make handwritten notes and later prepare a typed report, electronic recordings contain a permanent record of what police and suspects said and did (Moston and Stephenson, 1993). Finally, recordings are a valuable tool for training new police in proper interrogation techniques and for experienced police to self-evaluate and improve their methods (Westling and Waye, 1998).

All interrogations should be recorded to make them more 'transparent'. While there is a concern that recording an interrogation limits the interviewer's discretion or reduces the chance of achieving a confession from the suspect, research demonstrates that recording interrogations does not significantly lower the frequency of confessions (Geller, 1992). Investigators have found that the recordings can supplement the perceived strength and voluntariness of the evidence, while protecting the investigator against unfounded allegations of wrongdoing (Lassiter and Geers, 2004).

IN SUMMARY

The paradox of innocence shows that innocent people do confess to crimes they did not commit, sometimes creating false memories of their participation in the crime.

 CRITICAL THINKING AND APPLICATION QUESTIONS

1   Controlled laboratory scenarios designed to induce false confessions by hitting the Alt key on a keyboard or cheating have been criticised as being not very realistic and the 'crimes' do not have the consequences of a real-world confession. Design a better experiment to induce false confessions using college students that is both realistic and ethical.

2   Do you personally feel that you could be induced to make a false confession for a serious crime that you did not commit? If your answer is no, what are the critical differences between you and people who have made false confessions?

3   It appears that recording the interview will avoid many of the problems inherent in the interrogation process. However, researchers like Saul Kassin suggest that this is not as simple as it seems. What other variables can affect recording confessions?

WHY CONFESSIONS OVERRULE INNOCENCE AND EVIDENCE

FICTION: The outcome of the investigation is more important than the procedures used to obtain evidence.	*Versus*	**FACT:** The procedures underlying the investigation lay the foundation for admissible evidence.

Confessions are consistently one of the leading, and yet most misunderstood, causes of error in criminal justice systems and remain the most prejudicial source of false evidence leading to wrongful convictions. This section reviews the implications of empirical research for reducing the number of false confessions and improving the accuracy of confession evidence introduced against a defendant.

Innocence as a vulnerability

Why do confessions overrule innocence and evidence? A novel perspective is to consider innocence not as a state of mind that leads to trusting the integrity of suspect interviews, but as a vulnerability. Innocence is like being vulnerable because of internal characteristics (intellectual impairment, age) and situational characteristics (time spent under interrogation, threats, promises, presentation of false evidence, minimisation). Innocence is a vulnerable mental state that leads people to waive their rights to silence and legal counsel (Kassin, 2012). Unlike guilty suspects, innocent suspects are more direct in their interactions with police (Hartwig, Granhag and Strömwall, 2007). They offer alibis freely, unconcerned that slight inaccuracies cast doubt on their innocence (Olson and Charman, 2012) and they show less physical arousal during the stress of interrogation, unless they refuse to confess (because they are innocent). In this case, they show greater physiological arousal than both innocent and guilty suspects who confess (Madon et al., 2017).

The corruptive power of confessions

When it is innocence versus a confession, the confession triumphs. A confession not only overrules other evidence, but it can corrupt it as well. Once a suspect confesses, police often end the investigation and ignore alternative explanations. Yet, even after a confession, alibis are withdrawn, witnesses change stories, police ignore **exculpatory evidence** – evidence favourable to the defendant in a criminal trial that exonerates the defendant of guilt – and laboratory examiners reinterpret material. This happens even when the confession is contradicted by external evidence or is the product of a coercive interrogation (Drizin and Leo, 2004).

> **Exculpatory evidence**
> – Evidence favourable to the defendant in a criminal trial that exonerates the defendant of guilt.

This was the situation in the case of Barry Laughman, who had an IQ of 70 and was said to be functioning at the level of a 10-year-old. He was convicted of raping and murdering an elderly neighbour. He confessed after a state trooper convinced him that his fingerprints were found at the murder scene. After his confession, the police disregarded all other evidence. Neighbours offering alibis for Laughman were told they must be mistaken. His blood was type B, but the only blood at the crime scene was type A. Then the forensic expert proposed a novel (but scientifically flawed) theory: that bacterial degradation could have changed the blood type from B to A. Laughman spent 16 years in prison until DNA evidence finally cleared him (Perske, 2008).

Police-induced false confessions are difficult to identify because they often contain not only the admission of guilt, but a detailed narrative with information that only a person with guilty knowledge would have. So, where does an innocent suspect get this information? Garrett (2010) explored this question in an examination of 38 false confessions verified via DNA evidence. Thirty-six of these false confessions contained non-public information that only the perpetrator could have known. It appears that police had communicated these details unintentionally (or intentionally) to the suspect through leading questions, exposure to crime scene photographs, or escorted visits to the crime scene. Leo and Ofshe (1998) have recommended that investigators evaluate the suspect's post-admission explanation to determine the extent to which the details provided in the statement are consistent with known facts in the case. To accomplish this goal, Ives (2007) recommends that investigators withhold details of the case from the media or third parties that might otherwise contaminate a suspect's knowledge of case-related information. Finally, Sandoval (2003) recommends evaluating if any novel evidence was obtained during the interrogation that might independently corroborate the confession statement.

There is another mechanism by which confessions exert influence, and that is by tainting the perceptions of eyewitnesses, forensic experts and others entrusted to provide independent evidence to juries and judges. The criminal justice system trusts that different forms of evidence (trace evidence, interviews) are independent and do not influence each other during criminal investigations. But is this belief valid? The power of confirmation bias to overpower objective evidence should not be underestimated. Researchers examined cases of DNA exonerated cases comparing the kinds of errors made in wrongful convictions cases with false confessions and those without false confessions (Kassin, Bogart and Kerner, 2011). They found that more errors were made in 78 per cent of the false confession cases. Specifically, the false confession cases had more invalid or improper forensic science (63 per cent), mistaken eyewitness identification (29 per cent) and untruthful informants (19 per cent). Most suggestive of confirmation bias was their finding that, in 65 per cent of false confession cases, the confession was obtained at the beginning rather than later in the investigation.

Corroboration inflation – *The tendency for confessions to produce an illusion of support from other evidence.*

Turning from the sources of false confessions to their consequences, confession evidence can bias juries, judges, lay witnesses and forensic examiners. Like ripples in a pond, confessions spread their influence to other types of evidence, creating the illusion of validation. This effect is known as **corroboration inflation** – the tendency for confessions to produce an illusion of support from other evidence (Kassin, 2012). Ironically, even when confessions have turned out to be false, appeal courts have ruled that the other evidence is strong enough to support the conviction.

Redefining the role of the interrogator

The practice of seeking confessions is fundamentally flawed and it is time for new approaches. One model identifies deception based not on visible signs of emotional stress, but on 'cognitive load', which can lead liars to contradict themselves as they try to keep their stories straight (Sporer, 2016). Another approach is increased use of the PEACE procedure. For example, police in the UK conduct the open-ended interviews that journalists might use and are encouraged not to pursue confessions. Several other countries, including New Zealand and Australia, along with increasing parts of Canada, have adopted this method (Vrij, Fisher, Mann and Leal, 2006). They also record the entire interrogation to make the process transparent, something that 25 US states have also adopted. A final approach to avoid corroboration inflation is blind testing in forensic crime labs, and use of confession experts in court (Vallano and Winter, 2013).

IN SUMMARY

In the past, the ends justified the means and confessions often overruled innocence and evidence. We now understand the importance of fundamental procedures underlying the investigation and how they lay the foundation for admissible evidence.

 CRITICAL THINKING AND APPLICATION QUESTIONS

1   Your friend tells you that she was surprised that detectives named her as a suspect in a recent crime and have summoned her for an interview. She tells you that from her perspective, she is not worried because she is innocent. What would you tell her about her perspective?

2 Imagine that you have been hired as a consultant to the chief of investigations in a large city. What recommendations would you make to reduce the effects of the confirmation bias on the criminal justice system?

3 How does the concept of corroboration inflation explain how multiple sources of weak evidence supporting guilt can override a single strong source of innocence, such as DNA?

CHAPTER REVIEW

Most people reasonably believe that they would never confess to a crime they did not commit, so they evaluate others the same way, without an understanding of the influence of police interrogation practices, and the internal and external factors that lead an innocent person to confess. This is one reason why confessions impact verdicts more than other forms of evidence. Another is that the police, juries and forensic experts do not ignore confessions – and the confirmation bias continues even when confessions are retracted and judged to be the result of coercion.

Many kinds of evidence are used to make a case about a person's guilt or innocence. Each type of evidence has strengths and limitations but an overreliance on confession evidence stops the pursuit of empirical facts. It is important to remember that one reason that suspects are uncooperative is that they do not want to admit to the crime they committed, while another reason may be that they are innocent.

Claims that adversarial interrogation techniques can obtain forensically useful information from uncooperative suspects are flawed. These interrogation methods and their extreme form of torture are inefficient, ineffective and unethical. Unlike interrogations, inquisitorial interviews are performed by skilled professionals (O'Mara, 2016). Inquisitorial approaches like the PEACE method should be applied because they are effective, humane and grounded in empirical evidence.

NAMES TO KNOW

Saul Kassin

Pioneered the scientific study of false confessions and the effect confessions have on judges, juries, lay witnesses, forensic science examiners and the plea-bargaining process.

- Starr, D. (2019) The confession: A psychologist (Saul Kassin) has shown how police questioning can get innocent people to condemn themselves. *Science*, 364 (6445), 1022–6.

- Vrij, A., Meissner, C. A., Fisher, R. P., Kassin, S. M., Morgan, C. A. and Kleinman, S. M. (2017) Psychological perspectives on interrogation. *Perspectives on Psychological Science*, 12(6), 927–55.

Richard A. Leo

One of the leading experts in the world on police interrogation practices, the impact of Miranda, psychological coercion, false confessions and the wrongful conviction of the innocent.

- Leo, R. A. (2009) *Police Interrogation and American Justice*. Harvard University Press.
- Leo, R. A. and Thomas, G. C. (2012) *Confessions of Guilt: From Torture to Miranda and Beyond*. Oxford University Press.

Julia Shaw

Best known for her work in the areas of memory and criminal psychology and frequent TED talks.

- Shaw, J. (2017) *The Memory Illusion: Remembering, Forgetting, and the Science of False Memory*. Random House.
- Shaw, J. (2019) *Evil: The Science Behind Humanity's Dark Side*. Canongate Books.

PART III

GETTING TRUTHFUL INFORMATION

6 DETECTING CONCEALED INFORMATION AND DECEPTION

Chapter Introduction

Can you tell if someone is lying by their behaviour? Our journey begins with the search for reliable indicators of nonverbal deception. We explore one of the most controversial approaches to detecting lies: the polygraph. The controversy goes beyond just the test's accuracy and includes fears about replacing jurors and violating civil rights. Can this instrument detect lies or is it detecting something else? Next, we consider whether alternative counter-interrogation strategies can detect deception from a suspect's verbal statements. We complete our journey questioning whether we could or even should pursue the creation of a truth machine.

Learning Outcomes

The behaviour of lies: decoding behavioural deception
- Outline the attempts to find reliable indicators of nonverbal deception.

The tools of the trade: the polygraph
- Describe the theory and application of the core polygraph methods, such as the control question test and guilty knowledge test, and how these can be defeated via countermeasures.

The language of lies: decoding verbal deception
- Explain how the Strategic Use of Evidence (SUE) method exploits differences between liars and truth-tellers.

The quest for a truth machine
- Evaluate research that suggests that new technologies will enable us to create authentic truth machines.

THE BEHAVIOUR OF LIES: DECODING BEHAVIOURAL DECEPTION

FICTION: Everyone shows nonverbal signs of lying.

Versus

FACT: There are no nonverbal behaviours that are present in all liars and are absent in all truth-tellers.

From social media and online dating to fake news, identifying lies is a common task. But determining truth from lies can be a matter of life and death. From innocent people who have suffered unfair punishment because they were labelled as 'deceptive', to deaths from terrorist acts or pandemics that could have been prevented if the deception in planning and concealing information was detected.

CASE STUDY

The challenge of detecting deception

Princeton University welcomed Alexi Indris-Santana into their 1989 class based on his remarkable life story. With no formal schooling, Alexi had spent his adolescence entirely independent of family while living outdoors as an 18-year-old ranch hand in Utah. He was a self-made scholar and spent his free moments reading great works of philosophy, while sleeping under the stars alongside his horse 'Good Enough' (LeDuc, 1991). If that wasn't enough, he would often run in Utah's Mojave Desert, which led him to become an accomplished distance runner. Princeton University had received Alexi's brief application listing the books he had read, verified SAT scores, a reference from the ranch, and newspaper clippings of his outstanding high school running performance (Lofholm, [2006]2017). Based on his unique application and campus interview, he was accepted in the spring of 1988. However, he had to defer admission for a year to care for his ailing mother in Switzerland.

James Arthur Hogue (aka Alexi Indris-Santana) during his trial for forgery, theft and falsifying records

Source: Michael Abramson/The LIFE Images Collection/ Getty Images

In 1989, he entered the prestigious Ivy League university with enough financial aid to securely complete his education. Although he ate alone in the dining hall, he made friends, often entertaining a dozen women at once in his dorm room with glasses of wine. When asked why his bed was always neatly made, Alexi responded that he slept on the floor, because he was used to sleeping on the ground under the stars. After two years, he was earning high grades, a member of the track team and the exclusive Ivy Club (Samuels, 2001). It seemed that Princeton's faith in Alexi was confirmed.

However, Alexi's story was a lie. As it turned out, Alexi Indris-Santana was a pseudonym for James Arthur Hogue, a 31-year-old drifter, con-man and convicted thief. During a Princeton track meet, an old classmate from his brief time at Palo Alto High School had spotted him and alerted Princeton officials. History had repeated itself. Six years earlier, Hogue, who was then 25 years old, stole the identity of a deceased infant and enrolled in Palo Alto High School as a parentless student. He performed well on the track team until his true identity was discovered (Stannard, 2002).

Princeton University decided to act and on 26 February 1991 Hogue was arrested during class and charged with forgery, theft and falsifying records. Hogue pleaded guilty to third-degree theft for taking more than $40,000 in scholarship money and was sentenced to nine months in jail (Corzine and Tomlinson, 2018). The real reason Hogue deferred university admission for one year was revealed. It was not because his mother was dying, but because he had to serve nine months for theft charges before being paroled from Utah State Prison. In the years since, Hogue has been arrested several more times and his story has been recorded in a documentary called *Con Man* (Moss and Samuels, 2003).

Discussion Questions:

1   What do you think were Hogue's motivations for deceiving others? Were they simply to obtain a university degree or were they psychologically motivated?

2   Had Hogue been allowed to remain at Princeton University after his fraud was discovered, do you believe that he might well have been able to overcome his otherwise irrepressible tendency towards deception and criminality?

What makes a good liar?

Like all good liars, James Arthur Hogue was a natural performer who was good at acting, telling stories and offering convincing answers in almost any situation. He displayed the behaviours associated with being honest and likable from mirroring the posture of others to smiling. Hogue's preparation was important, because good liars are aware that what they say should be difficult to verify (Vrij, Granhag and Mann, 2010). At the same time, an effective liar must have a good memory to recall their earlier stories without contradicting themselves (Verigin, Meijer, Bogaard and Vrij, 2019). Finally, deceiving others is easier if the liar can suppress emotions like fear, guilt and delight (Decety and Jackson, 2004).

What are lies?

A **lie** is a statement that the liar believes is false made to intentionally deceive someone (Bok, 1989, 1999). Yet, although we are skilled at producing lies, we are terrible at detecting them. Bond and Depaulo (2006) found that in experimental situations, where guessing would produce 50 per cent correct judgements, subjects achieved only 54 per cent accuracy in discriminating lies from truths. Professional lie detectors, such as the police, polygraph examiners and judges, achieved 56–65 per cent (Aamodt and Custer, 2006), and rarely exceeded 70 per cent accuracy (Vrij, 2004; Vrij, Fisher and Blank, 2017). Studies from Sweden, the Netherlands and the UK have compared laypeople's and professionals' – police officers, judges, customs officers, prison guards and immigration officers – beliefs about the cues to deception. These studies found that professionals typically hold as many incorrect beliefs about deception as laypeople (Strömwall and Granhag, 2003; Strömwall, Granhag and Hartwig, 2004; Vrij and Semin, 1996). Additionally, both professionals and laypeople overestimated the number of cues that are actually associated with deception (Hartwig and Bond, 2014).

There are two reasons why we are such poor lie detectors. First, people often rely on the wrong cues when judging deception (Levine and McCornack, 2014; Vrij, 2019). Second, valid and reliable cues indicating deception are weak and hard to detect (Vrij and Turgeon, 2018).

Lie – A statement that the liar believes is false made to intentionally deceive someone.

The search for nonverbal cues of deception

Popular culture reflects the enduring belief that liars give themselves away through nonverbal behaviour. **Nonverbal communication** refers to any wordless communication (Knapp, Hall and Horgan, 2014). Unlike verbal and physiological measures of lie detection, nonverbal behaviour is found in every social encounter.

Global Perspectives

Worldwide beliefs about liars

Nonverbal communication – *Refers to gestures, facial expressions, tone of voice, eye contact (or lack thereof), body language, posture and other ways people can communicate without using language.*

Before reading further, answer the following question: How can you tell if someone is lying?

Check to see if your answer matches the Global Deception Research Team's (GDRT, 2006) findings. They asked this same question in 75 different countries and 43 different languages, gathering 11,157 responses. The most common belief about deception is that *liars avoid eye contact*. Specifically, 63.66 per cent of participants mentioned gaze aversion to tell when people are lying. This was followed by the idea that *liars are nervous* (28.15 per cent). Nervousness was viewed as physical cues, such as the perception of hand, arm and leg movements and shrugs, that increased during deception. Other common beliefs included that the *lies themselves are often incoherent* (25.30 per cent), and that *lying can be detected from movements of the liar's body* (25.04 per cent). Body movements include postural shifts, facial movements and fidgeting (GDRT, 2006).

However, none of these indicators have significant research support for detecting deception. Relying on inaccurate beliefs may lead to poor deception detection ability in interpersonal relationships, by juries, businesspeople and security professionals (Bond and DePaulo, 2006).

The belief that lies cause behaviours to leak is still the foundation of many police interrogation manuals (Vrij, 2019; Inbau, Reid, Buckley and Jayne, 2013; Vrij and Granhag, 2007). Many programmes taught invalid and unreliable nonverbal lie detection tools, such as the Behavioural Analysis Interview (Horvath, Blair and Buckley, 2008), and Ekman's approach of observing facial expressions and involuntary body language (Ekman, [1985]2009).

The belief that lies are easy to see is shown when jurors are asked to assess the truthfulness of a defendant's nonverbal behaviour (Vrij and Turgeon, 2018). These nonverbal behaviours include facial expressions, eye contact, body language, use of gestures, dress, grooming and level of confidence (Ogden, 2000). An example of this overreliance on behavioural indicators of deception is found in the Supreme Court of Queensland's (2016, p. 75) *Equal Treatment Benchbook*, where it is stated: 'An impressive witness according to Anglo-Australian culture will look his or her questioner in the eye and answer questions confidently and clearly.' This is one of many examples where the courts endorse the belief that eye contact, confidence and clear speech are reliable indicators of truthfulness.

Mental process theories: emotion and cognition

Some nonverbal approaches examine the mental processes involved in producing a deceptive statement. A common assumption of these approaches is that understanding the nonverbal behaviour of liars requires insight into internal mental states. The focus of these approaches is on emotional or cognitive processes.

The effect of emotions on behaviour

The foundation of emotional theories of deception is the belief in **behavioural leakage**. This belief began with Ekman and Friesen (1969), and is the failure to completely suppress emotions associated with deception, such as anxiety and fear, causing behavioural leakage cues in the face, arms, hands, legs and feet. Ekman ([1985]2009) explained that the leaked emotions are expressed via *micro-expressions* – facial expressions that occur within a fraction of a second. Behavioural leakage was a highly influential idea, producing the US TV drama *Lie to Me*, based partly on Ekman's life and work (Levine, Serota and Shulman, 2010). According to Ekman's ([1985]2009) model, liars also experience guilt and shame. However, many of Ekman's claims lack support (Bond, Levine and Hartwig, 2015; Lindquist et al., 2012). Ekman's theory does not define what emotions liars are supposed to feel and when they are supposed to feel them. Deception produces positive as well as negative emotional experiences and sometimes no emotions at all (Burgoon, 2018). According to the US National Research Council (2003), this approach confuses emotion and deception. Because of these problems, contemporary theories have focused on the cognitive processes of deception.

> **Behavioural leakage** – *The belief that liars produce unconscious behaviours that indicate emotions related to lying, such as fear and anxiety.*

The effect of cognitive load on behaviour

This approach focuses on understanding how lying is more cognitively demanding than telling the truth and how increased **cognitive load** affects nonverbal behaviour. Vrij, Semin and Bull (1996) reveal contradictory beliefs about body movements. Specifically, it is widely believed that deception is associated with an *increase* in movements; however, actual deception is associated with a *decrease* in movements. Observers expect increased movement with deception, assuming that liars feel nervous and will behave nervously when lying (Bogaard, Meijer, Vrij and Merckelbach, 2016). The explanation is that in an interview setting, lying is more cognitively demanding than telling the truth (Bird, Gretton, Cockerell and Heathcote, 2019; Driskell and Driskell, 2019). There is more evidence that people engaged in cognitively complex tasks make less (not more) hand and arm movements. Frosina et al. (2018) explain that the increased cognitive load reduces body language and overall animation. Some argue that this effect is found only in low-stakes laboratory experiments (Fitzpatrick and Bachenko, 2012), compared to high-stakes situations, such as police interviews and interviews with customs officials, which produce more tension. Hartwig and Bond (2014) investigated lie detection accuracy based on nonverbal cues by comparing high-stakes settings that cause strong emotions with those that do not. No difference was found in the accuracy of lie detection between these two settings.

> **Cognitive load** – *The amount of cognitive effort (or amount of information processing) required to perform a task.*

Why do we believe in nonverbal indicators of deception?

One of the simplest explanations for our belief in the power of nonverbal indicators of deception is that we do not receive enough feedback to learn from our experience and discover that our views are wrong. Specifically, we often discover that we have been lied to a long time after the interaction took place (Park et al., 2002).

PART III

How lies are really detected

We have all been on the receiving end of a lie. Try to remember a lie you detected in the past. Recall as much as you can about the situation in which the person lied to you. Describe the event where you were lied to. Where did it happen? What was the lie about? Can you recall what the person said to you? Now think about how you found out that the person had lied to you. What evidence revealed the lie? Finally, how much time passed between the time when the lie was told and when you knew that the person had lied?

These were the same questions asked by Park et al. (2002). Consider your evidence again. Was your evidence based on context or behaviour? If your experience matches their findings, you probably used contextual cues like third-party information (a friend told you about the lie), physical evidence (a text message or a photo), or the liar's confession. In the real world, lies are detected in people you know – friends 39.5 per cent, romantic partners 32.8 per cent, family 7.2 per cent, roommates 4.6 per cent and co-workers 4.6 per cent. Discovering the lie takes time. In their study, 4.1 per cent were detected in less than an hour, 20.6 per cent in less than a day, 20.6 per cent in less than a week, 20.6 per cent in less than one month, 15.5 per cent in less than one year, and 1.5 per cent were discovered more than one year after they were told!

Do these results match your experience? If so, you now have insight into the superiority of contextual cues over behavioural information when judging truthfulness.

Confirmation bias – *The tendency to interpret new evidence as confirmation of one's existing beliefs or theories.*

Another explanation is the power of stereotypes. Research shows that once stereotypical beliefs have been formed, for example the notion that liars display gaze aversion and excessive movements, they are difficult to change. For example, once incorrect beliefs are formed, people only seek information that confirms their beliefs – known as the **confirmation bias** (Nickerson, 1998) – and they perceive supporting evidence that does not exist – illusory correlations (Stroessner and Plaks 2001). For example, when observers were told that someone was lying, they overestimated the amount of gaze aversions the alleged liar actually displayed (Levine, Asada, and Park, 2006).

IN SUMMARY

Despite portrayals in the entertainment media, there are no valid, reliable or strong indicators of lying and we overestimate the relationship between nonverbal behaviour and deception.

CRITICAL THINKING AND APPLICATION QUESTIONS

1   Based on what we now know about the myths of nonverbal behaviour, if you were to coach a witness to behave in a believable manner for a jury trial, what would be your advice?

2   Why do observers mistake behaviours that relieve stress, such as neck touching, hand wringing and facial touching, for deception?

3   In some countries, it is instilled in children that when an authority figure is reprimanding them, they should avoid eye contact with that person. This shows that you are contrite and humble. How could this behaviour be misinterpreted in a legal setting, such as a police arrest or a courtroom?

THE TOOLS OF THE TRADE: THE POLYGRAPH

FICTION: The polygraph is based on scientific principles of physiological responses to lies.

Versus

FACT: The polygraph is built on anecdotal evidence and unproven theories and is designed to elicit confessions and admissions of guilt.

Countermeasures and the validity of the polygraph

Floyd 'Buzz' Fay sought revenge after he was falsely convicted of murder based on a failed polygraph test. Fay was accused and arrested for murder in Ohio, USA in 1978. The police had no motive or evidence and he knew it. They offered him a deal: take a lie detector test and if you pass, you go free; if you fail, the results would be used in court. The strategy, which, surprisingly, is still legal in some US states, seemed a sure thing to Fay, who was confident of his innocence. However, Fay failed the test, stood trial, and was sentenced to life in prison. Three years after the real killers were found, Fay was set free.

Fay believed the popular misunderstanding that polygraphs don't make mistakes and that the machines are impartial and unbiased. What he hadn't considered was the role of the person who interpreted the test results: the polygraph operator. The objectively achieved results gain any meaning they have only from the subjective evaluation of the polygraph operator (Vrij, 2000). Fay had also failed to consider the possibility that objective factors can be altered. 'I believed the polygraph worked', but years later, Fay added: 'Any criminal who knows how to beat a polygraph can beat it' (Radelet, Bedau and Putnam, 1994, p. 221).

During his two and a half years of wrongful imprisonment, he made himself a polygraph expert. Then he coached 27 men (who admitted their guilt to Fay) on how to apply countermeasures to beat the most popular format of the polygraph, the control question test. By artificially increasing his arousal by pressing his toes against the sole of his shoe, or having arousing thoughts during the control questions, after only twenty minutes of instruction, 23 of the inmates beat the machine (Ford, 2006).

Discussion Questions:

1   How did Floyd 'Buzz' Fay's knowledge that he was innocent work against him? What did he believe about the device that turned out to be false?

2   Evidence shows that strategies used to 'beat' polygraph tests, so-called 'countermeasures', may be effective. Should this information be classified to maintain the integrity of the device, or should this information be freely available to show the dangers of using the polygraph to measure deception?

For many in the law enforcement and intelligence communities, the polygraph is the most valued method for identifying criminals, spies and saboteurs when there is no direct evidence (Harris, 2018). It is widely used in many countries, for example Canada, Japan, Israel and the USA, for employment screening and investigating specific events. Yet the polygraph suffers from a polarising critique – it is viewed with either magical veneration or sceptical disdain.

The most common concern is the test's accuracy, while other concerns include fears about replacing jurors and violations of a person's civil rights. Even the description of the device is controversial. Some describe the polygraph as a 'lie detector' (Best, Hodgeon and Street, 2019), while others describe it as a 'fear detector' (Rutbeck-Goldman, 2017), or even an 'emotion detector' (Houston, Bee and Rimm, 2013). Also controversial is the effectiveness of the polygraph to detect deception. How do you measure effectiveness when research has yet to separate the placebo-like effects, that is, the subject's belief in the effectiveness of the procedure, from the actual relationship between deception and physiological responses?

What the polygraph measures and how

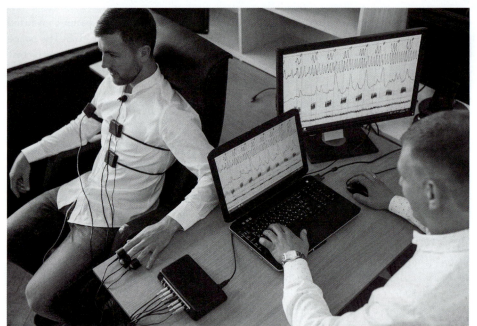

Source: iStock.com/standret

The polygraph uses a combination of medical devices that monitor biological changes

The 'polygraph' (meaning 'many writings') uses a combination of medical devices to monitor biological changes. Table 6.1 shows what the polygraph really measures.

Table 6.1: What does the polygraph measure?

What it measures	How it measures
Blood pressure/ heart rate	A blood-pressure cuff is placed around the subject's upper arm. The sound of blood pumping through the arm is converted into electrical signals
Galvanic skin resistance	Fingerplates, called 'galvanometers', are attached to two of the subject's fingers. They measure the skin's ability to conduct electricity. Since sweat has salt, it conducts electricity much more easily than when the fingers are dry
Breathing (pneumography)	Two hollow rubber tubes wrapped around the subject's chest and abdomen record respiratory movements. When the chest or abdominal muscles expand, the air inside the tubes is displaced and converted into electronic signals
Body movements	Sensors connected to the body record the movements of the arms and legs. This detects the use of physical countermeasures

The average polygraph test lasts two or three hours from beginning to end. The longest part of the polygraph test is the pretest interview, which lasts anywhere from 45 to 90 minutes (Grubin, 2010). This is then followed by the testing phase. Deceptive behaviour is supposed to trigger physiological changes that can be detected by a polygraph and interpreted by a trained examiner. There are two generally accepted procedures: the control question test (CQT) and the guilty knowledge test (GKT). They are shown in Table 6.2.

Table 6.2: Control question test versus guilty knowledge test

	Control question test	**Guilty knowledge test**
Detects	Emotional by-products of deception	Orienting responses
Theory	Lying creates an emotional response in guilty but not innocent subjects	Guilty subjects have knowledge of the crime, innocent subjects do not
Locations used	Canada, the USA, Israel	Japan

The control question test (CQT)

The control question test (CQT), sometimes known as the 'comparison question test', is the most used polygraph procedure (Cook and Mitschow, 2019). The rationale behind the CQT is that lying produces different emotions than telling the truth, and an emotional response is a natural reaction to threatening situations (Ekman, 2009). For the deceptive examinee, the questions about the crime are threatening and should produce a greater emotional response than the truthful examinee. Figure 6.1 shows the CQT procedure.

Figure 6.1: The CQT procedure

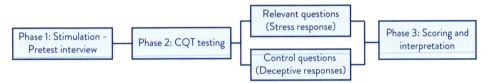

Phase 1: Stimulation: pretest interview

The goal is to convince the examinee that the technique is accurate and that the polygraph will detect every lie. The stimulation phase is meant to have different effects on innocent and guilty subjects. Theoretically, innocent subjects will have increased confidence in the machine, while guilty subjects will now have greater fear of guilt detection (Redlich and Meissner, 2009). But, if the test is valid, why do subjects need to be convinced? Imagine if, during an ophthalmologist visit, half the time was spent convincing you that their equipment really can detect vision problems.

Phase 2: CQT testing

During this phase, the examiner begins asking questions and recording physiological responses. There are two types of questions: relevant questions and control questions.

Relevant questions pertain to the crime under investigation, such as 'Did you kill the victim?', while **control questions** are unrelated to the crime and deal with issues concerning the examinee's moral character. Sometimes, these are called 'probable-lie questions', which are meant to be constructed and asked in such a way as to prompt the examinee to respond 'no' (Ginton, 2016) (Table 6.3).

Table 6.3: A typical CQT question sequence

Question category	*Yes or no* **response**
Control 1	Did you ever take something that did not belong to you? 'No'
Relevant 1	Did you take the money? 'No'
Control 2	Did you ever do something illegal or dishonest? 'No'
Relevant 2	Did you take the money from the safe? 'No'
Control 3	Have you ever lied to get out of trouble or to create problems for someone else? 'No'
Relevant 3	Did you participate in any way in the theft of the money? 'No'

For a valid CQT, two assumptions must be true. The first requires that innocent individuals are more responsive to control rather than relevant questions. The second is that guilty or deceptive individuals should respond more intensely to relevant than control questions (Ginton, 2019).

Phase 3: Scoring and interpretation

The physiological data is digitally stored, and software is used to calculate a probability statement of the chances that the person was telling the truth when responding (Olsen, Harris, Capps and Ansley, 1997).

Criticisms of the CQT

The main criticism of the CQT is the assumption that innocent suspects will display stronger reactions to the control questions than crime-relevant questions (Ben-Shakhar, 1991). Because the stress-inducing effect of control questions depends on the examiner's presentation, the accuracy of the test depends on the skills of the examiner, rather than on the test itself (Meijer and Verschuere, 2010).

Another problem is that guilty subjects may **habituate** – show a reduced response to a repeated stimulus – to the charges covered by the crime-relevant questions. This is because subjects are often given the lie detector test long after the crime was committed and only after their repeated denials to the relevant questions. With repeated presentation of emotionally charged questions, physical responses weaken over time. Therefore, the relevant questions on the CQT lose their impact and reduce the chances that guilty individuals will respond more strongly to relevant than control questions (Ben-Shakhar, 2002).

The guilty knowledge test (GKT)

The guilty knowledge test (GKT) is considered a superior polygraph testing method, due to its stronger scientific foundation (Ogawa, Matsuda, Tsuneoka and Verschuere, 2015).

While the CQT was developed by law enforcement agencies, psychologists developed the GKT. The GKT is most often used in Japan by the National Police (Matsuda, Ogawa and Tsuneoka, 2019).

The rationale behind the GKT is that the guilty subject has knowledge about the crime that innocent suspects do not. The subject reveals this concealed knowledge via the **orienting response** (Smith, Rypma and Wilson, 1981). This response is a spontaneous reaction to novel environmental stimuli (Lang, Bradley and Cuthbert, 1990). The reaction is like the 'cocktail party effect' (Cherry, 1953), when a subject's attention automatically focuses on familiar information, such as hearing your own name spoken aloud at a crowded cocktail party. This automatic response is difficult to suppress, and, unlike the CQT, it depends on cognitive not emotional factors (Ben-Shakhar and Furedy, 1990).

Orienting response – *A physiological response to a specific stimulus.*

The validity of the GKT relies on the assumption that only guilty suspects will remember the details of their crime perfectly, and only the offender knows detailed crime information. However, this might not always be true. For example, crimes of passion (those committed under impulse) and crimes committed by those diagnosed with mental impairments (schizophrenia) may not be remembered in detail and may not produce an orienting response (Meijer et al., 2016; Peth, Vossel and Gamer, 2012).

Figure 6.2: Steps in the GKT

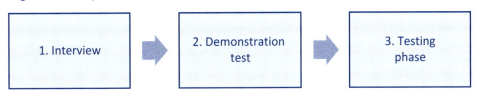

1. Interview → 2. Demonstration test → 3. Testing phase

As shown in Figure 6.2, the process starts with the interview, when the examiner evaluates what the examinee already knows about the details of the crime. Next, in the demonstration phase, the examiner demonstrates how the GKT questioning functions. The examinee is asked to select a card and memorise its number. Then the examiner presents card numbers sequentially, pausing 20–30 seconds between each number. During the card test, the examiner observes how the examinee responds physiologically to the questions, focusing on their reaction to their choice. Some instructions describe using marked cards, so the examiner knows which card was selected by the examinee (Synnott, Dietzel and Ioannou, 2015). At this point, the examinee should be convinced that the GKT test is valid and is ready to begin the actual test. The third step is the testing phase. The test begins with the presentation of a question with four to six response items. Only one of the items is related to the crime (see Table 6.4). The examiner reads each question and response choices, pausing 20–30 seconds between each item. This delay allows the examinee's psychological responses to return to baseline (Krapohl, McCloughan and Senter, 2009). Next, other questions are asked, changing the order of the items to remove presentation order bias (Matsuda, Ogawa and Tsuneoka, 2019). Based on the physical responses to the items, the examiner identifies which responses to a specific item are different from those to other items and infers that the examinee recognises a specific item relevant to the crime.

Table 6.4: Typical GKT question format

Question type	Question: The victim was struck with a
Irrelevant	hammer?
Relevant	cricket bat? ← *Guilty suspects should show greater orienting response to this item*
Irrelevant	pipe?
Irrelevant	chair?
Irrelevant	fist?

Criticism of the GKT

Unlike Japan, where the GKT is used regularly (Nakayma, 2002), there is resistance to perform field studies of the GKT because psychologists need the cooperation of the police to conduct such research. Although not a criticism, if law enforcement agencies switched to the GKT, it would acknowledge that they had been using a flawed technique and raise questions about convictions based on CQT procedures.

Another criticism is that the GKT only applies to a small percentage of specific incident investigations. To use this technique, investigators must withhold information from the news media (details incidental to the crime). If a crime receives media attention and innocent suspects gain knowledge of the crime's details, or the investigators do not have enough detailed knowledge of the crime, then the GKT is useless. Proponents counter that, if criminal investigations were conducted with the GKT in mind (as in Japan), then it could easily be applied on a large scale, like other forensic tools, such as fingerprints and DNA analysis (Lykken, 1998).

As you would expect, there are times when a polygraph examiner misreads a person's reaction to a question. The subjective nature of the test is why polygraph results are rarely admissible in court. Brett and Beary (1986) describe two ways that a response can be misinterpreted. The first is a false positive, when the response of a truthful person is determined to be deceptive. The second is a false negative, when the response of a deceptive person is determined to be truthful. If the polygraph examination is unbiased, one would expect an equal percentage of false positives and false negatives. Yet, Horvath (1977) found that laboratory-based studies show that false-positive errors occur more often than false-negative errors.

Use of countermeasures

Counter-measures – *When subjects deliberately manipulate their physical and mental responses during the examination.*

Countermeasures are when subjects deliberately manipulate their physical and mental responses during the examination (Honts, Raskin and Kirchera, 1994). Countermeasures include reducing reactivity, suppressing physiological reactions, and increasing physiological reactions (Gudjonsson, 1988).

Physical countermeasures

Physical countermeasures include behaviours that cause pain thus creating a physiological response, such as biting the tongue, lip or cheek, stepping on a tack inserted into the shoe, during the control or irrelevant questions (Table 6.5). This method is recommended for brief 'yes' or 'no' responses (which are most questions). However, some examiners have developed an effective 'counter-countermeasure' for this tactic – they ask the examinee to remove their shoes or give longer responses.

Table 6.5: Examples of physical countermeasures

Sedatives
Antiperspirant on fingertips
Tacks placed in the shoe
Biting tongue, lip or cheek

Mental countermeasures

While mental countermeasures are more secretive, they are also less effective and more difficult to learn (Honts, Devitt, Winbush and Kircher, 2007). These include mental distractions that reduce the subject's physiological response, such as counting backwards by seven. This creates a similar physical response to each question and leads to inconclusive test results. Examiners have developed counter-countermeasures via the use of filler questions. Examinees are supposed to answer 'yes' to fillers but 'no' to the other questions. This forces the examinee to listen and therefore process the questions.

Do countermeasures work?

Honts, Raskin, Kircher and Hodes (1988) found countermeasures ineffective against the CQT. When subjects are forced to use them spontaneously, the task quickly becomes overwhelming (Memon, Virj and Bull, 1998). Research supports the effectiveness of practised use of countermeasures to defeat the polygraph (Honts, Devitt, Winbush and Kircher, 2007). For example, researchers trained subjects for 30 minutes to use either physical countermeasures (biting the tongue or pressing the toes against the floor) or mental countermeasures (counting backwards by seven) during a control question polygraph test (Honts, Raskin and Kircher, 1994). While both physical and mental countermeasures were equally effective, that is, each enabled 50 per cent of the subjects to defeat the polygraph, the strongest effects were observed on cardiovascular measures. Furthermore, the countermeasures were difficult to detect either instrumentally or by observation. Experienced examiners correctly identified only 12 per cent of the physical and none of the mental countermeasures.

Admissibility in courts

In Europe, lie detector tests are not used as they are not regarded as reliable evidence and violate a person's right to remain silent (Meijer and van Koppen, 2017). In 1982, Australia's New South Wales District Court ruled that lie detector tests were inadmissible (Freckelton, 2004). In the USA, the use of the polygraph is barred in 30 of 50 states. Ironically, the most consistent opponent to polygraph admission in court is the US Federal government, which also happens to be the largest consumer of polygraph exams (Rutbeck-Goldman, 2017).

The original decision about the criteria to admit novel scientific procedures as evidence was *Frye* v. *United States* (293 F. 1013, D.C. Cir 1923). Frye was accused of murdering a doctor and he took a unigraph, which measured only systolic blood pressure. The examiner reported that Frye was truthful, and Frye moved to have that evidence admitted in court. The court ruled that before any scientific device could be admitted as evidence, it must first be accepted by the scientific community. In the 1920s, there was no published research on unigraphs, so the evidence was not admitted. Decades later, *United States* v. *Piccinonna*

(885 F.2d 1529, 11th Cir. 1989) allowed polygraph results to be admitted as long as at least one of two criteria were met, the two parties in the case agree, or the judge decides to allow it. Then, in 1993, the Supreme Court established the criteria for admissibility of scientific evidence, known as the 'Daubert ruling'. The case of *Daubert* v. *Merrell Dow Pharmaceuticals, Inc.* (113 S. Ct. 2786, 1993) established rules on expert testimony and how the judge should determine the validity of the expert witness. The court provided five guidelines a judge can use to help guide their decision (Table 6.6).

Table 6.6: Daubert guidelines for admitting new science

1. Has the technique been experimentally tested?
2. Has it been subjected to peer review and publication?
3. What is its known or potential error rate?
4. Are there established standards for controlling the technique?
5. Is it generally accepted in the relevant scientific community?

IN SUMMARY

The polygraph is designed to elicit confessions and admissions of guilt, but its reputation is built on anecdotal evidence and unproven theories. Because of its lack of scientific support, it is not admissible as evidence.

 ## CRITICAL THINKING AND APPLICATION QUESTIONS

1   Compare and contrast the CQT and the GKT methods, focusing on the differences between their theoretical assumptions and procedures.

2   Write a brief guide for beating the polygraph using countermeasures. Choose either the CQT or the GKT and describe *when* during the procedure you should apply physical and mental countermeasures.

3   Imagine you are a judge and the defence team intend to introduce the results of their truth machine as evidence of their client's innocence. Review the five essential questions you want to know about this machine to decide if it functions based on valid scientific principles from Table 6.6.

THE LANGUAGE OF LIES: DECODING VERBAL DECEPTION

FICTION: Liars are best detected by their nonverbal behaviour and polygraph responses.   *Versus*   **FACT:** The Strategic Use of Evidence approach is a valuable and reliable alternative to exploit differences between liars and truth-tellers.

Where were you exactly one month ago? Imagine if the police think you were involved in a crime and asked you to provide your alibi for that day. Like most people, you will find this difficult, and your alibi or explanation might even contradict the police's evidence. Even though you are innocent, forgetting the past and presenting conflicting evidence could make you look like a liar. This situation is not as strange as it seems because police are trained to rely on contradictions between suspects' statements and the available evidence to detect if suspects are lying (Hartwig, Granhag, Stromwall and Kronkvist, 2006; Luke et al., 2016). Exploiting these contradictions allows police to differentiate between truth-tellers and liars.

The Strategic Use of Evidence (SUE) framework

At the heart of the **Strategic Use of Evidence (SUE) framework** is the suspect's perceptions of the interviewer's knowledge, and how these perceptions affect the suspect's counter-interrogation strategies, and, in turn, their verbal responses (Granhag, 2010; Granhag and Hartwig, 2015). The process begins with establishing rapport and then asking open-ended questions. But these questions are about incriminating information the suspect does not know the investigators are aware of. Then the strategy shifts to asking questions the investigator already knows the answer to and watching how the suspect responds. This is followed by a 'free recall' stage, when the investigator asks the suspect to describe what happened on the day or time in question. This causes guilty subjects to avoid talking about incriminating evidence, while innocent subjects are more open to talk about all the evidence. This interview style is focused on information gathering as opposed to confrontation. While the goal is to discover new evidence, it is more about looking for signs of deception to use later when formulating key questions. While the SUE framework is not specifically designed to elicit a confession, it is possible that a suspect will confess during any stage of the interview.

> **Strategic Use of Evidence (SUE) framework –** *The presenting of evidence to exploit differences between guilty and innocent subjects' strategies during interviews.*

Strategic differences between liars and truth-tellers

The SUE approach is built on the findings that guilty and innocent subjects adopt different strategies to preserve their credibility during interviews (Luke et al., 2016). Specifically, guilty subjects make statements that contradict evidence. Furthermore, the contradictions increase when questioned without knowledge of the evidence against them.

The SUE approach examines **statement–evidence consistency** – when subjects change their statements to match the evidence, omitting and denying factual evidence. Unlike earlier passive methods of interviewing (PEACE, the cognitive interview), the SUE approach is an active approach to detect differences between liars and truth-tellers. The difference is the SUE approach shifts from examining emotional and behavioural differences to examining differences in cognitive strategies between the guilty and the innocent.

For example, a woman claims innocence in the murder of her husband, but her DNA is on the murder weapon, a kitchen knife. The evidence suggests she is lying. But if she is innocent, she would be more likely to admit that she had recently used the knife to prepare dinner and could reveal what food she prepared. If her alibi was that she was shopping for food when the murder happened, she could supply details about what was purchased, what was on sale, and even details about her interactions with the cashier on duty. While there may be gaps in her memory, the innocent suspect has no reason to withhold any of this information from the investigators.

On the other hand, if the woman was guilty of killing her husband, when the DNA evidence is presented, she would use avoidance strategies and produce few verifiable

> **Statement–evidence consistency –** *When subjects change their statements to match the evidence, by omitting and denying factual evidence.*

details. In this case, the guilty suspect knows the investigator has recovered DNA on the knife. What she does not know is that the investigator learned that she did not leave the house until an hour after she claimed she did, because surveillance cameras at the bank across from her house captured her car leaving her house later than she claimed. Although she can present a false story, it will not have the rich complex narrative about the shop that an innocent suspect could supply, even if she went there after the murder.

A real-world example of the analysis of statement–evidence consistency is the case of Susan Smith. Smith claimed that her two young children were kidnapped at gunpoint. The kidnapping in 1994 in Union County, South Carolina attracted worldwide attention and stirred racial tension after Smith initially told police that a black man had carjacked her and kidnapped her children. She tearfully pleaded for her children to be returned. But nine days later, she admitted pushing her car down the access ramp of John D. Long Lake with her two children buckled securely in the back seat (Gleick, 2001). However, before Smith was a suspect in her children's deaths, she told reporters, 'My children wanted me. They needed me. And now I can't help them' (Adams, 1996, p. 12). Her choice of past tense was strange because relatives normally speak of a missing person in the present tense (Parr and Stevenson, 2015). The fact that Smith used the past tense in this context suggested that she already viewed her missing children as dead (Adams, 1996). It was a small but significant contradiction in her story that led to her confession. Smith told police about stopping at a red light on Monarch Mills Road. She stated that she saw no other cars on the road, yet the light turned red, contradicting the fact that the light on Monarch Mills Road was always green and only turned red if it was triggered by a car on the cross street. Since she said there were no other cars on the road, there was no reason for her to come up to a red light (Chuck, 2015). This verbal contradiction and the strategic use of this evidence eventually led to Smith confessing that she drowned her children and fabricated the entire story.

Suspect counter-interrogation strategies

Counter-interrogation strategies are the methods interviewees use to convince the interviewer that they are telling the truth. The liar and truth-teller view the interview from different perspectives and motivations. For example, the interview is both a goal (being perceived as truthful) and a threat (being perceived as a liar). While liars are threatened that their concealed information *will* be revealed, truth-tellers are threatened that their truthful information will *not* be revealed.

The threats to the liar are greater under heavy cognitive load to conceal information. For example, unlike the innocent suspect, guilty suspects must make decisions about speaking or remaining silent, telling the truth, revealing or withholding the information, and how to respond to questions during the interview. To cope with these threats, liars adopt two strategies: escape (denial) and avoidance (avoid mentioning the incriminating evidence) (Alison et al., 2014).

Research on counter-interrogation strategies reveals that liars often report having a plan before the interview and avoid disclosing concealed information (Granhag, Hartwig, Giolla and Clemens, 2015). If unable to avoid responding, when confronted with direct questions, they use escape strategies like denial. Specifically, as part of their 'lie-script', liars tried to manage their concealed information by repeating simple stories while avoiding or denying incriminating information (Hartwig, Granhag, Strömwall and Doering, 2010). Meanwhile, if the truth-teller does have a strategy, it is to be verbally forthcoming and tell the truth like it happened (Strömwall, Hartwig and Granhag, 2006).

Tactical use of questions and disclosure strategies

How do you exploit the concealment strategies of liars to produce changes or revisions to their stories? In the SUE method, it is by the tactical use of questions and disclosure of evidence. First, let us explore the tactical use of questions. Granhag and Hartwig (2008) suggest that the interviewer should withhold relevant evidence, keeping the subject unaware of what the interviewer knows. Beginning with broad, open-ended, free recall questions, such as 'Tell me all about your visit to London', produced differences in the number of omissions in liars' statements. On the other hand, specific, direct questions, such as 'Did you take the Tube, Metro, or bus?', led to dishonest replies that contradicted the evidence. Granhag and Vrig (2010) explain that specific questions about the evidence eventually exhaust the guilty suspect's alternative explanations, and liars use more intense escape and denial strategies as the level of incriminating information increases (Jordan et al., 2012).

The second approach is the tactical use of disclosure of evidence. Research on the SUE framework examined both the timing and manner of evidence disclosure. In other words, when is it ideal to disclose the information and how should this information be presented to produce the greatest difference between the innocent and the guilty?

Related to the timing of disclosure, studies have manipulated the moment when the information is revealed to the subjects during the interview. Revealing information late in the interview is more effective than revealing it early (Dando, Bull, Ormerod and Sandham, 2013), or revealing pieces of evidence throughout the interview (Leahy-Harland and Bull, 2017). Ultimately, withholding the evidence until the end of the interview produced the most verbal differences between liars and truth-tellers in terms of statement–evidence consistency (Hartwig, Granhag, Strömwall and Kronkvist, 2006).

Related to the manner of evidence disclosure, the **evidence framing matrix** can be used (Granhag, Strömwall, Willén and Hartwig, 2013). The evidence framing matrix is a tool designed to tactically confront an interviewee with inconsistencies in their statements and available evidence (see Figure 6.3).

> **Evidence framing matrix** – A tool designed to tactically confront an interviewee with inconsistencies in their statements and available evidence.

Figure 6.3: The evidence framing matrix

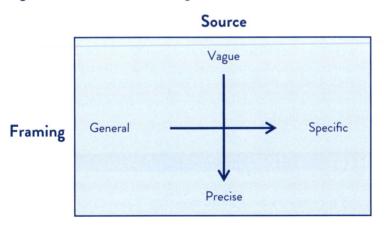

Generally, the tactic consists of revealing evidence with increasing strength and precision. Framing includes the way the suspect is told how the investigators know the evidence (the source) and the framing of the evidence (what they know). Interviewers adjust the way information is framed from general to specific and the source of the information from vague to precise. For example, the source can be revealed in a vague to precise manner; such as 'We have information that you visited London recently' to 'We have video of you entering King's Cross station on the morning of the crime.' The framing of information can also follow a general to specific format; for example, 'You were seen in London recently' to 'You were seen at King's Cross station' to 'You were seen on platform 9¾ at King's Cross Station.' The ultimate purpose of the evidence framing matrix is to structure the evidence disclosure in such a way that it creates greater challenges for liars than truth-tellers to tell a credible story. In other words, exploiting the concealment strategies of liars forces them to alter their stories.

Support for the SUE method

Granhag et al. (2013) showed the effectiveness for presenting evidence in an incremental fashion – moving from general and vague to specific and precise framing. Deceptive subjects revised their statements to make them fit the evidence as it was presented. The incrementally presented SUE proved to be the most effective interview technique, resulting in significant differences between guilty and innocent suspects for all three cues examined: statement–evidence inconsistency, within-statement inconsistency, and within-group inconsistency (Granhag, Rangmar and Strömwall, 2014).

As final support for the SUE method, researchers asked an intriguing question: 'How does the passage of time affect the consistency of verbal reports?' In their first experiment, subjects committed a theft (liars) or an innocent activity (truth-tellers) in a university bookshop (Sukumar, Wade and Hodgson, 2018). Subjects were questioned shortly after or two months later about their bookshop visit without informing them of the evidence implicating them in the theft. All subjects were not informed that they would be questioned about their activity later to prevent them from attending to the activity more closely than an everyday activity or rehearsing their memory of the activity in preparation for the interview. As expected, liars always contradicted the evidence more than truth-tellers. Next, they presented all the mock suspects' responses to an independent group of laypeople and asked them to rate subject deceptiveness. Liars were rated as more deceptive than truth-tellers after both time delays. The researchers suggest that liars' tendency to distance themselves from a crime is greater than any memory decay that truth-tellers experience two months after a crime. Eventually, the extent of a suspect's contradictions with the evidence indicate deception even after an extended time delay. Still unanswered is to what extent police interviewers and jurors adjust their deception judgements of suspects to account for the passage of time and its effect on the number of statement–evidence inconsistencies even an innocent truthful suspect might make.

IN SUMMARY

The strategic use of evidence is important in cases when the evidence indicates (but does not prove) the suspect's involvement in a crime. Research in this area is challenging and while it is impossible for anyone to detect lies in another person with 100 per cent accuracy, strategies such as the SUE framework improve the investigator's chances and offers alternative non-accusatory methods for the investigator's skillset.

CRITICAL THINKING AND APPLICATION QUESTIONS

1   Why is it more difficult to lie than tell the truth?

2   Where were you two days ago at 9 pm? Review your answer. Was it easier to identify people who could verify your story or provide empirical evidence to support your story? How would this affect you, if determining innocence relies only on empirical evidence?

3   Your roommate denies borrowing your car while you were sleeping. Although you have evidence (GPS coordinates, security camera footage, key found on their desk), you would like your roommate to confess to the incident. Describe how you would apply the SUE method's tactical use of disclosure of evidence to elicit a confession.

THE QUEST FOR A TRUTH MACHINE

FICTION: Lie detection has transitioned from a pseudoscience to an evidence-based discipline.

Versus

FACT: We have not made significant progress detecting deception and if we had, society would be very different.

The creation of a reliable truth machine would rewrite the rules of society. Imagine a world where lies simply did not work. People could still commit crimes, but not with the expectation that no one would know. In our criminal justice systems, there would be no need for judges and juries because rather than weighing the evidence, we would know the truth. A transformation of our society would happen if lie detectors become affordable, unobtrusive and used beyond court cases. Few people would invest in companies that did not freely subject their public statements and advertising to lie detection. Corrupt governments and politicians would have a much harder time staying in power. While not all conversations would happen under lie detection, the public would demand it of the important ones. It would still be possible to keep secrets, and to refuse to comment on specific topics, but it would no longer be common to pretend to tell the truth (Halprin, 1996).

There is a fundamental problem with detecting lies that technology has yet to overcome, and that is that there is no reliable relationship between any kind of external stimuli and your internal mental state (Iacano and Shakhar, 2019). The National Research Council (2003) concluded that when measuring physiological signs of deception, there is no evidence that heart rate, blood pressure, sweating and breathing indicate truths or lies. The ability to read thoughts and decipher emotions eludes science. Yet not all technology is unreliable and invalid (Saxe, 1991). The use of DNA and ballistics testing meets the criteria of valid and reliable science. Given the controversial nature and the potential societal impact of lie detection technology, the courts should apply the same scientific standards required for adoption of a medical test or device (Langleben and Moriarty, 2013).

India's quest for the ultimate truth machine

In 2008, Aditi Sharma was the first person convicted of murder based on a brain scan. Her charge was poisoning her former fiancé Udit Bharati with sweets dipped in arsenic. Judge Shalini Phansalkar-Joshi explained during sentencing that the brain scan conducted on Sharma left no doubt that she had 'experiential knowledge' of arsenic, the murder itself and the way Bharati was killed (Gaudet, 2011).

Police in India used a form of brain scanning called Brain Electrical Oscillations Signature Profiling (BEOSP) (Mukundan, Sumit and Chetan, 2017). During the test, the accused sits silently in a small, windowless room, wearing a skullcap with a set of 30 electrodes, which records/measures the components of electrical oscillations generated during remembrance of autobiographical episodes, which can occur only when one has acquired the experiences through participation in said activities. The accused listens to a series of statements – some of which are associated with the crime – and the assumption is that BEOSP reveals whether the suspect shows prior knowledge of a particular cue, for example, a murder weapon, or the injuries suffered by a victim.

It is believed that the new generation of tests based on brain scans are less fallible than traditional lie tests. The trouble is, the idea of futuristic brain-scanning evidence is extremely persuasive to a judge in a court of law, and even more so to a jury (Cox, 2016). The controversy lies in the idea that because the brain and mind are one, then every thought has a physical cause that can be detected and understood. But not everyone is convinced. In September 2008, India's National Institute of Mental Health and Neuroscience declared that brain scans of criminal suspects were unscientific and should not be used in investigations or as evidence in a court of law (Aggarwal, 2009).

Six months later, Aditi was released because the evidence of her possessing the arsenic-laced sweets was not compelling and could have been planted (Kein, 2008). The BEOSP evidence was not mentioned.

Can we measure intention?

The intention to act is a hidden process existing only in a person's mind. It is the moment that awareness of an impulse or decision to act surfaces (Alexander et al., 2016). We may never be able to measure intention, as most intentions are unconscious (Kihlstrom, 2019), and although we remember our behaviours, we are unaware of their causes (Skinner, 1986). Without the ability to predict what a person is thinking, the only objective way to measure intent is inference via a subject's actions or words (Rafter, 2008).

Similar issues arise when using new technologies such as lie (or truth) detectors to incriminate or exonerate defendants. Companies believe that they have (or will) perfect such techniques for lie detection and malingering (falsely exaggerating physical and/or psychological symptoms). The challenge is balancing the limited legal admissibility of these new technologies and marketing these techniques for use in legal proceedings, employment screening and national security investigations. Even if acceptable validity and reliability standards are met, their practical application remains elusive. For example, persuading a suspected terrorist insurgent to lie still in an fMRI chamber for questioning seems unrealistic (O'Mara, 2015).

Exploring the next generation of truth machines

In response to the lack of confidence in the reliability of the polygraph and lack of courtroom admissibility, new detection technologies are continually being introduced.

But are these new technologies an improvement on the polygraph or do they suffer from the same fundamental flaws? Table 6.7 shows a selection of some of these new methods and their theoretical perspectives. Despite these advances, the polygraph remains the standard truth test for most law enforcement and government agencies.

Table 6.7: Alternatives to the polygraph: new lie detection technologies

Technology	What it measures	Method	Lie detection theory
Eye-scanning lie detector (EyeDetect)	Pupil dilation and blink rate	An infrared camera observes the eye, capturing images 60 times a second while subject responds to questions	Deception creates emotional stress of the sympathetic division of the autonomic nervous system (the fight-or-flight response) and dilates the pupils
Eye-detection software and motion and pressure sensors (e.g. the AVATAR kiosk)	Changes in the eyes, voice, gestures and posture	Users face a screen in a kiosk and talk to an electronic interviewer. Sensors detect changes in eye movements, voice, posture and facial gestures	Machine learning and artificial intelligence, using a complex analytical algorithm, can determine truths from lies
Functional MRI lie detector (No Lie MRI and Cephos Corp.)	Regional blood flow changes in the brain during cognition	Functional magnetic resonance imaging (fMRI) of blood flow	Lying requires greater cognitive load and creates greater brain activation
Computer voice stress analysis and layered voice analysis	Changes in vocal patterns	Audio recording of interview responses to questions	Deception and concealment create micro-tremors in the voice

Will these new lie detection technologies ever be legally admissible?

The rise of new technologies raises two important questions. First, can these technologies accurately measure a person's past or even present mental state? Second, just because we can use them, should we? In response to both questions, the short answer is 'no'. No device has been able to reliably translate physiological responses, including brain activity, into mental states of mind. No device can differentiate guilt from anxiety, fear or anger (Iacono and Ben-Shakar, 2019; Synnott, Dietzel and Ioannou, 2015). Even with modern technology, we have not identified a physical marker of deception. This is similar to Carl Lashley's problem of trying to find the engram, the physical trace of a memory (see Chapter2).

For as long as there have been lies, there have been methods of lie detection and, over time, our talents for practising deception have outpaced our detection ability. To detect lies, some cultures developed rituals that invoke supernatural aid through sacred signs and totems. However, these techniques relied more on belief in their effectiveness to condemn the deceitful than their verified history of detecting liars. Science author Arthur C. Clarke describes this belief as: 'Any sufficiently advanced technology is indistinguishable from magic' (Clarke, 1985, p. 36). The problem with using magical tools is that their capabilities seem obvious, while their limitations do not. Magical thinking offers a convenient mental shortcut for an explanation, making it easier to believe in magic than to critically examine any conflicting evidence.

Problems occur when the inventors of these tools are more interested in marketing and production rather than research and verification. The dilemma is the seductive appeal of technology (Stronge, 2009). Ironically, in the courtroom, juries are less likely to question the results of a scientific test than the testimony of a witness. Consequently, admission of polygraph evidence is prohibited in most criminal justice systems.

Whether we rely on racing hearts or active neurons, the greatest obstacle is the practical application of these technologies. For example, how do you use these technologies on unwilling subjects, or subjects who lack the intention to deceive, or, in the case of psychological disorders, lack the conscious knowledge of their own deception? These technologies require a willing subject. The test is useless for an uncooperative subject who cannot be forced to submit to this test (Simpson, 2008). Physically cooperative subjects need to remain still for at least 10 minutes to produce usable fMRI data (Langleben, 2010).

Involuntarily restraining subjects would produce stress that overrides the subtle fMRI signal differences between lies and truth (Langleben, 2010). Because of this, the ethical and legal use of fMRI-based lie detection will be limited to cooperative volunteers seeking acquittal, or clearance after failing a polygraph test (Halber, 2007). Second, false positives persist due to the difficulty of detecting the intention to deceive. A lie, by its very definition, is when someone says something they know is false and intend to deceive (Ekman, [1985]2009). Currently, there is no way to directly measure levels of intention. Different applications may require different accuracy trade-offs. For example, false-positive rates not acceptable for incriminating evidence could be enough to demonstrate reasonable doubt (Halber, 2007). These techniques will produce more false positives as technology becomes more invasive. Ironically, these 'new' brain-scanning technologies suffer from the same problem as the polygraph – even truthful defendants can be nervous when interrogated (Grafton, Sinnott-Armstrong, Gazzaniga and Gazzaniga, 2006).

Finally, there is a lack of generalisability between laboratory and real-world experiments (Levine, 2018). Specifically, the subjects in these experiments are often given incentives to lie (money or credits), and there are no life-changing consequences at stake (Ekman, [1985]2009). Laboratory subjects, unlike defendants, are told to lie and they know that their lies will be exposed because we know the ground truth (Kircher, Horowitz and Raskin, 1988). Because these two situations are so different, we cannot extend the evidence accumulated in controlled experiments to actual trials (Nahari et al., 2019). Legal scholars and neuroscientists are interested and alarmed by fMRI's potential use in detecting liars. Kozel et al. (2009) used fMRI in their study, where subjects chose one of two objects (ring or watch) to 'steal' and placed it in their locker. Participant's brains were then scanned while being visually presented with a series of questions. They reported detecting the lies with 86 per cent accuracy. However, the study suffers from significant conflicts of interest, because the authors have pending patents and the researcher is the president and CEO of Cephos Corp. (offers fMRI-based deception detection services).

Vulnerability to countermeasures

Like the polygraph, current technologies are also vulnerable to physical and mental countermeasures. Ganis et al. (2011) demonstrated that physical countermeasures, such as making finger and other small movements during the critical questions, while in the fMRI chamber are effective. Researchers investigated whether purely mental countermeasures are effective (Hsu, Begliomini, Dall'Acqua and Ganis, 2019). They found that purely mental countermeasures, like mental distraction, are much more difficult to detect than physical countermeasures, and the participants did not need extensive training to overcome the fMRI results. These findings show that fMRI-based deception detection measures are vulnerable and should be applied with caution before using them in the field. Methods to defeat countermeasures, or at least to detect their use, need to be developed.

In conclusion, modern technologies applied to the task of lie detection suffer from the same pitfalls as previous technologies, namely a lack of valid and reliable results. If there is so much evidence that polygraphs do not detect lies, why is it still used? The *belief* in the polygraph's accuracy is important for eliciting confessions. The machine is useful as a prop. Saxe (1991) calls this the 'theater' of interrogation. A persuasive examiner can manipulate the subject's beliefs in the validity of the test through tricks and social pressure and convince them that they might as well confess.

The right to private thoughts

Neuroscience may one day reveal our intentions before we can act upon them. Even if neuroscientists are successful and decode the language of the brain, a final ethical dilemma arises, the issue of cognitive freedom. Specifically, this research is based on the assumption that human thought and behaviour are produced by physical processes in the brain. Therefore, if human behaviour is produced by the operation of physical mechanisms within the brain, then the intention, creation and communication of a lie are the result of measurable physical mechanisms (Farah, 2005). Should someone be held responsible if the physical mechanisms in their brain generate a lie? More importantly, if these lies are the results of physical processes beyond our control, what happens to our free will and responsibility (Blank, 1999)? Why is the concept of individual intent and responsibility important? The answer lies in the **retributive theory of punishment**. The retributive theory of punishment justifies the suffering of the offender on the basis of their voluntary decision to commit a crime (Walker, 1991). If the neuroscience continues to make progress in this area, we may discover that our behaviours are not voluntary (Altimus, 2017) and punishment is no longer an option.

Another question of ethics concerns the right to the privacy of one's thoughts. Neuroethicists called this concept **cognitive liberty** (Setentia, 2004). This is the idea that individuals have a right to privacy and must provide consent before their thought processes are measured (Boire, 2000). Attaining the ability to decipher human thoughts poses fundamental legal, ethical and social challenges. Determining whether or not it is legal to gain access or interfere with another person's neural activity is a violation of our basic rights against self-incrimination (Lenca, 2017). If prosecutors try to get the results of fMRI lie detection tests admitted into court, they can expect a challenge based on most countries' ban on self-incriminating testimony. But this right has already been circumvented. For example, the US Supreme Court has ruled that defendants can be forced to provide samples of their blood, saliva and other physical evidence that may incriminate them (*Maryland* v. *King*, 569 U.S. 435, 2013). Legal admissibility will depend on the answer to the question: Is a brain scan similar to giving testimony or giving a DNA sample?

Retributive theory of punishment – *Justifies a proportional response and suffering of the offender on the basis of their voluntary decision to commit a crime.*

Cognitive liberty – *The idea that individuals have a right to privacy and must provide consent before their thought processes are measured.*

PART III

IN SUMMARY

Unlike what is shown in the entertainment media, we have not made significant progress detecting deception. If we do, issues of legal admissibility, measuring intention and our fundamental rights to cognitive liberty will need to be addressed.

 CRITICAL THINKING AND APPLICATION QUESTIONS

1   How are new technologies different from the original polygraph? Research and investigate the claims of one of the new technologies like No Lie MRI and EyeDetect. Can you find unbiased peer-reviewed support for their claims?

2   Many countries screen airline passengers to detect their intention to commit a criminal act. What are the challenges for measuring a person's intention to commit a crime, a terrorist act or even a simple lie? Do you believe this is possible?

3   Imagine that an accurate and faultless lie detector exists, it has met all assessments of reliability and validity. What are the 'pros' and 'cons' of releasing this device into society? What changes would we expect in our daily social interactions, politics and the legal system.

CHAPTER REVIEW

Phrenology
– The study of the shape and size of the cranium as a supposed indication of character and mental abilities.

In our quest for the ultimate truth machine, we have discovered that no machine can determine if someone is lying or telling the truth. These technologies generate unacceptable levels of false positives (suggesting that truthful people are lying when they are not). Therefore, it will always be essential to verify the accuracy of a confession elicited by a polygraph test or its replacement. It is time to decide about the technology of lie detection. If it is a valid approach like DNA, then allow its use in the legal system, if it is not, then discard it and classify it in the same category as other pseudoscientific claims, including horoscopes, **phrenology** and extrasensory perception. Yet, we stubbornly remain uncommitted. On one hand, we cite the advantages of eliciting confessions and admissions of guilt. On the other hand, we cite the invasion of privacy, the cost of investigating large numbers of false-positive results and the harm done to innocent people. Also important is the chance that the most deceitful individuals are more motivated to effectively use countermeasures, and the false sense of security that comes from the use of an easily fooled screening tool. Finally, recent technologies are repeating the mistakes of the past with promises of accurate deception detection without research evidence or the support of psychological theory.

NAMES TO KNOW

Dan Ariely

Conducts research in behavioural economics on the irrational ways people behave, described in plain language.

• Ariely, D. (2009) *Predictably Irrational: The Hidden Forces That Shape Our Decisions.* Harper.

- Ariely, D. (2013) *The (Honest) Truth About Dishonesty: How We Lie to Everyone – Especially Ourselves.* Harper Perennial.

Aldert Vrij

Has conducted extensive research on nonverbal and verbal cues in deception and lie detection.

- Vrij, A. (2008) *Detecting Lies and Deceit: Pitfalls and Opportunities.* Wiley.

- Leal, S., Vrij, A., Deeb, H. and Kamermans, K. (2019) Encouraging interviewees to say more and deception: The ghostwriter method. *Legal and Criminological Psychology,* 24(2), 273–87.

Sean O'Mara

Has carried out research on brain systems affected by stress, anxiety, depression and motivation, and the application of brain science to interrogational torture and other public policy issues.

- O'Mara, S. (2015) *Why Torture Doesn't Work: The Neuroscience of Interrogation.* Harvard University Press.

- O'Mara, S. (2016) Mind games: What torture does to the brain. *Foreign Affairs,* 16 January. www.foreignaffairs.com/articles/2016-01-15/mind-games.

PART III

7 THE ART AND SCIENCE OF OFFENDER PROFILING

Chapter Introduction

Offender profiling is driven by popular interest and potential applications for a more effective criminal justice system. However, a shroud of secrecy often surrounds this practice that is at odds with a true scientific discipline. Our exploration begins with an overview of this fascinating process. Next, we examine the classic approach of criminal investigative analysis, followed by the more recent offender profiling approaches of investigative psychology, geographic profiling and crime linkage analysis. Our journey ends by weighing the evidence that offender profiling is either a method that provides valuable insights, commonsense explanations, or pseudoscientific predictions.

Learning Outcomes

Background and goals of offender profiling
- To be able to explain the five 'Ws' of offender profiling.

Criminal investigative analysis (CIA)
- Describe the steps and theoretical basis of criminal investigative analysis.

Investigative psychology, geographic profiling and crime linkage analysis
- Compare and contrast the methods and goals of investigative psychology, geographic profiling and crime linkage analysis.

Profiling: valuable insights, common sense or pseudoscience?
- Make a persuasive argument why offender profiling is or is not a science.

BACKGROUND AND GOALS OF OFFENDER PROFILING

FICTION: Offender profiling is the single best approach to identify criminal suspects.

Versus

FACT: There are many approaches to profile and predict criminal behaviour, but they may not be as effective as shown in the entertainment media.

CASE STUDY — Profiling the 'Mad Bomber'

Angry and resentful about events surrounding a workplace injury at Consolidated Edison, mechanic and electrician George Metesky planted 33 homemade explosives in the 1940s and 1950s in New York City's most crowded public spaces – theatres, terminals, subway stations, a bus depot and a library – injuring 15 and earning him the title the 'Mad Bomber'.

Desperate to find the culprit, the police contacted psychiatrist and criminologist Dr James A. Brussel. Using the evidence and known details from the case, Dr Brussel formed a profile of the characteristics and traits

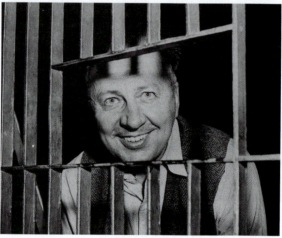

George Metesky grins from behind bars after his arrest as the 'Mad Bomber', having terrorised the New York area for over 16 years with his planted homemade bombs

Source: Bettmann/Getty Images

possessed by the culprit. He predicted the offender's demographic, physical and character traits, diagnosed him with psychological disorders, and even predicted that the offender would be wearing a double-breasted suit, buttoned. When police arrested George Metesky, at home, in his pyjamas, he changed into a double-breasted suit that he buttoned (Greenberg, 2011).

But that's not the end of the story. The real credit for finding the 'Mad Bomber' belongs not to profiling, but to Consolidated Edison's clerk Alice Kelly, who matched information from Metesky's letters in the newspaper with his workplace injury information in his personnel files.

Even though many of Dr Brussel's predictions were of little value in solving the crime, the story was the origin of offender profiling becoming an investigative tool (Cannell, 2017).

Discussion Questions:

1   Is this story more about the power of profiling or the power of anecdotal evidence?

2   Can you explain why George Metesky was identified by Alice Kelly's research and not Dr Brussels's profile?

History and goals of psychological profiling

Offender profiling is a process where crime scene information is used to make predictions about the behaviour and underlying traits of a suspect (Chifflet, 2015). Profiling criminal behaviour is considered the 'third wave' of investigative science; the first wave being the study of clues and the second wave being the study of the crime itself – body location, type of weapon used, time of day the crime was committed. A more contemporary perspective, **behavioural investigative advice**, describes the process as drawing inferences about an offender or offence from a detailed, behavioural examination of actions within a crime (Cole and Brown, 2014).

Offender profiling does not point to a specific person, rather, it is based on the probability that someone with certain characteristics is likely to have committed a certain type of crime (Miller, 2015). While specific physical characteristics (height, weight, age) are important, some profilers emphasise the personality and motivations of the offender, their common methods in committing crimes and handling their victims (Canter and Youngs, 2017).

Despite what is shown in entertainment media, profilers do not travel to incompetent police departments solving crimes or rescuing hostages from dangerous psychopaths (Muller, 2000). Offender profiling is still an evolving field of study, where its practitioners often do not agree on the methodology, procedures or even the basic terminology (Miller, 2015). There is no widely accepted definition of profiling, because every profiler can offer their own operational definition of what profiling involves (Kocsis and Palermo, 2013).

An essential part of the profiling process is building a theoretical foundation about classifying criminality. Similar to today's profilers, nineteenth-century Italian physician Cesare Lombroso, considered the father of *anthropological criminology* (or criminal anthropology), attempted to determine the origins and motivations of criminal behaviour (Palermo, 2018). Lombroso's study of criminals predicted that physical characteristics, such as a sloping forehead, ears of unusual size, asymmetry of the face and skull, could reveal criminal traits (Figure 7.1) (Gatti and Verde, 2012). Lombroso's flawed **atavistic** explanation of criminal behaviour declared that criminality was inherited, and that someone 'born criminal' could be identified by their physically inherited defects and confirming the criminal as a savage.

Figure 7.1: Criminal faces from Cesare Lombroso's *L'homme criminel*

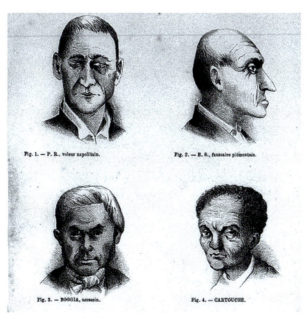

Source: Lombroso, C. (1888) *L'homme criminal: atlas.* Bocca Freres.

Offender profiling – *Identifying the offender by their personality and behaviour based on analysis of the crime committed.*

Behavioural investigative advice – *The process of drawing inferences about an offender or offence from a detailed, behavioural examination of actions within a crime.*

Atavistic – *Relating to or characterised by reversion to something ancient or ancestral; associated with biological theories of crime and Cesare Lombroso.*

PART III

The frightening implication of Lombroso's work was the idea that criminals could be identified merely by their 'criminal' facial features (Gibson, 2002). Remarkably, Lombroso's influence is still reflected in research investigating facial characteristics and sentencing inequities (Blair, Judd and Chapleau, 2004), and machine learning to discriminate criminals from non-criminals based on facial features, such as the curve of the lip or the distance between the corners of the inner part of the eye. Wu and Zhang (2016) imagine a dystopian future where computers could discriminate between criminals and non-criminals.

Systematic research into profiling began in Europe at the International Criminal Police Organization (Interpol) with the setting up in 1993 of the Analytical Criminal Intelligence Unit (ACIU), established to assess the nature and frequency of various criminal activities and develop techniques and methods for carrying out a complex analysis of criminal behaviour (Fahlman, 1999). The ACIU helps Interpol to use profiling to help its member countries combat crime by establishing the links between crimes and offenders and distributing that information for investigation by its member countries, thus providing law enforcement with valuable and actionable intelligence information. The US Federal Bureau of Investigation (FBI) popularised offender profiling with a list of very basic characteristics that the unknown offender possessed, such as age, gender and previous convictions (Winerman, 2004). Profiling became a major focus of the FBI in the 1970s, when the FBI's Behavioral Sciences Unit (now called the Behavioral Analysis Unit) was set up in 1972 to develop a profiling process, anchored in the premise that behaviour reflects personality.

The five 'Ws' of profiling

What is a profile used for?

Offender profiles are used to narrow a list of potential suspects, help investigators develop interviewing and interrogation strategies, and suggest directions the investigation should take (Dern, Dern, Horn and Horn, 2009). Profiles can also offer strategies for answering curious media requests for information, such as 'Who do you think committed this crime?' (Perri and Lichtenwald, 2009). Finally, information identifying a specific individual is rarely found in a profile (Douglas, Ressler, Burgess and Hartman, 1986).

When is a profile used?

In practice, offender profiling is used in the investigation, apprehension and prosecution phases of the criminal justice process. In the investigation phase, profiling determines whether crimes are related and is used to predict the personality and lifestyle characteristics of an unknown offender. In the apprehension phase, profiling is used to develop strategies to apprehend the unknown offender and to determine the chances that the offender's crime intensity will increase. Within this phase, profiling is used to predict where to look for an unknown serial offender, to determine what information should be included in a search warrant, and how the offender may react when caught. In the prosecution phase, offender profilers serve as experts in court to link crimes to offenders.

Profiles may be used when the manner of a person's death is unknown (see Table 7.1) or to determine insurance payments because most insurance policies are void if the death is determined to be suicide (Hebert, Crowley and Trudeau, 2017). Although the cause of a death may be clear, the manner may not. Consider a parachutist falling and dying from multiple impact injuries. A **psychological autopsy** – an investigative approach to establish whether an uncertain death was the result of natural causes, suicide, accident

Psychological autopsy – *An investigative approach to establish whether an uncertain death was the result of natural causes, suicide, accident or homicide.*

or homicide – would be carried out to determine whether the parachute malfunctioned (accident), whether the parachutist intentionally jumped with a bad parachute (suicide), whether the parachute had been intentionally tampered with (homicide), or whether the parachutist suffered a heart attack during the jump (natural) (Young, 1992).

Why is profiling used?

With advancing forensic science techniques, why is offender profiling still used? Unlike some offender profiles based on subjective impressions and assumptions, forensic science generates legally admissible objective evidence (Daeid, 2010). The primary reason seems to be that police *believe* that offender profiling works (Snook et al., 2008). Survey research in this area reveals interesting biases. Specifically, the results show that some officers believe that profiles are useful because they tend to reinforce their own opinions, increase their understanding of the offender and focus the investigation. Alternatively, some police are forced to consult a profiler to satisfy judicial requirements to use all available investigative options to solve the crime (Muller, 2000).

Where is profiling used?

Contrary to widespread belief, offender profiling has value beyond serial murder and sexual assault. It has potential applications for any crime that follows a predictable pattern of behaviours – arson, terrorist acts, burglary, shoplifting, robbery, internet crimes and bank fraud. A single act of murder (especially if it is spontaneous) is not a good candidate for profiling because the spontaneous nature of the crime makes it more difficult to interpret than a series of crimes that reflect similar actions or locations.

Who is qualified to profile?

A common stereotype of an offender profiler is of a peculiar intellectual outsider who solves crimes by relying on intuition and insight into the criminal mind. In reality, a profiler is typically a police investigator or consultant who examines evidence from the crime scene, victims and witnesses to construct an accurate psychological and demographic description of the offender (Woodworth and Porter, 2002). While the media often portrays profilers as professionally trained psychologists, detectives and psychics, there is no consensus about who is qualified to be a profiler. The simplest description is that anyone who calls themselves a profiler and has engaged in the practice of constructing a profile for a criminal investigation is a profiler (Kocsis, 2004). Alternatively, others argue that only individuals who have considerable investigative experience should be profilers (Hazelwood, Ressler, Depue and Douglas, 1995). Although some attempts have been made to create accreditation standards for profilers, such as the International Criminal Investigative Analysis Fellowship, there is still no universally recognised regulatory body that provides a professional offender profiler designation.

Hazelwood et al. (1995) describe the essential characteristics of a profiler as having a deep appreciation of the criminal mind, a basic understanding of psychology and investigative experience. For this reason, Hazelwood et al. (1995) have suggested that mental health professionals may not be qualified to profile. However, Gudjonsson and Copson (1997) argue that mental health professionals who engage in 'clinical' profiling displayed better profiling accuracy compared to other types of offender profilers. However, the most accurate profilers may not be the police, but statisticians applying their knowledge of probability. Fox and Farrington (2015) trained a police department to use statistical profiles in their investigations, while three neighbouring departments continued their standard policing techniques. One year later, the police department using the statistically based profiles solved over 260 per cent more crimes compared to the other departments.

The problem of interpreting vague statements

Find someone who has *not* read the following 13 statements. Read each one individually and ask the person to rate how well each statement describes their personality. If your subject is like most people, they will agree that most of these statements describe their personality.

These statements represent a common psychological phenomenon known as the 'Barnum effect' (also known as the 'Forer effect'). This is when an individual believes that personality descriptions apply specifically to them; for example, reading your horoscope in a newspaper and realising it's surprisingly accurate. It is easy to agree with these broad and general statements, but are any of them measurable? In the same way, an offender profile can be so vague and general that it cannot narrow down a list of possible suspects.

Evaluate each statement	Rating	
	'Like me'	'Not like me'
1. You have a great need for other people to like and admire you.		
2. You have a tendency to be critical of yourself.		
3. You have a great deal of unused capacity that you have not turned to your advantage.		
4. While you have some personality weaknesses, you are generally able to compensate for them.		
5. Your sexual adjustment has presented problems for you.		
6. Disciplined and self-controlled outside, you tend to be worrisome and insecure inside.		
7. At times you have serious doubts as to whether you have made the right decision or done the right thing.		
8. You prefer a certain amount of change and variety and become dissatisfied when hemmed in by restrictions and limitations.		
9. You pride yourself as an independent thinker and do not accept others' statements without satisfactory proof.		
10. You have found it unwise to be too frank in revealing yourself to others.		
11. At times you are extroverted, affable and sociable, while at other times you are introverted, wary and reserved.		
12. Some of your aspirations tend to be pretty unrealistic.		
13. Security is one of your major goals in life.		

Source: Reproduced from Forer, B. R. (1949) The fallacy of personal validation: A classroom demonstration of gullibility. *Journal of Abnormal and Social Psychology*, 44(1), 118–23. This work is now in the public domain.

The profile creation process

Most methods of offender profiling involve either inductive or deductive reasoning. Inductive reasoning uses criminological studies, the profiler's own experience, intuition and bias, stereotypes and generalisations to make inferences about a case (Petherick, 2014). In contrast, deductive reasoning begins with an assessment of the current case's physical evidence. Profilers using this approach must prove that all premises are true and valid before basing conclusions on them. This method is best suited for determining offender characteristics, while inductive reasoning can generate hypotheses (Petherick, 2014).

Holmes and Holmes (2008) outline three broad stages of offender profile creation, as shown in Figure 7.2.

Figure 7.2: Stages in profile creation

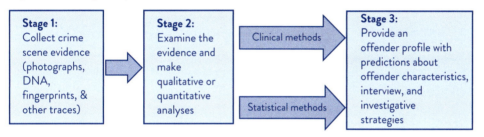

Collecting and examining evidence during stages 1 and 2 are common to all thorough investigations. In stage 3, profilers can take either a clinical or a statistical approach (Hicks and Sales, 2006). Most profilers focus on a clinically oriented approach, where they apply their knowledge, experience and intuition of criminal behaviour (West, 2000). Statistically oriented profilers use the results from a statistical analysis of the data, such as age, conviction frequency and gender, on offenders who have committed crimes that are similar to the crime being investigated (Canter, 2004; Jackson and Bekerian, 1997).

Offender profiling approaches can be divided into six broad categories (Table 7.1) (Bartol and Bartol, 2013). Although there is some overlap with these types, there are methodological and theoretical differences between the approaches.

Table 7.1: Profiling categories and methods

Category	Description	Similar methods
Crime scene profiling	Describes the significant behavioural, cognitive, emotional, lifestyle and demographic features of the crime scene to understand the motives or characteristics of the suspect	• Behavioural evidence analysis • Behavioural investigative advice • Criminal investigative analysis • Investigative psychology
Crime linkage	The process of linking two or more crimes together based on the crime scene behaviour shown by an offender	• Crime linkage analysis • Comparative case analysis

(continued)

Geographic profiling	Analyses locations connected to a series of crimes to determine the most probable area in which the offender lives	• Crime action profiling • Crime mapping • Geographic mapping
Psychological autopsy	Detailed description of psychological and background characteristics of a deceased person, to determine the cause of death. Important for insurance payments and national security issues	• Equivocal death analysis • Equivocal death psychological autopsy • Reconstructive psychological evaluation • Suicide psychological autopsy
Psychological profiling	Gathering of information on a known individual who poses a threat or is believed to be dangerous to explain the motivations of the suspect	• Diagnostic evaluation • Risk assessment • Threat assessment
Suspect-based profiling	Systematic collection of data on previous offenders to identify similar offenders	• Ethnic profiling • Racial profiling

The current status of offender profiling

Offender profiling has captured the public's fascination, with references to it appearing in all forms of entertainment media. Even those who claim to practise offender profiling state that it is both an art and a science (Bonn, 2015). However, the field is becoming more scientific by using psychology's statistical and research methods. Yet the barrier for accepting profiling testimony in the courtroom remains, due to the lack of scientific studies to support many profiling claims. To make matters worse, the field continues to lack agreement about its required expertise, ethics, methods of profiling and research needs (McGrath, 2000).

IN SUMMARY

There are many approaches to profile and predict criminal behaviour, but among the most effective are the statistically based methods that rely on empirical data to link the offender to the offence.

 CRITICAL THINKING AND APPLICATION QUESTIONS

1   In what ways are applications of DNA analyses to predict potential criminological characteristics similar to the chilling implications of Lombroso's theories of criminal typologies?

2   Name a character that portrays a profiler depicted in the entertainment media. Evaluate whether the character is shown using either empirically verifiable techniques or intuitive commonsense approaches.

3   Which categories of profiling methods (Table 7.1) do you believe are the most and least valid? Explain your selection.

CRIMINAL INVESTIGATIVE ANALYSIS (CIA)

FICTION: Criminal investigative analysis is a scientific approach that relies on crime scene evidence to find suspects.

Versus

FACT: Criminal investigative analysis relies on more than just crime scene evidence, it also assesses the personalities and risk levels of known suspects, and is often neither accurate nor scientific.

The Federal Bureau of Investigation's (FBI) **criminal investigative analysis (CIA)** approach identifies the personality traits, behavioural patterns, geographic habits and demographic features of an offender based on characteristics of the crime (Bartol and Bartol, 2016). The primary assumption is that an offender's personality is reflected in the crime scene. CIA includes a variety of services and advice provided by the FBI to law enforcement agencies. The FBI's method remains one of the most widely taught methods in the world today. It is customary practice for agents from various police forces around the world to travel overseas and take part in their training programmes. The FBI's style of profiling is presented more as a 'special art' (Canter, 2004) rather than a scientific endeavour and consists of four stages (Figure 7.3).

> **Criminal investigative analysis (CIA)** – *Investigative profiling tool used by the FBI to solve violent crimes, based on the premise that personality predicts behaviour.*

The FBI's shift from *crime scene analysis* to *criminal investigative analysis* was to make broader and less specific predictions about an offender's behaviour, avoiding specific assumptions about the personality traits and criminal motivations of a suspect. This shift reduced overreliance on subjective profiling information (motives and intentions) and mismanagement of resources that delays closing cases (Alison, Bennell, Mokros and Ormerod, 2002).

Generating an offender profile using CIA

Law enforcement procedures attempt to do more than describe a crime, rather investigators use the crime scene to generate hypotheses about the type of suspect who committed the crime; then they seek specific individuals who possess the characteristics of this type. The primary goal of CIA is to examine all the behavioural information and provide advice to the requesting agency, rather than become involved in the actual investigative process (Sparrow, 1991).

CIA is the most widely known of the profiling approaches, developed by the Behavioral Analysis Unit of the FBI and frequently exaggerated by the entertainment media (Rossmo, 2016). The four stages are shown in Figure 7.3 and then discussed in detail.

Figure 7.3: The four stages of criminal investigative analysis

| STAGE 1: Data assimilation | STAGE 2: Crime scene classification | STAGE 3: Crime scene reconstruction | STAGE 4: Profile generation |

Stage 1: Data assimilation

This first stage involves collecting crime-related information, including autopsy reports, photographs of the crime scene and deceased, anything that is likely to indicate what, how and why the crime happened (Canter, 2004). The goal of this stage is organising and arranging the information into meaningful patterns. Two patterns or categories of behaviours include identifying the **modus operandi** (MO, Latin for *mode of operating*) and the **signature**, such as ritualised or fantasy-based behaviours.

Modus operandi (MO) – *The particular way a person performs a particular task (mode of operating).*

The modus operandi is the offender's common method of committing crimes based on past experience. More simply, it is the method of committing the crime modified for success (Turvey, 1999). Examples of the modus operandi include the type of weapon used, time of day, where the crime was committed, and types of restraints used on the victim (Beauregard and Proulx, 2016).

The suspect's signature is a more complex and personalised ritual than the MO, and often serves the criminal's emotional and psychological needs (James and Proulx, 2016). Examples of signatures include the type of victim selected, the level and types of injuries to the victim, and any items, notes or objects or physical traces left at the crime scene (Pettigrew, 2019). Holmes and Holmes (1996) argue that the signature evidence is more important for linking crimes and for developing a suspect profile, because the suspect's MO may change due to situational circumstances, such as time of day, location, multiple eyewitness, but the signature does not.

Signature – *Specific and identifiable actions or characteristics of the suspect that reflect their emotional and psychological needs.*

The essential difference between the modus operandi and signature is that the modus operandi is something done to successfully complete the crime, while a signature is a ritual that is unique to the offender. Signatures are displayed in sports when superstitious behaviour rituals reveal unique player signatures. For example, in basketball, bouncing the ball three times before making a shot is a signature ritual, because it is not necessary to successfully complete the shot (Dömötör, Ruíz-Barquín and Szabo, 2016).

Stage 2: Crime scene classification

Based on the principle that criminal behaviour reflects personality, the CIA attempts to categorise the offender's behaviours into broad categories. These categories help to understand the psychological motivations influencing the offender's behaviours. During this stage, the information is structured, and an initial analysis of the crime is carried out. To standardise this process, the FBI developed its own *Crime Classification Manual* (Douglas, Burgess, Burgess and Ressler, 1992), which functions in a similar way to the system used by psychologists to classify mental illness (Katerndahl, Larme, Palmer and Amodei, 2005). This stage generates general classifications: the primary motive – sexual, financial or emotional – and the controversial organised/disorganised distinction.

Classifying motivations

Homicide – *The deliberate and unlawful killing of one person by another; murder.*

Intention determines whether a criminal **homicide** is classified as murder or manslaughter and at what degree: 'murder' when the homicide is the primary objective versus 'manslaughter' when it was secondary to another crime (Gillespie, 1989). Other motives can include criminal enterprise, emotional or selfish reasons and sexual motivations (DeHart and Mahoney, 1994).

The offender may kill out of self-defence or even compassion – mercy killings by disconnecting the life support system or intentionally overdosing a dying patient (Joldasbayevich, 2019). The motivation may be related to mental illness, with psychotic or paranoid reactions sometimes linked to assassinations, for example Sirhan Sirhan (Meloy, 1992) and Mark Chapman (Spitzberg and Cupach, 2003). Finally, sexual intention can serve as the motive for killing, such as the desire to engage in sex or torture, or other activities that have meaning solely for the offender (Keppel and Walter, 1999). Ultimately, the challenge with understanding intention is that different offenders do similar things for different reasons.

Classifying the organised/disorganised behaviours

The organised/disorganised classification system is presented in Table 7.2. This classification system is widely cited, despite weaknesses in its precision and reliability (Ressler et al., 1986; Kocsis and Palermo, 2007). Investigations into the FBI's organised/disorganised dichotomy have demonstrated that this classification scheme of serial killers does not withstand close empirical testing (Canter, Alison, Alison and Wentink, 2004).

Table 7.2: Characteristics of organised and disorganised serial offenders

Organised	Disorganised
• Plan all details, leave no clues	• Leave a weapon at the crime scene
• Use restraints	• Reposition the dead body
• Commit sexual acts with live victims	• Perform sexual acts with a dead body
• Use a car or a van	• No use of a vehicle
• Emphasise control over the victim by using manipulative or threatening techniques	• Keep the dead body and depersonalise it

However, researchers found support for the organised/disorganised types among a sample of 350 Canadian cases of sexual homicide (Mjanes, Beauregard and Martineau, 2017). Variables related to crime scene characteristics and the offenders' MOs were evaluated using 'latent class' analyses (a measurement model in which individuals can be classified into mutually exclusive and exhaustive types, or latent classes). Surprisingly, their results support the original dichotomy that sexual murderers can be separated into two distinct profiles, similar to the organised/disorganised dichotomy, in terms of the detection avoidance strategies, control, and type of violence used by the offender. Their latent class results also support the FBI model in relation to the offender's approach, sexual acts and postmortem activities.

Organised serial killers are those who plan their murders, target their victims, demonstrate self-control at the crime scene by leaving few clues, and sometimes engage in torture and dismemberment while acting out violent fantasies (Jackson and Bekerian, 1997). The typical example of the organised classification is the serial killer Ted Bundy. While abducting women from highly visible locations (ski lodge, campuses, beaches), he chose his victims according to specific, predetermined criteria. They were young, attractive and similar in appearance. His control of the victims was planned, beginning with clever manipulations such as feigning a broken arm in order to gain assistance, and escalated to using physical force and sexually abusing them after he killed them (Ramsland, 2013).

Disorganised serial killers are rare, and the disorganised murderer is less likely to plan the crime, instead behaving in a random manner and often obtaining their victims by chance (Canter et al., 2004). The disorganised pattern of behaviour may suggest psychosis (a break with reality) and they lack impulse control, do not plan their kills in advance, and are less selective about the physical characteristics of their victims (Warf and Waddell, 2002).

Although the organised/disorganised classification seems reasonable, most crime scene evidence falls along a continuum between the categories (Mjanes, Beauregard and Martineau, 2017). In response to this continuum of evidence, Douglas et al. (1992) introduced a third *mixed offender* category. There are a variety of reasons as to why

Organised serial killer – *A serial killer whose behaviours indicate above-average intelligence, performing premeditated, carefully planned crimes that leave little evidence.*

Disorganised serial killer – *A serial killer whose behaviours indicate below-average intelligence, performing unplanned crimes that leave evidence.*

offenders cannot easily be categorised as either organised or disorganised. For example, an attack may involve multiple offenders and unanticipated events, the victim may resist, or the offender's pattern of behaviour may change (Mjanes, Beauregard and Martineau, 2017). The addition of the mixed category raises doubts about the utility of the original two categories, making them only a theoretical proposal of no practical use.

The FBI developed the organised/disorganised dichotomy from interviews and case information from 36 murderers. However, the interviews were flawed because they lacked structure and uniformity. Also, the FBI agents did not select a random, or even large, sample of all offenders and then explore how they may be empirically divided into subgroups (Chan, 2015). These flaws raise the question of whether the organised/disorganised dichotomy represents an authentic typology of all serial murderers or only incarcerated serial murderers willing to be interviewed, thus missing those who refused to participate (Kocsis and Palermo, 2005).

Stage 3: Crime scene reconstruction

Stage three connects the chain of events before, during and after the commission of a crime (Rossmo, 2016). At this stage, the profiler tries to determine how people acted, how events happened, and how the offender planned and performed the crime. The profiler attempts to reconstruct the crime from the perspective of both the victim and the offender. Douglas and Olshaker (1997) describe this process as trying to 'walk in the shoes' of both the victim and the offender. Finally, common elements of the crime scene are linked with similar personality characteristics of the offenders, indicating unique offender characteristics (James, Crane and Hinchliffe, 2005). These include patterns of the wounds on the victim, such as bite marks, incisions and bruises, whether sexual acts were performed before or after death, and whether cannibalism or mutilation was practised on the body (Schlesinger, Kassen, Mesa and Pinizzotto, 2010).

Staging – leaving a victim's body in an unusual position – is considered a conscious criminal action by an offender to mislead an investigation or to protect the victim's character or the victim's family (Lupariello et al., 2018). Staging includes manipulating the scene around the body as well as positioning the body to make the scene appear to be something it is not (a suicide or accident) (Chancellor and Graham, 2014). On the other hand, if the crime scene alterations only serve the fantasy needs of the offender, they are considered part of the signature and then they are referred to as 'posing' (Bonn, 2014). Keppel and Weis (2004) found that both the staging of the crime and the posing of the victim are rare, finding only 1.3 per cent of victims are left in an unusual position, with 0.3 per cent classified as being posed and 0.1 per cent being staged.

Determining if the crime scene was staged may reveal the motives of the suspect. As investigators analyse crime scenes, the details may hold unique facts that serve no apparent purpose in the act of the crime, while obscuring the underlying motive of the crime. For example, trying to return the victim to a natural looking state may be related to the behavioural pattern of **undoing**, an attempt to symbolically reverse the murder. Examples of undoing involve the use of blankets to cover the victim's body, positioning the body, use of a bed or a couch, washing the body, using pillows, as well as removing clothing and adding other types of adornments (Russell, Schlesinger and Leon, 2017). Offenders who stage crime scenes often make mistakes because they assemble the scene to resemble what they believe it should look like. Rarely do they have enough time to fit every piece of the crime scene puzzle together in a logical manner. Consequently, discrepancies between forensic findings and the overall look of the crime scene appear. These discrepancies signal intentional staging (Hazelwood and Napier, 2004).

Staging –
When someone who has committed a crime makes the scene look like something it is not, for example a suicide or an accident.

Undoing –
A suspect's attempts to symbolically reverse the murder via crime scene staging.

To prevent this from happening, Palermo and Kocsis (2005) recommend examining all crime scene indicators separately, and then viewing them in context with the total picture. Crime scene indicators include all evidence of offender activity, such as method of entry, offender–victim interaction and body disposition.

Final clues for classification are souvenirs and trophies, distinguished by their symbolic motivation. A **trophy** is any item taken from the victim that symbolises the achievement of the crime. For example, serial killer Jeffrey Dahmer took body parts and photographs as trophies (Tithecott, 1997). A **souvenir** is a more psychologically significant item collected by the suspect to remember and re-experience the pleasurable elements of the crime (Miller, 2014).

Stage 4: Profile generation

Having evaluated and merged the information from the preceding stages, the profiler is now ready to hypothesise about the type of person who committed the crime. The preliminary narrative will usually include details relating to the suspect's sex, age, race, occupational skills, IQ, social interests, mental health status and family background (Kocsis, 2003). This final stage creates a profile that includes physical elements as well as identifiers related to personality (Turvey, 2012). Most crime scenes tell a story, with characters, a plot, a beginning, middle and a conclusion, and so should a good profile (Table 7.3).

> **Trophy** – Any item taken from the victim that symbolises the crime.

> **Souvenir** – Items collected by the suspect from the victim to remember and relive the pleasurable elements of the crime.

Table 7.3: List of elements to include in an offender profiling report

- Overview of established facts relevant to crime-related behaviour and victimology
- Opinion of the victim's lifestyle, situational risk, resistance and risk taken by offender to acquire victim
- Analysis of crime scene characteristics, location, point of contact
- Offender skill level, use of weapons, force, method of approach and control
- Types of actions – sexual, precautionary, contradictory
- Offender behaviours, items taken from victim, modus operandi, motivational reasons

Limitations of criminal investigative analysis

The controversy surrounding the organised and disorganised profiles is that rather than being based on quantitative data and statistical methods (Fox and Farrington, 2018), CIA methods often lack empirically validated scientific theories, using anecdotal evidence, intuition and unproven theories of human behaviour. Additionally, the research used to develop the CIA approach was based on a small and biased sample and did not rely on advanced statistical analysis. This creates a situation where profilers using the same crime scene analysis data produce different profiles. Finally, even when accuracy is defined by how many characteristics are correct on an offender profile or how valuable the analysis is to a law enforcement agency in obtaining useful investigative assistance, success is often a matter of serendipity rather than science.

IN SUMMARY

With a goal of identifying an offender, the four stages of criminal investigative analysis are based on assimilating data, classifying the type of crime, reconstructing the crime and generating a profile. The approach uses clinically oriented and intuitive approaches, often generating vague and subjective offender profiles.

CRITICAL THINKING AND APPLICATION QUESTIONS

1   What are the primary goals for each of the criminal investigative analysis stages?

2   Are the goals of each stage verifiable and based on empirical observations or do they rely more on speculation and intuition about the offender's motives?

3   Review the list of elements to include in an offender profile (Table 7.3). Select one element that provides the most valuable information for investigators and explain why you selected that element.

INVESTIGATIVE PSYCHOLOGY, GEOGRAPHIC PROFILING AND CRIME LINKAGE ANALYSIS

FICTION: Investigative psychology and criminal investigative analysis use the same profiling methods with the same levels of effectiveness.	*Versus*	**FACT:** Criminal investigative analysis uses less effective intuitive personality-based predictions, while investigative psychology uses more empirical, behaviour-based predictions.

Investigative psychology – Bottom-up approach to profiling developed by David Canter, who proposed that profiling should be based on psychological theory and research.

Origins of investigative psychology

Psychologist David Canter developed **investigative psychology**. Canter's approach is unique because it draws on the principles of **applied psychology** and **environmental psychology**. Specifically, the goal of this approach is to infer characteristics of an offender based on their behaviour during the crime.

Investigative psychology examines the complex interaction of factors that predict a crime by examining the power of situational forces, offender motivation, geographical location and the characteristics of the target. Underlying investigative psychology are three theories as to why suspects are compelled to commit a crime:

1   *routine activity theory:* if the situation is attractive (Schildkraut, Naman and Stafford, 2019)

2   *crime pattern theory:* if it occurs in a familiar environment (Bernasco, 2010)

3   *rational choice theory:* if it returns a desired reward (Osborne and Capellan, 2017).

Applied psychology – Using psychological methods and findings of scientific psychology to solve practical problems of human and animal behaviour and experience.

Unlike other approaches, there is an emphasis on empirical observations and statistical analysis (Carson and Bull, 2003). A strength of this approach is that its degree of reliability lies with the process rather than the individual profiler (Canter and Youngs, 2009). Another strength is its reliance on psychological theories and methodologies, 'showing how and why variations in criminal behaviour occur' (Dwyer, 2001). Canter (1994) devised the term 'investigative psychology' to show the many ways psychology contributes to criminal investigations beyond the bizarre crimes in which some form of psychopathology was clear (serial killing and serial rape).

Using investigative psychology to catch the 'Railway Killers'

David Mulcahy and his schoolfriend John Duffy became known as the 'Railway Killers' (also called the 'Railway Rapists') by targeting lone victims at railway stations in southeast England in the 1980s, raping and killing 19 women over five years. Three police forces pooled their resources to catch them, and enlisted the help of Dr David Canter, an expert in the field of geographic profiling. Canter examined the details of each crime and built a profile of the attacker's personality, habits and traits. His applied profile led to the prompt arrest, charge and conviction of John Duffy, one the killers.

Canter's starting point for this profile was the idea that a violent crime is a transaction between two people and therefore reveals something about the way the offender interacts with people. Canter identified two themes in regard to how the offender committed the crime. The first theme is how the offender deals with the victim. The second is how much strength or force was used. In John Duffy's case, a minimal amount of force was used because weaker victims were selected. The profile indicated that the rapist would live in the area near the attacks. Studying the cases over four years, Canter placed the cases on a map and overlaid this with the years on a transparent plastic film to reveal distinctive patterns in the locations and types of related crimes. This method was later developed into the circle theory of environmental range (Canter and Larkin, 1993), allowing Canter to speculate about where the killer might live (Palermo and Kocsis, 2005).

This was the first case in the UK to use behavioural characteristics to search for a criminal instead of purely forensic evidence from the crime scene and it was successful. Duffy matched 13 of the 17 observations made about the attacker's lifestyle and habits. Before Canter's profile, Duffy was one of 2,000 suspects, after the profiling he became one of two (Farquhar, 2016).

Environmental psychology – *Interdisciplinary field that examines how the interaction between individuals and their surroundings affects behaviour.*

PART III

Investigative psychology extends to areas that require investigation but that may not always be within the domain of law enforcement, including insurance fraud, malicious fire setting, terrorism, tax evasion or smuggling (Youngs, 2017).

Canter (1994) presents five broad approaches to profile offenders based on the interaction between the victim and the suspect (see Figure 7.4).

Figure 7.4: Investigative psychology's five approaches

Interpersonal coherence	Suspects will treat their victims in the same way they treat people in their day-to-day lives.
The significance of time and place	Time and location information provide clues about the offender's mobility and residence.
Criminal characteristics	Places suspects into broad categories, from which subcategories can be selected or developed.
Criminal career	Assessing whether the suspect previously engaged in criminal activity.
Forensic awareness	An assessment of the scene and evidence to determine if the suspect has knowledge of evidence gathering procedures used by the police (related to criminal career).

Five approaches of investigative psychology

Interpersonal coherence

**Interpersonal
coherence**
– There is a
consistency
between the
way suspects
interact with
their victims
and others in
their everyday
lives.

Interpersonal coherence assumes that suspects will treat their victims the same way they treat other people in their daily lives. For example, the suspect may select victims that have characteristics similar to significant people in their lives. This is similar to the way serial killers tend to attack the same ethnicity as themselves (Canter, 2004). Therefore, we should be able to determine the ethnicity of the suspect based on the victim. This theory also predicts that the suspect preys on people within their own subgroup, for example Ted Bundy murdered over 30 students while he himself was one (James, 2019).

The significance of time and place

**Geographic
profiling** –
The process
of analysing
locations
connected to a
series of crimes
to determine
probable areas
in which the
suspect lives.

Research on the spatial mobility of serial offenders has found that people make intentional and consistent decisions about the ways in which they meet suitable victims (Johnson, 2014; Bernasco, 2010). Because the offender chooses the time and place, they can reveal information about their personal life and schedule. The assumption is that the location selected by the offender is meaningful and they are not likely to commit crimes such as arson, rape and murder in unfamiliar locations. These crimes may be based on control fantasies, and the offender will not be able to perform them in strange environments without losing control over the victim. Therefore, the crimes will be committed in the same geographic area where the offender works or lives (Canter, 2004). In cases where the suspect travels, the destination represents a place that is emotionally significant or makes the suspect feel comfortable because they are familiar with the location's activities (Kocsis, Cooksey and Irwin, 2002).

Geographic profiling

Geographic profiling searches for patterns associated with different types of suspects. This approach searches geographic locations associated with spatial movements of a single serial offender (Bartol and Bartol, 2013). Essentially, investigative psychology is the 'who', and geographic profiling is the 'where' (MacKay, 1999).

Global Perspectives

Using geographic profiling to identify a modern art mystery

Who is Banksy? The internationally known graffiti artist known for ironic art first appeared on walls in Bristol before spreading to London and then around the world (Baker, 2008). Recently, his 2009 painting *Devolved Parliament* fetched £9.9 million at auction (O'Connor, 2019). But, like a superhero, his true identity remains a mystery. Using geographic profiling to analyse the spatial patterns of the 140 Banksy artworks, geographic profilers calculated the probability of finding the suspect's residence. Their analysis highlights areas associated with the residence of one prominent candidate supporting his identification as Banksy. (If you are curious, the results point to one residence and one candidate – Robin Gunningham.)

Most importantly, their findings support the use of geographic profiling in counterterrorism, based on the theory that minor 'terrorism-related acts' – like graffiti – could help find the bases of terrorists' operations before more serious incidents happen (Hauge, Stevenson, Rossmo and Le Comber, 2016).

Marauder –
Serial rapist
victim search
pattern
indicating that
the suspect
lives near
the offence
locations.

Rossmo (2006b) explains that geographic profiling is feasible when the same suspect has committed a minimum of five crimes, and the suspects are **marauders** (they live in the area of criminal activity), as opposed to **commuters**, who commit their crimes in different areas from their home (Paulsen, 2007; Canter and Larkin, 1993).

The hypothesis that serial offenders operate within an area where they feel comfortable (close to home or work) is known as the **circle theory of environmental range**. This hypothesis assumes that the crimes spread outwards from a central location. Therefore, using the distance from the two furthest locations as the diameter, a circle can be drawn encompassing most of the crime locations and locating the central home base (Wilson, Lincon and Kocisis, 1997).

Researchers tested the validity of the circle theory by studying a group of 53 German serial killers' decision making in relation to offence location. In 63 per cent of murders, the killer lived within 10 kilometres (6.214 miles) of the location where the body was found (Snook, Cullen, Mokros and Harbort, 2005). An earlier study found support for the circle hypothesis by examining the spatial behaviour of 54 US serial killers, each of whom had killed at least ten times. They measured the relationship between the offenders' home and the locations where they encountered their victims and disposed of the bodies. As expected, the serial killers were likely to encounter and abduct their victims close to their own home. Furthermore, as the number of killings increased, the offenders disposed of the bodies progressively closer to their home (Goodwin and Canter, 1997). Muller (2000) interprets this behaviour as a reflection of growing confidence with their ability to remain undetected.

Criminal characteristics

The assumption that offenders make consistent rational choices is essential for understanding the 'what' and the 'why' behind criminal actions. Categorising criminal characteristics involves examining offenders and crimes and investigating which differences lead to reliable classifications of the offenders. Understanding the classification structure of a deviant population is the foundation of theory building and the cornerstone of intervention, treatment, or predicting the causes of deviant behaviour patterns (Knight and Prentky, 1990).

Whether human or animal, predators select their victims using a series of complex cognitive decisions and strategies to find victims, subdue their prey and improve their killing efficiency (Canter, Coffey, Huntley and Missen, 2000; Stander, 1992). Borrowing classifications from the hunting methods used by the Serengeti lions (Schaller, 1972) and domestic burglary methods (Bennett and Wright, 1984), five victim search methods (see Figure 7.5) have been identified that describe the 'hunting patterns' of serial predatory offenders (Hewitt, Beauregard and Davies, 2016). The hunting process includes the victim search, choice, location of the encounter and attack site (Rossmo, 2006b).

Commuter – *A victim search pattern showing that the suspect commutes to offence locations.*

Circle theory of environmental range – *Using the geographical locations of a suspect's known offences to predict the approximate site of the offender's residential base.*

PART III

Figure 7.5: Victim search methods used by serial predatory sexual offenders

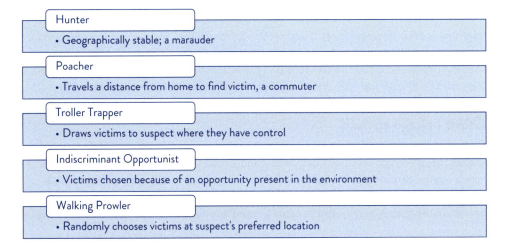

Hunter
• Geographically stable; a marauder

Poacher
• Travels a distance from home to find victim, a commuter

Troller Trapper
• Draws victims to suspect where they have control

Indiscriminant Opportunist
• Victims chosen because of an opportunity present in the environment

Walking Prowler
• Randomly chooses victims at suspect's preferred location

Rossmo (2000) describes three victim attack methods, raptor, stalker and ambusher. *Raptors* attack their victims immediately upon encounter, *stalkers* follow and watch their targets, waiting for an opportunity to attack, and *ambushers* attack victims by bringing them to a place where they have control (their residence or workplace). However, most suspects use only one or two attack behaviours (Rossmo, 2000). These attack behaviours are a useful tool for examining the spatial patterns of the attacker and are consistent (patterns observed in the USA are similar to those observed in South Africa), particularly in regard to hunting grounds, release sites and distance from an offender's home or work address (Lovell et al., 2017).

Criminal career

The characteristic crime scene appearances and behavioural patterns enable investigators to distinguish between different offenders committing the same types of crimes. Researchers describe the criminal career as an evolving process of persistent offending, beginning with a varied set of offences followed by a gradual process of specialisation over time (Lussier, McCuish, Deslauriers-Varin and Corrado, 2017). Crime specialisation in this context refers to criminal activity following a more predictable pattern and the range of criminal offences becoming more specific. Although serial offenders continually reshape their modus operandi to meet the demands of the crime, the signature aspect of their crimes remains a constant and distinctive part of each offender (Douglas and Munn, 1992).

Insights into the criminal careers of burglars were revealed by examining solved burglary cases in four police departments in Florida. Fox and Farrington (2012) used one police station as an experimental group and the three remaining as the controls. Profile analysis revealed four career path categories of burglaries; opportunistic, organised, disorganised and interpersonal. With the help of these statistically derived profile categories, the experimental police station more than tripled its arrest rate as compared to the three controls (Fox and Farrington, 2016).

Forensic awareness

With the rise in popularity of the true crime genre (Schwarz, 2019), many offenders have knowledge of forensic evidence collection and procedures. Investigators can use this information to narrow the list of offenders to those with records for prior offences (Muller, 2000). Awareness of factors that avoid detection and capture increases the possibility that the murder is a serial offence (Salfati and Bateman, 2005). Research in Sweden by Sturup (2018) found that planning and forensic awareness were more common in serial offences than in single offences. To avoid leaving evidence, experienced offenders are more likely to use condoms, incinerate human remains, wear gloves or remove objects that might have their fingerprints or blood on (Ferguson, 2019). However, the interpretation of motives is subjective (Kocsis and Middledorp, 2004). Valid alternative explanations are that the offender used a condom because he was afraid of infection, incinerates the body because of a fascination with fire or removed an object because of its value.

> **Crime linkage analysis** –
> *Linking a known offender to other unsolved crimes based on consistent and distinctive behaviours.*

Crime linkage analysis

Crime linkage analysis is the process of linking a known offender to one or more unsolved crimes based on high levels of consistency and distinctiveness in crime scene behaviours across a series of offences (Deslauriers-Varin and Beauregard, 2013). Focusing on statistical analysis of police data, crime linkage analysis reveals patterns in offending linking an unsolved crime to other behaviourally similar cases where the offender responsible is usually already known (Woodhams, Hollin and Bull, 2007; Bennell, Mugford, Ellingwood and Woodhams, 2014). The goal of crime linkage analysis is to develop decision-making support systems and proper resource allocation for use by investigators (Bennell et al., 2012). There is an increasing body of evidence that crime linkage analysis' emphasis on behavioural consistency and distinctiveness is increasing its empirical support (Woodhams et al., 2019).

Linking a series of crimes helps the police combine information from various crime scenes, potentially increasing the evidence against an offender (Davies and Woodhams, 2019). If a group of crimes are believed to have been committed by the same individual they can be investigated together, thus using limited police resources more efficiently. Finally, evidence of crimes being linked has been used as similar fact evidence in legal proceedings (Pakkanen, Santtila and Bosco, 2014). For example, in 2006, Themba Sukude, the Newcastle serial murderer and rapist, was the first person in South Africa's legal history to be convicted of crimes attributed to him through crime linkage analysis (Geldenhuys, 2019).

Crime linkage analysis has found consistent behaviours among serial offenders for child abduction (van Nevel and Bayless, 2016), arson (Santtila, Fritzon and Tamelander, 2004), sexual assault (Yokota et al., 2017), sexual homicide (Greenall and Wright, 2019) and burglary (Fox and Farrington, 2016; Bouhana, Johnson and Porter, 2016).

Comparing criminal investigative analysis and investigative psychology

Both CIA and investigative psychology are broad approaches that assume that the crime scene holds evidence of a suspect's relevant behaviours and this information reveals their distinctive characteristics. Although there are overlapping concepts between the CIA and investigative psychology approaches (modus operandi, staging, signature), investigative psychology is more empirical and less reliant on the intuitive and clinically focused CIA. The CIA approach is more of a 'top-down' or theory-driven approach, while investigative psychology is more of a 'bottom-up' or data-driven approach. Finally, investigative psychology distinguished itself by systematically exploring how offenders behaved during their offences and applying investigative techniques of geographic profiling and crime linkage analysis to find meaningful patterns of behaviour from large datasets (Howitt, 2009).

IN SUMMARY

Investigative psychology, geographic profiling and crime linkage analysis represent a significant shift towards empirical, behaviour-based predictions and away from subjective intuition-driven approaches of the past. The future of profiling relies more on the *process* and less on the *person*.

CRITICAL THINKING AND APPLICATION QUESTIONS

1   Compare and contrast the approaches of criminal investigative analysis and investigative psychology.

2   What are the consequences of using a vague offender profile for police, suspects and offenders? Hint: research the case of Colin Stagg and the murder of Rachel Nickell.

3   Review the five classifications of the victim search methods used by sexual offenders. Can you find examples from real life or entertainment media that use any of these hunting patterns?

OFFENDER PROFILING: VALUABLE INSIGHTS, COMMON SENSE OR PSEUDOSCIENCE?

FICTION: Offender profiling is a valid scientific approach for solving crimes and capturing criminals.

Versus

FACT: Most offender profiling approaches lack scientific rigour and the potential utility lies in linking suspects, behaviours and locations rather than identifying specific offenders.

The Unabomber: measuring the accuracy of profiling

Theodore J. Kaczynski was a gifted mathematical genius and won a Harvard University scholarship at the age of 16. Nine years later, in 1967, he became the youngest assistant professor of mathematics in the history of the University of California, Berkeley. But two years later, his brilliant mind and body travelled to a darker place. Kaczynski left society behind to live an isolated existence deep in the woods, where he taught himself survival skills, such as foraging for food and hunting game (McFadden, 1996).

Theodore Kaczynski was the youngest assistant professor of mathematics at the University of California before he became the infamous Unabomber

Source: Sygma/Getty Images

Forensic linguistics
– Applying linguistic knowledge, methods and insights to the forensic context of law, language, crime investigation, trial and judicial procedure.

From his remote location, the former mathematics professor cultivated a psychotic resentment of modern technology, which led him, eventually, to sending 16 homemade explosive devices to universities and airlines over the period 1978–95 (hence the code name UNiversity and Airline BOMBER or 'Unabomber'). The Unabomber killed three and injured many others, deliberately leaving a trail of false clues in a long-running mystery that stumped investigators for nearly 20 years. In 1980, the FBI's Behavioral Sciences Unit (now known as the Behavioral Analysis Unit) issued a psychological profile of the unidentified bomber. Upon Kaczynski's arrest, it was verified that only 22 per cent or 4 out of 18 profile predictions were correct (Kendall and Marx, 1996). The four correct predictions were that he was: a white male; reclusive (he bought his land deep in the mountains); had problems dealing with women; and he grew up near Chicago.

Ironically, it was not the psychological profile but Kaczynski's own words that led to his capture. After newspapers published his manifesto *Industrial Society and Its Future*, Kaczynski's sister-in-law (who he had never met) recognised the familiar writing and convinced her husband David Kaczynski to review the published manifesto. He also recognised the oddly familiar ideas and unique phrases used by his brother. Next, the FBI used **forensic linguistics** (Leonard, Ford and Christensen, 2017) to compare the writings of Ted Kaczynski and the Unabomber's manifesto. They found significant similarities in content, style and expression (Hitt, 2012; Kaczynski, 2015). Kaczynski was arrested on 3 April 1996 at his cabin. He is serving eight life sentences with no possibility of parole.

Discussion Questions:

1   Examine the four correct items from the FBI profile. Which of these could significantly reduce the pool of potential suspects?

2   Why do you think he was caught by forensic linguistics? Comment on the empirical nature of this approach.

When will offender profiling become an accepted science?

The path from a pseudoscientific discipline to an evidence-based discipline requires impartial empirical verification. Judicial and law enforcement agencies will remain sceptical of the work of offender profilers until they meet the standards of an accepted science (Deming, 2016). Techniques with a strong scientific basis such as forensic DNA are essential to modern criminal investigations and are widely accepted by judicial systems (Stern, Cuellar and Kaye, 2019). This is because forensic DNA analysis meets two important criteria for a science: the need for a **paradigm** and the requirement of **falsifiability**.

Examining the first criteria is simple. Any new discipline, such as psychological profiling, begins with conflicting theories that have no underlying basis. As the discipline matures, a paradigm (the theoretical foundation on which a theory rests) is formed and evaluated until it is replaced by a more effective paradigm (Kuhn, 1962; Orman, 2016). Unfortunately, many of the practices of profiling have developed without explanation of the underlying principles that support its predictions (Pinizzotto and Finkel, 1990). Psychological profiling has become a discipline without a paradigm binding the research together. Without this guiding principle, it is impossible for it to be considered a science. The lack of an overriding paradigm is reflected in the variety of approaches and language used to describe profiling (see Table 7.1) and this leads to the illusion of a science (Kocsis, 2010). But this reflects a deeper problem than terminology. This proliferation of methods lacks standardisation, and different procedures create different results and their continuous disagreement only helps the offenders of crimes (Kocsis, 2010).

The second criteria is falsifiability – to be considered scientific, a discipline like psychological profiling must be able to propose hypotheses that are empirically testable (Susser, 1986). Proving that a hypothesis is true is difficult because experimentation cannot provide proof of a hypothesis for every situation, but we can easily disprove hypotheses. Imagine if I told you that 'all swans are white'. Based on observation, most people would agree unless you are from Australia, in which case you would say 'I've seen a black swan!' Thus, a single black swan disproves the hypothesis that all swans are white (Taleb, 2010).

The concept of falsifiability is also important for legal reasons. If a psychological profile is going to be presented in a court of law, it would need to be submitted as expert evidence. While the standards for acceptance of expert evidence vary from country to country (Slobogin, 2006), most countries require that scientific theories can be tested, thus meeting the criterion of falsifiability (Odgers and Richardson, 1995).

Paradigm – A distinct set of theories, research methods and standards for what constitutes legitimate contributions to a field.

Falsifiability – A theory is scientific based on whether it can be disproved, a tool to distinguish between science and pseudoscience.

Daubert standard – *A rule of evidence about the admissibility of expert witness testimony in court (aka the Daubert test).*

To present profiling evidence in a court requires more than personal stories of successful profiles, it requires empirical proof. For example, the US federal court system maintains standards for the admissibility of scientific evidence using the **Daubert standard**, a set of guidelines for determining whether an expert's methodology is valid. The guidelines comprise five factors to be considered:

1   *Testability:* Are techniques and theories reliable and falsifiable?

2   *Peer review and publication* by the scientific community.

3   *Error rate:* The method's known error rate (the proportion of responses that are incorrect).

4   *Standard:* The existence and maintenance of standardised methods controlling its application.

5   *General acceptance:* Whether the method has widespread acceptance within the relevant scientific community (Jarman and Merkley, 2019).

Although the Daubert criteria only legally apply in the USA, these same standards are applied by courts in other countries, such as Australia, Canada, Italy, New Zealand and the UK (Ireland and Beaumont, 2015; Pakkanen, Santtila and Bosco, 2014).

How effective is offender profiling?

Successful profiling depends on the validity of three fundamental assumptions:

Homology – *The idea that similar offenders commit similar crimes.*

1   **Homology**: Similar crimes are committed by similar offenders.

2   **Behavioural consistency**: Repeat offenders will commit their crimes in the same way.

Behavioural consistency – *The tendency to behave in a manner that matches past decisions or behaviours.*

3   **Behavioural distinctiveness**: The way one offender behaves is different from that of another offender (Tonkin and Woodhams, 2017; Alison, McLean and Almond, 2007).

Homology

Behavioural distinctiveness – *The way one offender behaves is different from that of another offender.*

Homology assumes that if personality traits were the predictable causes of criminal behaviours, then offenders with the same personalities would show consistent behaviour across crimes (Bateman and Salfati, 2007). Homology is rooted in **trait theories** of personality, but the weakness of personality theory in general and trait theory specifically is its limited ability to predict behaviour from personality, that is, its predictive validity.

For personality traits to serve as valid predictors of human behaviour requires a long period of time, precise situations, and very specific measures of traits that a person scores extremely low or high. This means that different traits make for better predictors for different people (Monson, Hesley and Chernick, 1982). It is important to remember that no matter how good a predictor of personality a trait may be, it can still be overwhelmed by strong situational factors (Ganpat, van der Leun and Nieuwbeert, 2017).

Trait theory – *The idea that people have relatively stable personality characteristics that cause individuals to behave in predictable ways.*

Behavioural consistency

Behavioural consistency is the belief that behaviour is consistent across situations (Alison et al., 2002), although research shows the opposite is true (Mokros and Alison, 2002).

The **personality paradox** is the observation that while personality tends to remain the same over time, behaviour changes in different situations. When predicting behaviour, psychologists have known that situational factors contribute as much as and sometimes more than personality.

As support for the power of the situation to change behaviour, Shoda, Mischel and Wright (1994) examined the aggressive behaviour of children in a variety of situations at a summer camp. Most psychologists assumed that aggression was a stable trait, but the researchers found that children's responses varied depending on the details of the interaction. For example, the same child might consistently lash out when teased by a peer, but willingly submit to adult punishment.

There is some evidence supporting behavioural consistency by linking of crime scene behaviours and offender characteristics (DeLisi et al., 2019). Bateman and Salfati (2007) examined 450 serial murder cases to find out whether these offenders consistently performed the same behaviours across their crimes. They found that signatures or specific key behaviours are the consistent elements in an offender's behaviour across crimes.

> **Personality paradox** – The observation that a person's personality remains the same over time, while their behaviour can change in different situations.

Behavioural distinctiveness

Psychologists have spent decades searching for traits that exist independently of circumstance. What if personality cannot be separated from context? Imagine if only innate personality traits motivated burglaries. The burglar would randomly select their victim showing no preference for alarm systems, attack dogs, convenient methods of entry or signs of wealth (Jenkins, 1994).

Successful offenders change their behaviours (modus operandi) in response to situational cues, not their dispositional traits (Ekehammar, 1974). With this in mind, Mischel (1973) encouraged researchers to include situational factors in their experiments and look for the consistent behaviours that characterise an individual in a variety of contexts. Mischel describes the interactionist perspective as similar to the process used by a car mechanic. Imagine your car is making a loud screeching sound. The mechanic solves the problem by trying to identify the specific conditions that cause the noise. Is there a screech when the car is accelerating, or when shifting gears, or turning at slow speeds? Unless the mechanic can give the screeching sound a context, the mechanic will never find the cause. Mischel wanted psychologists to think like mechanics and examine people's responses under specific conditions. By including the situation as perceived by the individual and by analysing behaviour in its situational context, the consistent behaviours that characterise the individual can be found (Mischel, 1973).

Why is there still a belief in offender profiling?

Given the lack of valid and reliable research support, it is surprising that the public and police and even the US FBI (who teach this method) still have confidence in the power of offender profiling. The answer lies in how information about offender profiling is presented to people through stories and how consumers process that information.

The power of a story

The first explanation is based on the power of anecdotal evidence. Offender profiling stories in books, magazines and even peer reviewed journals often rely exclusively on a 'case study' or 'success stories' to illustrate profiling's successes. Snook et al. (2007)

conducted a narrative review of the offender profiling literature and found that anecdotal arguments were the most frequent source of knowledge (60 per cent of the articles).

There are at least three reasons why anecdotes alone are inadequate to prove the effectiveness of offender profiling. The first reason is the limited sampling size. An anecdote is a single case used to prove a point. The use of anecdotal evidence is often selective. When attempting to persuade others that offender profiling works, a profiler can select at least one example in which a profile appears to have helped investigators solve a crime. This selective use of only some evidence is a classic example of confirmation bias, the tendency to notice and remember information that lends support to our views about something. This tendency is common not only in the creation of an offender profile, but also in its interpretation (Ask and Granhag, 2005). Second, anecdotal evidence can exaggerate the usefulness of a profile in solving a case because anecdotes become exaggerated and distorted to make them seem more informative and entertaining (Shermer, 2008, 2017). Third, anecdotal evidence is notorious for being both ambiguous and unverifiable and therefore open to interpretation and misinterpretation (Alison, Smith, Eastman and Rainbow, 2003).

Repetition of the message

A second explanation is borrowed from the domain of advertising, that is, repetition of the message that 'profiling works' (Eisend and Schmidt, 2015). Repeating the message that offender profiling is 'an effective investigative tool' or that 'police actively seek the profiler's input' contributes to the false belief in the message that profiling works. Meta-analyses reveal that the message that offender 'profiling works' is clearly stated in 52 per cent of the 130 offender profiling articles, while only 3 per cent of articles clearly stated that offender profiling does not work (Snook et al., 2008).

Reporting only successes

A third explanation is reporting only the successful cases and not the unsuccessful ones. Profilers can create the false impression that their conclusions are highly accurate by overreporting their successes and underreporting their failures. Unfortunately, when the essential and relevant information is not reported, the public forms an impression based only on the biased information. Psychological research demonstrates that presenting only correct inferences leads people to overestimate the accuracy and usefulness of offender profiles (Anand and Sternthal, 1990; Muller, 2000).

Future directions of training and research in offender profiling

Unfortunately, the seductive promise of profiling popular today will remain with us in the future. Offender profiling is often a pseudoscientific practice with elements that show promise for effective application (geographic profiling and crime linkage analysis). What form it will take is uncertain, but future profiles should be built on empirical approaches that rely on advanced statistical analyses of large datasets (not the intuition or experiences of the author or a handful of cases) and undergo peer review before publication. Additionally, if offender profiles are allowed to be used in police investigations, they need to be evaluated for their effect on arrest rates in unsolved cases. Using proven experimental design principles will establish the known error rate and evaluate which profiling approaches are most effective when applied in real police investigations. This will reduce the large number of different offender profiling methods, increase the quality of offender profiles and the acceptance of profiling in the judicial system.

IN SUMMARY

Most offender profiling approaches lack the level of scientific rigour to pass the Daubert test. Part of the challenge is verifying the validity of three fundamental assumptions: homology, behavioural consistency and behavioural distinctiveness. A potential solution is applying crime linkage analysis, linking suspects with their behaviours and locations rather than identifying specific offenders.

 CRITICAL THINKING AND APPLICATION QUESTIONS

1   Is your personality or behaviour more stable and consistent over time? What evidence could you use to support your decision?

2   Find a consumer product that makes a claim of being effective, such as copper bracelets and increased health. Do their claims offer a theoretical explanation and are they falsifiable?

3   If offender profiling were to be accepted by the judicial system, what criteria would it have to meet to be accepted as a valid science?

PART III

CHAPTER REVIEW

Offender profiling is regarded as both an art (based on experience and intuition) and a science (based on empirical research that generates falsifiable hypotheses), lacking an underlying paradigm. Offender profiling often relies on anecdotal evidence and commonsense justifications based on outdated theories of personality (trait theory). In controlled situations, professional profilers perform no better than laypeople in predicting criminals' cognitive processes, physical attributes, offence behaviours, social habits and history. However, because of immense public belief in profiling as a practical technique, it must be recognised, although this belief can be modified through education. Criminal behaviour changes, and so should the field of offender profiling. The methods that offer the most promising direction are those relying on statically focused procedures linking patterns of behaviours. Given the extraordinary potential for valid and reliable profiling, we should remain optimistic yet sceptical. As the astronomer Carl Sagan (1986, p. 73) wrote: 'I believe that the extraordinary should certainly be pursued. But extraordinary claims require extraordinary evidence.'

NAMES TO KNOW

David Canter

An applied social psychologist, internationally known for developing the field of investigative psychology and environmental psychology. A number of TV documentaries have been built around his work, including his work on the psychological implications of places, human actions in fires and other emergencies, wayfinding in buildings and homelessness in London.

- Canter, D. and Youngs, D. (2009) *Investigative Psychology: Offender Profiling and the Analysis of Criminal Action*. Wiley.

- Canter, D. (2019) *Mapping Murder: The Secrets of Geographical Profiling*. Endeavour Media.

Richard N. Kocsis

A psychologist and criminologist, he is the author/co-author and editor of books, book chapters and articles on topics related to offender profiling, aberrant violent crime, forensic psychology/psychiatry and the law, political violence and counterterrorism. Over his career, he has served as an expert consultant to law enforcement, emergency and prosecution agencies as well as law firms.

- Kocsis, R. N. (2006) *Criminal Profiling: Principles and Practice*. Humana.
- Kocsis, R. N. and Palermo, G. B. (2013) Disentangling criminal profiling: Accuracy, homology, and the myth of trait-based profiling. *International Journal of Offender Therapy and Comparative Criminology*, 59(3), 313–32.

Kim Rossmo

Has researched and published in the areas of criminal investigations, the geography of crime, policing and offender profiling.

- Rossmo, K. (1999) *Geographic Profiling*. CRC Press.
- Rossmo, K. (2003) *Criminal Investigative Failures*. CRC Press.

8 ASSESSING FITNESS TO STAND TRIAL AND CRIMINAL RESPONSIBILITY

Chapter Introduction

Determining a person's mental state at the time of the offence (criminal responsibility) or at the time of trial (competency) are among the most challenging tasks confronting forensic psychologists. Also challenging is determining what psychological disorders are so severe that their presence excuses criminal behaviours. If this process were not difficult enough, there lurks the question: 'Is the person malingering?' Are they feigning a serious mental disorder to avoid a guilty verdict or a prison sentence? If the person is found to be legally insane, does the legal term 'insanity' meet the needs of current criminal justice systems, or do we need to replace the legal perspective with a medical one?

Learning Outcomes

Assessing fitness to stand trial
- Explain the legal and psychological challenges when assessing fitness to stand trial.

Assessing criminal responsibility
- Explain the legal and psychological challenges when assessing criminal responsibility.

Malingering and its detection
- Be able to identify malingering and the ways to measure it.

Neuroscience and the insanity defence: Do bad brains cause bad behaviour?
- Be able to describe the difference between a legal and a medical approach to evaluate criminal responsibility.

ASSESSING FITNESS TO STAND TRIAL

FICTION: Being 'unfit to stand trial' is equal to being found 'not guilty' and is equal to a 'get-out-of-jail-free card'.

Versus

FACT: Many defendants who are initially found to be unfit to stand trial become competent to stand trial through successful treatment or rehabilitation efforts, and those who are unlikely to become fit or those who are deemed dangerous are subject to commitment.

Determining a person's mental fitness at the time of the trial is important for the fair administration of justice. This is why forensic psychologists continually fight the misconception that if an individual is found 'unfit', it is the same as being found 'not guilty'. Being considered unfit to stand trial does not mean that the defendant will no longer be prosecuted for the crime for which they are charged. After an *unfit* defendant is restored to competency, they will return to the court system to enter a plea, have a trial, or in some manner decide their case. But, sometimes, a person who is not mentally fit to stand trial becomes lost in a legal limbo and spends more time incarcerated than if they had pleaded guilty. This was the case for an Aboriginal Australian man named Marlon Noble.

Global Perspectives

Marlon Noble: a victim of Western Australia's Criminal Law (Mentally Impaired Accused) Act

Marlon Noble was born in 1982 and suffered with meningitis at four months, leaving him with below-average intelligence, cognitive difficulties and problems expressing himself verbally. In December 2001, aged 19, he was charged with sexually assaulting two children. In 2002, Marlon first appeared in court, and was held in custody for assessment. He was assessed as mentally impaired. In March 2003, it was decided he was 'unfit to stand trial'.

Source: Copyright © Australian Human Rights Commission

Marlon Noble was found unfit to stand trial under the Criminal Law (Mentally Impaired Accused) Act 1996. He was accused of sex crimes and spent 10 years behind bars despite no trial or conviction

The court could then choose whether to release Marlon unconditionally, or make a custody order. The court decided to hold him in custody, and his case was transferred to Western Australia's Mentally Impaired Accused Review Board. The board decided to hold him in prison. He was not found guilty of any of the charges made against him. In June 2010, a forensic psychologist found that Marlon was now able to plead and stand trial with assistance. Marlon decided to plead not guilty to the charges. But this was not an option because the charges were withdrawn as of late 2010 because the alleged victims and their mother denied that Marlon had ever harmed them and supported his release. However, the Director of Public Prosecutions explained that because Marlon had been imprisoned for so long, he would not seek to continue with the charges.

In fact, Marlon was held much longer than if he had been found guilty of all charges. Marlon was imprisoned for 10 years without ever being found guilty of a crime. There appears to be no evidence that the crimes which it was alleged he committed had ever actually occurred (McGaughey, Tulich and Blagg, 2017). However, it was not intended that he stay in prison forever. In 2006, the Mentally Impaired Accused Review Board endorsed a five-stage plan for graduated release into the community. In November 2011, the board referred him to the national sex offender's registry, as it considered conditionally releasing him, even though he was never found guilty of any sexual offence, the charges were withdrawn, and the alleged victims do not seem to believe he sexually assaulted them.

Since this case, there have been revisions of policies and all Australian jurisdictions have mental health services in their prisons that are similar to the government mental health services that exist in the community. There are also dedicated forensic mental health hospitals to which acutely ill prisoners can be transferred (Clugston et al., 2018).

Fitness to stand trial across jurisdictions

Depending on your jurisdiction, the description of an individual's ability to represent themselves may differ. It is called **fitness to plead** in the UK and Australia, **fitness to stand trial** in Canada, and **competency to stand trial** in the USA. Regardless of the terminology, all jurisdictions have a common goal, which is to provide as many people as possible their day in court, while excluding individuals who are unable to understand legal procedures or assist in their defence (Golding, Roesch and Schreiber, 1984).

Fitness to stand trial ensures the integrity and fairness of the legal system. Although legal jurisdictions vary on the precise requirements and thresholds for fitness to stand trial (see Table 8.1), all jurisdictions assume that every person is mentally competent until legal proceedings decide otherwise. All jurisdictions recognise the importance of the defendant's ability to understand and assist legal counsel in order to participate in the legal process.

Jurisdictional differences in fitness to stand trial (Canada, the UK, the USA and Australia)

Across jurisdictions, fitness to stand trial is focused on four areas:

1   An appreciation of the charges and potential consequences, including the significance of the potential pleas.
2   An ability to understand the trial process.
3   A potential for the defendant to participate in that process.
4   The ability to work collaboratively with legal counsel on their defence.

As Table 8.1 shows, the descriptions and applications of this concept are different.

Fitness to plead – *The capacity of a defendant in criminal proceedings to comprehend the course of those proceedings.*

Fitness to stand trial – *The accused person is able to defend against the charge they are facing.*

Competence to stand trial – *The legally determined capacity of a criminal defendant to proceed with criminal judgement.*

Table 8.1: Jurisdictional differences in fitness to stand trial

Country	Label	Legal reference
Canada	Fitness to stand trial	Criminal Code of Canada (CCC)
Description		
Unable on account of mental disorder to conduct a defence at any stage of the proceedings before a verdict is rendered or to instruct counsel to do so, and, in particular, unable on account of mental disorder to: (1) understand the nature or object of the proceedings; (2) understand the possible consequences of the proceedings; or (3) communicate with counsel.		
UK	Fitness to plead	*Regina* v. *Pritchard* (7C and P303, 1836)
Description		
The Pritchard criteria: A finding of unfitness to plead involves demonstrating, 'on the balance of probabilities that the defendant is incapable of one or more of: (1) understanding the charges; (2) deciding whether to plead guilty or not; (3) exercising his right to challenge jurors; (4) instructing solicitors and counsel; (5) following the course of proceedings; and (6) giving evidence in his own defence' (Law Commission, 2010, p. 30). In Scotland, the test is based on *HMA* vs *Wilson*, and has two elements: to be able to instruct counsel and to understand and follow proceedings.		
USA	Competency to stand trial	*Dusky* v. *United States* (362 US. 402, 1960)
Description		
Whether the accused has sufficient present ability to consult with his lawyer with a reasonable degree of rational understanding and whether he has a rational as well as factual understanding of the proceedings against him.		
Australia	Fitness to stand trial	*R* v. *Presser* (VR 45, 1958)
Description		
'In the Australian Territories, New South Wales, Tasmania, Victoria and Western Australia, criteria for unfitness to stand trial include: a. being unable to understand the nature of the charge; or b. being unable to exercise a plea in relation to the charge; or c. unable to understand the nature of the proceedings; or d. unable to follow the evidence or the course of proceedings. South Australia does not incorporate an ability to plead the charge as an element of fitness to stand trial, and Queensland does not include elements a, c, & d, listed above as elements in its legislation' (Australian Psychological Society, n.d.)		

Source: Definition of the Pritchard Criteria from The Law Commission (2010). Reproduced with permission.

Principle of proportionality
– *The idea that the punishment of a certain crime should be in proportion to the severity of the crime.*

Fitness to stand trial is the most frequent referral issue facing forensic mental health professionals and consumes considerable resources in the process (Wood, Anderson and Glassmire, 2017). It can be viewed as a matter of threshold, where the degree of competence required varies according to the nature and legal impact of the offence. Specifically, it is about determining whether the person belongs within the criminal justice system or whether they should be detained in a non-penal institution without a determination of the person's legal liability. From the perspective of the law in the UK, the **principle of proportionality**, requiring greater cognitive capacity for complex decisions when the consequences are more serious, can be observed more clearly in healthcare settings than in the courtroom.

The right of a person *not* to be tried while incompetent is a fundamental right in most countries. Punishing a defendant who lacks the ability to understand the charges against them and the consequences of a trial is ineffective and immoral. In the same way that a person has the right to be physically present during their trial, they must also be mentally present. A defendant who is physically or mentally unfit cannot defend against a criminal charge. Importantly, impairments that affect mental functioning do not automatically mean that a defendant is not fit to stand trial, because a person with these impairments may meet the legal standards for competence. In the UK, a finding that a patient is unfit to plead may result in compulsory admission to a hospital for treatment under the Criminal Procedure (Insanity and Unfitness to Plead) Act 1991.

Why mental fitness matters

Legally determining a defendant's mental competency is important for three reasons: to preserve the dignity of the judicial process; to reduce the risk of mistaken convictions; and to protect defendants' decision-making autonomy. Morally, punishment is ineffective for a defendant who cannot understand the punishment and the reasons for imposing it. Table 8.2 summarises four legal reasons for trying only persons who are identified as mentally fit.

Table 8.2: Four legal reasons for trying only defendants who are fit to stand trial

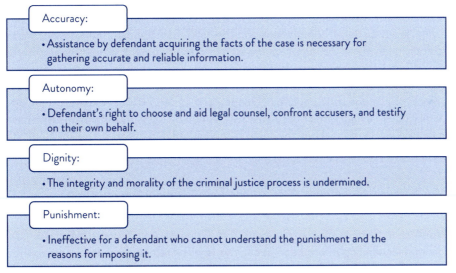

Source: Inspired by Hoge, S. K. (2016) Competence to stand trial: An overview. *Indian Journal of Psychiatry*, 58(2), S187–90.

How do forensic psychologists determine fitness to stand trial?

Measuring fitness to stand trial is the most common forensic evaluation requested by the courts (Pirelli, Gottdiener and Zaph, 2011; Blake, Ogloff and Chen, 2019). The process consists of a specialised forensic interview of the defendant along with a clinical interview that may include the administration of standardised forensic tests and assessments, and a review of materials related to the offence. The interviews typically take place in a jail, a community-based outpatient facility, or an institutional setting like a psychiatric hospital (Luxton and Lexcen, 2018). Forensic evaluators need to be mental health professionals who are trained to perform psycholegal assessments (APA, 2013b). As part of fitness to stand trial assessments, evaluators routinely offer opinions about the feasibility of restoration of fitness and recommendations about treatment for the restoration of fitness.

There are three common instruments to assess mental competency: the Evaluation of Competency to Stand Trial-Revised (ECST-R); the Competency Screening Test (CST); and the MacArthur Competence Assessment Tool-Criminal Adjudication (MacCAT-CA). Space permits only a brief overview of these forensic assessment instruments used in competency evaluations.

Evaluation of Competency to Stand Trial–Revised (ECST-R)

The Evaluation of Competency to Stand Trial–Revised (ECST-R) is a semi-structured interview designed to assess the factual understanding of the courtroom proceedings, rational understanding of the courtroom proceedings, and the ability to consult with counsel. The ECST-R provides screening for feigned incompetency to stand trial, with questions probing claimed impairment and symptoms related to competency issues (Rogers, Tillbrook and Sewell, 2004).

The Competency Screening Test (CST)

The Competency Screening Test (CST) is a 22-item, sentence-completion test measuring levels of legal comprehension. The CST has standardised administration (completion takes about 25 minutes) and standardised scoring. Examples of test items include: 'When I go to court, my lawyer will ...' and 'When they say a man is innocent until proven guilty, I ...'. Strengths of the CST include ease of administration and recognition of persons truly impaired (Denney and Tyner, 2010). Weaknesses include low validity due to a high rate of false positives, difficulty assessing defendants who have a high degree of cynicism about the system and limited and unproven reliability of the test (Brown, Haun, Zapf and Aiken, 2018).

The MacArthur Competence Assessment Tool-Criminal Adjudication (MacCAT-CA)

The MacArthur Competence Assessment Tool-Criminal Adjudication (MacCAT-CA) measures understanding information about the legal system and the legal process, the ability to reason, and the ability to appreciate one's own legal circumstances and situation (Hoge, Bonnie, Poythress and Monahan, 1999). The test uses a hypothetical vignette describing a bar fight between two men, Fred and Reggie, which results in an aggravated assault charge against Fred. The defendant is asked a series of questions about Fred's situation and how Fred might deal with various aspects of his case. The items are scored based on the reasons that the defendant provides for their judgement and whether they are plausible or implausible – grounded in reality or based on delusional beliefs (Poythress et al., 2002).

IN SUMMARY

A finding of 'unfit to stand trial' is not equal to being found 'not guilty'. Many defendants who are initially found unfit to stand trial later become competent to stand trial through successful treatment or rehabilitation efforts, and those unlikely to become fit, and are dangerous, are subject to sometimes longer commitment than if they were found mentally competent.

 CRITICAL THINKING AND APPLICATION QUESTIONS

1   Explain why competency to stand trial is important from both a legal *and* a moral perspective.

2   Imagine you are a forensic psychologist, interviewing a 19-year-old facing a charge related to car theft. They were evaluated for fitness to stand trial. You note that the defendant spoke very little and 'did not appear to be taking the evaluation seriously'. Outline your plan and questions for interviewing this person to assess their fitness to stand trial.

3   Many jurisdictions use a specific age to establish when a person is mature enough to stand trial. Are there better ways to ensure the competency of juveniles than relying only on their age?

ASSESSING CRIMINAL RESPONSIBILITY

FICTION: There are many individuals acquitted by reason of insanity who are not treated as severely in terms of the level of security of imprisonment and length of confinement as if they were found guilty of the same crime.

Versus

FACT: The reality of the insanity defence is that it is difficult to plead, seldom used and rarely successful.

Criminal responsibility is a person's ability to understand their conduct when the crime was committed. This is based on the idea that convicting an individual of a crime requires proving a guilty action with guilty intention. Without criminal intent during the act, no crime has occurred. For example, taking someone's phone while believing it is yours is not theft. In other words, what someone is thinking when committing a crime, or what is expected when the crime is committed, is important. However, criminal responsibility should not be confused with fitness to stand trial. While fitness to stand trial is concerned with the defendant's *present* mental capacity during trial, criminal responsibility refers to the defendant's *past* mental capacity during the offence (Feuerstein et al., 2005a). The challenge is figuring out what the defendant was thinking, feeling and doing at the time of the offence that happened weeks, months or even years earlier (Bartol and Bartol, 2016). But what about situations where a person commits an act, with intention, but was suffering from a condition impairing their ability to appreciate that they were doing something wrong, or were unable to control their behaviour, or both?

> **Criminal responsibility** – A person's ability to understand their conduct when the crime was committed.

The voluntary requirement of criminal responsibility

In 1987, Kenneth Parks was 23 years old. He had a wife, a five-month-old daughter, and a good relationship with his in-laws. His mother-in-law often described him as a 'gentle giant' (Brody, 1996). Suffering from a gambling addiction, marital problems and financial difficulties, Kenneth planned to reveal his troubles to his in-laws the next day. After falling asleep on the couch, Kenneth got up sometime after midnight, but did not awaken. While sleepwalking, he climbed into his car and drove 22 kilometres (14 miles) to his in-laws' home. He entered their house with a key they had given him and, using a tyre iron he brought with him, he beat his

Source: Frank Lennon/Toronto Star/Getty Images

Kenneth Parks leaving court a free man after being acquitted of sleepwalking homicide

mother-in-law to death. He then turned on her husband and tried to choke him to death but was unsuccessful. Parks roamed the house briefly afterwards, as confirmed by the teenage children, who reported hearing his 'grunting noises'.

Parks left and awoke at some point during his drive home and detoured to the police station, arriving at 4:45 am, covered in blood, and confessing to the police that he thought he had killed his in-laws (Popat and Winslade, 2015). The police said that he seemed distressed and was shaking. Despite deep cuts in the tendons in both hands, he did not appear to be in pain. This profound reduction in pain sensation is known as **dissociative analgesia**. Dissociative analgesia can occur during states of sleepwalking but also after drug use and in states of shock or great distress. This insensitivity to pain, the EEG indications of abnormal brain wave patterns during sleep, and his (and his relative's) history of sleepwalking led experts to believe that he committed these heinous acts while sleeping.

We assume that sleepwalkers are deeply asleep, but there are reports of hallucinations during sleepwalking (Zadra, Desautels, Petit and Montplaisir, 2013). These hallucinations explain his behaviour. He said he yelled 'kids, kids, kids' after hearing the teenage children yelling. But the children reported only hearing him make grunting noises. He also saw his in-laws' faces as sad, which may have been a hallucinatory state of mind (Diaz, 2018).

The Canadian court was sceptical at first, but while all parties agreed that he committed murder, there was no motive. The defence argued that a combination of external factors caused the killing and that it was doubtful that a similar combination of stress, insomnia and external factors would occur again (Brogaard and Marlow, 2012). The jury ruled that he was not responsible for his actions (*R. v. Parks*, 2 S.C.R. 871, 1992). The medical diagnosis was **non-insane automatism** – an act done by a sane person but without intention, awareness, or hatred (Schenck and Mahowald, 1995; Kramers-Olen, 2019). Because he was found not guilty, he

Dissociative analgesia – *A profound reduction of pain sensation.*

Non-insane automatism – *An act done by a sane person but without intention, awareness, or hatred.*

was not sentenced to a psychiatric hospital and he was not judged insane because it was an involuntary act. Instead, he walked out of the courtroom free. Parks was prescribed medication and never had another episode of his sleepwalking violence (Adam, 2010).

Discussion Questions:

1   The border between justification and excuse is not always clear, but the distinction is useful. Consider the nature of Kenneth Parks' defence. Is his reason a justification or an excuse?

2   Parks' complete lack of consciousness during sleepwalking led to his acquittal from criminal responsibility. But what if Parks stopped taking his medication and had a similar violent episode while sleepwalking? Should he be held criminally responsible?

Mental states and criminal responsibility

Kenneth Parks' story shows the importance of considering voluntary intention when assigning responsibility for a person's actions (Gordon and Fondacaro, 2018). Criminal responsibility has two parts, a cognitive (rational thinking) component and a volitional (intentional behaviour) component (see Figure 8.1). First, a defendant must have the ability to form criminal intent or the understanding that the conduct was wrong or evil by society's standards (Bartol and Bartol, 2016). Second, the defendant must have control over their conduct, which was *not* the case with the sleepwalking Kenneth Parks.

Figure 8.1: Criminal responsibility

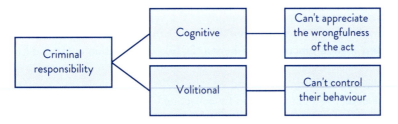

Establishing criminal intention – **mens rea** – is the key to defining fault and justifying punishment (Child, 2019). The challenge is how to define a 'voluntary' or 'intentional' act in a logical and useful way (Zacharski, 2018). As shown in Table 8.3, assigning blame rests on the level of intentionality from purposeful to blameless. Australia's solution is to designate elements of intention or mens rea as 'fault elements' and **actus reus** as 'physical elements' (Badar, 2013). In China, criminal responsibility is divided into three levels: the whole responsibility, diminished responsibility and irresponsibility (Cai et al., 2014). The American Law Institute's Model Penal Code divides intention into five sublevels, each reflecting a different level of responsibility for a crime (Dubber, 2011).

Mens rea – *Latin for 'guilty mind', it is the mental element of a person's intention to commit a crime.*

Actus reus – *The Latin term for 'guilty act', used to describe a criminal act that was the result of voluntary bodily movement.*

Table 8.3: Varying mental states within a single theme

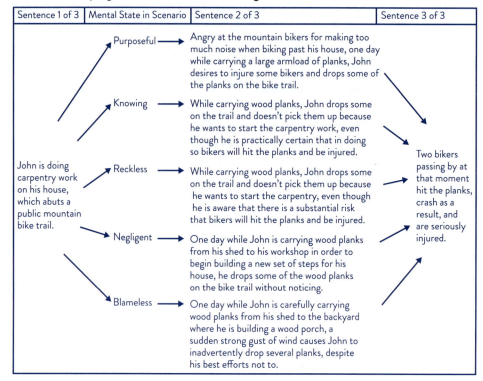

Sentence 1 of 3	Mental State in Scenario	Sentence 2 of 3	Sentence 3 of 3
John is doing carpentry work on his house, which abuts a public mountain bike trail.	Purposeful	Angry at the mountain bikers for making too much noise when biking past his house, one day while carrying a large armload of planks, John desires to injure some bikers and drops some of the planks on the bike trail.	Two bikers passing by at that moment hit the planks, crash as a result, and are seriously injured.
	Knowing	While carrying wood planks, John drops some on the trail and doesn't pick them up because he wants to start the carpentry work, even though he is practically certain that in doing so bikers will hit the planks and be injured.	
	Reckless	While carrying wood planks, John drops some on the trail and doesn't pick them up because he wants to start the carpentry, even though he is aware that there is a substantial risk that bikers will hit the planks and be injured.	
	Negligent	One day while John is carrying wood planks from his shed to his workshop in order to begin building a new set of steps for his house, he drops some of the wood planks on the bike trail without noticing.	
	Blameless	One day while John is carefully carrying wood planks from his shed to the backyard where he is building a wood porch, a sudden strong gust of wind causes John to inadvertently drop several planks, despite his best efforts not to.	

Source: Shen, F. X., Hoffman, M. B., Jones, O. D., Greene, J. D. and Marois, R. (2011) Sorting guilty minds. *New York University Law Review*, 86, 1306–60. Reproduced with permission.

Evaluation of criminal responsibility and sanity

Clinical evaluations are imperfect even under the best circumstances, such as when the forensic psychologist is working with a voluntary, truthful and willing client and the focus is on present mental functioning (Ahonen, 2019). The situation is more difficult when evaluating criminal responsibility, focusing on a specific point in time in the past, with an unwilling client (Gottfried, Schenk and Vitacco, 2016). The forensic psychologist operates more like a detective than a clinician by collecting information from many sources. The sources are varied, including investigative evidence collected by the police, interviews with defendants, and information collected from third parties who may have knowledge relevant to the defendant's behaviour and functioning at or near the time of the offence (Goldstein, Morse and Shapiro, 2003). Other sources include social media, and the use of body and dashboard cameras (Vitacco, Gottfried and Batastini, 2018).

The essential job of the forensic psychologist is to translate legal terms into psychological concepts for objective evaluation (Goldstein, Morse and Shapiro, 2003). While there are many standardised tools available, one approach is to apply the Rogers Criminal Responsibility Assessment Scale (R-CRAS). This measures the defendant's cognitive and volitional impairment at the time of the offence (Rogers and Fiduccia, 2015). However, general psychological assessment measures, such as the Minnesota Multiphasic Personality Inventory (MMPI) and the Personality Assessment Inventory, are used more often (Neal and Grisso, 2014).

Who is exempt from criminal responsibility?

There are two classes of individuals who are excused from judgements of criminal responsibility because of characteristics that make them unable to make appropriate moral and legal judgements. Therefore, they are incapable of behaving appropriately and benefiting from corrective punishment.

The first class of individuals is children, who, because of a lack of life experience, and mental or emotional immaturity, are considered not accountable in the way that adults are held accountable for their behaviour (Yaffe, 2018; Roman, 2019). The rationale behind the age of accountability laws are the same as those behind the insanity defence (Caton, Golding and Fincham, 1987). The second class of individuals (and the focus of our exploration) is those with significant mental disorders whose symptoms contribute to their 'criminal behaviour' in specific ways that society excuses them from moral culpability (criminal responsibility).

From determining criminal responsibility to determining 'sanity'

Now that we have addressed the legal question of assigning criminal responsibility, let us turn to the concept of determining sanity. While a judge determines fitness to stand trial (competency) before a trial begins, a jury determines insanity at the end of trial with the verdict. The insanity defence is based on the assumption that the majority of people are sane and choose to follow the law, but some people cannot be held accountable because mental disease or impairment denies them the ability to make a rational or voluntary choice (Asokan, 2016). Such individuals need special treatment as opposed to prison because punishment is unlikely to prevent future antisocial conduct (Clark, 2015). It is important to remember that the insanity defence is used most often to mitigate the level of punishment (Perlin, 2017).

While the insanity defence is a legal doctrine, at its core it is the expression of a moral principle that individuals should not be punished for their criminal actions if they lack the ability to engage in rational thinking and voluntary behaviours (Schouten, 2012). It is the role of the court, not the psychologist, to determine whether a defendant is insane. Yet psychologists are asked to offer their opinion on the mental status of the defendant at the time of the crime. The term *legal insanity* refers to the 'mental state' of a person at the time of committing a crime and nothing else (Math, Kumar and Moirangthem, 2015). This is purely a legal concept and is unrelated to a psychiatric diagnosis.

Regardless of the precise legal standard, the insanity defence is rarely raised and rarely successful. It is used in only about 1 per cent of cases in the USA and is successful less than 25 per cent of the time (Schouten, 2012). In the UK, there are approximately 30 insanity pleas annually (Connett, 2016). Finally, the fact that most highly publicised cases involve murder disguises the true demographics: 60–70 per cent of insanity pleas are for crimes other than murder (Lyon, 2018). They range from assault to shoplifting (Perlin, 2017). All these myths contribute to the belief that criminals can avoid punishment by claiming insanity.

Insanity defence legislation

Insanity defence standards are constantly evolving within the greater cultural context. These revisions change not only our laws but also the vocabulary of psychology. For example, the mental condition once labelled 'insanity' in the nineteenth century was renamed 'mental illness' in the twentieth, and then 'neurobiological disease' in the twenty-first century (Meynen, 2014; Focquaert, 2018; Szasz, 1997).

Since ancient Rome, legal codes distinguished between those who were 'lunatics' and not accountable and those who were sane and responsible (Eigen, 1995). Terminology such as 'criminally insane', 'crazy' and 'mad' perpetuates the myth that most people with serious mental illness are dangerous. Due to the stigma associated with the term 'insanity', jurisdictions have altered the language of the law. For example, in South Australia, the insanity defence is known as the 'defence of mental incompetence' (Wondermagen, 2014). People view the mentally ill differently than the physically ill. A broken arm is something someone recovers from, but mental illness allegedly endures forever. A person with a broken arm is seen as less threatening than a person with schizophrenia (Rosenhan, 1973).

The wild beast standard

The 'wild beast' standard for insanity was based on the idea that a 'man must be totally deprived of his understanding and memory so as not to know what he is doing, no more than an infant, brute or a wild beast' (Melton, Petrila, Poythress and Slobogin, 1997, p. 190). This 'wild beast' standard was the insanity requirement of England's courts for over a hundred years and any defendant who attempted to use the defence had to prove that they lacked the minimum understanding of a wild animal (or infant) (Platt and Diamond, 1965).

The 'right versus wrong' standard

The Daniel McNaughton case is the key to the beginning of behavioural science in the courtroom. The guidelines for evaluating the criminal responsibility for defendants claiming to be insane were established in the British courts in the case of McNaughton in 1843 (Dalby, 2006). McNaughton was acting under delusions of persecution and paranoia, believing that the prime minister was the cause of all the personal and financial hardships that he endured. Believing that he was attacking the prime minister of England (Sir Robert Peel), he shot and mortally wounded Edward Drummond, the prime minister's private secretary. During his trial, nine witnesses testified that he was insane, and the jury acquitted him, finding him 'not guilty by reason of insanity' (West and Walk, 1977).

> **McNaughton rule** – A test to determine whether a person was sane when committing a crime and therefore responsible.

Queen Victoria was not pleased with this outcome and asked the House of Lords to review the verdict with a panel of judges. The principles the judges expounded is now known as the **McNaughton rule**, which became the basis of the law governing legal responsibility in cases of insanity in England and most of the Western world (West and Walk, 1977). Under the McNaughton rule, defendants are not guilty by reason of insanity if, at the time of a crime, they were afflicted with a 'disease of the mind as to not know the nature and quality of the act he was doing; or if he knew it, that he did not know what he was doing was wrong' (McNaughton, 1843, cited in Rogers, Seman and Clark, 1986, p. 67). (Note: McNaughton's name is often misspelled as M'Naghten, but is verified as McNaughton by his own signature; see Diamond, 1964.)

The intention of the McNaughton rule was to limit the insanity defence to cognitive insanity. By focusing on the 'understandability of right and wrong' and an 'intellectual' rather than a moral definition, the issues of lack of control and irresistible drives or impulses were ignored (Asokan, 2007). Moran (1977) offers another point of view, suggesting that the insanity verdict discredited McNaughton and the political ideas he represented by interpreting his act as the product of a diseased mind.

Impact of the McNaughton rule

The McNaughton rule quickly spread around the globe, and today influences current insanity regulations (Hanganu-Bresch, 2019). These include:

> **Product test** – A person may be found insane if the criminal act was a product of a mental disease.

- The **product test**, wherein a person may be found insane if the criminal act was a product of a mental disease (Moore, 2015).

- The **irresistible impulse** test, wherein a person should not be held criminally liable for their actions that broke the law, because they could not control those actions, even if they knew them to be wrong (Donohue, Arya, Fitch and Hammen, 2008).

- The **cognitive impairment of moral reasoning**, wherein a person was insane if they could not appreciate that their actions were wrong. In other words, they lack the capacity to know that society considers their actions to be wrong (Rix, 2016).

APPLY IT

The challenge of labelling abnormal behaviour

How do mental health professionals decide when a person's thinking or behaviour is not normal? They typically use four criteria to make this judgement. If a person's thinking or behaviour meets one or more of these criteria, this does not mean that a person is suffering from a psychological disorder, only that the behaviour is abnormal. Remember, the definitions of normality can vary by person, place, time, culture and situation. They can be thought of as the four 'Ds' (Davis, 2009):

Is the person's thinking or behaviour

1   *Deviant:* Is it a deviation from normal or considered rare?

2   *Dysfunctional:* Does it prevent the person from successfully adapting to life's demands?

3   *Distressful:* Is the person concerned about their thoughts or behaviour?

4   *Dangerous:* Is the person a danger to self or to others?

Here are some examples for you to evaluate.

Thinking or behaviour	Deviant	Dysfunctional	Distressful	Dangerous
Starring in a reality show	Yes	No	Maybe	No
Hearing voices when no one is around				
Participating in extreme sports				
Afraid to leave home				

Not guilty by reason of insanity (NGRI)

Variants of the **not guilty by reason of insanity (NGRI)** defence are used in Australia, Europe (except for Sweden), Canada and the USA (except for Kansas, Montana, Idaho and Utah). In most European jurisdictions, the NGRI defence can be raised in one of three ways:

1   The defendant can claim they were insane.

2   The defendant can raise a defence of **automatism**, where the judge decides it was insanity instead.

3   The defendant can raise a plea of **diminished responsibility**, where the judge or prosecution show that the insanity plea is more appropriate (VanDercar and Resnick, 2018).

However the plea of insanity is reached, the same test is used each time, as laid out in the McNaughton rule.

Irresistible impulse – *A person should not be held responsible, because they could not control their actions.*

Cognitive impairment of moral reasoning – *A person was insane if they could not appreciate that their actions were wrong.*

Not guilty by reason of insanity (NGRI) – *Admitting the crime but claiming to be mentally disturbed at the time and lacking the intention to commit the crime.*

Automatism – *The performance of actions without conscious thought or intention.*

PART III

Diminished responsibility – *An unbalanced mental state used as grounds for a reduced charge, but that does not classify them as insane.*

A frequent misconception is that the NGRI verdict frees the defendant. However, although individuals found not guilty by reason of insanity are technically acquitted of the crime with which they were charged, most of these individuals are sent to psychiatric hospitals for confinement and treatment of their mental disorder (Minhas, 2017). Unfortunately, the length of confinement frequently varies by jurisdiction and the seriousness of the offence is associated with lower rates of release (Douzenis, 2016; Silver, 1995). The unsettling conclusion is that punishment may be a higher priority than treatment and the defendant may serve a longer sentence in a psychiatric hospital than if they did not receive the NGRI verdict (Testa and West, 2010; Dirks-Linhorst and Kondrat, 2012; Vitacco et al., 2018).

IN SUMMARY

The myth is that the insanity defence represents a legal loophole and a person acquitted by reason of insanity is not treated as severely in terms of the level of security of imprisonment and length of confinement as if they were found guilty of the same crime. The reality of the insanity defence is that it is difficult to plead, seldom used and almost never successful. As a result, many jurisdictions have moved away from the legal concept of measuring sanity retrospectively. But failure to recognise the insanity defence has dire consequences, including sending mentally ill people to prison, which undermines society's theories of punishment.

 ## CRITICAL THINKING AND APPLICATION QUESTIONS

1   If a defendant uses the defence of *temporary* insanity, stating that they were insane at the time of the crime but are now sane, is the defendant responsible for their crime?

2   It can be argued that people should be punished for the harms they cause, regardless of their mental functioning. Explain why being mentally ill excuses (or does not excuse) someone from criminal guilt.

3   Imagine a jurisdiction that decided that everyone, regardless of their mental state, age or incapacity, was responsible for their legal offences. List some of the possible consequences of this decision.

MALINGERING AND ITS DETECTION

FICTION: Mental illness is easy to fake and difficult to detect.

Versus

FACT: Forensic psychologists have strategies to detect malingering and verify the true nature of the defendant.

Cosa Nostra crime boss Vincent 'the Chin' Gigante deceived psychiatric evaluators for years by feigning schizophrenia. By talking to parking meters and always wearing a bathrobe and pyjamas in public, he maintained this ruse during evaluations of his competency to stand trial for racketeering (De Stefano, 2006; Resnick and Knoll, 2005). If you are curious, the nickname 'the Chin' comes from an edict not to utter his name in public, so instead people referred to him by rubbing their chins (Rashbaum, 2005). The behaviour of 'the Chin' shows that no other syndrome is as easy to describe, yet so difficult to diagnose as malingering.

Although not classified as a mental illness, **malingering** is 'the intentional production of false or grossly exaggerated physical or psychological symptoms, motivated by external incentives' (APA, 2013a, p. 726). While defining malingering is easy, detecting malingering is difficult. For example, the DSM criteria results in accurate identification only 13.6– 20.1 per cent of the time, with 79.9–84.6 per cent of individuals wrongly classified as malingering (false positives) (Walczyk, Sewell and DiBenedetto, 2018). Australian psychologists retrospectively estimated malingering base rates in a psycholegal context to be 5–10 per cent (Yoxall, Bahr and Baring, 2010). This estimate is similar to that found by Sullivan, Lange and Dawes (2005), but lower than North American estimates of 8 per cent (Cornell and Hawk, 1989) to 17.5 per cent (McDermott, Dualan and Scott, 2013) among samples of individuals in pretrial evaluations or settings. In many jurisdictions (the USA, Australia, the UK and South Africa), the criminal trial process is delayed while a defendant who is found to lack competence to stand trial is treated and restored to competence. Defendants often misunderstand the process and think that a finding that they are not competent means that the charges will be dropped (Feuerstein et al., 2005b). Compared to those genuinely suffering from psychiatric disorders, malingerers present symptoms and other patterns of behaviour that are rare, exaggerated or atypical (Walczyk, Sewell and DiBenedetto, 2018).

> **Malingering –** *The intentional production of false or grossly exaggerated physical or psychological symptoms.*

When does malingering occur?

During the criminal justice process, individuals are tempted to feign mental illness during their fitness to stand trial and assessment of criminal responsibility phases and while attempting to influence the penalty phase of the sentence – mitigating factors upon the jury or judge's decisions (Iverson, Franzen and Hammond, 1993).

The **adaptational model of malingering** proposed by Rogers (1990) states that malingerers engage in a 'cost–benefit analysis' during assessment. Malingering is more likely to occur when the evaluation is perceived as confrontational, the personal stakes are very high, and no other alternatives appear to be practical. In the context of this model, individuals malinger based on their estimate of success in obtaining the desired external incentives, that is, a reduced penalty (Velsor and Rogers, 2018).

> **Adaptational model of malingering –** *The idea that malingerers engage in a cost–benefit analysis during assessment.*

Psychologists accept a great responsibility when assessing malingering (Weiss and van Dell, 2017). Their goal is to decrease the chances that malingerers avoid detection and evade their responsibilities to the criminal justice system. However, the misclassification of a person with a mental disorder is a serious mistake. In prison, for example, inmates may feign mental illness to do 'easier time' or obtain drugs (Jones et al., 2017). On the other hand, malingering in prison may also be an adaptive response by a mentally ill inmate to gain scarce and difficult-to-obtain mental health resources (Kupers, 2004). Failure to detect malingering in cases of fitness to stand trial or criminal responsibility can delay prosecution for months or years, resulting in unnecessary hospitalisations. It also allows malingerers to be moved from secure jails and prisons to less secure psychiatric facilities from which escape is easier (Soliman and Resnick, 2010).

Clinical versus forensic settings

In a clinical setting, there is the possibility of a misclassification of malingering. Diagnoses similar to malingering include pathological lying (pseudologia fantastica) (Frierson and

Kaustubh, 2018), giving inappropriate or misleading answers to questions (e.g., Ganser's syndrome) (Debeyne, Haekens and Peuskens, 2016), personality disorders (borderline, antisocial, histrionic, and narcissistic) (Hong, Pirnie and Shobassy, 2019) and **factitious disorder** (Bass and Wade, 2019). Both malingering and factitious disorder involve feigning physical or psychological illness. The motivation for feigning associated with factitious disorder is a desire to assume the sick role. The motivation is internal, such as the need for attention or to reduce loneliness (APA, 2013a; Jimenez et al., 2019). In malingering, external incentives are tangible. An example is a case in which a criminal defendant feigns mental illness in an attempt to be designated incompetent so as not to be punished (Resnick, 1999). On the other hand, a patient with factitious disorder who repeatedly injects insulin to induce hypoglycaemia may jeopardise their own wellbeing – a high personal cost just to assume the sick role (Jimenez et al., 2019).

In a forensic setting, the examiner must be aware of attempts to malinger to obtain external incentives. These incentives include feigning mental illness to avoid going to trial, or feigning symptoms in order to be found insane and therefore not fit to stand trial. Malingering is also referred to as 'faking bad' and reverse malingering as 'faking good' (Lurati, 2015; Meyer and Wynn, 2018). In addition to feigning or exaggerating mental illness (faking bad), forensic psychologists are likely to meet examinees who fake good, trying to show themselves in a positive light. For example, parents involved in a child custody dispute are reluctant to reveal even the most minor faults about themselves, fearing that it may jeopardise their chances of gaining custody of their children (Redondo et al., 2018; Arce, Fariña, Seijo and Novo, 2015). Similarly, applicants for law enforcement positions and police officers referred for a fitness-for-duty evaluation may attempt to fake good (Lurati, 2015).

The problem with labels

In addition to the problem of not identifying individuals who are malingering, there are also very serious consequences for misclassifying malingering when the individual is being truthful (**false positives**). Labelling an individual as a malingerer can be stigmatising and negatively impact the individual for the rest of their lives (Boone, 2011). Labelling someone as malingering can have legal implications. Therefore, some forensic psychologists recommend that the label 'malingering' be reserved for cases where the evidence for the diagnosis is undeniable (Young, 2014).

CASE STUDY   Malingering and the dangers of diagnostic labels

Psychologist David Rosenhan ran a now-famous experiment, sending undercover participants (*pseudopatients*), who were told to feign auditory hallucinations, to various psychiatric hospitals to see if the psychiatrists could tell that they were feigning mental illness. They could not.

Rosenhan's (1973) experiment began when his participants assumed false names and professions and set up appointments at hospitals claiming that they had been hearing strange voices muttering words like 'thud'. Not only was every pseudopatient admitted, but all except one received a diagnosis of schizophrenia (the other diagnosis was 'manic-depressive psychosis'). After admission, the pseudopatients acted normally and told staff that they felt fine and had not experienced any more hallucinations. During their stay, they were prescribed more than 2,000 pills, including antipsychotics and antidepressants, which were discarded. None of them were ever identified by the hospital staff. But the actual patients often had no trouble detecting them, accusing the pseudopatients of faking, with some patients stating:

'You're not crazy. You're a journalist or a professor' (Gaughwin, 2011). In fact, hospital staff would observe normal behaviour on the part of the pseudopatients and characterise it as abnormal. For example, Rosenhan instructed the pseudopatients to take notes on their experiences. A nurse observing this behaviour wrote in a daily report that the 'patient engages in writing behaviour'. Their hospitalisations ranged from 7 to 52 days. All were forced to admit to having a mental illness and agree to take antipsychotic drugs as a condition of their release (Spitzer, 1975).

Rosenhan's classic experiment applies to medical and legal situations where a diagnosis is a label that shapes our explanations of behaviour (Cummins, 2020). Once a person is labelled, we reframe their behaviour so that it matches our diagnosis. Rosenhan rebuked the admitting staff for misdiagnosing his confederates/pseudopatients. However, in their defence, they rarely need to suspect malingering in clinical settings and approach clinical interviews with a trusting and therapeutic nature.

In a provocative twist, insulted hospital administrators challenged Rosenhan to send more pseudopatients to their hospitals for detection. Rosenhan agreed and, in the following weeks, out of 250 new patients, the staff identified 41 as potential pseudopatients. Rosenhan had sent *no* pseudopatients to the hospital (Frances, 2013).

Discussion Questions:

1   In Rosenhan's study, why were the hospital patients able to identify the pseudopatients but the staff were not? Consider the different perspectives and expectations of patients and medical personnel.

2   Why do we label people with an illness? Rosenhan (1973) criticises the psychiatric assumption that 'once a schizophrenic, always a schizophrenic', regardless of whether a patient was in remission. Do you believe that this is the common assumption regarding mental illness? What evidence can you present to support or refute this question?

Experiments like Rosenhan's feed the false belief that mental illness can be easily feigned. After all, if psychiatrists and other trained medical personnel can be fooled, then why not judges and juries? Rosenhan's experiment also shows that labels such as 'insane', 'incompetent' and 'mentally ill' alter our perceptions of people with mental impairments and can become a self-fulfilling prophesy (Merckelbach and Merten, 2012).

Ways of detecting malingering

Reliably diagnosing malingered mental illness is complex, requiring the psychologist to consider data beyond the patient interview (Resnick, 1999). The benchmark for the detection of malingered psychosis involves expert clinical assessment augmented by standardised psychometric testing (Pierre, 2019). Forensic psychologists rely on their clinical skills and psychological tests to detect the presence and extent of malingering during an evaluation. Most tests that are designed to detect malingering assume that the examinee is naive and will exaggerate or produce symptoms not generally seen in clinical populations (Singh, Avasthi and Grover, 2007). There are two main categories of malingering: psychiatric symptoms and cognitive impairment (Roesch, Zaph and Hart, 2010). Malingering psychiatric symptoms requires pretending to experience symptoms of a mental illness, while malingering cognitive impairment involves pretending to suffer from memory or other impairments (Rodes, 2018).

The forensic interview

The interview begins with open-ended questions, to allow patients to report symptoms in their own words. The interview is critical in the assessment of malingering; if responses trigger suspicion of malingering, interviewers should be cautious in how they frame questions, avoiding leading questions that might give defendants clues about how a genuine syndrome reveals itself. The challenge of this phase of the interview is to carefully phrase the initial inquiries about the client's symptoms to avoid suggesting the correct responses. For example, 'How are you today?' versus 'Do you have any strange thoughts, visions or other hallucinations?' As the interview progresses, it proceeds to more detailed questions of specific symptoms (Rogers, Gillis, Dickens and Bagby, 1991). After defendants are given a chance to report symptoms in their own words, interviewers can ask specific, detailed questions that help to characterise symptoms as typical or atypical. More signs of feigning are individuals who endorse rare or implausible symptoms. Logically, because rare symptoms occur very infrequently, even severely disturbed patients almost never report improbable symptoms (Thompson, LeBourgeois, Black, 2004).

Rogers, Gillis, Bagba and Monteiro (1991) recommend several essential steps during this phase of the process. Surprisingly, they recommend not confronting the malingerer with the suspicion of lying in order to conduct an objective evaluation. Their rationale is that defendants are likely to become defensive if they perceive any doubt and putting them on their guard decreases the ability to uncover evidence of malingering. Rogers (2008, p. 61) cautions that 'malingerers may attempt to take control of the interview and behave in an intimidating or hostile manner'. Furthermore, in a defensive reaction, they may accuse the psychiatrist of inferring that they are faking, although Rogers (2008) indicates that such behaviour is rare in genuinely psychotic individuals. Another strategy malingerer's use is feigning intellectual deficits, in the belief that it will make their story more genuine. For example, Resnick and Knoll (2005) cite the example of a man who had a college education and alleged that he did not know the colours of his country's flag.

Psychiatric malingering detection strategies

Assessment instruments used to detect psychiatric malingering include the Structured Interview of Reported Symptoms (SIRS-2), the Minnesota Multiphasic Personality Inventory-2-Restructured Form (MMPI-2-RF) and the Miller Forensic Assessment of Symptoms Test (M-FAST). These three instruments are now briefly described.

Structured Interview of Reported Symptoms (SIRS-2)

Forensic psychologists can evaluate the potential for malingering in a structured interview format using the second version of the Structured Interview of Reported Symptoms (SIRS-2). The SIRS-2 was developed to assess deliberate distortions in the self-report of symptoms (Rogers, Sewell and Gillard, 2010) and is the most commonly used and best validated assessment tool in the forensic detection of malingering (Becke et al., 2019). The updated SIRS-2 helps evaluate feigning of psychiatric symptoms with questions about rare symptoms, uncommon symptom pairing, atypical symptoms, and other indices involving excessive symptom reporting (Dixon, 1995). The primary focus of the SIRS-2 is on the evaluation of feigning and the manner in which it is likely to occur, such as an exaggeration of symptom severity rather than just creating false symptoms (Edens, Poythress and Watkins-Clay, 2007).

Minnesota Multiphasic Personality Inventory-2-Restructured Form (MMPI-2-RF)

The Minnesota Multiphasic Personality Inventory-2-Restructured Form (MMPI-2-RF) is one of the most widely used personality inventories (Sellbom, 2019). The MMPI-2-RF, a new version of the MMPI-2, was published in 2008. The MMPI-2-RF uses an empirical keying approach, which means that the scales, or categories, were derived by selecting items that were endorsed by patients known to have been diagnosed with certain pathologies (Ben-Porath and Tellegen, 2011). This test is a 338-item, true/false self-report measure of a person's psychological state. It has validity scales (or 'lie' scales) that assess lying, defensiveness, faking good and faking bad among others (Goldsworthy and Donders, 2019). These scales make it very difficult to fake the MMPI-2-RF results. This test has a 'lie' scale of 15 items measuring social desirability, the tendency for respondents to give answers that are socially desirable or socially acceptable, but not necessarily true. The MMPI-2-RF has a scale known as the 'Fb' scale that seeks to detect 'faking bad' response styles (Butcher et al., 1989; Pelfrey, 2004). This technique offers the ability to differentiate between people instructed to malinger and actual psychiatric patients (Iverson, Frazen and Hammond, 1993).

Miller Forensic Assessment of Symptoms Test (M-FAST)

The Miller Forensic Assessment of Symptoms Test (M-FAST) is a 25-item structured interview (Miller, 2001) that can be administered in 5–10 minutes. The measure is more useful because of its interview format (the reading level of the test taker is irrelevant) and its brief administration time. The test uses an interesting approach of measuring reported versus observed behaviours, extreme symptoms, rare combinations and unusual hallucinations (Detullio, Messer, Kennedy and Millen, 2019). What makes the M-FAST different is its three additional scales. It measures reported speed of onset of mental illness (unusual symptom course), the tendency of malingerers to believe that they should be viewed negatively by others (negative image), and the chance likelihood that malingerers will endorse symptoms that they believe will make them appear mentally ill (suggestibility) (Vitacco, Rogers, Babel and Munizza, 2007). The M-FAST includes items that represent these detection strategies along with items that reflect actual symptoms of mental illness (Miller, 2004). The M-FAST was developed at a forensic hospital with patients who were either found NGRI or incompetent to stand trial. In all the samples, the M-FAST effectively discriminated between genuine psychiatric patients and those who were found to be faking mental illness for secondary gain (Miller, 2001).

Tests to detect cognitive malingering detection strategies

Unlike the tests of psychological impairment, cognitive tests of malingering focus on excessive memory impairment and unexpected patterns of responses. Responses detected by these strategies include performance failures on items that are typically achievable by persons with actual cognitive impairments and the detection of failure rates that are statistically unlikely. Two such tests are briefly described here.

The Test of Memory Malingering (TOMM)

The Test of Memory Malingering (TOMM) is a visual recognition test designed to distinguish between malingered and true memory impairments. Research has found the TOMM to be sensitive to malingering and insensitive to a wide variety of neurological impairments, which makes it very reliable (Brand, Webermann, Snyder and Kaliush, 2019). The TOMM has 50 items and consists of two memory learning trials, with each trial followed by an assessment of recognition memory. The theory behind the TOMM is to present cognitive tasks that malingerers incorrectly believe impaired individuals are incapable of completing accurately (Martin et al., 2019). The test shows the subject a series of line drawings followed by a recognition assessment in which each drawing is presented alongside a foil. The subject is asked to identify the previously presented drawing and given feedback about the correctness of their response.

> **False negatives** – *A test result that incorrectly indicates that a particular condition or attribute is absent.*

Word Memory Test (WMT)

The Word Memory Test (WMT) applies the learning principle that memory recognition performance is better than recall (Tversky, 1973). Individuals attempting to malinger do not account for this learning principle in their efforts to deceive. The test presents the participant with 20 pairs of semantically related words during two learning trials. Scoring is accomplished by comparing the number of words recognised consistently across the immediate and delayed trials (Armistead-Jehle, Green, Gervais and Hungerford, 2015). However, Pella et al. (2012) warn that the WMT may be particularly vulnerable to coaching, resulting in a high rate of **false negatives**.

IN SUMMARY

There is no perfect method to identify malingering, and its detection and management raise procedural, ethical and legal questions. The detection of malingering requires strong clinical insight as well as sound psychological assessment. Tests have been developed to assist the forensic psychologist in identifying malingering. However, no single test should be used as the basis for a forensic decision. Rather, a battery of tests combined with interviews and third-party reports can assist the examiner in developing an informed opinion.

 CRITICAL THINKING AND APPLICATION QUESTIONS

1   As a forensic psychologist, consider the practical, ethical and legal issues that might arise when assessing an 80-year-old defendant who is malingering because he will receive a life sentence if convicted of his crime.

2   If you ran the Rosenhan study today, would you find the same results? Has the way we admit and assess people who may suffer from a mental impairment changed? You may want to research the intake procedures used by hospitals in your jurisdiction and country.

3   How much do you believe that those who assess defendants for malingering are biased by knowledge of the defendant's crime? How could you redesign the assessment procedures to avoid bias from contaminating the malingering assessment procedure?

NEUROSCIENCE AND THE INSANITY DEFENSE: DO BAD BRAINS CAUSE BAD BEHAVIOUR?

FICTION: All people can behave rationally and make rational decisions.

Versus

FACT: Rational thought and behaviour is not the default for all people and human behaviour cannot be separated from human biology.

For over 100 years, the term 'insanity' has been retired from the medical vocabulary, yet despite advancements in neuroscience, we still adhere to the original standards of the legal insanity defence (Weiss, Freidman, Hatters and Shand, 2019). The legal insanity defence was created to understand the defendant's mind when mental illness was misunderstood and rarely acknowledged (Walker, 1985). Yet there is a large gap between the psychological and legal understanding of mental illness (Math, Kumar and Moirangthem, 2015). Presently, many mental impairments are now considered brain disorders arising from physical causes, such as chemical imbalances and traumatic brain injury (Angermeyer, Holzinger, Carta and Schomerus, 2011; Rose, 2016). On the one hand, some have called for a neurological defence on the grounds that brain diseases may excuse the crime (Nestor, 2019; Marcopulos, Welner and Campbell, 2019; Redding, 2006), while others express concern that brain images mislead juries, giving them the mistaken impression that the brain is entirely responsible for human behaviour. This perspective offers an excuse for criminal behaviours based on any brain abnormality in the defendant (Hardcastle and Lamb, 2018; Morse, 2004; Rachul and Zarzeczny, 2012).

Neuroscience can be used as a source of knowledge to improve the accuracy of the psycholegal assumptions that support criminal responsibility (LaDuke, Locklair and Heilbrun, 2018; Rose, 2000). The introduction of neuroscientific data by forensic experts in criminal trials can be used to evaluate an offender's dangerousness, rather than their responsibility (Gkotsi and Gasser, 2016). But when does our ability to control dangerous thoughts and behaviours begin and end? This was the essential question behind the actions of Charles Whitman.

CASE STUDY

Charles Whitman and the neuroscience of free will

It was after much thought that I decided to kill my wife, Kathy, tonight ... I love her dearly, and she has been as fine a wife to me as any man could ever hope to have. I cannot rationaly [sic] pinpoint any specific reason for doing this ... I intend to kill her as painlessly as possible. (Holmes and Holmes, 2010, p. 74)

In 1966, Charles Whitman wrote a letter confessing his plan to kill his wife. In the letter, Whitman described suffering from overwhelming violent impulses and tremendous headaches. At the end of his letter, for similarly unknown reasons, Whitman then added that he intended to kill his mother. This he did. Having killed his wife and his mother, and after a night's rest, he took the lift to the 28th floor of the University of Texas Tower. With an assortment of rifles, he began targeting people in the vicinity. Altogether, Whitman killed 14 people and wounded 31 in 96 minutes, before he was killed by police officers (Colloff, 2016).

PART III

As a child, Whitman was very bright, scoring in the highest 1 per cent on the Stanford-Binet IQ test (Eagleman, 2011). He joined the Marines and was an accomplished marksman. In his early twenties he got married, bought a dog and enrolled at the University of Texas. However, unbeknown to Whitman, a tumour was growing deep within his brain. By 1966, the 25-year-old Whitman was suffering from severe headaches and consulted a therapist at the university to discuss the concerns he had over his mental health (Ponder, 2018). The evening before the killings, Whitman had sat at his typewriter and composed a suicide note:

> I don't really understand myself these days. I am supposed to be an average reasonable and intelligent young man. However, lately (I can't recall when it started) I have been a victim of many unusual and irrational thoughts. (Burka, 1986, p. 169)

In the letter, Whitman also indicated that he wanted his brain examined after his death to check for signs of a physical cause of mental illness (Lavergne, 1997). His request was granted, and it showed that he had a tumour, nestled between his thalamus, hypothalamus and amygdala. All three structures are related to emotional responding and control (Blair, 2016).

Research shows that tumours located in these regions can trigger 'intermittent explosive disorder', a disorder characterised by recurrent and severe aggressive behaviour with symptoms eerily similar to those of Whitman (Gouveia et al., 2019; Fanning, Coleman, Lee and Coccaro, 2018; Coccaro et al., 2015). Although his actions seemed planned and deliberate, given what we now know about his condition, it is hard to confirm that he was acting under his own free will (Madhusoodanan, Ting, Farah and Ugur, 2015). The letters written by Whitman on the eve of his killing spree provide a terrifying view into a mind losing the ability to understand good, bad and other people.

Discussion Questions:

1   Does the discovery of Charles Whitman's tumour change your beliefs about the senseless murders he committed? Specifically, if he survived, would it affect the type of sentence you would find appropriate for his crime?

2   Would it be dangerous to conclude that people with brain tumours are free of guilt, and that they should not be responsible for their crimes? Under what conditions would you hold someone responsible for their behaviour?

3   Are there any similar medical conditions that affect a person's ability to control their behaviour and thus their blameworthiness? Should we see similar subjects as patients or offenders, or both?

Diagnosing mental illness

Modern methods of diagnosing a mental illness involve rigorously identifying symptoms according to a standardised diagnostic classification system. These systems provide reliable psychiatric diagnoses. Two widely accepted methods include the *International Statistical Classification of Diseases and Related Health Problems* (ICD-11) and the *Diagnostic and Statistical Manual of Mental Disorders*, 5th edition, DSM-5 (APA, 2013a). The ICD-11 includes a section classifying mental and behavioural disorders (Chapter V).

How will advances in neuroscience affect the insanity defence?

Theoretically, any mental or medical condition could serve as a basis for an insanity defence, although most countries limit the conditions that can be considered for that purpose (Szasz, 1986; Yamamoto, Maeder and Fenwick, 2017). In many jurisdictions, for example the UK, Australia, the USA and Canada, to be released from responsibility for your behaviour, the condition must impede your cognition or your freedom of intention, or, in rare cases, both. For example, the highest rate of impaired decision making among psychiatric disorders is schizophrenia, followed by depression and bipolar disorder (Sorrentino, 2014).

As our understanding of the human brain improves, judges and juries are challenged by questions of biological responsibility and free will. This new understanding is causing changes in both our laws and society (Meynen, 2018). The research field studying the impact of neuroscience on the law and legal practices is called **neurolaw** (Hoffman, 2018). Neuroscientists assume that the essential ingredients of our human condition, including free will, empathy and morality, are the predictable consequences of immense assemblies of communicating neurons (Mobbs, Lau, Jones and Frith, 2007).

The presence of abnormal brain function due to injury, tumour and epilepsy has been used successfully as the basis for an insanity defence in criminal cases for hundreds of years (Mobbs, Lau, Jones and Frith, 2007). The key to the success of these defences lies in the concrete and observable nature of the abnormality: judges and juries can see the tumour on a brain scan, and may be presented with evidence that the criminal behaviour did not occur before the injury or that it stops after treatment (Matthews, 2004). The relationship between brain injury and behavioural abnormalities associated with criminal behaviour (aggression, violence, impulsivity and apathy) is found among incarcerated groups (Farrer and Hedges, 2011) and juvenile offenders (Farrer, Frost and Hedges, 2013).

Neurolaw – *The research field studying the impact of neuroscience on the law and legal practices.*

Three examples of brain changes that led to behavioural changes

Examples of the brain–behaviour relationship show that even slight changes in the balance of brain chemistry can cause large and unexpected changes in behaviour (Ott and Nieder, 2019). For example, small amounts of the drug Mirapex (pramipexole) dramatically changed the lives of Parkinson's patients. Sufferers of Parkinson's disease have brains that lack the neurotransmitter dopamine and pramipexole works by increasing what dopamine is left. However, dopamine plays two roles: besides helping people move again, it also motivates the brain towards food, drink, mating and other behaviours useful for survival (Robinson et al., 2015). Because of dopamine's role in rewarding behaviours, it changes our ability to make rational decisions (Ott and Nieder, 2019). It triggers compulsive behaviours like overeating, drug addiction and gambling. Under the influence of Mirapex, many of these patients, who had never gambled before, became compulsive gamblers, some gambling for days at a time, others losing hundreds of thousands of dollars in a few months. One patient was a 63-year-old man who previously gambled at casinos once every three months with no overspending. Under the effect of the medication, he gambled two to three times per week, with an 'incredible compulsion' even when he 'logically knew it was time to quit'. He described this as a 'unique behaviour' and stated that he 'had never experienced anything like this before' (Dodd et al. 2005, p. 1378). For some, the addictive behaviours included compulsive drinking, eating and hypersexuality (Johnson et al., 2011). Fortunately, the negative effects of the drug are reversible and lowering the dose makes the compulsive behaviours disappear.

Another example that illustrates the relationship between changes in the brain and behaviour is that of a 40-year-old schoolteacher who suddenly developed a voracious interest in child pornography and sexually propositioned his prepubescent stepdaughter and all the female staff of the treatment programme to which he was sentenced. After complaining of worsening headaches, he underwent a brain scan, which revealed an egg-sized tumour pressing on the right frontal lobe. When surgeons removed it, the lewd behaviour and paedophilia faded away (Eagleman, 2011). But, a year after his brain surgery, his paedophilic behaviour returned. Brain scans revealed that the first surgery did not remove the entire tumour and it was regrowing. After the removal of the remaining tumour, his behaviour again returned to normal (Slobogin, 2017).

A third example of the brain–behaviour relationship is the role our frontal lobes play in making rational choices and predicting the consequences of our actions (Ling, Umbach and Raine, 2019; Brower and Price, 2001). When the frontal lobes are damaged, people make startlingly poor choices (Fuster, 2015), for example those diagnosed with *frontotemporal dementia*, a disease similar to Alzheimer's except the frontal and temporal lobes of the brain degenerate (Besnard et al., 2017). The loss of brain tissue is followed by the loss of impulse control (Roberts, Henry and Molenberghs, 2018). Often to the frustration and embarrassment of their loved ones, these patients begin shoplifting in front of security personnel, removing their clothing in public, and become physically or sexually violent (Neary, Snowden and Mann, 2005). Individuals with frontotemporal dementia often end up in front of a judge where their representative must explain that the violation was not their fault because much of their brain is gone and there is no medical treatment. We know that this specific disease is related to this type of behaviour because 42 per cent of frontotemporal dementia patients engage in criminal behaviour as compared with only 15 per cent of Alzheimer's patients (Liljegren et al., 2019).

These three cases illustrate how neuroscience evidence relates to the definition of legal insanity. The outcome raises questions about how changes in brain structure and chemistry influence behaviour and judgement. The challenge is proving to the judicial system that these changes *cause* the individual to lose the ability to control impulses or anticipate the consequences of their choices.

Ways that neuroscience can improve and inform the concept of legal sanity

It is time that neuroscience and the law spoke the same language about issues of criminal responsibility, punishment and rehabilitation. Without this conversation, the insanity defence will collapse, given the restrictions on its use and its frequent lack of success (Gooding and Bennet, 2018; Meynen, 2016). The insanity defence should continue to play a role in our legal conception of moral blameworthiness and there are ways that neuroscience can create more effective and efficient systems.

Using neuroscience to determine the blameworthiness of an offender is controversial (Chambon and Bigenwald, 2019; Morse, 2019). Some question the extent of its utility, arguing that neuroscience is unrelated to legal matters or only useful for confirming evidence of a legal impairment proved through other means (Maoz and Yaffe, 2016; Fuchs, 2006). Others argue that neuroscience shows that most offenders lack control over their behaviour (Bonicalzi and Haggard, 2019). In between are those who advocate adopting a balanced perspective between the fields of neuroscience and law by accepting pragmatic strategies for combating mass incarceration and recidivism (Anderson and Kiehl, 2020; Nestor, 2019).

First, neuroscience holds the promise of explaining the operations of the mind in terms of the physical operations of the brain. Therefore, neuroscience can support diagnoses of mental illness by providing reproducible, biological evidence about individuals with neurological illness or injury (Moriarty, 2016). For example, most jurisdictions have minimum ages of accountability, such as age 10 in Australia and the UK and age 12 in Canada and the USA. These legal policies guiding responsibility and autonomy are based on decades old neuroscience research showing that brain structures and the communication between them continue to change into early adulthood, affecting impulsiveness and judgement (Johnson and Giedd, 2015; Lebel and Beaulieu, 2011). If more research develops along these lines, then the legal system would be more receptive of legal insanity (Delmage, 2014).

Second, developing neuroscience has the potential to show the relationship between irrational thinking and abnormal behaviour. For example, increases in brain injuries from combat (Hardy, Kennedy, Reid and Cooper, 2020; Chen and Zhao, 2019) and sports (Golden and Zusman, 2019; Finkel and Bieniek, 2019) have led to research demonstrating the relationship between brain injury, rational thoughts and voluntary behaviour. This data could help develop appropriate strategies for sentencing, where criminals are removed from public interaction, but their sentencing is customised with new opportunities for brain-based rehabilitation (Geraldo et al., 2018; Day et al., 2016).

Third, developing neuroscience will shape our opinions about moral blameworthiness in the legal system and the appropriate use of treatment and punishment. To do this, the focus should shift from the current backward-looking assessment of criminal responsibility used to determine insanity to a forward-looking treatment of the person with mental impairment. As Eagleman (2011) states, the questions now focus on using neuroscience to predict the chances of repeating criminal behaviours and the potential for change. For example, individuals with frontal lobe brain damage who cannot control their actions and emotions should receive post-sentence treatment instead of incarceration (Lamparello, 2011).

Finally, any mature criminal justice system must recognise that because of serious mental illness some people are not responsible for their behaviours. Punishing these people the same way we punish those who act reasonably and responsibly makes neither logical nor moral sense (Keram, 2002; Janofsky et al., 2014). Perhaps the road to insanity defence reform is about our readiness to accept a justice system that values the consistent application of compassion and justice, regardless of the circumstances of the defendant (Bonnie, 1983).

IN SUMMARY

Rational thought and behaviour are not the norm for all people and human behaviour cannot be separated from human biology. The emerging field of neurolaw questions our biological responsibility and free will. This changes the way we think about criminal responsibility, punishment and rehabilitation.

 ## CRITICAL THINKING AND APPLICATION QUESTIONS

1   Is the definition of legal insanity too broad or too narrow? For your argument, think about cases when defendants cannot appreciate the wrongfulness of their actions and defendants who cannot control their behaviours.

2   Given the advances in medical knowledge since the McNaughton rule was established, do we still need an 'insanity defence'? Would individuals with severe mental illness suffer more or less without it?

3   Should we treat mental disorders merely as brain diseases? What are the pros and cons of taking this position?

CHAPTER REVIEW

In this chapter, we have explored empirical knowledge about the insanity defence, its level of use, and what happens to those who are acquitted by reason of insanity. The reality of the insanity defence is that it is difficult to plead, seldom used and almost never successful. Paradoxically, public concern is that the insanity defence is a loophole through which offenders escape punishment for illegal acts. The public belief in this myth is poorly aligned with reality, where the layperson overestimates the use and success of the insanity defence and underestimates the extent to which insanity acquitters are confined upon acquittal. The answer to merging these two opposite opinions lies in rejecting proposals to abolish the insanity defence, in favour of proposals to narrow it and shift the burden of proof to the defendant. This conservative approach adequately responds to public concern about possible misuse of the insanity defence and is compatible with the basic doctrines and principles of law.

NAMES TO KNOW

Michael Perlin

An internationally recognised expert on mental disability law and how the legal system deals with individuals with mental disorders or intellectual disability.

- Perlin, M. L. (2013) *A Prescription for Dignity: Rethinking Criminal Justice and Mental Disability Law*. Ashgate.

- Perlin, M. L. (2000) *The Hidden Prejudice: Mental Disability on Trial*. APA.

V.S. Ramachandran

His investigations into phantom limb pain, synaesthesia and other brain disorders offer explanations into the philosophical questions about the nature of self and human consciousness. His book *Phantoms in the Brain* (1998) about rare neurological disorders was adapted as a miniseries on BBC TV.

- Ramachandran, V. S. (2007) 3 clues to understanding your brain. TED Talks; (2009) The neurons that shaped civilization. TED Talks.

- Ramachandran, V. S. (2012) *The Tell-Tale Brain: A Neuroscientist's Quest for What Makes Us Human*. W.W. Norton & Company.

- Ramachandran, V. S. (2004) *A Brief Tour of Human Consciousness: From Impostor Poodles to Purple Numbers*. Pi Press.

David Eagleman

Directs the non-profit Center for Science & Law, which seeks to align the legal system with modern neuroscience. He is known for his work on brain plasticity, time perception, synaesthesia and neurolaw.

- Eagleman, D. M. (2015) Can we create new senses for humans? TED Talks.

- Eagleman, D. M. (2012) *Incognito: The Secret Lives of the Brain*. Knopf Doubleday.

- Eagleman, D. M. (2004) Neuroscience: The where and when of intention. *Science*, 303(5661), 1144–6.

PART IV

APPLYING PSYCHOLOGY TO FORENSIC TECHNIQUES

9 CORRECTIONAL PSYCHOLOGY: RISK ASSESSMENT, THREAT AND RECIDIVISM

Chapter Introduction

In the justice system there are many risks to assess. A prison officer assesses whether a depressed inmate is suicidal. A parole board assesses the likelihood of an inmate adjusting to life in the community and correctional psychologists assess an offender's progress in rehabilitation. The effectiveness of rehabilitation depends on how offenders are treated, and it is time to make a choice. We can punish offenders more severely and risk changing them for the worse, or we can apply psychological principles to help people change for the better. Can we predict reoffending? A close examination of different programmes shows potential if applied in the correct manner. Perhaps the best way is based on the risk they present, what they need, and in what kinds of environments they should be placed.

Learning Outcomes

What are the purposes of punishment?
- Explain the purposes of punishment from a deterrence perspective.

Psychological effects of imprisonment
- Explain the effects of incarceration and the psychological impact of institutionalisation.

The psychology behind effective prison rehabilitation programmes
- Demonstrate how different perspectives on rehabilitation can be effectively applied to change criminal behaviour in prisons.

Reducing recidivism: the risk-needs-responsivity model
- Describe how the components of the risk-needs-responsivity model are applied to reduce recidivism.

WHAT ARE THE PURPOSES OF PUNISHMENT?

FICTION: Prisons are designed to change behaviour with punishing consequences.

Versus

FACT: Punishment is not the most effective approach for lasting behaviour change.

CASE STUDY

Do prisons have to be ugly to be effective?

Source: Fairfax Media/Getty Images

A high-risk management cell at Goulburn Correctional Centre, New South Wales, Australia

Static security – *A prison philosophy to maintain safety using an environment designed to prevent improper behaviour.*

Dynamic security – *A prison philosophy using interpersonal relationships between the staff and the inmates as the primary factor in maintaining safety.*

The Goulburn Correctional Centre in Australia and Halden Prison in Norway are both maximum-security prisons. The psychological theories behind these maximum-security prisons are vastly different. Goulburn Correctional Centre was designed to manage behaviour and combat prison violence and riots (Grant and Jewkes, 2015). Inmates eat all their meals alone in their cell and spend only an hour a day out of their cell. Goulburn prison relies on **static security** designed to prevent an inmate with bad intentions from enacting them. Inmates are monitored by cameras, contained by remote-controlled doors, prevented from vandalism or weapon-making by tamper-proof furniture, and burdened by shackles with officer escorts when moved. The officers are trained to control offenders with as little interaction as possible, minimising the risk of altercation (Abdel-Salam and Sunde, 2018).

In contrast, Halden Prison is designed to simulate a village where offenders can consider themselves part of a society, just as if they were outside prison. Halden Prison relies on **dynamic security** to foster interpersonal relationships between the staff and the inmates and maintain safety by preventing dangerous behaviours from happening in the first place (Farley and Pike, 2016). The guard stations are small, which encourages guards to spend more time in common rooms with the inmates. Inmates can be watched via surveillance cameras on the prison grounds, but they often move unaccompanied by guards. This requires trust, which the administrators believe is crucial for rehabilitation.

Which prison's rehabilitation approach is the most successful? One way to measure success is by measuring the rate of **recidivism** – criminal acts that result in rearrest, reconviction or a return to prison (Lovell, Johnson and Cain, 2007). In Norway, only 20 per cent of offenders returned to prison after release between 2015 and 2018, compared with 54 per cent in Australia and 76 per cent in the USA (Walmsley, 2018; Australian Institute of Criminology, 2019; Alper, Durose and Markman, 2018). If the goal of incarceration is to reduce recidivism, then Halden Prison's approach is the most successful.

> **Recidivism** –
> *The tendency of a convicted criminal to reoffend.*

Discussion Questions:

1   Imagine spending 23 hours per day in a cell in the Goulburn Correctional Centre. What strategies would you use to cope with this environment? What would the passage of time feel like?

2   Is Halden Prison too comfortable for offenders? What information is your response based on? *Remember your response to this question as you read about the theories of punishment in this chapter to see where your perspective lies.*

Punishment and behaviour change

Many jurisdictions with growing rates of incarceration and longer sentences have seen a hardening of public attitudes towards crime. As a result, most criminal justice systems rely nearly exclusively on punishment as the mechanism for reducing crime and reoffending (Carvalho, Chamberlen and Duff, 2019). An example is the US's 'tough on crime' era beginning in the 1980s that increased prison populations and resulted in the highest incarceration rates in the world (Shjarback and Young, 2018), and to a lesser extent Australia's similar mandatory minimum sentencing policies (Lovell, Guthrie, Simpson and Butler, 2018; Mackay, 2015). The purpose of these stricter policies was to punish more individuals more severely. Massive capital investment expanded prisons and changed sentencing laws, including mandatory sentences (Sundt, Schwaeble and Merritt, 2017), mandatory minimum sentences (Tonry, 2018) and habitual offender laws – the three strikes law in the USA (DeVault, Miller and Griffin, 2016).

Universally, prison is one of the most severe forms of punishment, but is this punishment effective? While punishment does effectively suppress unwanted behaviour, rewards are still the preferred choice because punishment has the following limitations:

- Any behaviour change resulting from punishment is often temporary (Ateah, Secco and Woodgate, 2003).

- The punished behaviour often reappears when the punishment is withdrawn (Skinner, 1953; Gershoff, 2002).

- Punishment can produce aggression (King et al., 2018) and learned helplessness (Seligman, 1972).

- Punishment does not teach alternative behaviours to do, but only what behaviours *not* to do (Gendreau, 1996).

Why do we put people in prison? Is it to protect society, rehabilitate or punish? There is no right answer because a case can be made for each of these options (Kunen, 2017). When evaluating the reasons for prisons, we begin by exploring the theories of punishment.

PART IV

Theories of punishment

Theories of punishment can be viewed from two broad perspectives: utilitarian and retributive. While the **utilitarian perspective** punishes offenders to discourage future wrong behaviour, the **retributive perspective** punishes offenders because they deserve to be punished (Collica-Cox and Sullivan, 2017). From a utilitarian perspective, laws should maximise society's happiness and because crime and punishment reduce happiness, they should be minimised (Viner, 1949). The utilitarian perspective recognises that punishment should not be limitless but in proportion to the severity of the crime. For example, in a bank robbery, the person with the gun receives more punishment and blame than the driver of the getaway car. In contrast, the retributive perspective focuses on the crime itself as the reason for imposing punishment. If humans have free will and make rational decisions, then a person who makes a conscious choice to offend should be punished (Ezorsky, 2015). Retribution is the idea that it is fair, reasonable and correct to reward evil with evil (Webster and Saucier, 2015).

Figure 9.1: Perspectives and theories of punishment

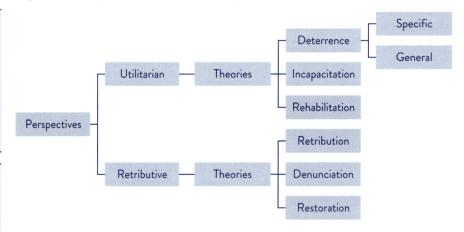

As shown in Figure 9.1, the first three theories fall under the utilitarian category and the last three under the retributive category:

- **Deterrence theory** believes that the threat of punishment will discourage people from committing crime (Lee and McCrary, 2017). From the utilitarian perspective, deterrence operates on two levels: **specific deterrence** – the effectiveness of punishment to motivate an *individual* to change their future behaviour and **general deterrence** – the effectiveness of individual punishment to prevent *others* from committing crime (Fehr, 2019).

- **Incapacitation theory** suggests that holding individuals in prison will prevent them from committing new crimes (Pereboom, 2018; Augustyn and McGloin, 2017). Related to incarceration, there is an important distinction. Individuals behind bars cannot commit additional crimes – this is incarceration as *incapacitation*. Before committing a crime, an individual may fear incarceration and refrain from committing future crimes – this is incarceration as *deterrence* (Nagin, 2013).

Utilitarian perspective – Punishing discourages future wrongful behaviour.

Retributive perspective – Punishing offenders because they deserve to be punished.

Deterrence theory – The threat of punishment will discourage people from committing crime.

Specific deterrence – The punishment should prevent the same person from committing crimes.

General deterrence – The punishment should prevent other people from committing criminal actions.

- **Rehabilitation theory** suggests that directing offenders to treatment or training programmes will change the individual, thus keeping them from committing new offences (Moss, Lee, Berman and Rung, 2019).

- **Retribution theory** suggests that a person who makes an intentional decision to violate laws should be punished for their decision so that the person can pay their debt to society (Hanna, 2019).

- **Denunciation theory** suggests that punishing someone publicly prevents others from committing the same offence due to the stigma associated with it (Bergemann, 2017).

- **Restoration theory** emphasises repairing the harm caused by criminal behaviour; crime causes harm and justice should repair that harm (Silva and Samimi, 2018).

Among the theories of punishment, deterrence offers the strongest pragmatic and theoretical foundation for many criminal justice policies and programmes (Chalfin and McCrary, 2017).

Deterrence theory

The everyday work of individuals employed in law enforcement, corrections and other parts of the criminal justice system involves identifying, capturing, prosecuting, sentencing and incarcerating offenders. The function of these activities is deterring individuals from committing illegal activity in the first place (Lee and McCrary, 2017). Deterrence is important not only because it results in lower crime but also because, relative to incapacitation, it is less expensive (Hylton, 2019). The effectiveness of deterrence to reduce crime is difficult to measure because people obey laws for other reasons, such as religious beliefs, moral beliefs or physical incapacitation (Chalfin and McCrary, 2017). Deterrence theory is a process of influence (Figure 9.2).

Figure 9.2: The process of deterrence

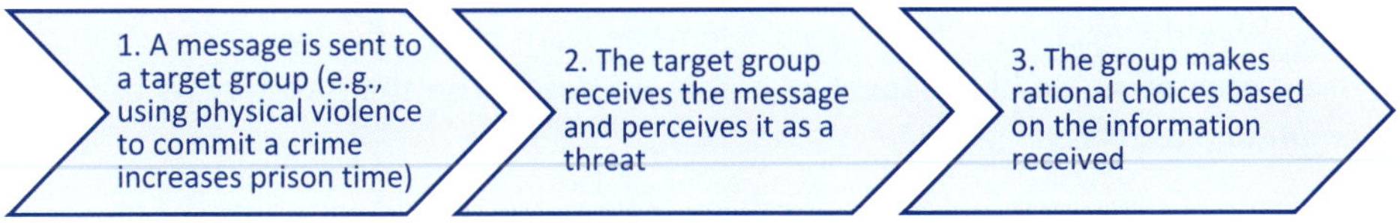

1. A message is sent to a target group (e.g., using physical violence to commit a crime increases prison time)

2. The target group receives the message and perceives it as a threat

3. The group makes rational choices based on the information received

Among the three processes, the first is the easiest to enact. Most people are aware that it is wrong to harm another person or steal and so on, although they may not be aware of the specific penalties for crimes other than incarceration. Parts two and three are more challenging. It is assumed that everyone will be threatened by the penalty for the crime; however, this is not always true. For some individuals, being arrested and serving time in jail or prison is a way of life (Paterline and Orr, 2016), while others do not make rational choices, especially while under the influence of drugs and/or alcohol (Chapman et al., 2010). This is why consciously planned crimes are more easily deterred than those caused by substance misuse or sudden unexpected emotional reactions (Chalfin and McCrary, 2017).

Incapacitation theory – *Holding individuals in prison prevents those individuals from committing new crimes.*

Rehabilitation theory – *Directing offenders to treatment or training programmes changes that individual and keeps them from committing new offences.*

Retribution theory – *A theory of punishment that when an offender breaks the law, justice requires that they suffer in return.*

Denunciation theory – *Punishing someone publicly will prevent others from committing the offence.*

PART IV

Three components of deterrence theory

Individuals respond to changes in the certainty, severity and celerity of punishment. **Celerity of punishment** refers to the effectiveness of the speed of punishment in reducing illicit behaviour (Buckenmaier, Dimant, Posten and Ulrich, 2019). A punishment imposed immediately after an offence is more effective than one that is delayed (Dušek, 2015). **Severity of punishment** is an important component because a rational person might commit a crime that brings a benefit even if punishment is swift when the consequence is insignificant. **Certainty of punishment** applies to the likelihood of being caught. The threat of a severe punishment is not effective if there is no possibility of ever being caught. These approaches have the potential to increase deterrence but are they equally effective?

- *Celerity:* Punishment is most effective if it immediately follows the behaviour (Dušek, 2015). However, prison sentences often occur long after the crime has been committed, explaining why sending people to prison does not always reduce criminal behaviour (Church, 1963). Celerity effectiveness weakens when the punishment is delayed, even by a matter of minutes or seconds (Banks and Vogel-Sprott, 1965; Camp, Raymond and Church, 1967). Unfortunately, attempts to increase the speed of consequences often face legal due process challenges (fair treatment through the normal judicial system) and busy court systems (Roberts and Irwin-Rogers, 2015; Selke, 1983).

- *Severity:* Severe punishment was once believed to be the best solution to deterring criminal behaviour (Antunes and Hunt, 1974). As a result, many jurisdictions use severe sanctions to deter crime (Tomlinson, 2016). Early research supported the theory that severe punishments deterred crime, for example in reducing drunk driving (Hansen, 2015), and homicides (Antunes and Hunt, 1974). However, when research expanded beyond these two areas, there was a surprise: more severe penalties were associated with *increased* rates of rape, assault, larceny, robbery, burglary and car theft (Darley, 2005). The severity of punishment did not deter these crimes, and severe prison sentences (particularly long sentences) are unlikely to deter future crime. They may have the opposite effect because inmates learn more effective crime strategies from each other, and time spent in prison can desensitise them to threats of future imprisonment (Nagin, 2013).

- *Certainty:* Certainty refers to the possibility of being caught and punished. The effects of certainty of punishment are more consistent than the severity of punishment (Carroll and Weaver, 2018; Mungan, 2019). However, increasing the certainty that an offender will be caught requires more enforcement efforts and a change in police practices. Additionally, because punishment achieves greater results when it is consistently applied, it is difficult to administer a punishment every single time a behaviour occurs (Husak, 2017). For example, people often continue to drive over the speed limit even after receiving a speeding ticket because the behaviour is inconsistently punished (Skinner, 1971).

IN SUMMARY

Increasing the severity of punishment has done little to deter crime. Punishment does not permanently alter criminal behaviour; it merely suppresses it and eventually leads to increases in criminal behaviours. The relationship between the severity of punishment and the deterrence of future crimes is influenced by the length, severity and speed of sentencing. In fact, the experience of incarceration may have lasting psychological effects that prevent changes in behaviour.

 ### CRITICAL THINKING AND APPLICATION QUESTIONS

1   One of the arguments against using punishment to change behaviour is that it does not eliminate criminal behaviour but temporarily suppresses it. How could you evaluate this hypothesis? Design a study that examines the potential for punishment to create lasting behaviour change in people.

2   Would incapacitation be an effective strategy to deal with the small percentage of individuals who commit the most crimes? In other words, should we consider incarcerating these individuals when they are young and early in their criminal careers? What legal, ethical and developmental problems would this strategy present?

3   Imagine you control your local criminal justice system and are given the power to *maximise* each of the three components of deterrence – celerity, severity and certainty. Choose a specific crime, such as shoplifting, bank robbery or speeding, and explain how *your* system would manage violations.

PSYCHOLOGICAL EFFECTS OF IMPRISONMENT AND INSTITUTIONALISATION

FICTION: Longer and harsher prison sentences will eventually rehabilitate even the most hardened criminal.	*Versus*	**FACT:** Longer and harsher prison sentences change people in ways that make returning to society difficult and sometimes impossible.

American jails as modern-day asylums

In 2018, the US Bureau of Justice Statistics reported that 14 per cent of prisoners in state and federal facilities and 26 per cent in jails met the criteria for having serious mental health conditions (Lyon, 2019). In the USA, people with mental illnesses are often sent to jail for minor crimes because, unlike prisons, which house those convicted of and sentenced for a crime, jails must accept anyone arrested, including those suffering a mental health crisis (Harpster, 2018). Most are not violent, but they cost more to house, are more likely to commit suicide and to be placed in solitary confinement than their counterparts without mental illness (AbuDagga et al., 2016). Their victimisation risk is higher and often their mental health deteriorates (Roth, 2018). The result is a cycle of untreated people with mental illness being sent to jail where their illnesses are undiagnosed, increasing the chances of committing future crimes upon release (Prins, 2014).

PART IV

Mental illness in America's jails

Jamycheal Mitchell was arrested in April 2015 for stealing less than five dollars' worth of food from a local store. He believed the store was owned by his father so he could take what he wanted. Mitchell's beliefs were a delusion because he experienced both schizophrenia and bipolar disorder. He ended up in a local jail (Harki, 2018). To restore his competency so that Mitchell could stand trial, a judge ordered him to a state mental hospital, but the order was lost twice. The jail attendants tried using an emergency order, but the local mental health representative arrived when Mitchell was in court and never returned. Mitchell's condition deteriorated. Wearing only a simple smock, he was given few clothes to prevent self-harm. Mitchell was rarely permitted to leave his cell. Family members and even other inmates begged for help for him, but none came (Hammel, 2019). Further, Mitchell was regularly denied food and access to psychotropic medications (medications capable of affecting the mind, emotions and behaviour). In a desperate plea for help, Mitchell flooded his cell with an overflowing toilet – a frequent way to have some control over the environment and gain attention – resulting in his water being turned off. On 19 August 2015, Mitchell died alone in his cell, 40–50 pounds lighter, with faeces on the walls and urine on the floor, still awaiting transfer to the state mental health hospital (Lithwick, 2016). The official cause of death was 'wasting disease' (Case 2:16-cv-00229-RBS-LRL, 2016).

Discussion Questions:

1   Why are the mentally ill mistreated more frequently than those without mental illness?

2   Does your local jurisdiction offer any kind of early interventions to keep people with mental illness from going to jail in the first place?

Adaptation and change in the prison environment

Prisonisation
– The process of accepting the culture and social life of prison society.

Imagine having no choice of who to be with, where to go and what to eat. You are separated from your friends and family and surrounded by threats and suspicion with no personal space to call your own. To cope with this environment, your only choice is to adapt and change. This adaptation is called **prisonisation**, where inmates accept the culture of prison society.

The psychological study of personality once believed that our personalities remain stable into adulthood (Roberts and Mroczek, 2008). However, current research shows that despite their relative stability, our habits, emotions, behaviours and thoughts do change in important ways. It is inevitable that time spent in a highly structured, yet socially threatening environment leads to significant long-lasting personality changes (Penson, Ruchensky, Morey and Edens, 2018). The problem is that the personality changes that help the offender survive in prison, such as a lack of trust, hypervigilance and aggression, are counterproductive outside prison.

Post-incarceration syndrome
– A cluster of institutionalised personality traits, including social–sensory disorientation and alienation.

The prison environment changes personality through the loss of choice and privacy, heightened fear and wearing a mask of emotionless invulnerability by acting impenetrable, tough and aloof (Shlosberg, Ho and Mandery, 2018). Exposure to the prison environment contributes to institutionalised personality traits, social–sensory disorientation and alienation, known as **post-incarceration syndrome**, when released (Stearns, Swanson and

Etie, 2019). This syndrome is similar to the concept of **institutionalisation**, when some offenders find it impossible to cope with the world outside prison upon their release, having adapted to the norms and values of prison life.

The effects of sensory and social isolation

Some prisons can be an impoverished environment with few physical, mental and social activities. This environment can create both 'physiological stress' induced by a lack of stimuli (Maschi, Viola and Koskinen, 2015), and 'psychological stress' induced by a lack of human interaction (Haney, 2017).

Approximately 84,000 offenders in the USA live in solitary confinement, while other major industrialised countries, such as Japan, Germany and France, each hold approximately 60,000 offenders in solitary confinement (Johner, 2019). Within Europe, the maximum duration of solitary confinement allowed varies. For example, in Belgium 8 days is the maximum permissible duration, while Finland allows 14 days; Poland, England and Wales allow 28; France and Estonia allow 45; and Ireland allows up to 60 (Payne-James, Beynon and Vieira, 2017; Lamb, 2015).

We have known about the effects of solitary confinement since the penitentiary system began in the early nineteenth century. The system used in North America, Europe and Australia involved an almost exclusive reliance on solitary confinement as a means of incarceration (Rothman, 1971). Penitentiaries were created and named under the root word 'penitence', and giving offenders a space where they are forced to be alone with their thoughts was believed to reform their character and promote their penitence (Kass, 2019).

Shortly after the widespread use of this approach, reports began to appear of mental disorders among offenders, including hallucinations, dementia and monomania – excessive concentration on a single object or idea (Smith, 2006). Social isolation effects continued after offenders were released into the general population of the prison. Isolated inmates had difficulty adjusting due to social anxiety and social atrophy, and often reported continuing bizarre and disturbing subjective sensory and social experiences after leaving isolation (Bennion, 2015).

> **Institutionali-sation** – *Difficulty coping with society after release from prison, having adapted to the norms and values of prison life.*

PART IV

Global Perspectives

Exploring the human impact of solitary confinement

In a case that would gain worldwide attention, Albert Woodfox was convicted of armed robbery in 1971 and sentenced to 50 years in jail, to be served at the Louisiana State Penitentiary (known as Angola Prison). He was 26 years old. Then, in 1972, Woodfox was convicted on questionable racially and politically motivated charges of murdering a guard during a prison riot. Woodfox and another inmate, Herman Wallace, both African American

Source: ALAIN JOCARD/AFP/Getty Images

Albert Woodfox spent the longest period of solitary confinement in US prison history – a total of 43 years and 10 months

men, were found guilty by an all-white jury. The trial included the testimonies from three inmates recruited by promises of favourable treatment. A fingerprint was the only physical evidence presented at the trial and it cleared both Woodfox and Wallace.

For 23 hours a day, Woodfox endured four decades of isolation in a 2 x 3 metre cell (6 x 9 feet), with one hour of solitary shackled exercise a day. Pacing became his method of coping, lasting from minutes to hours. He would pace to relieve tension, pace to sleep, pace to drive the fear of going insane out of his mind. He would pace so much that during the sweltering summer months, a puddle of water ran the length of his cell (Woodfox, 2019).

Finally, in June 2015, the courts demanded his immediate and unconditional release. After serving *43 years* in solitary confinement, Woodfox was released on his 69th birthday. Woodfox should not have remained in solitary confinement; his behaviour was commendable, and his records showed that he had posed no risk to himself or others. Woodfox was denied opportunities for participation in rehabilitation programmes. Amnesty International and the United Nations both deemed Woodfox's imprisonment 'inhumane' (Amnesty International UK, 2018).

Upon release, Woodfox turned to activism, maintaining his vow to be the voice and face of the people hidden behind the walls of prisons (Pilkington, 2016).

Albert Woodfox's tragic story shows that solitary confinement is not just used for dangerous offenders. Solitary confinement is also used to isolate detainees during the pretrial stage of investigation, sometimes as part of a coercive interrogation strategy. For example, solitary confinement for pretrial detainees has been a part of Scandinavian prison practice for many years (Pratt and Eriksson, 2011). It is also used to isolate offenders with mental illnesses (Cochran, Toman, Mears and Bales, 2018). Another use is protecting vulnerable inmates from others. This was the case with Brenton Tarrant, a white supremacist shooter who killed 50 Muslim worshippers in a mosque in Christchurch, New Zealand in 2019. For his protection, he is spending the rest of his life in isolation. In a prison where 80 percent of inmates are Māori or Pacific Islanders and he is a white supremacist, isolation is his best protection (Muller, 2019).

The experience of solitude is found in many circumstances, including polar station expeditions (Ramachandran, John Paul and Mandal, 2019), real and simulated space missions (Golden, Chu-Hsiang and Kozlowski, 2017), on board submarines (Brasher, Dew, Kilminster and Bridger, 2009) and long-distance drivers (Apostolopoulos, Sönmez, Hege and Lemke, 2016). All these isolated experiences produce a range of similar psychological effects (Table 9.1).

Table 9.1: Psychological symptoms of extreme solitary confinement

Anxiety	Persistent low level of anxiety, fear of impending death, panic attacks (Haney, 2017)
Depression	Emotional flatness/blunting and the loss of ability to feel emotions, mood swings, hopelessness, social withdrawal, loss of initiation of activity or ideas, apathy, lethargy, major depression (Arrigo and Bullock, 2007)
Anger	Irritability and hostility, poor impulse control, outbursts of physical and verbal violence against others, self and objects, unprovoked anger (Kovács, Kun, Griffiths and Demetrovics, 2019; Reiter and Blair, 2015)
Cognitive disturbances	Poor concentration and memory, obsessive thoughts, disorientation (Smith, 2006; Metzner and Fellner, 2010)

Perceptual distortions	Hypersensitivity to noises and smells, distortions of sensation (walls closing in), disorientation in time and space, hallucinations affecting all five senses (objects or people appearing in the cell, or hearing voices) (Catalano et al., 2003; Grassian and Friedman, 1986)
Paranoia and psychosis	Recurrent and persistent thoughts, often of a violent and vengeful character (directed against prison staff), paranoid ideas (often persecutory), psychotic episodes, psychotic depression (Haney, 2018; Cloud, Drucker, Browne and Parsons, 2015)
Self-harm	Self-mutilation and cutting, suicide attempts (Vinokur and Levine, 2019; Kaba et al., 2014)
Sleep disturbances	Circadian rhythm sleep difficulties due to a lack of activity and the effects of continual exposure to artificial light (Acar, Öğülmüş and Boysan, 2019; Grassian, 2006)

Suicide prevention and alternatives to solitary confinement

Prison suicide is an international problem, and rates of suicide in offenders are higher than in the general population (Fazel, Ramesh and Hawton, 2017). Offenders are a very high-risk group for suicide (Favril and O'Connor, 2019), and those in solitary confinement are even more at risk (Barlett, Frater and Hyde, 2018). Within the US prison population, the leading cause of death is suicide, and depression and hopelessness are the greatest risk factors (Phillips, Padfield and Gelsthorpe, 2018). Larney et al. (2012) found that traumatic brain injury, symptoms of depression, and childhood abuse and trauma were among the most frequent predictors of suicide attempts among Australian prisoners. According to Kaba et al. (2014), the combination of solitary confinement and having a diagnosable mental illness increases the chances of committing serious self-injury.

Most suicides in prisons occur when an inmate is isolated from staff and fellow inmates. If solitary confinement is the only available option for housing the suicidal inmate, constant observation should be maintained (Way et al., 2005). Ideally, the suicidal inmate should be housed in a dormitory or shared cell setting. In some facilities, social support is provided through the use of specially trained inmate 'buddies' or 'listeners', which improves the wellbeing of potentially suicidal inmates (Junker, Beeler and Bates, 2005).

Another alternative is the UK's **close supervision centres**, where the most dangerous offenders are given more control of their environment, rather than less. Offenders have access to libraries, mental health treatment and exercise. They can earn credits for privileges like phone calls, exercise and access to cooking facilities. They can express complaints, and monthly reports review offenders' progress in the units (Johner, 2019).

Close supervision centres – *Units where disruptive, challenging and dangerous offenders are managed within small and highly supervised units.*

Ineffectiveness of solitary confinement

Solitary confinement requires more time and more money, and causes more harm while not deterring inmates from committing further violence on release into the larger prison population (Almasy and Holcombe, 2019). Even short-term solitary confinement increases later misconduct (Medrano, Ozkan and Morris, 2017). Inmates who have spent time in solitary confinement are more likely to reoffend than those who serve their sentence in a prison's general population (Mendrano, Ozkan and Morris, 2017).

More than 40 years ago, the European Commission on Human Rights condemned severe solitary confinement as a form of inhumane treatment, which cannot be justified by the requirements of security (Lamb, 2015). There is a growing realisation that the conditions of the prison itself are the source of the violence and not the offender. Rather than isolating the 'problem offender' from the rest of the inmates in a crowded prison, it is more effective to change the problem conditions (Resnik, VanCleave, Harrington and Petchenik, 2019). A review of the list of mental health outcomes in Table 9.1 strengthens the message that solitary confinement is an excessive punishment that lacks rehabilitative purpose (Morris, 2015). The United Nations Standard Minimum Rules for the Treatment of Offenders, also known as the 'Nelson Mandela Rules', classify confinement more than 15 consecutive days equal to torture or other cruel, inhuman or degrading treatment (UNODC, 2015).

IN SUMMARY

Many inmates are destined to fail. They are told to conduct themselves as independent subjects while under total control. They are told to reflect on the consequences of their actions in a situation that produces cognitive impairment and mental stress or illness. The belief that a person in confinement is reflecting about their actions and will somehow understand how to manage situations differently in the future is not realistic. They are told to achieve an ethical and social transformation in a situation that blocks social and ethical relationships with others. Human beings require social interaction and meaningful activity, and solitary confinement provides only isolation and idleness, leading to mental deterioration.

 CRITICAL THINKING AND APPLICATION QUESTIONS

1   Are the core values of your self-identity independent of how others define you? What aspects of prison would force you to change your identity to adapt to this environment?

2   Knowing what the research says about the power of prison situations to have a destructive effect on human nature, what recommendations would you make about changing the prison system in your country?

3   Solitary confinement is a form of punishment that has limited effectiveness. What are the reasons that this approach is ineffective for changing behaviour?

THE PSYCHOLOGY BEHIND EFFECTIVE PRISON REHABILITATION PROGRAMMES

FICTION: Criminals are born bad and punishment is the only way to teach offenders that their behaviour is unacceptable.

Versus

FACT: The same psychological principles behind learned criminal behaviours can be applied to unlearn them.

Rehabilitation programmes

Ideally, preparation for release begins on the first day of imprisonment (Gideon and Sung, 2011). Altschuler and Bilchik (2014) recommend three overlapping opportunities for developing successful re-entry:

1   During admission into prison

2   When transitioning from prison settings and reintegrating into the community

3   In the community.

More time between completing rehabilitation programmes and release corresponds with reduced chances of returning to prison (Papp, Wooldredge and Pompoco, 2019). To increase the amount of time in rehabilitation, successful programmes are integrated into the daily prison routine and extend beyond incarceration. This is the case in the prison systems of Norway, Denmark and Finland (Ward et al., 2013). These prison systems have successfully deterred future crimes by integrating rehabilitation programmes as part of inmates' daily routine. As a result, Nordic countries have significantly lower recidivism rates compared to other countries (Gideon and Sing, 2011).

Preparing for **desistance** – the process by which a person arrives at a state of non-offending – is the responsibility of prisons to provide the skills needed to lead crime-free lives after release (Ortiz and Jackey, 2019). There are a variety of rehabilitation programmes to teach inmates skills for successful community reintegration, including those focused on education (McCorkel and Defina, 2019), vocational training (Newton et al., 2016), substance abuse treatment (Kelly, Welsh and Stanley, 2019), parenting (Dodson, Cabage and McMillan, 2019), anger management (Laursen and Henriksen, 2019), mental health counselling (Irina, Tobias, Reinhard and Manuela, 2019), physical health and recreation (Link, Ward and Stansfield, 2019), faith-based efforts (Stansfield, O'Connor and Duncan, 2018), and animal training (Cooke, 2019). The skills can be characterised by their overlapping perspectives (Figure 9.3).

Successful rehabilitation programmes reduce the frequency of criminal behaviour by addressing the inmate's needs or deficits (Schnepel, 2018). Rehabilitation lowers recidivism and shields society from crimes (Ganapathy, 2018). However, belief in the power of rehabilitation after prison is not always widespread. Sometimes, the released offender is met with anger, as was the case of Jason Owen from London. Owen was sentenced to six years in prison for playing a part in the death of 17-month-old Peter Connelly, known as 'Baby P' (Lake, 2018). On his release six years later, *The Sun* newspaper launched a campaign to find him, suggesting that readers contact the newspaper if they had information about his location, stating that the 'brute mingles with shoppers', as he tried to find a job (Wells, 2011). This example shows a cycle of prejudice promoting future recidivism, which is then cited by newspapers as 'proof' that criminals cannot be rehabilitated. As a cruel self-fulfilling prophecy, Jason Owen returned to prison in 2013 for breaching the conditions of his release (Mortimer, 2017).

Desistance
– The process by which a person arrives at a state of non-offending.

PART IV

The ABC of rehabilitation programmes

Rehabilitation and desistance are about fostering lasting behaviour change, and this process of change often starts with changing attitudes. One way to categorise rehabilitation programmes is their focus on changing **a**ffect, **b**ehaviour, or **c**ognitions (the ABC model of attitude change; Figure 9.3):

• Affective programmes focus on changing a person's feelings and emotions.

• Behavioural programmes focus on changing maladaptive behaviours.

• Cognitive programmes focus on changing maladaptive beliefs and knowledge.

Figure 9.3: The ABC perspective on rehabilitation programmes

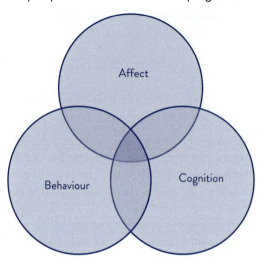

Affective-focused rehabilitation programmes

The Good Lives Model (GLM)

The Good Lives Model (GLM) is a strengths-based approach applying inmates' strongest values and goals to motivate them to lead better lives. Understanding what motivates human behaviour provides prison administrators with a useful tool for managing inmates, since it helps explain both good and bad behaviour. The GLM helps inmates develop and implement meaningful life plans that are incompatible with future offending (Walgrave, Ward and Zinsstag, 2019). Also, the focus on pursuing meaningful goals enables individuals to develop more optimistic outlooks for themselves and their future (Andrews, Bonta and Wormith, 2011). Other components include the idea that inmates, like all humans, value certain states of mind, personal characteristics and experiences. These are defined as **primary goods** – activities, experiences and situations that are intrinsically motivating and increase fulfilment and happiness (Wincup, 2019). Attaining primary goods is associated with higher levels of wellbeing and their absence is associated with increased rates of psychological problems (Ward and Maruna, 2007). The GLM model has become increasingly popular in sexual offending treatment programmes (McGrath et al., 2010).

> **Primary goods**
> – Activities, experiences and situations that are intrinsically motivating and increase fulfilment and happiness.

Behaviour-focused rehabilitation programmes

Contingency management approaches

Contingency management refers to a type of behavioural therapy in which individuals are 'reinforced', or rewarded, for evidence of positive behavioural change (Petry, 2011). Most programmes use positive reinforcement of prosocial and positive behaviours, such as punctuality, participation, completion of programme tasks. In a **meta-analysis**, researchers found that contingency management programmes significantly increased a variety of behaviours, for example prosocial behaviours, education attainment, work assignments completion, in prison settings and are offered as an alternative to solitary confinement (Gendreau, Listwan, Kuhns and Exum, 2014).

> **Meta-analysis**
> – A statistical procedure for combining data from multiple studies.

Three examples of contingency management programmes in prisons

Token economies are one of the earliest methods used with inmates. It is a procedure where tokens or points are earned for 'good' behaviour and can be exchanged for tangible goods, such as money and material goods, desirable activities, such as sports, recreation, TV and time for socialisation, social reinforcers like praise and approval, and sometimes early prison release (Lagorio and Yanagita, 2015). Token economies have a high degree of structure and immediate rewards, and are effective with higher risk, unmotivated inmates who have been unresponsive to prison authorities (Walker, Pann, Shapiro and van Hasselt, 2016). The challenges include overcoming the practical difficulties of finding an effective level of motivating reward, tracking tokens and points, and weaning the individual off the token system for release into society (Wexler, 1973).

Positive behaviour interventions and supports is a behaviour management system used to understand what maintains an individual's challenging behaviours (aggression and violence) and uses applied behavioural analysis to then change those behaviours. It is based on the idea that inappropriate behaviours are difficult to change because they serve a purpose and are reinforced by the environment (Jolivette and Nelson, 2017). An advantage of this approach is that it reduces aggression without relying on medication, restraint and seclusion, while ultimately reducing recidivism (Tolisano, Sondik and Dike, 2017).

Project BRITE (Behavioural Reinforcement to Increase Treatment Engagement) tested the impact of a positive behavioural reinforcement intervention on inmates' engagement in 2010 during a 12-week intensive outpatient prison-based drug treatment programme. Inmates who enrolled in these programmes received positive behavioural reinforcement contingent upon attending and taking part in regularly scheduled group sessions and completing treatment-related tasks. Applying positive reinforcement in a timely and systematic manner, Project BRITE increased inmate engagement in the treatment programmes, and demonstrated decreased drug use and recidivism (Burdon et al., 2013).

> **Token economies** – Rewarding good behaviour with symbols or points that can be exchanged for something desired.

Cognitive-based programmes

Cognitive behavioural therapy (CBT)

Cognitive behavioural therapy (CBT) helps individuals become aware of their thoughts and behaviours and make positive changes to them. CBT focuses on how 'criminal thinking' contributes to criminal behaviour. For example, distorted cognitions can include misinterpretation of social cues, feelings of dominance and entitlement, and a lack of moral reasoning (Lipsey and Landenberger, 2006). Therefore, CBT develops skills to recognise distorted or unrealistic thinking, and then change the distorted thoughts or beliefs to reduce the problem behaviour (Clark, Landenberger and Lipsey, 2005).

APPLY IT

How CBT is used to reduce negative thinking

Negative thinking can lead to negative consequences, especially when based on false beliefs or a few selective facts. Ultimately, negative thinking can turn into automatic thinking through repetition (Kahneman, 2011).

Examples include the following:

- *All-or-none thinking:* 'I have to do things perfectly, and anything less is failure.'

- *Focusing on the negatives:* 'Nothing goes my way. It feels like one disappointment after another.'

- *Negative self-labelling:* 'I'm a failure. If people knew the real me, they would not like me. I am flawed.'

- *Catastrophising:* 'If something is going to happen, it'll probably be the worst-case scenario.'

PART IV

To experience how CBT examines the recurring negative themes in automatic thoughts, think about a situation you're having difficulty coping with and then respond to each of the six questions below:

1. *The situation and initial thoughts:* Describe the situation that led to your unpleasant feelings.

2. *Consider the consequences:* Why do you want to change this thinking? What will be the consequences if you do not change?

3. *Challenge your initial thought:* How successful has this thinking been for you in the past?

4. *Negative thinking:* Summarise the kind of negative thinking behind your initial thought. Identify one or more of the basic types of negative thinking: all-or-none thinking, focusing on the negatives, negative self-labelling and catastrophising.

5. *Alternative thinking and action plans:* How could you have managed the situation differently? How can you prepare for the situation in the future? Write a list of strengths you bring to the situation.

6. *Improvement:* Do you feel slightly better or more optimistic? This step reinforces the idea that if you change your thinking, you will change your behaviour.

Examples of CBT programmes

Reasoning and rehabilitation

Reasoning and rehabilitation is often used with violent and antisocial offenders in Canada, the UK and the USA (Wilkinson, 2005). This approach directly addresses the thoughts leading to criminal behaviour. It reduces recidivism by treating the issues that led to an individual committing a criminal act. This approach teaches inmates to deal with their concerns directly rather than coping with their anger and other emotions by engaging in risky or violent behaviour. The reasoning and rehabilitation programme aims to help participants reframe these thoughts and alter their behaviours accordingly by teaching them cognitive skills in the following areas: lateral thinking, social skills and values education. A meta-analysis of this approach found a 14 per cent reduction in recidivism in inmates who participated in the programme (Joy Tong and Farrington, 2006).

Aggression replacement training

Aggression replacement training (ART) is a multimodal programme that replaces antisocial behaviours by actively teaching desirable behaviours (Feindler, Engel and Gerber, 2016). This programme produces significant increases in constructive social behaviours and moral reasoning, while decreasing impulsivity and antisocial behaviour (Feindler, 2016). ART features three coordinated and integrated components – social skills training, anger control and moral reasoning (Ensafdaran, Karhé, Njad and Arshadi, 2019).

Thinking for a change (T4C)

Thinking for a change (T4C) is a CBT programme that includes cognitive restructuring, social skills development, and the development of problem-solving skills to help individuals take control of their lives by taking control of their thinking (Bush, Glick, Taymans and Guevara, 2011). The foundation of T4C is the use of CBT principles through group sessions, developing interpersonal communication skills and altering patterns of thought that lead to problem behaviours. Lessons on cognitive self-change provide participants with a process for self-reflection, concentrating on uncovering antisocial thoughts, feelings, attitudes and beliefs. Social skills lessons prepare participants to engage in prosocial interactions based on self-understanding and awareness of the impact their actions may have on others. Finally, critical thinking skills provide participants with a step-by-step process to address the challenges and stressful situations they may encounter. Support for this approach is offered by Lowenkamp, Hubbard, Makarios and Latessa (2009), who found significantly fewer offenders reoffended in the T4C group than a control group.

Global Perspectives

Cognitive behaviour therapy for sex offenders

The sex offender treatment programme is a cognitive behavioural psychological group-based intervention used in the UK since 1992. It involves assessment, evaluation, professional counselling, perpetrator treatment groups (active and maintenance) and intensive supervision of sex offenders, either within residential facilities or under intensive supervision. The goal of treatment is to reduce the risk of reoffending and make self-management possible (Lösel et al., 2020). But does it work? Mews, Di Bella and Purver (2017) compared prisoners who took part in the 180 hours of group sessions before their later release from prison with matched offenders who did not participate in the programme. Unfortunately, they found that a greater number of treated sex offenders committed at least one sexual reoffence (10 per cent compared with 8 per cent) and committed at least one child image reoffence when compared with the matched comparison offenders (4.4 per cent compared with 2.9 per cent).

What was the explanation? Sharing stories during group treatment may normalise sex offender behaviour, reduce its stigma or allow sharing of contacts and sources associated with sexual offending (Mews, Di Bella and Purver, 2017). The replacement therapies still involve group sessions, but the inmates are no longer required to discuss their own offences (Casciani, 2017).

PART IV

IN SUMMARY

Eventually, almost all offenders are released, and rehabilitation and desistance should be the primary responsibilities of prisons. Psychological research provides developed and developing tools to promote lasting behavioural change whether from an affective, behavioural or cognitive perspective.

? CRITICAL THINKING AND APPLICATION QUESTIONS

1   Affective models of rehabilitation like the GLM model, have been shown to motivate people to engage in rehabilitation programmes. How important is the role of affective or emotional states in long-term behavioural change?

2   A critique of behavioural management approaches is that they only manage behaviour but not the causes of those behaviours – like turning off a fire alarm, but not dousing the fire. Reviewing the three examples of contingency management programmes used in prisons, do you believe that this criticism is valid?

3   The goal of cognitive behaviour therapy is to alter behaviour by changing patterns of thoughts and beliefs. Do you believe that changing our thoughts and feelings affects our behaviours or does changing behaviour affect our thoughts and feelings? Support your response with a unique example from your own experience.

REDUCING RECIDIVISM: THE RISK-NEEDS-RESPONSIVITY MODEL

FICTION: Reducing recidivism is beyond the control of the criminal justice system.

Versus

FACT: The risk-needs-responsivity model has been used with increasing success to assess and rehabilitate offenders.

ASSESSING RECIDIVISM

Recidivism rates vary because of different procedures and definitions. For example, the US Bureau of Justice Statistics found that most offenders (82 per cent) are rearrested within the first three years of release (Alper Durose and Markman, 2018). In Canada, the two-year rate is 23.4 per cent (Correctional Service Canada, 2019), while in the UK, the three-year rate is 29 per cent (Ministry of Justice, 2019). In Australia, the rate is 45.6 per cent (Sentencing Advisory Council, 2018), and in South Africa, recidivism rates are between 84 per cent and 95 per cent (Herbig and Hesselink, 2013; Ngabonziza and Singh, 2012).

Jurisdictions are releasing offenders earlier because of prison crowding and rising detention costs (Scott, 2017; Bodenhorn, 2016). This has created a renewed emphasis on rehabilitation to reduce recidivism because almost all offenders are eventually returned to society. Recidivism in this context is relapsing into criminal behaviour with a prior conviction (Hanson and Morton-Bourgon, 2005). Releasing offenders requires using information about the risks of recidivism revealed during trial and incarceration to make informed decisions about whom to release and when to release them.

Three popular approaches for reducing incarceration rates include:

1   Send fewer people to prison – place offenders on probation or in diversion programmes like drug treatment facilities

2   Shorten prison sentences – allow inmates to serve a portion of their prison sentence on parole or grant them early release by allowing them to earn time off their prison sentence

3   Divert low-level drug offenders from prison or grant nonviolent offenders early release (Fabelo and Thompson, 2015).

The challenge is determining the offender's risk to the community. However, calculating the risk based only on the crime is not always the best strategy (Chaiken, Chaiken and Rhodes, 1994). For example, an offender with no history of violence, who poses a low risk for future violence, might be convicted of a violent crime, such as driving a getaway car for someone who committed armed robbery. Alternatively, an offender with a history of violence might be sentenced to prison for a nonviolent crime or have a violent offence reduced to a nonviolent offence from a plea deal.

Predicting future violence for people within the criminal justice system can be approached from a clinical judgement, actuarial assessment or a structured professional judgement. Many professionals rely on their clinical professional judgement to understand and manage violence. While this approach utilises their clinical experience, it is vulnerable to cognitive and situational biases. In contrast, actuarial assessment involves the statistical estimation of the risk of violence based on patterns of behaviours that perpetuate criminal behaviours and recidivism in various offender groups (Pham et al., 2019). Structured professional judgement relies on professional experience with a structured checklist. This approach reduces the limitations of unstructured clinical and actuarial assessment while retaining the strengths of each (Brook, 2017). Although an improvement on unstructured assessment, structured applications have significant limitations, highlighting the importance of a multimethod approach to violence risk assessment (Hart, Douglas and Guy, 2017). The actuarial and structural approaches are covered in more detail in Chapter 12.

Assessing risk and needs factors

Risk and needs assessment instruments for predicting recidivism measure offender's specific needs that, if addressed, will reduce the likelihood of future criminal activity. These factors, known as risk factors, are divided into two categories: static and dynamic (Table 9.2). **Static risk factors** cannot be altered through treatment programmes, while **dynamic risk factors** can. Latessa and Lowenkamp (2005) compare this risk assessment approach to the risk factors associated with having a heart attack. Static risk factors include your age, sex and family history of heart problems. Dynamic risk factors include your weight, amount of exercise, blood pressure, stress, cholesterol level and whether you are a smoker. Understanding your level of risk of having a heart attack involves examining all these static and dynamic factors. However, to lower the risk of having a heart attack, targeting the dynamic factors is more effective.

Table 9.2: Static and dynamic risk factors for recidivism

Static factors	Dynamic factors
Age at first arrest	Current age
Gender	Education level
Past addiction and substance abuse	Current addiction and substance abuse
Previous history of mental health problems	Marital status
History of violating terms of supervision (parole or probation)	Employment status

A range of models have been developed for predicting recidivism by focusing on educational (Ahmed et al., 2019; Ginsburg, 2019) or vocational deficits (Fajonyomi, 2019), substance abuse (Kelly, Welsh and Stanley, 2019) or **criminogenic thinking** – patterns of thought that perpetuate criminal behaviour (Carr, Rosenfeld and Rotter, 2019). However, the most successful model has been the risk-needs-responsivity model.

Static risk factors – *Risk factors that predict recidivism but cannot be altered through treatment programmes.*

Dynamic risk factors – *Risk factors that predict recidivism and can be altered through treatment programmes.*

Criminogenic thinking – *Patterns of thought that perpetuate criminal behaviour.*

PART IV

The risk-needs-responsivity (RNR) model

It was once believed that nothing worked to reduce recidivism (Cullen, 2013) and, traditionally, assessing offender risk was a matter of professional judgement. During intake, prison staff would determine which offenders were likely to be a security risk based on their own experience. These assessments were used to assign inmates to the appropriate institution based on their risk determination. Over time, the limitations of using subjective, intuitive professional judgement became obvious (Whittington et al., 2013).

A more effective approach is the risk-needs-responsivity (RNR) model. The model is used in the field of criminology to develop recommendations for how offenders should be assessed based on the risk they present, what they need, and what kinds of environments they should be placed in to reduce recidivism. The RNR model is considered the best model for determining offender treatment and has yielded some of the most effective risk assessment tools. Bonta and Andrews (2007) emphasise that the RNR model has had global success because it stresses the importance of matching the style and mode of intervention to the offender's characteristics (Andrews, Bonta and Wormith, 2011).

Generally, the RNR model predicts that personality and situational factors interact to create values, thoughts and temperament orientations that are favourable to criminal conduct (Smith, Gendreau and Swartz, 2009). Therefore, the tendency for criminal behaviour involves thinking and response patterns that are learned and reinforced. Specifically, the RNR model identifies the most important risk factors for changing criminal behaviours (Andrews and Bonta, 2010). Assessing risk typically consists of a series of questions during intake to guide interviews with offenders and measure their risk of recidivism. This data is collected during the interview and is supplemented with information from official records (criminal history). The RNR instrument generates a total score that places the offender into a risk category ('low', 'moderate' or 'high') (James, 2018).

The rehabilitative principles of RNR

The RNR model has three main rehabilitative principles: assessing *risk*, addressing criminogenic *needs*, and providing treatment that is *responsive* to the offender's abilities.

Risk principle: Who should receive treatment?

The risk principle relies on two assumptions: the risk of criminal behaviour can be predicted using reliable and validated risk assessment methods, and the level of intervention should be matched with the risk level of the offender. The risk principle states that high-risk offenders need to be placed in programmes that provide more intensive treatment and services, while low-risk offenders should receive minimal or sometimes no intervention (VanBenchoten, Bentley, Gregoire and Lowencamp, 2016). Importantly, inappropriate matching of treatment intensity with offender risk level can result in increased criminal behaviour.

Needs principle: What needs should be addressed?

The needs principle suggests that treatment programmes should focus on criminogenic needs, those factors directly relating to offending behaviour that are responsive to change (Andrews and Bonta, 2010). Wilpert et al. (2018) identified eight factors that predict recidivism (Table 9.3), which they call the 'central eight'. They further divided the central eight into the 'big four' and the 'moderate four'. A review of the relationship between risk and need factors and criminal behaviour found that both the 'big four' and the 'moderate four' risk factors were statistically significant predictors of future offending (Andrews and Bonta, 2010). However, the 'big four' are more strongly associated with recidivism than the 'moderate four' (Papp, Campbell and Anderson, 2018). Generally, the more of the eight risk factors programmes include, the greater the reduction in recidivism (Viglione, 2018; Johnson and Cullen, 2015).

Table 9.3: The 'central eight' risk and needs factors

Risk/needs factors	Indicator
The big four	
History of antisocial behaviour	Early involvement in antisocial activities (convictions, charges, misconduct, use of weapons/serious threats, imprisonment), being arrested at a young age, a large number of prior offences, and rule violations while on conditional release
Antisocial personality pattern	Displaying behaviour that is impulsive, adventurous, pleasure-seeking, impulsivity (mood swings, irritability, inconsistency) and anger management problems (expressions of negative, hostile affect)
Antisocial cognition	Holding attitudes, beliefs and values favourable to crime. Identifying with criminals, negative attitudes towards the law and justice system, belief that crime yields rewards, rationalises criminal behaviour (the victim deserved it)
Antisocial associates	Associating with pro-criminal others (gangs) and avoiding anti-criminal others. Associates who have a criminal record or are involved in criminal activities, as well as a lack of prosocial associates
The moderate four	
Family and marital circumstances	Poor quality relationship between parent and child (juvenile offenders) or spouses. Instability/conflict in relationships with partner, parents/carers and other family members
School/employment	Problems with performance at and interest/involvement in education and employment
Leisure/recreation	Lack of involvement in prosocial leisure activities
Substance abuse	Alcohol and drug abuse and/or dependence in present (last year) or past

Source: Wilpert, J., van Horn, J. E. and Moonmann, C. (2018) Comparing the central eight risk factors: Do they differ across age groups of sex offenders? *International Journal of Offender Therapy and Comparative Criminology*, 62(13), 4278–94. Adapted with permission.

Responsivity principle: How should services be delivered?

The responsivity principle states that rehabilitative programmes should be delivered in ways that are consistent with the ability and learning styles of the offender. This principle is divided into two elements. The first is **general responsivity**, the idea that cognitive behavioural and social learning theories are the most effective form of intervention. General responsivity calls

General responsivity – *The idea that cognitive behavioural and social learning theories are the most effective form of intervention.*

Specific responsivity – *The idea that treatment should take into account the relevant characteristics of the individual.*

for the use of cognitive behavioural approaches for treatment because these approaches are the most effective approach with offenders as a whole (Hoge, 2016). The second is **specific responsivity**, the idea that treatment should take into account the relevant characteristics of the individual – the offender's preferences, motivations, personality, age, gender, ethnicity and cultural identification (Taxman, 2014). Specific responsivity acknowledges that non-criminogenic needs (age) may help or hinder the provision of treatment, thus they should be individually addressed to reduce recidivism (Higley, Lloyd and Serin, 2019).

Limitations of the RNR approach

The use of the RNR approach has its limitations, among them is the risk of false positives (inmates identified as 'high risk' but do not reoffend) and false negatives (inmates identified as 'low risk' but do reoffend) (Vitopoulos, Peterson-Badali, Brown and Skilling, 2019; Taxman, 2014).

IN SUMMARY

The RNR model serves as a crucial resource to help jurisdictions allocate offenders into appropriate services, including what services need to exist. Reducing criminal behaviour and improving public safety can be achieved by matching offenders to services that are consistent with the behaviours that drive their criminal activity. The RNR model can help determine the effective distribution of treatment services to offenders in prisons with the needs of the offender as guidance.

 CRITICAL THINKING AND APPLICATION QUESTIONS

1   We looked at how static and dynamic factors can be understood in terms of the way they can predict a heart attack. Create a unique example that demonstrates how static and dynamic factors can be used to predict another event.

2   Estimate the most effective and the least effective of the three approaches for reducing incarceration rates. These are: send fewer people to prison; shorten prison sentences; and divert low-level drug offenders from prison or grant nonviolent offenders early release.

3   Review Table 9.3, which lists the 'central eight' risk and needs factors. Rank the factors along a continuum from the most dynamic to the most static. Does your ranking agree with the order presented in the table? Explain the similarity or difference.

CHAPTER REVIEW

Correctional psychology reveals that punitive strategies are ineffective in reducing recidivism and wasteful of human potential and monetary resources. Old ideas are being contested. Is solitary confinement necessary to manage offenders? Do prisons have to be ugly to be effective? New ideas are being embraced, such as gender-sensitive approaches for female offenders; community partnerships as a core feature of reintegration strategies; new technologies to give offenders more choice and access to education, family, leisure and self-development; innovative treatment approaches for inmates suffering from drug addiction and mental illness; effective programmes and interventions are also being adapted to suit different cultural contexts. Future application of the RNR approach will shift perspectives from retribution to rehabilitation, punishment to reformation, and condemnation to reasoning.

NAMES TO KNOW

Yvonne Jewkes

Has over twenty years' experience in ethnographic prison research. Her research investigates the various aspects of prisons and imprisonment.

- Jewkes, Y. (2015) *Media and Crime* (3rd edn). Sage.

- Jewkes, Y., Crewe, B. and Bennett, J. (2016) *The Handbook on Prisons* (2nd edn). Routledge.

Ian O'Donnell

His work reframes scholarly debates about prolonged solitary confinement. Other related areas include criminal justice policy, sentencing, penal reform, imprisonment, history of crime and punishment.

- O'Donnell, I. (2018) The art of imprisonment. *Crime, Media, Culture: An International Journal*, 15(3), 559–60.

- O'Donnell, I. (2016) The survival secrets of solitaries. *British Psychological Society*, 29(3), 184–7.

Tony Ward

Investigates desistance and reintegration processes in offenders, cognition and evolutionary approaches to crime, and ethical issues in forensic and correctional psychology, and is the developer of the Good Lives Model.

- Ward, T., Durrant, R. and Sullivan, J. (2019) (eds) Understanding crime. *Psychology, Crime & Law*, 25, 527–711.

- Ward, T. and Willis, G. (2018) The rehabilitation of offenders: Good lives and risk reduction. In G. Davis and A. Beech (eds) *Forensic Psychology* (3rd edn). Wiley-Blackwell.

PART IV

10 POLICE PSYCHOLOGY

Chapter Introduction

Deciding to use physical force is among the most important decisions a police officer can make. Frequently, these decisions are made during extreme, dangerous and uncertain circumstances after other options, such as negotiation, have failed. Additional stress happens when these encounters are often captured on video for media scrutiny and criticism, with little understanding of the laws governing these interactions or the policies guiding the officers' decisions. The unique culture surrounding law enforcement has been detrimental to the psychological health of police, where asking for help has traditionally been seen as a sign of weakness, but informed psychological research is changing this tradition.

Learning Outcomes

Police use of force

- Explain the causes and prevention strategies with use of force decisions during critical incidents.

The art of crisis negotiation

- Apply the five-step BISM approach to a sample hostage negotiation scenario.

Psychological effects of acute stress on performance

- Explain the effects of acute stress response on performance.

Psychological effects of chronic stress on performance

- Explain the connection between the organisational stressors of policing and the psychological effects of chronic stress.

POLICE USE OF FORCE

FICTION: Because police work is dangerous, force is a necessary part of the job.

Versus

FACT: The use of force is rare because most situations can be de-escalated through more effective methods.

CASE STUDY

Is lethal force sometimes the only choice?

Sammy Yatim died on the morning of 27 July 2013, in Toronto, Canada. Yatim, carrying a 12 cm (4.7 in) switchblade knife in a streetcar (tram), threatened passengers and ordered them to leave. Officer James Forcillo and his Sergeant Dan Pravica arrived. From the front of the streetcar, Forcillo called for a Taser, believing that the situation could be contained (Alamenciak, 2013). Several times, both officers ordered Yatim to drop the knife. After Yatim started advancing towards them, Officer

Sammy Yatim's mother protesting her son's death by Toronto police

Forcillo fired three shots from his pistol, forcing Yatim to the ground. When Yatim started to get up, several seconds later, Forcillo fired six more shots. Thirty seconds later, Pravica tasered Yatim. Surveillance video shows that Yatim was lying on the floor when the last six shots were fired.

A use of force expert believed Yatim presented no imminent threat requiring the use of deadly force by Forcillo (O'Neil, 2016). During his trial, the prosecution asked Forcillo why he had not put more effort into de-escalating the situation to avoid violence. Forcillo responded that pulling out his firearm in response to Yatim's knife was 'a form of **de-escalation**'. In support of the defence, a police college instructor testified that Forcillo was out of options when he shot Yatim (Pagliaro, 2015). Officer Forcillo served on the Toronto police force for six years and is the seventh officer to be charged with manslaughter (Hough, 2014).

Discussion Questions:

1   Define 'excessive use of force'. According to *your* definition, which parts of this story show excessive use of force?

2   Was shooting Yatim a form of self-defence? What are the arguments for and against this position?

De-escalation
– Stabilising a situation to reduce the immediate threat and obtain more time, options or resources.

Reasonable versus excessive use of force

Using force is both necessary and allowed under specific circumstances, such as self-defence or defence of another individual or group, to allow officers to protect the communities they serve. Police can assert force through their physical presence, verbal directions, or physical strength and training (Paoline and Terrill, 2007, 2011). For example, when police respond to a call to check a business for intruders, the reason the police are called is not just to investigate, but because if the police find an intruder, they can physically force them to leave. The challenge is using a reasonable level of force. Reasonable use of force is equal to the seriousness of the threat and uses the minimum amount required for police officers to perform their job. Excessive use of force is when the amount of force exceeds the seriousness of the threat and the minimum amount required to control the situation (Stoughton, Noble and Alpert, 2020).

One strategy is to implement the effective use of force policies. These are policies that regulate the levels and types of force that police are allowed to use against citizens. They are important because they are used to train police, guide their encounters with the community and establish if force is being used in an excessive manner (Perkins and Bourgeois, 2006).

Obasogie and Newman (2017) identified five core features of force policies (Table 10.1).

Table 10.1: Five core features of force policies

Feature	Description
A force continuum	Applying a range of actions to increase or decrease force equal to the level of resistance
De-escalation tactics	Actions, such as warnings and verbal persuasion, that minimise the likelihood of the need to use force during an incident and increase the likelihood of voluntary compliance
Exhaustion of alternatives	Using physical force only after all other reasonable alternatives have been exhausted
Proportionality of force	The countering force should be equal to the threatened physical harm, when faced with a threat to safety
Continual reassessment	Constantly assess the situation and changing circumstances to modify the use of appropriate force

Source: Obasogie, O. K. and Newman, Z. (2017) Police violence, use of force policies, and public health. *American Journal of Law and Medicine*, 43(2/3), 279–95. Adapted with permission.

The European Convention on Human Rights offers a good example of a force policy. The policy describes the acceptable use of force as 'reasonable' in the circumstances and appropriate if it is 'absolutely necessary for a purpose permitted by law' and 'the amount of force used is reasonable and proportionate' (Mowbray, 2016). This requires a consideration of the degree of force used. Any excessive use of force by a police officer is unlawful and an officer could thus be prosecuted under criminal law (Mowbray, 2016).

The rise of terrorism has changed our views on the use of force. For example, Kennison and Loumansky (2007) believe that traditional policing styles in the UK are based on notions of reasonableness, compromise and respect for the individual's rights. A central principle of our consent to be policed is the thoughtful and rare use of force, which is based on a continuum ranging from negotiation at one extreme to lethal consequences at the other. However, since the introduction of Operation Kratos (tactics developed by London's Metropolitan Police for dealing with suspected suicide bombers), the nature of policing is changing (Smith, 2012). Traditional reactive policing styles have given way to a proactive military approach. The consequence is that military styles of policing using overt displays of force tend to ignore civil rights and make more mistakes (Miller and Sabir, 2012).

Psychological theories of force focus on the social production of violence, the interaction among officers and the interaction between officers and civilians.

Racial explanations for the use of force

Do racial stereotypes bias police use of force? Researchers used a simple video game to examine the effect of ethnicity on 'shoot/don't shoot' situation decisions (Correll, Park, Judd and Wittenbrink, 2002). This scenario assumes that the decision-making process necessary to start shooting also applies to the decision to stop shooting. The researchers used black or white targets holding guns or other non-threatening objects, appearing in complex backgrounds. The white university student participants shot armed targets more often and more quickly if they were black rather than white, and refrained from shooting more often when the target was white. White participants' most common mistakes were shooting an unarmed black target and not shooting an armed white target. However, this biased pattern is more complicated than it seems. Correll et al. (2007) included a sample of experienced police officers with university students. Like other studies, officers showed evidence of bias in their reaction times to black or white targets. But, the police officers showed no evidence of racial bias in their ultimate decisions to shoot. In other words, although their response times showed bias, suggesting that officers activated racial stereotypes, their ultimate decisions revealed no bias. They reacted more quickly to armed black targets and unarmed white targets, in other words, targets that aligned with racial stereotypes. But, unlike university students, those biases in their reaction times did not translate to their ultimate decision to shoot or not shoot. The officers' intense training functioned as a safeguard.

Still, this was only part of the story. In a more recent study, Sim, Correll and Sadler (2013) explored how training and expertise might reduce bias, and when the beneficial effects of training might fail. They found that a sample of highly trained special unit officers, who regularly interact with minority gang members, were more likely to show racial bias in their decision to shoot. When race is unrelated to the presence/absence of a weapon, training may eliminate bias as participants learn to focus on diagnostic object information (gun vs. no gun). But, when training promotes the use of racial cues, it reinforces the use of stereotypes.

The social dynamics of police–civilian interactions

Violence does not occur as an isolated act, but as part of a process – usually, as a progression from relative calm to increasing tension to peak escalation, climaxing in a sudden and violent act or series of actions. Instead of viewing police use of deadly force incidents as single 'shoot/don't shoot' decisions, Binder and Scharf (1980) portrayed police–citizen encounters as a series of events and decisions extending back in time before the deadly force decision is made. In their model, violent police–citizen encounters are a product of consecutive decisions and behaviours by either police officer or citizen, or both. The mutual contributions in the encounter have the potential for increasing or decreasing violence. Binder and Scharf (1980) analysed the relative importance of events taking place at the beginning, middle and end of police–citizen transactions and proposed a four-phase model for evaluating and identifying outcomes (Figure 10.1).

Figure 10.1: Four phases of the police–citizen encounter

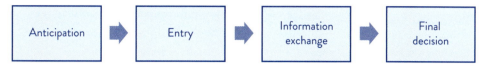

The four phases are as follows:

1   *Anticipation*: the moment when the officer becomes aware of the problem. This is usually a dispatch from the radio, observation of a problem, or receiving information from any source. The nature of the problem and indications of its seriousness influence an officer's response.

2   *Entry*: the officer arrives on the scene and makes a first appraisal of the situation. The entry phase establishes police authority, the tone of the police response and clarifies expectations for the citizen.

3   *Information exchange*: the officer gathers facts from suspects, victims and witnesses. Binder and Scharf (1980) note that this phase can last anywhere from one second ('Police … show me your hands!') to hours or even days of negotiation.

4   *Final decision*: the officer identifies the problem and applies a solution. This final phase includes the officer's decision to use force.

Each of these phases, and the actions taken by all actors within each phase, influences the final outcome. In a study conducted 12 years later, Fridell and Binder (1992) found that the information exchange phase of an encounter determined whether a potentially violent situation ended in deadly force. An important finding was that deadly force situations often involve uncertainty and surprise. Therefore, clear communication between officers and citizens is important. The ultimate lesson is that police are not limited to reacting in the final moment to a suspect's threatening behaviour, but they can take steps at the beginning of an encounter to create positive outcomes.

A cycle of escalation

Understanding violence requires an understanding of the interactions between aggressor and victim. In the same way, our analyses of police use of force cannot focus only on the actions of the citizen, or only on the actions of the police. In most jurisdictions, resistance is the primary legal justification for the police use of force, and a citizen's demeanour is an important predictor of police actions (Boivin, 2017). Sykes and Brent (1980) found officers typically reassert their control using verbal force and increase their response if the citizen disrespects the officer's authority. Excessive force is the result of a cycle of violence between the police and the citizen.

Profiles of violence-prone officers

Police psychologists play a role in identifying officers at risk for excessive force. In a classic study, Scrivner (1994) surveyed police psychologists about the characteristics of officers accused of using excessive force. Five distinct risk profiles predicting excessive force emerged from their responses (Table 10.2). The categories revealed that excessive force is a result of both individual personality traits and organisational influences.

PART IV

Table 10.2: Five predictors of officers at chronic risk for excessive force

Personality disorders	Antisocial, narcissistic, paranoid personality or abusive tendencies
Previous job-related experience	Previous use of excessive force in career
Problems at early stages in their police careers	Immaturity, low frustration tolerance, impulsive
Inappropriate patrol styles	Authoritarian policing style and sensitive to challenge and provocation
Personal problems	Separation, divorce, or loss of status

Source: Based on Scrivner, E. M. (1994) *Controlling Police Use of Excessive Force: The Role of the Police Psychologist.* National Institute of Justice.

When lethal force is unavoidable

'Suicide by police' is when a suicidal individual purposely provokes police officers to shoot and kill them (Dewey et al., 2013). Mohandie, Meloy and Collins (2009) examined the characteristics of 707 suicide by police cases in Canadian and US officer-involved shootings. They found that 80 per cent of these individuals had a weapon, which was a firearm 60 per cent of the time. Additionally, 46 per cent of those with a firearm fired at the police during the encounter. Finally, only 19 per cent pretended to have a weapon to achieve their suicidal intentions (Mohandie, Meloy and Collins, 2009).

Suicide by police: ideology or psychology?

Anton Lundin Pettersson was a lonely, isolated and angry 21-year-old. On the morning of 22 October 2015, Pettersson left his apartment carrying a long sword and dagger. He was dressed all in black, from his Nazi Second World War helmet and face mask, to his long coat and boots (Erlandsson and Reid Meloy, 2018). Pettersson was preparing to attack the Kronan School in Trollhättan, Sweden. An hour before the attack, he had messaged his online friend about his expectation to die and how he hated himself and hoped the police would aim straight (Kolankiewicz, 2018). Pettersson entered the school looking like the Star Wars villain Darth Vader.

At first, eyewitnesses thought that it was a Halloween prank, but then Pettersson fatally struck 20-year-old teaching assistant Lavin Eskandar with his sword. Pettersson then stabbed Ahmed Hassan, who later died in the hospital. Then, while wandering the halls, Pettersson posed with two students who thought he was playing a prank and took a picture of Pettersson while blood dripped from his sword. Shortly after, 42-year-old teacher Nazir Amso was stabbed after he asked Pettersson to remove his mask.

The attack was certainly a suicide by police scenario. To help the police officers' aim, he brought firing range targets, intending to fasten them to his chest but he did not have time. When the police arrived and ordered Pettersson to drop the sword, he responded by raising it. He was hit by a single shot and later died in the hospital.

The Second World War helmet and military manner led the police to conclude that his motivation was racism. Further supporting this conclusion was his choice of school, because of its location in a neighbourhood with a high immigrant population (Crouch, 2015). However, he was not just ideologically motivated. In their psychological autopsy, Erlandsson and Reid Meloy (2018) present convincing evidence that Pettersson was clinically depressed. The evidence includes the scars on his arms (from earlier attempts to self-harm), his suicide by police letter and his internet search history of suicide. The outcome of the story is that Pettersson's behaviours may represent a dangerous combination of mental illness and racial ideology (Reid Meloy and Yakeley, 2014).

IN SUMMARY

The use of force is an important part of policing, but the skill of applying force in proportion to the threat requires clear use of force policies and effective training. However, restrictive use of force policies are effective, but they must support officer safety.

CRITICAL THINKING AND APPLICATION QUESTIONS

1   Review Figure 10.1. How do the first three phases of the police–citizen encounter contribute to the last phase?

2   Research incidents of 'suicide by police'. Is there more evidence supporting the theory that 'suicide by police' incidents are an act of psychological desperation or the theory that they are acts of political declaration?

3   Why is it difficult to determine when the use of force is excessive?

THE ART OF CRISIS NEGOTIATION

FICTION: Tactical assaults are the most effective use of police resources for dealing with crisis situations.	*Versus*	**FACT:** Psychological strategies are the most effective use of police resources for dealing with crisis situations.

Global Perspectives

The 'Sydney siege' and the need for hostage negotiation skills

'They have not negotiated, they've done nothing. They have left us here to die!' This is part of the phone conversation from a hostage during the 16-hour Sydney hostage crisis. In 2014, a lone shooter, Man Haron Monis, held 18 customers and employees hostage in the Lindt chocolate café in Sydney, Australia. During the siege, no significant effort was made to negotiate with Monis, as would normally be expected in a hostage situation, in order to build a relationship with the gunman and persuade them to surrender. Instead, Monis received no encouragement or assistance from trained police negotiators (Salna, 2016). The standoff ended quickly when a gunshot was heard from inside and police officers from the Tactical Operations Unit stormed the café. Hostage Tori Johnson was killed by Monis and hostage Katrina Dawson was killed by a police bullet ricochet. Monis was also killed (Ralson, 2015). Police were criticised for the deaths of hostages and the lack of negotiation during the siege (Feneley, 2015).

The 'Sydney siege' illustrates the importance of negotiation strategies. The art of crisis negotiation has been described as a 'complex verbal dance between the negotiator and the subject' (Kellin and McMurtry, 2007, p. 30). This skill is one of the most important developments in law enforcement and police psychology. Our exploration focuses on how police train to apply this skill and the modifications necessary to meet the dynamics of the situation and perpetrator motivations, traits and characteristics.

The role of the police negotiator

Police officers are trained to react appropriately in violent situations. They need to analyse a great deal of information in a short amount of time before deciding to protect themselves,

PART IV

the victims and even the perpetrator. These situations typically involve one or more armed or potentially armed individuals, who refuse to surrender and behave dangerously towards themselves (suicidal intentions) and/or others (violent/homicidal intentions), who barricade themselves, alone or with others (hostages, accomplices), or climb a high structure (bridge, utility tower, building) in order to solve their personal and/or domestic problems (Morewitz, 2019). In situations like these, brute force tactical assaults are not the most effective strategic solutions.

Law enforcement professionals in many countries increasingly rely on negotiation as a peaceful alternative to tactical assault. Today's police officer has become the wedge between peaceful surrender and active conflict because, when emotion is high, rational thinking and the ability to identify non-violent solutions are compromised. The first goal of negotiation is to stabilise the situation and decrease emotion.

A crisis, by its very nature, means that time is short and the stakes are high, and rise with every word and every gesture (Gardner, 2015). Given such a heavy responsibility, it is crucial to consider the characteristics required for successful negotiation. Surveys of crisis negotiators list the skills of active listening, displays of empathy, effective communication, and staying calm as the most important characteristics. On the other hand, being confrontational, arguing, yelling and interrupting are behaviours to be avoided (Johnson, Thompson, Hall and Meyer, 2018).

Police negotiators assume that the offender is rational and views the officer involved as credible. If either of these assumptions are absent, then negotiation will fail to persuade the offender to change their behaviour. During a state of crisis, when coping and social support mechanisms fail, at least one of these assumptions must be restored. In these situations, the Behavioural Influence Stairway Model provides the officer with an approach to re-establish social support, thus returning the individual to a rational state of mind, and to demonstrate empathy, thus gaining trust and credibility (Vecchi, Wong, Wong and Markey, 2019).

The Behavioural Influence Stairway Model (BISM)

The Behavioural Influence Stairway Model (BISM) is a systematic, multistep model designed to produce a peaceful, non-lethal resolution of critical incidents (Vecchi, van Hasselt and Romano, 2005). The BISM is used in situations such as domestic violence (Morewitz, 2019; Ireland, 2017), hostage negotiations (Vecchi, van Hasselt and Romano, 2005), persons in crisis (Vecchi, Wong, Wong and Markey, 2019) and terrorism (Ireland and Vecchi, 2009).

Figure 10.2: The five steps of the Behavioural Influence Stairway Model (BISM)

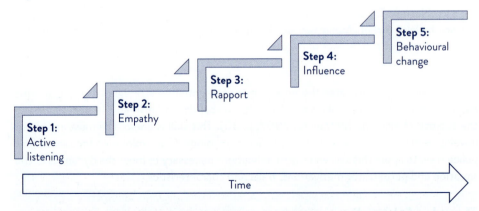

Source: Ireland, C. A. & Vecchi, G. M. (2009). The Behavioral Influence Stairway Model (BISM): a framework for managing terrorist crisis situations? *Behavioral Sciences of Terrorism and Political Aggression*, 1(3), 203–218. Adapted by permission of Taylor & Francis Ltd, www.tandfonline.com on behalf of Society for Terrorism Research.

The BISM model outlines a process for developing a relationship between the police negotiator and the individual in crisis (hostage taker, suicidal individual), which concludes with the negotiator influencing the decisions of the counterpart. The model has five steps that are to be completed in succession to cause behavioural change. For example, a negotiator must successfully listen (Step 1) before they can express empathy (Step 2).

Step 1: Active listening

Active listening, the first step of the BISM, establishes the foundation for the next steps and applies a collection of techniques aimed at establishing a relationship between the negotiator and the offender. Humanistic psychologist Carl Rogers described active listening as a means of communication to perceive the world from another person's frame of reference and communicate to that person what we have perceived. A person's **frame of reference** includes their experience, values, feelings and perceptions (Rogers, 1975). Active listening is a group of affective and effective skills. The affective components build rapport and trust, while the effective components gather vital information. Table 10.3 presents the 'PRIME SOS' **mnemonic** to help remember these.

Frame of reference – *A person's unique experiences, values, feelings and perceptions.*

Mnemonic – *Any learning technique that aids information retention or retrieval.*

Table 10.3: Active listening skills of the BISM: using the 'PRIME SOS' mnemonic

Paraphrase	Repeat what the person said in a shorter format, in your own words, to increase clarity
Reflect and mirror	Repeat the last few words the person said. If the person ended by saying, 'nothing has worked', you would say, 'Nothing has worked?'
'I' messages	Use personal disclosure to connect an emotion or experience to the context of what the subject is describing: 'I feel … when you … because …'
Minimal encouragers	Use simple verbal and nonverbal cues to the subject, indicating attention to what the subject is saying and experiencing: 'Yeah.' 'Uh-huh.' 'When?' 'And?' 'Really?' 'You do?'
Emotion labelling	Identify the emotions the subject is feeling: 'You seem …', 'I hear …'
Summarise	Combine the content of paraphrasing with emotion labelling into the negotiator's own words
Open-ended questions	These prompt the subject to expand on their concerns and perspectives and encourage clarification: 'I really want to understand this. Can you give me an example?'
Silence	Silence before a meaningful comment creates anticipation in the subject, while silence after creates reflection

Source: Adapted with permission from Thompson, J. (2016) Crisis negotiation: How to talk to someone you're worried about. Available at https://afsp.org/crisis-negotiation-talk-someone-youre-worried-about.

Step 2: Empathy

The goal of empathy, the second step in the BISM, is for the negotiator to show that they understand the beliefs, feelings and motives of the other person (Vecchi, 2009). This is an important part of advancing the relationship between the negotiator and the other person, and can be achieved with a tone of voice that is genuine and using phrases that convey

PART IV

interest in and concern for the other person. An example of an empathic statement would be: 'I understand how hard losing your house would be.' It is important to note that this is different than expressing sympathy, which can indicate pity. During a crisis, the goal is to establish a relationship via effective communication. Expressing empathy is difficult because we rarely listen intently to another's experience without judgement, advice or analysis (Rogers, 1975).

Step 3: Rapport

Rapport, the third step of the BISM, builds on the negotiator's active listening and expressions of empathy, and aims to establish a connection with the other party, and increase trust between the parties. The negotiator continues to build rapport through conversation that focuses on three social negotiation strategies to justify, blame, or excuse the crisis (Kim, Cundiff and Choi, 2015):

1   Applying two Freudian **defence mechanisms** of rationalisation and projection can increase rapport. First, by using **rationalisation** – when the controversial behaviours or feelings are justified and explained in a rational or logical manner to avoid the true explanation: an example would be: 'You sound like a good person who's been through a bad situation'; and second, by **projection** of blame – attributing unwanted thoughts, feelings and motives onto another person (Strentz, 2017).

2   **Minimisation** – downplaying the significance of an event or emotion – although typically associated with interrogation, is a common strategy in dealing with feelings of guilt. For example, appealing to the suspect's self-interest and their conscience (Kelly, Russano, Miller and Redlich, 2019).

3   **Collaboration** – using social negotiation to find common ground to reduce real or perceived differences. At this point, the person in crisis is ready to be influenced by the police and be persuaded to change their behaviour (van Hasselt et al., 2006).

Step 4: Influence

Being able to influence another person means producing an effect without direct authority or force (Vecchi, 2009). Once rapport has been established, the negotiator is in a position to begin to make suggestions to the other person, explore potential and realistic solutions to the conflict, and consider the likely alternatives available to the other side. More simply stated, the negotiator has earned the credibility to suggest a course of action to the person in crisis as a result of their collaborative problem solving (Vecchi, van Hasselt and Romano, 2005).

Step 5: Behavioural change

A hostage taker typically has only four possible options: surrender, escape, suicide, or killing hostages. Only the first option is preferred by law enforcement, although nonviolent escape at least spares hostages and may enable authorities to track the suspect down later. Surrender depends on how well the negotiator completed the first four steps of the BISM. Ultimately, the aim of crisis negotiation is to demonstrate that the method chosen by the perpetrator, namely the taking of a hostage, is not an effective strategy for dealing with their problem (Hatcher, Mohandie, Turner and Gelles, 1998).

Defence mechanisms – Unconscious strategies used to decrease anxiety arising from unacceptable thoughts, feelings or behaviours.

Rationalisation – When controversial behaviours or feelings are justified to avoid the true explanation.

Projection – Attributing unwanted thoughts, feelings and motives onto another person.

Minimisation – Downplaying the significance of an event or emotion.

Collaboration – Using social negotiation to find common ground to reduce real or perceived differences.

Role playing hostage negotiation

Read the following scenario:

> The divorce was final, and after enduring months of stalking and harassment, Linda filed
> a court order against David, the father of her child. This order prevented David from
> contacting Linda or their daughter. David responded by kidnapping Linda and their child from
> the daughter's school. Authorities traced his phone and found David holding them hostage at
> gunpoint in a hotel room.

How many of the active listening skills in Table 10.3 can you apply in responding to the following four
statements/responses from David?

1   'I'm not going to just let her take my daughter away from me.'

2   'I'm so tired of trying to get Linda to come back to me.'

3   'You don't understand, my daughter is all I have.'

4   'I can't take it anymore.'

Hostage taker categories

Knowing that the hostage taker is motivated by personal (emotional), criminal
(instrumental), or social/political (ideological) issues requires different negotiation tactics.

Hostile and aggressive hostage takers

Reasons for hostile behaviour include pathological anger, narcissistic rage, post-traumatic
stress disorder, brain trauma, substance abuse and life crises (Allen and Anderson, 2017).
One of the most common characteristics of aggressive and hostile individuals is that they
plan their aggression to gain control of the situation, while keeping others off balance.
This creates an advantage from which they can exploit weaknesses (Johnson et al., 2018).
Therefore, when dealing with a hostile and aggressive hostage taker, calm active listening is
a priority. Not reacting to provocations allows the negotiator to depersonalise the situation
and turn from being reactive to being proactive.

Hostage takers with mental illness

Most people in this category who take hostages represent the diagnostic categories of
schizophrenia, depression and antisocial personality disorder (Borum and Strentz, 1992).
It is important to remember that while many of those involved in hostage incidents may
suffer from mental health problems, this does not mean that many of those suffering from
mental health problems are likely to take hostages (Miller, 2007).

Schizophrenia spectrum disorder

Schizophrenia spectrum disorder is one of the most challenging disorders because
of the disruption and disorganisation in thinking and behaviour, impaired emotional
experience and expression, and the presence of delusions (false beliefs) and hallucinations
(false perceptions) (Tandon et al., 2013). Most hallucinations are **auditory persecutory
hallucinations** that involve hearing voices that degrade and demean the subject (Iwashiro
et al., 2019). These subjects are usually in a state of extreme fear and agitation in response

**Auditory
persecutory
hallucinations**
*– Hearing
voices that
degrade and
demean the
subject.*

PART IV

to these hallucinations. The second most common type of hallucination is the **command hallucination**, which orders the subject to do something (Pontillo et al., 2016). In this situation, where the underlying emotion is likely to be some combination of fear and anger, the application of calming techniques is appropriate. Because these individuals are less responsive to normal emotional cues, many of the active listening approaches are ineffective. In these situations, rapport emerges from the subject's need to explain their motives, which may or may not be grounded in reality. In this case, acknowledging the content of the delusion, while trying to understand the subject's frame of reference, and keeping the focus on present reality is more effective (Mothersill, Knee-Zaska and Donohoe, 2016).

> **Command hallucination**
> – *Hearing voices ordering the subject to do something.*

Depression

Subjects suffering from depression may be hopeless, suicidal and dangerous because they have 'nothing to lose' by harming their hostages. If a hostage has a history with the offender, such as a disliked employer or estranged family member, there may be no demands, other than an audience for their act of desperate revenge (Guszkowski and van Hasselt, 2017). They may be unresponsive to the dynamics of negotiation, simply due to emotional and behavioural apathy – a feeling of 'nothing left to live for'. Hostage negotiators should begin and end with open-ended questions that allow silence before the response. If this approach is not effective, then they should use direct, closed-ended questions that reflect feelings. Finally, if the subject mentions suicide, the negotiator should address it directly, while keeping in mind that the ultimate goal is to end the crisis and not engage in therapy (Knowles, 2016).

Antisocial personality disorder

Antisocial personality disorder is characterised by selfish, irresponsible behaviour, which is often impulsive or aggressive, ignoring any harm or distress caused to other people. A challenge for creating rapport with this category of hostage taker is their inability to maintain long-term social and personal relationships (Edens et al., 2015). Unlike other personality disorders, antisocial personality disorder is distinguished by a lack of conscience, reflected in ruthless and remorseless behaviour. Hostage takers suffering this form of mental disorder are skilful at manipulating and intimidating those around them (Black, 2015). In this case, any information gathered during the first steps in the BISM should be verified using external sources.

IN SUMMARY

Crisis negotiation is complex, and the Behavioural Influence Stairway Model is an effective model to begin the negotiation process and consider the development of clear approaches and tactics that are relevant for the presenting situation. Exploration of the presenting traits, characteristics and behaviour of the hostage taker is an important focus, which requires careful consideration and thought on behalf of the crisis negotiator. Thus, to be truly effective, negotiators need to connect the art and science of crisis management to insights on personality and psychopathology offered by mental health professionals.

CRITICAL THINKING AND APPLICATION QUESTIONS

1   Describe a virtual environment hostage simulation that could be used to train people in the BISM approach. Explain how the simulation would be standardised and realistic.

2   Examine Table 10.3 and rank the eight BISM active listening skills from the easiest to the hardest to apply. What made the most difficult techniques so challenging?

3   In what ways could the BISM be modified to accommodate people suffering from mental illness?

PSYCHOLOGICAL EFFECTS OF ACUTE STRESS ON PERFORMANCE

FICTION: Fate determines the critical differences in the functioning of police officers who perform well in the face of danger and those who fail.	*Versus*	**FACT:** Research shows that understanding the psychophysiological effects of stress can be applied to enhance police performance.

One critical incident with four different responses

The critical incident took place on 16 September 2016 on a two-lane road outside the US town of Tulsa, Oklahoma. Police cameras captured the encounter between police officer Betty Shelby and 40-year-old motorist Terence Crutcher. The video footage showed Crutcher continuously reaching into his pocket, refusing to show his hands, walking towards his vehicle despite being told to stop, and then trying to reach into his vehicle.

There were four police officers at the scene and four different responses. Officer Shelby fired her gun, another officer deployed a Taser, a third pointed his gun at Crutcher but chose not to fire, and the fourth did nothing more than rest one hand on his gun belt while using the other to operate a microphone (Juozapavicius, 2016).

Crutcher lay bleeding in the street as officers moved in to check him for weapons and administer first aid. But they were too late and he was pronounced dead at the hospital. Police found a vial of phencyclidine (a drug used illegally for its hallucinogenic effects) in the driver's side-door pocket, and no weapons on his body or in his car (Stack, 2016). Shelby claimed self-defence as her reason for shooting because she thought he was reaching into his car for what might have been a weapon. It was the first time Shelby had fired her gun in the line of duty. She was arrested for manslaughter. However, because the jury could not conclude that she went beyond her duties and training as a police officer, she was later acquitted (Ellis, 2017).

Discussion Questions:

1   When police shoot an unarmed suspect, it is often ruled as justified if the officer's fear of severe harm in that moment is reasonable. Some say that this principle of objective reasonableness acts as a shield against post-action review for police officers. Where do you stand on this issue?

2   Based on their behaviour, explain the story from the different perspectives of the other police officers at the scene?

Acute stress and police performance

The case of Betty Shelby reveals how stress affects police officer performance during a critical incident. This section explores how intense critical incident stress changes a police officer's awareness and performance.

Police performance research reveals that psychological and physiological stress responses during critical incidents can produce both negative and positive outcomes (Arble, Daugherty and Arnetz, 2019). A **critical incident** is an event stressful enough to overwhelm an individual's usual coping skills (Mitchell and Bray, 1990). These include any threatening situations to a person's life or safety, or exposure to the death or injury of another as a result of an accident, suicide or crime (Jacobsson, Backteman-Erlanson, Brulin and Hörnsten, 2015). The greater the degree of uncertainty an individual feels about an outcome, the greater the anxiety and stress.

Imagine a police officer responding to a report of another officer in urgent need of help. As she races to the scene, her mouth is dry, her heart races as tension in her arms and shoulders rise. As she gets closer to the situation, her breathing quickens and she begins sweating. Before arriving at the scene, her body is preparing for the demands of what may happen. Her symptoms are due to the fight-or-flight response – the stress response (Cannon, 1932). Police routinely face unpredictable, unexpected and uncontrollable events, all of which increase the threatening nature of a situation (Sapolsky, 2015). Over time, these challenges can cause physical, emotional and social consequences associated with reduced performance during critical incidents (Arble, Daugherty and Arnetz, 2018). The mistakes made during these moments carry great psychological weight and their emotional consequences increase the chance of future mistakes (Leino, Selin, Summala and Virtanen, 2011).

Stress is an imbalance between a threatening physical or psychological demand and the ability to meet the demand. The body reacts to these threats with physical, cognitive and emotional responses (Ross and Murphy, 2017). The stressful demands of police work include dealing with immediate life-or-death decisions, human misery, people in crisis and long, unpredictable hours. If this was not enough, there are strict legal procedures and societal responsibilities (Korre et al., 2014). Meanwhile, during a stress reaction, the police officer is expected to maintain vigilance, dynamic threat assessment, sound judgement and appropriate tactical decision making. Instead, stress-induced emotions (fear and anger), perceptual anomalies (tunnel vision, auditory exclusion, altered sense of space and time), memory loss and distracting thoughts can cause maladaptive behaviours – freezing, automatic reactions, dissociation – sometimes with tragic consequences (Fenici, Brisinda and Sorbo, 2011).

Examining the psychophysiological responses of an officer's behaviour under critical tactical stress is important because any potential threat (real or imagined) can trigger the release of stress hormones. Stress hormones such as adrenaline and glucocorticoids increase heart rate and energy level. The process begins with the physiological stress response of the **sympathetic nervous system (SNS)** and ends with the activation of the **parasympathetic nervous system (PNS)**, which is responsible for returning the body back to a normal level of functioning. Stress hormones speed thinking and mobilise energy, while the SNS turns off everything that is not essential to surviving, such as digestion, growth and reproduction (Sapolsky, 2015). A police officer's stress response depends on the intensity, nature and duration of the stressor, and internal factors –coping skills, physical and mental resiliency (Joëls and Baram, 2009). According to McGrath (1970), as cited in Blankenship (2007), the stress response consists of four interrelated stages (Figure 10.3).

Critical incident – An event stressful enough to overwhelm an individual's usual coping skills.

Stress – An imbalance between an important or threatening physical or psychological demand and the ability to meet the demand.

Sympathetic nervous system (SNS) – A part of the nervous system that serves to accelerate the heart rate, constrict blood vessels and raise blood pressure.

Parasympathetic nervous system (PNS) – Responsible for returning the body back to a normal level of functioning.

Figure 10.3: The four-stage stress process

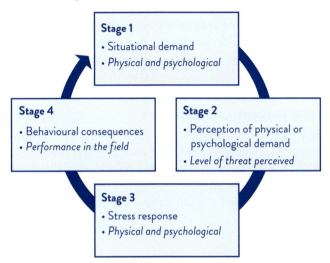

Source: Based on Blankenship, B. T. (2007). The stress process in physical education. *Journal of Physical Education, Recreation & Dance,* 78(6), 39–44.

The four-stage stress process can be described as follows:

- Stage 1 starts with *situational demands* (stressors). The demand can be physical, such as chasing a suspect, or psychological, feeling anxiety when stopping a suspected stolen vehicle.

- Stage 2 describes an *individual's perception of the physical or psychological demand* and their capabilities to meet the demand. Stress can be perceived as facilitative (helpful) or debilitative (harmful). Two police officers may view pursuing a stolen vehicle differently. One officer may view the situation as an opportunity to apply their training and perceive the chase as motivating and exciting, while another officer may view the same situation as a threat. This stress is a product of the perceived imbalance between the demands placed on the officer (having to demonstrate driving skills) and their ability to meet those demands.

- Stage 3 describes the *individual's physical and psychological response to the perception of the situation*. If the police officer perceives an imbalance in their ability to meet the stressful challenge, they will feel threatened and display increased physical signs of stress (changes in muscle tension, concentration, blood pressure).

- Stage 4 is the *behaviour of the police officer in the field while under stress*. In McGrath's model, the final stage feeds back into the first. If a police officer becomes overly threatened and performs poorly in the field in front of other officers, the negative social evaluation becomes an added demand on the individual (stage 1). The stress process then becomes a cycle (Rauch, Fink and Hatak, 2018).

An understanding of the stress cycle enables police psychologists to target efforts to reduce stress (Büssing and Glaser, 2000). If a police psychologist is asked to develop a stress management programme, stage 1 of the model suggests that psychologists should determine what demands are placed on the police force, such as unrealistic workloads, changing shifts, or lack of training. An analysis of stage 2 might lead the psychologist to question who is experiencing the most stress, such as individuals working longer hours and those with certain personality dispositions. Stage 3 requires studying the reactions of individual police to increased stress, such as increased somatic anxiety, attention and concentration problems. Offering physical activity or other means of stress management is an appropriate intervention. Stage 4 analysis focuses on the officer's behavioural reaction to increased stress, such as absenteeism, reduced productivity, or decreased job satisfaction.

Acute stress and perceptual distortions

The physiological effects of critical incident stress affect performance in life-and-death scenarios. Stress responses can distort police officers' auditory, visual, motor coordination and time perception. While the stress response can never be eliminated, properly prepared officers will be able to anticipate and identify these responses in themselves and others and can initiate safeguards to limit or control the effects of stress on task performance.

Auditory distortions

Auditory exclusion
– A form of temporary hearing loss occurring during high levels of stress.

Arthwhol and Christensen (1997) found that 88 per cent of officers experienced a distortion of sound during a police shooting. One form of distortion is **auditory exclusion** – a form of temporary hearing loss occurring under high stress. Police officer Betty Shelby (from the previous case study) claimed 'auditory exclusion' for her lack of awareness of other officers around her (Hutchinson and Ghebremedhin, 2018). This narrowing of auditory focus is similar to the visual experience of tunnel vision under high stress. Auditory exclusion occurs only during the physiological changes associated with the fight-or-flight reaction and not when an individual is voluntarily participating in an intense form of exercise (Jafari, Kolb and Mohajerani, 2017). A more extreme example is **inattentional deafness** – a temporary deafness to normal environmental sounds, such as speech (Raveh and Lavie, 2015). Experiencing inattentional deafness happens during intense levels of visual focus and cognitive processing (Murphy and Greene, 2015).

Inattentional deafness
– A temporary deafness for normal environmental sounds, such as speech.

Visual and attention distortions

The stress response alters vision in three ways; restricted peripheral vision (tunnel vision), distance-only eyesight and forced binocular vision (Rogers and Landers, 2005; Olson, 1998). Reduced peripheral vision is caused by vasoconstriction of the blood vessels on the periphery of the retina where motion detection occurs (Rogers, Rushton and Warren, 2017). Peripheral vision is important for maintaining situational awareness. For example, police officers' shooting accuracy decreased significantly when they performed in high-anxiety conditions in which opponents returned fire using coloured soap cartridges. Even trained officers focused on the immediate threat (soap cartridges) when confronted with life-threatening situations at the expense of potentially life-threatening cues in peripheral vision (Nieuwenhuys and Oudejans, 2010).

Stress-induced visual distortions affect shooting accuracy when targets are at close range. SNS arousal causes the pupils to dilate and can impair daytime visual acuity, contrast sensitivity and increased glare sensitivity (Wood et al., 2003). SNS disrupts monocular vision and reduces the ability to focus on a gun sight (Klinger and Brunson, 2009). Additionally, police no longer looked straight at the opponent and blinked more often, which increased the amount of time they had their eyes closed. The overall effect of stress on performance was that police officers' behaviour became less efficient and more stimulus focused (Nieuwenhuys and Oudejans, 2010).

Continuous visual information feedback during aiming and shooting is crucial for effective perceptual–motor performance. The visual gaze behaviour of police during high-stress circumstances reveals that they focused more on threat-related and task-irrelevant stimuli (opponent's gun or face) than during the low-stress condition (Nieuwenhuys and Oudejans, 2010). However, Vickers and Lewinski (2012) showed that experience plays a role in efficient visual processing. Experienced police officers had more visual fixations on task-relevant locations (locations where a gun could be hidden) and were ready to fire earlier than novices, resulting in better shooting performance. In contrast, novice police officers shifted their gaze away from the opponent to their own gun during shooting.

Motor coordination

Police officers seldom shoot accurately during tactical shooting situations (Vila and Morrison, 1994) and reduced motor coordination under stress can be explained by three causes:

1   Reduced attention affects movement execution (action).

2   While gross motor skills (larger movements) become enhanced during stress (Giessing et al., 2019), fine motor skills (pulling the trigger of gun smoothly and precisely aiming at a target) become increasingly difficult under stress.

3   Research reveals that shooting accuracy is affected by increased heart rate variability (Thompson et al., 2015).

Stress affects two brain structures that coordinate movement. Stress can reduce the role of the *prefrontal cortex*, which controls fine coordination, planning and decision making (Arnsten, 2009). Another structure is the *cerebellum*, which controls learning and performance of complex automatic motor sequences (aiming and shooting of a weapon). Research shows that even a single exposure to acute stress affects information processing in these brain areas (Savtchouk and Liu, 2011).

This effect was demonstrated in the case of officer Johannes Mehserle's experience in San Francisco, California on New Year's Day, 2009. In the presence of a hostile crowd, Mehserle and officer Anthony Pirone were trying to control suspect Oscar Grant. Grant was actively resisting while Pirone had Grant's head and shoulders pinned down with his knee. Meanwhile, Mehserle was trying to pull Grant's hand out from under his body to handcuff him. Mehserle twice announced his intention to Taser Grant. However, he drew his Sig Sauer P226 pistol with his right hand – not his yellow Taser, which was on the left front of his body in a cross-draw position – partially stood, and fired a single, fatal shot into Grant's back (Bulwa and Swan, 2018). This mistake is called a **slip-and-capture error**. These are mistakes that are made when you think you are doing one action, but you are actually doing another (Martin, 2016). Mehserle had less practice drawing a Taser (only about a dozen times) and none in stressful circumstances. By contrast, he had practised drawing his handgun at least 50 times a week and had developed a strong automatic motor response (Martinelli, 2010). In effect, the intended behaviour (normally coordinated by the prefrontal cortex) 'slips off' the path you wanted it to go because it is 'captured' by a stronger, more practised response (controlled by the cerebellum) and sent in a different direction.

Slip-and-capture error – *Mistakes that are made when you think you are doing one action, but you actually are doing another.*

Time distortion

Performance change under stress is affected by distortions in the perception of time. Ninety four per cent of officers involved in shooting incidents described some altered perception of reality either before or during the firing of their weapons (Klinger and

Brunson, 2009). The feeling of slow-moving time was reported 67 per cent and the feeling of time moving faster 15 per cent (Solomon and Horn, 1986). One explanation is that attention is dedicated to task-relevant activities (aiming the weapon, tracking the target) and attention to time-based cues is minimised. This distorts both the perception of the passage of time and the memory of events (Hancock and Weaver, 2005).

Cognitive effects

Cognitive processes and well-rehearsed behaviours required in police work are affected differently by stress. Specifically, cognitive functions that require greater mental resources are vulnerable to disruption. One example of this is the decision to discharge a weapon. Nieuwenhuys and Oudejans (2017) found that during stressful situations, police are more likely to decide to fire their weapon and have lower shot accuracy (Nieuwenhuys and Oudejans, 2017). Acute stress impairs complex and intentional behaviours, but *not* reflexive self-defence behaviours (Renden, Savelsbergh and Oudejans, 2017).

IN SUMMARY

For the safety of the police and public, it is important to understand the effects of police officer physiological arousal (acute stress response) on tactical and communication skills during a critical incident. Research demonstrates that extensive practice and repetition allows police officers to use well-rehearsed tactical procedures while under threat, thus translating physiological arousal into decisive and effective tactical responding.

 ## CRITICAL THINKING AND APPLICATION QUESTIONS

1   Define stress and identify how the four stages of the stress process can be used to guide police training.

2   What are some of the reasons the same situation produces a different behavioural response in different individuals?

3   Discuss the relationship between a police officer's cognitive interpretation of stress as facilitative or debilitative and their performance.

PSYCHOLOGICAL EFFECTS OF CHRONIC STRESS ON PERFORMANCE

| **FICTION:** Policing culture breeds toughness and buffers the effects of stress. | *Versus* | **FACT:** Police culture contributes to the chronic effects of stress especially during critical incidents. |

The 'onion field' murders

On the night of 9 March 1963, the three-word police code 'Six Zebra Four' echoed over the police airwaves in a desperate search for two missing officers. Earlier that night, Los Angeles Police Department officers Ian Campbell and Karl Hettinger pulled over a vehicle for making an illegal U-turn. However, they did not know that the occupants, Gregory Powell and Jimmy Lee Smith, had recently committed a string of robberies, and were each carrying a concealed gun. Powell, the driver, pulled a gun on officer Campbell, who 'calmly told his partner, "He has a gun in my back. Give him your gun."' The two officers were then forced into Powell's car and driven to a secluded onion field (Mendoza, 2013). They shot and killed Campbell in front of Hettinger, but as they were preparing to kill Hettinger, a cloud obscured the moonlight. In the darkness and confusion, Hettinger escaped, running nearly seven kilometres (four miles) to reach the safety of a farmhouse (Malnic, 1994). Not only was Hettinger victimised by watching his partner murdered, but he was second-guessed by his colleagues because he escaped and survived while his partner did not.

After the incident, Hettinger was forced to admit blame for his lack of courage by visiting other police departments and describing the incident and the consequences for surrendering his weapon. Being forced to recount the details over and over simply reinforced his anguish and the feeling that he was responsible for Campbell's death (Harpold and Feemster, 2002). His experience inspired the controversial 'Hettinger Memorandum', that told officers never to give up their weapons. The memo suggested that Campbell could have prevented his own death and implied that both Campbell and Hettinger were cowards (Oliver, 2002).

At the time, there was no support for police enduring situations like this. There were no police psychologists, family education programmes or peer support, because of the belief that enduring emotional and physical trauma was just part of the job and should be ignored, eventually fading with time. Since the days of the 'onion field' incident, we now know about the psychological trauma that critical incidents like these can cause (Krajicek, 2008).

Discussion Questions:

1　　Why do you think Hettinger's police colleagues questioned his motives for escape?

2　　What do you think is the effect of reviewing traumatic experiences without proper psychological or even emotional support?

Sources of chronic stress

This section explores the sources of stress and their consequences for police officers. Police officers are considered to be at higher risk for developing mental health disturbances because of chronic exposure to critical incidents and organisational stress during their career. Policing is a psychologically stressful work environment and consequences can range from developing a cynical view of life, burnout and low job satisfaction (Brady, 2017) to PTSD (APA, 2013), depression (Jenkins et al., 2019) and suicide ideation (Violanti et al., 2019).

Operational stressors – *Stresses related to tasks related to the job of policing.*

Organisational stressors – *Stresses related to the culture of policing.*

The stressors in policing can be divided into **operational stressors** – stress of doing the job – and **organisational stressors** – stress related to the culture of policing (Stancel et al., 2019). Operational stressors include work schedules, court work, lack of time spent with family and friends, traumatic events, and threats to physical and psychological health (Violanti et al., 2016). Organisational stressors include bureaucracy and co-worker relations, inconsistencies in leadership, participation in decision making, and the perception of having to prove yourself to the organisation (McCreary, Fong and Groll, 2017). Despite more research attention on acute situations and events, such as attending accidents and exposure to violence, organisational sources of job stress are better predictors of police distress than acute and potentially traumatic incidents (LaMontagne et al., 2016).

The police culture

Police culture is a source of stress and sometimes celebration (Bleakley, 2019). Authority and power are vested in police officers as representatives of their jurisdictions; they have guns, Tasers, handcuffs, batons and uniforms (Delsol, 2015). They take charge, give orders and can limit citizen freedoms (by making arrests and the power to stop and search). Police officers often divide their world into 'us' and 'them' (everyone not a police officer) and believe that only other officers can understand them (Rose and Unnithan, 2015). There is also a stigma attached to admitting psychological difficulties and seeking help (Stuart, 2017). This stigma is the result of requiring officers to exercise a high degree of control and suppress emotions. Officers avoid seeking professional help because they expect to have their weapon taken away, or to be ignored for career advancement. They may also fear having a history of psychological problems becoming part of their permanent record, being shunned by their fellow officers, and being distrusted by those in command (Bullock and Garland, 2018).

Fitness-for-duty evaluations (FFDEs)

Law enforcement is a unique population and ensuring public safety requires that officers are mentally, emotionally and physically stable and considered 'fit for duty' to perform effectively. Reasons for undergoing fitness-for-duty evaluations (FFDEs) may include drug and alcohol abuse, emotional disturbances, violence or threats of violence, poor judgement, and abuse of authority. Some indicators may include threats to self or others, suicide attempts, psychiatric hospitalisations, or observed symptoms – unusual irritability and suspiciousness, which may be due to depression, anxiety, or other psychological conditions. Most FFDEs concern impulse control, substance abuse, or general observations about employee behaviour, such as withdrawal from contact with work peers and irritability (Mayer and Corey, 2017). A fitness-for-duty programme can prevent the occurrence of more serious problems. But, once a problem has been identified, the situation should be referred to a psychological services unit if one exists, internal affairs, or an employee assistance programme (Fischler et al., 2011). Regardless of jurisdiction (Australia, Canada, Europe, the UK or the USA), every law enforcement officer undergoes FFDEs that entail a combination of psychological testing and interviewing. Failing the evaluation may result in job loss or suspension. An unintended consequence is that most officers are hesitant to seek help with mental, emotional, relational or even physical issues because it could result in their inability to work (Miller, 2006).

Source: Ollie Millington/Getty Images

All police undergo FFDEs to determine whether they can function in a manner conducive to public safety and the safety of fellow officers

Mental health symptoms following critical incident exposures

Policing places officers at high risk of exposure to situations that could lead to trauma and stress-related disorders, such as acute stress disorder (ASD) and post-traumatic stress disorder (PTSD), following exposure to critical incidents (Birch, Vickers, Kennedy and Galovic, 2017).

Acute stress disorder (ASD)

Police facing traumatic and frequent stressors are at an increased risk of experiencing an acute stress response (Ehlers et al., 2013). An acute stress response during or immediately after traumatic stress involves biological and psychological responses – hyperarousal, anger/irritability, sadness, numbing, nightmares and intrusive thoughts (APA, n.d.; Marin et al., 2019). While these responses are normal, some police develop more serious impairments requiring assessment and treatment, for example acute stress disorder (ASD) (Morina, Wicherts, Lobbrecht and Priebe, 2014). ASD may be a way to identify police who require immediate treatment, rather than as a tool for highlighting those at risk of developing later PTSD (Bryant, 2011). ASD can be identified in individuals starting three days after an event and includes multiple symptoms – intrusions, negative mood, dissociation, avoidance and arousal (Meiser-Stedman et al., 2017). ASD is different from a typical stress response due to the persistent severity of symptoms beyond the timeframe of an acute stress reaction. Although ASD diagnosis was established to predict later PTSD, longitudinal studies indicate that ASD is not an accurate predictor of PTSD (Bryant, 2018).

Post-traumatic stress disorder (PTSD)

Post-traumatic stress disorder (PTSD) may occur when a person is exposed to one or more traumatic events. The potential long-term effects of PTSD in police officers may lead to behavioural dysfunction such as substance abuse, aggression and suicide. Symptoms of PTSD include re-experiencing trauma, avoidance, negative cognitions and mood, and arousal – often manifested by aggressiveness, sleep problems, recklessness, or self-destructive behaviour (APA, 2013a). Individuals with PTSD symptoms are more likely to experience other psychological conditions, including depression, suicidal ideation, substance abuse and social phobias (Marchand et al., 2015). It is not surprising that officers with PTSD symptoms also report reduced quality of life, poorer health, increased sick leave, more frequent medical appointments, and higher hospital admissions compared to officers without PTSD symptoms (Martin, Marchand, Boyer and Martin, 2009). Furthermore, officers who were exposed to multiple traumatic incidents experienced more severe symptoms compared to those who reported relatively few traumatic events (Violanti et al., 2017).

Trauma intervention strategies

Trauma-related problem intervention can happen during three periods; primary, secondary and tertiary (Figure 10.4):

- *Primary prevention* methods are proactive actions that prepare for future traumatic events.

- *Secondary prevention* methods modify an officer's response to stressors by intervening with the trauma survivor soon after exposure but before the development of post-trauma symptoms.

- *Tertiary prevention* methods are reactive and minimise the effects of stress-related problems once they have already occurred.

Figure 10.4: Three levels of trauma intervention strategies

Primary prevention strategies

Preparing for traumatic events increases psychological coping strategies and reduces a stressor's unpredictability and uncontrollability (Meichenbaum, 2017). Primary approaches have less social stigma because they cultivate good mental and behavioural health rather than treatment of mental illness. Police also need to use the best possible behavioural tactics during potentially traumatic encounters. Stressful arousal can interfere with adaptive behaviour, resulting in aggression, escape or freezing, all of which can have negative consequences (Paton, 2006). Teaching officers to engage in optimal police tactics while they prepare for potential threats leads to better police performance in the field (Arnetz et al., 2009). Preparing for threats includes the use of imaginal rehearsal

(Arble et al., 2017). Senior officers trained 32 police academy officers to engage in imaginal rehearsal of specific dangerous situations while using optimal police tactics and healthy emotional reactions. After their first year of fieldwork, 22 officers were reassessed. Compared to pretraining, these officers showed significant increases in the use of positive reframing and humour, and significant reductions in anxiety and alcohol use over the year and trauma symptoms did not increase.

Another primary approach is mindfulness behavioural training to increase resilience. **Psychological resilience** is a process of positive adaptation to acute and chronic stress (Mlinac and Schwabenbauer, 2018), and resilience may be a key mechanism that controls the impact of stress (Horn, Charney and Feder, 2016). **Mindfulness** is an active state of awareness of one's immediate experiences, and may counter the tendency to avoid emotions and thoughts, and break maladaptive patterns (Kudesia, 2019). Among police officers, greater mindfulness predicts less depression over the first year of service and improves symptoms of depression and anxiety, while also enhancing general psychological functioning (Williams, Ciarrochi and Deane, 2010; Gardner and Moore, 2012). Mindfulness-based resilience training increased resilience, mental and physical health, and reduced burnout among police (Christopher et al., 2016).

Secondary management strategies

Secondary management strategies take place shortly after traumatic exposure but before the development of post-trauma symptoms. Secondary interventions are concerned with the rapid detection and management of experienced stress, and the enhancement of police ability to manage stressful conditions more effectively. This approach focuses on increasing police awareness, knowledge, skills and coping resources (Duffy, Avalos and Dowling, 2015). Unfortunately, one of the most commonly used interventions, a critical incident stress debriefing, has limited empirical support; evidence suggests this approach is not helpful and may even be harmful to participants (Brucia, Cordova and Ruzek, 2017).

Police culture is resistant to accepting emotional support, fearing that it could interfere with the officer's reputation and job duties (Evans et al., 2013; Bell and Eski, 2016). Seeking support from non-police sources has limitations for the officer, from concerns about the individual's ability to understand and cope with often horrific incidents, and from family and friends, feelings of discomfort and worry about the officer's safety (Waters and Ussery, 2007). Yet humour is an accepted form of coping for police officers (Gayadeen and Phillips, 2016). Most police officers prefer to talk about difficult or challenging events with others who have similar experiences (Andersen and Papazoglou, 2015). Peer support is a crucial resource and they are often the first to notice when colleagues show symptoms of psychological distress (Bohl-Penrod and Clark, 2017). Unlike mental health professionals, peer supporters are perceived as more credible. Contact with peers gives police the encouragement, help and support they need to enlist the services of mental health professionals (a tertiary resource). Peer support is particularly important to women and minority police officers (Hartley, Mnatsakanova, Burchfiel and Violanti, 2014).

Tertiary reactive strategies

Tertiary interventions are reactive strategies that treat established trauma reactions with interventions such as psychological counselling and therapy (Ehlers et al., 2013). Such treatments are often seen as stigmatising by police and are underutilised (Stuart, 2017), except in the case of service dogs (Vincent et al., 2019). Regrettably, the tertiary approach can leave officers with months or years of distress and social and professional dysfunction before they can find relief.

Psychological resilience – The ability to mentally or emotionally cope with a crisis or to return to pre-crisis status quickly.

Mindfulness – An active state of awareness of one's immediate experiences.

PART IV

IN SUMMARY

Investigating police stress responses allows the design of more effective stress management strategies for these critical incidents and improves performance and coping with work-related stress. Coping with stress is a skill, requiring continued practice, updated training and external resources, such as psychological services, post-trauma intervention and peer support.

 CRITICAL THINKING AND APPLICATION QUESTIONS

1   Describe a situation when you or someone you know has demonstrated resilience. Do you see resilience as being a quality that someone can learn or develop? If so, how?

2   Think of one or two situations that have recently occurred in which you experienced stress. Analyse whether it was the situation or your personality traits that caused the stress response.

3   As a forensic psychologist, what elements of a stress management programme for police would be appropriate at the primary, secondary and tertiary levels?

CHAPTER REVIEW

Police psychology applies behavioural science principles to the concerns of police officers. While use of force is a necessary tool for police, the skill of when and how to use force in a proportional manner is more important. In the same way, understanding the psychophysiological reactions during acute stress can help police cope with the normal reactions to stress and improve efficiency. Long-term chronic stress can increase vulnerability to mental health problems unless shielded by empirically supported stress prevention approaches. Finally, principles of social psychology connect the art of crisis management to insights on personality and psychopathology.

NAMES TO KNOW

Robert Sapolsky

A professor of biological sciences and neurology and neurological sciences, he investigates the physiological effects of stress on health.

- Sapolsky, R. (2004) *Why Zebras Don't Get Ulcers* (3rd edn). Holt Paperbacks.

- Sapolsky, R. (2017) *Behave: The Biology of Humans at Our Best and Worst*. Penguin Books.

John Violanti

An internationally known expert on police stress, he is a retired NYPD officer and conducts research on officer safety and wellness issues.

- Violanti, J. M., Charles, L. E., McCanlies, E., Hartley, T. A., Baughman, P. et al. (2017) Police stressors and health: A state-of-the-art review. *Policing: An International Journal of Police Strategies & Management*, 40(4), 642–56.

• Allison, P., Mnatsakanova, A., McCanlies, E., Fekedulegn, D., Hartley, T. A., Andrew, M. E. and Violanti, J. M. (2019). Police stress and depressive symptoms: Role of coping and hardiness. Policing: An International Journal.

Judith P. Andersen

A health psychologist specialising in the psychophysiology of stress-related mental and physical health issues, by working with populations exposed to severe and chronic stress, including combat soldiers and police.

• Andersen, J. P., Papazoglou, K. and Collins, P. (2018) Exploring the association between authoritarianism, compassion fatigue, and compassion satisfaction among police officers. *International Journal of Criminal Justice Sciences*, 13(2), 403–17.

• Andersen, J. P. and Gustafsberg, H. (2016) A training method to improve police use of force decision making: A randomized controlled trial. *Sage Open*, 6(2), 1–13.

11 THE PSYCHOLOGY BEHIND JURY DECISION MAKING

Chapter Introduction

It is a unique challenge; finding a group of strangers to comprehend complex, confusing and sometimes contradictory evidence, to understand and apply laws, and to collectively reach a verdict. It is also an ideal opportunity for psychological investigation. We begin by reviewing the purpose and origins of juries and the methods of investigating what goes on behind closed doors. Research into the secret lives of juries investigates whether jury verdicts can be predicted from juror characteristics. If they can, then can their verdicts be manipulated? Next, we examine the question 'can individual jurors be unbiased?' by exploring how a juror and juries make their decisions.

Learning Outcomes

Investigating the secret lives of juries

- Present a clear argument outlining the case for and against jury secrecy.

Predicting verdicts from juror characteristics

- Support or refute the argument that juror verdicts can be predicted based on juror characteristics.

How individual jurors interpret evidence

- Describe the effect of different variables on individual juror's assessment of evidence.

The story behind jury deliberations

- Defend the argument that a group of people will make better decisions than a single individual.

INVESTIGATING THE SECRET LIVES OF JURIES

FICTION: Juries are like any other group and reach the same verdict with or without secrecy.	*Versus*	**FACT:** The secrecy of juror identity and deliberations both helps and hinders verdict deliberation.

Why do we have juries?

Why should we trust a group of inexperienced people to sit in judgement on our most serious criminal trials? Research has shown that layperson participation in the legal system and collective wisdom are essential for a transparent and fair system of justice (Pyo, 2018). Ironically, the democratisation of jury service has raised questions about jurors' ability to deliver justice fairly and predictably. Specifically, some raise concerns that laypeople are unable to understand complex evidence, are swayed by sympathy, and award extravagant sums of money for trivial claims (Greene, 2009).

Juries are drawn from the local population to create representative participation, although the exact way juries are formed varies across jurisdictions. Many jurisdictions use juries of ordinary citizens selected randomly from the community, while others, including most of Continental Europe, draw on a pool of lay judges or expert jurors selected through local elections or as political appointments (Jackson and Kovalev, 2006). The use of juries in criminal and some civil cases is widespread but declining (Bornstein and Greene, 2011).

Many countries use the term 'juror' for any layperson who takes part in legal decision making. Jurors are often selected randomly from the general population, but there are exceptions. In their survey of lay participation, Jackson and Kovalev (2006) distinguish five approaches to lay legal decision making. These five models show differences in how countries use laypeople in legal decision making (Table 11.1).

Table 11.1: Types of juries around the world

Model	Description	Jurisdictions
The Continental jury	An all-citizen jury that gives exclusive determination of guilt to the jury	The UK, the USA, Canada, Australia, New Zealand and 40 other nations
Collaborative court models: a mixture of lay citizens and law-trained judges who usually decide both guilt and sentence in criminal cases		
The German collaborative court	A professional judge and two lay assessors Citizens are appointed as members of the court and sit at the head of the courtroom with the professional judge	Austria, Bulgaria, Croatia, Czech Republic, Denmark, Estonia, Finland, Germany, Hungary, Latvia, Macedonia, Norway, Poland, Serbia, Slovakia, Slovenia, Sweden, Switzerland and Ukraine
The French collaborative court	Three professional judges and nine lay assessors Citizens are randomly selected from the population to be jurors	France. But Italy, Greece and Portugal use a combination of both French and German features in their systems

The expert assessor collaborative court	Members of the community with special expertise thought to be relevant to a case sit with one or more law-trained judges to decide the outcome Used for complex criminal cases	Croatia, France, Germany, Iceland, the Netherlands, and Norway have some variation of this system in place
The lay judge model	Lay judges without formal legal training sit either individually or in small groups to decide the outcomes of legal cases Used most frequently in lower courts and minor cases	The USA, France, England and Scotland

Source: Jackson, J. D. and Kovalev, N. P. (2006) Lay adjudication and human rights in Europe. *Columbia Journal of European Law*, 13(1), 83–123. Adapted with permission.

The vanishing jury trial: a global phenomenon

The entertainment industry frequently produces legal dramas showing juries in action (Marder, 2017; Grossman, 2019), perpetuating the belief that jury trials are the norm, but their use is, in fact, declining (Galanter, 2016).

In the USA, among federal defendants in 1997, 3,200 were convicted in jury trials, but, by 2015, jury convictions had dropped to 1,650 (Weiser, 2016). In June 2015, the Norwegian parliament proposed a bill repealing the jury system and replacing it with a mixed panel of professional and lay judges (Jackson and Kovalev, 2016).

Jury trials are disappearing because they are time-consuming and expensive (Conrad and Clements, 2018; Michael, 2018), the issues they must weigh up are increasingly complex (DNA and random match probability) and jury service is perceived as a burden on jurors (Lerner, 2015). In Australia, the accused are incentivised to give up their right to a trial by jury due to sentence discounting for pleading guilty before trial (Hunter, Roberts, Young and Dixon, 2016). Sweden is exploring alternatives to the traditional jury called 'Nämndemän'.

'Nämndemän': Sweden's tripartite solution to the jury

Serious criminal cases in Sweden are decided by a professional judge in collaboration with three lay jurors, that is, Nämndemän, who are randomly drawn from a pool of eligible lay jurors. Nämndemän are politically affiliated, appointed officials who serve on many trials during a four-year term. Most Swedish citizens over the age of 18 who do not have criminal records are eligible to become Nämndemän. However, the jury pool is drawn only from individuals who consent to serve. Working as a lay judge typically requires 10–15 days per year, and most are unemployed or retired. In the courtroom, each Nämndemän listens to the proceedings and may ask more questions. After the hearing, the judge and the Nämndemän discuss the verdict and sentence, and express their opinions. Each lay judge's opinion is equal to the presiding judge. A defendant is convicted if the majority finds them guilty, even if the presiding professional judge believes the defendant should be acquitted (Anwar, Bayer and Hjalmarsson, 2018).

A brief history of trial by jury

The modern jury was born in eleventh-century England, when courts called the defendant's neighbours to testify (Simon, 1980). This practice evolved into asking the witnesses to determine whether the facts called for a verdict of guilty or not guilty (Turner, 1968). By the fourteenth century, the jury and the group of people who testified were kept distinct. Jury members were chosen not for their knowledge of the case but because of their ignorance. The idea of a jury of one's peers and of an impartial jury developed in the early eighteenth century, but in a different form than the present. For example, jury selection was not a random process, because frequently the local authorities picked the jurors. Because of this practice, challenging and excluding jurors on grounds of bias also developed during this period. By the middle of the eighteenth century, the jury was similar in composition and function to what we would recognise today (Erlanger, 1969; Klerman, 2018).

The secret lives of juries

What takes place in the jury room is generally a well-kept secret. No one can challenge a jury verdict by obtaining evidence about jury discussions, even if jurors accuse each other of legal misunderstandings or ignoring the judge's instructions.

Sometimes, the identities of jurors must remain secret. Keeping jury identities secret is rare because this reduces the transparency of the legal process. Keeping juror's identities secret is important in cases of terrorism (Donohue, 2006), organised crime (Liptak, 2002), or any situation where there are concerns about juror safety, harassment and outside influence (Langhoder, 2005). However, while juror identities may not remain secret, their deliberations are. Sometimes, the case demands that the jury is sequestered and confined to a location where they can be shielded from outside distractions while their deliberations are ongoing. Unfortunately, sequestration is expensive and may place jurors under unnecessary stress and may not deter juror misconduct (Levine, 1995).

Juror deliberations are secret because juries serve a broader purpose: they infuse a trial with community values, and they promote a sense of authenticity (King, 1996). Yet, free speech advocates argue that private jury deliberations undermine the transparency of legal systems. They worry that juries that decide others' fates while cloaked in secrecy will not be accountable for their verdicts or will render verdicts differently (Jackson, 2016). Anonymity may create biased juries, according to the findings of jury simulation research (Gans, 2017). For example, Hazelwood and Brigham (1998) used a mock jury experiment to examine anonymity on juror decision making and found that anonymous juries imposed harsher punishments and showed higher rates of conviction (70 per cent) than non-anonymous juries (40 per cent).

Secrecy is important because jurors should be able to debate freely without fear of exposure to public ridicule, contempt or hatred (Aaron, 1986), while also protecting them from outside influences (harassment). Many jurisdictions, such as Australia, Canada, the UK and the USA, forbid jurors from disclosing any information relating to their deliberations (Horan and Israel, 2016). Without secrecy, people would be reluctant to serve. Also, it ensures that the verdict is final, and enables jurors to bring unpopular verdicts, while preventing unreliable disclosure by jurors (Barrett, Libling and Barkai, 2019). It is also important that cases are completed. If the entire process were made public, it would raise endless rounds of appeals and even public discussion (Chopra and Ogloff, 2000).

However, this secrecy means that few research studies can investigate the jury system, leaving us dangerously unaware of its problems. For example, jurors conducting online independent research on defendants have caused mistrials – a trial ruled invalid through an error in the proceedings or when the jury cannot agree on a verdict (Daftary-Kapur and

Penrod, 2018). It is possible that most jurors are conducting online research from the first day of selection, but we have no idea because we cannot ask them (Liou and Tran, 2019).

Arguments in favour of disclosing jury deliberations are that it makes juries more accountable, and that it would be easier to inquire into the reliability of convictions and thus remedy injustices (Budworth, Ryan and Bartels, 2017). It would show where reform is needed and educate the public about the opaque jury process (Brooks, 2017).

The Chicago Jury Project: the beginning (and end) of jury research

Jury research began (and ended) in 1953 with the Chicago Jury Project, an innovative effort to study the US legal system using behavioural science (Broeder, 1958; Campbell, Chao, Robertson and Yokum, 2015). The scandal began when researchers from the University of Chicago recorded six jury deliberations. Although the recordings were approved by legal counsel and the judge, the jurors themselves were unaware that the heating units in the jury room held concealed microphones (Kalven and Zeisel, 1966). Unfortunately, the recordings became national news and were viewed as a violation of the tradition of a secret trial by jury (Cornwell, 2010). These events led to legislation prohibiting this practice (Katz, 1972), closing the door to the jury room to researchers for the next 50 years (and it is only now starting to reopen). Researchers were forced to seek alternative methods for studying jury deliberation and subsequently invented the *mock jury approach* (Hans, 2015; Diamond, 2018).

Juror B37

Source: Pool/Getty Images

George Zimmerman found not guilty of second-degree murder in the death of Trayvon Martin. Juror B37 suggests that the jury decision process was flawed

What happens during jury deliberations? Juror B37 (name withheld for privacy) offers a peek into the secret world of jury deliberation. The case involved the *State of Florida* v. *George Zimmerman*, who was charged with second-degree murder in the shooting of 17-year-old Trayvon Martin (Botelho, 2012). Two days after the jury acquitted Zimmerman, Juror B37 was interviewed on television (in shadow to conceal her identity). Juror B37 disclosed that initially some jurors were determined to find Zimmerman guilty of something, and the jury struggled to understand the court's confusing instructions. During the interview, Juror B37 emphatically stated that race played no role in the fatal shooting of Martin, while making remarks that suggested otherwise (Brown and Beekman, 2013; Nolan, 2013). The story ends with an interesting twist; 48 hours after the verdict, Juror B37 announced that she was represented by a literary agent who was ready to put together a book about her experience (Kovera, 2019).

Discussion Questions:

1 Should jurors' identities remain private even after the verdict is revealed?

2 Do you believe that jurors can remain unbiased if they plan to profit from their experience?

3 Should jurors be allowed to discuss their deliberations after they have delivered their verdict?

How is data collected about juries?

If we cannot study the workings of real juries via experiments and field studies, we must rely on alternative techniques that attempt to gain some understanding of the juror experience in the courtroom and how jurors individually and collectively determine the guilt or innocence of the accused (Table 11.2).

Table 11.2: Most frequent jury investigation approaches

Technique	Advantages	Disadvantages
Mock juries using simulated trials	Allows control of extraneous variables	Generalisability to real juries is questioned
Interviews and surveys of ex-jurors	Real juries and large sample size	Cognitive biases of respondents
Archival study of jury verdicts	Rich source of data and real deliberations	Limited number of variables, case differences

Mock juries and simulated trials

A *simulated trial* is a presentation of a false abbreviated trial (over several hours rather than several days or weeks) to a group of individuals acting as jurors, followed by juror feedback to determine how jurors would react in the actual trial. Trial simulations:

• try to weigh the strengths and weaknesses of the case

• evaluate the impact of testimonial and non-testimonial evidence

• evaluate the trial strategy and tactics

• estimate the range of verdicts that a jury might return (Ellison and Munro, 2015).

Like the members of a focus group, the mock jurors are screened to ensure that they are representative of the types of jurors the defence attorney would face in the real trial (Ruva and Guenther, 2015).

A sampling of recent mock jury studies reveals a wide range of applications from measuring jury perception of complicated evidence (Remmel, Glenn and Cox, 2019), and juror note taking during trials (Lorek, Centifanti, Lyons and Thorley, 2019), to the effect of the physical attractiveness of the defendant on mock jurors (Beaver, Boccio, Smith and Ferguson, 2019). Meta-analysis research supports the validity of mock juries, finding no significant difference in guilty verdicts, guilt ratings of the defendant, and damage awards between real and simulated juries (Bornstein et al., 2017).

Critics argue that jury simulations lack authenticity, particularly because of their use of student mock jurors, and that this limits both the external and ecological validity of their findings. **External validity** refers to whether a research finding in one experiment would be found in another experiment with different participants and procedures (Ziemke and Brodsky, 2015a). This is different from **ecological validity**, which asks whether a research finding represents what happens in everyday life (Breu and Brook, 2007; Bornstein, 1999). Ecological validity is a concern when policy decisions are based on the results of simulation studies (Bornstein and Greene, 2011). Unfortunately, no matter how realistic the simulation, the participants are aware that their decisions have no genuine consequences (Bornstein and McCabe, 2005).

Post-verdict interviews

Post-verdict interviews are a form of self-report research using interviews or surveys of ex-jurors about their verdict. Typically, this approach is used to investigate the jury's verdict (McCarthy, 2018), in order to understand what influenced jurors and thereby improve future trial tactics (Rowe and McCann, 2018).

An advantage of interviews and surveys is that they are inexpensive tools that can reach more subjects than experiments or observation (McDonald, 2008). Post-verdict interviews and surveys can be performed quickly so a researcher can obtain results in days or weeks (Paulhus and Vazire, 2007). Furthermore, the interviews and surveys can be collected privately and anonymised to protect sensitive information and promote truthful responses (Osberg, 1989).

The disadvantages of this approach are rooted in the complex psychological processes underlying self-report. For example, self-reported answers may be exaggerated, and jurors may be embarrassed to reveal private details of their experience, because of **social desirability**. Jurors may not be able to evaluate their subjective experiences accurately (how did you feel after the jury voted?) (Goffin and Boyd, 2009). Jurors may give a different response to questions based on their earlier responses and respond in a predictable way – known as **response bias**. For example, if a juror is first asked about possible racial bias during the deliberations, and is then asked if there were any reasons that the decision may not have been valid. Additionally, only those jurors who are willing to respond are included in the data. This is a form of **sampling bias** that questions whether the responding jurors represent all the jurors. It is important to remember that self-report measures are a valid but limited way to draw conclusions about juror behaviour.

Archival analysis of jury verdicts

In the archival approach, jury verdicts are sampled from court records and analysed to identify relationships between verdicts and case characteristics (Ventresca and Mohr, 2017). Examples of this approach include examining jury decisions about child sexual abuse (Read, Connolly and Welsh, 2006), acceptance of confession evidence (Kassin, Redlich, Alceste and Luke, 2018) and capital punishment (Devine and Kelly, 2015).

An advantage of the archival research method is that the data has already been collected. In addition, the data can be easy and inexpensive to review. Finally, the data in archives can be useful for answering questions in longitudinal studies, such as changing attitudes of juries towards drug-related offences (Ventresca and Mohr, 2017).

External validity – Asks whether a research finding in one experiment would be found in another experiment with different participants and procedures.

Ecological validity – Asks whether a research finding represents what happens in everyday life.

Social desirability – The tendency to present one's self in a manner that will be viewed favourably by others.

Response bias – When jurors respond to questions based on their earlier responses and respond in a predictable way.

Sampling bias – A sample collected in such a way that it does not represent the population it was drawn from.

PART IV

The disadvantages of using archival research is that the data may not match the research question, so the data may have to be recoded to answer a new question (Terrovitis, Mamoulis and Kalnis, 2011). Also, the data may lack detail, or has been inconsistently recorded and is missing potentially relevant information. This is because the data records *what* juries have done and not *why* they did it (L'Eplattenier, 2009).

IN SUMMARY

Juries serve multiple purposes from rendering a verdict to infusing democratic principles into the legal system. However, our knowledge of the realities of jury deliberation is limited because of their secret nature. Fortunately, we have alternative methods of investigation.

 ## CRITICAL THINKING AND APPLICATION QUESTIONS

1   Imagine a TV show that displayed actual jury deliberations as they happen: *Real juries in real time with X!* (name your preferred host). What effects would a show like this have on potential jurors, juror behaviour and verdict outcomes?

2   Find the information for serving on a jury in your local community. A quick search of your local jurisdiction under 'FAQ jury duty' should locate the information. How are jurors selected and what is expected of their service?

3   What are the advantages and disadvantages of revealing juror deliberations after a verdict?

PREDICTING VERDICTS FROM JUROR CHARACTERISTICS

FICTION: Legal procedures can create fair and impartial juries.	*Versus*	**FACT:** Juries are not impartial and many of our legal manipulations to create more fair and balanced juries often have the opposite effect.

At the heart of our justice system lives the myth that all people receive an unbiased trial from an impartial jury. Legal systems in all jurisdictions assume that jurors can make decisions that are free from bias. But is this assumption true? In this section we examine the empirical support for the belief that juries are or can be impartial.

Sources of jury bias

Jury selection

In countries with adversarial legal systems – where advocates for each side are set against each other, while a judge ensures that the rules of the court and the law are followed, such as Australia, Canada, the UK and the USA – the use of pretrial hearings for identifying potential juror bias is common, although how these hearings are conducted varies greatly between jurisdictions (Brooks, 2017). To ensure that juries include jurors who are unbiased, potential jurors are selected in a pretrial procedure called **voir dire**, a French term meaning 'to speak the truth'. During this process, potential jurors respond to questions that ascertain whether they have knowledge or biases that could interfere with their ability to evaluate the evidence fairly (Kovera and Austin, 2016). **Challenges for cause** are reserved for blatant expressions of bias and are agreed upon by both prosecution and defence. **Peremptory challenges** allow dismissal of a potential juror by the defence or prosecution for many reasons that do not need to be expressed but may be tactical, or the attorney angered the juror during questioning (Collett and Kovera, 2003). The effectiveness of the voir dire approach for detecting prospective juror biases is questionable (Kovera and Austin, 2016). Specifically, the desired outcome is to identify jurors who can be fair and impartial. However, which jurors are considered fair and impartial is different for the prosecution and defence.

Other jurisdictions may not begin with voir dire. For example, although Australia, Canada and the UK have a right to a jury trial in criminal cases, there is no voir dire questioning of prospective jurors as a part of jury selection. Rather, in these three countries, the first 12 people whose names have been randomly selected are seated in the jury box (Marder, 2015). After the jurors are seated, challenge for cause or peremptory challenges may be used (Collett and Kovera, 2003).

Scientific jury selection (SJS) offers the promise of predicting verdict preferences based on juror characteristics (Oostinga and Willmott, 2017). However, few juror characteristics are consistently good predictors of juror verdict preferences (Devine, Krouse, Cavanaugh and Basora, 2016; Devine and Macken, 2016). Strier (1999) identifies three controversial issues concerning SJS:

1   It is difficult to measure the effectiveness of SJS by analysing court cases, because it is not possible to claim with any certainty that a favourable verdict is completely due to scientific jury selection.

2   The fairness of scientific jury selection. If SJS is effective – able to affect the direction of the verdict – then its use would produce biased and predictable juries.

3   The fairness question persists. It is important to maintain a perception of fairness, and even if SJS is not effective, it gives the impression of interference with the jury process.

Jury demographics

Demographic differences, such as sex, education, income, religion and ethnicity, may explain why jurors who are exposed to the same evidence react differently because of pre-existing differences (Diamond, 1990). Demographic composition of the jury is important to the fairness of the trial. But demographic fairness is difficult to define. For example, is a demographically fair jury one that is similar to the defendant, different, or a jury that is representative of the community (Golash, 1992)?

Voir dire – A preliminary examination of a witness or a juror by a judge or legal counsel.

Challenge for cause – Request that a prospective juror be dismissed because there is reason to believe that the person is biased or prejudiced in some way.

Peremptory challenges – A defendant's or legal counsel's objection to a proposed juror, made without needing to give a reason.

Scientific jury selection (SJS) – The use of social science techniques and expertise to choose favourable juries during a criminal or civil trial.

PART IV

Jury–defendant similarity

A consistent finding is a **jury–defendant similarity bias**. This is when jury demographic factors interact with defendant characteristics to produce a bias in favour of defendants who are similar to the jury in some relevant respect (Englich, 2009). Supporting this idea, research has found that greater difference in socioeconomic status between juries and defendants was positively related to greater chance of conviction, longer incarceration times and higher ratings of guilt (Adler, 1973; Gleason and Harris, 1975; Freeman, 2006). Similarity of the gender of the jury also predicts verdicts. Male-dominated juries awarded higher damages to male plaintiffs, while female-dominated juries awarded larger amounts to female plaintiffs (Nagel and Weitzman, 1972).

Sex and sexual orientation

The research on sex differences in jury research is complex. For example, using mock trials, Blue and Hirschhorn (2009) found that women are likely to be more critical of female witnesses and more sensitive to male attorneys' treatment of women in the courtroom. One of their strongest findings is that female jurors reacted to trial evidence with stronger emotions, and they devoted more time to reviewing the evidence than male jurors.

Verdicts in rape trials are influenced by the attitudes, beliefs and biases about rape that jurors bring into the courtroom, which includes the negative attitudes that jurors and society might hold towards rape victims (Olson, 2017). Grubb and Harrower (2008) examined attribution of fault to the victim or attacker in the UK and found that men engage in victim blaming more often than women. To better understand such attitudes, researchers in the USA examined gender differences in individuals' beliefs about rape victims – victim responsibility and blame attributions and rape minimising attitudes (Hockett, Smith, Klausing and Saucier, 2016). Their meta-analysis showed that, overall, men perceived rape victims more negatively than women.

Evidence of juror sex differences was discovered in the Capital Jury Project. This project investigated the decision making of jurors in death penalty cases in the USA. The Capital Jury Project was conducted by a consortium of scholars who collected extensive interview data from nearly 1,200 jurors serving in 353 death penalty trials (Devine and Kelly, 2015). The Capital Jury Project found that jurors make life-and-death punishment decisions early in the trial, misunderstand sentencing guidelines, and often deny their responsibility for the punishment given to a defendant (Bowers, 1996). Two questions about juror experience revealed interesting sex differences: 'Did you find the experience emotionally upsetting?' 'During the trial or right after it, did you have any trouble sleeping, have any bad dreams or nightmares, or lose your appetite?' Overall, more females found the experience emotionally upsetting and suffered sleep and other problems because of their jury service. Specifically, females were more likely to comment about seeing the crime scene evidence presented at trial, feeling isolated and being frustrated with being sequestered. Females also mentioned suffering from long-term side effects, fearing reprisal, seeking counselling, refusing to serve again, and regretting their decisions more than males. Finally, females mentioned experiencing dreams or nightmares, feeling drained, stressed and strained, and using prescription drugs, alcohol or smoking more after the trial because of their jury service (Antonio, 2008).

Negative effects of sexual orientation bias have been found in the courtroom setting. Jurors have been found to treat gay and lesbian victims of crime more negatively than similarly defined heterosexual victims (Davies, Rogers and Whitelegg, 2009; Petsko and Bodenhausen, 2019). More detailed investigation examined mock jurors' reactions to a sexual abuse case involving a male teacher and a 10-year-old child (Wiley and Bottoms,

2009). Because gay men are sometimes stereotyped as child molesters, they portrayed defendant sexual orientation as either gay or straight and the victim as either a boy or a girl. Jurors made more pro-prosecution decisions in cases involving a gay versus a straight defendant, particularly when the victim was a boy. In boy victim cases, jurors' emotional feelings of moral outrage towards the defendant mediated these effects. On average, women jurors were more pro-prosecution than were men. Although limited by the use of mock juries, these studies suggest that juries are assessing victim credibility based on the sexual orientation of the victim.

Race and ethnicity

Research supports the hypothesis that mock jurors differently judge black versus white defendants, even when the evidence against these defendants is exactly the same (Jones and Kaplan, 2003). Specifically, jurors tend to make more severe guilt judgements when defendants are charged with crimes that are associated with their racial group (Jones and Kaplan, 2003; Maeder, Yamamoto, McManus and Capaldi, 2016). This finding supports the existence of a **race–crime congruency bias** in juror decision making. This bias describes jurors' tendency to think in ways that disadvantage blacks relative to whites for stereotypically black crimes, like gang violence, but that also disadvantage whites relative to blacks for stereotypically white crimes, like insider trading (Petsko and Bodenhausen, 2019).

Fortunately, racial prejudice effects can be reduced. Sommers (2009) found that any aspect of a trial, such as the balance of a jury's racial composition, that leads white mock jurors to be concerned about racial bias reduces the influence of the defendant's race. In general, racially mixed juries show different patterns of deliberation strategies, better communication, and are viewed by the public as more authentic than all-white or mostly white juries (Gau, 2016). Another study examined this effect in more detail by comparing all-white and racially mixed mock jury deliberations (Stevenson, Lytle, Baumholser and McCracken, 2017). The researchers found that interracial juries triggered more social anxiety and self-monitoring. The mock jurors spent more time developing their response in racially mixed juries than all-white juries. Deliberation analyses showed that racially diverse juries share a wider range of information than all-white juries. The effect of diversity was not limited to information exchange, because even before discussion, whites in diverse juries (as opposed to homogeneous groups) were more lenient towards the black defendant (Sommers, 2006).

Difference in social cognition

Social cognition is a subtopic of social psychology that focuses on how jurors process, store and apply information about other people and the courtroom environment (Nosek and Riskind, 2016). Social cognitive processes can be grouped into three domains:

- *social perception*: the perceptual processing of social information, such as faces and emotional expressions
- *social understanding*: understanding others' cognitive or emotional states
- *social decision making*: planning behaviours that consider your own and others' goals (Arioli, Crespi and Canessa, 2018).

Emotional responses

In New Zealand, the trial of Michael Curran, accused of murdering toddler Aaliyah Morrissey, showed photographs so graphic that jurors reacted by crying and vomiting

---

Race–crime congruency bias – *A tendency to condemn black men more than white men for stereotypically black crimes but to do the reverse for stereotypically white crimes.*

Social cognition – *A field that focuses on how people process, store and apply information about other people and social situations.*

PART IV

(Rowan, 2007). Will jurors' heightened emotions prejudice their judgements against a defendant? Emotion is linked with cognitive decision-making processes and its impact varies depending on the type of emotion and legal judgement.

Believing that instructing jurors to ignore their feelings removes emotion from jury deliberations oversimplifies human decision making (Phalen, Nadler and Salerno, 2019). Many factors influence the emotional channels of juror decision making. For example, when mock jurors heard a murder defendant labelled a 'terrorist', they were more angry and more likely to find him guilty relative to those who heard the same evidence but did not hear this label (Goodman-Delahunty, Martschuk and Ockenden, 2016). Neuroimaging evidence suggests that these emotion-driven reactions may overwhelm cognitive processing of the evidence, showing that jurors exposed to emotional stimuli display an expected increase in emotion but also decreased overall cognitive processing (Salerno and Bottoms, 2009).

Individual emotional reactions may be related to different verdicts. Georges, Wiener and Keller (2013) examined dynamic emotional responses during a mock death penalty trial. During the trial, feelings of anger and disgust increased during the assessment of guilt phase of the trial. Anger and disgust are associated with a desire to punish (Salerno and Peter-Hagene, 2013; Molho et al., 2017) and a need to assign blame (Keltner, Ellsworth and Edwards, 1993). Juror experience of negative emotions, like moral outrage (Salerno and Peter-Hagene, 2013), disgust (Salerno, 2017) and anger (Nuñez, Schweitzer, Chai and Myers, 2015), can lead mock jurors to find a defendant guilty. Even anticipated feelings can influence jurors' punishment decisions. Mock jurors who anticipated experiencing more positive feelings as a result of imposing a death sentence were more likely to sentence a defendant to death than those who anticipated feeling fewer positive feelings (Wiener, Georges and Cargas, 2014).

Mock jury studies reveal reasons why feeling negative emotions might lead to greater convictions and punitiveness. One explanation is that mock jurors' level of anger reduces the effects of **mitigating evidence** – evidence that reduces the perceived severity of the crime (Georges, Wiener and Keller, 2013), causing jurors to judge a defendant's actions as more intentional (Nuñez, Myers, Wilkowski and Schweitzer, 2017). Not all emotions have the same effect, however; juror empathy for the defendant reduces convictions (Sjöberg, 2015), while sympathy and sadness have a negligible effect on verdicts and damage awards (Feigenson, Park and Salovey, 1997).

Mitigating evidence – *Evidence that reduces the perceived severity of the crime.*

Implicit bias

What if individual jurors are not aware of their biases? When questioned by legal counsel, they would be unable to reveal these hidden prejudices. **Implicit social cognitions** are unconscious attitudes or stereotypes that affect our understanding, actions and decisions (Nosek, Hawkins and Frazier, 2011). So influential was this idea that on 10 March 2017, the Western District of Washington (2017) adopted criminal jury instructions that discuss unconscious bias. But they may have acted too quickly, because research suggests that the implicit bias effect on jurors may be an illusion (Forscher et al., 2019).

Implicit social cognition is based on the idea that if memories that are not accessible to awareness can influence our actions, associations can also influence our attitudes and behaviour. Individual differences in associations of concepts could allow researchers to understand attitudes that cannot be measured through traditional self-report methods due to lack of awareness or social desirability bias (Greenwald and Banaji, 1995). A computer-based measure was developed, known as the Implicit Association Test (IAT). This test requires that users rapidly categorise two target concepts with an attribute, such as the concepts 'male' and 'female' with the attribute 'logical', such that easier pairings (faster responses) are interpreted as more strongly associated in memory than difficult pairings (slower responses) (Lane, Banaji, Nosek and Greenwald, 2007).

Implicit social cognitions – *The attitudes or stereotypes that affect our understanding, actions and decisions in an unconscious manner.*

However, there are doubts about whether the IAT measures hidden prejudice or just familiarity with stereotypical concepts (Fiedler and Bluemke, 2005; Fiedler, Messner and Bluemke, 2006) and whether the test predicts real-world behaviour, a concept known as **predictive validity**. Finally, Forscher et al. (2019) applied a meta-analysis, which shows only small correlations between IAT scores and behavioural outcomes. Overall, there is a lack of evidence that most persons have deeply held negative associations that can lead to subtle discrimination without conscious awareness.

Predictive validity – *The extent to which a test predicts real-world behaviour.*

IN SUMMARY

Despite decades of research in scientific jury selection, analysis of the demographic characteristics of jurors, and measures of implicit social cognition, we still do not know how individual differences in jurors translate into predictable verdicts.

 CRITICAL THINKING AND APPLICATION QUESTIONS

1   Imagine if scientific jury selection was an accepted science and for the right price a jury could be selected that would guarantee a favourable verdict for the prosecution or defence. What problems would this create for legal systems that rely on juries?

2   Describe any other juror demographic characteristics not mentioned, which you believe would be a valid predictor of juror verdict behaviour and need further investigation.

3   The concept of 'implicit social cognition' suggests that our unconscious beliefs, attitudes or prejudices affect our behaviours. Design a study to test the validity of this concept without using the Implicit Association Test.

HOW INDIVIDUAL JURORS INTERPRET EVIDENCE

FICTION: Juries make their decisions based only on the strength of the evidence presented.	*Versus*	**FACT:** When the evidence is not clear, juries use information from outside the trial to make decisions.

Juries make decisions about guilt, damages, liability and occasionally sentencing. In most trials, the evidence alone determines those decisions, but other variables sometimes influence their verdicts. Some of these variables are associated with the trial but are not part of the admissible evidence, including definitions of legal terms and pretrial publicity. One benefit of *rules of evidence* – the legal principles that govern the proof of facts in a legal proceeding – is to ensure that the facts that juries see are challenged and scrutinised. When jurors use *extra-evidentiary evidence* (outside information), that benefit is lost. In this section we explore the ways jurors evaluate trial evidence.

Differences between judges and juries

Critics of the jury system want to eliminate the role of the jury in deciding legal cases, recommending instead that jury decision making be replaced with judicial decision making (Klerman, 2018). This criticism indicates a lack of understanding of the roles played by

PART IV

judges and juries. Juries function as triers of fact, while judges function as triers of law. Judges are legally trained professionals, while jurors are not. Although the jury could include members with legal training, most jurors are legal novices. While, in many jurisdictions, the trial judge sits and deliberates alone, jury members can pool their experiences and opinions and correct misunderstandings, because jurors, unlike judges, must reach a group decision. Finally, the judge is experienced in the procedures of trials and the juror is not. Generally, judges agree with jury verdicts 75–80 per cent of the time (Eisenberg et al., 2005). Both judges and juries are most influenced by the strength of the evidence presented during the trial (Devine, 2012; Robbennolot, 2005).

Global Perspectives

South Korea's unique judge and jury alliance

Since July 2012, South Korea has been experimenting with trials by jury to encourage greater democracy and generate more legitimacy for the Korean courts. The nine-member jury decides by majority rule for defendants charged with sentences of more than one year. Three differences make these jury deliberations unique:

A courtroom at South Korea's Constitutional Court with a nine-member lay jury system making legal decisions of guilt and sentencing with the judge

1   The jurors receive opinions from the judge overseeing the case.

2   The jury's decision is nonbinding – the judge may disregard it.

3   Besides deciding guilt and innocence, the jury gives an opinion about sentencing. This is different from most jurisdictions, where the jury does not usually influence punishment but only guilt (Hans, 2014).

This system offers a unique judge–jury relationship by combining both the independent phase of jury deliberations and fact finding with opportunities to interact with the judge under specific circumstances. However, this system has many features that still allow South Korean judges to exert significant influence over the outcome. The nonbinding nature of the jury decisions may become a problem. Research shows when juror decisions are only advisory, jurors felt less responsible for the sentencing decision, and they reported deliberating more quickly and less toughly, compared to jurors whose decision was binding (Bowers, 1994).

Influence is a problem during the pretrial stage. Even after a defendant moves for a jury trial, South Korean judges may decide not to honour the request and proceed instead to a bench trial. Furthermore, they are able to constantly introduce their opinions and conclusions because they can participate in jury deliberations. Even after trial, South Korean judges may set aside a jury verdict because jury verdicts are only advisory and not binding. If the judiciary intends to enhance its credibility, it should clearly define the role of judges in jury trials and make way for true civil participation (Rose, 2017).

Strength of evidence –
The quantity and quality of evidence presented during a trial.

Strength of evidence

The strongest determining factor of the jury's verdict is the strength of evidence against the defendant. The **strength of evidence** is the quantity and quality of evidence presented during a trial. In a field study investigating the decisions of real juries, and in dozens of experimental studies with mock jurors, the strength of evidence has been systematically varied by providing evidence (Brown, Rodriguez, Gretak and Berry, 2017), withholding evidence (De La Fuente, De La Fuente and García, 2003) or altering the presentation of evidence (Arscott, Morgan, Meakin and French, 2017). Devine et al. (2009) found that the strength of the prosecution's evidence was a stronger predictor of jury conviction than either jury deliberation or **extra-evidentiary factors** – factors affecting jury decision making that are not from the admissible evidence presented at trial. Beyond this finding, the more interesting question is: How do juries decide when the evidence is weak or even ambiguous?

The liberation hypothesis

How much are juries influenced by extraneous information unrelated to the evidence? Kalven and Zeisel (1966) proposed an answer known as the **liberation hypothesis**. Where the evidence is weak or contradictory or the offence is less severe, juries are liberated to use extralegal factors, such as considering legal fees, attractiveness of the defendant or prior convictions, in reaching their decisions.

Psychological explanations for the liberation hypothesis

Viewing jurors as active information processors means that more than just the evidence and legal guidelines influence their decision making. Cognitive explanations of attitude change explain why jurors choose to rely on extra-evidentiary information when the prosecution's evidence is only moderately strong. **Dual process theories** propose that jurors are using two information-processing strategies, or 'routes' (Eagly and Chaiken, 1993; Petty and Cacioppo, 1986) (Figure 11.1):

- A *central route* involves organised and effortful processing to analyse and evaluate evidence based on the merits of the underlying arguments.

- A *peripheral route* uses less intensive processing by relying on heuristics (mental shortcuts) to evaluate evidence. Although some heuristics are useful – they save time or make the task manageable – sometimes they lead to poor decisions – the heuristics jurors apply may rely on information they are instructed not to use, ignore crucial evidentiary points, and make inappropriate inferences.

Figure 11.1: Dual process model of juror decision making

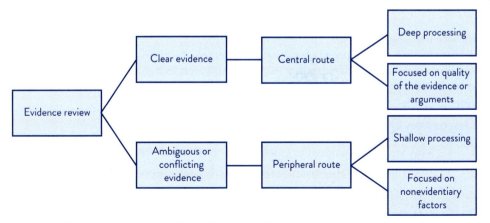

Source: Inspired by Petty, R. E. and Cacioppo, J. T. (1986) The Elaboration Likelihood Model of Persuasion. *Advances in Experimental Social Psychology*, 19, 123–205.

Extra-evidentiary factors – *Factors affecting jury decision making that are not from the admissible evidence presented at trial.*

Liberation hypothesis – *When the evidence is weak or contradictory, jurors use extralegal factors in reaching their decisions.*

Dual process theories – *Propose that jurors are using two information-processing strategies, or 'routes', to understand evidence.*

PART IV

Applying this dual process theory suggests that when an individual elaborates on a given message or argument, it becomes more persuasive. Petty, Cacioppo and Kasmer (2015) argue that jurors use the central route strategy when they are given clear evidence of guilt and view the decision as important. However, when jurors are trying to understand complex and conflicting evidence, they are unable to choose a verdict using the logic and reasoning approach of the central route and are susceptible to extraneous influences and follow the peripheral route (Curley, MacLean, Murray and Laybourn, 2019).

The problems of pretrial publicity (PTP)

Prejudicial pretrial publicity (PTP) is a source of juror bias, but not all publicity is a problem. The problem is when media coverage reveals critical issues that would be discussed during trial, and information that would be excluded from trial, such as a defendant's criminal record. Another problem is that to obtain a jury of peers, the jurors are drawn from the same communities where the media coverage is most prevalent, making it more likely that the jurors viewed the PTP and are biased.

Exposure to pretrial publicity causes jurors to evaluate evidence from a biased perspective, as occurred in the US case of Steven Avery, which was the subject of the Netflix true crime documentary web TV series *Making a Murderer* (Ricciardi and Demos, 2015), examining the conflict between Avery and the Manitowoc County legal system. After spending 18 years in prison for a wrongful conviction, Avery was arrested again and found guilty of the murder of Teresa Halbach. During the Avery trial, both the prosecutor and the police frequently updated the public via press conferences and interviews with news outlets; during these exchanges, the public was informed of various crime details, such as when and where the victim's body and car were found, how interrogations were going, and why they believed the suspect was guilty (Ricciardi and Demos, 2015). Due to the controversial nature of the case and its popularity associated with the documentary series, researchers used this event to evaluate the influence of PTP on decisions concerning a defendant's guilt or innocence. An online survey showed that those who had watched the TV documentary series were significantly more likely to claim that Avery was innocent than those who had not (Rodriguez et al., 2019).

Google mistrials: pretrial publicity in the internet age

"Well, I was curious."
(juror caught Googling defendant's name during trial: Schwartz, 2009)

This juror's reply to the judge shows the potential danger of curiosity and convenient internet access. The defendant was accused of selling illegal prescriptions through pharmacies on the internet. During the trial, the judge found that eight jurors researched the lawyers and defendant, read online news articles about the case, searched Wikipedia for legal definitions, and searched for excluded evidence. A mistrial was granted, as well as a motion to dismiss the indictments against the defendant, based on rampant juror misconduct (Fallon, 2010).

Discussion Questions:

1   Why are jurors tempted to conduct their own outside research?

2   If you were the judge, how would you balance the need for controlling juror access to information with individual freedom to use the internet?

3   Information flows both ways, so do you think that jurors also cause problems for a fair trial when they use the internet as an outlet for their private opinions?

This case study is not an isolated incident:

- In the UK, a juror used her Facebook page to hold a poll because she could not decide whether or not the defendant was guilty (Mastro, 2011).

- In Australia, jurors 'anonymously' shared details of their deliberations in the comments section of a blog receiving more than 5 million hits during the trial, including prominent prosecutors (Horan, 2012).

These cases show that using social media creates problems for impartiality. The information that jurors access may be irrelevant yet could alter the course of their final verdict. The question is whether the knowledge produces bias and whether it can be detected during juror questioning or controlled with judicial instructions.

Today's jurors reflexively seek out information online (news websites, social media). How often jurors access the internet during a trial is unknown because jurors are unlikely to report their violations. The spontaneous use of the internet shows that jurors rely less on collective common sense and more on verifying initial reactions about the evidence. But does this behaviour make today's jurors more biased? Hope, Memon and McGeorge (2004) believe this individual verification of the evidence creates a sense of confirmation bias. The juror's interpretation of new evidence becomes distorted by biased interpretation to confirm previously learned information.

Is a juror using the internet for research considered misconduct? Marder (2014; Hogg, 2019) believes that this behaviour shows a clear disregard for judicial instructions to rely only on the evidence presented in court. But Hoffmeister and Watts (2018) offer another perspective, suggesting that jurors are trying to gain information about the defendant's background and the circumstances of the case to better understand the law and legal terms. Their intention is to be fair and accurate in their decision making. From this perspective, using the internet is a distorted sense of responsibility to make the 'right' decision.

To remove a juror from the jury and declare a mistrial, the judge must examine the type of information that resulted from internet use, the stage of the trial when the misconduct occurred, whether the extralegal information obtained was shared with other jurors, and whether it is related to a critical aspect of the case (McGee, 2010; Dawson, Banks, Vermeer and Shelton, 2018; Braun, 2017). For example, internet research to look up the meaning of a word might not be considered prejudicial, but research that leads to a juror discovering a prior conviction of a defendant requires intervention (Daftary-Kapur and Penrod, 2018).

Juror comprehension of instructions

Jury instructions are a set of legal rules that jurors should follow when deciding a case. They guide jurors as to how to decide who is guilty and how to consider certain types of evidence – direct versus indirect evidence. The challenge is meeting the contradictory needs, providing clear instructions for jurors, while also providing enough detail to reduce the chances of the case going to the Court of Appeal. If the jury is not instructed correctly, this can form the basis for an appeal. Unfortunately, this has led to complex jury instruction processes that may be poorly understood by jurors (Gibbons, 2017). Juror comprehension of judicial instructions ranges from 50 to 70 per cent (Devine, 2012), and understanding legal terminology, such as 'reasonable doubt' or 'circumstantial evidence', ranges from 25 to 70 per cent (Ellsworth and Reifman, 2000).

Simplified instructions improve comprehension, but a meta-analysis of 75 studies reveals that the process is more complex (Baguley, McKimmie and Masser, 2017). While reducing conceptual complexity increased juries' application of instructions to their decision, other changes, such as reducing the amount of information, did not.

Solutions for improving comprehension include providing jurors with trial transcripts, juror note taking, allowing juror questions, plain language directions and structured decision aids – routes to verdict (Chalmers and Leverick, 2018). Additionally, repetition and timing of instructions is important. Diamond and Doorley (2015; Alvarez, Miller and Bornstein, 2016) recommend providing jury instructions at the beginning of the trial, not just at the end, to guide jurors' interpretation of the evidence.

Juror comprehension of scientific evidence

Plain language may not be enough to ensure juror comprehension. Another way to present complex evidence is through expert witnesses – a person who testifies at a trial because of special knowledge or ability in a field that is relevant to the case. Psychologists, as expert witnesses, present the results of psychological assessments of individuals, testify about the results of psychological research on a topic relevant to a case, or offer opinions about the appropriateness of procedures used in the course of the investigation that led to the court case (Marion, Kaplan and Cutler, 2019; Milroy, 2017). The expert's authoritative power to sway jurors may be related to the jury's reactions to the symbols of authority that trigger this response. According to Cialdini (2009), the expert's opinion is only half the story: juries pay attention to the expert witness's title and clothing.

Jurors are often challenged to identify reliable and valid scientific research (Koeler, Schweizer, Saks and McQuiston, 2016). Expert testimony helps jurors to be more sceptical of and sensitive to scientific evidence (Laub, Kimbrough and Bornstein, 2016). For example, Jones and Penrod (2016) showed that an expert could teach jurors to notice variations in the quality of confession evidence, such as whether the confession is consistent or inconsistent with the crime evidence. Other studies show that opposing experts can improve jurors' sensitivity to the strength of scientific evidence (Jones and Kovera, 2015), but some studies show it can create a general scepticism of all experts (Levett and Kovera, 2008).

The use of expert witnesses in civil trials is sometimes criticised because they are often used by both sides to advocate different positions, and it is left up to a jury to decide which expert witness to believe. Although experts are legally prohibited from expressing their opinion of submitted evidence until after they are hired, sometimes a party can surmise beforehand, because of reputation or prior cases, that the testimony will be favourable. Such experts are sometimes disparagingly referred to as 'hired guns' (Ziemke and Brodsky, 2015b).

IN SUMMARY

Jurors process evidence through different channels of information, some of which are influenced by extra-evidentiary factors. Increased understanding of these factors will lead to better understanding about juror decision making and interventions to achieve more objective and fair trials.

 CRITICAL THINKING AND APPLICATION QUESTIONS

1   Should jurors be allowed to submit questions to the judge during the trial? Answer this question from both the juror's and the judge's perspective. *Remember that the judge may not always be allowed to respond to a question because it may bias the jury.*

2   What specific social media do you consider to have the most influence on juror bias? Other than taking away access to the internet and sequestering the jury, is there any way to convince the jury to limit their access only to information presented during the trial?

3   Given the controversy of juror ability to understand complex scientific and technical legal terminology, should we replace the traditional jury of laypeople with professional jurors?

THE STORY BEHIND JURY DELIBERATIONS

FICTION: Jury deliberation is a simple task of counting votes to decide which evidence was the strongest.	*Versus*	**FACT:** Jury deliberation involves complex social dynamics and cognitive principles to create a plausible story.

In 90 per cent of trials, the majority position at the beginning of deliberation becomes the jury verdict at the end (Bornstein and Greene, 2011). However, sometimes the evidence is unclear and, in these cases, juries must find rational ways to reconstruct the truth, based on facts and without relying on extralegal factors. This section explores the psychological processes juries use to produce an understandable story of the case.

Understanding evidence and decision alternatives

Juries apply two distinct and opposing deliberation styles: verdict-driven and evidence-driven. **Verdict-driven juries** vote early and structure their discussion around the available verdict options, trying to find the most acceptable option. This approach involves fewer participants and silences those who are not in agreement. **Evidence-driven juries** spend more time evaluating the evidence. They vote less often, relying on a final vote to confirm their evaluation of the evidence. The evidence-driven deliberation approach offers individual jurors more influence because jurors with different recall of the facts or who hold a minority opinion can offer alternative interpretations about the nature of the evidence (Lieberman and Krauss, 2009). Marder (1986) identifies gender differences in style preference; male jurors preferred the verdict-driven style and female jurors preferred the evidence-driven style.

> **Verdict-driven juries** – *When juries vote early and structure the discussion around available verdict options.*

> **Evidence-driven juries** – *Juries that spend more time evaluating the evidence instead of the verdict.*

The story model

A trial typically involves contradictory accounts of past events and, often, uncertainty about future events as well, such as criminal defendants' dangerousness or civil plaintiffs' pain and suffering. Research on how jurors make sense of this conflicting information shows that they actively evaluate conflicting claims and construct a story that provides a plausible interpretation of the evidence (Pennington and Hastie, 1992). This process is known as the *story model*, where jurors attempt to assemble the evidence into a reasonable narrative that is consistent with the facts of the case and makes sense, given their existing knowledge. Creating stories helps juries make sense of uncommon, uncertain, or novel situations (Pennington and Hastie, 1992).

During jury deliberation, jurors collaborate to create a description of what actually happened by combining stories told during the trial with stories from their own lives

PART IV

(Conley and Conley, 2009). This storyline is constantly challenged and revised during deliberation. Cammiss (2006) described the process as a 'flattening' of the story to fit legal criteria, where the jury spends their time and effort sifting related from unrelated facts. To create a coherent story, the jury assembles the evidence, arguments and testimony into a recognisable story (Holstein, 1985; Saletta et al., 2020). Stories combine the jury's skills, knowledge and memories and promote trust and communication, while strengthening the jury's identity and group relationships (Bietti, Tilston and Bangerter, 2019).

The ritual of jury deliberation

Interaction ritual chain – *Successful rituals create symbols of group membership and increase emotional energy, while failed rituals drain emotional energy.*

Stories evolve as they are shaped by both the storyteller and the audience, who may respond, debate or add more information (Ochs and Capps, 2009). Jury deliberation is a form of an **interaction ritual chain**; during deliberation, jurors develop a conversational ritual of presenting, evaluating, accepting and ignoring various elements of a story. They develop a shared collaborative rhythm and focus to their discussion, resulting in a sense of unity and shared emotion (Baker, 2019; Collins, 2014). A positive feedback cycle is created that leads to greater feelings of solidarity (Rossner, 2019).

Cognitive aspects of deliberation

Cognitively, the story model approach helps jurors process complicated information in several ways. Jurors use these stories as a framework for analysing evidence and arguments. The story becomes a filter to decide what evidence is relevant and a memory tool (mnemonic) to retain more information. Finally, the story approach persuades other jurors to change their verdicts during deliberation (Jay et al., 2019).

Creating a story about the evidence relies on the ability of jurors to combine three types of knowledge (Devine and Macken, 2016):

1   Case-specific information acquired during the trial, such as witness statements during trial.

2   Information about similar events, such as a similar crime in the juror's community.

3   Expectations about what makes a complete and believable story, such as human actions are goal driven.

The effectiveness of the story approach is explained by our reliance on cognitive schema – patterns of thought that organise information. These schema function as filters through which individuals identify people and situations quickly. For jurors, these schemas take the form of preconceptions and personal knowledge of the world to construct stories from trial evidence and fill in missing details to increase the story's consistency. This cognitive processing helps jurors apply their common sense and community values to inform judgements about a case (Vallano and McQuiston, 2018).

Collaborative inhibition

Collaborative inhibition – *A phenomenon that causes members of a collaborative group to remember less information than an equal number of single individuals.*

Jury deliberation assumes that even if human memory is unreliable, the collaborative efforts of the jury will compensate for its individual flaws. However, this does not seem to be true. Groups typically do not recall as much information as the same number of individuals working alone and sometimes do not correct the memory errors of their members, known as **collaborative inhibition** (Betts and Hinsz, 2010). Pritchard and Keenan (2002) contrasted the memories of jurors before and after a mock jury deliberation. Overall, deliberation resulted in only a slight memory improvement. Interestingly, those most likely to change their verdict because of deliberation were not those who had the least accurate memories, but those who had the least confidence in their memories. Unfortunately, collaboration increases confidence in both correct and incorrect memory judgements (Clark, Stephenson and Kniveton, 1990).

The jury setting seems designed to encourage collaborative inhibition rather than reduce it (Hinsz, Betts, Sánchez-Manzanares and Tindale, 2020). For example, collaborative inhibition disappears in long-term couples (Grysman, Harris, Barnier and Savage, 2020), but juries consist of unrelated individuals. Group size matters, as groups of only two do not show collaborative inhibition (Thorley and Dewhurst, 2007), while most juries range from 6 to 12 individuals. *Social loafing* – the tendency of individuals to put forth less effort when they are part of a group – contributes as well. Some members will leave the task of remembering to others. Finally, memory retrieval blockage also plays a part, where one person uses a retrieval strategy that is only effective for the individual and reduces the memory retrieval of the group (Betts and Hinsz, 2010).

Group polarisation

Group polarisation happens during discussion, when a jury – initially leaning towards a certain opinion – moves further in the direction they initially agreed on (Sunstein, 2009; Jung et al., 2019). For example, a jury whose members are likely, before deliberation, to find a defendant not guilty will likely render a verdict of not guilty; a jury whose members want to award punitive damages will likely award a greater amount than the original amount. Group polarisation occurs even when the group is not physically together. Social media platforms, such as Instagram, Twitter and Facebook, demonstrate that as long as the group of individuals begins with the same fundamental opinion on the topic and a consistent dialogue is maintained, group polarisation happens (Yardi and Danah, 2010).

> **Group polarisation** – *Happens during discussion, when a jury – initially leaning towards a certain opinion – moves further in the direction they initially agreed on.*

PART IV

Experiencing group polarisation

Read the following story:

> Chris Smith was driving home after meeting friends for some drinks. On the way home, his mobile phone (cell phone) slid out of his pocket and under the seat. He glanced down to see where it had fallen and by the time he looked up it was too late; his car mounted the curb, killing a pedestrian. Tests revealed that Chris's alcohol level was slightly above the legal limit. This was his second arrest for drink driving.

If you were to sentence Chris to prison, how long would you recommend? Write down your answer. Now join other people who read this story and, as a group, discuss the case and make a unanimous decision about the length of Chris's sentence. Calculate the average sentence length before discussion, by finding the average of the individual decisions, and compare it with the group's decision. Did you find evidence of group polarisation?

The psychological roots of group polarisation

A pair of theories explain how group polarisation works. Social comparison theory concerns individual jurors comparing their views with the jury, while informational influence theory focuses on how individual jurors try to persuade the jury.

Social comparison theory
– Group polarisation occurs because of our desire to gain acceptance and be perceived in a favourable way by the group.

Social comparison theory (also known as 'normative social influence theory') states that group polarisation occurs because of our desire to gain acceptance and be perceived in a favourable way by the group. Jurors compare their own ideas with those held by the rest of the jury; they observe and evaluate what verdicts and evidence the group values and prefers. To gain acceptance, individual jurors take a position that is similar to the jury but slightly more extreme. In doing so, individual jurors support the group's beliefs, while still promoting their individuality and reflecting the group ideal (Gerber, Wheeler and Suls, 2018).

Informational influence theory (also known as 'persuasive argument theory') states that individuals become more convinced of their views when they hear novel arguments in support of their position (Arvan, 2019). The jury polarises as jurors spend more time discussing and making better arguments for the side they prefer (prosecution or defence). This behaviour is a form of confirmation bias, where jurors selectively seek information confirming their pre-existing beliefs, while ignoring or minimising conflicting information (Kassin, Dror and Kukucka, 2013).

Informational influence theory – Individuals become more convinced of their views when they hear novel arguments in support of their position.

The role of personality in jury deliberation

Personality traits are stable patterns of thoughts, emotions and behaviours, and understanding their role during juror deliberation is important (Roberts, Wood and Smith, 2005). The *five-factor model of personality* is a framework for describing the so-called 'Big Five' personality traits (Barrick and Mount, 1991; Goldberg, 1990). The model uses five personality traits based on self-descriptions (Table 11.3).

Table 11.3: Five-factor model of personality

Trait	High score	Low score
Openness	Imaginative, curious, flexible	Practical, conventional, prefers routine
Conscientiousness	Hardworking, dependable, organised	Impulsive, careless, disorganised
Extraversion	Sociable, assertive, talkative	Quiet, reserved, withdrawn
Agreeableness	Trusting, tolerant, helpful	Critical, uncooperative, suspicious
Neuroticism	Anxious, depressed and other negative emotions	Calm, even-tempered, secure

Source: Barrick, M. R. and Mount, M. K. (1991) The big five personality dimensions and job performance: A meta-analysis. *Personnel Psychology*, 44(1), 1–26. Adapted with permission.

It should be pointed out that some researchers have reservations about the five-factor model, specifically its imprecise specification of these dimensions (Novikova and Vorobyeva, 2019; Livneh and Livneh, 1989). Some researchers suggest that more than five dimensions are needed to encompass the domain of personality. To examine patterns of influence, Marcus, Lyons and Guyton (2000) administered the five-factor model to actual jurors. Jurors reporting high levels of conscientiousness were most likely to report being influenced by other jurors, and jurors reporting high levels of openness were least likely to report being influenced. Extraversion was the only trait associated with perceptions of being influential, with extraverted jurors being perceived as much more influential than introverted jurors.

In a similar study using real jurors, researchers found that high levels of juror extraversion were associated with not guilty verdicts or verdicts in favour of defendants (Clark, Boccaccini, Caillouet and Chaplin, 2007). Juror extraversion was also correlated with longer deliberation times and perceived foreperson (a juror selected by the other jurors to preside over the jury) influence (when jurors were polled) in criminal cases. Extraversion is associated with being selected as a jury foreperson and extraverted forepersons were associated with longer jury deliberation times.

IN SUMMARY

We examined the psychological processes jurors apply when individual jurors reason collectively. Research reveals that the social, cognitive and interpersonal dynamics of the jury affect their decisions.

CRITICAL THINKING AND APPLICATION QUESTIONS

1   How does a group discussion persuade individuals to change their minds?

2   Given what we know about cognitive and social influences on jury deliberation, write instructions for the jury about how they should deliberate to reach a verdict that addresses these issues in clear language.

3   Does your personal experience with collaborative inhibition (when members of a collaborative group remember less information than an equal number of single individuals) support or refute this theory?

CHAPTER REVIEW

Jury trials play a centrally important role in the criminal justice system, and they are also of interest to psychologists. How individual jurors perceive, interpret and remember evidence, as well as the group processes involved in jury deliberation, can be described in terms of fundamental psychological concepts. Juror research raises issues about how the internet is changing the nature of trials and strategies to cope with modern jury–media relationships. Juries provide a real-world laboratory for examining theoretical issues related to reasoning, memory, judgement, decision making, stereotyping, persuasion and group behaviour.

NAMES TO KNOW

Shari Seidman Diamond

An expert on jury behaviour, jury process and legal decision making, including the use of science by the courts.

• Diamond, S. S. (2018) Coping with modern challenges and anticipating the future of criminal jury trials: Criminal juries in the 21st century. *Psychological Science and the Law*, 297–315.

• Diamond, S. S. and Rose, M. R. (2018) The contemporary American jury. *Annual Review of Law and Social Science*, 14, 239–58.

Liana Peter-Hagene

Investigates the role of extralegal psychological factors, such as emotions, attitudes and regulatory processes, that affect jurors' decision making in criminal cases.

• Peter-Hagene, L. (2019) Jurors' cognitive depletion and performance during jury deliberation as a function of jury diversity and defendant race. *Law and Human Behavior*, 43(3), 232–49.

• Salerno, J. M. and Peter-Hagene, L. C. (2015) One angry woman: Anger expression increases influence for men, but decreases influence for women, during group deliberation. *Law and Human Behavior*, 39(6), 581–92.

Margaret Bull Kovera

Investigates eyewitness identification, jury decision making and scientific evidence.

• Kovera, M. B. (ed.) (2017) *The Psychology of Juries*. APA.

• Kovera, M. B. and Levett, L. M. (2015) Jury decision making. In B. L. Cutler and P. A. Zapf (eds) APA *Handbook of Forensic Psychology*, vol. 2: *Criminal Investigation, Adjudication, and Sentencing Outcomes* (pp. 271–311). APA.

12 PSYCHOLOGICAL ASPECTS OF VIOLENCE AND AGGRESSION

Chapter Introduction

Violence takes many forms. We see innocent people abused by those who should protect them, and people exploited, humiliated and injured by their intimate partners. We see people killed in mass murders with tragic frequency, and despite mass media coverage, the cause remains a mystery. We see small groups of violent people terrorise others and ask how a rational person can sacrifice their family, identity and sometimes their life for a belief system. A better understanding of the psychological motivations behind these violent behaviours will help us recognise the warning signs in order to intervene and save lives.

Learning Outcomes

In search of violent patterns

- Describe violence and the evolution of risk assessment methods.

Intimate partner violence

- Explain the multifaceted nature of interpersonal violence.

Mass murder and risk assessment

- Describe alternative approaches to profiling mass murderers.

The psychology of terrorism

- Apply the theories of terrorism using the three-phase process of joining an extreme group.

IN SEARCH OF VIOLENT PATTERNS

FICTION: Worldwide violence is increasing and cannot be predicted.

Versus

FACT: Worldwide violence is decreasing and the patterns and trends across many forms of violence can be predicted.

CASE STUDY

Premeditated violence

Fifteen-year-old William Cornick collapsed on holiday in Cornwall, England after which he was diagnosed with diabetes. Later, he was upset at not being able to join the Army because of his diabetes. During Christmas 2013, he sent a Facebook message to a friend in which he first mentioned 'brutally murdering' Ann Maguire, his Spanish teacher at Corpus Christi Catholic College in Leeds. Cornick disliked Maguire and posted a Facebook message to his friends to see if any of them would murder Maguire for him for a payment of £10 and film the attack (Pidd, 2017).

In April 2014, Cornick attended lessons as normal. After morning break, he went to the top floor for his Spanish lesson. Halfway through the lesson, he stabbed Maguire seven times in the back and neck with a 21 cm (8.3 inch) knife. A pathologist's report found that there were no defensive injuries and she had been stabbed after being 'taken by surprise', with the fatal wound being 'stab wound three' to her jugular (Hurst, 2017). Psychiatrists said that Cornick had 'a gross lack of empathy for his victim and a degree of callousness rarely seen in clinical practice' and that he presented a risk of serious harm to the public. He was imprisoned at Leeds Crown Court for a minimum of 20 years. He has never shown any remorse for his actions (Christodoulou, 2019). After sentencing, there was concern that the minimum sentence length was excessive because the brain of a 15-year-old is not mature (Steinberg, 2017).

Discussion Questions:

1   With all the clues about his intentions, why do you think none of the people who Cornick told said anything?

2   Explain the causes of Cornick's murderous behaviour from a biological, social and developmental perspective.

3   Do you agree with the concern that Cornick's 15-year-old brain was too immature to understand the consequences of his actions?

Defining violence and aggression

The case of William Cornick shows violent aggression intending to harm another person. In these situations, the offender believes that the behaviour will cause harm and the potential victim is motivated to avoid the aggressions. These kinds of aggressive behaviours can be direct, hitting, threatening, or mocking a person, or indirect, gossiping or cyberbullying. Although the negative outcomes of direct physical aggression are more obvious, indirect aggression also has consequences.

Violence can be viewed by its affective and predatory intentions. Meloy (2006) identifies these affective and predatory modes of violence. **Affective violence** is an instinctual, defensive and reactive form of violence to a perceived threat, and the goal of

Affective violence – *An instinctual, defensive and reactive form of violence to a perceived threat.*

affective violence is threat reduction. On the other hand, **predatory violence** is a planned or purposeful form of violence, where there is no perceived threat, it is attack focused and the goals are variable (Hoffer, Hargreaves-Cormany, Muirhead and Meloy, 2018).

Violent behaviour is direct and has extreme consequences (death or injury). However, not all forms of aggression are violent, but all forms of violence are aggressive. All forms of aggression and violence appear as social behaviour and involve an interaction between at least two persons. These criteria exclude violence directed at inanimate objects without the intention to harm another person (hitting a wall), aggressive emotions (hate and rage), or cognitions (attitudes or beliefs about violence).

Violence has many causes, including frustration, exposure to violent media, violence in the home or neighbourhood and a tendency to view others' actions as hostile even when they are not. Certain situations also increase the risk of aggression, such as drinking alcohol, being insulted and other provocations, and environmental factors like heat and overcrowding.

The problem with 'random' acts of violence

Many extraordinary events, from winning lotteries to coincidental meetings, do happen and occur partially or fully by chance. Yet we confuse random events with low-probability events, assuming outcomes cannot be predicted (Teigen and Keren, 2020). In the same way, a 'random' act of violence means that there is no discernible pattern, while the media portray patterns of violence as unpredictable, pointless and increasing (Best, 1999).

If violence were unpredictable, it could happen to anyone at any time and anyone could be either a victim or a perpetrator of violence. Yet research on violence reveals many discernible social patterns, such as violence is typically perpetrated by younger males (Manley et al., 2017; Fox, Levin and Quinet, 2012). Although there are crimes with random victims – a stray bullet hitting an unintended target – most are not. In fact, a pattern emerges that negative social experiences such as negative peer and family influences, poverty, substance abuse, mental illness and many other issues increase the chances of becoming a violent offender and/or a victim of a violent crime (Lanier, 2018).

If violence were pointless, it would lack purpose or rational motives on the part of violent offenders. While the loss of human life is indeed pointless, there is usually a motivating goal behind violent actions, at least from the offender's perspective. This belief encourages people to think that there are no recognisable patterns in terms of who the victims and offenders of crimes are and that there are no consistent targets that are disproportionately attacked. The problem is that perceived randomness disguises real offender motivations and causes. Finally, labelling these actions as 'random' distorts and exaggerates the level of risk in society and increases fear. This causes people to believe that acts of violence are more likely to happen than they are (Madfis, 2016).

Labelling violent acts as behaviours typical of a certain group does not prevent future incidents. To understand violence, it is important to investigate how seemingly irrational and pointless crimes may be rational and meaningful for the offender (Walters, 2016; Winter, 2019). Understanding the behaviour from the perspective of the offender is to see that their actions have purpose. This is the argument behind **rational choice theory**: offenders are rational thinkers, who consider the costs and benefits of multiple paths or options and choose the course of action with the greatest perceived benefit or least cost (Cornish and Clarke, 1987; Hodwitz, 2020; Meenaghan et al., 2020). For example, two offenders plan a burglary by entering a home at night when the family is on holiday. The burglars made a rational decision by weighing the means and benefits, and making a decision to violate the law despite the punishment if caught. The idea that offenders commit crime out of a rational choice of self-benefit has found empirical evidence supporting its effectiveness in explaining propensity towards violence. For example, in a study examining sibling fights,

Predatory violence – *A planned or purposeful form of violence where there is no perceived threat.*

Rational choice theory – *Offenders are rational in their decision making, and despite the consequences, the benefits of committing the crime outweigh the punishment.*

researchers showed that the probability of the younger sibling (usually the less powerful actor) starting a fight increased in the presence of their parents, as the chances of self-preservation in such cases are higher (Felson, 1983).

The final problem with 'random' acts of violence is portraying violence as more malevolent and increasing. In fact, global rates of violence are decreasing (Spagat and van Weezel, 2020; van Dijk, Tseloni and Farrell, 2012; Eisner, Nivette, Murray and Krisch, 2016). For example, in the USA, there has been a decrease in general crime and violent crime since the high rates of crime in the 1990s (Weiss, Santos, Testa and Kumar, 2016; Tcherni-Buzzeo, 2019). While there are local fluctuations in violence and crime rates, there is a global trend of decline (Pinker, 2011). The theory that the twentieth century was the most violent in history lacks support (Pinker, 2012). We are likely to think that modern-day life is more violent because historical records from recent eras are more complete, and because the human mind overestimates the frequency of vivid, memorable events – the **availability heuristic**. What would have been called a 'heroic conquest' might be classified as 'genocide' today and their leaders prosecuted as war criminals. However, some argue that Pinker's perspective of moral progress is wishful thinking and the long peace is merely a statistical sampling error – choosing samples that do not represent the population of data (Gray, 2011). Specifically, Pinker's declining violence argument is based more on data concerning violent events, such as homicide and deaths on the battlefield. In discussing such data, Bessel (2018) questions the reliability and comparability of these violent events over time. In the end, Pinker's argument may be more about the growing public sensitivity towards many forms of violence, including sexual violence, for which there is considerable evidence (Adeyemi, 2020).

Availability heuristic – *A mental shortcut relying on immediate examples that come to a person's mind when evaluating a topic, concept or decision.*

Global Perspectives

Treating violence like a disease

Exposure to violence increases a person's risk of adopting violent behaviour themselves. Violent behaviour transmits and spreads based on exposure – just like a disease epidemic. This evocative idea is the driving force behind the global organisation Cure Violence Global (https://cvg.org). Public health methods have been extremely successful in reducing violence in communities

Cure Violence Global prevents the spread of violence by using methods associated with disease control

Source: Cure Violence Global

around the world. The *epidemic control method* for reducing violence utilises trained, supervised and supported specialised community-based health workers who:

- chart areas with the highest incidence of transmission of symptoms or 'disease'
- reach out to those who have early or more developed signs
- reduce the likelihood of further events
- detect and treat close contacts and others at next highest risk.

This works for violence as it works for tuberculosis or Ebola (Slutkin, 2017).

Violence risk assessment

Estimating an individual's future risk of violence is important for the safety of the community and individual treatment. Risk assessment is used in mental health, community and criminal justice settings, where the importance of accuracy is crucial. The results of violence risk assessments are often used for decisions about mental health and criminal detention and sentencing considerations. The approaches to risk assessment fall on a continuum from purely clinical to actuarial approaches. Clinical decision making relies on the ability of the assessor, with the subjective conclusions based on the clinician's knowledge and experience. In comparison, pure actuarial risk assessments rely solely on data and probability in the absence of human experience (Mills, 2017).

Three generations of risk management tools

Risk assessment methods have progressed through three generations of techniques, from unstructured clinical judgements, actuarial risk assessment instruments to the current structured professional judgement (SPJ) tools combining clinical and actuarial approaches.

First generation of risk assessment: unstructured clinical judgements

Initial predictions of violence risk were clinical opinions of a violent individual's circumstances based on the clinician's hypotheses about the causes of violent behaviour and their own experiences. Although this approach is built on the expertise of the clinician, it proved no better than chance when predicting future violence (Brook, 2017). This approach has been questioned since the early 1970s when Ennis and Litwack (1974) cast doubt on its reliability and validity. Another problem was the influence psychiatric experts have in the courtroom. At commitment hearings, psychiatrists are encouraged to offer their opinions on the key issues: Is the prospective patient 'mentally ill', 'dangerous' or 'in need of care and treatment'? Psychiatrists are also allowed to describe the potential patient using technical terminology and psychiatric diagnoses. Yet, there are varying levels of training and experience in expert testimony and assessor susceptibility to bias (Shepherd and Sullivan, 2017).

Second generation of risk assessment: actuarial risk assessment instruments

Actuarial risk assessment instruments require the assessor to respond to the presence or absence of preset factors to determine the future risk of using violence. The accumulation of multiple risk factors increases the individual's future risk of the use of violence. As data is gathered, individual scores are compared to population scores and group norms. The data is directly linked to outcome variables and provides a statistically valid risk category predicting the use of future violence by an individual (Harris and Rice, 2007). Although the use of statistical probability is a valid approach for the weather and life insurance, actuarial risk assessment instruments are prone to both group and individual errors (Hart and Cooke, 2013). The problem is that actuarial assessment of violence provides a probability estimate based on static factors, such as criminal history or past substance abuse. According to researchers, static factors are less useful for planning treatment because they cannot be changed through interventions (O'Shea, Picchioni and Dickens, 2016). Additionally, many of the instruments developed for static factors are time-consuming, rely on historical factors and predict violence in the long term (Lorettu, Nivoli, Milia and Nivoli, 2020).

Third generation of risk assessment: structured professional judgement (SPJ)

While the earlier clinical and actuarial approaches can provide a prediction of violent reoffending in categorical or numerical terms, structured professional judgement (SPJ) is a combination of actuarial and clinical decision making providing an empirical basis for clinical observations. The SPJ approach is similar to actuarial approaches, scoring risk factors as absent (0), somewhat present (2) and higher overall scores, which are related to an increased future risk of an individual's propensity to be violent. In practice, a numerical presentation of the risk level is not recommended, with best practice guidelines to present the risk category with an explanation (De Bortoli, Ogloff, Coles and Dolan, 2017). The advantage of this approach is that SPJ tools guide the assessor to consider a range of factors, form a judgement of risk and assist with case treatment interventions. Although still somewhat subjective, the SPJ approach identifies treatment targets and guides risk management based on a set of structured guidelines and summary risk ratings (Falzer, 2013). Unlike purely actuarial approaches, the SPJ approach includes dynamic factors such as attitudinal, behavioural and social issues, resulting in a risk assessment with more factors that can be altered, unlike static factors. This helps predict an individual's future capacity for violence and provides guidance for the selection of appropriate interventions. By relying on structured clinical judgement of known correlates of risk for violence, SPJ provides a fuller picture of an individual's circumstances, risk factors and targeted areas or needs to reduce future reoffending (Singh, Fazel, Gueorguieva and Buchanan, 2014).

The future of violence risk assessment

Future violence risk assessment is likely to shift from cross-sectional risk prediction to ongoing clinical monitoring using technology, such as the analysis of social media and telemetry to report physiological markers of intoxication and abnormal mood states. The intrusiveness of these methods would have to be balanced with their effectiveness in reducing violence. However, any new methods should be assessed by their predictive ability and reliable evidence that they can actually reduce violence and that the reduction is not at an unacceptable cost to social freedom.

IN SUMMARY

Violence is an intentional act to commit harm. The media portray violence as unpredictable, pointless and increasing. Unstructured clinical judgement of violence risk lacks reliability, by relying on personal intuition or opinion, while structured professional judgement (SPJ) relies on structured assessment based on historical factors or observable factors (or both) that can be placed into probability risk categories. Unstructured clinical judgement is less reliable and valid compared with SPJ.

 CRITICAL THINKING AND APPLICATION QUESTIONS

1   Crime requires three things: motivated offenders (criminals), suitable targets (victims) and the absence of capable guardians to prevent the act. Apply the epidemic control model at any of these points to 'cure' crime in your local jurisdiction.

2   Imagine if we discovered that violent behaviours were caused solely by *external environmental* causes. How would this change our perspectives about people who commit violent acts?

3   Imagine if we discovered that violent behaviours were caused solely by *internal dispositional* causes. How would this change our perspectives about people who commit violent acts?

INTIMATE PARTNER VIOLENCE

FICTION: Intimate partner violence is physical abuse instigated by the victim.	*Versus*	**FACT:** Most intimate partner violence is psychological, and the victim is blameless.

CASE STUDY

The tragic case of Zahra Abrahimzadeh

Ziaolleh Abrahimzadeh and his wife Zahra migrated to Australia from Iran in 1997 ready to start a new life and family. But, by 2009, life was abusive and controlled. Zahra and her children, Arman, Atena and Anita, were living in constant fear of Ziaolleh. On a particularly bad day, Ziaolleh in a mad rage brandished a knife and threatened to kill them all. When Ziaolleh left for work the next morning, they had a chance to escape. With only time to pack what they needed, they fled. With no confidence that a restraining order would keep her husband away, Zahra contacted the police, who supplied a safe house run by the Central Domestic Violence Service. During the 12 months the family spent on the run, they were careful about who they contacted and the information they shared (Abrahimzadeh, 2019).

Meanwhile, Ziaolleh continued to stalk his family, by securing visitation rights to his youngest daughter, through whom he relayed threats that he would kill her mother for leaving him. On 21 March 2010, Zahra and her daughter Atena were enjoying a rare night out together on Persian New Year's Eve at the Adelaide Convention Centre. Discovering via social media that Zahra was at the event, Ziaolleh casually walked into the building and then ran behind where Zahra sat. In front of 300 witnesses, he stabbed Zahra eight times in the torso, neck and chest, continuing to plunge the knife even as she fell forward (Fewster, 2014).

At trial, Justice John Sulan noted that Ziaolleh had been both an abusive husband and father who had relentlessly sought revenge on Zahra because she refused to stop divorce proceedings. Courageously, all three children – whom the judge praised as impressive witnesses – testified against their father. He received a minimum sentence of 26 years.

Five years later, Arman and his sisters opened the Zahra Foundation (www.zahrafoundation. org.au), which aims to help break the cycle of domestic and family violence. It funds a five-week financial literacy course offered through domestic violence services. It covers saving and budgeting, managing debts and repayments, along with the basics of loans and credit (Novak, 2015).

Discussion Questions:

1   In what ways is the experience of violence different for immigrants to a country?

2   Although Ziaolleh Abrahimzadeh was subject to a restraining order for 13 months, between contacting the police to report the domestic violence and the date of Zahra's death, Ziaolleh was never arrested by the criminal justice system for his alleged offending. What effect do you think this had on him?

The heart-breaking story of Zahra Abrahimzadeh is just one more example of intimate partner violence (McMahon and McGorrery, 2016). Intimate partner violence is violence that occurs when one partner uses physical or psychological means to dominate and control the other (Kelly and Johnson, 2008), and includes physical, sexual, psychological, spiritual, economic and social abuse (Miller and McCaw, 2019; Miles, 2016; Stylianou, 2018). Intimate partner violence occurs in intimate heterosexual and same-sex relationships (Whitehead, Dawson and Hotton, 2020). It can be perpetrated by a current or past partner and is a chronic syndrome characterised not only by episodes of physical violence but also by the emotional and psychological abuse that perpetrators use to maintain control over their partners (Ali and McGarry, 2020).

Intimate partner violence is one part in the typology of interpersonal violence. This typology distinguishes four modes in which abuse may be inflicted: physical, sexual, psychological and economic. It further divides the general definition of interpersonal violence into subtypes according to the victim–perpetrator relationship. Many forms of violence may occur simultaneously, so they are not mutually exclusive. We will focus on intimate partner violence.

Psychological and physical consequences of intimate partner violence

The mental and physical health consequences of intimate partner violence include chronic pain, difficulty sleeping, activity limitations, depression, anxiety, PTSD and low self-esteem (Black et al., 2011). The impact of intimate partner violence ranges from short-term physical effects to severe long-term psychological effects, such as depression, post-traumatic stress symptoms and suicidal tendencies (Chang et al., 2018). According to the World Health Organization (WHO, 2013), women experience physical or sexual abuse in higher proportions in Southeast Asia (37.7 per cent), the Eastern Mediterranean region (37 per cent) and Africa (36.6 per cent), while the lowest rates are estimated to be in the Americas (29.8 per cent), Europe (25.4 per cent) and the Western Pacific region (26.4 per cent).

Why don't victims of intimate partner violence leave?

When it is a realistic choice, it is best for victims to escape their abusers. However, this is not the case in all situations. When abuse victims are able to safely escape and remain free from their abuser, they often survive with long-lasting and sometimes permanent effects on their mental and physical health, their relationships with friends, family and children, and their economic wellbeing (Black et al., 2011).

Abusers repeatedly go to extremes to prevent the victim from leaving. Often, leaving an abuser is the most dangerous time for a victim of domestic violence. In interviews with men who have killed their wives, either threats of separation by their partner or actual separations were most often the precipitating events that led to murder (Rezey, 2020; Tjaden and Thoennes, 2000; McKay et al., 2018).

A victim's reasons for staying with their abusers are complex and, in most cases, are based on the belief that their abuser will follow through with the threats they have used to keep them trapped. Some of the reasons include: the abuser will hurt or kill them; they will hurt or kill the children; they will win custody of the children; they will harm or kill pets (McDonald et al., 2019; Wuerch et al., 2020) or others; they will ruin their victim financially. The victim may not be able to safely escape or protect those they love. Researchers found that 20 per cent of homicide victims were not the domestic violence victims themselves, but family members, friends, neighbours, persons who intervened, law enforcement responders, or bystanders (Smith, Fowler and Niolon, 2014).

Tactics of abuse

Every relationship differs, but there are common tactics used by abusers to gain and maintain power and control over the victim. Physical, sexual, psychological and financial abuse are briefly described.

Physical abuse

Physical violence is the intentional use of physical force that has the potential to cause death, injury or harm (Breiding et al., 2015). Physical injuries are often indicators of intimate partner violence (Reginelli et al., 2020). Violence most often results in injuries that strike the head, neck and face (Lee, 2009; Ochs, Neuenschwander and Dodson, 1996). Researchers examined different assault mechanisms of face lesions of 950 patients and discovered that violence was the most frequent cause of craniofacial fractures (Hussain, Wijetunge, Grubnic and Jackson, 1994).

Defensive wounds are also a sign of interpersonal violence and are often used by police to determine which person was the assailant and which was the victim (Payne-James, Stark, Nittis and Sheasby, 2020). The most obvious defence wounds on the upper limbs are incised wounds, that is, wounds that are longer than they are deep (Payne-James, Stark, Nittis and Sheasby, 2020). Rouse (1994) investigated 156 deaths from stabbing and found that incised wounds to the hands are the most common form of defensive injury.

Sexual abuse

Sexual violence includes non-consensual sexual contact and non-consensual non-contact acts of a sexual nature, such as voyeurism and sexual harassment (Basile and Saltzman, 2002). Acts qualify as sexual violence if they are committed against someone who is unable to consent or refuse, because of age, disability, misuse of authority or threats of violence. Sexual coercion is forcing (or attempting to force) another individual through violence, threats, verbal insistence, deception, cultural expectations or economic circumstances to engage in sexual behaviour against their will (Snow, Alonzo, Servedio and Prum, 2019).

Psychological abuse

Psychological violence is defined as the use of both verbal and nonverbal communication with the intention to mentally or emotionally harm and/or exert control over your partner (CDC, 2014). The subtype of psychological violence (compared to physical and sexual violence) is estimated to be the most common form of intimate partner violence in the USA (Black et al., 2011) and Europe (EUAFR, 2014), affecting between 35 and 49 per cent of men and women. These findings have led some European countries to criminalise psychological violence as an independent offence, making it equally punishable as physical violence, for example Norway (Vatnar, Friestad and Bjørkly, 2019) and England (McGorrery and McMahon, 2019). Acts of psychological violence are found along a continuum from aggression (yelling and insults) to coercion (threats and isolation) (Lagdon, Armour and Stringer, 2014).

Psychological abuse is associated with both emotional and behavioural problems such as depression and antisocial behaviours, as well as impairments in future relationships (Arslan, 2016). According to the US National Intimate Partner and Sexual Violence

Survey (Black et al., 2011), 40 per cent of women experienced violence such as insults or name calling at least once in their lifetime and 41 per cent had experienced coercive control in their lifetime. Psychological violence can be experienced separately but can also occur with other forms of maltreatment (Hughes and Cossar, 2016). In fact, psychological violence has been identified as a significant predictor of physical violence in romantic relationships (Frye and Karney, 2006), and the impact of psychological violence may be more significant than physical abuse (Hattery and Smith, 2016). Thus, according to Hughes and Cossar (2016), psychological violence could be the most common form of abuse with long-lasting impact. Moreover, although studies have focused on psychological violence in adulthood, fewer have focused on psychological violence as experienced during adolescence (Arslan, 2016).

Financial abuse

A hidden form of abuse perpetrated within intimate partner relationships is economic abuse, also referred to as 'financial abuse'. Although identified as the foundation of coercive control, economic abuse has only recently been viewed as distinct from emotional and psychological abuse (Stylianou, Postmus and McMahon, 2013). It is difficult to establish the prevalence of economic abuse, because victims may have difficulty distinguishing economically abusive patterns from the economic insecurity they experience as women. This difficulty is related to the gendered nature of care, the undervaluing of women's paid and unpaid work and workforce discrimination (López-Mosquera, 2016; Bruns, 2019; Auspurg, Hinz and Sauer, 2017). Unlike physical abuse, economic abuse is harder to identify. It leaves its victims helpless and without resources, both during and after the abuse. This forces the victim to either risk staying in an abusive relationship, or risk becoming homeless and facing poverty (Postmus et al., 2020). By blocking or controlling access to financial assets, abusers can coerce their victims into staying with them or coming back if they try to leave, locking them into a cycle of abuse (Stylianou, Postmus and McMahon, 2013). In fact, lacking financial knowledge or resources is the primary indicator of whether a victim will stay, leave or return to an abusive relationship (Postmus et al., 2020; Postmus, Plummer and Stylianou, 2016).

Predictors of intimate partner violence

Risk factors predicting intimate partner violence are not direct causes, but they are characteristics associated with an increased chance that a problem behaviour will occur. It is important to note that the presence of a risk factor does not mean that the behaviour will necessarily occur, only that the chances of it occurring are greater.

Unlike many health problems, there are few social and demographic characteristics that define risk groups for intimate partner violence. Poverty is the exception and increases risk through effects on conflict, women's power and male identity. Lower income women have higher rates of intimate partner violence than do higher income women (Grose et al., 2019). Women who are more empowered educationally, economically and socially are most protected. However, below this high level the relationship disappears, and less educated women have higher rates of intimate partner violence than do more educated women (Bhona et al., 2019). Furthermore, couples with income, educational or occupational status disparities have higher rates of intimate partner violence than do couples with no status disparity. Related to this, unmarried, cohabiting couples have higher rates of intimate partner violence than do married couples (Kenney and McLanahan, 2006). Also, experiencing and/or seeing violence in one's family of origin increases one's chances of being a perpetrator or victim of intimate partner violence (Haj-Yahia, Sousa and Lugassi, 2019). Finally, research suggests that persons with a disability are at greater risk of violence (Stern, van der Heijden and Dunkle, 2019). Researchers are exploring the male experience of intimate partner violence from their female partners (Bates and Weare, 2020; Powney and Graham-Kevan, 2019). Surveys of male victims found that their most distressing experiences were from the control their female partners exerted over them. These experiences included gaslighting, isolating from friends and family, control over basic freedom, and the fear or uncertainty of living with the abuse in day-to-day life (Bates, 2020).

Violence is often used to resolve a crisis of male identity, whether caused by poverty or an inability to control women. In addition, research shows that wife assault is more common in families where power is concentrated in the hands of the husband or male partner and the husband makes most of the decisions regarding family finances and strictly controls when and where his wife or female partner goes (Lydiah, Casper, Ngare and Immaculate, 2019).

Alcohol consumption increases the risk of violence (Cogan and Ballinger, 2006; Vitoria-Estruch, Romero-Martínez, Lila and Moya-Albiol, 2018). Male-to-female aggression is eleven times more likely on days when perpetrators drink alcohol (Fals-Stewart, Leonard and Birchler, 2005). Intimate partner violence offenders are five times more likely than non-offenders to consume alcohol (Luthra and Gidycz, 2006). Additionally, Thompson and Kingree (2006) found that alcohol-consuming offenders are more likely to cause significant physical injury to their partners compared with sober offenders. These findings support recommendations for addressing alcohol abuse and intimate partner violence at the same time (Lira et al., 2019; Klostermann and Fals-Stewart, 2006).

IN SUMMARY

Intimate partner violence is a specific type of interpersonal violence where the abuser uses physical, sexual, psychological and economic tactics to maintain control of the victim. Predictors of intimate partner violence include social, cultural, financial and substance abuse.

CRITICAL THINKING AND APPLICATION QUESTIONS

1   Why is leaving the most dangerous time for a victim of intimate partner violence?

2   Describe ways to counter the risk factors for intimate partner violence.

3   Why are victims of intimate partner violence sometimes blamed for the abusive treatment they receive?

MASS MURDER AND RISK ASSESSMENT

FICTION: School shootings are an epidemic driven by lone revenge-motivated offenders.

Versus

FACT: School shootings are rare. The offenders are not always loners motivated by revenge.

The father of a boy who died at the Columbine massacre at an anti-gun protest in reaction to the Columbine mass shooting

Eric Harris, 18, and Dylan Klebold, 17, made a video in their school video production class called 'Hitmen for hire', in which they dressed in trench coats, carried improvised guns and pretended to kill school athletes. They did it again with real guns five months later. On 20 April 1999, they murdered 12 students and a teacher and wounded 23 other students and teachers before killing themselves at Columbine High School in Littleton, USA (Cullen, 2009). In hindsight, there were clues that this tragic event was about to happen. The pair had planned the massacre for around a year. Prior to the attack, Harris posted online threats that included the declaration, 'I'm coming for EVERYONE soon and I will be armed to the f-----g teeth and I WILL shoot to kill ... All I want to do is kill and injure as many of you ... as I can' (Columbine Review Commission, 2001, p. 92). Klebold submitted a creative writing essay about a fictional mass shooting of 'preps' that ended with the assertion, 'I understood his actions' (Cullen, 2009). Law enforcement had contacted the offenders at least 15 times and were shown the evidence from Harris's website that he threatened to kill others, including a classmate, and had acquired weapons (Columbine Review Commission, 2001). Harris and Klebold also used their schoolwork to foreshadow the massacre. They both displayed themes of violence in their creative writing projects. Harris wrote a paper on school shootings and a poem from the perspective of a bullet. Klebold wrote a short story about a man killing students, which worried his teacher so much that she alerted his parents (Altheide, 2009). Harris told his friend Brooks Brown to go home just minutes prior to the shooting. Brown did not report Harris's odd behaviour to anyone prior to the shooting.

Unfortunately, the Columbine shootings have attained a mythical existence and have influenced subsequent rampages (the Columbine effect) and 'Columbine' has become a slogan for mass shootings (Larkin, 2009).

In this section, we will explore the idea that instead of trying to identify potential shooters like Eric Harris and Dylan Klebold, perhaps we should be listening to the clues they share about their actions.

What is a mass murder?

Although all mass murders are tragic and well publicised, the total number over the past 50 years is still small compared with other violent crimes like homicide (Booty et al., 2019). In fact, mass murders are different from other types of homicides, and mass murders have specific classifications (Table 12.1).

Table 12.1: Homicide typologies

Classification	Description
Serial killer	Multiple victims over a variety of locations and has a cooling off period between kills
Spree killer	Multiple victims over a variety of locations all occurring within a single period of time
Mass murderer	Multiple victims intentionally killed in a single location and a single period of time
	• *Family annihilator:* Kills family and themselves
	• *Set-and-run killer:* Concerned with escape before the deaths occur (bombs, fires, poisoning a food source)
	• *Rampage killer or pseudocommando:* Warrior mentality, on a mission of revenge for a perceived wrong

Source: Definitions of 'serial', 'spree' and 'mass murderer' from Kop, Read and Walker (2019), definitions of 'family annihilator', 'set-and-run killer' and 'rampage killer' from Dietz (1986).

Mass shooting describes a specific form of mass murderer, sometimes referred to as an 'active shooter' or 'rampage shooter'. In these incidents, offenders fire their weapons in public places with the intention of harming multiple victims. These incidents do not include gang conflicts, robberies or other conventional crimes (Lankford, 2016). While public mass shootings are traditionally defined as four or more victims being killed, active shootings have no minimum threshold (Fox and Levin, 2015). An active shooter is an armed person who has used deadly force and continues to do so with unrestricted access to additional victims (Fox and Levin, 2015).

Germany's worst mass shooting tragedy

On 26 April 2002, 19-year-old Robert Steinhäuser stormed the Gutenberg-Gymnasium secondary school in Erfut, Eastern Germany wearing a black mask and carrying a pistol and a shotgun. Unlike most rampage shooters, Steinhäuser ignored students and specifically targeted teachers. His attack occurred during a major examination and it was believed that Steinhäuser's vengeful rage stemmed from his expulsion from school for presenting a forged medical certificate after some days absent from school. Without the proper qualifications, he would have limited job prospects.

His rampage preparations began the year before with intense target practice at an Erfurt gun club and with a first-person shooter video game. During his rampage, Steinhäuser killed 16 people in the massacre – 12 teachers, an administrator, a police officer and two students who were unintentionally killed by shots fired through a locked door (Fahr, 2007). Steinhäuser killed himself as armed police prepared to break into the classroom where he had taken refuge. From the first shot to Steinhäuser's suicide, the tragic event lasted no more than 20 minutes (Hooper, 2002). After the rampage, around 700 students were diagnosed with PTSD, about 100 of whom were still under treatment a year later (Schattauer, 2012).

The tragedy shattered Germany's assumption that its gun control was the strictest in Europe and that rampage murders like these only happen in America. After the shooting, the German government adopted a youth protection law, giving police the ability to attack shooters without waiting for a SEK unit (special operational unit), began regulating violent video games, and changed access to firearms by adding psychological evaluations (Ritzheimer, 2016).

Predicting attacks is challenging because of the statistically rare nature of these events. For example, the USA has significantly more mass shooters than the rest of the world, yet there are a million people who do not commit a public mass shooting for every individual that does (Blair and Schweit, 2014). Finding those at risk in a population this size is nearly impossible. For example, many public mass shooters own guns and suffer from mental health problems, but most gun owners and people with mental illness are not violent (Madfis, 2014). Therefore, incidents with such a low base rate are difficult to predict; however, threats of violence are a potential problem. Once a threat is made, having a fair, rational and standardised method of evaluating and responding is vital.

Lankford and Madfis (2018) have devised a checklist of three warning signs that law enforcement can use to determine whether an at-risk individual appears to:

1   have suicidal motives or apathy that might eliminate fear of consequences

2   be able to justify their attack because of a perception of being persecuted

3   have a desire to gain attention or attain celebrity status through killing.

While checklists and catalogues of warning behaviours work for events that have a higher probability of occurring (shoplifting and speeding), in practice, creating a list of warning signs to predict the next school shooter is unwise and even potentially dangerous. These types of lists are often publicised by the media and can unfairly stigmatise and label many nonviolent students as potentially dangerous. In fact, many adolescents display some of the behaviours and personality traits included on these lists without ever committing acts of violence. Perhaps the answer lies in exploring these questions: How did a student reach the belief that killing others is the answer? Were there signs before their actions? Even if there is not a checklist of traits, perhaps there was a list of clues that signalled a need for help.

Leakage –
When offenders intentionally or unintentionally reveal insights into their thoughts or feelings that suggest impending targeted violence.

Leakage of threat intention

The answer to prevention is not profiling active shooters but allowing them to identify themselves. In the weeks and months before an attack, many active shooters engage in behaviours that may signal impending violence. While some of these behaviours are intentionally concealed, others are observable and if recognised and reported may prevent an attack. This situation is described as **leakage** and is when a shooter intentionally or unintentionally reveals clues about their future actions via feelings, thoughts, fantasies, attitudes or intentions. These clues range from subtle threats, boasts or predictions to ultimatums and manifestos (O'Toole, 2000). Generally, a threat is an intention to do harm to someone. Threats can be spoken, written or symbolic – motioning with one's hands as though shooting at another person.

Threat levels can be classified according to their level of risk, as shown in Table 12.2. The specific plausible details are important. The details can include the identity of the victim, the reason and the method. Specific details can indicate that substantial thought, planning and preparation has already occurred, suggesting that the threatener will follow through on the threat. In some cases, the distinction between threat levels may not be clear. More information about the threat or threatener is needed. This approach helps identify the most serious threats to act upon quickly.

Table 12.2: Levels of threat and risk criteria

Low	Medium	High
A threat that poses a minimal risk	*A threat that could be conducted, although it may not be realistic*	*A threat that appears to pose an imminent and serious danger to the safety of others*
• Vague and indirect • Not realistic • Information content in the threat is inconsistent, lacks detail and suggests that the person is unlikely to act	• Direct and more concrete, the wording shows more deliberation for conducting the action • General indication of place and time (but not detailed) • Vague reference to preparation (the availability of a weapon, or plot from a movie) • A specific statement that the threat is real	• Threat is direct, detailed specific and plausible • Threat shows concrete steps to take to complete the task – statements indicating that the threatener has acquired or practised with a weapon or has the victim under surveillance

Source: O'Toole, M. E. (2009) *The School Shooter: A Threat Assessment Perspective.* Diane Publishing Company.

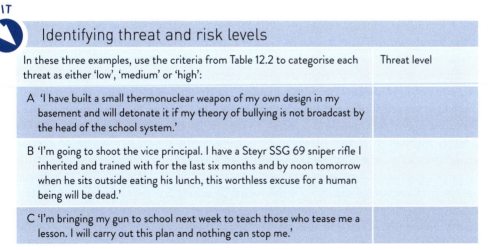

APPLY IT

Identifying threat and risk levels

In these three examples, use the criteria from Table 12.2 to categorise each threat as either 'low', 'medium' or 'high':	Threat level
A 'I have built a small thermonuclear weapon of my own design in my basement and will detonate it if my theory of bullying is not broadcast by the head of the school system.'	
B 'I'm going to shoot the vice principal. I have a Steyr SSG 69 sniper rifle I inherited and trained with for the last six months and by noon tomorrow when he sits outside eating his lunch, this worthless excuse for a human being will be dead.'	
C 'I'm bringing my gun to school next week to teach those who tease me a lesson. I will carry out this plan and nothing can stop me.'	

Answers: A = Low, B = High, C = Medium

Leakage is common; the US Secret Service found that in 81 per cent of cases, 'at least one person had information that the attacker was thinking about or planning the school attack, and in 59 per cent of cases, more than one person knew that the attacker was thinking about or planning an attack' (Vossekuil et al., 2002, p. 25). Investigations of public mass murderers from 1990 to 2014 found that 58 per cent engaged in some form of leakage (Silver, Horgan and Gill, 2018). Research of active shooters from 2000 to 2013 found that 56 per cent openly expressed their violent thoughts or intent before attacking (Silver, Simons and Craun, 2018). Detailed analysis reveals that leakage is more common among younger offenders (Silver, Simons and Craun, 2018; Vossekuil et al., 2002), is sometimes communicated directly to the targets themselves (Meloy, 2014; Meloy, Hoffmann, Roshdi and Guldimann, 2014; Meloy, Hoffmann, Guldimann and James, 2012), and takes many different forms – verbal statements, written statements and social media communications (Madfis, 2014, 2018; Meloy et al., 2001; Silver, Simons and Craun, 2018).

In a novel approach, Lankford, Adkins and Madfis (2019) compared the deadliest mass shootings with active shooters who killed fewer victims, and found that the deadliest mass shooters engaged in leakage about their violent thoughts/intentions (87 per cent) more often than other active shooters (52 per cent). Also, signalling specific interest in mass killing (one of the most severe forms of intention) was more common among the deadliest mass shooters (80 per cent). Perhaps because of the intensity of their crime, the deadliest perpetrators' concerning behaviour was reported to law enforcement prior to the attack much more frequently (80 per cent) than other active shooters' concerning behaviour (34 per cent).

Prevention by public reporting

Bystander effect – *When the presence of others discourages an individual from intervening during an emergency.*

Unfortunately, friends and family members of the active shooter may not recognise the behaviour as dangerous and resist reporting a friend or family member as a potential killer. In the USA, from 2010 to 2013, only 41 per cent of active shooters were reported because of their concerning behaviours (Silver, Simons and Craun, 2018; Lankford and Madfis, 2018). Why were people hesitant to report? One explanation is the **bystander effect** (Latané and Darley, 1969). Specifically, people are uncomfortable speaking up against things that seem wrong, because speaking places the burden of responsibility on them (Madfis, 2014). Additionally, the perception of *diffused responsibility*, where people often assume that others will respond, also decreases the chances of reporting (Mathes and Kahn, 1975). Finally, people may not communicate their knowledge about leakage if the threats are ambiguous, such as innocent jokes or comments. This is why improved education about warning signs is important (Hoffman, 2017; Madfis, 2014, 2018).

Encouraging people to report dangerous behaviours may seem as simple as the US Department of Homeland Security's approach, an 'If you see something, say something' campaign to distribute surveillance responsibilities to the public (Reeves, 2012). The challenge is that people are willing to report the behaviour of strangers, but not a family member, friend or co-worker. This behaviour is shown in research on averted school massacres, where students who observed leakage were more likely to report the threatening behaviour of acquaintances than close friends (Madfis, 2014). A better approach to encourage reporting is the model of *suicide prevention*. Suicide prevention education has successfully encouraged family members and friends to recommend that at-risk individuals voluntarily seek psychological treatment. Furthermore, in extreme cases, they have also called law enforcement to conduct welfare checks that can result in the individual being taken into custody. Appeals and education to protect the person they care about by calling the police and saving both the person at risk and potential victims have been successful (McGillivray et al., 2020). When it comes to reporting potential mass shooters, calling the police could save both the at-risk individual's life and the lives of potential victims (Kissner, 2016; Lankford, Adkins and Madfis, 2019).

IN SUMMARY

Common myths about school shootings are perpetuated by stereotypes and sensational news coverage. While there is no single profile that accurately describes the typical shooter, research suggests that most active shooter events were preventable based on leaked information revealed by the shooter in advance. The deadliest mass shooters show more warning signs and are reported to law enforcement more often than other active shooters. Future prevention efforts should encourage the public to report warning signs to law enforcement to evaluate and investigate potential threats.

CRITICAL THINKING AND APPLICATION QUESTIONS

1   Design a school safety campaign that would encourage students to prevent school shootings.

2   Why is profiling mass shooters difficult?

3   How is the suicide prevention model effective for preventing mass shooters?

THE PSYCHOLOGICAL IMPACT OF TERRORISM

FICTION: Terrorists are psychologically deviant.	*Versus*	**FACT:** Terrorists do not deviate from the population in terms of psychopathology.

The hidden world of Islamic State brides

Tempted by the false promises of an Islamic utopia, empowerment and adoring husbands, Shamima Begum, 16, Kadiza Sultana, 17, and Amira Abase, 16, secretly fled the UK in 2015 to join the jihadist group, the so-called 'Islamic State'. This group is also referred to as Isis (Islamic State of Iraq and al-Sham) or Isil (Islamic State of Iraq and the Levant), but in 2014 Isis declared the establishment of a 'caliphate', the so-called 'Islamic State' (IS) (Irshaid, 2015). The three girls were among an estimated 550 women from Western countries who had travelled to join the Islamic State. After arriving in the Islamic city of Raqqa, they were married to fighters approved by Islamic State – including an Australian and a US national – and two became widows within months (Saltman and Smith, 2015).

Why some people are drawn to violent Islamic extremist groups is uncertain. But what is certain is the Islamic State's shrewd recruitment tactics of exploiting their vulnerabilities, frustrations and dreams, as well as meeting needs the West has failed to address. The Islamic State tactics include appealing to different female profiles, using girl-to-girl recruitment strategies, gendered imagery and iconic memes (Bennhold, 2015). Recruits are promised the fulfilment of their religious duty, the experience of deep and meaningful belonging and sisterhood, and an exciting adventure in which they can find true romance, as well as being empowered (Speckhard, 2017).

Like their male counterparts, female recruits often feel isolated, a sense of persecution and have idealistic goals of a utopian 'caliphate' where they can belong. The targeting of women is crucial for building a functioning Islamic State with successive generations moulded to an ideology. These women may present as much of a threat to the West as the men. Less likely to be killed and more likely to lose a spouse in combat, they may try to return home, indoctrinated and embittered (Patel-Carstairs, 2019).

What is terrorism and violent extremism?

Recruitment and radicalisation can affect the vulnerable and with the added leverage of social media, terrorism is a global concern posing a significant threat to the security of citizens (Magen, 2018). Terrorism is a controversial and subjective term with multiple definitions, one of which relates to the use or threat of violence against civilians and the state, or symbols thereof, in order to create fear and achieve political, economic, religious or ideological goals (Moghaddam et al., 2016). Throughout this section, the definition of a terrorist act is taken from the Global Terrorism Database (2019, p. 10):

> the threatened or actual use of illegal force and violence by a non-state actor to attain a political, economic, religious, or social goal through fear, coercion, or intimidation.

However, the difference between the fear created by terrorism and the deaths caused by terrorism is no accident. The purpose of terrorism is to spread fear, panic and anxiety. It is not just an enemy or an event (Pinker, 2012). Terrorists use these emotions to seek publicity and attention for political, ideological or religious causes.

Understanding why people engage in terrorism is challenging. Our typical methods of study are limited because terrorists do not volunteer for experiments nor are they easy to study in a laboratory. Asking someone why they join a group that is extremely different provides only the expected ideological answers. Part of the difficulty is that there can be many types of extremism. For example, mountain climbers qualify as extreme because they take risks that few people are willing to undertake. Some addictions like gambling and substance abuse are extreme. Even behaviours like mass murder and altruistic self-sacrifice are extreme. For these reasons, perspective is important, because one group's terrorist is another group's freedom fighter.

What is radicalisation?

People voluntarily join terrorist groups based on a range of motivations, including: the search for group-based identity; the ideological appeal of the group; perceived exclusion or cultural threat; the potential for economic gain or long-term economic stability; the prospect of fame, glory, or respect; and personal connections, including family and friendship networks (Darden, 2019).

Radicalisation is a process and not a state of being. Thinking of radicalisation as a process increases our understanding of the radicalisation journey. The terms 'radicalisation', 'radicalise' and 'radical' are often used in a way that suggests their meaning is obvious. This leads to using the terms in a circular logic. For example, a 'radical' is someone who has radical ideas or who has become 'radicalised'. While there is no single definition of radicalisation, one attempt by the UK government is: 'the process by which people come to support terrorism and violent extremism and, in some cases, then to join terrorist groups' (HM Government, 2009, p. 82). At the individual level, Smith (2018, p. i) describes the radicalisation process as 'embracing a terrorist belief system that identifies others or groups as enemies and justifies engaging in violence against them'. These definitions are concerned that an emerging adult's radicalisation involves only choosing violent jihad or acts of violence. However, people may develop radical views without supporting violence, and many people's views might be considered extreme by others (Bartlett and Miller, 2012). Furthermore, research has failed to find psychopathology, personality features or economic deprivation profiles of people who become radicalised and/or engaged in terrorism (Horgan, 2003; McGilloway, Ghosh and Bhui, 2015).

While individuals may not share common characteristics, many radical groups do (Bergen, van Feddes, Pels and Doosje, 2015). Radical groups often share a common belief that society has serious problems and they are dissatisfied with the way the current institution is dealing with their problems (Doosje, van den Bos and Loseman, 2013). They believe that the institutions do not manage or care about their grievances. This perspective often leads to distrust and a lack of belief in the legitimacy of authorities. Another characteristic of radical groups is that they consider their own group's norms superior to other groups (Doosje et al., 2012). This creates an ideology that embraces violence as a solution (Reicher and Haslam, 2016).

A model of radicalisation

An effective approach is to ask how a person decided to engage in terroristic activity. Viewing terrorism in terms of the psychological principles of group dynamics and cognitive processes – such as our subconscious fear of death and our desire for meaning and personal significance – may help to explain some aspects of terrorist actions and our reactions to them. Figure 12.1 presents a process model of radicalisation inspired by the 'staircase model of terrorism' (Moghaddam, 2005). This model provides three phases of terrorism induction:

- Phase 1: Characterised by a sensitivity to a radical ideology.

- Phase 2: Social cohesion is enhanced as the individual joins a radical group.

- Phase 3: The individual is ready to act on behalf of the group's ideology.

At each phase are three increasing levels of influence (individual, group and society). The advantage of this model is its focus on the role of social cohesion and polarisation in the radicalisation process.

Figure 12.1: The process of radicalisation

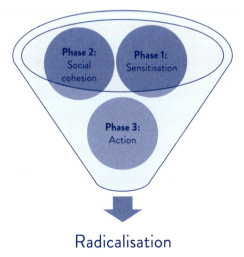

Source: Inspired by Moghaddam (2005) and Doosje et al. (2016).

Phase 1: Sensitisation to radical ideology

The sensitisation phase explores the psychological motivations within the individual that may influence their radicalisation process. In the first study of its kind, Horgan (2003) interviewed 60 former terrorists to identify their motivations. His evocative findings revealed how leaders influence people's decision to adopt roles, such as the role of suicide bomber. The former terrorists revealed that individuals sensitive to terrorist recruitment and radicalisation tend to feel angry and disenfranchised. They feel the need to act rather than just talk about the problem and believe that engaging in violence is not always immoral. Finally, they believe that joining a movement offers social and psychological rewards such as adventure, camaraderie and an increased sense of identity. Many of these motivations are also associated with young people who are the primary recruits of many terror organisations.

Due to biological aspects and psychosocial factors during the process of maturation, juveniles and adolescents are especially vulnerable to the radicalisation efforts of so-called 'jihadist ideologues'. In some cases, young people join terrorist groups because they are deceived, trafficked, kidnapped or forcibly recruited (Heinke and Persson, 2016). Others join terrorist groups voluntarily because of: the appeal of a group-based identity; perceptions of exclusion, grievances, or cultural threats; the promise of economic stability; the prospect of fame, glory, or respect; and personal connections, including family and friendship networks (Magen, 2018).

Quest for significance theory – *Extreme behaviour for an ideological cause is more likely under conditions that induce a search for meaning and social recognition.*

During this first phase, a crucial motivation is the 'quest for significance', sometimes brought about by feelings of unimportance caused by a loss of status, humiliation, or unfair treatment (Milla, Putra and Umam, 2019). The **quest for significance theory** assumes that radicalisation into violent extremism requires three basic ingredients: the need, the narrative and the network (Kruglanski et al., 2018). Needs are about the desires to gain respect, competence, esteem and meaning in life. The narrative is the story that justifies the use of violence; specifically, when oppressed individuals are drawn to a collective cause as a way to cure their feelings of insignificance. For example, a person could fail at an important life goal or experience deep humiliation, and later find extremism for a socially valued cause attractive as it lifts them from their feeling of inferiority (Pedahzur, 2005). The last requirement is a network of people who support that narrative, leading individuals to believe that the violence-justifying narrative is morally acceptable.

Phase 2: Social cohesion

The social cohesion phase relies on the processes of social dynamics and desire for group cohesion. The decision to join violent extremist groups has been described as a 'transformative trigger' (Wilner and Dubouloz, 2010), or 'turning point'. In such situations, the person may be particularly prone to identity transformation. This transformation is explained by **social identity theory** (Tajfel and Turner, 1979; Hogg, 2016), which says that our identity is defined by the groups to which we belong, such as our identity as a 'student', 'athlete' or 'Liverpool supporter'. Our sense of who we are and how we relate to others and our worldviews are constructed by our membership of groups. Simply stated, people who commit terrorist acts associate with others who commit terrorist acts (Smith, 2008). For example, 70 per cent of the people who join al-Qaeda do so with friends, and about 20 per cent do so with relatives (Sageman, 2008). Group cohesion gives recruits a sense of belonging, respect and heroism by fighting for an honourable cause (Rashed, Piorkowski and McCulloh, 2019).

Social identity theory – *That part of an individual's self-concept which derives from knowledge of the person's membership in a social group.*

A state of uncertainty may make an individual open to identification with a group whose radical views, including demonisation of another group, provide a new sense of certainty, possibly including a justification for violent action against the other group. The **uncertainty–identity theory** provides an explanation for the attractiveness of joining groups. While some degree of uncertainty can be rewarding and exciting (a challenging opportunity to grow), too much is uncomfortable. This is particularly true when we are uncertain about our identity, what we should think, how we should behave, and how we should interact with others in a given context. An effective way to resolve uncertainty is identifying with a group. Group membership offers a social identity that describes and prescribes perceptions, attitudes and behaviours that define the group. It also allows you to predict how others will think of and interact with you. In this way, group membership resolves self-uncertainty and offers a solution for identity by providing consensual support for our perceptions, feelings, attitudes and behaviours (Choi and Hogg, 2020; Hogg and Mahajan, 2018).

Violent extremist groups are better suited to reduce uncertainty than other groups. These groups have a strong sense of **entitativity** – the perception of a group as a single entity, distinct from its individual members. Violent extremists groups meet this criterion because they provide a shared fate, common goals and shared attributes (Choi, Jackson and Gelfand, 2018; Hamilton and Sherman, 1996). Their distinctiveness is sometimes expressed as a 'sacred canopy' of religious beliefs providing a sense of certainty about the world, the self and the future, such as life after death and rewards in heaven (Griffin, 2012). Such groups provide clear social identity information and when experiencing uncertainty, people identify more strongly with high entitativity groups (Hogg et al., 2007).

Paradoxically, an unconscious fear of death may supply the motivation for terrorism. Underlying the continuing existence of our species is our fear of death. Because death is inevitable, contemplating our own mortality creates anxiety about our existence – *existential anxiety*. According to **terror management theory**, existential anxiety is resolved by seeking out others to confirm our worldview, by group membership (Arrowood, and Cox, 2020; Greenberg, Solomon and Pyszczynski, 1997; van Kessel, den Heyer and Schimel, 2020). This theory states that death anxiety drives people to adopt worldviews that protect their sense of self-esteem, allowing them to believe that they play an important role in a meaningful world (Ramya and Roshanara, 2020). Reminding people of their mortality – the ultimate frustration of the need for control and meaning – led to aggressive behaviour against the worldview of threatening others (McGregor et al., 1998) and increased support for suicide bombing (Pyszczynski, Motyl and Abdollahi, 2009).

To examine if terror management theory could reduce conflict between the Middle East and the West, researchers compared subjects in the USA, Iran and Israel. In all three countries, the participants were subtly reminded of their mortality and primed to adhere to their group identity (Abdollahi, Henthorn and Pyszczynski, 2010). All participants were more likely to support the bombing of the outgroup: Iranians were more likely to support suicide bombing against Westerners, Americans were more likely to advocate military force to battle Islamic extremists, while Israelis were more likely to condone violence against Palestinians.

Phase 3: Action

During the action phase, the individual is ready to perform on behalf of the group's ideology, such as planning an attack. This is when the violent act is performed. It is important to stress the vast gulf between terrorist ideology and terrorist action. As Moskalenko and McCauley (2011, p. 5) have observed: 'Polls in Muslim countries indicate that *millions*

Uncertainty–identity theory – *People identify with social groups to decrease feelings of self-related uncertainty.*

Entitativity – *The perception of a group as a single entity, distinct from its individual members.*

Terror management theory – *A type of defensive human thinking and behaviour that stems from an awareness and fear of death.*

PART IV

sympathise with jihadist goals or justify terrorist attacks. But Muslim terrorists number only in the *thousands*. The challenge is to explain how only one in a thousand with radical beliefs is involved in radical action.'

To be as effective as possible, any inhibition about killing innocent people must be overcome. This is accomplished by inflating the differences between the ingroup and the outgroup, the perceived enemy. The call to action requires a change in the beliefs of those outside the group. According to **moral disengagement theory** (Bandura, 1999), individuals engage in hatred towards outgroups if they can justify their conduct as having a moral or ideological purpose. Analysis of suicide terrorists' farewell videos and interviewing mothers of deceased suicide bombers found that the most frequently stated reasons for suicide terrorism were ideological (Kruglanski et al., 2009). When moral disengagement happens, outgroups become dehumanised, which further limits communication between ingroups and outgroups. The lack of further contact enhances the process and fuels the motivation for violence and commitment to violent organisations.

> **Moral disengagement theory** – *The process of convincing the self that ethical standards do not apply to oneself in a particular context.*

Current approaches and future directions

Despite heavy investment in counterterrorism, Western governments have struggled to offer practical solutions and continue to struggle to measure the impact of countering violent extremism. The current opinion is that either religious authorities should debate extremists into submission using theological arguments, or psychologists should determine and treat the underlying mental health issues of the radicalisation process to break the bond between the individual and their extremist ideology or group. Understanding radicalisation as an issue that relates to identity and agency does not exclude religion as a valid part of an explanation of radicalisation (Stephens and Sieckelinck, 2019). Both approaches are ineffective for tackling a psychological process (radicalisation). Another assumption is that people become radicalised by exposure to certain kinds of thoughts and ideas, which increases their risk for involvement in terrorism. Interviews with former terrorists show that that logic does not hold in most cases, as intuitive as it might seem. This concept of radicalisation is not effective. Psychologists need to counter violent extremism by addressing the specific developmental situation of young people, and combine education, social integration and individual appreciation with counter ideology programmes to identify individuals who have disengaged from terrorism.

IN SUMMARY

The causes and methods to counter violent extremism are still developing. Profiling pathological and personality characteristics has failed and the success of deradicalisation programmes is still unknown. Future approaches need to address radicalisation by focusing on the many resilient individuals who disengage from terrorism and question the effectiveness of earlier policies (not negotiating with terrorists) (Mertes, Mazei and Hüffmeier, 2020).

CRITICAL THINKING AND APPLICATION QUESTIONS

1   What is the purpose of terrorism and why is its impact mainly psychological?

2   Examine any of the theories presented under the three phases of the process of radicalisation and find a current research article that investigates their impact on the study of terrorism.

3   Why have earlier counterterrorism tactics failed to reduce incidents of terrorism?

CHAPTER REVIEW

Violence is an intentional act to commit harm that has purpose and a pattern. Surprisingly, most forms of violence are decreasing. Yet some forms of violence, like intimate partner violence, are resistant to change and need more support for its victims. Meanwhile, mass murder and terrorism incidents have low prevalence, making actuarial approaches ineffective at identifying predictive patterns in the data. Future approaches should adopt a multifaceted approach borrowing from social dynamics, developmental psychology and education. If hate, prejudice and violence are learned, then perhaps someday they can be unlearned.

NAMES TO KNOW

Stephen Pinker

Conducts research on language and cognition, and writes for publications such as *The New York Times*, *Time* and *The Atlantic*.

- Pinker, S. (2011) *The Better Angels of our Nature*. Viking.
- Pinker, S. (2018) *Enlightenment Now: The Case for Reason, Science, Humanism, and Progress*. Viking.

Rachel Jewkes

Has led research in South Africa and globally on the intersection of gender inequity and gender-based violence and health, and is the author of over 300 peer-reviewed journal articles, reports, training manuals and book chapters.

- Jewkes, R., Fulu, E., Naved, R. T., Chirwa, E., Dunkle, K. et al. (2017) Women's and men's report of past-year prevalence of intimate partner violence and rape and women's risk factors for intimate partner violence: A multicountry cross-sectional study in Asia and the Pacific. *PLoS Medicine*, 14(9), e1002381.
- Jewkes, R. (2002) Intimate partner violence: Causes and prevention. *The Lancet*, 359(9315), 1423–9.

Thomas A. Pyszczynski

His research is focused primarily on terror management theory, which is concerned with the role of self-esteem and cultural belief systems in providing protection against core human fears, especially the fear of death.

- Pyszczynski, T., Kesebir, P. and Lockett, M. (2019) A terror management theory perspective on human motivation. In R. M. Ryan (ed.) *The Oxford Handbook of Human Motivation* (2nd edn). Oxford University Press.
- Pyszczynski, T., Solomon, S. and Greenberg, J. (2003) *In the Wake of 9/11: The Psychology of Terror*. APA.

PART IV

13 FORENSIC VICTIMOLOGY

Chapter Introduction

Every crime has three parts: the crime, the offender and the victim. Our exploration begins by studying the third part, the victim of crime. Studying the crime's victims provides information to help reduce crime. Our focus on the victim reveals the strange psychological paradox of blaming victims for the crimes they have suffered. As we investigate victims of crimes related to social media, we see that many more people are victimised not in a physical space, but a virtual one. Our investigation of cyberstalking raises the evocative question of whether the same rules apply in a virtual space as a physical one. Finally, victims of crime are often told to seek 'closure' to end their grief. But does this concept really exist or is it a myth? We will investigate this idea in the context of capital punishment, which may be the ultimate form of closure.

Learning Outcomes

Forensic victimology
- Explain why learning about the victims of crime can help reduce crime.

The psychology behind victim blaming
- Compare and contrast effective and ineffective strategies for coping with violent crime.

The effects of social media on victimisation
- Compare and contrast the effects of the virtual world of social media with the real world of social dynamics.

Searching for psychological closure
- Explain why achieving closure is a myth.

FORENSIC VICTIMOLOGY

FICTION: Victims and offenders have unpredictable motivations that prevent predictions of risk.	*Versus*	**FACT:** Like offenders, victims have similar motivations that offer predictions of risk.

What is forensic victimology?

Research on violent crime focuses on the offender or the offensive behaviour, but the third element of violent crime, the victim, is also important. Originally, the Latin term *victima* was used to describe individuals or animals whose lives were destined to be sacrificed to please a god (Burgess, 2017). Historically, the word did not imply pain or suffering. However, by the nineteenth century, the word 'victim' was associated with the notion of harm or loss in general (Spalek, 2017). Throughout this chapter, the term 'victim' will be used to describe anyone who suffers harm or loss, either at their own hands or at the hands of others (Karmen, 2004).

General victimology examines victims and victimisation, as well as the relationship between victims and offenders, and includes those who have been harmed by crime, accidents, natural disasters, wars and other life-threatening events. The goals of general victimology often relate to the restoration of a victim's losses – financial, material and emotional – and advocate for empowering victims, returning the victims to the state they were in prior to suffering harm or loss, and making them feel secure and satisfied that justice has been served (Nugent, Williams and Umbreit, 2004).

Forensic victimology has a different focus – it examines victims of crime to answer investigative and legal questions. Forensic victimology is an applied discipline examining victim evidence in a scientific manner. The assessments from this perspective search for patterns, themes and associations that reveal an overall risk assessment for the victim (Petherick, 2019). Although forensic victimology does not seek to assist with victim advocacy or promote victim sympathy, the collected evidence and interpretations may be used by others for these purposes. The roles of the forensic victimologist include:

- supporting or refuting claims of victimisation
- developing offender modus operandi and motives
- establishing investigative suspect pools
- assisting with the investigative linkage of unsolved cases (Turvey and Petherick, 2009).

> **General victimology** – The study of all victims, not just victims of crime.

> **Forensic victimology** – The examination of victims of crime to solve investigative and legal questions.

A brief history of victimology

Three distinct time periods define the history of the victim's role in the criminal justice system: the golden age, the dark age and the re-emergence of the victim (Moriarty and Jerin, 1998).

The golden age

Formal criminal justice systems are new. In the past, it was the responsibility of the victim and the victim's relatives to deal with the offenders (Schafer, 1977). The term 'golden age' implies that this was a time when victims held influence over offenders. They did, but at a cost. Without written laws and established governments, there existed only tribal laws. In tribal laws, the victims determined the punishments for unlawful actions that others committed against them or their property. Without judges, trials and jails, it was up to the victims or their survivors to decide what actions to take against the offender (Doerner and Lab, 2005). Personal retribution was the primary way to resolve criminal matters, and victims actively sought revenge or demanded compensation for their losses directly from those who wronged them (Karmen, 2007). The victim could seek compensation without any pre-established burden of proof. This created situations where the only evidence was the victim's word against the accused. In these circumstances, determining fault and consequences depended on the strength of the victim's character and their level of influence (Doerner and Lab, 2005).

As tribes grew, individual victim-oriented solutions became difficult to use because sometimes entire families and tribes suffered from crime. For example, if the offender was not available for punishment, their relatives might have to assume the responsibility for the harms caused to the victim(s). Tragically, like ripples in a pond, a single crime had the potential to affect many people and successive generations. When successive generations pay for the crimes, insults or injuries of previous victims, the resulting vendettas can lead to 'blood feuds' between families or tribes for harms that may not have happened (Karmen, 2012).

While victim-oriented justice promotes strong loyalty between family, tribe and culture, it does not resolve crimes. Holding an individual responsible for another's crime extended the effects of the original crime to innocent people. This creates cycles of victimisation, as groups fought each other out of perceived retribution and vengeance. Rather than helping the victim, victim-driven justice makes the situation worse; as is the case of 'blood marriages', a victim-oriented remedy for the problems of crime, debt and related blood feuds. Blood marriages mix the blood from both sides to end the need for retaliation (Tang, 2007).

Blood feuds and blood marriage in South Sudan

In the state of Eastern Equatoria in South Sudan, the solution to a blood feud is often a blood marriage. Without prisons, this tradition for resolving disputes and solving conflicts is still practised today. This was the case for eight-year-old Atia Odongi, whose brother killed a man during a cattle dispute. As compensation, Atia was given to the man's family. Atia was married to a son in her new family when she turned nine, and then given to a younger brother when that man died. Often, the new family exploits the girls given in blood marriage. Atia's life became one of constant abuse and servitude. The new family's desire to replace their murdered family member often results in repeated sexual abuse (Rhodes, 2017).

The dark age

The dark age of victimology emerged from formal laws and state governments. As economies grew and became more stable, there was greater urbanisation and industrialisation. The former tribal systems of victim-oriented laws faded as populations grew (Karmen, 2007).

As these new forms of offender-oriented (as opposed to victim-oriented) systems grew, the offences were viewed as being perpetrated against the laws of the state or king and not just the victim. The focus shifted from victim rights and restoration to offender rights and punishments. As these formal systems of laws and regulations spread, victim involvement declined until they served as only witnesses for the police and prosecution in the courts (Doerner and Lab, 2005). As a result, the modern criminal justice system

PART IV

evolved to benefit society, not just individual victims. In fact, the goal of the criminal justice system was separating offenders from society through deterrence and harsh punishments to ultimately reduce victimisation (Turvey, 2013).

Re-emergence of the victim

In the 1950s and 1960s, there was an awareness that the people affected by crime were rarely involved in the criminal justice process (Karmen, 2007). Gradually, an understanding took hold that 'the victims were forgotten figures in the criminal justice process whose needs and wants had been systematically overlooked but merited attention' (Karmen, 2007, p. 27). Importantly, there was a growing awareness that victims were being neglected as a source of information about crime and criminals. While victims' rights were gaining attention, victimology, in its early years, did not try to address the needs of victims and alleviate their suffering. Instead, victimology tried to understand the victim's role in the criminal act, their relationship with the offender and culpability (Doerner and Lab, 2005).

Victim precipitation

Victim precipitation (*not victim blaming*) is a controversial theory claiming that victims sometimes initiate the actions that lead to their harm or loss. According to this theory, some victims (whether they realise it or not) invite abuse through their personalities, attitudes or actions. Specifically, the characteristics or conduct of the victim make them, to a certain degree, culpable for the misdeeds of others (Suonpää and Savolainen, 2019). Make no mistake, victims cannot and should not be blamed for their aggressors' actions, and aggressors should be held accountable for their crimes. Victim precipitation is important to study because research shows that it happens with some frequency, and therefore cannot be ignored simply because it is unpleasant (Petherick, 2017). Whether victims influence the context that increases chances of victimisation is an empirical question, and two reasons drive this position:

> **Victim precipitation –** *A controversial theory claiming that victims sometimes initiate the actions that lead to their harm or loss.*

1   The lack of scientific, data-driven evidence to support the exclusion of the victim precipitation model.

2   The potentially harmful premise of its replacement, the perpetrator predation model (Cortina, 2017).

Studying victim precipitation is useful because a better understanding of the role victims play in crime could help provide more effective support for them and reduce victimisation and revictimisation. Although there are cases where the crime would have occurred regardless of the victim's actions, there are also cases where the opposite is true. This perspective helps us understand that some victims can be offenders and some offenders can also be victims (Muftić and Hunt, 2013). Therefore, studying victim precipitation allows us to understand how the victim and offender are connected. This includes efforts to understand how the physical and emotional experiences of each party are perceived. Finally, while not excusing the offender, a deeper analysis of victim precipitation provides a full accounting of the offender's responsibility in the commission of the crime, thus giving insights into the offender's motivations and intentions (North and Smith, 2018).

Predicting crime risk: the seven-factor model

Researchers have begun to recognise the value of improving our knowledge of victims and their unique role in the criminal process. Several models have been proposed to help explain the characteristics of both offenders and victims, and the way in which these characteristics influence the risk of offending and/or becoming a victim of a criminal act. The seven-factor typology of victim characteristics is the latest iteration of these typological models and represents an empirically founded culmination of several previous victim typologies (Petherick and Ferguson, 2012; Brotto, Sinnamon and Petherick, 2017).

An empirical evaluation of victim typologies presented by Brotto, Sinnamon and Petherick (2017) reveals evidence for the seven-factor typology of victim characteristics (Table 13.1). The seven-factor approach to study victim characteristics has been shown to have a strong ability to predict the type of crime that specific victim characteristics are likely to experience. This is the first typology to show predictive utility for victimisation risk. The seven victim types are based on 160 male and female victims of personal violence, that is, intimate partner violence, sexual assault, physical assault and stalking (Brotto, Sinnamon and Petherick, 2017).

Table 13.1: The seven-factor model of victim motivational characteristics

Victim orientation	Victim description	Risk of victimisation
1. Reassurance-oriented victims	Low self-esteem, poor social skills and antisocial behaviours. High in fear of rejection, abandonment, feelings of failure, and need for reassurance	Related to a belief that abuse is deserved, they have or will be subjected to repeated victimisation. For these victims, the psychological cost of the abuse is less important than the emotional cost of being alone
2. Assertive-oriented victims	Driven by low self-esteem and a dominating personality, they make themselves feel better by making others feel worse	Using dominance, control and humiliation may result in those receiving this treatment responding aggressively
3. Anger-retaliatory oriented victims	Possessing a great deal of rage towards others, from feelings of inadequacy, failure and blaming others for their problems	Their overt aggression may bring out aggression in others
4. Pervasively oriented victims	A generalised state of anger that is pervasive and targets anyone	Their pervasive anger creates isolation and lack of support
5. Excitation-oriented victims	High in masochistic and sadistic traits. Likely to engage in high-risk, antisocial and self-harming behaviours	Exposure to harm or loss in sadomasochistic activity or self-harm (cutting or scarification)
6. Materially oriented victims	Engages in behaviours that provide material or personal gain through the acquisition of money or personal goods	A lack of financial resources leads them to stay with an abusive but financially controlling partner
7. Preservation-oriented victims	Engages in retaliatory behaviours against an oppressor. Alternatively, they may display submissive behaviours and avoid risky behaviours such as separation	The retaliatory and preservation behaviours can create events where they cannot complete their retaliation and become the victim rather than the aggressor

Source: Brotto, G. L., Sinnamon, G. and Petherick, W. (2017) Victimology and predicting victims of personal violence. In W. Petherick and G. Sinnamon (eds) *The Psychology of Criminal and Antisocial Behavior: Victim and Offender Perspectives* (pp. 79–144). Elsevier. Adapted with permission.

Just as with offender motivation typologies, there is no sharp division between victim motivations. They are not mutually exclusive, and any given person may show multiple behaviours in a single instance, or multiple motivations over multiple instances. The following motivations are not intended to blame the victim or portray the victim in a negative light, they are intended only to show situations involving increased harm or loss.

Reassurance-oriented victim type and risk of being stalked

The reassurance-oriented victim type is at a higher risk of being stalked. It is likely that the stalker will be a partner or ex-partner whose motivation is the continuation of the relationship. This kind of stalking behaviour represents 75–80 per cent of stalking behaviour (Løkkegaard, Hansen, Wolf and Elklit, 2019). While surveillance-oriented behaviours were most frequently reported by both males and females (Chan and Sheridan, 2019), the primary motive is to maintain control over a weaker victim. In this situation, the victim is afraid of ending the relationship and afraid of retaliation. Similar to victims of intimate partner violence, stalking victims are likely to be influenced by low self-esteem, denial of the seriousness of the offence, inability to trust others, and an unhealthy dependency on the stalker (Johnson and Thompson, 2016; McEwan, Daffern, MacKenzie and Ogloff, 2017).

Anger-retaliatory, excitation and preservation-oriented victim types

Individuals with the characteristics of anger or excitation, or self-preservation-oriented types are at a significantly higher risk of becoming a victim of multiple crimes of intimate partner violence. Research supports the relationship between increased victimisation risk and personal characteristics associated with higher engagement with violent behaviour, lower self-control, anger, aggression, masochism, fear and desperation (Brotto, Sinnamon and Petherick, 2017). Additionally, the 'anger' and 'excitation' types share a characteristic engagement with antisocial and high-risk behaviour, which also increases victimisation risk (Petherick and Sinnamon, 2016).

Preservation-oriented victim risks for intimate partner violence

The preservation-oriented victim type has the highest risk of becoming a victim of intimate partner violence (Brotto, Sinnamon and Petherick, 2017). In this situation, one of the most prominent characteristics is financial abuse. In fact, financial abuse and despair are common reasons for victims to stay in an abusive relationship (Postmus et al., 2020). Economic abuse is a form of control when the person is denied access to finances and has no financial independence (Morgan and Chadwick, 2009). This form of abuse primarily affects women and often leads to the victim being 'trapped' in a violent relationship because of financial despair (Kutin, Russell and Reid, 2017).

Another characteristic of the preservation orientation is using self-protective behaviours like avoiding separation to reduce the chances of being harmed. Separation is a risk factor for intimate partner violence (Spencer and Stith, 2020; Logan and Walker, 2004). For example, in addition to experiencing lethal or non-lethal forms of physical violence and psychological abuse, many women who try to leave, or who have left their partners, are sexually assaulted (DeKeseredy, Rogness and Schwartz, 2004). Leaving a violent partner increases the risk of more severe or even fatal outcomes (Cleak, Schofield, Axelsen and Bickerdike, 2018). Homicide rates are higher for women who have separated from their partners than for women in ongoing relationships (Ellis, 2017); however, this heightened risk of homicide following a separation is not found for men (Johnson and Hotton, 2003). Additionally, researchers found that 85 per cent of wives and 77 per cent of husbands reported abuse, including emotional abuse and coercive control, during separation (Beck, Walsh, Mechanic and Taylor, 2010). However, more research is still needed, because it may be that violence follows separation, or the decision to separate is due to violence (Cardinali et al., 2018).

Staying with the abusive partner is a form of self-preservation and the cost of being victimised is less than the retaliation received when leaving, in terms of physical abuse or financial hardship. Yet, Eriksson and Ulmestig (2017) describe how intertwined women's experiences of financial abuse are with other forms of abuse; from the immediate monetary impact causing poverty and affecting their ability to have a reasonable standard of living to causing health problems and damaging their self-esteem and ability to work and engage in social life.

IN SUMMARY

Crimes involve both offenders *and* victims. Contemporary approaches recognise the value in improving our knowledge of victims and their unique role in the criminal process. The seven-factor model offers a predictive capability to identify victims of crime before they occur. It is essential to remember the risk of moving from victim characteristics to the more hostile position of victim blame. Used compassionately, and being aware of this risk, this approach is a powerful tool to identify victim risk and inform programmes and policies to educate and protect those most at risk.

 CRITICAL THINKING AND APPLICATION QUESTIONS

1   Describe how forensic victimology differs from other types of victimology.

2   Describe four ways that forensic victimologists serve investigations and court proceedings.

3   How do the factors of the seven-factor model of victim characteristics relate to crimes of interpersonal violence?

THE PSYCHOLOGY BEHIND VICTIM BLAMING

| **FICTION:** Victims are never blamed for the crimes they suffer. | *Versus* | **FACT:** Victims are often blamed for the crimes they suffer. |

CASE STUDY

Death by texting

Conrad Roy was only 18 years old when he died by suicide on 13 July 2014. Conrad had previously tried to kill himself in October 2012 after his parents divorced. But things seemed to be improving as Conrad met his future girlfriend Michelle Carter in Florida that same year. After their initial encounter, their relationship became mainly digital, sharing intimate thoughts via text messages and emails. They bonded over their shared experiences of clinical depression and previous suicide attempts. After learning that he was planning to kill himself, Michelle repeatedly tried discouraging him, even urging him to get professional help.

Michelle Carter during trial for involuntary manslaughter for encouraging Conrad Roy to kill himself in July 2014

Source: Boston Globe/Getty Images

Then, in June 2014, their relationship changed after Conrad texted Michelle suggesting they act like Romeo and Juliet, checking that she understood they had each killed themselves. After this, Michelle started thinking that it might be a 'good thing to help him die'. In their thousands of text messages, Conrad confided that he wanted to end it all. In some of the texts, Michelle offered specific advice, such as: 'Why don't you just drink bleach?' 'Hang yourself' and 'Jump over a building, stab yourself, idk. There's a lot of ways.' She also wrote to him: 'You just need to do it, Conrad … No more pushing it off. No more waiting' (Spargo, 2019).

Conrad prepared to end his life by carbon monoxide poisoning in his truck (Li, 2019). He exchanged text messages with Michelle all day leading up to his death. They talked on the phone while he was sitting in his truck and slowly dying from the increasing level of toxic gas. But, as Conrad started to feel the effects of the gas, he became frightened and got out of his truck. Conrad heard Michelle's voice for the last time as she told him to 'get back in' the truck (Main, 2019).

The prosecution alleged that she harassed Conrad to his death to receive the attention that being the girlfriend of the boy who killed himself would bring. The defence said it was a question of her freedom of speech and that she was not responsible for Conrad's behaviour (Finn, 2020).

Michelle's digital relationship with Conrad raises the following questions: Did 17-year-old Michelle Carter's actions really play a pivotal role in Conrad Roy's death by suicide? Could she have stopped him? Could she have called for help? We will never know, because she did nothing.

Discussion Questions:

1   How much blame for Conrad Roy's death does Michelle Carter deserve? Is she the offender, the victim or something in between?

2   Do you think that the nature of their mainly digital relationship was partially to blame?

The case of Conrad Roy and Michelle Carter shows how the digital age has changed the dynamics of relationships. Their relationship is an example of **digital dating abuse**, which includes the physical, sexual or psychological/emotional violence that occurs between romantic partners using texting, social media and related online media (Hinduja and Patchin, 2020). But, in this tragic story, who the victim is and who is to blame shifts depending on our perspective. But the bigger question is: 'Why do we feel the need to blame a victim for their suffering?'

How do we assign blame?

Generally, issues of intentionality and preventability are important contributions to moral judgements of blame. The tendency to blame the victim may be programmed into the human mind at a basic level. Ask yourself if you have ever wondered whether the victims of a crime or accident had done something to set themselves up for their tragedy? At the heart of how we assign blame is the **Path Model of Blame**, which follows a series of information-processing steps that are necessary for assigning blame (Malle, Guglielmo and Monroe, 2014). Assigning blame begins with reviewing information about who or what caused the event; if it is determined that the person caused the event (as opposed to a natural event), then a decision about whether the act was caused intentionally is made. If it is determined that the act was intentional, then the person's reasons or justifications are reviewed, but if it is determined that it was unintentional, then information about whether the person could have prevented the event (capacity to prevent) and should have prevented it (obligation to prevent) is used. Sometimes, the victim is blamed because of misunderstood causality; for example, how problematic behaviours on the part of the victim, such as poor academic performance, alcohol, or drug abuse, are viewed. It is important to emphasise that these behaviours may be the direct *result* of a sexual assault, not the *cause* of it.

Intentionality amplifies blame judgements, as shown by Ames and Fiske (2015). Their research asked 80 participants to read a vignette about a company CEO who had either accidentally or intentionally made a poor investment that resulted in lower pay for his employees. Those who thought the CEO had intentionally made the mistake rated the harm done to his employees as 39 per cent greater than those who thought it was accidental.

Why do victims sometimes receive sympathy for their suffering and at other times scorn and blame? Surprisingly, victims are blamed by offenders, friends, family, professionals and even themselves (Peter-Hagene and Ullman, 2018). For example, in 2014, the dean of student affairs at Patrick Henry College in Virginia, USA responded to a student's sexual assault complaint as follows: 'You are in part responsible for what happened, because you put yourself in a compromising situation ... actions have consequences' (Feldman, 2014). This kind of treatment of victims can cause **secondary victimisation**, which results in added trauma beyond the original traumatic experience (Mendonça, Gouveia-Pereira and Miranda, 2016).

Explanations of victim blaming

Cognitive dissonance

Cognitive dissonance is the state of having conflicting thoughts, beliefs or attitudes, especially relating to behavioural decisions and attitude change (Festinger, 1957); in other words, it is the discomfort felt by a person who holds conflicting ideas, beliefs or values at the same time. Cognitive dissonance was first investigated by Leon Festinger, during a participant observation study of a cult which believed that the earth was going to be destroyed by a flood, and what happened to its members – particularly the really

Digital dating abuse – *The physical, sexual or psychological/ emotional violence that occurs between romantic partners using texting, social media and related online media.*

Path Model of Blame – *A series of information-processing steps that are necessary for the assignment of blame.*

Secondary victimisation – *Victim-blaming behaviours and insensitive attitudes that traumatise victims of violence.*

PART IV

committed ones who had given up their homes and jobs to work for the cult – when the flood did not happen. While fringe members were more inclined to recognise that they had made fools of themselves and 'put it down to experience', committed members were more likely to reinterpret the evidence to show that they were right all along (the earth was not destroyed because of the faithfulness of the cult members).

Offenders using controlling violence often blame their victim, with over 70 per cent of abused women reporting being blamed by their abuser for their own abuse (Anderson et al., 2003). Offenders do this to justify their behaviour and reduce the cognitive dissonance that comes from hurting another person (Goldner, 1999). For example, in one study, a husband gave a typical excuse for hitting his wife: 'She wasn't changing, she was still not shutting up when I told her to shut up' (Whiting, Oka and Fife, 2012, p. 8). Unfortunately, despite a growing number of victim support organisations and improved legislation to support and empower victims of crime (Ryan, 2019), victims of intimate partner violence still face a range of stereotypical and victim-blaming attitudes when disclosing their experiences.

The ideal victim theory

Empathy and support seems to be reserved only for innocent and vulnerable victims (Kogut, 2011), and public perceptions of innocence vary with different types of victims and victimisation (Dunn, 2010). Sometimes, victims are less likely to be believed or receive media attention (Jewkes, 2015) if they do not fit 'ideal victim' status (Greer, 2017). The example in this situation is one where the alleged offender is better known and presumably better loved than the alleged victim, who did not fit the 'ideal' categories of being weak, respectable, blameless or hurt by an evil entity. Rather than take the victim's claims at face value, many commenters dismiss or attack the victim, which is a common response to those reporting victimisation from a known offender (Edwards, Dardis and Gidycz, 2012).

The concept of the 'ideal victim' states that in order for a victim to be seen as innocent and worthy of social reactions that involve empathy and support, a victim has to be seen as:

- weak or vulnerable
- involved in a respectable activity at the time of victimisation
- blameless in the circumstances of their victimisation

while the offender is dominant to the victim, and can be described in negative terms and is unknown to them (Christie, 1986).

The ideal victim also has its opposite; the drunken athletic young man robbed in a seedy bar by those he was associating with. This example emphasises moral responsibility: he should not have gone to such a bar, he should not have got drunk, and he should not have associated with those types of people (Lindgren and Nikolic-Ristanovic, 2011).

The need for predictability

Hindsight bias – The tendency of people to overestimate their ability to have predicted an outcome that could not have been predicted.

Research on cognitive biases has demonstrated the existence of a **hindsight bias** – the tendency of people to overestimate their ability to have predicted an outcome that could not possibly have been predicted. We selectively recall information that confirms what we know to be true and we try to create a narrative that makes sense out of the information we have (van Boekel, Varma and Varma, 2017). When this narrative is easy to create, we interpret that to mean that the outcome must have been foreseeable. To examine hindsight bias's effect on victim blaming, researchers asked participants to read two different versions of a story. In one version, a character was raped at the end, and the other had a neutral ending. Those who read the version with the assault were more likely to blame the victim, because they selected evidence that could retroactively support this conclusion (Janoff-Bulman, Timko and Carli, 1985). This 'I knew-it-all-along' bias happens when people claim reasons to make events seem predictable, even if they were not.

The need for fairness and justice

The idea that people get what they deserve and deserve what they get is the belief behind the **just-world hypothesis**, a common cognitive bias in which individuals believe that the world operates in a fair and predictable manner (Lerner and Miller, 1978). Applying the just-world hypothesis gives people a feeling that the world is stable, orderly and controllable (Lerner, 1980; Donat, Wolgast and Dalbert, 2018). Unfortunately, just-world beliefs are a primary driving force behind victim-blaming attitudes. Blaming is related to the concept of 'victim derogation', which involves unwarranted judgements that those who have suffered must have deserved their plight, even if there is little or no evidence to that effect (Hafer, Bègue, Choma and Dempsey, 2005).

> **Just-world hypothesis**
> – A cognitive bias in which individuals believe that the world operates in a fair and just manner.

The just-world hypothesis suggests that people treat victims badly out of a desire to support their beliefs in justice. For example, when participants read scenarios involving rape, belief in a just world emerges as a powerful predicator of which individuals will place greater blame on the victim (their clothing or the time of day brought it upon them) and lesser blame placed on the offender (Strömwall, Alfredsson and Landström, 2013). On the societal level, individual endorsement of the just-world hypothesis has consistently predicted opposition to social equality, such as discrimination against the LGBTQ+ community (Hettinger and Vandello, 2014), the homeless (Baumgartner, Bauer and Bui, 2012), and blaming the elderly for their poor health and dire financial circumstances, resulting in lower rates of helping behaviour (MacLean and Chown, 1988).

Can we reduce victim blaming?

Blaming victims sacrifices another person's wellbeing for our own. This belief ignores the reality that the offender is responsible for acts of crime and violence, not the victim. Fortunately, victim blaming is not inevitable, and the solution is empathy. Evidence indicates that fostering empathy towards abuse survivors reduces the endorsement of harmful victim-blaming attitudes that these individuals may otherwise carry with them (Latshaw, 2015). This idea was supported in a study where college students completed a series of psychological tests measuring sexism, belief in a just world and their levels of empathy. The results showed that people with greater empathy tended to view survivors of rape through a more positive lens, while those with less empathy tended to view survivors more negatively (Sakalli-Uğurlu, Yalçın and Glick, 2007).

IN SUMMARY

Victim blaming is the attitude which suggests that the victim rather than the offender bears responsibility for the crime. Blaming victims marginalises the survivor, minimises the criminal act, and makes people less likely to come forward and report what has happened to them. Victim blaming occurs when it is assumed that an individual did something to provoke the violence by actions, words or dress. Many people would rather believe that someone caused their own misfortune because it makes the world seem a safer place, but victim blaming is a major reason that survivors of sexual and intimate partner violence do not report their assaults.

CRITICAL THINKING AND APPLICATION QUESTIONS

1   Are the cognitive explanations of victim blaming, such as cognitive dissonance, the ideal victim, hindsight bias and the just-world hypothesis, based on conscious or unconscious thinking? Support your response with examples.

2   Outline an effective programme for prospective juries to reduce victim blaming. For ideas, read the article by Clevenger, Navarro and Gregory (2017) (see References).

3   Based on the Path Model of Blame, will humans blame robots and other artificially intelligent machines for their actions?

THE EFFECTS OF SOCIAL MEDIA ON VICTIMISATION

FICTION: Cyberstalking has less psychological impact than crimes in the real world.	*Versus*	**FACT:** Cyberstalking is at the very least equal in psychological impact if not more so due to its speed, range and lasting effects.

CASE STUDY

Social media stalking

Ellie Flynn and her friends live in the UK and frequently post the highlights of their daily lives online. But what she did not know was that, for nearly a decade, all her pictures, posts and tweets were leading a double life. Since the information from their social media accounts were stolen, Flynn and her friends have been approached by strangers who insist they know them. In one unnerving confrontation, a stranger appeared at her university residence looking for the person he met online (Flynn, 2015). Flynn and her friends' pictures are used by people using the same first name but different last names – Ellie Flynn became Ellie Rose and her friend Chia became Chia Colarossi.

There are over 60 fake profiles on every social media format. One fake site has produced over 36,000 tweets impersonating Flynn and her friends. The impersonator is following her closely and reposts Flynn's pictures and tweets almost as quickly as she creates them. Worse still, people have been using the stolen photos to *catfish* people for the past decade. This happens when a stranger takes pictures from social media accounts and uses the same pictures under a different, fake name (Hartney, 2018).

Although this sinister world of stalker-like obsession appears harmless and amusing, these profiles are used to send victims to the person's actual location. Although most of these encounters end without incident, this might not always happen. Another important issue is the damage these duplicate online profiles do to the victim's reputation. In case you are wondering, Flynn and her friends asked Facebook and Twitter to remove the fraudulent accounts, and they have succeeded in some cases, but more fake accounts appear. They have even messaged the fake profilers to try to get whoever is behind this to stop and yet the imitation game continues (Moore, 2015).

Discussion Questions:

1   What would motivate someone to obsessively re-create another person's life?

2   Is this type of behaviour illegal in your jurisdiction?

3   What are the costs associated with using another person's online identity?

Ellie Flynn's experience is a new form of cyberstalking, but is cyberstalking any different than offline stalking? Here we examine the criminological risks arising from the use of technology, and the psychological motivations and consequences underlying these behaviours. The real and digital worlds share the same psychosocial dynamics that can turn friends, acquaintances and lovers into adversaries, aggressors and victims. For a growing number of people, life is experienced through an online platform and access to the internet is now seen as a human right by many countries (Howell and West, 2016). As people spend more time using social media, they become more comfortable disclosing personal information about themselves, which increases the risk of becoming a victim of cyberstalking (Welsh and Lavoie, 2012).

Cyberstalking

Cyberstalking describes a collection of behaviours in which an individual uses digital technology to harass individuals, groups of individuals or organisations. This includes persistent unwanted contact of an offensive/threatening nature, monitoring data, damaging data or equipment, damaging a reputation and encouraging others to join in (Bocij, 2018). Types of cyberstalking include:

- mail bombing – sending a large number of messages to the victim's email address or mobile phone

- spamming

- identity theft

- gaining access to the victim's computer, infecting the victim's computer with a virus (McFarlane and Bocij, 2003)

- posting sexualised content along with the victim's name and contact details on the internet (Wolak, Finkelhor, Walsh and Treitman, 2017)

- using GPS to track the victim (Sargent, Krauss, Jouriles and McDonald, 2016; Groban, 2016)

- using social media platforms to embarrass, humiliate and isolate victims (Woodlock, 2017)

- and, recently, non-consensual pornography – revenge porn (Magaldi, Sales and Paul, 2020).

> **Cyberstalking** – A constellation of behaviours in which one individual uses digital technology to harass individuals, groups of individuals or organisations.

Cyberstalking harms its victims, in both their personal and professional lives. Victims have been known to experience severe depression, a variety of employment issues, including humiliation in the workplace and difficulty securing and succeeding at employment, and even suicide (Mafa, Kang'ethe and Chikadzi, 2020).

Social networking and online gaming sites are used as conduits for stalking and online harassment (Fox and Tang, 2017; Hilvert-Bruce and Neill, 2020; Chadha, Steiner, Vitak and Ashktorab, 2020), and even visiting social networking sites leads to increased chances of becoming a victim of cyberstalking (Kraft and Wang, 2010). Technology both enables and invites antisocial behaviour from individuals who might never take part in these activities. One explanation is that the psychological, social and technological characteristics of the internet combine to lower inhibitions and establish new norms of behaviour (Garg and Pahuja, 2020). For example, the anonymity offered by the internet enables people to participate in activities such as encouraging violence against others with little fear of retaliation (cyberaggression). Four categories of cyberstalking have been identified, as shown in Table 13.2 (McFarlane and Bocij, 2003).

Table 13.2: Four motivation categories of cyberstalking offenders

Vindictive cyberstalkers	Characterised by relentless harassment of their victim without a specific reason. Frequently suffering from a psychological disorder
Composed cyberstalkers	Motivated to cause victim distress, goal is to cause constant annoyance and irritation to the targeted victim. No desire to establish a relationship with the victim
Intimate cyberstalkers	Characterised by the desire to attract the attention or affection of their victim. Usually have detailed knowledge of the person being targeted
Collective cyberstalkers	A group of individuals harassing their victims through the use of communication technology

Source: Inspired by McFarlane, L. and Bocij, P. (2003) An exploration of predatory behaviour in cyberspace: Towards a typology of cyberstalkers. *First Monday*, 8(9).

Is cyberstalking different than offline stalking?

Is stalking in the digital realm worse than in the real world? The initial effects may be stronger online than offline. For example, in the virtual world, flirting causes stronger physical and sexual reactions than when experienced in a face-to-face interaction (Alapack, Blichfeldt and Elden, 2005). An explanation is the lack of physical presence creates more uninhibited digital interactions where users share their most intimate thoughts and desires without restraint (Abbasi, 2018; Carter, 2015; Cravens and Whiting, 2014).

In the offline world, stranger stalking is rare, and most cases involve stalkers trying to establish a romantic relationship with the victim (Thomas, Purcell, Pathé and Mullen, 2008). However, in the digital world, stranger cyberstalking is more common (Cuenca-Piqueras, Fernández-Prados and González-Moreno, 2020), with various estimates suggesting it makes up more than 40 per cent of all cases (Fisher and Sloan, 2013). In many of these cases, the cyberstalker lacks basic victim information (gender and location) (Bocij and McFarlane, 2003), so they are unlikely to be an intimacy seeker or incompetent suitor. Instead, they are more likely to be following a deliberate course of action with the aim of causing distress or other harm to the victim (a vindictive cyberstalker). Unlike offline stalking, cyberstalking does not require physical proximity (Nobles, Reyns, Fox and Fisher, 2014) or even an online victim, because cyberstalkers can recruit others to harass or threaten their victims offline (Shimizu, 2013; Woodlock, 2017).

An unanswered question is whether cyberstalking is different from offline stalking or whether it is merely stalking in a virtual medium. Some studies found considerable differences between (offline) stalking and cyberstalking; for example, a higher frequency of male victims of cyberstalking compared to offline stalking (Spitzberg and Hoobler, 2002), and strangers as the most frequent type of offenders in cyberstalking but not in offline stalking (Ahlgrim and Terrance, 2018). These results suggest that online environments attract offenders who would not stalk individuals in the real world. On the other hand, there is evidence that technology is frequently used by both females and males to monitor intimate partners (Kodellas, Giannakoulopoulos and Floros, 2010), and that online social networking sites like Facebook facilitate relational intrusion-like behaviours (D'Ovidio and Doyle, 2003). Similarly, some studies report ex-partners as the most frequent category of cyberstalkers (Cravens and Whiting, 2014), comparable to rates of offline stalking. Sheridan and Grant (2007) found cyberstalking to be indistinguishable from offline stalking in many situations and the negative impact of cyberstalking on the victims' wellbeing appears similar to that of offline stalking.

APPLY IT

Are you cyberstalking?	'Yes' or 'no'
1. Checked my partner's email account to see who they were talking to or emailing without my partner's knowledge.	
2. Kept tabs on the whereabouts of my partner using social media.	
3. Checked my partner's phone to see who they were talking to or texting without my partner's permission.	
4. Checked or tracked my partner's internet activity without their permission.	
5. Used my partner's social media account to view their activity without my partner's permission.	
6. Sent repeated online messages or texts asking about my partner's location or activities.	
7. Used GPS technology to track my partner's location without my partner's permission.	
8. Took information or images from my partner's phone, email or social media profile without their permission.	

Source: Watkins, L. E., Maldonado, R. C. and DiLillo, D. (2018) The Cyber Aggression in Relationships Scale: A new multidimensional measure of technology-based intimate partner aggression. *Assessment*, 25(5), 608–26. Adapted with permission.

Transitions between online and offline stalking

In many cases, the offender makes use of both online and offline stalking techniques (Maple et al., 2012; Sheridan and Grant, 2007). Researchers have also reported that it is common for cyberstalking to begin with the issuing of threats, and escalate to physical assault (Todd, Bryce and Franqueira, 2020; Bocij, Griffiths and McFarlane, 2002). Dreßing et al. (2014) found that victims in only one-fourth of the cases classified as cyberstalking experienced only cyberstalking; 42 per cent reported the simultaneous onset of both online and offline stalking. Specifically, 16.5 per cent of cyberstalking cases were followed by methods of offline stalking and 15.8 per cent of cases of offline stalking were used first, followed by online stalking. Cyberstalking victims also reported violent physical attacks – grabbed or held down, 12 per cent, hit with the hand, 8.8 per cent, and attacked with objects, 3.8 per cent.

Theories explaining cyberstalking

Theories of cyberstalking range from behavioural conditioning, evolutionary theories, relational goal theory and psychodynamic theories.

Reward and reinforcement come in many forms, and how the reward is given alters behaviour. Decades ago, B. F. Skinner demonstrated the effects of schedules of reinforcement on behaviour (James and Tunney, 2017), finding that some schedules are more addictive than others. One of the most addictive patterns is the **variable ratio schedule** – a type of operant conditioning reinforcement schedule where reward reinforcement is given after an unpredictable (variable) number of responses. This schedule of reinforcement explains many forms of behavioural addictions, including gambling, drug addiction and stalking. Specifically, the stalker (both online and offline) receives reinforcement (contact with their victim, real or virtual) at an unpredictable rate.

Variable ratio schedule – *A type of operant conditioning reinforcement schedule where reward reinforcement is given after an unpredictable (variable) number of responses.*

According to the **evolutionary approach**, stalking evolved to solve problems related to mating and within gender competition (Korkodeilou, 2020).

Relational goal theory states that obsessive online pursuers link the goal of having a particular relationship to higher-order goals, such as happiness and self-worth (Cupach, Spitzberg, Bolingbroke and Tellitocci, 2011). In the case of stalking, the goal becomes creating a relationship with the victim because their happiness and self-worth becomes increasingly dependent upon it. If this goal is blocked (the relationship ends), the stalker experiences frustration and anger. Frequent responses include ruminating about their failed goal and a persistent pursuit of the goal/person, with increasing levels of pursuit to achieve their goal (Spitzberg, Cupach, Hannawa and Crowley, 2014).

If we apply a psychodynamic perspective using **attachment theory**, those who stalk tend to have attachment issues from childhood disruptions, such as an emotionally or physically absent carer, or childhood trauma in the form of abuse. Applied to stalking, individuals with insecure-anxious attachment styles resort to stalking and other threatening behaviours to reduce the anxiety experienced from previous rejection or abandonment. Unfortunately, the increased emotional distance or unavailability of the pursued person creates more intense and desperate attempts to repair the relationship (Patton, Nobles and Fox, 2010; Almeida, Ramalho, Belmira Fernandes and Guarda, 2019).

The cyberstalking process

Bocij's (2018) Online Victimisation Intervention and Reduction (OVIAR) Model shows the general progression of cyberstalking in discrete stages that can escalate in frequency and intensity (Figure 13.1). The purpose of the model is to find points of intervention to focus resources and break the cyberstalking cycle. The model assumes that the cyberstalker is a rational decision maker intending to achieve a specific goal (relationship, harming the victim) (Bocij, 2018).

Figure 13.1: The Online Victimisation Intervention and Reduction (OVIAR) Model

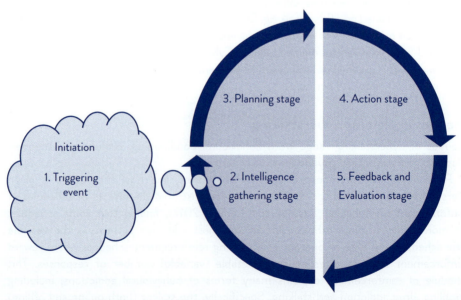

Source: Bocij, P. (2018) OVIAR: Towards a model for cyberstalking intervention and reduction. *International Journal of Emerging Trends in Social Sciences,* 4(2), 58–66. Adapted with permission.

The OVIAR model has five stages:

1   The initiation stage, where the cyberstalker chooses to pursue the victim. This decision is often based on a single **triggering event** (Bocij, 2005). In many cases, the triggering event is obvious, such as when a relationship ends, beginning when one partner moves out of the shared dwelling, or when legal documentation finalising the relationship is received (Taylor, 2018). However, sometimes the triggering event may be something insignificant to the victim, but very significant to the cyberstalker (Smoker and March, 2017).

2   During the **intelligence-gathering stage**, information about the victim is gathered to plan further actions. The more information discovered about the victim, the more opportunities become available in terms of actions to take against the victim. The information-gathering process can range from an unstructured and informal search using publicly available search tools, to a more formal and organised approach and sometimes illegal approach (MacFarlane and Bocij, 2003). These more advanced approaches include the covert installation of spyware to monitor the victim's internet devices and capture information from webcam images, text messages, passwords and other sensitive data (Tonellotto, 2020). In this way, every moment can be tracked – messages stating future plans and locations, emails sent to a domestic violence shelter (Harkin, Molnar and Vowles, 2020; Chatterjee et al., 2018).

3   During the **planning stage**, the cyberstalker selects the course of action based on the information collected during the previous intelligence-gathering stage. Actions chosen are often based on a range of limiting factors, which include technical skills, resources, level of motivation, the fear of being caught, time pressures and the amount of effort needed to carry out a given action.

4   In the **action stage**, the plan is conducted and sometimes altered in response to the victim's reactions.

5   During the **feedback and evaluation stage**, the cyberstalker evaluates their level of satisfaction, which results in three possible courses of action:

– *unsatisfactory feedback* may cause the cyberstalker to lose interest in the current victim. Unlike offline stalking, the cyberstalker may find the feedback less gratifying and rewarding (Reyns and Fisher, 2018).

– *satisfactory feedback* results in continuing the cycle of cyberstalking.

– *unsatisfying feedback* (or even unexpectedly satisfying feedback) may cause escalation to more extreme forms of cyberstalking moving into the physical world.

Unlike other crimes, cyberstalking offers immediate rewards and gratification, which motivates greater intelligence gathering, planning and stalking (Runions, Bak and Shaw, 2017; Reyns, 2019). Part of the explanation is that immediate rewards are extremely addictive (Chóliz, 2010). Even the *anticipation* of a reward (downloading stolen mobile phone images) releases behaviourally reinforcing neurotransmitters like dopamine, a common basis of addiction (Linnet, 2019). The faster reward makes cyberstalking behaviour more addictive than offline stalking.

Triggering event – *In the OVIAR model, the initial event that causes the cyberstalker to notice the victim.*

Intelligence-gathering stage – *Second stage in the OVIAR model, where information about the victim is gathered to plan further actions.*

Planning stage – *Third stage in the OVIAR model, where the cyberstalker selects the course of action.*

Action stage – *Fourth stage in the OVIAR model, where the plan is conducted and sometimes altered in response to the victim's reactions.*

PART IV

Feedback and evaluation stage – *Fifth stage in the OVIAR model, where the cyberstalker evaluates their level of satisfaction with their action.*

Cyberstalking interventions

The OVIAR model can be used to identify intervention opportunities to disrupt a cyberstalker's activities by focusing on the initiation, intelligence-gathering and feedback and evaluation stages.

During the initiation stage, avoiding a potential cyberstalker's attention and thus preventing the pursuit of the victim in the first place is easier than attempting to intervene after the cycle becomes routine behaviour. At this stage, recommendations include using gender neutral internet identifiers – email addresses and screen names.

Once the cyberstalker selects a victim, they enter the intelligence-planning stage. Disrupting the intelligence-planning-action-feedback cycle can be achieved by controlling the information available online. This limits the number of actions available to the cyberstalker, making it difficult to develop a profile of the victim. Two approaches to this are separating various aspects of a person's online life by using different usernames for each online account. Another is to use misdirection and intentionally enter incorrect information such as gender or location information used by search engines (Odebade, Welsh, Mthunzi and Benkhelifa, 2017).

Intervening later, during the evaluation and feedback stage, might cause the cyberstalker to lose interest in the victim more quickly. Specifically, starving the cyberstalker of feedback may cause them to lose interest in the victim, although there is still a risk that the harassment might escalate. This is supported in part by studies of offline stalking, which have shown that actions involving communication with stalkers, such as attempting to reason with them or even taking legal action, do little to discourage them and may even make matters worse (Logan and Walker, 2017).

Behaviour sequence analysis – *A method for understanding the dynamic relationship between progressions of behaviours and social interactions occurring over time.*

Future solutions may come from behaviour sequence analysis. Researchers moved beyond risk factors for stalking to mapping the temporal dynamics of stalking using the **behaviour sequence analysis** method (Quinn-Evans, Keatley, Arntfield and Sheridan, 2019). They analysed the sequence of stalker and victim interaction over time, for example the frequency and type of interactions and the intensity of responses, using detailed accounts of stalking in online forums containing both stalker behaviour and decisions made by victims. Their surprising findings were that victims need not perform many behaviours for stalkers to continue with their actions and many behaviour transactions occurred before victims felt there was a significant problem.

An understudied avenue in cyberstalking research is related to what occurs after the victimisation (Reyns and Fissel, 2020). With this in mind, the future of stalking convictions lies in digital forensics. *Digital forensics* is an investigation and analysis technique to gather and preserve evidence from a computing device in a way that is suitable for presentation in a court of law (Frommholz et al., 2016). The goal is to locate the cyberstalking evidence with the aid of artificial intelligence technology, report to law enforcement, and find the identity of the stalker. Research is shifting its focus on how to proactively detect and prevent this kind of crime (Feng, Asante, Short and Abeykoon, 2017).

IN SUMMARY

Cyberstalking takes many forms, but the psychological motivations and consequences are, in many ways, more intense than offline stalking. Understanding how cyberstalkers make decisions can provide opportunities to intervene, prevent and discourage further acts of harassment against victims.

CRITICAL THINKING AND APPLICATION QUESTIONS

1. Is cyberstalking different from stalking or is it a variant of stalking behaviour?

2. Review Table 13.2. Apply the explanations of cyberstalking to explain one of the four categories.

3. How much responsibility should the victim of cyberstalking assume?

SEARCHING FOR PSYCHOLOGICAL CLOSURE

FICTION: Pursuing psychological closure is a way for victims of crime to find an end to their grief and mental suffering.

Versus

FACT: Pursuing psychological closure may create greater intensity of grief and anguish for crime victims.

Malaysia Airlines Flight 370 departed from Kuala Lumpur on 8 March 2014. Having climbed to a cruising altitude of 35,000 feet, the crew broadcast the message 'Goodnight, Malaysia 370' calmly, with no sign that something catastrophic was about to happen (Llewelyn, 2020). Two minutes later, the plane and all 227 passengers and 12 crew members disappeared from the radar. The disappearance of Flight 370 is one of the greatest aviation mysteries of all time. The idea that a plane with modern instruments and redundant communications could simply vanish seems impossible (Langewiesche, 2019). The loss devastated families on four continents and the search for the missing airplane became the costliest in aviation history, never providing what those who grieved wanted most, a feeling of 'closure'.

The tragedy of Flight 370 shows that life sometimes denies us the sense of an ending or closure. But what exactly is closure and why do we tell victims of tragic and traumatic events to search for it to overcome their grief and loss?

Psychological closure is a comforting or satisfying feeling of finality to an event with an ambiguous ending. But there are more dimensions to this concept. Closure is a process that can be viewed as partial, in the sense that suffering remains. We can distinguish several types of closure (Armour and Umbreit 2007), including:

- judicial – the imprisonment of an offender
- emotional – forgiving and letting go of emotional anger towards the offender
- psychological – completing rituals to honour the victim.

Closure is a convenient way to refer to a group of ambiguous but related concepts about victims and their families – finality, catharsis, peace, relief, satisfaction and justice. Its use offers the hope of healing (Armour and Umbreit, 2007). Because the concept of 'closure' is so ambiguous, it's easy to use, but difficult to measure (Madeira, 2010).

The idea of closure first appeared in the 1920s as part of Gestalt psychology (Gestalt is German for 'whole') to explain the way we organise our perceptions (Guberman, 2015). Gestalt psychologists discovered that humans have a natural tendency to close incomplete diagrams, such as a partially open square, in order to gain a gestalt, or a whole picture. For

Psychological closure – *A comforting or satisfying feeling of finality to an event with an ambiguous ending.*

PART IV

example, Figure 13.2 does *not* show a white square, but only four circles with a quarter of their circumference missing. Because of our need for closure, we perceive a white square. The term has evolved and now refers to a psychological state where all uncertainty is resolved.

Figure 13.2: Closure and the perception of a square

Another aspect of closure is letting go of painful memories. However, there is no evidence that memories are ever permanently lost (except by permanent organic brain damage). The creation of memories results in actual physical changes in the brain (Kandel, 2007). This finding means that the right cue can trigger a resurgence of memories. How much of the original emotions and feelings resurface depends on the intensity and depth of rehearsal of the original event. The triggered memory may range from a minor distraction to a severe intrusion, such as PTSD (Herz, 2016; Palmer, 2019). Expecting memories to fade in intensity over time reflects our experiences with everyday memories. For example, Habermas and Berger (2011) showed that everyday narratives of common emotional experiences become less emotionally focused and recounted from a more distant perspective. Similarly, Beike and Writh-Beaument (2010) proposed that life events are typically remembered with a satisfying sense of closure when there is decreased emotional detail in the reconstructed episodic memory. However, emotion-focused retelling of experiences increases emotional detail and decreases the sense of closure. Focusing on the emotional components makes the memory feel more present and active. Unfortunately, these intense emotion-focused memories are the same type that victims of crime are often forced to rehearse in the pursuit of closure.

The Need for Closure Scale (NFCS)

While the goal of achieving complete closure may be unrealistic, it is clear that many people have a need to reach a conclusion or find a resolution. With this in mind, Webster and Kruglanski (1994) developed the Need for Closure Scale (NFCS) – a standardised measure of variation in need for cognitive closure. The scale measures the extent to which a person, faced with a decision or judgement, wants any answer, as compared to confusion and ambiguity. The basic idea is that people high in need for closure are more likely to enjoy clear stories with uncomplicated moral endings and feel uncomfortable with ambiguity over important issues. Typical statements in the NFCS include: 'I think that having clear rules and order at work is essential for success', 'I don't like situations that are uncertain', and 'I dislike questions which could be answered in many different ways' (Kruglanski et al., 1997). Kruglanski (1990) states that two connected tendencies underlie the NFCS: the urgency tendency to seize on closure quickly, and the permanence tendency to maintain a state of closure. Both tendencies serve to avoid the unpleasant lack of closure, the first by ending this state quickly, and the second by keeping it from recurring (Evans et al., 2017). This desire for cognitive closure varies along a continuum, with a strong need to achieve closure at one end and a high need to avoid closure at the other end. A person's level of need for closure is not stable: when we feel comfortable and safe, our level of need for closure decreases; when we feel threatened, it increases. Finally, critique and scepticism concerning this scale have surfaced. Neuberg, Judice and West (1997) cite the scale's lack of **discriminant validity**, which determines if two measures that should not be related are actually not related. For example, the NFCS measures both the need for cognitive closure and the desire for structure (Neuberg, Judice and West, 1997).

> **Discriminant validity** – *Determining if two measures that should not be related are actually not related.*

The false promise of closure

This search for closure can be profoundly unsatisfying and telling victims of traumatic experiences to 'find closure' reflects the attitude that victims should 'get over it', that trauma and grief are temporary and that a final resolution is possible (Spungen, 1998). The risk for victims is that closure may lead to secondary victimisation.

The promise that psychological closure will alleviate symptoms of grief, anger and sadness is offered to victims as the solution for their suffering. However, if the symptoms are not relieved promptly, the cause of the failure to achieve closure is projected onto the victim. Descriptions of victims not 'working hard enough' or 'not wanting to let go of the experience' reflect this blame. Victims of crime are given the expectation that closure will result in a meaningful engagement in life once they are able to 'let go' or leave their issue permanently in the past (Bandes, 2019). The need to work through stages of grief or the traumatic loss of a loved one becomes a false promise of resolution and closure. Blaming the victim for their inability to overcome their memories of the traumatic event creates self-blame. Alternatively, one could argue that if it is an important life event, why would we not search for a way to remain connected to the one who is loved and was lost?

There are victims who have suffered a type of loss that is fundamentally open ended, an ambiguous loss. **Ambiguous loss** is a type of loss when a loved one disappears in body, such as soldiers missing in action or the passengers and crew of Flight 370, or mind – dementias like Alzheimer's (Pauline and Boss, 2009). Ambiguous loss offers no opportunity for closure. Without the verification of death, there are no rituals of support for the suffering or memorials for the missing. Instead, victims experiencing ambiguous loss are often criticised for not finding closure while being trapped between hope and despair (Boss, 2018). Instead of closure, the therapeutic goal is to help people find meaning despite the lack of definitive information and finality. Hope lies in increasing a person's tolerance for ambiguity (Boss, 2010).

> **Ambiguous loss** – *A type of loss without closure when a loved one disappears in body or mind.*

The ultimate closure: the death penalty

The concept of closure has been enthusiastically embraced by many jurisdictions as a legitimate psychological state and one that the criminal justice system ought to help victims reach. In the context of the death penalty, the concept of closure has changed the way we talk about the rationale for the death penalty. It has changed what both survivors and jurors in death penalty cases expect to feel (Bandes, 2019).

Although the death penalty represents an attempt at complete closure, a death sentence in the USA or Japan is not a clear expression of finality but a perpetual delay of the last word. In Japan and the USA, the death penalty really means an average of 10 years in prison with an indeterminate chance of release through reversal or commutation, and with the possibility of execution sometime in the future (McLeod, 2016; Johnson, 2020).

The controversial connection of closure with the death penalty (Armour and Umbreit, 2012) resulted from mass media coverage and criminal justice system practice, as prosecutors argue to juries that family members can gain closure from the execution of their loved one's killer, or that executions heal social or communal wounds (Meade, 1996; Bandes, 2004). Before 1989, closure was rarely mentioned by the media in combination with the death penalty; in 1989, the two were mentioned in the same context only once (Zimring, 2003). Beginning in 1993, however, the frequency with which closure was mentioned in the context of the death penalty grew to 500 mentions in 2001, when an ABC News/Washington Post poll found that 60 per cent of respondents strongly or moderately agreed with the statement that the death penalty was fair because it gave closure to victims' family members (Zimring, 2003).

The popularity of closure increased, despite empirical research on deterrence showing that the death penalty has failed (Madeira, 2010; Steiker and Steiker, 2020). The death penalty is often described as the only punishment that provides true justice and closure for a victim's family and friends, who are also known as 'co-victims' (Gross and Matheson, 2002). A **co-victim** is anyone, such as a spouse or partner, child, sibling, extended family member or friend, who has been impacted by the death of a loved one by homicide (Reed, Dabney, Tapp and Ishoy, 2019). Research has indicated that most co-victims reported feelings of emptiness and their sense of closure was minimal, with only 2.5 per cent responding that they achieved true closure in the wake of an execution (Vollum, Longmire and Buffington-Vollum, 2004).

Co-victim
– Anyone who has been impacted by the death of a loved one by homicide.

Global Perspectives

The death penalty in Japan

In Japan and many other countries, executions used to be staged in public so that rulers could communicate to their subjects the extent of their political power (Martschukat, 2005). Today, a cloak of secrecy protects Japan's system of capital punishment from outside examination and review. The justification of secrecy is that it ensures that executions are as impersonal and non-controversial as possible (Johnson, 2020). The secrecy surrounding capital punishment in Japan helps explain the absence of controversy over execution methods (Kita and Johnson, 2014).

Source: JIJI PRESS/AFP/Getty Images

A rare glimpse of the execution room inside a Tokyo prison. The square outline on the floor is a trapdoor that opens to enable hanging of the prisoner

Secrecy includes the day and time of executions. Prisoners are given no warning or just a few hours' notice. This causes death row inmates to live for decades in fear that every day is their last. To reduce the chance of protest and debate, no advanced notice is given to their families, legal representatives or the media. In some cases, even the members of the execution team are given little prior notification, partly out of concern that if told in advance they may not show up for work (Hodge, 2018). To deter research and reporting about capital punishment, scholars and reporters are denied access to most official death penalty documents (Johnson, 2020). Rarely are outside citizens and media allowed to view the gallows where all prisoners are hung. An exception was in 2010, when Japanese authorities allowed select reporters a 30-minute visit to the glass-walled execution room in the Tokyo Detention House (Lane, 2015). There is also the secrecy of lay judges, who are not legally permitted to disclose information about their experiences during trials (Weitzdörfer, Shiroshita and Padfield, 2018). This forced silence prevents the public from knowing and talking about how decisions about capital punishment are made.

Radelet (2015) found improved physical and psychological health for co-victims, as well as greater satisfaction with the justice system, when life sentences were given, rather than the death penalty. This finding is explained as the survivors prefer the finality of a life sentence, and the obscurity into which the defendant will quickly fall, to the continued uncertainty and publicity around the death penalty. Researchers have found that victims' families believe closure to be a myth and often find the executions unsatisfying, except when the offender enjoys great media visibility when alive so that the execution has a silencing effect, as was the case of Oklahoma City bomber Timothy McVeigh's execution by lethal injection in 2001 (Armour, 2012).

IN SUMMARY

Psychological closure is an ambiguous concept with no discernible ending, resisting definition due to its unique and personal nature. Encouraging victims of crime to seek closure does not provide an end to their grief and may increase the tendency of others to blame them. Seeking closure for the victim offers an easy solution in the death penalty debate because of the moral retribution it seems to offer. However, without any empirical method to investigate closure, we cannot say that those who support seeking psychological closure are right or wrong.

 CRITICAL THINKING AND APPLICATION QUESTIONS

1   Why is the concept of 'closure' so challenging to measure?

2   What kinds of situations cause ambiguous closure and what seems to be the best approach to help victims cope with this situation?

3   Why does the death penalty as practised in the USA and Japan fail to provide co-victims with a feeling of closure?

CHAPTER REVIEW

Forensic victimisation is an essential complement to the study of offender behaviour. Learning about the role of the victim in relation to the offender allows analysis of their interactions and risk assessment. It is important to remember that victims are sometimes victimised twice by being held responsible for being a victim of crime. This is the case for the victims of abuse via social media. These victims are also being blamed for their suffering. Yet, the psychological rules that govern many behaviours, from cyberstalking to cyberaggression, function in the same way in the digital and offline worlds. Lastly, victims are told to seek closure, an ambiguous concept that promises a quick end to psychological suffering. Unfortunately, if the symptoms (grief, depression) persist, blame is placed on the victim for their continued mental anguish and loss.

NAMES TO KNOW

Wayne Petherick

Investigates stalking and is developing a response–outcome model to better understand the response style of victims of stalking and how this may perpetuate the cycle of harassment.

- Petherick, W., Turvey, B. E. and Ferguson, C. E. (eds) (2009) *Forensic Criminology.* Academic Press.

- Petherick, W. and Ferguson, C. (2014) Forensic victimology. In W. Petherick (ed.) *Applied Crime Analysis: A Social Science Approach to Understanding Crime, Criminals, and Victims* (pp. 62–80). Elsevier.

Paul Bocij

Research interests are cyberstalking and educational technology, especially computer-based assessment and computer-based learning.

- Bocij, P. (2002) Victims of cyberstalking: An exploratory study of harassment perpetrated via the Internet. *First Monday*, 8(10). DOI: 10.5210/fm.v8i10.1086.

- MacFarlane, L. and Bocij, P. (2003) An exploration of predatory behaviour in cyberspace: Towards a typology of cyberstalkers. *First Monday*, 8(9). DOI: https://doi.org/10.5210/fm.v8i9.1076.

Pauline Boss

A researcher in the field of ambiguous loss and coping with unresolved grief.

- Boss, P. (2009) *Ambiguous Loss: Learning to Live with Unresolved Grief.* Harvard University Press.

- Boss, P. (2010) The trauma and complicated grief of ambiguous loss. *Pastoral Psychology*, 59(2), 137–45.

GLOSSARY

Absolute-relative judgement theory: A strategy found in sequential line-ups when witnesses compare faces from memory rather than to each other.

Acquiescence bias: The tendency for respondents to agree with statements regardless of their content.

Action stage: Fourth stage in the OVIAR model where the plan is conducted and sometimes altered in response to the victim's reactions.

Actus reus: The Latin term used to describe a criminal act that was the result of voluntary bodily movement.

Adaptational model of malingering: The idea that malingerers engage in a cost–benefit analysis during assessment.

Adverse childhood experiences (ACE) score: The frequency of distinct types of abuse, neglect and other adverse experiences during childhood.

Affective violence: An instinctual, defensive and reactive form of violence to a perceived threat.

Ambiguous loss: A type of loss without closure when a loved one disappears in mind or body.

Amygdala: An almond-shaped brain structure responsible for the response to and memory of emotions, especially fear.

Anecdotal evidence: Evidence based on non-systematic methods such as examining personal experiences and opinions rather than facts.

Apophenia: Perceiving connections and meaningfulness in unrelated things, that is, patternicity.

Applied psychology: Using psychological methods and findings of scientific psychology to solve practical problems of human and animal behaviour and experience.

Ask-and-answer procedure: A series of quick closed-ended questions.

Atavistic: Relating to or characterised by reversion to something ancient or ancestral; associated with biological theories of crime and Cesare Lombroso.

Attachment theory: Stalkers have attachment issues from childhood disruptions, such as an emotionally or physically absent carer, or childhood trauma in the form of abuse.

Auditory exclusion: A form of temporary hearing loss occurring during high levels of stress.

Auditory persecutory hallucinations: Hearing voices that degrade and demean the subject.

Autism spectrum disorder (ASD): Impairments in social communication and interaction and difficulties in verbal and nonverbal communication.

Automatism: The performance of actions without conscious thought or intention.

Availability heuristic: A mental shortcut relying on immediate examples that come to a person's mind when evaluating a topic, concept or decision.

Behaviour sequence analysis: A method for understanding the dynamic relationship between progressions of behaviours and social interactions occurring over time.

Behavioural consistency: The tendency to behave in a manner that matches past decisions or behaviours.

Behavioural distinctiveness: The way one offender behaves is different from that of another offender.

Behavioural investigative advice: The process of drawing inferences about an offender or offence from a detailed, behavioural examination of actions within a crime.

Behavioural leakage: The belief that liars produce unconscious behaviours that indicate emotions related to lying, such as fear and anxiety.

Burnout: The physical and emotional exhaustion associated with increased workload and institutional stress.

Bystander effect: When the presence of others discourages an individual from intervening during an emergency.

Causation: When changes in the value of one variable cause changes in the value of another variable.

Celerity of punishment: Faster punishment is more effective in reducing illicit behaviour.

Certainty of punishment: The greater the perception of being caught, the less likely someone will engage in illicit behaviour.

Challenge for cause: Request that a prospective juror be dismissed because there is a reason to believe the person is biased or prejudiced in some way.

Change blindness: When a change in a visual stimulus is introduced and the observer does not notice it.

Childhood amnesia: The inability of adults to remember episodic experiences that occurred prior to age three.

Circle theory of environmental range: Using the geographical locations of a suspect's known offences to predict the approximate site of the offender's residential base.

Close supervision centres: Units where the disruptive, challenging and dangerous offenders are managed within small and highly supervised units.

Coerced-compliant false confession: When an innocent person believes that the immediate benefits of confession outweigh the long-term costs.

Coerced-internalised false confession: When an innocent person falsely confesses to a crime truly believing that they are responsible for the criminal act.

Cognitive dissonance: An anxiety-producing situation where our attitudes, beliefs and behaviours are inconsistent, requiring a change to restore consistency.

Cognitive impairment: When a person has trouble remembering, learning new things, concentrating, or making decisions that affect their everyday life.

Cognitive impairment of moral reasoning: A person was insane if they could not appreciate that their actions were wrong.

Cognitive interview: Interview process to enhance retrieval of information from the perspective of eyewitnesses' memory.

Cognitive liberty: The idea that individuals have a right to privacy and must provide consent before their thought processes are measured.

Cognitive load: The amount of cognitive effort (or amount of information processing) required to perform a task.

Cognitive schemas: Patterns of thought that organise information.

Collaboration: Using social negotiation to find common ground to reduce real or perceived differences.

Collaborative inhibition: A phenomenon that causes members of a collaborative group to remember less information than an equal number of single individuals.

Command hallucination: Hearing voices ordering the subject to do something.

Commuter: A victim search pattern showing that the suspect commutes to offence locations.

Compassion fatigue: The emotional residue or strain of exposure from working with those suffering from the consequences of traumatic events.

Competence to stand trial: The legally determined capacity of a criminal defendant to proceed with criminal judgement.

Competency: The ability to deliver reliable testimony.

Confederate: A person who is an accomplice helping the experimenter.

Confession: A detailed statement that admits all the facts necessary for the conviction of a crime.

Confirmation bias: The tendency to interpret new evidence as confirmation of one's existing beliefs or theories.

Control questions: Questions that are unrelated to the crime and deal with issues concerning the examinee's moral character.

Correlation: A statistical technique that tells us how strongly a pair of variables are linearly related and change together.

Corroboration inflation: The tendency for confessions to produce an illusion of support from other evidence.

Counter-interrogation strategies: The methods interviewees use to convince the interviewer that they are telling the truth.

Countermeasures: When subjects deliberately manipulate their physical and mental responses during the examination.

Co-victim: Anyone who has been impacted by the death of a loved one by homicide.

Credibility: The degree to which a judge or jury believes that the witness can deliver honest and accurate testimony.

Crime linkage: Linking crimes based on the similarities in the behaviours of the offenders or as inferred from the crime scene.

Crime linkage analysis: Linking a known offender to other unsolved crimes based on consistent and distinctive behaviours.

Criminal investigative analysis (CIA): Investigative profiling tool used by the FBI to solve violent crimes, based on the premise that personality predicts behaviour.

Criminal responsibility: A person's ability to understand their conduct when the crime was committed.

Criminogenic thinking: Patterns of thought that perpetuate criminal behaviour.

Critical incident: An event stressful enough to overwhelm an individual's usual coping skills.

Cross-race effect: The tendency to more easily recognise faces of the race one is most familiar with, which is most often one's own race.

Cue utilisation hypothesis: As arousal increases, attention narrows, blocking encoding information.

Cyberstalking: A constellation of behaviours in which one individual uses digital technology to harass individuals, groups of individuals, or organisations.

Daubert standard: A rule of evidence about the admissibility of expert witness testimony in court (aka the Daubert test).

De-escalation: Stabilising a situation to reduce the immediate threat and obtain more time, options or resources.

Defence mechanisms: Unconscious strategies used to decrease anxiety arising from unacceptable thoughts, feelings or behaviours.

Delayed response latency: An increased length of time between the last word of the interviewer's question and the first word of the subject's response.

Demand characteristics: Subtle cues that communicate the interviewer's expectations.

Dementia: A decline in intellectual ability, including significant impairment of memory and other cognitive functions.

Denunciation theory: Punishing someone publicly will prevent others from committing the offence.

Desistance: The process by which a person arrives at a state of non-offending.

Deterrence theory: The threat of punishment will discourage people from committing crime.

Diagnostic feature detection theory: Simultaneous line-ups lead to better discriminability because viewing all line-up suspects together allows witnesses to compare specific features in each face.

Digital dating abuse: The physical, sexual or psychological/emotional violence that occurs between romantic partners using texting, social media and related online media.

Diminished responsibility: An unbalanced mental state used as grounds for a reduced charge, but that does not classify them as insane.

Discriminant validity: Determining if two measures that should not be related are actually not related.

Disorganised serial killer: A serial killer whose behaviours indicate below-average intelligence, performing unplanned crimes that leave evidence.

Dissociative analgesia: A profound reduction of pain sensation.

Double-blind procedure: Neither the eyewitness nor the line-up administrator knows the identity of the suspect.

Dual process theories: Propose that jurors are using two information-processing strategies, or 'routes', to understand evidence.

Dynamic risk factors: Risk factors that predict recidivism and can be altered through treatment programmes.

Dynamic security: A prison philosophy using interpersonal relationships between the staff and the inmates as the primary factor in maintaining safety.

Ecological validity: Asks whether a research finding represents what happens in everyday life.

Empirical evidence: Evidence based on the systematic use of observation and measurement.

Encoding specificity: Memory is better when conditions during retrieval match those when the memory was stored.

Engram: The physical trace of a memory in the brain.

Entitativity: The perception of a group as a single entity, distinct from its individual members.

Environmental psychology: Interdisciplinary field that examines how the interaction between individuals and their surroundings affects behaviour.

Episodic memory: A person's unique autobiographical memory of a specific event.

Estimator variables: Variables that affect the accuracy of eyewitness identifications, but cannot be controlled by the criminal justice system.

Evidence-driven juries: Juries that spend more time evaluating the evidence instead of the verdict.

Evidence framing matrix: A tool designed to tactically confront an interviewee with inconsistencies in their statements and available evidence.

Evolutionary approach: Darwinian perspective that stalking evolved to solve problems related to mating and within gender competition.

Exculpatory evidence: Evidence favourable to the defendant in a criminal trial that exonerates the defendant of guilt.

Executive dysfunction: Disruption to the efficacy of executive functions, the cognitive processes that regulate, control and manage thoughts and actions.

Expressive aphasia: The inability to produce language while language comprehension remains intact.

External validity: Asks whether a research finding in one experiment would be found in another experiment with different participants and procedures.

Extra-evidentiary factors: Factors affecting jury decision making that are not from the admissible evidence presented at trial.

Factitious disorder: A psychiatric disorder in which sufferers intentionally fabricate physical or psychological symptoms in order to assume the role of the patient, without any obvious gain.

False memory: The memory for an event that never occurred.

False negatives: A test result that incorrectly indicates that a particular condition or attribute is *absent*.

False positives: A test result that incorrectly indicates that a particular condition or attribute is *present*.

Falsifiability: A theory is scientific based on whether it can be disproved, a tool to distinguish between science and pseudoscience.

Feedback and evaluation stage: Fifth stage in the OVIAR model where the cyberstalker evaluates their level of satisfaction with their action.

Field study: Research where the confines of a laboratory setting are abandoned in favour of a natural setting.

Fight-or-flight response: A physiological reaction that prepares our bodies to stay and fight or to flee when threatened.

Fitness to plead: The capacity of a defendant in criminal proceedings to comprehend the course of those proceedings.

Fitness to stand trial: The accused person is able to defend against the charge they are facing.

Flashbulb memory: A vivid, enduring memory associated with a personally significant and emotional event.

Foils: Also known as line-up fillers (an innocent person in a police line-up), they test an eyewitness's recognition memory.

Foot-in-the-door technique: After agreeing to a small request, people find it easier to agree to a bigger one.

Forensic interview: A structured conversation to elicit detailed information about event(s) a child may have experienced or witnessed.

Forensic linguistics: Applying linguistic knowledge, methods and insights to the forensic context of law, language, crime investigation, trial and judicial procedure.

Forensic psychology: A field of psychology that applies the production and application of psychological knowledge to criminal justice systems.

Forensic victimology: The examination of victims of crime to solve investigative and legal questions.

Frame of reference: A person's unique experiences, values, feelings and perceptions.

Fundamental attribution error: Attributing other people's behaviour to internal causes, while underestimating the importance of external causes.

General deterrence: The punishment should prevent other people from committing criminal actions.

General responsivity: The idea that cognitive behavioural and social learning theories are the most effective form of intervention.

General victimology: The study of all victims, not just victims of crime.

Geographic profiling: The process of analysing locations connected to a series of crimes to determine probable areas in which the suspect lives.

Group polarisation: Happens during discussion, when a jury – initially leaning towards a certain opinion – moves further in the direction they initially agreed on.

Habituate: Reduced responding to a repeated stimulus.

Heuristics: Mental shortcuts that evolve from experience.

Hindsight bias: The tendency of people to overestimate their ability to have predicted an outcome that could not have been predicted.

Hippocampus: A brain structure responsible for consolidating memories.

Homicide: The deliberate and unlawful killing of one person by another; murder.

Homology: The idea that similar offenders commit similar crimes.

Illusion of transparency: A tendency for people to overestimate the degree to which their personal mental state is known by others.

Implicit social cognitions: The attitudes or stereotypes that affect our understanding, actions and decisions in an unconscious manner.

Inattentional deafness: A temporary deafness for normal environmental sounds, such as speech.

Incapacitation theory: Holding individuals in prison prevents those individuals from committing new crimes.

Informational influence theory: Individuals become more convinced of their views when they hear novel arguments in support of their position.

Institutionalisation: Difficulty coping with society after release from prison, having adapted to the norms and values of prison life.

Intelligence-gathering stage: Second stage in the OVIAR model, where information about the victim is gathered to plan further actions.

Interaction ritual chain: Successful rituals create symbols of group membership and increase emotional energy, while failed rituals drain emotional energy.

Interpersonal coherence: There is a consistency between the way suspects interact with their victims and others in their everyday lives.

Interrogational torture: Torture for the purpose of extracting information.

Investigative psychology: Bottom-up approach to profiling developed by David Canter, who proposed that profiling should be based in psychological theory and research.

Irresistible impulse: A person should not be held responsible, because they could not control their actions.

Jury–defendant similarity bias: Jury demographic factors interact with defendant characteristics creating a bias in favour of defendants who are similar to the jury.

Just-world hypothesis: A cognitive bias in which individuals believe that the world operates in a fair and just manner.

Leading questions: Questions that assume a specific answer.

Leakage: When offenders intentionally or unintentionally reveal insights into their thoughts or feelings that suggest impending targeted violence.

Legal competency: The mental ability of an individual to understand and participate in legal proceedings.

Liberation hypothesis: When the evidence is weak or contradictory, jurors use extralegal factors in reaching their decisions.

Lie: A statement that the liar believes is false made to intentionally deceive someone.

Line-up superiority hypothesis: The belief that live presentation of line-up members yields the best eyewitness identification outcomes.

McNaughton rule: A test to determine whether a person was sane when committing a crime and therefore responsible.

Malingering: The intentional production of false or grossly exaggerated physical or psychological symptoms.

Marauder: Serial rapist victim search pattern indicating that the suspect lives near the offence locations.

Mens rea: Latin for 'guilty mind', it is the mental element of a person's intention to commit a crime.

Meta-analysis: A statistical procedure for combining data from multiple studies.

Mindfulness: An active state of awareness of one's immediate experiences.

Minimisation: Downplaying the significance of an event or emotion.

Minimisation approach: Interrogation in which an interrogator tries to alleviate a suspect's anxiety associated with confessing to a crime.

Mitigating evidence: Evidence that reduces the perceived severity of the crime to be weaker.

Mnemonic: Any learning technique that aids information retention or retrieval.

Modus operandi: The particular way a person performs a particular task (mode of operation).

Moral disengagement theory: The process of convincing the self that ethical standards do not apply to oneself in a particular context.

Moral distress: A conflict between our deepest values and the work we are required to do.

Multiple trace theory: Every memory has many unique components that can be activated with the proper cue.

Negative punishment: Taking something good or desirable away to reduce the occurrence of a particular behaviour.

Negative reinforcement: Taking something bad or undesirable away to increase the occurrence of a particular behaviour.

Neurolaw: The research field studying the impact of neuroscience on the law and legal practices.

Non-insane automatism: An act done by a sane person but without intention, awareness, or hatred.

Nonverbal communication: Refers to gestures, facial expressions, tone of voice, eye contact (or lack thereof), body language, posture and other ways people can communicate without using language.

Norm of reciprocity: Social rule when people feel an obligation to return a favour.

Not guilty by reason of insanity (NGRI): Admitting the crime but claiming to be mentally disturbed at the time and lacking the intention to commit the crime.

Offender profiling: Identifying the perpetrator of a crime by their personality and behaviour based on analysis of the crime committed.

Operational stressors: Stresses related to tasks related to the job of policing.

Organisational stressors: Stresses related to the culture of policing.

Organised serial killer: A serial killer whose behaviours indicate above-average intelligence, performing premeditated, carefully planned crimes that leave little evidence.

Orienting response: A physiological response to a specific stimulus.

Paradigm: A distinct set of theories, research methods, and standards for what constitutes legitimate contributions to a field.

Paradox of innocence: When an innocent person is more likely to confess to committing a crime than a guilty suspect.

Parasympathetic nervous system (PNS): Responsible for returning the body back to a normal level of functioning.

Path Model of Blame: A series of information-processing steps that are necessary for the assignment of blame.

PEACE model of interviewing: PEACE stands for Preparation and planning, Engage and explain, Account (clarify and challenge), Closure, Evaluate. The model assumes that a relaxed subject with whom the interviewer has rapport is more likely to cooperate.

Peremptory challenges: A defendant's or legal counsel's objection to a proposed juror, made without needing to give a reason.

Personality paradox: The observation that a person's personality remains the same over time, while their behaviour can change in different situations.

Phrenology: The study of the shape and size of the cranium as a supposed indication of character and mental abilities.

Planning stage: Third stage in the OVIAR model where the cyberstalker selects the course of action.

Positive punishment: Giving something bad or undesirable to reduce the occurrence of a particular behaviour.

Positive reinforcement: Giving something good or desirable to increase the occurrence of a particular behaviour.

Post-incarceration syndrome: A cluster of institutionalised personality traits, including social–sensory disorientation and alienation.

Predatory violence: A planned or purposeful form of violence where there is no perceived threat.

Predictive validity: The extent to which a test predicts real-world behaviour.

Primary goods: Activities, experiences and situations that are intrinsically motivating and increase fulfilment and happiness.

Principle of proportionality: The idea that the punishment of a certain crime should be in proportion to the severity of the crime.

Prisonisation: The process of accepting the culture and social life of prison society.

Product test: A person may be found insane if the criminal act was a product of a mental disease.

Projection: Attributing unwanted thoughts, feelings and motives onto another person.

Pseudoscience: Claims or beliefs that are misrepresented as being derived from the use of the scientific method.

Psychological autopsy: An investigative approach to establish whether an uncertain death was the result of natural causes, suicide, accident or homicide.

Psychological closure: A comforting or satisfying feeling of finality to an event with an ambiguous ending.

Psychological resilience: The ability to mentally or emotionally cope with a crisis or to return to pre-crisis status quickly.

Psychology: The scientific study of the mind and behaviour.

Quest for significance theory: Extreme behaviour for an ideological cause is more likely under conditions that induce a search for meaning and social recognition.

Race–crime congruency bias: A tendency to condemn black men more than white men for stereotypically black crimes but to do the reverse for stereotypically white crimes.

Rational choice theory: Offenders are rational in their decision making, and despite the consequences, the benefits of committing the crime outweigh the punishment.

Rationalisation: When controversial behaviours or feelings are justified to avoid the true explanation.

Recidivism: The tendency of a convicted criminal to reoffend.

Registered intermediary: Specialists who help vulnerable people communicate more effectively during a police interview and when giving evidence at trial.

Rehabilitation theory: Directing offenders to treatment or training programmes changes that individual and keeps them from committing new offences.

Relational goal theory: Obsessive online cyberstalkers link the goal of having a relationship to higher-order goals, such as happiness and self-worth.

Relevant questions: Questions that pertain to the crime under investigation, such as 'Did you kill the victim?'

Reminiscence bump: The tendency for older adults to have increased recollection for events that occurred during their adolescence and early adulthood.

Response bias: When jurors respond to questions based on their earlier responses and respond in a predictable way.

Restoration theory: Repairing the harm caused by criminal behaviour.

Retributive perspective: Punishing offenders because they deserve to be punished.

Retributive theory of punishment: Justifies a proportional response and suffering of the offender on the basis of their voluntary decision to commit a crime.

Rumble stage: The initial signs of distress displayed in ASD before expressing intense behaviours from stimulus overload.

Sampling bias: A sample collected in such a way that it does not represent the population it was drawn from.

Scientific jury selection (SJS): The use of social science techniques and expertise to choose favourable juries during a criminal or civil trial.

Secondary trauma: Indirect exposure to a trauma through a first-hand account or narrative of a traumatic event.

Secondary victimisation: Victim-blaming behaviours and insensitive attitudes that traumatise victims of violence.

Severity of punishment: Greater intensity of punishment is more effective in reducing illicit behaviour.

Signature: A specific and identifiable action or characteristics of the suspect that reflects their emotional and psychological needs.

Silencing response: A process of psychological withdrawal where children are unintentionally silenced because the information shared is too distressing.

Slip-and-capture error: Mistakes that are made when you think you are doing one action, but you actually are doing another.

Social cognition: A field that focuses on how people process, store and apply information about other people and social situations.

Social communication impairment: A disorder characterised by difficulties with the use of verbal and nonverbal language for social purposes.

Social comparison theory: Group polarisation occurs because of our desire to gain acceptance and be perceived in a favourable way by the group.

Social desirability: The tendency to present one's self in a manner that will be viewed favourably by others.

Social identity theory: That part of an individual's self-concept which derives from knowledge of the person's membership in a social group.

Source monitoring error: A type of memory error where a specific remembered experience is incorrectly thought to be the source of the memory.

Souvenir: Items collected by the suspect from the victim to remember and relive the pleasurable elements of the crime.

Specific deterrence: The punishment should prevent the same person from committing crimes.

Specific responsivity: The idea that treatment should take into account the relevant characteristics of the individual.

Spreading activation model of semantic memory: Networks of associated ideas are linked together and spread from one node to another.

Staging: When someone who has committed a crime makes the scene look like something it is not, for example a suicide or an accident.

Statement–evidence consistency: When subjects change their statements to match the evidence, by omitting and denying factual evidence.

Static risk factors: Risk factors that predict recidivism but cannot be altered through treatment programmes.

Static security: A prison philosophy to maintain safety using an environment designed to prevent improper behaviour.

Stimming: A behavioural coping response involving repetitive and calming behaviours that can involve any of the senses.

Strategic use of evidence (SUE) framework: Presenting evidence to exploit differences between guilty and innocent subjects' strategies during interviews.

Strength of evidence: The quantity and quality of evidence presented during a trial.

Stress: An imbalance between an important or threatening physical or psychological demand and the ability to meet the demand.

Suggestive questioning: Introducing new information into an interview when the child has not already provided that information.

Sundowning: Symptoms of confusion and agitation that worsen in the late afternoon and evening and improve earlier in the day.

Sympathetic nervous system (SNS): A part of the nervous system that serves to accelerate the heart rate, constrict blood vessels and raise blood pressure.

System variables: Variables affecting the accuracy of eyewitness identifications, under control of the criminal justice system.

Task support hypothesis: The idea that situations can be created for individuals with autism that capitalise on their areas of strength – in the case of memory, creating situations that increase their ability to remember.

Terror management theory: A type of defensive human thinking and behaviour that stems from an awareness and fear of death.

Terroristic torture: Torture used as a warning by sending a message to people.

The fruit of the poisonous tree: A legal metaphor stating that evidence obtained as the result of a coerced statement is inadmissible.

Theory of mind: Understanding the mental states of others and recognising that those mental states differ from our own.

Third degree: The first degree is arrest, the second is transportation to jail and the third degree is interrogation with physical pain.

Ticking bomb scenario: A hypothetical reason to justify the use of torture.

Tip-of-the-tongue phenomenon: Failure to recall a specific word or term with awareness that they know the word or term.

Token economies: Rewarding good behaviour with symbols or points that can be exchanged for something desired.

Trait theory: The idea that people have relatively stable personality characteristics that cause individuals to behave in predictable ways.

Triggering event: The initial event that causes the cyberstalker to notice the victim in the OVIAR model.

Trophy: Any item taken from the victim that symbolises the crime.

Uncertainty–identity theory: People identify with social groups to decrease feelings of self-related uncertainty.

Unconscious transference effect: When an eyewitness to a crime misidentifies a familiar but innocent person from a police line-up.

Undoing: A suspect's attempts to symbolically reverse the murder via crime scene staging.

Utilitarian perspective: Punishing discourages future wrongful behaviour.

Variable ratio schedule: A type of operant conditioning reinforcement schedule where reward reinforcement is given after an unpredictable (variable) number of responses.

Verdict-driven juries: When juries vote early and structure the discussion around available verdict options.

Victim precipitation: A controversial theory claiming that victims sometimes initiate the actions that lead to their harm or loss.

Voir dire: A preliminary examination of a witness or a juror by a judge or legal counsel.

Voluntary false confession: When a person falsely confesses to a crime without any pressure or coercion.

Weapon focus effect: An eyewitness's concentration on a weapon to the exclusion of other details of a crime.

REFERENCES

Aamodt, M. G. and Custer, H. (2006) Who can best catch a liar? *The Forensic Examiner*, 15(1), 6–11.

Aaron, D. (1986) The First Amendment and post-verdict interviews. *Columbia Journal of Law & Society Problems*, 20, 203.

Abbasi, I. S. (2018) Social media and committed relationships: What factors make our romantic relationship vulnerable? *Social Science Computer Review*, 1–10. https://doi.org/10.1177/0894439318770609.

Abdel-Salam, S. and Sunde, H. M. (2018) Enhancing the role of correctional officers in American prisons. *Federal Sentencing Reporter*, 31(1), 67–74.

Abdollahi, A., Henthorn, C. and Pyszczynski, T. (2010) Experimental peace psychology: Priming consensus mitigates aggression against outgroups under mortality salience. *Behavioral Sciences of Terrorism and Political Aggression*, 2(1), 30–7.

Abrahimzadeh, A. (2019) My father tracked down my mother and killed her as hundreds of people witnessed. *Insight*, 2 November. Available at www.sbs.com.au/news/insight/my-father-tracked-down-my-mother-and-killed-her-as-hundreds-of-people-witnessed.

AbuDagga, A., Wolfe, S., Carome, M., Phatdouang, A. and Torrey, E. F. (2016) *Individuals with Serious Mental Illnesses in County Jails: A Survey of Jail Staff's Perspectives*. Treatment Advocacy Center.

Acar, Ö. F., Öğülmüş, S. and Boysan, M. (2019) Associations between circadian preferences, sleep quality, dissociation, post-traumatic cognitions, and post-traumatic stress disorder (PTSD) among incarcerated offenders. *Sleep and Hypnosis: A Journal of Clinical Neuroscience and Psychopathology*, 21(3), 201–19.

ACE Study (2018) *The Adverse Childhood Experiences Study*. Centers for Disease Control and Prevention, National Center for Injury Prevention and Control, Division of Violence Prevention.

Ackerman, R. and Koriat, A. (2011) Response latency as a predictor of the accuracy of children's reports. *Journal of Experimental Psychology*, 17, 406–17.

Adam, L. (2010) The science of defending sleepwalkers who kill. BBC Radio 4, 25 March. Available at news.bbc.co.uk/2/hi/health/8583408.stm.

Adams, S. (2009) Double jeopardy killer Mario Celaire jailed for life. TheTelegraph.com. Available at www.telegraph.co.uk/news/uknews/law-and-order/5734931/Double-jeopardy-killer-Mario-Celaire-jailed-for-life.html.

Adams, S. H. (1996) Statement analysis: What do suspects' words really reveal? *FBI Enforcement Bulletin*, 65(10), 12–20.

Adams, W. C. (2015) Conducting semi-structured interviews. In K. E. Newcomer, H. P. Hatry and J. S. Wholey (eds) *Handbook of Practical Program Evaluation* (4th edn, pp. 492–505). Jossey-Bass.

Adeyemi, O. E. (2019) Gender and victimization: A global analysis of vulnerability. In J. O. Ayodele (ed.) *Global Perspectives on Victimization Analysis and Prevention* (pp. 114–33). IGI Global.

Adler, F. (1973) Socioeconomic factors influencing jury verdicts. *New York University Review of Law & Social Change*, 3, 1–10.

Adler, N., Nadler, B., Eviater, Z. and Shamay-Tsoory, S. G. (2010) The relationship between theory of mind and autobiographical memory in high-functioning autism and Asperger syndrome. *Psychiatry Research*, 30, 178(1), 214–16.

Aggarwal, N. K. (2009) Neuroimaging, culture, and forensic psychiatry. *Journal of the American Academy of Psychiatry and the Law*, 37(2) 239–44.

Agneswaran, A. (2018) Exploring the experiences of registered intermediaries and police officers in UK of working with adult witnesses with intellectual disabilities. Doctoral dissertation, Manchester Metropolitan University.

Ahern, E. C., Andrews, S. J., Stolzenberg, S. N. and Lyon, T. D. (2018) The productivity of wh- prompts in child forensic interviews. *Journal of Interpersonal Violence*, 33(13), 2007–15.

Ahlgrim, B. and Terrance, C. (2018) Perceptions of cyberstalking: impact of perpetrator gender and cyberstalker/victim relationship. *Journal of Interpersonal Violence*, 0886260518784590.

Ahmed, R., Johnson, M., Caudill, C., Diedrich, N., Mains, D. and Key, A. (2019) Cons and pros: Prison education through the eyes of the prison educated, *Review of Communication*, 19(1), 69–76.

Ahonen, L. (2019) Crazy, mad, insane, or mentally ill? In L. Ahonen, *Violence and Mental Illness: An Overview* (pp. 11–20). Springer.

Aizpurua, A., Garcia-Bajos, E. and Migueles, M. (2011) False recognition and source attribution for actions of an emotional event in older and younger adults. *Experimental Aging Research*, 37, 310–29.

Alamenciak, T. (2013) Who was Sammy Yatim? *The Star*, 24 August. Available at www.thestar.com/news/crime/2013/08/24/who_was_sammy_yatim.html.

Alapack, R., Blichfeldt, M. F. and Elden, A. (2005) Flirting on the internet and the hickey: A hermeneutic. *CyberPsychology & Behavior*, 8(1), 52–61.

Alberini, C. M. and Travaglia, A. (2017) Infantile amnesia: A critical period of learning to learn and remember. *Journal of Neuroscience*, 37(24), 5783–95.

Alexander, P., Schlegel, A., Sinnott-Armstrong, W., Roskies, A. L., Wheatley, T. and Tse, P. U. (2016) Readiness potentials driven by non-motoric processes. *Consciousness and Cognition*, 39, 38–47.

Ali, P. and McGarry, J. (2020) Classifications of domestic violence and abuse. In P. Ali and J. McGarry (eds) *Domestic Violence in Health Contexts: A Guide for Healthcare Professions* (pp. 35–49). Springer.

Alison, L., Kebbell, M. and Lewis, P. (2006) Considerations for experts in assessing the credibility of re-covered memories of child sexual abuse. *Psychology, Public Policy, and Law*, 12(4), 419–41.

Alison, L., McLean, C. and Almond, L. (2007) Profiling suspects. In T. Newburn, T. Williamson and A. Wright (eds) *Handbook of Criminal Investigation* (pp. 493–576). Routledge.

Alison, L., Bennell, C., Mokros, A. and Ormerod, D. (2002) The personality paradox in offender profiling: A theoretical review of the processes involved in deriving background characteristics from crime scene actions. *Psychology, Public Policy, and Law*, 8(1), 115–35.

Alison, L., Smith, M. D., Eastman, O. and Rainbow, L. (2003) Toulmin's philosophy of argument and its relevance to offender profiling. *Psychology, Crime & Law*, 9(2), 173–83.

Alison, L., Alison, E., Noone, G., Elntib, S., Waring, S. and Christiansen, P. (2014) Whatever you say, say nothing: Individual differences in counter interrogation tactics amongst a field sample of

right wing, AQ inspired and paramilitary terrorist. *Personality and Individual Differences*, 68, 170–5.

Allen, J. J. and Anderson, C. A. (2017) Aggression and violence: Definitions and distinctions. In P. Sturmey, *The Wiley Handbook of Violence and Aggression* (pp. 1–14). Wiley Blackwell.

Allen, K. (2018) Police use Taser on 87-year-old woman cutting dandelions with a knife. CNN, 17 August. Available at www.cnn.com/2018/08/16/us/georgia-police-taser-woman-dandelions-knife/index.html.

Allison, M., Wright, A. M. and Holliday, R. E. (2010) Police officers' perceptions of older eyewitnesses. *Legal and Criminological Psychology*, 10(2), https://doi.org/10.1348/135532505X37001.

Almasy, S. and Holcombe, M. (2019) A federal offender believed to have spent the longest time in solitary confinement has died. Cnn.com, 23 May. Available at www.cnn.com/2019/05/23/us/colorado-thomas-silverstein-dies/index.html.

Almeida, I., Ramalho, A., Belmira Fernandes, M. and Guarda, R. (2019) Adult attachment as a risk factor for intimate partner violence. *Annals of Medicine*, 51(sup1), 187.

Alper, A., Durose, M. R. and Markman, J. (2018) *2018 Update on Prisoner Recidivism: A 9-Year Follow-up Period (2005–2014)*. US Department of Justice. Available at www.bjs.gov/content/pub/pdf/18upr9yfup0514.pdf.

ALRC (Australian Law Reform Commission) (1986) *Recognition of Aboriginal Customary Laws*. Report no. 31. www.alrc.gov.au/publications/report-31.

Altheide, D. L. (2009) The Columbine shootings and the discourse of fear. *American Behavioral Scientist*, 52(10), 1354–70.

Altimus, C. M. (2017) Neuroscience has the power to change the criminal justice system. *eNeuro*, 3(6), doi: 10.1523/ENEURO.0362-16.2016.

Altman, C. M., Schreiber Compo, N., McQuiston, D., Hagsand, A. V. and Cervera, J. (2018) Witnesses' memory for events and faces under elevated levels of intoxication. *Memory*, 26, 946–59.

Altschuler, D. and Bilchik, S. (2014) *Critical Elements of Juvenile Reentry in Research and Practice*. CSG Justice Center. Available at https://csgjusticecenter.org/wp-content/uploads/2014/04/4.18.14_Critical-Elements-of-Juvenile-Reentry.pdf.

Alvarez, M. J., Miller, M. K. and Bornstein, B. H. (2016) 'It will be your duty …': The psychology of criminal jury instructions. In M. K. Miller and B. H. Bornstein (eds) *Advances in Psychology and Law* (pp. 119–58). Springer.

Alzheimer's Association (2006) *Alzheimer's Disease: Guide for Law Enforcement*. Available at www.alz.org/

national/documents/SafeReturn_lawenforcement. pdf.

Alzheimer's Association (2019) Alzheimer's disease facts and figures. Available at www.alz.org/media/Documents/alzheimers-facts-and-figures-2019-r.pdf.

Amendola, K. L. and Wixted, J. T. (2015) Comparing the diagnostic accuracy of suspect identifications made by actual eyewitnesses from simultaneous and sequential lineups in a randomized field trial. *Journal of Experimental Criminology*, 11(2), 263–84.

American Bar Association (2002) *The Child Witness in Criminal Cases*. Task Force on Child Witnesses of the American Bar Association Criminal Justice Section.

Ames, D. L. and Fiske, S. T. (2015) Perceived intent motivates people to magnify observed harms. *Proceedings of the National Academy of Sciences*, 112(12), 3599–605.

Amnesty International UK (2018) Albert Woodfox freed after 43 years in solitary confinement. 12 January. Available at www.amnesty.org.uk/albert-woodfox-free-louisiana-usa-after-43-years-solitary-confinement-us.

Anand, P. and Sternthal, B. (1990) Ease of message processing as a moderator of repetition effects in advertising. *Journal of Marketing Research, 27*(3), 345–53.

Andersen, J. P. and Papazoglou, K. (2015) Compassion fatigue and compassion satisfaction among police officers: An understudied topic. *International Journal of Emergency Mental Health and Human Resilience*, 17(3), 661–3.

Anderson, C. A., Lepper, M. R. and Ross, L. (1980) Perseverance of social theories: The role of explanation in the persistence of discredited information. Journal of Personality and Social Psychology, 39, 1037–49.

Anderson, D. A. (2002) Constructing representations of Karl Spencer Lashley. *Journal of the History of the Behavioral Sciences*, 38(3), 225–45.

Anderson, J. N. (2013) The Corner House Forensic Interview Protocol: An evolution in practice for almost 25 years. *APSAC Advisor*, 4, 2–7.

Anderson, M. A., Gillig, P. M., Sitaker, M., McCloskey, K., Malloy, K. and Grigsby, N. (2003) 'Why doesn't she just leave?': A descriptive study of victim reported impediments to her safety. *Journal of Family Violence*, 18(3), 151–5.

Anderson, N. E. and Kiehl, K. A. (2020) Re-wiring guilt: How advancing neuroscience encourages strategic interventions over retributive justice. *Frontiers in Psychology*, 11. https://doi.org/10.3389/fpsyg.2020.00390.

Andrews, D. A. and Bonta, J. (2010) *The Psychology of Criminal Conduct* (5th edn). Elsevier.

Andrews, D. A., Bonta, J. and Wormith, S. (2011) The risk-need-responsivity (RNR) model: Does adding the Good Lives Model contribute to effective crime prevention? *Criminal Justice and Behavior*, 38(7), 735–55.

Andrews, S. J., Lamb, M. E. and Lyon, T. D. (2015) The effects of question repetition on responses when prosecutors and defense attorneys question children alleging sexual abuse in court. *Law and Human Behavior*, 39(6), 559–70.

Angermeyer, M., Holzinger, A., Carta, M. and Schomerus, G. (2011) Biogenetic explanations and public acceptance of mental illness: Systematic review of population studies. *British Journal of Psychiatry*, 199(5), 367–72.

Antonio, M. E. (2008) Stress and the capital jury: How male and female jurors react to serving on a murder trial. *The Justice System Journal*, 29(3), 396–407.

Antunes, G. and Hunt, L. A. (1974) The impact of certainty and severity of punishment on levels of crime in American states: An extended analysis. *Journal of Criminal Law and Criminology*, 64(4), 486–93.

Anwar, S., Bayer, P. and Hjalmarsson, R. (2018) Politics in the courtroom: Political ideology and jury decision making. *Journal of the European Economic Association*, 17(3), 834–75.

APA (American Psychiatric Association (2013a) *Diagnostic and Statistical Manual of Mental Disorders, 5th Edition: DSM-5*. APA.

APA (2013b) Specialty guidelines for forensic psychology. *American Psychologist*, 68(1), 7–19.

APA (2018) Why we're susceptible to fake news – and how to defend against it. *Skeptical Inquirer*, 42(6), 8–9.

APA (n.d.) Recovering emotionally from disaster. Available at www.apa.org/helpcenter/recoveringdisasters.aspx.

Apostolopoulos, Y., Sönmez, S., Hege, A. and Lemke, M. (2016) Work strain, social isolation and mental health of long-haul truckers. *Occupational Therapy in Mental Health*, 32(1), 50–69.

APS (Australian Psychological Society) (n.d.) Ethical guidelines on reporting abuse and neglect, and criminal activity. APS.

APSAC (American Professional Society on the Abuse of Children) (2012) *Practice Guidelines: Forensic Interviewing in Cases of Suspected Child Abuse*. APSAC.

Aransih, M. P. and Edison, R. E. (2019) The naturalness of biological movement by individuals with autism spectrum conditions: Taking neurotypical individuals' viewpoint. *Open Access Macedonian Journal of Medical Sciences*, 7(16), 2574–8.

Arble, E. P., Daugherty, A. M. and Arnetz, B. B. (2018) Models of first responder coping: Police officers as a unique population. *Stress and Health*, 34, 612–21.

Arble, E. P., Daugherty, A. M. and Arnetz, B. B. (2019) Differential effects of physiological arousal following acute stress on police officer performance in a simulated critical incident. *Frontiers in Psychology*, 10, 759. https://doi.org/10.3389/fpsyg.2019.00759.

Arble, E., Lumley, M. A., Pole, N., Blessman, J. and Arnetz, B. B. (2017) Refinement and preliminary testing of an imagery-based program to improve coping and performance and prevent trauma among urban police officers. *Journal of Police and Criminal Psychology*, 32(1), 1–10.

Arce, R., Fariña, F., Seijo, D. and Novo, M. (2015) Assessing impression management with the MMPI-2 in child custody litigation. *Assessment*, 22(6), 769–77.

Arioli, M., Crespi, C. and Canessa, N. (2018) Social cognition through the lens of cognitive and clinical neuroscience. *BioMed Research International*, 4(13), 1–14.

Arkowitz, H. and Lilienfeld, S. O. (2009) Lunacy and the full moon: Does a full moon really trigger strange behaviour? *Scientific American*, 20(1), 64–5.

Armistead-Jehle, P., Green, P., Gervais, R. O. and Hungerford, L. D. (2015) An examination of the word memory test as a measure of memory. *Applied Neuropsychology Adult*, 22(6), 415–26.

Armour, M. P. (2012) Assessing the impact of the ultimate penal sanction on homicide survivors: A two state comparison. *Marquette Law Review*, 96(1), 1–131.

Armour, M. P. and Umbreit, M. S. (2007) Ultimate penal sanction and 'closure' for survivors of homicide victims. *Marquette Law Review*, 91(1), 381–424.

Armour, M. P. and Umbreit, M. S. (2012) Survivors of homicide victims: Factors that influence their well-being. *Journal of Forensic Social Work*, 2(2/3), 74–93.

Arnetz, B. B., Nevedal, D. C., Lumley, M. A., Backman, L. and Lublin, A. (2009) Trauma resilience training for police: Psychophysiological and performance effects. *Journal of Police and Criminal Psychology*, 24(1), 1–9.

Arnsten, A. F. (2009) Stress signaling pathways that impair prefrontal cortex structure and function. *Nature Reviews Neuroscience*, 10, 410–22.

Aronoff, J., Lynn, S. J. and Malinoski, P. (2000) Are cultic environments psychologically harmful? *Clinical Psychology Review*, 20(1), 91–111.

Arrigo, B. A. and Bullock, J. L. (2007) The psychological effects of solitary confinement on offenders in supermax units: Reviewing what we know and recommending what should change. *International Journal of Offender Therapy and Comparative Criminology*, 52(6), 622–40.

Arrowood, R. B. and Cox, C. R. (2020) Terror management theory: A practical review of research and application. *Brill Research Perspectives in Religion and Psychology*, 2(1), 1–83.

Arscott, E., Morgan, R., Meakin, G. and French, J. (2017) Understanding forensic expert evaluative evidence: A study of the perception of verbal expressions of the strength of evidence. *Science & Justice*, 57(3), 221–7.

Arslan, G. (2016) Psychological maltreatment, emotional and behavioral problems in adolescents: The mediating role of resilience and self-esteem. *Child Abuse & Neglect: The International Journal*, 52, 200–9.

Artwohl, A. and Christensen, L. W. (1997) *Deadly Force Encounters: What Cops Need To Know to Mentally and Physically Prepare for and Survive a Gunfight*. Paladin Press.

Arvan, M. (2019) The dark side of morality: Group polarization and moral epistemology. *The Philosophical Forum*, 50(1), 87–115.

Asch, S. E. (1955) Opinions and social pressure. *Scientific American*, 193, 31–5.

Ask, K. and Granhag, A. (2005) Motivational sources of confirmation bias in criminal investigations: the need for cognitive closure. *Journal of Investigative Psychology and Offender Profiling*, 2(1), 43–63.

Asokan, T. V. (2007) Daniel McNaughton (1813–1865). *Indian Journal of Psychiatry*, 49(3), 223–4.

Asokan, T. V. (2016) The insanity defence: Related issues. *Indian Journal of Psychiatry*, 58(Suppl 2), S191–8.

Ateah, C. A., Secco, L. M. and Woodgate, R. L. (2003) The risks and alternatives to physical punishment with children. *Journal of Pediatric Health Care*, 17(3), 126–32.

Atkinson, A. P., Dittrich, W. H., Gemmell, A. J. and Young, A. W. (2004) Emotion perception from dynamic and static body expressions in point-light and full-light displays. *Perception*, 33(6), 717–46.

Augustyn, M. B. and McGloin, J. M. (2017) Revisiting juvenile waiver: Integrating the incapacitation experience. *Criminology*, 56(1), 1–224.

Auspurg, K., Hinz, T. and Sauer, C. (2017) Why should women get less? Evidence on the gender pay gap from multifactorial survey experiments. *American Sociological Review*, 82(1), 179–210.

Australian Institute of Criminology (2019) *Recidivism rates*. Available at https://aic.gov.au/publications/rpp/rpp107/recidivism-rates.

Australian Law Reform Commission (2015) *Traditional Rights and Freedoms: Encroachments by Commonwealth Law*. ALRC Interim Report 127.

Australian Psychological Society (n.d.) Mental impairment and fitness to stand trial. Information sheet, College of Forensic Psychologists. Available at https://groups.psychology.org.au/Assets/Files/Mental-impairment-and-ftness-to-stand-trial.pdf.

Aykan, S. and Nalçacı, E. (2018) Assessing theory of mind by humor: The Humor Comprehension and Appreciation Test (ToM-HCAT). *Frontiers in Psychology*, 9, 1470. doi:10.3389/fpsyg.2018.01470.

Azar, S. (2000) Preventing burnout in professionals and paraprofessionals who work with child abuse and neglect cases: A cognitive behavioral approach to supervision. *Journal of Clinical Psychology*, 56(5), 643–63.

Azzopardia, C., Eirichb, R., Rashb, C. L., MacDonald, S. and Madigan, S. (2019) A meta-analysis of the prevalence of child sexual abuse disclosure in forensic settings. *Child Abuse and Neglect*, 93, 291–304.

Badar, M. E. (2013) *The Concept of Mens Rea in International Criminal Law: The Case for a Unified Approach*. Bloomsbury.

Baguley, C. M., McKimmie, B. M. and Masser, B. M. (2017) Deconstructing the simplification of jury instructions: How simplifying the features of complexity affects jurors' application of instructions. *Law and Human Behavior*, 41(3), 284–304.

Baker, L. (2008) Banksy: Off the wall. *Daily Telegraph*, 28 March. Available at www.telegraph.co.uk/culture/art/3672135/Banksy-off-the-wall.html.

Baker, W. E. (2019) Emotional energy, relational energy, and organizational energy: toward a multilevel model. *Annual Review of Organizational Psychology and Organizational Behavior*, 6, 373–95.

Bala, N., Ramakrishnan, K., Lindsay, R. and Lee, K. (2005) Judicial assessment of the credibility of child witnesses. *Alberta Law Review*, 42(4), 995–1017.

Baldwin, J. (1993) Police interviewing techniques: Establishing truth or proof? *British Journal of Criminology*, 33(3), 325–52.

Bandes, S. A. (2004) Fear factor: The role of the media in covering and shaping the death penalty. *Ohio State Journal of Criminal Law*, 1, 585–97.

Bandes, S. A. (2019) Closure in the criminal courtroom: The birth and strange career of an emotion. In S. A. Bandes et al. (eds) *Research Handbook on Law and Emotion*. Edward Elgar.

Bandura, A. (1999) Moral disengagement in the perpetration of inhumanities. *Personality and Social Psychology Review*, 3(3), 193–209.

Banks, R. K. and Vogel-Sprott, M. (1965) Effect of delayed punishment on an immediately rewarded response in humans. *Journal of Experimental Psychology*, 70, 357–9.

Baranowsky, A. B. (2002) The silencing response in clinical practice: On the road to dialogue. In C. R. Figley (ed.) *Treating Compassion Fatigue* (pp. 155–70). Brunner-Routledge.

Barlow, H. (1972) Single units and sensation: A neuron doctrine for perceptual psychology? *Perception*, 1, 371–94.

Barnett, B. (2005) Perfect mother or artist of obscenity? Narrative and myth in a qualitative analysis of press coverage of the Andrea Yates murders. *Journal of Communication Inquiry*, 29(1), 9–29.

Baron-Cohen, S. (1989) The autistic child's theory of mind: a case of specific developmental delay. *Journal of Child Psychology and Psychiatry*, 30, 285–97.

Barrett, D. A., Libling, J. J. and Barkai, Y. (2019) Opening the door to jury room secrets after Peña-Rodriguez. *Litigation*, 45(4), 1–6.

Barrick, M. R. and Mount, M. K. (1991) The big five personality dimensions and job performance: A meta-analysis. *Personnel Psychology*, 44(1), 1–26.

Barry-Walsh, J. B and Mullen, P. E. (2004) Forensic aspects of Asperger's syndrome. *Journal of Forensic Psychiatry and Psychology*, 15, 96–107.

Bartlett, A., Frater, A. and Hyde, S. (2018) Suicide and the criminal justice system: A more complete picture. *The Lancet Psychiatry*, 5(2), 106–7.

Bartlett, F. C. (1932) *Remembering: A Study in Experimental and Social Psychology*. Cambridge University Press.

Bartlett, J. and Miller, C. (2012) The edge of violence: Towards telling the difference between violent and non-violent radicalization. *Terrorism and Political Violence*, 24(1), 1–21.

Bartol, C. R. and Bartol, A. M. (2013) *Criminal and Behavioral Profiling*. Sage.

Bartol, C. R. and Bartol, A. M. (2016) *Criminal Behavior: A Psychological Approach* (11th edn). Pearson.

Basile, K. C. and Saltzman, L. E. (2002) *Sexual Violence Surveillance: Uniform Definitions and Recommended Data Elements*. CDC.

Bass, C. and Wade, D. T. (2019) Malingering and factitious disorder. *Practical Neurology*, 19(2), 96–105.

Bateman, A. L. and Salfati, C. G. (2007) An examination of behavioral consistency using individual behaviors or groups of behaviors in serial homicide. *Behavioral Sciences and the Law*, 25, 527–44.

Bates, E. A. (2020) 'Walking on egg shells': A qualitative examination of men's experiences of intimate partner violence. *Psychology of Men & Masculinities*, 21(1), 13–24.

Bates, E. A. and Weare, S. (2020) Sexual violence as a form of abuse in men's experiences of female-perpetrated intimate partner violence. *Journal* of Contemporary Criminal Justice, https://doi.org/10.1177/1043986220936115.

Bauer, P. J. and Larkina, M. (2014) Childhood amnesia in the making: Different distributions of autobiographical memories in children and adults. *Journal of Experimental Psychology: General*, 143(2), 597–611.

Bauer, T. K., Bender, S., Heining, J. and Schmidt, C. M. (2013) The lunar cycle, sunspots and the frequency of births in Germany, 1920–1989. *Economics & Human Biology*, 11(4), 545–50.

Baumgartner, B. J., Bauer, L. M. and Bui, K. T. (2012) Reactions to homelessness: Social, cultural, and psychological sources of discrimination. *Psi Chi Journal of Psychological Research*, 17(1), 26–34.

Beacher, F., Daly, E., Simmons, A., Prasher, V., Morris, R. et al. (2009) Alzheimer's disease and Down's syndrome: An in vivo MRI study. *Psychological Medicine*, 39(4), 675–84.

Beauregard, E. and Proulx, J. (2016) Models of modus operandi in sexual offending: A criminological perspective. In D. P. Boer (ed.) *The Wiley Handbook on the Theories, Assessment and Treatment of Sexual Offending* (pp. 337–56). Wiley-Blackwell.

Beaver, K. M., Boccio, C., Smith, S. and Ferguson, C. J. (2019) Physical attractiveness and criminal justice processing: Results from a longitudinal sample of youth and young adults. *Psychiatry, Psychology and Law*, 26(4), 669–81.

Bebko, J. M., Rhee, T., McMorris, C. A. and Ncube, B. L. (2015) Spontaneous strategy use in children with autism spectrum disorder: the roles of metamemory and language skills. *Frontiers in Psychology*, 6(182), 1–10.

Beck, C. J., Walsh, M. E., Mechanic, M. B. and Taylor, C. S. (2010) Mediator assessment, documentation, and disposition of child custody cases involving intimate partner abuse: A naturalistic evaluation of one county's practices. *Law and Human Behaviour*, 34(3), 227–40.

Becke, M., Fuermaier, B. M., Buehren, J., Weisbrod, M., Aschenbrenner, S. et al. (2019) Utility of the Structured Interview of Reported Symptoms (SIRS-2) in detecting feigned adult attention-deficit/hyperactivity disorder. *Journal of Clinical and Experimental Neuropsychology*, 41(8), 786–802.

Beike, D. and Wirth-Beaumont, E. (2005) Psychological closure as a memory phenomenon. *Memory*, 13(6), 574–93.

Bell, B. E. and Loftus, E. (1989) Trivial persuasion in the courtroom: The power of (a few) minor details. *Journal of Personality and Social Psychology*, 56, 669–79.

Bell, S. and Eski, Y. (2016) 'Break a leg – it's all in the mind': Police officers' attitudes towards colleagues with mental health issues. *Policing: A Journal of Policy and Practice*, 10(2), 95–101.

Bellamy, K., Dowse, R., Ostini, R., Martini, N. and Kairuz, T. (2019) Preferences of resettled refugees on pictograms describing common symptoms of illness. *Journal of Immigrant & Minority Health*, 22(1), 216–19.

Benford, P. and Standen, P. J. (2010) The use of email-facilitated interviewing with higher functioning autistic people participating in a grounded theory study. *International Journal of Social Research Methodology*, 14(5), 353–68.

Benjamin, L. T. and Baker, D. B. (2004) The psychological profession in the 21st century. In L. T. Benjamin and D. B. Baker, *From Séance to Science: A History of the Profession of Psychology in America* (pp. 200–04). Wadsworth/Thomson Learning.

Bennell, C., Mugford, R., Ellingwood, H. and Woodhams, J. (2014) Linking crimes using behavioural clues: Current levels of linking accuracy and strategies for moving forward. *Journal of Investigative Psychology and Offender Profiling*, 11(1), 29–56.

Bennell, C., Snook, B., Macdonald, S., House, J. C. and Taylor, P. J. (2012) Computerized crime linkage systems: A critical review and research agenda. *Criminal Justice and Behavior*, 39, 620–34.

Bennett, M., Webster, A. A., Goodall, E. and Rowland, S. (2018) Challenging the public's perception of life on autism spectrum: The impact of the vaccination myth. In M. Bennett et al. (eds) *Life on the Autism Spectrum: Translating Myths and Misconceptions into Positive Futures* (pp. 37–60). Springer.

Bennett, T. and Wright, R. (1984) *Burglars on Burglary: Prevention and the Offender*. Gower.

Bennhold, K. (2015) How Islamic State lured three UK teenagers. *The Irish Times*, 18 August. Available at www.irishtimes.com/news/world/middle-east/how-islamic-state-lured-three-uk-teenagers-1.2320836.

Bennion, E. (2015) Banning the bing: Why extreme solitary confinement is cruel and far too usual punishment. *Indiana Law Journal*, 90(2), 741–86.

Ben-Porath, Y. S. and Tellegen, A. (2011) *Minnesota Multiphasic Personality Inventory-2-Restructured Form: Manual for Administration, Scoring and Interpretation*. University of Minnesota Press.

Ben-Shakhar, G. (1991) Clinical judgment and decision-making in CQT-polygraph: A comparison with other pseudoscientific applications in psychology. *Integrative Physiological and Behavioral Sciences*, 26(3), 232–40.

Ben-Shakhar, G. (2002) A critical review of the Control Questions Test (CQT). In M. Keiner (ed.) *Handbook of Polygraph Testing* (pp. 103–26). Academic Press.

Ben-Shakhar, G. and Furedy, J. J. (1990) The detection of deception: A psychophysiological, specific-effects-oriented perspective. In G. Ben-Shakhar and J. J. Furedy, *Theories and Applications in the Detection of Deception* (pp. 92–100). Springer.

Bergemann, P. (2017) Denunciation and social control. *American Sociological Review*, 82(2), 384–406.

Bergen, D., van Feddes, A. R., Pels, T. and Doosje, B. (2015) Collective identity factors and the attitude to ethnic or religious in-group violence in Muslim youth of Turkish and Moroccan descent. *International Journal of Intercultural Relations*, 47, 89–100.

Bering, J. (2019) Conversations with my dead mother: Why we see signs and omens in everyday events. *Skeptic*, 24(2), 16–19.

Berlow, A. (2007) What happened in Norfolk? *The New York Times Magazine*, 19 August. Available at www.nytimes.com/2007/08/19/magazine/19Norfolk-t.html.

Bernasco, W. (2010) A sentimental journey to crime: Effects of residential history on crime location choice. *Criminology*, 48(2), 389–416.

Berresheim, A. and Weber, A. (2003) Structured witness interviewing and its effectiveness. *Kriminalistik*, 57, 757–71.

Besnard, D., Le Gall, V., Chauviré, G., Aubin, F. and Etcharry-Bouyx, P. and Allain, P. (2017) Discrepancy between social and nonsocial decision-making under uncertainty following prefrontal lobe damage: The impact of an interactionist approach. *Social Neuroscience*, 12(4), 430–47.

Bessel, R. (2018) Assessing violence in the modern world. *Historical Reflections/Réflexions Historiques*, 44(1), 66–77.

Best, G., Hodgeon, J. and Street, C. (2019) How contemporary theory informs lie detection accuracy and bias. *Crime Security and Society*, 1(2). DOI: 10.5920/css.555.

Best, J. (1999) *Random Violence: How we Talk about New Crimes and New Victims*. University of California Press.

Bethell, C. D., Newacheck, P., Hawes, E. and Halfon, N. (2014) Experiences: Assessing the impact on health and school engagement and the mitigating role of resilience. *Health Affairs (Project Hope)*, 33(12), 2106–15.

Betts, K. R. and Hinsz, V. B. (2010) Collaborative group memory: Processes, performance, and techniques for improvement. *Social and Personality Psychology Compass*, 4(2), 119–30.

Bhona, F. M., Gebara, C. F., Noto, A. R., Vieira, M. D. and Lourenço, L. M. (2019) Socioeconomic factors and intimate partner violence: A household survey. *Trends in Psychology*, 27(1), 205–18.

Bietti, L. M., Tilston, O. and Bangerter, A. (2019) Storytelling as adaptive collective sensemaking. *Topics in Cognitive Science*, 11(4), 710–32.

Billings, J. F., Taylor, T. Burns, J., Corey, D. L. and Garven, S. and Wood, J. (2007) Can reinforcement induce children to falsely incriminate themselves? *Law and Human Behavior*, 31, 125–39.

Binder, A. and Scharf, P. (1980) The violent police-citizen encounter. *The Annals of the American Academy of Political and Social Science*, 452(1), 111–21.

Birch, P., Vickers, M. H., Kennedy, M. and Galovic, S. (2017) Wellbeing, occupational justice and police practice: an 'affirming environment'? *Police Practice and Research*, 18(1), 26–36.

Bird, L., Gretton, M., Cockerell, R. and Heathcote, A. (2019) The cognitive load of narrative lies. *Applied Cognitive Psychology*, 33(5), 936–42.

Bjorklund, D. F. (2000) *False-memory Creation in Children and Adults: Theory, Research, and Implications*. Lawrence Erlbaum.

Black, D. W. (2015) The natural history of antisocial personality disorder. *Canadian Journal of Psychiatry*, 60(7), 309–14.

Black, M. C., Basile, K. C., Breiding, M. J., Smith, S. G., Walters, M. L. et al. (2011) *The National Intimate Partner and Sexual Violence Survey (NISVS): 2010 Summary Report*. National Center for Injury Prevention and Control, CDC.

Blackburn, E. (2002) *Broken Lives*. Hardie Grant Publishing.

Blair, I. V., Judd, C. M. and Chapleau, K. M. (2004) The influence of Afrocentric facial features in criminal sentencing. *Psychological Science*, 15(10), 674–9.

Blair, J. P. and Schweit, K. W. (2014) *A Study of Active Shooter Incidents, 2000–2013*. Texas State University and Federal Bureau of Investigation, US Department of Justice.

Blair, R. (2016) The neurobiology of impulsive aggression. *Journal of Child Adolescent Psychopharmacology*, 26(1), 4–9.

Blake, G. A., Ogloff, J. R. and Chen, W. S. (2019) Meta-analysis of second generation competency to stand trial assessment measures: Preliminary findings. *International Journal of Law and Psychiatry*, 64, 238–49.

Blank, R. H. (1999) *Brain Policy: How the New Neuroscience Will Change our Lives and Politics*. Georgetown University Press.

Blankenship, B. T. (2007) The stress process in physical education. *Journal of Physical Education, Recreation & Dance*, 78(6), 39–44.

Bleakley, P. (2019) A thin-slice of institutionalised police brutality: A tradition of excessive force in the Chicago Police Department. *Criminal Law Forum*, 30(4), 425–49.

Blizard, R. A. and Shaw, M. (2019) Lost-in-the-mall: False memory or false defense? *Journal of Child Custody*, 16(1), 20–41.

Block, S., Foster, M. E., Pierce, M. W., Berkoff, M. C., Runyan, D. K. (2013) Multiple forensic interviews during investigations of child sexual abuse: A cost-effectiveness analysis. *Applied Developmental Science*, 17(4), 174–83.

Blue, L. and Hirschhorn, R. B. (2009) The psychology of women's influence on juries. *The Advocate*, 49, 47–9.

Boag, S. (2006) Freudian repression, the common view, and pathological science. *Review of General Psychology*, 10(1), 74–86.

Boal, M. and Ellison, M. (producers) and Bigelow, K. (director) (2012) *Zero Dark Thirty* [Motion Picture]. Columbia Pictures.

Bocij, P. (2005) Reactive stalking: A new perspective on victimisation. *Journal of Forensic Practice*, 7(1), 23–34.

Bocij, P. (2018) OVIAR: Towards a model for cyberstalking intervention and reduction. *International Journal of Emerging Trends in Social Sciences*, 4(2), 58–66.

Bocij, P. and McFarlane, L. (2003) Cyberstalking: The technology of hate. *The Police Journal*, 76(3), 204–21.

Bocij, P., Griffiths, M. D. and McFarlane, L. (2002) Cyberstalking: A new challenge for criminal law. *The Criminal Lawyer*, 122, 3–5.

Bodenhorn, A. (2016) Prison crowding, recidivism, and early release in early Rhode Island. *Explorations in Economic History*, 59, 55–74.

Bodine, L. (2014) $7.75 million settlement for father wrongly jailed for daughter's murder. *The Trial Lawyer*, 19 March. Available at www.thenationaltriallawyers.org/2014/03/7-75-settlement-father-wrongly-jailed-murder/.

Bogaard, G., Meijer, E. H., Vrij, A. and Merckelbach, H. (2016) Strong, but wrong: Lay people's and police officers' beliefs about verbal and nonverbal cues to deception. *PloS One*, 11(6), e0156615. doi: 10.1371/journal.pone.0156615.

Bohl-Penrod, N. K. and Clark, D. W. (2017) Peer support in public safety organizations. In C. L. Mitchell and E. H. Dorian (eds) *Police Psychology and its Growing Impact on Modern Law Enforcement* (pp. 237–50). IGI Global.

Boire, R. G. (2000) On cognitive liberty. *Journal of Cognitive Liberties*, 1, 7–13.

Boivin, R. (2017) Correlates of subject(ive) resistance in police use-of-force situations. *Policing: An International Journal of Police Strategies & Management*, 40(4), 719–32.

Bok, S. (1989) *Secrets: On the Ethics of Concealment and Revelation*. Vintage.

Bok, S. (1999) *Lying: Moral Choice in Public and Private Life*. Vintage.

Bonach, K. and Heckert, A. (2012) Predictors of secondary traumatic stress among children's advocacy center forensic interviewers. *Journal of Child Sex Abuse*, 21(3), 295–314.

Bond, C. F. and DePaulo, B. M. (2006) Accuracy of deception judgments. *Personality and Social Psychology Review*, 10, 214–34.

Bond, C. F., Levine, T. R. and Hartwig, M. (2015) New findings in nonverbal lie detection. In P. A. Granhag, A. Vrij and B. Verschuere (eds) *Deception Detection: Current Challenges and New Directions* (pp. 37–58). Wiley-Blackwell.

Bonicalzi, S. and Haggard, P. (2019) Responsibility between neuroscience and criminal law: The control component of criminal liability. *Rivista internazionale di Filosofia e Psicologia*, 10(2), 103–19.

Bonkiewicz, O. L. (2019) Notes from the field: Peer support – a valuable tool in assisting mental health consumers after a crisis. Available from https://nij.ojp.gov/topics/articles/notes-field-peer-support-valuable-tool-assisting-mental-health-consumers-after.

Bonn, S. A. (2014) *Why We Love Serial Killers: The Curious Appeal of the World's Most Savage Murderers*. Skyhorse.

Bonn, S. A. (2015) Is criminal profiling a science, art, or magic? *Psychology Today*, 4 May. Available at www.psychologytoday.com/us/blog/wicked-deeds/201505/is-criminal-profiling-science-art-or-magic.

Bonnie, R. J. (1983) The moral basis of the insanity defense. *American Bar Association Journal*, 69(2), 194–7.

Bonta, J. and Andrews, D. A. (2007) Risk-need-responsivity model for offender assessment and rehabilitation. *Rehabilitation*, 6(1), 1–22.

Bonta, J. and Wormith, J. S. (2018) Adult offender assessment and classification in custodial settings. In J. D. Wooldredge and P. Smith (eds) *The Oxford Handbook of Prisons and Imprisonment* (pp. 397–424). Oxford University Press.

Boone, K. B. (2011) Somatoform disorders, factitious disorder, and malingering. In M. R. Schoenberg and J. G. Scott (eds) *The Little Black Book of Neuropsychology* (pp. 551–66). Springer.

Booty, M., O'Dwyer, J., Webster, D., McCourt, A. and Crifasi, C. (2019) Describing a 'mass shooting': The role of databases in understanding burden. *Injury Epidemiology*, 6(1), 47.

Bornstein, B. H. (1999) The ecological validity of jury simulations: Is the jury still out? *Law and Human Behavior*, 23(1), 75–91.

Bornstein, B. H. and Greene, E. (2011) Jury decision making: Implications for and from psychology.

Current Directions in Psychological Science, 20(1), 63–7.

Bornstein, B. H. and McCabe, S. G. (2005) Jurors of the absurd? The role of consequentiality in jury simulation research. *Florida State University Law Review*, 32, 443–67.

Bornstein, B. H., Golding, J. M., Neuschatz, J. Kimbrough, C., Reed, K. et al. (2017) Mock juror sampling issues in jury simulation research: A meta-analysis. *Law and Human Behavior*, 41(1), 13–28.

Boroditsky, L. and Gaby, A. (2010) Remembrances of times east: Absolute spatial representations of time in an Australian Aboriginal community. *Psychological Science*, 21(11), 1635–39.

Borum, R. and Strentz, T. (1992) The borderline personality. *FBI Law Enforcement Bulletin,* 61, 6–10.

Boss, P. (2010) The trauma and complicated grief of ambiguous loss. *Pastoral Psychology,* 59(2), 137–45.

Boss, P. (2018) Building resilience: The example of ambiguous loss. In B. Huppertz, *Approaches to Psychic Trauma: Theory and Practice*, Rowman & Littlefield.

Botelho, G. (2012) What happened the night Trayvon Martin died. CNN.com, 23 May. Available at www.cnn.com/2012/05/18/justice/florida-teen-shooting-details/index.html.

Bottoms, B.L., Quas, J.A. and Davis, S.L. (2007) The influence of the interviewer provided social support on children's suggestibility, memory and disclosures. In M. E. Pipe, M. E. Lamb, Y. Orbach and A. C. Cederborg (eds) *Child Sexual Abuse: Disclosure, Delay, and Denial* (pp. 135–57). Erlbaum.

Boudry, M. and Braeckman, J. (2012) How convenient! The epistemic rationale of self-validating belief systems. *Philosophical Psychology*, 25(3), 341–64.

Bouhana, N., Johnson, S. D. and Porter, M. (2016) Consistency and specificity in burglars who commit prolific residential burglary: Testing the core assumptions underpinning behavioral crime linkage. *Legal and Criminological Psychology*, 21(1), 77–94.

Bowers, W. J. (1994) The capital jury project: Rationale, design, and preview of early findings. *Indiana Law Journal*, 70, 1043–102.

Bowers, W. J. (1996) The capital jury: Is it tilted toward death? *Judicature*, 79(5), 220–3.

Bowler, D. M., Gaigg, S. B. and Gardiner, J. M. (2008) Effects of related and unrelated context on recall and recognition by adults with high-functioning autism spectrum disorder. *Neuropsychologia*, 46(4), 993–9.

Bowler, D. M., Gaigg, S. B. and Gardiner, J. M. (2015) Brief report: The role of task support in the spatial and temporal source memory of adults with autism spectrum disorder. *Journal of Autism and Developmental Disorders*, 45(8), 2613–17.

Bowmaker, J. K. (1998) Visual pigments and molecular genetics of color blindness. *News in Physiological Sciences*, 13, 63–9.

Brady, P. Q. (2017) Crimes against caring: Exploring the risk of secondary traumatic stress, burnout, and compassion satisfaction among child exploitation investigators. *Journal of Police and Criminal Psychology*, 32(4), 305–18.

Brand, B. L., Webermann, A. R., Snyder, B. L. and Kaliush, P. R. (2019) Detecting clinical and simulated dissociative identity disorder with the Test of Memory Malingering. *Psychological Trauma: Theory, Research, Practice, and Policy*, 11(5), 513–20.

Brasher, K. S., Dew, A. B., Kilminster, S. and Bridger, R. S. (2009) Occupational stress in submariners: The impact of isolated and confined work on psychological well-being. *Ergonomics*, 53(3), 305–13.

Braun, K. (2017) Yesterday is history, tomorrow is a mystery: The fate of the Australian jury system in the age of social media dependency. *University of New South Wales Law Journal*, 40(40), 1634–62.

Breiding, M., Basile, K. C., Smith, S. G., Black, M. C. and Mahendra, R. R. (2015) *Intimate Partner Violence Surveillance: Uniform Definitions and Recommended Data Elements*. Version 2.0. CDC.

Brett, A. S. and Beary, P. M. (1986) Predictive power of the polygraph: Can the 'lie detector' really detect liars? *The Lancet*, 1(8480), 544–7.

Breu, D. L. and Brook, B. (2007) 'Mock' mock juries: A field experiment on the ecological validity of jury simulations. *Law & Psychology Review*, 31, 77–92.

Brewer, N. (2006) Uses and abuses of eyewitness identification confidence. *Legal and Criminological Psychology*, 11, 3–23.

Brewer, N., Weber, N. and Guerin, N. (2019) Police lineups of the future? *American Psychologist*, 75(1), 76–91.

Brewer, N., Weber, N., Wootton, D. and Lindsay, D. S. (2012) Identifying the bad guy in a lineup using confidence judgments under deadline pressure. *Psychological Science*, 23(10), 1208–14.

Brezis, R. S. (2015) Memory integration in the autobiographical narratives of individuals with autism. *Frontiers in Human Neuroscience*, 9(76). https://doi.org/10.3389/fnhum.2015.00076.

Bride, B. E. (2007) Prevalence of secondary traumatic stress among social workers. *Social Work*, 52(1), 63–70.

Brody, J. E. (1996) When can killers claim sleepwalking as a legal defense? *The New York Times*, 16 January. Available at www.nytimes.com/1996/01/16/science/when-can-killers-claim-sleepwalking-as-a-legal-defense.html.

Broeder, D. (1958) The University of Chicago Jury Project. *Nebraska Law Review*, 38, 744–60.

Brogaard, B. and Marlow, K. (2012) Sleep driving and sleep killing. *Psychology Today*, 13 December. Available at www.psychologytoday.com/us/blog/the-superhuman-mind/201212/sleep-driving-and-sleep-killing.

Brook, M. (2017) Structured approaches to violence risk assessment: A critical review. *Psychiatric Annals*, 47(9), 454–9.

Brooks, T. (2017) The right to trial by jury. In T. Brooks (ed.) *The Right to a Fair Trial* (pp. 83–98). Routledge.

Brotto, G. L., Sinnamon, G. and Petherick, W. (2017) Victimology and predicting victims of personal violence. In W. Petherick and G. Sinnamon (eds) *The Psychology of Criminal and Antisocial Behavior: Victim and Offender Perspectives* (pp. 79–144). Academic Press.

Brower, M. C. and Price, B. H. (2001) Neuropsychiatry of frontal lobe dysfunction in violent and criminal behavior: A critical review. *Journal Neurology Neurosurgery Psychiatry*, 71(6), 720–6.

Brown, J., Haun, J., Zapf, P. A. and Aiken, T. (2018) FASD and Competency to Stand Trial (CST): An exploratory review. In E. Jonsson, S. Clarren and I. Binnie (eds) *Ethical and Legal Perspectives in Fetal Alcohol Spectrum Disorders (FASD)* (Ch. 12). Springer.

Brown, M., Rodriguez, D. N., Gretak, A. P. and Berry, M. A. (2017) Preliminary evidence for how the behavioral immune system predicts juror decision-making. *Evolutionary Psychological Science*, 3(4), 325–34.

Brown, S. R. and Beekman, D. (2013) Juror B37 says George Zimmerman feared for his life in his fatal encounter with Trayvon Martin. *Daily News*, 16 July.

Brubacher, S. P., Roberts, K. P. and Powell, M. (2011) Effects of practicing episodic versus scripted recall on children's subsequent narratives of a repeated event. *Psychology, Public Policy, and Law*, 17(2), 286–314.

Brucia, E., Cordova, M. J. and Ruzek, J. I. (2017) Critical incident interventions: Crisis response and debriefing. In C. L. Mitchell and E. H. Dorian, *Police Psychology and Its Growing Impact on Modern Law Enforcement* (pp. 119–42). IGI Global.

Bruck, M., Ceci, S. J., Francoer, E. and Barr, R. J. (1995) I hardly cried when I got my shot! Influencing children's reports about a visit to their pediatrician. *Child Development*, 66, 193–208.

Bruck, M., Ceci, S. J., Melnyk, L. and Finkelberg, D. (1999) The effect of interviewer bias on the accuracy of children's reports and interviewer's reports. Paper presented at the biennial meeting of the Society for Research in Child Development. Albuquerque.

Bruns, B. (2019) Changes in workplace heterogeneity and how they widen the gender wage gap. *American Economic Journal: Applied Economics*, 11(2), 74–113.

Bryant, R. A. (2011) Acute stress disorder as a predictor of posttraumatic stress disorder: A systematic review. *Journal of Clinical Psychiatry*, 72(2), 233–9.

Bryant, R. A. (2018) The current evidence for acute stress disorder. *Current Psychiatry Reports*, 20(12), 111. DOI: 10.1007/s11920-018-0976-x.

Buckenmaier, J., Dimant, E., Posten, A. and Ulrich, S. (2019) Efficient Institutions and Effective Deterrence: On Timing and Uncertainty of Punishment, PPE Working Papers 0010. Available at http://dx.doi.org/10.2139/ssrn.3300563.

Budworth, B., Ryan, T. and Bartels, L. (2017) Reigniting the lamp: The case for including people who are blind or deaf as jurors. *University of Western Australia Law Review*, 42(2), 29–55.

Bufacchi, V. and Arrigo, M. J. (2006) Torture, terrorism and the state: A refutation of the ticking-bomb argument. *Journal of Applied Philosophy*, 23, 355–73.

Bull, R. (2010) The investigative interviewing of children and other vulnerable witnesses: Psychological research and working/professional practice. *Legal and Criminological Psychology*, 15, 5–23.

Bull, R. (2011) The investigative interviewing of children and other vulnerable witnesses: Psychological research and working/professional practice. *Legal and Criminological Psychology*, 15(1), 1–157.

Bull, R. and Milne, R. (2004) Attempts to improve the police interviewing of suspects. In G. D. Lassiter (ed.) *Interrogations, Confessions, and Entrapment* (pp. 182–96). Kluwer Academic.

Bullock, K. and Garland, J. (2018) Police officers, mental (ill-) health and spoiled identity. *Criminology & Criminal Justice*, 18(2), 173–89.

Bulwa, D. and Swan, R. (2018) 10 years since Oscar Grant's death: What happened at Fruitvale Station? *The San Francisco Chronicle*, 28 December. Available at www.sfchronicle.com/bayarea/article/10-years-since-Oscar-Grant-s-death-What-13489585.php.

Burdon, W. M., St. De Lore, J., Dang, J. Warda, U. S. and Prendergast, M. L. (2013) Psychosocial functioning among inmates in prison-based drug treatment: Results from Project BRITE. *Journal of Experimental Criminology*, 9(1), 45–64.

Burgess, A. W. (2017) *Victimology: Theories and Applications*. Jones & Bartlett Learning.

Burgoon, J. K. (2018) Microexpressions are not the best way to catch a liar. *Frontiers in Psychology*, 9, 1672, https://doi.org/10.3389/fpsyg.2018.

Burka, P. (1986) Madman on the tower: Charles Whitman 20 years later. *Texas Monthly*, August, 109–69.

Bush, J., Glick, B., Taymans, J. and Guevara, M. (2011) *Thinking for a Change: Integrated Cognitive Behavior Change Program, Version 3.1.* US Department of Justice, National Institute of Corrections.

Büssing, A. and Glaser, J. (2000) Four-stage process model of the core factors of burnout: The role of work stressors and work-related resources. *Work & Stress*, 14(4), 329–46.

Butcher, J. N., Dahlstrom, W. G., Graham, J. R., Tellegen, A. and Kaemmer, B. (1989) *Minnesota Multiphasic Personality Inventory –2 (MMPI-2): Manual for Administration and Scoring.* University of Minnesota Press.

Butler, E., Fukurai, H., Dimitrius, J. and Krooth, R. (2001) *Anatomy of the McMartin Child Molestation Case.* University Press of America.

Cahill, L. and Alkireb, M. T. (2003) Epinephrine enhancement of human memory consolidation: Interaction with arousal at encoding. *Neurobiology of Learning and Memory*, 79(2), 194–8.

Cai, W., Zhang, Q., Fuyin, H., Wei, G., Tang, T. and Liu, C. (2014) The reliability and validity of the rating scale of criminal responsibility for mentally disordered offenders. *Forensic Science International*, 236, 146–50.

Cammiss, S. (2006) 'He goes off and I think he took the child': Narrative (re) production in the courtroom. *King's Law Journal*, 17(1), 71–95.

Camp, D. S., Raymond, G. A. and Church, R. M. (1967) Temporal relationship between response and punishment. *Journal of Experimental Psychology*, 74(1), 114–23.

Campbell, J., Chao, B., Robertson, C. and Yokum, D. V. (2015) Countering the plaintiff's anchor: Jury simulations to evaluate damages arguments. *Iowa Law Review*, 101, 543–71.

Campbell, S. M., Ulrich, C. M. and Grady, C. (2018) A broader understanding of moral distress. In C. M. Ulrich and C. Grady (eds) *Moral Distress in the Health Professions* (pp. 59–77). Springer.

Campos, L. and Alonso-Quecuty, M. L. (1999) The cognitive interview: Much more than simply 'try again'. *Psychology, Crime & Law*, 5(1/2), 47–59.

Can, S. N. and Saribas, D. (2019) An argumentative tool for facilitating critical evaluation. *Science & Education*, 28(6/7), 669–87.

Candel, I., Merckelbach, H., Loyen, S. and Reyskens, H. (2005) 'I hit the Shift-key and then the computer crashed': Children and false admissions. *Personality and Individual Differences*, 38(6), 1381–7.

Cannell, M. (2017) Unmasking the Mad Bomber. *Smithsonian Magazine*, April. Available at www.smithsonianmag.com/history/unmasking-the-mad-bomber-180962469/.

Cannon, W. B. (1932) *The Wisdom of the Body.* W. W. Norton.

Canter, D. V. (1994) *Criminal Shadows: Inside the Mind of the Serial Killer.* HarperCollins.

Canter, D. V. (2004) Offender profiling and investigative psychology. *Journal of Investigative Psychology and Offender Profiling*, 1, 1–15.

Canter, D. V. and Larkin, P. (1993) The environmental range of serial rapists. *Journal of Environmental Psychology*, 13(1), 63–9.

Canter, D. V. and Youngs, D. (2009) *Investigative Psychology: Offender Profiling and the Analysis of Criminal Action.* John Wiley & Sons.

Canter, D. V. and Youngs, D. (2017) *Principles of Geographical Offender Profiling.* Routledge.

Canter, D. V., Alison, L. J., Alison, E. and Wentink, N. (2004) The organized/disorganized typology of serial murder: Myth or model? *Psychology, Public Policy, and Law*, 10(3), 293–320.

Canter, D. V., Coffey, T., Huntley, M. and Missen, C. (2000) Predicting serial killers home base using a decision-support system. *Journal of Quantitative Criminology*, 16(4), 457–78.

Cardinali, P., Migliorini, L., Giribone, F., Bizzi, F. and Cavanna, D. (2018) Domestic violence in separated couples in Italian context: Communalities and singularities of women and men experiences. *Frontiers in Psychology*, 9, 1602. https://doi.org/10.3389/fpsyg.2018.01602.

Carlson, C. A. and Carlson, M. A. (2014) An evaluation of perpetrator distinctiveness, weapon presence, and lineup presentation using ROC analysis. *Journal of Applied Research in Memory and Cognition*, 3, 45–53.

Carlson, C. A., Gronlund, S. D. and Clark, S. E. (2008) Lineup composition, suspect position, and the sequential lineup advantage. *Journal of Experimental Psychology: Applied*, 14, 118–28.

Carr, N. (2010) Chaos theory. *Wired Magazine*, 18 June, 112–18.

Carr, W. A., Rosenfeld, B. and Rotter, M. (2019) Criminal thinking as a risk factor for psychiatric inpatient aggression. *International Journal of Forensic Mental Health*, 18(4), 389–99.

Carroll, J. and Weaver, F. (2018) Shoplifters' perceptions of crime opportunities: A process-tracing study. In M. Scott, *The Reasoning Criminal: Rational Choice Perspectives on Offending* (Ch. 2). Routledge.

Carson, D. and Bull, R. (2003) *Handbook of Psychology in Legal Contexts.* Wiley.

Carter, Z. A. (2015) Married and previously married men and women perceptions of communication on Facebook with the opposite sex: How communicating through Facebook can be damaging to marriages. Doctoral dissertation.

Carvalho, H., Chamberlen, A. and Duff, A. (eds) (2019) The problem of punishment: Renewing critique, *Social & Legal Studies*, 28(1), 3–9.

Casciani, D. (2017) Sex offender treatment in prison led to more offending. BBC News, 30 June. Available at www.bbc.com/news/uk-40460637.

Catalano, G., Houston, S. H., Catalano, M. C., Butera, A. S., Jennings, S. M. and Hakala, M. S. (2003) Anxiety and depression in hospitalized patients in resistant organism isolation. *Southern Medical Journal*, 96(2), 141–51.

Caton, R. F., Golding, S. L. and Fincham, F. D. (1987) Implicit theories of criminal responsibility: Decision making and the insanity defense. *Law and Human Behavior*, 11(3), 207–32.

Cattell, J. M. (1895) Measurements of the accuracy of recollection. *Science*, 2(49), 761–66.

CDC (Centers for Disease Control and Prevention) (2012) Adverse Childhood Experiences (ACEs). CDC. Available at www.cdc.gov/ace/.

CDC (2014) *Understanding Intimate Partner Violence Fact Sheet*. Available at www.cdc.gov/ViolencePrevention/pdf/IPV-FactSheet.pdf.

Chadha, K., Steiner, L., Vitak, J. and Ashktorab, Z. (2020) Women's responses to online harassment. *International Journal of Communication*, 14, 239–57.

Chaiken, J., Chaiken, M. and Rhodes, W. (1994) Predicting violent behavior and classifying violent offenders. *Understanding and Preventing Violence*, 4, 217–95.

Chalfin, A. and McCrary, J. (2017) Criminal deterrence: A review of the literature. *Journal of Economic Literature*, 55(1), 5–48.

Chalmers, J. and Leverick, F. (2018) *Methods of Conveying Information to Jurors: An Evidence Review*. Scottish Government.

Chambon, V. and Bigenwald, A. (2019) Criminal responsibility and neuroscience: No revolution yet. *Frontiers in Psychology*, 10, 1406. https://doi.org/10.3389/fpsyg.2019.01406.

Chan, H. C. and Sheridan, L. (2019) Who are the stalking victims? Exploring the victimization experiences and psychosocial characteristics of young male and female adults in Hong Kong. *Journal of Interpersonal Violence*, 0886260519889938.

Chan, O. (2015) *Understanding Sexual Homicide Offenders: An Integrated Approach*. Springer.

Chancellor, A. S. and Graham, G. D. (2014) Staged crime scenes: crime scene clues to suspect misdirection of the investigation. *Investigative Science Journal*, 6(1), 19–34.

Chang, E. C., Yu, E. A., Kahle, E. R., Du, Y., Chang, O. D. et al. (2018) The relationship between domestic partner violence and suicidal behaviors in an adult community sample: examining hope agency and pathways as protective factors. *Violence against Women*, 24(12), 1399–412.

Chapman, M., Collins, S., Flygare, C., Hunt, D., Kuck-Jalbert, S. et al. (2010) *Adam II: 2009 Annual Report*. Office of National Drug Control. Washington, DC.

Chatterjee, R., Doerfler, P., Orgad, H., Havron, S., Palmer, J. et al. (2018) The spyware used in intimate partner violence. In *2018 IEEE Symposium on Security and Privacy (SP)* (pp. 441–58). IEEE.

Chaudhari, N. K., Mori, R., Garg, S., Rathwa, V. and Shah, J. (2018) Lunar phases and suicide: A prospective study. *International Journal of Medical Toxicology & Legal Medicine*, 21(1/2), 1–2.

Chen, Y. and Zhao, H. (2019) Post-traumatic stress disorder: Relationship to traumatic brain injury and approach to forensic psychiatry evaluation. *Journal of Forensic Science and Medicine*, 5(1), 33–9.

Cheol-Hong, M. (2017) Automatic detection and labeling of self-stimulatory behavioral patterns in children with autism spectrum disorder. Engineering in Medicine and Biology Society 39th Annual International Conference of the IEEE, 279-82. DOI: 10.1109/EMBC.2017.8036816.

Cherry, E. C. (1953) Some experiments on the recognition of speech, with one and with two ears. *Journal of the Acoustical Society of America*, 25(5), 975–9.

Cherry, K. and Mattiuzzi, P. G. (2010) *The Everything Psychology Book: Explore the Human Psyche and Understand Why We Do The Things We Do*. Simon and Schuster.

Chifflet, P. (2015) Questioning the validity of criminal profiling: An evidence-based approach. *Australian and New Zealand Journal of Criminology*, 48, 238–55.

Child, J. (2019) Defence of a basic voluntary act requirement in criminal law from philosophies of action. *New Criminal Law Review*, 24(1), 1–30.

Choi, E. U. and Hogg, M. A. (2020) Self-uncertainty and group identification: A meta-analysis. *Group Processes & Intergroup Relations*, 23(4), 483–501.

Choi, K., Lee, J. L. and Chun, Y. T. (2017) Voice phishing fraud and its modus operandi. *Security Journal*, 30(2), 454–66.

Choi, V. K., Jackson, J. C. and Gelfand, M. J. (2018) The role of entitativity in perpetuating cycles of violence. *Behavioural and Brain Sciences*, 41. DOI: https://doi.org/10.1017/S0140525X18002042.

Chóliz, M. (2010) Experimental analysis of the game in pathological gamblers: Effect of the immediacy of the reward in slot machines. *Journal of Gambling Studies*, 26(2), 249–56.

Chopra, S. R. and Ogloff, J. R. (2000) Evaluating jury secrecy: Implications for academic research and juror stress. *Criminal Law Quarterly*, 44, 190–222.

Christiansen, J. R. (1987) Testimony of child witnesses: Fact, fantasy, and the influence of pretrial interviews. *Washington Law Review*, 62(4), 705–21.

Christie, N. (1986) The ideal victim. In E. Fattah (ed.) *From Crime Policy to Victim Policy* (pp. 17–30). Macmillan.

Christodoulou, H. (2019) 'I DON'T GIVE A S***' Chilling words of twisted teen killer William Cornick, 15, after knifing his beloved teacher Ann Maguire to death in front of horrified classmates. *The Sun*, 10 May. Available at www.thesun.co.uk/news/9043554/teen-killer-william-cornick-chilling-words/.

Christopher, M. S., Goerling, R. J., Rogers, B. S., Hunsinger, M., Baron, G. et al. (2016) A pilot study evaluating the effectiveness of a mindfulness-based intervention on cortisol awakening response and health outcomes among law enforcement officers. *Journal of Police and Criminal Psychology*, 31(1), 15–28.

Chryssides, G. D. (2016) The devil at Heaven's Gate: Rethinking the study of religion in the age of cyberspace. In G. D. Chryssides (ed.) *Heaven's Gate: Postmodernity and Popular Culture in a Suicide Group* (pp. 117–50). Routledge.

Chuck, E. (2015) Susan Smith, mother who killed kids: 'Something went very wrong that night'. US News, 23 July. Available at www.nbcnews.com/news/us-news/susan-smith-mother-who-killed-kids-something-went-very-wrong-n397051.

Church, C., Alisanski, S. and Amanullah, S. (2000) The social behavioral and academic experiences of children with Asperger syndrome. *Focus on Autism and Other Developmental Disabilities*, 15, 12–20.

Church, R. M. (1963) The varied effects of punishment on behavior. *Psychological Review*, 70(5), 369–402.

Cialdini, R. B. (2009) *Influence: Science and Practice* (vol. 4). Pearson.

Clare, I. and Gudjonsson, G. (1993) Interrogative suggestibility, confabulation, and acquiescence in people with mild learning disabilities (mental handicap): Implications for reliability during police interrogations. *British Journal of Clinical Psychology*, 32(3), 295–301.

Clark, E. (2015) Mad literature: Insane asylums in nineteenth century America. *Arizona Journal of Interdisciplinary Studies*, 4, 42–65.

Clark, J., Boccaccini, M. T., Caillouet, B. and Chaplin, W. F. (2007) Five factor model personality traits, jury selection, and case outcomes in criminal and civil cases. *Criminal Justice and Behavior*, 34(5), 641–60.

Clark, L., Landenberger, N. A. and Lipsey, M. (2005) The positive effects of cognitive-behavioral programs for offenders: A meta-analysis of factors associated with effective treatment. *Journal of Experimental Criminology*, 1, 451–76.

Clark, N. K., Stephenson, G. M. and Kniveton, B. H. (1990) Social remembering: Quantitative aspects of individual and collaborative remembering by police officers and students. *British Journal of Psychology*, 81(1), 73–94.

Clarke, A. C. (1985) *Profiles of the Future: An Inquiry into the Limits of the Possible* (rev. edn). Harper & Row.

Clarke, C. and Milne, R. (2017) Interviewing suspects in England and Wales. In D. Walsh, G. E. Oxburgh, A. D. Redlich and T. Myklebust (eds) *International Developments and Practices in Investigative Interviewing and Interrogation* (pp. 133–50). Routledge.

Cleak, H., Schofield, M. J., Axelsen, L. and Bickerdike, A. (2018) Screening for partner violence among family mediation clients: Differentiating types of abuse. *Journal of Interpersonal Violence*, 33(7), 1118–46.

Clevenger, S., Navarro, J. N. and Gregory, L. K. (2017) Seeing life in their shoes: Fostering empathy toward victims of interpersonal violence through five active learning activities. *Journal of Criminal Justice Education*, 28(3), 393–410.

Cloud, D. H., Drucker, E., Browne, A. and Parsons, J. (2015) Public health and solitary confinement in the United States. *American Journal of Public Health*, 105, 18–26.

Clugston, B., Perrin, M., Davidson, F., Heffernan, E. and Kinner, S. (2018) *Prison Mental Health Services: A Comparison of Australian Jurisdictions*. Griffith University.

Coccaro, E. F., Lee, R., McCloskey, M., Csernansky, J. G. and Wang, L. (2015) Morphometric analysis of amygdala and hippocampus shape in impulsively aggressive and healthy control subjects. *Journal of Psychiatric Research*, 69, 80–6.

Cochran, J. C., Toman, E. L., Mears, D. P. and Bales, W. D. (2018) Solitary confinement as punishment: Examining in-prison sanctioning disparities, *Justice Quarterly*, 35(3), 381–411.

Cogan, R. and Ballinger, B. C. III (2006) Alcohol problems and the differentiation of partner, stranger, and general violence. *Journal of Interpersonal Violence*, 21(7), 924–35.

Cohen, D. (2009) Emerging from a coma, Kara saw her attacker stride up to her hospital bed. Here's how she brought him to justice. *The Evening Standard*. Available at www.questia.com/newspaper/1G1-207027805/emerging-from-a-coma-kara-saw-her-attacker-stride.

Cole, T. and Brown, J. (2014) Behavioural investigative advice: Assistance to investigative decision-making in difficult-to-detect murder. *Journal of Investigative Psychology and Offender Profiling*, 11(3), 191–220.

Collett, M. E. and Kovera, M. B. (2003) The effects of British and American trial procedures on the quality of juror decision-making. *Law and Human Behavior*, 27(4), 403–22.

Collica-Cox, K. and Sullivan, L. (2017) Why retribution matters: Progression not regression. *Theory in Action*, 10(2), 41–57.

Collings, S. J. (2017) The value of anatomical dolls in the psychological assessment of child sexual abuse: An evaluation of available empirical evidence. *Child Abuse Research in South Africa*, 18(2), 21–9.

Collins, A. M. and Loftus, E. (1975) A spreading activation theory of semantic processing. *Psychological Review*, 82(6), 407–28.

Collins, K., Harker, N. and Antonopoulos, G.A. (2016) The impact of the registered intermediary on adults' perceptions of child witnesses: Evidence from a mock cross examination. *European Journal on Criminal Policy and Research*, 23(2), 211–25.

Collins, R. (2014) Interaction ritual chains and collective effervescence. In C. von Scheve and M. Salmela (eds) *Collective Emotions* (pp. 299–311).Oxford University Press.

Colloff, M. F., Wade, K. A. and Strange, D. (2016) Unfair lineups make witnesses more likely to confuse innocent and guilty suspects. *Psychological Science*, 27(9), 1227–39.

Colloff, P. (2016) The reckoning. *Texas Monthly*, March. Available at https://features.texasmonthly.com/editorial/the-reckoning/.

Columbine Review Commission (2001) *The Report of Governor Bill Owens' Columbine Review Commission*. Columbine Review Commission.

Conley, R. and Conley, J. (2009) Stories from the jury room: How jurors use narrative to process evidence. In A. Sarat (ed.) *Studies in Law, Politics and Society* (pp. 25–56). Emerald.

Connett, D. (2016) Too many people unfit to plead face criminal trials, says Law Commission. *Independent*, 10 January. Available at independent.co.uk/news/uk/crime/too-many-people-unfit-to-plead-face-criminal-trials-says-law-commission-a6805191.html.

Connors, C. J., Patry, M. W. and Smith, S. M. (2019) The Mr. Big technique on trial by jury, *Psychology, Crime & Law*, 25(1), 1–22.

Conrad, R. J. Jr and Clements, K. L. (2018) The vanishing criminal jury trial: From trial judges to sentencing judges. *George Washington Law Review*, 86, 99–167.

Conway, M. A. (1995) *Essays in Cognitive Psychology: Flashbulb Memories*. Lawrence Erlbaum.

Conway, M. A. (2002) Sensory-perceptual episodic memory and its context: Autobiographical memory. In A. Baddeley, J. P. Aggleton and M. A. Conway (eds) *Episodic Memory: New Directions in Research* (pp. 53–70). Oxford University Press.

Cook, J. L. (2016) From movement kinematics to social cognition: The case of autism. *Philosophical Transactions of the Royal Society B: Biological Sciences*, 371(1693), 20150372. doi: 10.1098/rstb.2015.0372.

Cook, J. L., Blakemore, S. J. and Press, C. (2013) Atypical basic movement kinematics in autism spectrum conditions. *Brain*, 136(9), 2816–24.

Cook, L. G. and Mitschow, L. C. (2019) Beyond the polygraph: Deception detection and the autonomic nervous system. *Federal Practitioner*, 36(7), 316–21.

Cooke, B. J. (2019) Exploring types of programs: Dog rescue, rehabilitation and training. In M. Jalongo (ed.) *Prison Dog Programs*. Springer.

Cooke, M. (2004) *Caught in the Middle: Indigenous Interpreters and Customary Law*. Background paper no. 2. Perth: Law Reform Commission of Western Australia.

Cooke, P. J., Day, M. R. and Mulcahy, H. (2019) Dementia and elder abuse: Understanding public health nurses' experiences. *Journal of Nursing Education and Practice*, 9(7), 57–66.

Cooper, A. (2018) Jaymes Todd formally pleads guilty to murdering Eurydice Dixon. *The Age*, November 13. Available at www.theage.com.au/national/victoria/jaymes-todd-formally-pleads-guilty-to-murdering-eurydice-dixon-20181113-p50fo2.html.

Cooper, C. and Livingston, G. (2016) Intervening to reduce elder abuse: challenges for research. *Age and Ageing*, 45(2), 184–5.

Cooper, P. and Mattison, M. (2017) Intermediaries, vulnerable people, and the quality of evidence: An international comparison of three versions of the English intermediary model. *International Journal of Evidence & Proof*, 21(4), 351–70.

Cornell, D. G. and Hawk, G. L. (1989) Clinical presentation of malingerers diagnosed by experienced forensic psychologists. *Law and Human Behavior*, 13, 375–83.

Cornish, D. B. and Clarke, R. V. (1987) Understanding crime displacement: An application of rational choice theory. *Criminology*, 25(4), 933–48.

Cornwell, E. Y. (2010) Opening and closing the jury room door: A sociohistorical consideration of the 1955 Chicago Jury Project scandal. *Justice System Journal*, 31(1), 49–73.

Correctional Service Canada (2019) *A Comprehensive Study of Recidivism Rates among Canadian Federal Offenders*. Available at www.csc-scc.gc.ca/005/008/092/err-19-02-en.pdf.

Correll, J., Park, B., Judd, C. M. and Wittenbrink, B. (2002) The police officer's dilemma: Using ethnicity to disambiguate potentially threatening individuals. *Journal of Personality and Social Psychology*, 83(6), 1314–29.

Correll, J., Park, B., Judd, C. M., Wittenbrink, B., Sadler, M. S. and Keesee, T. (2007) Across the thin blue line: Police officers and racial bias in the decision to shoot. *Journal of Personality and Social Psychology*, 92(6), 1006–23.

Cortina, L. M. (2017) From victim precipitation to perpetrator predation: Toward a new paradigm for understanding workplace aggression. In N. A. Bowling and M. S. Hershcovis (eds) *Research and Theory on Workplace Aggression* (pp. 121–35). Cambridge University Press.

Corzine, D. and Tomlinson, B. (2018) The strange case of James Arthur Hogue. *Princeton Alumni Weekly*, 27 July. Available at https://paw.princeton.edu/article/strange-case-james-arthur-hogue.

Cox, D. (2016) Can your brain reveal you are a liar? BBC, 25 January. Available at www.bbc.com/future/story/20160125-is-it-wise-that-the-police-have-started-scanning-brains.

Craik, F. I. (2020) Remembering: An activity of mind and brain. *Annual Review of Psychology*, 71, 1–24.

Crane, L., Goddard, L. and Pring, L. (2013) Autobiographical memory in adults with autism spectrum disorder: the role of depressed mood, rumination, working memory and theory of mind. *Autism*, 17(2), 205–19.

Cravens, J. D. and Whiting, J. B. (2014) Clinical implications of internet infidelity: Where Facebook fits in. *American Journal of Family Therapy*, 42(4), 325–39.

Crouch, D. (2015) Swedish police say school attack was racist, as refugee rules tightened. *The Guardian*, 23 October. Available at www.theguardian.com/world/2015/oct/23/swedish-police-treat-school-attack-as-racist-as-government-plans-to-stem-refugees.

Crundall, D., Chapman, P., Phelps, N. and Underwood, G. (2003) Eye movements and hazard perception in police pursuit and emergency response driving. *Journal of Experimental Psychology: Applied*, 9(3), 163–74.

Cuenca-Piqueras, C., Fernández-Prados, J. S. and González-Moreno, M. J. (2020) Face-to-face versus online harassment of European women: Importance of date and place of birth. *Sexuality & Culture*, 24(1), 157–73.

Cullen, D. (2009) *Columbine*. Twelve.

Cullen, F. T. (2013) Rehabilitation: Beyond nothing works. *Crime and Justice*, 42(1), 299–376.

Cummins, I. (2020) Rereading Rosenhan. *Illness, Crisis & Loss*, 28(1), 38–50.

Cupach, W. R., Spitzberg, B. H., Bolingbroke, C. M. and Tellitocci, B. S. (2011) Persistence of attempts to reconcile a terminated romantic relationship: A partial test of relational goal pursuit theory. *Communication Reports*, 24(2), 99–115.

Curley, L. J., MacLean, R., Murray, J. and Laybourn, P. (2019) Decision science: A new hope. *Psychological Reports*, 122(6), 2417–39.

Cuypers, E. and Flanagan, R. J. (2018) The interpretation of hair analysis for drugs and drug metabolites. *Clinical Toxicology*, 56(2), 90–100.

D'Ovidio, R. and Doyle, J. (2003) A study on cyberstalking: Understanding investigative hurdles. *FBI Law Enforcement Bulletin*, 72(3), 10–17.

Daeid, N. N. (2010) *Fifty Years of Forensic Science.* Wiley.

Daftary-Kapur, T. and Penrod, S. D. (2018) Pre- and midtrial publicity in the age of internet and social media. In C. Najdowski and M. Stevenson (eds) *Criminal Juries in the 21st Century: Contemporary Issues, Psychological Science, and the Law* (pp. 155–72). Oxford University Press.

Dagan, S. W., Ben-Porat, A. and Itzhaky, H. (2016) Child protection workers dealing with child abuse: The contribution of personal, social and organizational resources to secondary traumatization. *Child Abuse & Neglect*, 51, 203–11.

Dalby, J. T. (2006) The case of Daniel McNaughton: Let's get the story straight. *American Journal of Forensic Psychiatry*, 27(4), 17–32.

Dalton, P. Doolittle, N. and Breslin, P. A. (2002) Gender specific induction of enhanced sensitivity to odors. *Nature Neuroscience*, 5(3), 199–200.

Dando, C. J., Wilcock, R. and Milne, R. (2008) The cognitive interview: Inexperienced police officer's perceptions of their witness interviewing behavior. *Legal and Criminological Psychology*, 13(1), 59–70.

Dando, C. J., Bull, R., Ormerod, T. C. and Sandham, A. L. (2013) Helping to sort the liars from the truth-tellers: The gradual revelation of information during investigative interviews. *Legal and Criminological Psychology*, 20(1), 114–28.

Dando, C. J., Ormerod, T. C., Wilcock, R. and Milne, R. (2011) When help becomes hindrance: Unexpected errors of omission and commission in eyewitness memory resulting from change temporal order at retrieval? *Cognition*, 121(3), 416–21.

Danzig, D. (2012) Countering the Jack Bauer effect: An examination of how to limit the influence of TV's most popular, and most brutal, hero. In M. Flynn and F. Salek (eds) *Screening Torture: Media Representations of State Terror and Political*

Domination (pp. 21–33). Columbia University Press.

Darden, J. T. (2019) *Tackling Terrorists' Exploitation of Youth*. American Enterprise Institute.

Darley, J. M. (2005) On the unlikely prospect of reducing crime rates by increasing severity of prison sentences. *Journal of Law and Policy*, 13(1), 189–208.

Darling, S., Valentine, T., and Memon, A. (2008) Selection of lineup foils in operational contexts. *Applied Cognitive Psychology*, 22(2), 159–69.

Davidson, M. (2017) Vaccination as a cause of autism: Myths and controversies. *Dialogues in Clinical Neuroscience*, 19(4), 403–7.

Davies, K. and Woodhams, J. (2019) The practice of crime linkage: A review of the literature. *Journal of Investigative Psychology and Offender Profiling*, 16(3), 169–200.

Davies, M., Rogers, P. and Whitelegg, L. (2009) Effects of victim gender, victim sexual orientation, victim response and respondent gender on judgements of blame in a hypothetical adolescent rape. *Legal and Criminological Psychology*, 14, 331–8.

Davis, S. L. and Bottoms, B. L. (2002) Effects of social support on children's eyewitness reports: A test of the underlying mechanism. *Law and Human Behavior*, 26, 185–215.

Davis, T. (2009) Conceptualizing psychiatric disorders using 'four D's' of diagnoses. *Internet Journal of Psychiatry*, 1(1), https://ispub.com/IJPSY/1/1/5049.

Davis, W. (2016) Heaven's Gate: A study of religious obedience. In G. D. Chryssides (ed.) *Heaven's Gate: Postmodernity and Popular Culture in a Suicide Group* (pp. 89–116). Routledge.

Dawson, J. C., Banks, D., Vermeer, M. and Shelton, S. R. (2018) *Strategies to Mitigate the Impact of Electronic Communication and Electronic Devices on the Right to a Fair Trial*. RAND.

Day, J., Gillespie, D. C., Rooney, A. G., Bulbeck, H. J., Zienius, K. et al. (2016) Neurocognitive deficits and neurocognitive rehabilitation in adult brain tumors. *Current Treatment Options in Neurology*, 18(5), 22. doi: 10.1007/s11940-016-0406-5.

Debeyne, M., Haekens, A. and Peuskens, H. (2016) 'Giving inappropriate and/or misleading answers': Is the era of the Ganser syndrome finally over? *Tijdschr Psychiatry*, 58(9), 659–62.

De Bortoli, L., Ogloff, J., Coles, J. and Dolan, M. (2017) Towards best practice: combining evidence-based research, structured assessment and professional judgement. *Child & Family Social Work*, 22(2), 660–9.

Decety, J. and Jackson, P. L. (2004) The functional architecture of human empathy. *Behavioral and Cognitive Neuroscience Review*, 3(2), 71–100.

DeHart, D. D. and Mahoney, J. M. (1994) The serial murderer's motivations: An interdisciplinary review. *OMEGA: Journal of Death and Dying*, 29(1), 29–45.

DeKeseredy, W. S., Rogness, M. and Schwartz, M. D. (2004) Separation/divorce sexual assault: The current state of social scientific knowledge. *Aggression and Violent Behaviour*, 9(6), 675–91.

De La Fuente, L., De La Fuente, E. I. and García, J. (2003) Effects of pretrial juror bias, strength of evidence and deliberation process on juror decisions: New validity evidence of the Juror Bias Scale scores. *Psychology, Crime and Law*, 9(2), 197–209.

Delahunty, J. G., Martschuk, N. and Dhami, M. K. (2014) Interviewing high value detainees: Securing cooperation and disclosures, *Applied Cognitive Psychology*, 28(6), 883–97.

DeLisi, M., Bunga, R., Heirigs, M. H., Erickson, J. H. and Hochstetler, A. (2019) The past is prologue: Criminal specialization continuity in the delinquent career. *Youth Violence and Juvenile Justice*, 17(4), 335–53.

Delmage, E. (2014) The minimum age of criminal responsibility: A medico-legal perspective. *Youth Justice*, 13(2), 102–10.

Delsol, R. (2015) *Stop and Search: The Anatomy of a Police Power*. Springer.

DeMatteo, D., Fairfax-Columbo, J. and Desai, A. (2019) *Becoming a Forensic Psychologist*. Routledge.

Deming, D. (2016) Do extraordinary claims require extraordinary evidence? *Philosophia*, 44(4), 1319–31.

Denney, R. L. and Tyner, E. A. (2010) Criminal law, competency, insanity, and dangerousness: Competency to proceed. In A. M. Horton Jr and L. C. Hartlage (eds) *The Handbook of Forensic Neuropsychology* (2nd edn, pp. 211–33). Springer.

Denno, D. W. (2003) Who is Andrea Yates?: A short story about insanity. *Duke Journal of Gender Law & Policy*, 10, 1.

Dent, H. R. and Stephenson, G. M. (1979) An experimental study of the effectiveness of different techniques of questioning child witnesses. *British Journal of Social and Clinical Psychology*, 18(1), 1–137.

Dern, H., Dern, C., Horn, A. and Horn, U. (2009) The fire behind the smoke: A reply to Snook and colleagues. *Criminal Justice and Behavior*, 36, 1085–90.

Dershowitz, A. (2006) Should we fight terror with torture? *Independent*, 3 July. Available at www.independent.co.uk/news/world/americas/alan-dershowitz-should-we-fight-terror-with-torture-6096463.html.

Desaunay, P., Briant, A. R., Bowler, D. M., Ring, M., Gérardin, P. et al. (2020) Memory in autism spectrum disorder: A meta-analysis of experimental studies. *Psychological Bulletin*, 146(5), 377–410.

Deslauriers-Varin, N. and Beauregard, E. (2013) Investigating offending consistency of geographic and environmental factors among serial sex offenders: A comparison of multiple analytical strategies. *Criminal Justice and Behavior*, 40(2), 156–79.

DeStefano, F. and Shimabukuro, T. T. (2019) The MMR vaccine and autism. *Annual Review of Virology*, 6(1), 585–600.

De Stefano, G. (2006) *An Offer we Can't Refuse: The Mafia in the Mind of America*. Faber & Faber/Farrar, Straus and Giroux.

Detullio, D., Messer, S. C., Kennedy, T. D. and Millen, D. H. (2019) A meta-analysis of the Miller Forensic Assessment of Symptoms Test (M-FAST). *Psychological Assessment*, 31(11), 1319–28.

Devaney, T. (1996) Unequal justice: The case for Johnny Lee Wilson. *Journal for Peace and Justice Studies*, 7(1), 99–103.

DeVault, A., Miller, M. K. and Griffin, T. (2016) Crime control theater: Past, present, and future. *Psychology, Public Policy, and Law*, 22(4), 341–8.

Devine, D. J. (2012) Effects of trial context. In D. J. Devine, *Jury Decision Making: The State of the Science* (pp. 68–90). New York University Press.

Devine, D. J. and Kelly, C. E. (2015) Life or death: An examination of jury sentencing with the Capital Jury Project database. *Psychology, Public Policy, and Law*, 21(4), 393–406.

Devine, D. J. and Macken, S. (2016) Scientific evidence and juror decision making: Theory, empirical research, and future directions. In M. K. Miller and B. H. Bornstein (eds) *Advances in Psychology and Law* (pp. 95–139). Springer.

Devine, D. J., Krouse, P. C., Cavanaugh, C. M. and Basora, J. C. (2016) Evidentiary, extraevidentiary, and deliberation process predictors of real jury verdicts. *Law and Human Behavior*, 40(6), 670–82.

Devine, D. J., Buddenbaum, J., Houp, S., Studebaker, N. and Stolle, D. P. (2009) Strength of evidence, extraevidentiary influence, and the liberation hypothesis: Data from the field. *Law and Human Behavior*, 33(2), 136–48.

Dewey, L., Allwood, M., Fava, J., Arias, E., Pinizzotto, A. and Schlesinger, L. (2013) Suicide by cop: Clinical risks and subtypes. *Archives of Suicide Research*, 17(4), 448–61.

Dewsbury, D. A. (2002) Constructing representations of Karl Spencer Lashley. *Journal of the History of the Behavioral Sciences*, 38(3), 225–45.

Dhami, M. K., Goodman-Delahunty, J. and Desai, S. (2017) Development of an information sheet providing rapport advice for interpreters in police interviews. *Police Practice and Research*, 18(3), 291–305.

Diamond, A. (2013) Executive functions. *Annual Review of Psychology*, 64, 135–68.

Diamond, B. L. (1964) On the spelling of Daniel M'Naghten's name. *Ohio State Law Journal*, 25, 84.

Diamond, S. S. (1990) Scientific jury selection: What social scientists know and do not know. *Judicature*, 73(4), 178–83.

Diamond, S. S. (2018) Jury research. In T. Grisso and S. L. Brodsky (eds) *The Roots of Modern Psychology and Law: A Narrative History* (pp. 61–77). Oxford University Press.

Diamond, S. S. and Doorley, F. (2015) What a (very) smart trial judge knows about juries. *DePaul Law Review*, 64(2), 373–92.

Diaz, N. A. (2018) Sleep disorders. In R. Tampi, D. Tampi and L. Boyle (eds) *Psychiatric Disorders Late in Life*. Springer.

Dickinson, J. J., Brubacher, S. P. and Poole, D. A. (2015) Children's performance on ground rules questions: Implications for forensic interviewing. *Law and Human Behavior*, 39(1), 87–97.

Dietz, P. E. (1986) Mass, serial and sensational homicides. *Bulletin of the New York Academy of Medicine*, 62(5), 477–91.

Dirks-Linhorst, P. A. and Kondrat, D. (2012) Tough on crime or beating the system: An evaluation of Missouri Department of Mental Health's not guilty by reason of insanity. *Homicide Studies*, 16(2), 129–50.

Dixon, D. N. (1995) Test review of the Structured Interview of Reported Symptoms. In J. C. Conoley and J. C. Impara (eds) *The Twelfth Mental Measurements Yearbook*. Buros Institute of Mental Measurements.

Dobson, R. (2002) An exceptional man: Stephen Hawking has survived almost 40 years with a disease that usually kills people 14 months after diagnosis. *British Medical Journal*, 324(7352), 1478.

Dockterman, E. (2014) What the torture report reveals about *Zero Dark Thirty*. *Time*, 10 December. Available at https://time.com/3627694/torture-report-zero-dark-thirty/.

Dodd, M. L., Klos, K. J., Bower, J. H., Geda, Y. E., Josephs, K. A. and Ahlskog, J. E. (2005) Pathological gambling caused by drugs used to treat Parkinson Disease. *Archives of Neurology*, 62(9), 1377–81.

Dodson, K. D., Cabage, L. N. and McMillan, S. M. (2019) Mothering behind bars: Evaluating the effectiveness of prison nursery programs on recidivism reduction. *The Prison Journal*, 99(5), 572–92.

Doerner, W. and Lab, S. (2005) *Victimology* (3rd edn). Lexis-Nexis.

Domingo, J., Treder, M., Kerrén, C. and Wimber, M. (2019) Evidence that neural information flow is reversed between object perception and object reconstruction from memory. *Nature Communications*, 10(1), 179, doi: 10.1038/s41467-018-08080-2.

Dömötör, Z., Ruíz-Barquín, R. and Szabo, A. (2016) Superstitious behavior in sport: A literature review. *Scandinavian Journal of Psychology*, 57(4), 368–82.

Donat, M., Wolgast, A. and Dalbert, C. (2018) Belief in a just world as a resource of victimized students. *Social Justice Research*, 31(2), 133–51.

Donohue, A., Arya, V., Fitch, L. and Hammen, D. (2008) Legal insanity: Assessment of the inability to refrain. *Psychiatry*, 5(3), 58–66.

Donohue, L. K. (2006) Terrorism and trial by jury: The vices and virtues of British and American criminal law. *Stanford Law Review*, 59, 1321–64.

Doosje, B., van den Bos, K. and Loseman, A. (2013) Radicalization process of Islamic youth in the Netherlands: The role of uncertainty, perceived injustice and perceived group threat. *Journal of Social Issues*, 69, 586–604.

Doosje, B., van den Bos, K., Loseman, A., Feddes, A. R. and Mann, L. (2012) 'My in-group is superior!': Susceptibility for radical right-wing attitudes and behaviors in Dutch youth. *Negotiation Conflict Manage Resolution*, 5, 253–68.

Doosje, B., Moghaddam, F. M., Kruglanski, A. W., De Wolf, A., Mann, L. and Feddes, A. R. (2016) Terrorism, radicalization and de-radicalization. *Current Opinion in Psychology*, 11, 79–84.

Douglas, J. E. and Munn, C. (1992) Violent crime scene analysis: Modus operandi, signature, and staging. *FBI Law Enforcement Bulletin*, 61(2), 1–10.

Douglas, J. E. and Olshaker, M. (1997) *Journey into Darkness*. Simon & Schuster.

Douglas, J. E., Burgess, A. W., Burgess, A. G. and Ressler, R. K. (eds) (1992) *Crime Classification Manual*. Lexington Books/Macmillan.

Douglas, J. E., Ressler, R. K., Burgess, A. W. and Hartman, C. R. (1986) Criminal profiling from crime scene analysis. *Behavioral Sciences & the Law*, 4(4), 401–21.

Douglass, A. B. and Smalarz, L. (2019) Post-identification feedback to eyewitnesses: Implications for system variable reform. In B. Bornstein and M. Miller (eds) *Advances in Psychology and Law*, vol. 4 (pp. 101–36). Springer.

Douzenis, A. (2016) The importance of the patients deemed not guilty by reason of insanity for the psychiatric reform. *Psychiatriki*, 27(3), 165–8.

Dreßing, H., Bailer, J., Anders, A., Wagner, H. and Gallas, C. (2014) Cyberstalking in a large sample of social network users: Prevalence, characteristics, and impact upon victims. *Cyberpsychology, Behavior, and Social Networking*, 17(2), 61–7.

Dressler, J. (2002) *Understanding Criminal Procedure* (3rd edn). Lexis Nexis.

Driskell, T. and Driskell, J. E. (2019) Got theory? Multitasking, cognitive load, and deception. In T. Docan-Morgan (ed.) *The Palgrave Handbook of Deceptive Communication* (pp. 145–65). Palgrave Macmillan.

Drizin, S. A. and Leo, R. A. (2004) The problem of false confessions in the post-DNA world. *North Carolina Law Review*, 82, 891–1007.

Drozd, L., Saini, M. A. and Vellucci-Cook, K. (2019) Trauma and child custody disputes: Screening, assessment and interventions. In L. R. Greenberg, B. J. Fidler and M. A. Saini (eds) *Evidence-informed Interventions for Court-involved Families: Promoting Healthy Coping and Development* (pp. 260–81). Oxford University Press.

Dubber, M. D. (2011) *The American Law Institute's Model Penal Code and European Criminal Law*. Maklu.

Dudai, Y. (2004) The neurobiology of consolidation, or how stable is the engram? *Annual Review of Psychology*, 55, 51–86.

Duffy, E., Avalos, G. and Dowling, M. (2015) Secondary traumatic stress among emergency nurses: A cross-sectional study. *International Emergency Nursing*, 23(2), 53–8.

Dunn, J. L. (2010) *Judging Victims: Why We Stigmatize Survivors, and How They Reclaim Respect*. Lynne Rienner.

Duron, J. F. and Cheung, M. (2016) Impact of repeated questioning on interviewers: Learning from a forensic interview training project. *Journal of Child Sexual Abuse*, 25(4), 347–62.

Duron, J. F. and Remko, F. S. (2015) Considerations for pursuing multiple session forensic interviews in child sexual abuse investigations. *Journal of Child Sexual Abuse*, 10, 1–21.

Dušek, L. (2015) Time to punishment: The effects of a shorter criminal procedure on crime rates. *International Review of Law and Economics*, 43, 134–47.

Dwyer, D. (2001) *Angles on Criminal Psychology*. Nelson Thornes.

Eagleman, D. (2011) The brain on trial. *The Atlantic*, July/August. Available at www.theatlantic.com/magazine/archive/2011/07/the-brain-on-trial/308520/.

Eagly, A. and Chaiken, S. (1993) *The Psychology of Attitudes*. Harcourt Brace.

Earhart, B., La Rooy, D. and Lamb, M. (2016) Assessing the quality of forensic interviews with child witnesses. In W. O'Donohue and M. Fanetti (eds) *Forensic Interviews Regarding Child Sexual Abuse: A Guide to Evidence-Based Practice* (pp. 317–35). Springer.

Easterbrook, J. A. (1959) The effect of emotion on cue utilization and the organization of behavior. *Psychological Review*, 66(3), 183–201.

Easton, P. (2002) Yates details how she killed her kids. MyPlainview.com, 8 March. Available at www.myplainview.com/news/article/Yates-details-how-she-killed-her-kids-8742016.php.

Edens, J. F., Poythress, N. G. and Watkins-Clay, M. M. (2007) Detection of malingering in psychiatric unit and general population prison inmates: A comparison of the PAI, SIMS, and SIRS. *Journal of Personality*, 88(1), 33–42.

Edens, J. F., Kelley, S. E., Lilienfeld, S. O., Skeem, J. L. and Douglas, K. S. (2015) DSM-5 antisocial personality disorder: Predictive validity in a prison sample. *Law and Human Behavior*, 39(2), 123–9.

Edey, R., Cook, J., Brewer, R., Johnson, M. H., Bird, G. and Press, C. (2016) Interaction takes two: Typical adults exhibit mind-blindness towards those with autism spectrum disorder. *Journal of Abnormal Psychology*, 125(7), 879–85.

Edwards, K. M., Dardis, C. M. and Gidycz, C. A. (2012) College women's disclosure of partner abuse to peers: A mixed methodological study. *Feminism & Psychology*, 22, 507–17.

Ehlers, A., Grey, N., Wild, J., Stott, R., Liness, S. et al. (2013) Implementation of cognitive therapy for PTSD in routine clinical care: Effectiveness and moderators of outcome in a consecutive sample. *Behaviour Research and Therapy*, 51(11), 742–52.

Eigen, J. P. (1995) *Witnessing Insanity: Madness and Mad doctors in the English Court.* Yale University Press.

Eisenberg, P. (2019) The cognitive interview and enhanced cognitive interview in financial forensics and investigations. *SSRN Electronic Journal*, 1, 55–64.

Eisenberg, T., Hannaford-Agor, P.L., Hans, V.P., Waters, N.L., Munsterman, G.T. et al. (2005) Judge jury agreement in criminal cases: A partial replication of Kalven and Zeisel's The American Jury. *Journal of Empirical Legal Studies*, 2(1), 171–206.

Eisend, M. and Schmidt, S. (2015) Advertising repetition: A meta-analysis on effective frequency in advertising. *Journal of Advertising*, 44(4), 415–28.

Eisner, M., Nivette, A., Murray, A. L. and Krisch, M. (2016) Achieving population-level violence declines: Implications of the international crime drop for prevention programming. *Journal of Public Health Policy*, 37(1), 66–80.

Ekehammar, B. (1974) Interactionism in personality from a historical perspective. *Psychological Bulletin*, 81(12), 1026–48.

Ekman, P. ([1985]2009) *Telling Lies: Clues to Deceit in the Marketplace, Politics and Marriage* (rev. edn). W. W. Norton.

Ekman, P. and Friesen, W. V. (1969) The repertoire of nonverbal behavior: Categories, origins, usage, and coding. *Semiotica*, 1(1), 49–98.

Ellis, D. (2017) Marital separation and lethal male partner violence. *Violence against Women*, 23(4), 503–19.

Ellis, R. (2017) Tulsa jury foreman: shooting of unarmed black man 'tragic but justifiable'. CNN, 21 May. Available at http://edition.cnn.com/2017/05/19/us/tusla-officer-shooting-jury-letter-explanation/index.html.

Ellis, T. and Hamai, K. (2017) Homicide in Japan. In F. Brookman, E. R. Maguire and M. Maguire (eds) *The Handbook of Homicide* (pp. 388–411). Wiley-Blackwell.

Ellison, K. W. and Buckhout, R. (1981) *Psychology and Criminal Justice.* Harper & Row.

Ellison, L. and Munro, V. E. (2015) 'Telling tales': Exploring narratives of life and law within the (mock) jury room. *Legal Studies*, 35(2), 201–25.

Ellsworth, P.C. and Reifman, A. (2000) Juror comprehension and public policy: Perceived problems and proposed solutions. *Psychology, Public Policy, and Law*, 6, 788–821.

Enang, I., Murray, J., Dougall, N., Wooff, A., Heyman, I. and Aston, E. (2019) Defining and assessing vulnerability within law enforcement and public health organizations: A scoping review. *Health & Justice*, 7(2), 1–13.

Enders, A. M. and Smallpage, S. M. (2019) Who are conspiracy theorists? A comprehensive approach to explaining conspiracy beliefs. *Social Science Quarterly*, 100(6), 2017–32.

Engle, R. W. (2010) Role of working-memory capacity in cognitive control. *Current Anthropology*, 51(S1), S17–26.

Englich, B. (2009) Heuristic strategies and persistent biases in sentencing decisions. In M. E. Oswald, S. Bieneck and J. Hupfeld-Heinemann (eds) *Social Psychology of Punishment of Crime* (pp. 295–314). Wiley.

Ennis, B. J. and Litwack, T. R. (1974) Psychiatry and the presumption of expertise: Flipping coins in the courtroom. *California Law Review*, 62, 693–752.

Ensafdaran, F., Karhé, B., Njad, S. B. and Arshadi, N. (2019) Efficacy of different versions of aggression replacement training (ART): A review. *Aggression and Violent Behavior*, 47, 230–7.

Eriksson, M. and Ulmestig, R. (2017) 'It's not all about money': Toward a more comprehensive understanding of financial abuse in the context of VAW. *Journal of Interpersonal Violence*, 28, 808–28.

Erlandsson, Å. and Reid Meloy, J. (2018) The Swedish school attack in Trollhättan. *Journal of Forensic Sciences*, 63(6), 1917–27.

Erlanger, H. S. (1969) Jury research in America: Its past and future. *Law & Society Review*, 4, 345–70.

Ermers, R. (2018) *Honor Related Violence: A New Social Psychological Perspective.* Routledge.

EUAFR (European Union Agency for Fundamental Rights) (2014) *Violence against Women, an EU-wide Survey: Main Results.* Vienna: European Union Agency for Fundamental Rights.

European Commission (2011) Fair trial rights: Suspects to receive a 'letter of rights' in criminal proceedings following European Parliament vote. European Commission Press Release, 13 December. Available at https://ec.europa.eu/commission/presscorner/detail/en/IP_11_1534.

Evans, A. D. and Lyon, T. D. (2012) Assessing children's competency to take the oath in court: The influence of question type on children's accuracy. *Law and Human Behavior*, 36(3), 195–205.

Evans, J. R., Meissner, C. A., Brandon, S. E., Russano, M. B. and Kleinman, S. M. (2010) Criminal versus HUMINT interrogations: The importance of psychological science to improving interrogative practice. *The Journal of Psychiatry & Law*, 38, 215–49.

Evans, N. J., Rae, B., Bushmakin, M., Rubin, M. and Brown, S. D. (2017) Need for closure is associated with urgency in perceptual decision-making. *Memory & Cognition*, 45(7), 1193–205.

Evans, R., Pistrang, N. and Billings, J. (2013) Police officers' experiences of supportive and unsupportive social interactions following traumatic incidents. *European Journal of Psychotraumatology*, 4(1), 1–9.

Everson, M. D. and Boat, B. W. (1994) Putting the anatomical doll controversy in perspective: An examination of the major uses and criticisms of the dolls in child sexual abuse evaluations. *Child Abuse & Neglect*, 18(2), 113–29.

Ewin, R. (2015) The vulnerable and intimidated witness: a socio-legal analysis of special measures. *Journal of Applied Psychology and Social Science*, 1(2), 31–54.

Ezorsky, G. (2015) *Philosophical Perspectives on Punishment* (2nd edn). SUNY Press.

Fabelo, T. and Thompson, T. (2015) Reducing incarceration rates: When science meets political realities. *Issues in Science and Technology*, 32(1), 98–108.

Fahlman, R. C. (1999) Intelligence led policing and the key role of criminal intelligence analysis: Preparing for the 21st century. *Journal of the Australian Institute of Professional Intelligence Officers*, 8(1), 23–35.

Fahr, A. (2007) Expressing the inexpressible: US and German coverage of the school. In R. Adelmann, A. Fahr and I. Katenhusen (eds) *Visual Culture Revisited: German and American Perspectives on Visual Culture* (pp. 115–25). Herbert von Halem.

Fajonyomi, A. (2019) Strategic learning ideologies in prison education programs, *International Journal of Lifelong Education*, 38(1), 124–6.

Faller, K. C. (2007) Questioning techniques. In K. C. Faller (ed.) *Interviewing Children about Sexual Abuse: Controversies and Best Practice* (pp. 90–109). Oxford University Press.

Faller, K. C. (2015) Forty years of forensic interviewing of children suspected of sexual abuse, 1974–2014: Historical benchmarks. *Social Sciences*, 4, 34–65.

Faller, K. C. and Hewitt, S. (2007) Special considerations for cases involving young children. In K. C. Faller (ed.) *Interviewing Children about Sexual Abuse: Controversies and Best Practice* (pp. 142–51). Oxford University Press.

Faller, K. C., Cordisco-Steele, L. and Nelson-Gardell, D. (2010) Allegations of sexual abuse of a child: what to do when a single forensic interview isn't enough. *Journal of Child Sexual Abuse*, 19(5), 572–89.

Fallon, T. J. (2010) Mistrial in 140 characters or less? How the internet and social networking are undermining the American jury system and what can be done to fix it. *Hofstra Law Review*, 38(3), 935–69.

Fals-Stewart, W., Leonard, K. E. and Birchler, G. R. (2005) The occurrence of male-to-female intimate partner violence on days of men's drinking: The moderating effects of antisocial personality disorder. *Journal of Consulting and Clinical Psychology*, 73(2), 239–48.

Falzer, P. R. (2013) Valuing structured professional judgment: Predictive validity, decision-making, and the clinical-actuarial conflict. *Behavioral Sciences & the Law*, 31(1), 40–54.

Fanning, J. R., Coleman, M., Lee, R. and Coccaro, E. F. (2018) Subtypes of aggression in intermittent explosive disorder. *Journal of Psychiatric Research*, 109, 164–72.

Farah, M. J. (2005) Neuroethics: the practical and the philosophical. *Trends in Cognitive Sciences*, 9(1), 34–40.

Farley, H. and Pike, A. (2016) Engaging offenders in education: Reducing risk and recidivism. *Advancing Corrections: Journal of the International Corrections and Prisons Association*, 1, 65–73.

Farquhar, S. (2016) *Dangerous Place: The Story of the Railway Murders.* The History Press.

Farrer, T. J. and Hedges, D. W. (2011) Prevalence of traumatic brain injury in incarcerated groups compared to the general population: A meta-analysis. *Progress in Neuro-pharmacology and Biological Psychiatry*, 35(2), 390–4.

Farrer, T. J., Frost, J. R. and Hedges, D. W. (2013) Prevalence of traumatic brain injury in juvenile offenders: A meta-analysis, *Child Neuropsychology*, 19(3), 225–34.

Farringer, A. J., Duriez, S. A., Manchak, S. M. and Sullivan, C. C. (2019) Adherence to 'What Works': Examining trends across 14 years of correctional program assessment. *Corrections*, 1–19.

Fashing, I. A., Ask, K. and Granhag, P. A. (2004) The man behind the mask: Accuracy and predictors of eyewitness offender descriptions. *Journal of Applied Psychology*, 89, 722–9.

Favril, L. and O'Connor, R. C. (2019) Distinguishing offenders who think about suicide from those who attempt suicide. *Psychological Medicine*, http://hdl.handle.net/1854/LU-8635307.

Fazel, S., Ramesh, T. and Hawton, K. (2017) Suicide in prisons: An international study of prevalence and contributory factors. *The Lancet Psychiatry*, 4(12), 946–52.

Fehr, C. (2019) Instrumental rationality and general deterrence. *Alberta Law Review*, 57, 53–69.

Feigenson, N., Park, J. and Salovey, P. (1997) Effect of blameworthiness and outcome severity on attributions of responsibility and damage awards in comparative negligence cases. *Law and Human Behavior*, 21(6), 597–617.

Feindler, E. (2016) Program evaluation challenges: Is Aggression Replacement Training (ART) effective?. *Journal of Psychology*, 4(2), 21–36.

Feindler, E., Engel, E. and Gerber, M. (2016) Program evaluation challenges: Is aggression replacement training (ART) effective? *Journal of Psychology and Behavioral Science*, 4(2), 1–10.

Feldman, K. (2014) Sexual assault at God's Harvard. *New Republic*, February. Available at www.newrepublic.com/article/116623/sexual-assault-patrick-henry-college-gods-Harvard.

Felitti, V. J., Anda, R. F., Nordenberg, D., Williamson, D. F., Spitz, A. M. et al. (1998) Relationship of childhood abuse and household dysfunction to many of the leading causes of death in adults. *American Journal of Preventive Medicine*, 14(4), 245–58.

Felson, R. B. (1983) Aggression and violence between siblings. *Social Psychology Quarterly*, 271–85.

Feneley, R. (2015) Police divided over strategy during Lindt cafe siege in Martin Place, Sydney. *The Sydney Morning Herald*, 11 January. Available at www.smh.com.au/national/police-divided-over-strategy-during-lindt-cafe-siege-in-martin-place-sydney-20150111-12lykf.html.

Feng, X., Asante, A., Short, E. and Abeykoon, I. (2017) Cyberstalking issues. In IEEE CyberSciTech, 15th DASC, 15th IEEE PICom, 3rd IEEE DataCom (pp. 373–6). IEEE.

Fenici, R., Brisinda, D. and Sorbo, A. R. (2011) Methods for real-time assessment of operational stress during realistic police tactical training. In J. Kitaeff (ed.) *Handbook of Police Psychology* (pp. 295–319). Routledge.

Ferbinteanu, J. (2019) Memory systems 2018: Towards a new paradigm. *Neurobiology of Learning and Memory*, 157, 61–78.

Ferguson, C. (2019) Forensically aware offenders and homicide investigations: Challenges, opportunities and impacts. *Australian Journal of Forensic Sciences*, 51(1), S128–31.

Festinger, L. (1957) *A Theory of Cognitive Dissonance*. Stanford University Press.

Feuerstein, S., Coric, V., Fortunati, F., Southwick, S., Temporini, H. and Morgan, C. A. (2005b) Malingering and forensic psychiatry. *Psychiatry*, 2(12), 25–8.

Feuerstein, S., Fortunati, F., Morgan, C. A., Coric, V., Temporini, H. and Southwick, S. (2005a) The insanity defense. *Psychiatry*, 2(9), 24–5.

Fewster, S. (2014) SA Police lashed by coroner over actions before murder of Zahra Abrahimzadeh. *The Advertiser*, 6 July. Available at www.adelaidenow.com.au/news/south-australia/sa-police-lashed-by-coroner-over-actions-before-murder-of-zahra-abrahimzadeh/news-story/8803d03fb2ca038ed4757f967ecd35c9.

Fiedler, K. and Bluemke, M. (2005) Faking the IAT: Aided and unaided response control on the Implicit Association Tests. *Basic and Applied Social Psychology*, 27(4), 307–16.

Fiedler, K., Messner, C. and Bluemke, M. (2006) Unresolved problems with the 'I', the 'A', and the 'T': A logical and psychometric critique of the Implicit Association Test (IAT). *European Review of Social Psychology*, 17(1), 74–147.

Finkel, A. M. and Bieniek, K. F. (2019) A quantitative risk assessment for chronic traumatic encephalopathy (CTE) in football: How public health science evaluates evidence, *Human and Ecological Risk Assessment: An International Journal*, 25(3), 564–89.

Finn, N. (2020) The latest twists in the Michelle Carter case 5 years after her boyfriend's death by suicide. E News, 23 January. Available at www.eonline.com/news/1114677/the-latest-twists-in-the-michelle-carter-case-5-years-after-her-boyfriend-s-death-by-suicide.

Firstman, R. and Salpeter, J. (2008) *A Criminal Injustice: A True Crime, a False Confession, and the Fight to Free Marty Tankleff*. Ballantine Books.

Fischler, G. L., McElroy, H. K., Miller, L., Saxe-Clifford, S., Stewart, C. O. and Zelig, M. (2011) The role of psychological fitness-for-duty evaluations in law enforcement. *The Police Chief*, 78(8), 72–8.

Fisher, B. S. and Sloan, J. J. (2013) *Campus Crime: Legal, Social, and Policy Perspectives*. Charles C. Thomas.

Fisher, R. P. (1995) Interviewing victims and witnesses of crime. *Psychology, Public Policy, and Law*, 1, 732–64.

Fisher, R. P. and Geiselman, R. E. (1992) *Memory Enhancing Techniques for Investigative Interviewing: The Cognitive Interview*. Charles C. Thomas.

Fisher, R. P. and Schreiber, N. (2017) Interview protocols to improve eyewitness memory. In M. P. Toglia, J. D. Read, and R. C. Lindsay (eds) *The Handbook of Eyewitness Psychology*: vol. I, *Memory for Events* (pp. 53–80). Psychology Press.

Fisher, R. P., Brewer, N. and Mitchell, G. (2009) The relation between consistency and accuracy of eyewitness testimony: Legal versus cognitive explanations. In T. Williamson, R. Bull and T. Valentine (eds) *Handbook of Psychology of Investigative Interviewing: Current Developments and Future Directions* (Ch. 8). John Wiley & Sons.

Fisher, R. P., Geiselman, R. E. and Amador, M. (1989) Field test of the cognitive interview: Enhancing the recollection of actual victims and witnesses of crime. *Journal of Applied Psychology*, 74, 722–7.

Fisher, R. P., Geiselman, R. E. and Raymond, D. S. (1987) Critical analysis of police interviewing techniques. *Journal of Police Science and Administration*, 15, 177–85.

Fisher, R. P., Milne, R. and Bull, R. (2011) Interviewing cooperative witnesses. *Current Directions in Psychological Science*, 20(1), 16–19.

Fitzgerald, R. J., Price, H. L. and Valentine, T. (2018) Eyewitness identification: Live, photo, and video lineups. *Psychology, Public Policy, and Law*, 24(3), 307–25.

Fitzpatrick, E. and Bachenko, J. (2012) Building a data collection for deception research. In E. Fitzpatrick, J. Bachenko and T. Fornaciari (eds) *Proceedings of the Workshop on Computational Approaches to Deception Detection* (pp. 31–8). Association for Computational Linguistics.

Flavell, J. (1996) Piaget's legacy. *Psychological Science*, 7(4), 200–3.

Fleer, M. (2019) Scientific playworlds: A model of teaching science in play-based settings. *Research in Science Education*, 49(5), 1257–78.

Flexser, A. J. and Tulving, E. (1978) Retrieval independence in recognition and recall. *Psychological Review*, 85(3), 153–71.

Flynn, E. (2015) Someone's been using my Facebook photos to 'catfish' people for nearly a decade. Vice. com, 21 January. Available at www.vice.com/en_us/ article/mv5zbn/someones-been-using-my-identity-to-catfish-people-for-nearly-ten-years-930.

Focquaert, F. (2018) Neurobiology and crime: A neuro-ethical perspective. *Journal of Criminal Justice*. DOI: 10.1016/j.jcrimjus.2018.01.001.

Ford, E. B. (2006) Lie detection: Historical, neuropsychiatric and legal dimensions. *International Journal of Law and Psychiatry*, 29, 159–77.

Forer, B. R. (1949) The fallacy of personal validation: A classroom demonstration of gullibility. *Journal of Abnormal and Social Psychology*, 44(1), 118–23.

Forscher, P. S., Lai, C. K., Axt, J. R., Ebersole, C. R., Herman, M. et al. (2019) A meta-analysis of procedures to change implicit measures. *Journal of Personality and Social Psychology*, 117(3), 522–59.

Fox, B. and Farrington, D. P. (2012) Creating burglary profiles using latent class analysis: A new approach to offender profiling. *Criminal Justice and Behavior*, 39(12), 1582–611.

Fox, B. H. and Farrington, D. P. (2015) An experimental evaluation on the utility of burglary profiles applied in active police investigations. *Criminal Justice and Behavior*, 42(2), 156–75.

Fox, B. H. and Farrington, D. P. (2016) Behavioral consistency among serial burglars: Evaluating offense style specialization using three analytical approaches. *Crime & Delinquency*, 62(9), 1123–58.

Fox, B. and Farrington, D. P. (2018) What have we learned from offender profiling? A systematic review and meta-analysis of 40 years of research. *Psychological Bulletin*, 144(12), 1247–74.

Fox, J. A. and Levin, J. (2015) Mass confusion concerning mass murder. *The Criminologist*, 40(1), 8–11.

Fox, J. A., Levin, J. and Quinet, K. (2018) *The Will to Kill: Making Sense of Senseless Murder* (5th edn). Sage.

Fox, J. and Tang, W. Y. (2017) Women's experiences with general and sexual harassment in online video games: Rumination, organizational responsiveness, withdrawal, and coping strategies. *New Media & Society*, 19(8), 1290–307.

Frances, A. (2013) The new crisis of confidence in psychiatric diagnosis. *Annals of Internal Medicine*, 159(10), 720–1.

Freckelton, I. (2004) The closing of the coffin on forensic polygraph evidence for Australia: Mallard v The Queen [2003] WASCA 296. *Psychiatry, Psychology and Law*, 11(2), 359–66.

Freedheim, D. K. (2003) *Handbook of Psychology*, vol. 1, *History of Psychology*. John Wiley & Sons.

Freedman, J. L. and Fraser, S. C. (1966) Compliance without pressure: The foot-in-the-door technique. *Journal of Personality and Social Psychology*, 4(2), 195–202.

Freeman, N. J. (2006) Socioeconomic status and belief in a just world: Sentencing of criminal defendants 1. *Journal of Applied Social Psychology, 36*(10), 2379–94.

Freire, A., Lee, K., Williamson, K. S., Stuart, S. J. and Lindsay, R. C. (2004) Lineup identification by children: Effects of clothing bias. *Law and Human Behavior, 28*(3), 339–54.

Freud, S. (1973) *The Psychopathology of Everyday Life*, in the *Standard Edition of the Complete Psychological Works of Sigmund Freud.* Hogarth Press.

Fridell, L. A. and Binder, A. (1992) Police officer decision making in potentially violent confrontations. *Journal of Criminal Justice, 20*(5), 385–99.

Friedman, R. D. and Ceci, S. J. (2000) The suggestibility of children: Scientific research and legal implications. *Cornell Law Review, 86*(1), 33–108.

Frierson, R. L. and Kaustubh, J. G. (2018) Implications of pseudologia fantastica in criminal forensic evaluations: A review and case report. *Journal of Forensic Science, 63*(3). DOI:10.1111/1556-4029.13616.

Frith, U. (2001) Mind blindness and the brain in autism. *Neuron, 32*(6), 969–79.

Frommholz, I., Al-Khateeb, H. M., Potthast, M., Ghasem, Z., Shukla, M. and Short, E. (2016) On textual analysis and machine learning for cyberstalking detection. *Datenbank-Spektrum, 16*(2), 127–35.

Frosina, P., Logue, M., Book, A., Huizinga, T., Amos, S. and Stark, S. (2018) The effect of cognitive load on nonverbal behavior in the cognitive interview for suspects. *Personality and Individual Differences, 130,* 51–8.

Frye, N. E. and Karney, B. R. (2006) The context of aggressive behavior in marriage: A longitudinal study of newlyweds. *Journal of Family Psychology, 20,* 12–20.

Fuchs, T. (2006) Ethical issues in neuroscience. *Current Opinion in Psychiatry, 19*(6), 600–7.

Fyfe, S., Williams, C., Mason, O. J. and Pickup, G. J. (2008) Apophenia, theory of mind and schizotypy: Perceiving meaning and intentionality in randomness. *Cortex, 44*(10), 1316–25.

Gagnier, C. and Collin-Vézina, D. (2016) The disclosure experiences of male child sexual abuse survivors. *Journal of Child Sexual Abuse, 25*(2), 221–41.

Gaigg, S. B. and Bowler, D. M. (2008) Free recall and forgetting of emotionally arousing words in autism spectrum disorder. *Neuropsychologia, 46*(9), 2336–43.

Gaigg, S. B., Gardiner, J. M. and Bowler, D. M. (2008) Free recall in autism spectrum disorder: The role of relational and item-specific encoding. *Neuropsychologia, 46*(4), 983–92.

Galanter, M. (2016) The decline of trials in a legalizing society. *Valparaiso University Law Review, 51,* 559–77.

Galanti, M. (2002) The Andrea Yates trial: What is wrong with this picture? *Cardozo Women's Law Journal, 9,* 345.

Ganapathy, N. (2018) Rehabilitation, reintegration, and recidivism: A theoretical and methodological reflection. *Asia Pacific Journal of Social Work and Development, 28*(3), 154–67.

Ganis, G., Rosenfeld, J. P., Meixner, J., Kievit, R. A. and Schendan, H.E. (2011) Lying in the scanner: Covert countermeasures disrupt deception detection by functional magnetic resonance imaging. *Neuroimaging, 55*(1), 312–19.

Ganpat, S. M., van der Leun, J. and Nieuwbeert, P. (2017) The relationship between a person's criminal history, immediate situational factors, and lethal versus non-lethal events. *Journal of Interpersonal Violence, 32*(17), 2535–65.

Gans, J. (2017) *The Ouija Board Jurors: Mystery, Mischief and Misery in the Jury System.* Waterside Press.

Gardner, C. (2015) Medicine's uncanny valley: The problem of standardizing empathy. *The Lancet, 386*(9998), 1032–3.

Gardner, F. L. and Moore, Z. E. (2012) Mindfulness and acceptance models in sport psychology: A decade of basic and applied scientific advancements. *Canadian Psychology/Psychologie Canadienne, 53*(4), 309–18.

Garg, P. and Pahuja, S. (2020) Social media: Concept, role, categories, trends, social media and AI, impact on youth, careers, recommendations. In S. Alavi and V. Ahuja (eds) *Managing Social Media Practices in the Digital Economy* (pp. 172–92). IGI Global.

Garret, B. L. (2010) The substance of false confessions. *Stanford Law Review, 62*(4), 1051–118.

Garrett, B. and Monahan, J. (2019) Assessing risk: The use of risk assessment in sentencing. *Judicature, 103*(2), 42–9.

Garvin, S., Wood, J. M., Malpass, R. S. and Shaw, J. S. (1998) More than suggestion: The effect of interviewing techniques from the McMartin preschool case. *Journal of Applied Psychology, 83*(3), 347–59.

Gatti, U. and Verde, A. (2012) Cesare Lombroso: Methodological ambiguities and brilliant intuitions. *International Journal of Law & Psychiatry, 35*(1), 19–26.

Gau, J. M. (2016) A jury of whose peers? The impact of selection procedures on racial composition and the prevalence of majority-white juries. *Journal of Crime and Justice, 39*(1), 75–87.

Gaudet, L. M. (2011) Brain fingerprinting, scientific evidence and Daubert: A cautionary lesson from India, *Jurimetrics Journal, 51,* 293–318.

Gaughwin, P. (2011) On being insane in medico-legal places: The importance of taking a complete history in forensic mental health assessment. *Psychiatry, Psychology and Law*, 12(1), 298–310.

Gay, P. (2006) *Freud: A Life for Our Time*. W. W. Norton & Company.

Gayadeen, S. M. and Phillips, S. W. (2016) Donut time: The use of humor across the police work environment. *Journal of Organizational Ethnography*, 5(1), 44–59.

GDRT (Global Deception Research Team) (2006) A world of lies. *Journal of Cross-Cultural Psychology*, 37(1), 60–74.

Gearty, C. (2007) Terrorism and human rights. *Government and Opposition*, 42(3), 340–62.

Geiselman, R. E., Fisher, R., MacKinnon, D. and Holland, H. L. (1985) Eyewitness memory enhancement in the police interview: Cognitive retrieval mnemonics versus hypnosis. *Journal of Applied Psychology*, 70(2), 401–12.

Geiselman, R. E., Fisher, R. P., Firstenberg, I., Hutton, L. A., Sullivan, S. J. et al. (1984) Enhancement of eyewitness memory: An empirical evaluation of a cognitive interview. *Journal of Police Science and Administration*, 12, 74–80.

Geldenhuys, K. (2019) Linkage analysis: When there is a lack of forensic evidence. *Servamus Community-based Safety and Security Magazine*, 112(11), 38–40.

Geller, W. A. (1992) *Police Videotaping of Suspect Interrogations and Confessions: A Preliminary Examination of Issues and Practices. A Report to the National Institute of Justice*. US Department of Justice. Available at www.springerlink.com/content/23638u3777622757/fulltext.pdf.

Gendreau, P. (1996) The principles of effective interventions with offenders. In A. T. Harland (ed.) *Choosing Correctional Options that Work: Defining the Demand and Evaluating the Supply* (pp. 117–30). Sage.

Gendreau, P., Listwan, S. J., Kuhns, J. B. and Exum, M. L. (2014) Making offenders accountable: Are contingency management programs the answer? *Criminal Justice and Behavior*, 41(9), 1097–102.

Genschow, O., Klomfar, S., d'Haene, I. and Brass, M. (2018) Mimicking and anticipating others' actions is linked to social information processing. *PLoS ONE*, 13(3). doi.org/10.1371/journal.pone.0193743.

Georges, L. C., Wiener, R. L. and Keller, S. R. (2013) The angry juror: Sentencing decisions in first-degree murder. *Applied Cognitive Psychology*, 27(2), 156–66.

Gerace, A., Day, A., Casey, S. and Mohr, P. (2017) 'I think, you think': Understanding the importance of self-reflection to the taking of another person's perspective. *Journal of Relationships Research*, 8, 1–19.

Geraldo, A. R., Coelho, B., Ramião, E., Castro-Caldas, A. and Barbosa, F. (2018) Efficacy of ICT-based neurocognitive rehabilitation programs for acquired brain injury. *European Psychologist*, 23(3), 250–64.

Gerber, J. P., Wheeler, L. and Suls, J. (2018) A social comparison theory meta-analysis 60+ years on. *Psychological Bulletin*, 144(2), 177–97.

Gershoff, E. T. (2002) Corporal punishment by parents and associated child behaviors and experiences: A meta-analytic and theoretical review. *Psychological Bulletin*, 128, 539–79.

Gianvanni, E. and Sharman, S. J. (2015) Psychologists as expert witnesses in Australian courtrooms, *Psychiatry, Psychology and Law*, 22(6), 1–7.

Gibbons, J. (2017) Towards clearer jury instructions. *Language and Law/Linguagem e Direito*, 4(1), 142–60.

Gibson, M. (2002) *Born to Crime: Cesare Lombroso and the Origins of Biological Criminology*. Praeger.

Gideon, L. and Sung, H. E. (2011) *Rethinking Corrections: Rehabilitation, Reentry, and Reintegration*. Sage.

Giessing, L., Frenkel, M. O., Zinner, C., Rummel, J., Nieuwenhuys, A. et al. (2019) Effects of coping-related traits and psychophysiological stress responses on police recruits' shooting behavior in reality-based scenarios. *Frontiers in Psychology*, 10. doi: 10.3389/fpsyg.2019.01523.

Gilbert, D. T. and Malone, P. S. (1995) The correspondence bias. *Psychological Bulletin*, 117, 21–38.

Gilbert, L. K., Breiding, M. J., Merrick, M. T., Parks, S. E., Thompson, W. W. et al. (2019) Childhood adversity and adult chronic disease: An update from ten states and the District of Columbia, 2010. *American Journal of Preventive Medicine*, 48(3), 345–9.

Gillespie, C. K. (1989) *Justifiable Homicide: Battered Women, Self-defense, and the Law*. Ohio State University Press.

Gilovich, T., Savitsky, K. and Husted, M. V. (1998) The illusion of transparency: Biased assessments of others' ability to read one's emotional states. *Journal of Personality and Social Psychology*, 75, 332–46.

Ginsburg, R. (2019) *Critical Perspectives of Teaching in Prison: Students and Instructors on Pedagogy behind the Wall*. Routledge.

Ginton, A. (2016) Examining different types of comparison questions in a field study of CQT polygraph technique: Theoretical and practical implications. *Journal of Investigative Psychology and Offender Profiling*, 14(1), 1–13.

Ginton, A. (2019) Essentials of the relevant issue gravity (rig) strength: A theoretical framework for understanding the comparison question test (CQT). *European Polygraph*, 13(4), 181–201.

Gkotsi, G. M. and Gasser, J. (2016) Neuroscience in forensic psychiatry: From responsibility to dangerousness. Ethical and legal implications of using neuroscience for dangerousness assessments. *International Journal of Law and Psychiatry*, 46, 58–67.

Glazebrook, P. R. (1972) The necessity plea in English criminal law. *The Cambridge Law Journal*, 30(1), 87–119.

Gleason, J. M. and Harris, V. A. (1975) Race, socio-economic status, and perceived similarity as determinants of judgements by simulated jurors. *Social Behavior and Personality: An International Journal*, 3(2), 175–80.

Gleick, E. (2001) Sex, betrayal, and murder. *Time*, 24 June. Available at http://content.time.com/time/magazine/article/0,9171,134423,00.html.

Glick, M. (2011) *The Instructional Leader and the Brain: Using Neuroscience to Inform Practice*. Sage.

Global Terrorism Database (2019) *Codebook: Inclusion Criteria and Variables*. START. Available at www.start.umd.edu/gtd/downloads/Codebook.pdf.

Goffin, R. D. and Boyd, A. C. (2009) Faking and personality assessment in personnel selection: Advancing models of faking. *Canadian Psychology/Psychologie Canadienne*, 50, 151–60.

Gohara, M. S. (2006) A lie for a lie: False confessions and the case for reconsidering the legality of deceptive interrogation techniques. *Fordham Urban Law Journal*, 33, 791–842.

Golash, D. (1992) Race, fairness, and jury selection. *Behavioral Sciences & the Law*, 10(2), 155–77.

Goldberg, D. A. (2010) Freud's traumatic memory: Reclaiming seduction theory and revisiting Oedipus. *Psychoanalytic Quarterly*, 79, 532–8.

Goldberg, L. R. (1990) An alternative 'description of personality': The Big-Five factor structure. *Journal of Personality and Social Psychology*, 59, 1216–29.

Golden, C. J. and Zusman, M. R. (2019) Prologue and introduction to CTE and aggression. In C. J. Golden and M. R. Zusman, *Chronic Traumatic Encephalopathy (CTE): Impact on Brains, Emotions and Cognition* (pp. 1–10). Springer.

Golden, S. J., Chu-Hsiang, C. and Kozlowski, S. W. (2017) Teams in isolated, confined, and extreme (ICE) environments: Review and integration. *Journal of Organizational Behavior*, 39(6). https://doi.org/10.1002/job.2288.

Golding, S. L., Roesch, R. and Schreiber, J. (1984) Assessment and conceptualization of competency to stand trial: Preliminary data on the Interdisciplinary Fitness Interview. *Law and Human Behavior*, 8(3/4), 321–34.

Goldner, V. (1999) Morality and multiplicity: Perspectives on the treatment of violence in intimate life. *Journal of Marital and Family Therapy*, 25(3), 325–36.

Goldstein, A. M., Morse, S. J. and Shapiro, D. L. (2003) Evaluation of criminal responsibility. In A. M. Goldstein (ed.) *Handbook of Psychology*: vol. 11. *Forensic Psychology* (pp. 381–406). Wiley.

Goldstein, M. L. (2016) *Ethical Issues in Child Custody Evaluations*. In M. L. Goldstein (ed.) *Handbook of Child Custody* (pp. 3–9). Springer.

Goldstein, R. L. (1983) Sigmund Freud: Forensic psychiatrist. *Journal of the American Academy of Psychiatry and the Law Online*, 11(3), 273–77.

Goldsworthy, R. and Donders, J. (2019) MMPI-2-RF patterns after traumatic brain injury. *Psychological Assessment*, 31(9), 1145–53.

Gooding, P. and Bennet, T. (2018) The abolition of the insanity defense in Sweden and the United Nations Convention on the Rights of Persons with Disabilities: Human rights brinksmanship or evidence it won't work? *New Criminal Law Review: An International and Interdisciplinary Journal*, 21(1), 141–69.

Goodman, G. S. and Melinder, A. (2010) Child witness research and forensic interviews of young children: A review. *Legal and Criminological Psychology*, 12(1), 1–19.

Goodman, G. S., Aman, C. and Hirschman, J. (1987) Child sexual and physical abuse: Children's testimony. In S. J. Ceci, D. F. Ross and M. P. Toglia (eds) *Children's Eyewitness Memory* (pp. 1–23). Springer.

Goodman, G. S., Simona, G., Quas, J. A., Edelstein, R. S., Alexander, K. W., et al. (2003) A prospective study of memory for child sexual abuse: New findings relevant to the repressed-memory controversy. *Psychological Science*, 14(2), 113–118.

Goodman-Delahunty, J., Martschuk, N. and Dhami, M. K. (2014) Interviewing high value detainees: Securing cooperation and disclosures. *Applied Cognitive Psychology*, 28(6), 883–97.

Goodman-Delahunty, J., Martschuk, N. and Ockenden, E. (2016) Effects of terrorist charges and threatening conduct on mock jurors' decisions. *Psychiatry, Psychology and Law*, 23(5), 696–708.

Goodwin, M. and Canter, D. (1997) Encounter and death: The spatial behavior of U.S. serial killers. *Policing: An International Journal of Police Strategy and Management*, 20, 24–38.

Gordon, H. M., Lyon, T. D. and Lee, K. (2014) Social and cognitive factors associated with children's secret-keeping for a parent. *Child Development*, 85(6), 2374–88.

Gordon, N. S. and Fondacaro, M. R. (2018) Rethinking the voluntary act requirement: Implications from neuroscience and behavioral science research. *Behavioral Science and the Law*, 36(4), https://doi.org/10.1002/bsl.2352.

Gorvin, J. J. and Roberts, M. S. (1994) Lunar phases and psychiatric hospital admissions. *Psychological Reports*, 75(3suppl), 1435–40.

Gottfried, E. D., Schenk, A. M. and Vitacco, M. J. (2016) Retrospectively assessing for feigning in criminal responsibility evaluations: Recommendations for clinical practice. *Journal of Forensic Psychology Practice*, 16(2), 118–28.

Gouveia, F. V., Hamani, C., Fonoff, E. T., Brentani, H., Alho, E. J. et al. (2019) Amygdala and hypothalamus: Historical overview with focus on aggression, *Neurosurgery*, 85(1), 11–30.

Grafton, S. T., Sinnott-Armstrong, W., Gazzaniga, S. I. and Gazzaniga, M. S. (2006) Brain scans go legal. *Scientific American Mind*, 17, 30–7.

Granhag, P. A. (2010) The Strategic Use of Evidence (SUE) Technique: A Scientific Perspective. Paper presented at HIG Research Symposium: Interrogation in the European Union.

Granhag, P. A. and Hartwig, M. (2008) A new theoretical perspective on deception detection: On the psychology of instrumental mind-reading. *Psychology, Crime & Law*, 14(3), 189–200.

Granhag, P. A. and Hartwig, M. (2015) The strategic use of evidence technique: A conceptual overview. In P. A. Granhag, A. Vrij and B. Verschuere (eds) *Deception Detection: Current Challenges and Cognitive Approaches* (pp. 231–51). Wiley-Blackwell.

Granhag, P. A. and Vrij, A. (2011) Introduction: What works in investigative psychology? *Legal and Criminological Psychology*, 15(1), 1–159.

Granhag, P. A. and Vrij, A. (2017) Interviewing to detect deception. In P. A. Granhag (ed.) *Forensic Psychology in Context* (pp. 75–93). Willan.

Granhag, P. A., Kleinman, S. M. and Oleszkiewicz, S. (2016) The Scharff technique: On how to effectively elicit intelligence from human sources. *International Journal of Intelligence and Counter Intelligence*, 29(1), 132–50.

Granhag, P. A., Montecinos, S. C. and Oleszkiewicz, S. (2015) Eliciting intelligence from sources: The first scientific test of the Scharff technique. *Legal and Criminological Psychology*, 20, 96–113.

Granhag, P. A., Rangmar, J. and Strömwall, L. A. (2014) Small cells of suspects: Eliciting cues to deception by strategic interviewing. *Journal of Investigative Psychology and Offender Profiling*, 12(2), 127–41.

Granhag, P. A., Hartwig, M., Giolla, E. M. and Clemens, F. (2015) Suspects' verbal counter-interrogation strategies: Towards an integrative model. In P. A. Granhag, A. Vrij and B. Verschuere (eds) *Deception Detection: New Challenges and Cognitive Approaches* (pp. 293–314). Wiley-Blackwell.

Granhag, P. A., Strömwall, L. A., Willén, R. M. and Hartwig, M. (2013) Eliciting cues to deception by tactical disclosure of evidence: The first test of the Evidence Framing Matrix. *Legal and Criminological Psychology*, 18(2), 341–55.

Grant, E. and Jewkes, Y. (2015) Finally fit for purpose: The evolution of Australian prison architecture. *The Prison Journal*, 95(2), 223–43.

Grassian, S. (2006) Psychiatric effects of solitary confinement. *Washington University Journal of Law and Policy*, 22, 325–84.

Grassian, S. and Friedman, N. (1986) Effects of sensory deprivation in psychiatric seclusion and solitary confinement. *International Journal of Law and Psychiatry*, 8, 49–65.

Gray, D. E. (1995) Lay conceptions of autism: Parents' explanatory models. *Medical Anthropology*, 16, 99–118.

Gray, J. (2011) Delusions of peace. *Prospect Magazine*. Available at www.prospectmagazine.co.uk/magazine/john-gray-steven-pinker-violence-review.

Greenall, P. V. and Wright, M. (2019) Stranger sexual homicide: An exploratory behavioral analysis of offender crime scene actions. *Journal of Sexual Aggression*, 1–15.

Greenberg, J., Solomon, S. and Pyszczynski, T. (1997) Terror management theory of self-esteem and cultural worldviews: Empirical assessments and conceptual refinements. In M. P. Zanna (ed.) *Advances in Experimental Social Psychology* (pp. 61–139). Academic Press.

Greenberg, M. M. (2011) *The Mad Bomber of New York: The Extraordinary True Story of the Manhunt that Paralyzed a City*. Union Square Press.

Greene, A. J. (2010) Making connections. *Scientific American Mind*, 21(3), 22–9.

Greene, E. (2009) Psychological issues in civil trials. In J. D. Lieberman and D. A. Krauss (eds) *Jury Psychology: Social Aspects of the Trial Process* (vol. 1, pp. 183–205). Ashgate.

Greenwald, A. G. and Banaji, M. R. (1995) Implicit social cognition: Attitudes, self-esteem, and stereotypes. *Psychological Review*, 102(1), 4–27.

Greer, C. (2017) News media, victims, and crime. In P. Davies, C. Francis and C. Greer (eds) *Victims, Crime, and Society* (pp. 20–49). Sage.

Griffin, R. (2012) The hybrid metapolitics of religious terrorism. In R. Griffin (ed.) *Terrorist's Creed* (pp. 158–72). Palgrave Macmillan.

Griffiths, A. and Milne, R. (2006) Will it all end in tiers? Police interviews with suspects in Britain. In T. Williamson (ed.) *Investigative Interviewing* (pp. 167–89). Willan.

Griffiths, A. and Rachlew, A. (2018) From interrogation to investigative interviewing: The application of psychology. In A. Griffiths and R. Milne (eds) *The Psychology of Criminal Investigation* (pp. 154–78). Routledge.

Grinnell, R. (2018) Just-world hypothesis. *Psych Central.* Available at https://psychcentral.com/encyclopedia/just-world-hypothesis/.

Grisso, T. (2003) *Evaluating Competencies: Forensic Assessment and Instruments* (2nd edn). Kluwer Academic/Plenum.

Groban, M. S. (2016) Intimate partner cyberstalking: Terrorizing intimate partners with 21st Century technology. *United States Attorneys' Bulletin*, 64(3), 12–16.

Grogan, C. and Woody, W. D. (2016) Forensic psychology. In W. D. Woody, R. L. Miller and W. J. Wozniak (eds) *Psychological Specialties in Historical Context: Enriching the Classroom Experience for Teachers and Students* (pp. 430–45). Society for the Teaching of Psychology.

Grose, R. G., Roof, K. A., Semenza, D. C., Leroux, X. and Yount, K. M. (2019) Mental health, empowerment, and violence against young women in lower-income countries: A review of reviews. *Aggression and Violent Behavior*, 46, 25–36.

Gross, C. G. (2002) Genealogy of the 'grandmother cell'. *Neuroscientist*, 8(5), 512–18.

Gross, S. R. and Matheson, D. J. (2002) What they say at the end: Capital victims' families and the press. *Cornell Law Review*, 88(2), 486–516.

Grossman, N. (2019) Just looking: Justice as seen in Hollywood courtroom films. *Law, Culture and the Humanities*, 15(1), 62–105.

Grove, W. M., Zald, D. H., Lebow, B. S., Snitz, B. E. and Nelson, C. (2000) Clinical versus mechanical prediction: A meta-analysis. *Psychological Assessment*, 12(1), 19–30.

Grubb, A. and Harrower, J. (2008) Attribution of blame in cases of rape: An analysis of participant gender, type of rape and perceived similarity to the victim. *Aggression and Violent Behavior*, 13(5), 396–405.

Grubin, D. (2010) The polygraph and forensic psychiatry. *Journal of the American Academy Psychiatry and the Law*, 38, 446–51.

Grysman, A., Harris, C. B., Barnier, A. J. and Savage, G. (2020) Long-married couples recall their wedding day: the influence of collaboration and gender on autobiographical memory recall. *Memory*, 28(1), 18–33.

Guberman, S. (2015) On Gestalt theory principles. *Gestalt Theory*, 37(1), 25–44.

Gudjonsson, G. H. (1988) How to defeat the polygraph tests. In A. Gale (ed.) *The Polygraph Test: Truth, Lies and Science* (pp. 126–36). Sage.

Gudjonsson, G. H. (2003) *The Psychology of Interrogations and Confessions: A Handbook*. John Wiley.

Gudjonsson, G. H. (2010) Psychological vulnerabilities during police interviews: Why are they important? *Legal and Criminological Psychology*, 15(2), 161–75.

Gudjonsson, G. H. and Copson, G. (1997) The role of the expert in criminal investigation. In J. L. Jackson and D. A. Bekerian (eds) *Offender Profiling: Theory, Research and Practice* (pp. 61–76). John Wiley & Sons.

Gudjonsson, G. H. and Grisso, T. (2008) Legal competencies in relation to confession evidence. In A. R. Felthouse and H. Sass (eds) *International Handbook on Psychopathic Disorders and the Law* (vol. 2, pp. 177–87). Wiley.

Gudjonsson, G. H. and Haward, L. R. (2016) *Forensic Psychology: A Guide to Practice*. Routledge.

Gustafsson, P. U., Lindholm, T. and Jönsson, F. U. (2019) Predicting accuracy in eyewitness testimonies with memory retrieval effort and confidence. *Frontiers in Psychology*, 10, 1–10.

Guszkowski, K. N. and van Hasselt, V. B. (2017) Crisis (hostage) negotiations. In V. B. Van Hasselt and M. L. Bourke (eds) *Handbook of Behavioral Criminology* (pp. 591–610). Springer.

Haas, S. M. and Smith, J. (2019) Core correctional practice: The role of the working alliance in offender rehabilitation. In P. Ugwudike et al. (eds) *The Routledge Companion to Rehabilitative Work in Criminal Justice* (pp. 339–51). Routledge.

Habermas, T. and Berger, N. (2011) Retelling everyday emotional events: Condensation, distancing, and closure. *Cognition and Emotion*, 25(2), 206–19.

Hackel, J. (2014) Torture doesn't work – so here's what does. *The World*, 10 December. Available at www.pri.org/stories/2014-12-10/former-army-interrogator-says-his-techniques-were-never-enhanced.

Hackman, S. L., Raitt, F. and Black, S. (eds) (2019) *The Expert Witness, Forensic Science, and the Criminal Justice Systems of the UK*. CRC Press.

Hafer, C. L., Bègue, L., Choma, B. L. and Dempsey, J. L. (2005) Belief in a just world and commitment to long-term deserved outcomes. *Social Justice Research*, 18(4), 429–44.

Haj-Yahia, M. M., Sousa, C. A. and Lugassi, R. (2019) The relationship between exposure to violence in the family of origin during childhood, psychological distress, and perpetrating violence in intimate relationships among male university students. *Journal of Interpersonal Violence*, doi: 10.1177/0886260519843280.

Hala, S., Rasmussen, C. and Henderson, A. M. (2005) Three types of source monitoring by children with and without autism: the role of executive function. *Journal of Autism and Developmental Disorders*, 35(1), 75–89.

Halber, D. (2007) Scientists swear a good lie detector is hard to find. MIT Tech Talk. Available at http://news.mit.edu//2007/techtalk51-17.pdf.

Hale, M. (1980) *Human Science and Social Order*. Temple University Press.

Halprin, J. (1996) *The Truth Machine*. Del Rey.

Hamilton, D. L. and Sherman, S. J. (1996) Perceiving persons and groups. *Psychological Review*, 103(2), 336–55.

Hamilton, I. S. (2006) *An Asperger Dictionary of Everyday Expressions* (2nd edn). Jessica Kingsley.

Hammel, T. (2019) Bell mental health-jail bill inspired by Jamycheal Mitchell case. *The Daily Progress*, 24 February. Available at www.dailyprogress.com/news/state/bell-mental-health-jail-bill-inspired-by-jamycheal-mitchell-case/article_2399791e-389c-11e9-861b-8f05853434af.html.

Hancock, P. and Weaver, J. (2005) On time distortion under stress. *Theoretical Issues in Ergonomics Science*, 6(2), 193–211.

Haney, C. (2017) 'Madness' and penal confinement: Some observations on mental illness and prison pain. *Punishment and Society*, 19(3), 310–26.

Haney, C. (2018) The psychological effects of solitary confinement: A systematic critique. *Crime and Justice*, 47(1), 365–416.

Hanganu-Bresch, C. (2019) Public perceptions of moral insanity in the 19th century. *The Journal of Nervous and Mental Disease*, 207(9), 805–14.

Hanna, N. (2019) Hitting retributivism where it hurts. *Criminal Law and Philosophy*, 13(1), 109–27.

Hans, V. P. (2014) Reflections on the Korean jury trial. *Journal of Korean Law*, 14(1), 81–115.

Hans, V. P. (2015) Jury research ethics and the integrity of jury deliberations. In J. Kleinig and J. P. Levine (eds) *Jury Ethics: Juror Conduct and Jury Dynamics* (pp. 261–88). Routledge.

Hansen, B. (2015) Punishment and deterrence: Evidence from drunk driving. *American Economic Review*, 105(4), 1581–717.

Hanson, R. K. and Morton-Bourgon, K. E. (2005) The characteristics of persistent sexual offenders: A meta-analysis. *Journal of Consulting and Clinical Psychology*, 73, 1154–63.

Hanson, R. K., Babchishin, K. M., Helmus, L. M., Thornton, D. and Phenix, A. (2017) Communicating the results of criterion referenced prediction measures: Risk categories for the Static-99R and Static-2002R sexual offender risk assessment tools. *Psychological Assessment*, 29(5), 582.

Hansson, S. O. (2013) Defining pseudoscience and science. In M. Boudry and M. Pigliucci (eds) *Philosophy of Pseudoscience: Reconsidering the Demarcation Problem* (pp. 61–77). University of Chicago Press.

Happé, F., Booth, R., Charlton, R. and Hughes, C. (2006) Executive function deficits in autism spectrum disorders and attention-deficit/hyperactivity disorder: Examining profiles across domains and ages. *Brain Cognition*, 61(1), 25–39.

Hardcastle, V. G. and Lamb, E. (2018) What difference do brain images make in US criminal trials? *Journal of Evaluation in Clinical Practice*, 24(4), 909–15.

Hardy, M., Kennedy, J., Reid, M. and Cooper, D. (2020) Differences in posttraumatic stress disorder, depression, and attribution of symptoms in service members with combat versus noncombat mild traumatic brain injury. *Journal of Head Trauma Rehabilitation*, 35(1), 37–45.

Harki, G. (2018) Horrific deaths, brutal treatment: Mental illness in America's jails. *The Virginian-Pilot*, 23 August. Available at www.pilotonline.com/projects/jail-crisis/article_5ba8a112-974e-11e8-ba17-b734814f14db.html-2.

Harkin, D., Molnar, A. and Vowles, E. (2020) The commodification of mobile phone surveillance: An analysis of the consumer spyware industry. *Crime, Media, Culture*, 16(1), 33–60.

Harper, C. A., Hogue, T. E. and Bartels, R. M. (2017) Attitudes towards sexual offenders: What do we know, and why are they important? *Aggression and Violent Behaviour*, 34, 201–13.

Harpold, J. A. and Feemster, S. L. (2002) Negative influences of police stress. *FBI Law Enforcement Bulletin*, 71(1), 1–7.

Harpster, N. T. (2018) Jails compared to prisons. In V. B. Worley and R. M. Worley (eds) *American Prisons and Jails: An Encyclopedia of Controversies and Trends*, 2 vols. ABC-CLIO.

Harris, G. T. and Rice, M. E. (2007) Adjusting actuarial violence risk assessments based on aging or the passage of time. *Criminal Justice and Behavior*, 34(3), 297–313.

Harris, M. (2018) The lie generator: Inside the black mirror world of polygraph job screenings. *Wired Magazine*, 1 October. Available at www.wired.com/story/inside-polygraph-job-screening-black-mirror/.

Harris, S. (2010) Toward a better way to interview child victims of sexual abuse. *NIJ Journal*, 267, 12–15. Available at www.ncjrs.gov/pdffiles1/nij/233282.pdf.

Hart, S. D. and Cooke, D. J. (2013) Another look at the (im-)precision of individual risk estimates made using actuarial risk assessment instruments. *Behavioral Sciences & the Law*, 31(1), 81–102.

Hart, S. D., Douglas, K. S. and Guy, L. S. (2017) The structured professional judgement approach to violence risk assessment: Origins, nature, and advances. In D. P. Boer et al. (eds) *The Wiley Handbook on the Theories, Assessment, and Treatment of Sexual Offending* (pp. 643–66). Wiley-Blackwell.

Hartley, T. A., Mnatsakanova, A., Burchfiel, C. M. and Violanti, J. M. (2014) Stressors and associated health effects for women police officers. In J. M. Violanti (ed.) *Dying for the Job: Police Work Exposure and Health* (pp. 93–114). Charles C. Thomas.

Hartney, T. (2018) Likeness used as bait in catfishing: How can hidden victims of catfishing reel in relief? *Minnesota Journal of Science & Technology*, 19, 277–303.

Hartwig, M. and Bond, C. F. Jr (2014) Lie detection from multiple cues: A meta-analysis. *Applied Cognitive Psychology*, 28(5), 661–76.

Hartwig, M., Granhag, P. A. and Strömwall, L. A. (2007) Guilty and innocent suspects' strategies during police interrogations. *Psychology, Crime & Law*, 13(2), 213–27.

Hartwig, M., Granhag, P. A., Strömwall, L. A. and Doering, N. (2010) Impression and information management: On the strategic self-regulation of innocent and guilty suspects. *Open Criminology Journal*, 3, 10–26.

Hartwig, M., Granhag, P. A., Strömwall, L. A. and Kronkvist, O. (2006) Strategic use of evidence during police interviews: When training to detect deception works. *Law and Human Behavior*, 30(5), 603–19.

Harvey, I. (2018) The most controversial case of sleepwalking homicide in history. The Vintage News. com, 23 October. Available at www.thevintagenews.com/2018/10/23/homicidal-sleepwalking/.

Hassan, S. (2000) *Releasing the Bonds: Empowering People to Thrive for Themselves*. Freedom of Mind Press.

Hatcher, C., Mohandie, K., Turner, J. and Gelles, M. G. (1998) The role of the psychologist in crisis/hostage negotiations. *Behavioral Sciences & the Law*, 16(4), 455–72.

Hattery, A. and Smith, E. (2016) *The Social Dynamics of Family Violence*. Westview Press.

Hauge, M. V., Stevenson, M. D., Rossmo, D. K. and Le Comber, S. C. (2016) Tagging Banksy: Using geographic profiling to investigate a modern art mystery. *Journal of Spatial Science*, 61(1), 185–90.

Hazelwood, L. D. and Brigham, J. C. (1998) The effects of juror anonymity on jury verdicts. *Law & Human Behavior*, 22(6), 695–713.

Hazelwood, R. R. and Napier, M. R. (2004) Crime scene staging and its detection. *International Journal of Offender Therapy and Comparative Criminology*, 48(6), 744–59.

Hazelwood, R. R., Ressler, R. K., Depue, R. L. and Douglas, J. C. (1995) Criminal investigative analysis: An overview. In A. W. Burgess and R. R. Hazelwood (eds) *Practical Aspects of Rape Investigation: A Multidisciplinary Approach* (2nd edn, pp. 115–26). CRC Press.

Hearnshaw, L. S. (2020) *The Shaping of Modern Psychology: An Historical Introduction*. Routledge.

Hebert, D. J., Crowley, G. R. and Trudeau, N. (2017) Compensating suicide. *Journal of Private Enterprise*, 33(4), 45–60.

Heinke, D. H. and Persson, M. (2016) Youth specific factors in radicalization. *Defence Against Terrorism Review*, 8, 53–66.

Henkel, L. A. (2013) Do older adults change their eyewitness reports when re-questioned? *Journals of Gerontology, Series B: Psychological Sciences and Social Sciences*, 69(3), 356–65.

Henkel, L. A. and Coffman, K. J. (2004) Memory distortions in coerced false confessions: A source monitoring framework analysis. *Applied Cognitive Psychology*, 18(5), 567–88.

Henkel, L. A., Coffman, K. J. and Dailey, E. (2008) A survey of people's beliefs and attitudes about false confessions. *Behavioral Sciences & the Law*, 26(5), 555–84.

Herbert, W. (2009) Witness for the prosecution. Association for Psychological Science, 9 January. Available at www.psychologicalscience.org/onlyhuman/2009/01/witness-for-prosecution.cfm.

Herbig, F. J. and Hesselink, A. M. (2013) Seeing the person, not just the number: Needs-based rehabilitation of offenders in South Africa. *SA Crime Quarterly*, 4(9), 29–37.

Herman, J. L. (1992) *Trauma and Recovery: The Aftermath of Violence from Domestic Abuse to Political Terror*. Basic Books.

Hershkowitz, I. (2009) Socioemotional factors in child sexual abuse investigations. *Child Maltreatment*, 14, 172–81.

Hershkowitz, I., Horowitz, D. and Lamb, M. E. (2005) Trends in children's disclosure of abuse in Israel: A national study. *Child Abuse & Neglect*, 29, 1203–14.

Hershkowitz, I., Lamb, M. E., Katz, C. and Malloy, L. C. (2015) Does enhanced rapport-building alter the dynamics of investigative interviews with suspected victims of intra-familial abuse? *Journal of Police and Criminal Psychology*, 30(1), 6–14.

Herz, R. S. (2016) The role of odor-evoked memory in psychological and physiological health. *Brain Sciences*, 6(3), 22. doi: 10.3390/brainsci6030022.

Hess, C. W. (1994) Sleep disorders and dementia. *Praxis*, 86, 1343–49.

Hettinger, V. E. and Vandello, J. A. (2014) Balance without equality: Just world beliefs, the gay affluence myth, and support for gay rights. *Social Justice Research*, 27(4), 444–63.

Hewitt, A. N., Beauregard, E. and Davies, G. (2016) An empirical examination of the victim-search methods utilized by serial stranger sexual offenders: A classification approach. *Journal of Interpersonal Violence*, 34(21/22), DOI: 10.1177/0886260516675921.

Hicks, S. J., and Sales, B. D. (2006) *Criminal Profiling: Developing an Effective Science and Practice.* APA.

Higley, C. A., Lloyd, C. D. and Serin, R. (2019) Age and motivation can be specific responsivity features that moderate the relationship between risk and rehabilitation outcome. *Law and Human Behavior*, 43(6), 558–67.

Hill, E. L. (2004) Evaluating the theory of executive dysfunction in autism. *Developmental Review*, 24, 189–233.

Hilvert-Bruce, Z. and Neill, J. T. (2020) I'm just trolling: The role of normative beliefs in aggressive behaviour in online gaming. *Computers in Human Behaviour*, 102, 303–11.

Hinduja, S. and Patchin, J. W. (2020) Digital dating abuse among a national sample of US youth. *Journal of Interpersonal Violence*. DOI: 10.1177/0886260519897344.

Hines, N. (2009) Double jeopardy killer Mario Celaire gets minimum of 23 years jail. *The Times*. Available at www.thetimes.co.uk/article/double-jeopardy-killer-mario-celaire-gets-minimum-of-23-years-jail-dlrxvnm9jth.

Hinsz, V. B., Betts, K. R., Sánchez-Manzanares, M. and Tindale, R. S. (2020) How interacting groups remember: Implications for learning by groups and organizations. In L. Argote and J. M. Levine (eds) *The Oxford Handbook of Group and Organizational Learning.* Oxford University Press.

Hinz, T. and Pezdek, K. (2001) The effect of exposure to multiple lineups on face identification accuracy. *Law and Human Behavior*, 25(2), 185–98.

Hitt, J. (2012) Words on trial: Can linguistics solve crimes that stump the police? *The New Yorker*, July 23. Available at www.newyorker.com/magazine/2012/07/23/words-on-trial.

HM Government (2009) *Pursue, Prevent, Protect, Prepare: The United Kingdom's Strategy for Countering International Terrorism.* Available at https://assets.publishing.service.gov.uk/government/uploads/system/uploads/attachment_data/file/228644/7547.pdf.

Hobbs, D. (2019) Faces in the clouds: Criminology, epochalism, apophenia and transnational organized crime. In T. Hall and V. Scalia (eds) *A Research Agenda for Global Crime.* Edward Elgar.

Hockett, J. M., Smith, S. J., Klausing, C. D. and Saucier, D. A. (2016) Rape myth consistency and gender differences in perceiving rape victims: A meta-analysis. *Violence against Women*, 22(2), 139–67.

Hodge, M. (2018) Japan's death row executes inmates without any warning. *New York Post*, 6 July. Available at nypost.com/2018/07/06/japans-death-row-executes-inmates-without-any-warning/.

Hodwitz, O. (2020) Threats to aviation: Modeling effectiveness. *Journal of Applied Security Research*, 1–23.

Hoffer, T., Hargreaves-Cormany, H., Muirhead, Y. and Meloy, J. R. (2018) Comparison of affective and predatory offenders. In T. Hoffer, H. Hargreaves-Cormany, Y. Muirhead and J. R. Meloy (eds) *Violence in Animal Cruelty Offenders* (pp. 93–4). Springer.

Hoffman, M. B. (2018) Nine neurolaw predictions. *New Criminal Law Review: An International and Interdisciplinary Journal*, 21(2), 212–46.

Hoffmann, J. (2017) The Virginia Tech massacre as a starting point for threat assessment programs in European universities. *Journal of Threat Assessment and Management*, 4, 112–17.

Hoffmeister, T. and Watts, A. C. (2018) Social media, the internet, and trial by jury. *Annual Review of Law and Social Science*, 14, 259–70.

Hoge, R. D. (2016) Risk, need, and responsivity in juveniles. In K. Heilbrun (ed.) *APA Handbook of Psychology and Juvenile Justice* (pp. 179–96). APA.

Hoge, S. K. (2016) Competence to stand trial: An overview. *Indian Journal of Psychiatry*, 58(2), 187–90.

Hoge, S. K., Bonnie, R. J., Poythress, N. and Monahan, J. (1999) *The MacArthur Competence Assessment Tool: Criminal Adjudication.* Psychological Assessment Resources.

Hogg, K. W. (2019) Runaway jurors. *Western Journal of Legal Studies*, 9(1), 1–14.

Hogg, M. A. (2016) Social identity theory. In S. McKeown et al. (eds) *Understanding Peace and Conflict Through Social Identity Theory* (pp. 3–17). Springer.

Hogg, M. A. and Mahajan, N. (2018) Domains of self-uncertainty and their relationship to group identification. *Journal of Theoretical Social Psychology*, 2(3), 67–75.

Hogg, M. A., Sherman, D. K., Dierselhuis, J., Maitner, A. T. and Moffitt, G. (2007) Uncertainty, entitativity, and group identification. *Journal of Experimental Social Psychology*, 43(1), 135–42.

Holmberg, U. and Christianson, S. (2002) Murderers' and sexual offenders' experiences of police interviews and their inclination to admit or deny crimes. *Behavioral Sciences & the Law*, 20, 31–45.

Holmes, R. M. and Holmes, S. T. (1996) *Profiling Violent Crimes: An Investigative Tool* (2nd edn). Sage.

Holmes, R. M. and Holmes, S. T. (2010) *Serial Murder* (3rd edn). Sage.

Holstein, J. A. (1985) Jurors' interpretations and jury decision making. *Law and Human Behavior*, 9(1), 83–100.

Home Office (2019) *CODE C: Revised: Code of Practice for the Detention, Treatment and Questioning of Persons by Police Officers*. TSO. Available at https://assets. publishing.service.gov.uk/government/uploads/system/uploads/attachment_data/file/826813/PACE-Code-C_2019.pdf.

Hong, V., Pirnie, L. and Shobassy, A. (2019) Antisocial and borderline personality disorders in the emergency department: Conceptualizing and managing 'malingered' or 'exaggerated' symptoms. *Current Behavioural Neuroscience Reports*, 1–6.

Honts, C. R., Raskin, D. C. and Kirchera, J. C. (1994) Mental and physical countermeasures reduce the accuracy of polygraph tests. *Journal of Applied Psychology*, 79(2), 252–9.

Honts, C. R., Devitt, M. K., Winbush, M. and Kircher, J. C. (2007) Mental and physical countermeasures reduce the accuracy of the concealed knowledge test. *Psychophysiology*, 33(1), 84–92.

Honts, C. R., Raskin, D. C., Kircher, J. C. and Hodes, R. L. (1988) Effects of spontaneous countermeasures on the physiological detection of deception. *Journal of Police Science and Administration*, 16, 91–4.

Hooper, J. (2002) How teacher stopped the school slaughter. *The Guardian*, 28 April. Available at www.theguardian.com/world/2002/apr/28/schools. education.

Hope, L., Memon, A. and McGeorge, P. (2004) Understanding pretrial publicity: Predecisional distortion of evidence by mock jurors. *Journal of Experimental Psychology: Applied*, 10(2), 111–19.

Horan, J. (2012) *Juries in the 21st Century*. Federation Press.

Horan, J. and Israel, M. (2016) Beyond the legal barriers: Institutional gatekeeping and real jury research. *Australian & New Zealand Journal of Criminology*, 49(3), 422–36.

Horgan, J. (2003) The search for the terrorist personality. In A. Silke (ed.) *Terrorists, Victims and Society: Psychological Perspectives on Terrorism and its Consequences* (pp. 3–27). Wiley.

Horn, S. R., Charney, D. S. and Feder, A. (2016) Understanding resilience: new approaches for preventing and treating PTSD. *Experimental Neurology*, 284, 119–32.

Horton, A. M. Jr and Soper, H. V. (2019) Forensic psychology: practice issues. In G. Goldstein, D. N. Allen and J. DeLuca (eds) *Handbook of Psychological Assessment* (4th edn, pp. 533–50). Academic Press.

Horvath, F. S. (1977) The effect of selected variables in interpretation of polygraph records. *Journal of Applied Psychology*, 62(2), 127–36.

Horvath, F. S., Blair, J. P. and Buckley, J. P. (2008) The behavioral analysis interview: Clarifying the practice, theory and understanding of its use and effectiveness. *International Journal of Police Science and Management*, 10(1), 101–18.

Hough, J. (2014) Sammy Yatim's family sues Toronto police for $8-million for using 'excessive' force the night of streetcar shooting. *National Post*, 23 July. Available at https://nationalpost.com/news/toronto/sammy-yatims-family-sues-toronto-police-for-8-million-for-using-excessive-force-the-night-of-streetcar-shooting.

Houston, J. P., Bee, H. and Rimm, D. C. (2013) *Invitation to Psychology*. Academic Press.

Howe, K. L. (2019) Unravelling the nature of early (autobiographical) memory. *Memory*, 27(1), 115–21.

Howell, C. and West, D. (2016) *The Internet as a Human Right*. Brookings Institution.

Howitt, D. (2009) *Introduction to Forensic and Criminal Psychology*. Pearson.

Hsu, C. W., Begliomini, C., Dall'Acqua, T. and Ganis, G. (2019) The effect of mental countermeasures on neuroimaging-based concealed information tests. *Human Brain Mapping*, 40(10), 2899–916.

Hudson, C. A., Vrij, A., Akehurst, L. and Hope, L. (2019) The devil is in the detail: Deception and consistency over repeated interviews. *Psychology, Crime & Law*, 25(7), 752–70.

Huff, R. C., Rattner, A., Sagarin, E. and MacNamara, D. E. (1986) Guilty until proved innocent: Wrongful conviction and public policy. *Crime Delinquency*, 32(4), 518–44.

Hughes, M. and Cossar, J. (2016) The relationship between maternal childhood emotional abuse/neglect and parenting outcomes: A systematic review. *Child Abuse Review*, 25, 31–45.

Hulse, L. M. and Memon, A. (2006) Fatal impact? The effects of emotional arousal and weapon presence on police officers' memories for a simulated crime. *Legal and Criminological Psychology*, 11(2), 313–25.

Hunter, J., Roberts, P., Young, S. N. and Dixon, D. (eds) (2016) *The Integrity of Criminal Process: From Theory into Practice*. Bloomsbury.

Hurst, P. (2017) Ann Maguire inquest: 'He's stabbed me in the neck... I'm dying', teacher gasped after fatal knife attack by student. *The Independent*, 17 November. Available at www.independent.co.uk/

news/uk/crime/ann-maguire-inquest-latest-will-cornick-knife-attack-last-words-stabbed-me-dying-leeds-a8059991.html.

Husak, D. N. (2017) Kinds of Punishment. Available at https://ssrn.com/abstract=2979458.

Hussain, K., Wijetunge, D. B., Grubnic, S. and Jackson, I. T. (1994) A comprehensive analysis of craniofacial trauma. *Journal of Trauma*, 36(1), 34–47.

Hutchinson, B. and Ghebremedhin, S. (2018) Officer who killed unarmed black man responds to critics of her 'critical incident' course. ABC News, 29 August. Available at https://abcnews.go.com/US/protest-erupts-critical-incident-class-taught-oklahoma-officer/story?id=57448147.

Hylton, K. N. (2019) Economic theory of criminal law. Boston University School of Law, Law and Economics Research Paper No. 19. https://papers.ssrn.com/sol3/papers.cfm?abstract_id=3382512.

Hyman, I., Husband, T. and Billings, J. F. (1995) False memories of childhood experiences. *Applied Cognitive Psychology*, 9, 181–97.

Iacono, W. G. and Ben-Shakhar, G. (2019) Current status of forensic lie detection with the comparison question technique: An update of the 2003 National Academy of Sciences report on polygraph testing. *Law and Human Behavior*, 43(1), 86–98.

IACP's Alzheimer's Initiatives (2019) *A Guide to Law Enforcement on Voluntary Registry Programs for Vulnerable Populations*. Available at www.theiacp.org/sites/default/files/all/a/Alz%20Voluntary%20Registry.pdf.

Inbau, F. E., Reid, J. E. and Buckley, J. P. (1986) *Criminal Investigation and Confessions*. Williams and Wilkins.

Inbau, F. E., Reid, J. E., Buckley, J. P. and Jayne, B. C. (2013) *Criminal Interrogation and Confessions* (5th edn). Jones & Bartlett Learning.

Innocence Project (2018) *Innocence Project*. Available at www.innocenceproject.org/.

Innocence Project (2020) DNA Exonerations in the United States. Available at www.innocenceproject.org/dna-exonerations-in-the-united-states/.

Ireland, C. A. (2017) Assessment of hostage situations and their perpetrators: In the context of domestic violence. In K. Browne et al. (eds) *Assessments in Forensic Practice: A Handbook* (pp. 319–32). Wiley & Sons.

Ireland, C. A. and Vecchi, G. M. (2009) The Behavioral Influence Stairway Model (BISM): A framework for managing terrorist crisis situations? *Behavioral Sciences of Terrorism and Political Aggression*, 1(3), 203–18.

Ireland, J. and Beaumont, J. (2015) Admitting scientific expert evidence in the UK: Reliability challenges and the need for revised criteria – proposing an abridged Daubert. *Journal of Forensic Practice*, 17(1), 3–12.

Irina, F., Tobias, V., Reinhard, E. and Manuela, D. (2019) Prison mental healthcare: Recent developments and future challenges. *Current Opinion in Psychiatry*, 32(4), 342–7.

Irshaid, F. (2015) Isis, Isil, IS or Daesh? One group, many names. *BBC News*, 2 December. Available at www.bbc.co.uk/news/world-middle-east-27994277.

Iverson, G. I., Franzen, M. D. and Hammond, J. A. (1995) Examination of inmates' ability to malinger on the MMPI-2. *Psychological Assessment*, 7, 118–21.

Ives, D. E. (2007) Preventing false confessions: Is Oickle up to the task? *San Diego Law Review*, 44, 477–90.

Iwashiro, N., Takano, Y., Natsubori, T., Aoki, Y., Yahata, N. et al. (2019) Aberrant attentive and inattentive brain activity to auditory negative words, and its relation to persecutory delusion in patients with schizophrenia. *Neuropsychiatric Disease and Treatment*, 15, 491–502.

Jackman, T. (2017) 'Norfolk 4,' wrongly convicted of rape and murder, pardoned by Gov. McAuliffe. *Washington Post*, 21 March. Available at www.washingtonpost.com/news/true-crime/wp/2017/03/21/norfolk-4-wrongly-convicted-of-rape-and-murder-pardoned-by-gov-mcauliffe/?utm_term=.2fe95322333c.

Jackson, J. (2016) Unbecoming jurors and unreasoned verdicts: Realising integrity in the jury room. In J. Hunter et al. (eds) *The Integrity of Criminal Process: From Theory Into Practice* (pp. 281–308). Hart.

Jackson, J. D. and Kovalev, N. P. (2006) Lay adjudication and human rights in Europe. *Columbia Journal of European Law*, 13(1), 83–123.

Jackson, J. D. and Kovalev, N. P. (2016) Lay adjudication in Europe: The rise and fall of the traditional jury. *Oñati Socio-legal Series*, 6(2), 368–95.

Jackson, J. L. and Bekerian, D. A. (1997) Does offender profiling have a role to play? In J. L. Jackson and D. A. Bekerian (eds) *Offender Profiling: Theory, Research and Practice* (pp. 1–7). John Wiley.

Jacobsson, A., Backteman-Erlanson, S., Brulin, C. and Hörnsten, Å. (2015) Experiences of critical incidents among female and male firefighters. *International Emergency Nursing*, 23(2), 100–4.

Jafari, Z., Kolb, B. E. and Mohajerani, M. H. (2017) Effect of acute stress on auditory processing: A systematic review of human studies. *Reviews in the Neurosciences*, 28(1), 1–13.

James, J. and Proulx, J. (2016) The modus operandi of serial and nonserial sexual murderers: A systematic review. *Aggression and Violent Behavior*, 31, 200–18.

James, J., Crane, J. and Hinchliffe, J. A. (2005) Injury assessment, documentation, and interpretation. In M. M. Stark (ed.) *Clinical Forensic Medicine: A Physician's Guide* (2nd edn, pp. 127–58). Humana Press.

James, N. (2018) *Risk and Needs Assessment in the Federal Prison System*. Congressional Research

Service. 7-5700. Available at https://fas.org/sgp/crs/misc/R44087.pdf.

James, R. J. and Tunney, R. J. (2017) The need for a behavioural analysis of behavioural addictions. *Clinical Psychology Review*, 52, 69–76.

James, V. (2019) Denying the darkness: Exploring the discourses of neutralization of Bundy, Gacy, and Dahmer. *Societies*, 9(46), 1–17.

Jameton, A. (1993) Dilemmas of moral distress: Moral responsibility and nursing practice. *AWHONN's Clinical Issues in Perinatal and Women's Health Nursing*, 4(4), 542–51.

Janoff-Bulman, R., Timko, C. and Carli, L. L. (1985) Cognitive biases in blaming the victim. *Journal of Experimental Social Psychology*, 21(2), 161–77.

Janofsky, J. S., Hanson, A., Candilis, P. J., Myers, W. C., Zonana, H. et al. (2014) AAPL practice guideline for forensic psychiatric evaluation of defendants raising the insanity defense. *Journal of the American Academy of Psychiatry and the Law*, 42, S3–76.

Jansari, A. and Parkin, A. J. (1996) Things that go bump in your life: Explaining the reminiscence bump in autobiographical memory. *Psychology and Aging*, 11(1), 85–91.

Janssen, S. M., Kristo, G., Rouw, R. and Murre, J. M. (2015) The relation between verbal and visuospatial memory and autobiographical memory. *Consciousness and Cognition*, 31, 12–23.

Jay, A. C., Stone, C. B., Meksin, R., Merck, C., Gordon, N. S. and Hirst, W. (2019) The mnemonic consequences of jurors' selective retrieval during deliberation. *Topics in Cognitive Science*, 11(4). https://doi.org/10.1111/tops.12435.

Jenkins, E. N., Allison, P., Innes, K., Violanti, J. M. and Andrew, M. E. (2019) Depressive symptoms among police officers: Associations with personality and psychosocial factors. *Journal of Police and Criminal Psychology*, 34(1), 67–77.

Jewkes, Y. (2015) *Media and Crime* (3rd edn). Sage.

Jian, Z., Zhang, W., Tian, L., Fan, W. and Zhong, Y. (2019) Self-deception reduces cognitive load: The role of involuntary conscious memory impairment. *Frontiers in Psychology*, 10, https://doi.org/10.3389/fpsyg.2019.01718.

Jimenez, X.F., Nkanginieme, N., Dhand, N., Karafa, M. and Salerno, K. (2019) Clinical, demographic, psychological, and behavioral features of factitious disorder: A retrospective analysis. *General Hospital Psychiatry*, 63, 93–5.

Joëls, M. and Baram, T. Z. (2009) The neuro-symphony of stress. *Nature Reviews Neuroscience*, 10(6), 459–66.

Johner, D. (2019) 'One is the loneliest number': A comparison of solitary confinement practices in the United States informed anger management. *Penn State Journal of Law & International Affairs*, 7(1), 230–50.

Johnson, C. L. and Cullen, F. T. (2015) Offender reentry programs. *Crime and Justice*, 44(1), 517–75.

Johnson, D. T. (2020) Why does Japan retain capital punishment? In D. T. Johnson, *The Culture of Capital Punishment in Japan* (pp. 1–18). Palgrave Pivot.

Johnson, E. F. and Thompson, C. M. (2016) Factors associated with stalking persistence. *Psychology, Crime & Law*, 22(9), 879–902.

Johnson, H. and Hotton, T. (2003) Losing control: Homicide risk in estranged and intact intimate relationships. *Homicide Studies*, 7(1), 58–84.

Johnson, K. E., Thompson, J., Hall, J. A. and Meyer, C. (2018) Crisis (hostage) negotiators weigh in: The skills, behaviors, and qualities that characterize an expert crisis negotiator. *Police Practice and Research*, 19(5), 472–89.

Johnson, M. K., Hashtroudi, S. and Lindsay, D. S. (1993) Source monitoring. *Psychological Bulletin*, 114(1), 3–28.

Johnson, P. S., Madden, G. J., Brewer, A. T., Pinkston, J. W. and Fowler, S. C. (2011) Effects of acute pramipexole on preference for gambling-like schedules of reinforcement in rats. *Psychopharmacology*, 213(1), 11–18.

Johnson, S. B. and Giedd, J. N. (2015) Normal brain development and child/adolescent policy. In J. Clausen and N. Levy (eds) *Handbook of Neuroethics* (pp. 1721–35). Springer.

Johnson, S. D. (2014) How do offenders choose where to offend? Perspectives from animal foraging. *Legal and Criminological Psychology*, 19, 193–210.

Joldasbayevich, R. M. (2019) Legal analysis of termination of legal capacity of a citizen. *International Journal of Research*, 6(11), 374–9.

Jolivette, K. and Nelson, M. C. (2017) Adapting positive behavioral interventions and supports for secure juvenile justice settings: Improving facility-wide behavior. *Behavioral Disorders*, 36(1), 28–42.

Jones, A. M. and Kovera, M. B. (2015) A demonstrative helps opposing expert testimony sensitize jurors to the validity of scientific evidence. *Journal of Forensic Psychology Practice*, 15(5), 401–22.

Jones, A. M. and Penrod, S. (2016) Can expert testimony sensitize jurors to coercive interrogation tactics? *Journal of Forensic Psychology Practice*, 16(5), 393–409.

Jones, C., Otey, A. J., Papadmos, T. J., Cook, C. H., Stawicki, S. P. and Evans, D. C. (2017) Association between intentional ingestion of foreign objects and psychiatric disease among prisoners: A retrospective study. *International Journal of Academic Medicine*, 3, 16–22.

Jones, C. E. (2013) I am Ronald Cotton: Teaching wrongful convictions in a criminal law class. *Ohio State Journal of Criminal Law*, 10(2), 609–11.

Jones, C. S. and Kaplan, M. F. (2003) The effects of racially stereotypical crimes on juror decision-making and information-processing strategies. *Basic and Applied Social Psychology*, 25(1), 1–13.

Jones, D. (2010) Beyond waterboarding, the sciences of interrogation. *New Scientist*, 205(2750), 40–3.

Jones, L. M., Cross, T. P., Walsh, W. A. and Simone, M. (2005) Criminal investigations of child abuse: The research behind 'best practices.' *Trauma, Violence and Abuse*, 6(3), 254–68.

Jones, R. and Elliot, T. (2005) Capacity to give evidence in court: Issues that may arise when a client with dementia is a victim of crime. *Psychiatric Bulletin*, 29, 324–6.

Jordan, S., Hartwig, M., Wallace, B., Dawson, E. and Xhihani, A. (2012) Early versus late disclosure of evidence: Effects on verbal cues to deception, confessions, and lie catcher's accuracy. *Journal of investigative Psychology and Offender Profiling*, 9, 1–2.

Joy Tong, L. S. and Farrington, D. P. (2006) How effective is the 'reasoning and rehabilitation' program in reducing reoffending? A meta-analysis of evaluations in four countries. *Psychology, Crime and Law*, 12(1), 3–24.

Judges, D. P. (2000) Two cheers for the department of justice's eyewitness evidence: A guide for law enforcement. *Arkansas Law Review*, 53(37), 231, 243–44.

Jung, J., Grim, P., Singer, D. J., Bramson, A., Berger, W. J. et al. (2019) A multidisciplinary understanding of polarization. *American Psychologist*, 74(3), 301–14.

Junker, G., Beeler, A. and Bates, J. (2005) Using trained inmate observers for suicide watch in a federal correctional setting: A win–win solution. *Psychological Services*, 2(1), 20–7.

Juozapavicius, J. (2016) Tulsa police say man had no gun; video shows he had hands up. ABC, 19 September. Available at https://apnews.com/d579b4424f3a4494ae5c5b31b12e54b3.

Jenkins, P. (1994) *Using Murder: The Social Construction of Serial Homicide*. Aldine de Gruyter.

Kaba, F., Lewis, A., Glowa-Kollisch, S., Hadler, J., Lee, D. et al. (2014) Solitary confinement and risk of self-harm among jail inmates. *American Journal of Public Health*, 104, 442–7.

Kaczynski, D. (2015) *Every Last Tie: The Story of the Unabomber and his Family*. Duke University Press.

Kahneman, D. (2011) *Thinking, Fast and Slow*. Farrar, Straus and Giroux.

Kalven, H. and Zeisel, H. (1966) *The American Jury*. University of Chicago Press.

Kandel, E. R. (2007) *In Search of Memory: The Emergence of a New Science of Mind*. WW Norton & Company.

Kane, L. and Pagliaro, J. (2013) Tasering of 80-year-old woman with dementia alarms experts. *The Star*, 13 September. Available at www.thestar.com/news/crime/2013/09/06/tasering_of_80yearold_woman_with_dementia_alarms_experts.html.

Kane, R. J. and White, M. D. (2015) TASER Exposure and cognitive impairment: Implications for valid Miranda waivers and the timing of police custodial interrogations. *Criminology & Public Policy*, 15(1), doi: 10.1111/1745-9133.12173.

Karably, K. and Zabrucky, K. M. (2009) Children's metamemory: A review of the literature and implications for the classroom. *International Electronic Journal of Elementary Education*, 2(1), 32–52.

Karlén, M. H. (2017) Interviewing intoxicated witnesses: Memory performance in theory and practice. *Scandinavian Journal of Psychology*, 59(2), 105–242.

Karlsen, C. F. (1989) *The Devil in the Shape of a Woman: Witchcraft in Colonial New England*. Vintage.

Karmen, A. (2004) *Crime Victims: An Introduction to Victimology* (5th edn). Wadsworth/Thomson Learning.

Karmen, A. (2007) *Crime Victims: An Introduction to Victimology* (6th edn). Thomson/Wadsworth.

Karmen, A. (2012) *Crime Victims: An Introduction to Victimology* (8th edn). Cengage Learning.

Kass, L. (2019) Penitence, external and internal sound at the eastern state penitentiary: 1830–1850. *International Journal of Listening*, 33(3), 133–7.

Kassin, S. M. (2008a) Confession evidence: Common sense myths and misconceptions. *Criminal Justice and Behavior*, 35, 1309–22.

Kassin, S. M. (2008b) False confessions: Causes, consequences, and implications for reform. *Current Directions in Psychological Science*, 17(40), 249–53.

Kassin, S. M. (2012) Why confessions trump innocence. *American Psychologist*, 67(6), 431–45.

Kassin, S.M. (2017) False confessions: How can psychology so basic be so counterintuitive? *American Psychologist*, 72(9), 951–64.

Kassin, S. M. and Gudjonsson, G. H. (2004) The psychology of confessions: A review of the literature and issues. *Psychological Science in the Public Interest*, 5, 33–67.

Kassin, S. M. and Kiechel, K. (1996) The social psychology of false confessions: Compliance, internalization, and confabulation. *Psychological Science*, 7, 125–8.

Kassin, S. M. and McNall, K. (1991) Police interrogations and confessions: Communicating promises and threats by pragmatic implication. *Law and Human Behavior*, 15(3), 233–51.

Kassin, S. M. and Neumann, K. (1997) On the power of confession evidence: An experimental test of the fundamental difference hypothesis. *Law and Human Behavior*, 21(5), 469–84.

Kassin, S. M. and Sukel, H. (1997) Coerced confessions and the jury: An experimental test of the 'harmless error' rule. *Law and Human Behavior*, 21(1), 27–46.

Kassin, S. M. and Wrightsman, L. S. (1985) Confession evidence. In S. M. Kassin and L. S. Wrightsman (eds) *The Psychology of Evidence and Trial Procedure* (pp. 67–94). Sage.

Kassin, S. M., Bogart, D. and Kerner, J. (2011) Confessions that corrupt: Evidence from the DNA exoneration case files. *Psychological Science*, 23(1), 41–5.

Kassin, S. M., Dror, I. E. and Kukucka, J. (2013) The forensic confirmation bias: Problems, perspectives, and proposed solutions. *Journal of Applied Research in Memory and Cognition*, 2(1), 42–52.

Kassin, S. M., Redlich, A. D., Alceste, F. and Luke, T. J. (2018) On the general acceptance of confessions research: Opinions of the scientific community. *American Psychologist*, 73(1), 63–80.

Kassin, S. M., Drizin, S. A., Grisso, T., Gudjonsson, G. H., Leo, R. A. and Redlich, A. D. (2010a) Police-induced confessions, risk factors, and recommendations: Looking ahead. *Law and Human Behavior*, 34(1), 49–52.

Kassin, S. M., Drizin, S. A., Grisso, T., Gudjonsson, G. H., Leo, R. A. and Redlich, A. D. (2010b) Police-induced confessions: Risk factors and recommendations. *Law of Human Behavior*, 34(1), 3–38.

Katerndahl, D. A., Larme, A. C., Palmer, R. F. and Amodei, N. (2005) Reflections on DSM classification and its utility in primary care: Case studies in 'mental disorders'. *Primary Care Companion to the Journal of Clinical Psychiatry*, 7(3), 91–9.

Katz, J. (ed.) (1972) *Experimentation with Human Beings*. Russell Sage Foundation.

Kavedžija, I. (2016) The age of decline? Anxieties about ageing in Japan. *Ethnos*, 81(2), 214–37.

Kebbell, M. R. and Hatton, C. (1999) People with mental retardation as witnesses in court: A review. *American Journal of Mental Retardation*, 37(3), 179–87.

Kebbell, M. R. and Wagstaff, G. F. (1997) Why do the police interview eyewitnesses? Interview objectives and the evaluation of eyewitness performance. *Journal of Psychology*, 131(6), 595–601.

Kebbell, M. R. and Wagstaff, G. F. (1999) *Face Value: Evaluating the Accuracy of Eyewitness Information*. London: Home Office.

Kebbell, M., Hurren, E. and Mazerolle, P. (2006) *An Investigation into the Effective and Ethical Interviewing of Suspected Sex Offenders*. Australian Institute of Criminology.

Keenan, K. and Brockman, J. (2011) *Mr. Big: Exposing Undercover Investigations in Canada*. Fernwood Publishing.

Kein, B. (2008) India's judges overrule scientists on 'guilty brain' tech. *Wired Magazine*, 17 October. Available at www.wired.com/2008/10/indias-judges-o/.

Kellin, B. and McMurtry, C. (2007) STEPS – Structured Tactical Engagement Process: A model for crisis negotiation. *Journal of Police Crisis Negotiations*, 7(2), 29–51.

Kelly, C. E., Welsh, W. N. and Stanley, J. N. (2019) The treatment group and recidivism: A multilevel analysis of prison-based substance abuse treatment. *The Prison Journal*, 99(5), 515–34.

Kelly, C. E., Russano, M. B., Miller, J. C. and Redlich, A. D. (2019) On the road (to admission): Engaging suspects with minimization. *Psychology, Public Policy, and Law*, 25(3), 166–80.

Kelly, I. W., Rotton, J. and Culver, R. (1985) The moon was full, and nothing happened. *Skeptical Inquirer*, 11, 129–33.

Kelly, J. B. and Johnson, M. P. (2008) Differentiation among types of intimate partner violence: Research update and implications for interventions. *Family Court Review*, 46(3), 476–99.

Keltner, D., Ellsworth, P. C. and Edwards, K. (1993) Beyond simple pessimism: Effects of sadness and anger on social perception. *Journal of Personality and Social Psychology*, 64(5), 740–52.

Kemp, R., Towell, N. and Pike, G. (1997) When seeing should not be believing: Photographs, credit cards and fraud. *Applied Cognitive Psychology*, 11, 211–22.

Kendall, P. and Marx, G. (1996) Unabomber profile is loose fit with suspect. *Chicago Tribune*, 8 April. Available at www.chicagotribune.com/news/ct-xpm-1996-04-08-9604080080-story.html 009.

Kenney, C. T. and McLanahan, S. S. (2006) Why are cohabiting relationships more violent than marriages? *Demography*, 43(1), 127–40.

Kennison, P. and Loumansky, A. (2007) Shoot to kill: Understanding police use of force in combatting suicide terrorism. *Crime, Law and Social Change*, 47(3), 151–68.

Keppel, R. D. and Walter, R. (1999) Profiling killers: A revised classification model for understanding sexual murder. *International Journal of Offender Therapy and Comparative Criminology*, 43(4), 417–37.

Keppel, R. D. and Weis, J. G. (2004) The rarity of 'unusual' dispositions of victim bodies: Staging and posing. *Journal of Forensic Sciences*, 49, 1308–12.

Keram, E. A. (2002) The insanity defense and game theory: Reflections on Texas v. Yates. *Journal of the American Academy of Psychiatry and the Law*, 30(4), 470–3.

Khachiyants, N., Trinkle, D., Son, S. J. and Kim, K. Y. (2011) Sundown syndrome in persons with dementia: an update. *Psychiatry Investigation*, 8(4), 275–87.

Kidd, W. R. (1940) *Police Interrogation*. R. V. Basuino.

Kihlstrom, J. F. (2019) The motivational unconscious. *Social and Personality Psychology Compass*, 13(4), e12466. https://doi.org/10.1111/spc3.12466.

Kim, K., Cundiff, N. L. and Choi, S. B. (2015) Emotional intelligence and negotiation outcomes: Mediating effects of rapport, negotiation strategy, and judgment accuracy. *Group Decision and Negotiation*, 24(3), 477–93.

Kim, S. H. and Lee, T. W. (2014) A study of the relationship between compassion fatigue, somatization and silencing response among hospital nurses: Focusing on the mediating effects of silencing response. *Korean Journal of Adult Nursing*, 26(3), 362–71.

King, A. R., Ratzak, A., Ballantyne, S., Knutson, S., Russell, T. D. et al. (2018) Differentiating corporal punishment from physical abuse in the prediction of lifetime aggression. *Aggressive Behavior*, 44(3), 306–15.

King, N. J. (1996) Nameless justice: The case for the routine use of anonymous juries in criminal trials. *Vanderbilt Law Review*, 49, 123, 126–9.

Kipps, C. M. and Hodges, J. R. (2005) Cognitive assessment for clinicians. *Journal of Neurology, Neurosurgery and Psychiatry*, 76(Suppl I): i22–30.

Kircher, J. C., Horowitz, S. W. and Raskin, D. C. (1988) Meta-analysis of mock crime studies of the control question polygraph technique. *Law and Human Behavior*, 12(1), 79–89.

Kissner, J. (2016) Are active shootings temporally contagious? An empirical assessment. *Journal of Police and Criminal Psychology*, 31(1), 48–58.

Kita, M. and Johnson, D. T. (2014) Framing capital punishment in Japan: Avoidance, ambivalence, and atonement. *Asian Journal of Criminology*, 9(3), 221–40.

Klemfuss, J. Z. and Ceci, S. J. (2012) Legal and psychological perspectives on children's competence to testify in court. *Developmental Review*, 32(2), 268–86.

Klerman, D. (2018) Was the jury ever self-informing? In M. Mulholland (ed.) *Judicial Tribunals in England and Europe, 1200-1700* (pp. 58–80). Manchester University Press.

Klinger, D. A. and Brunson, R. K. (2009) Police officers' perceptual distortions during lethal force situations: Informing the reasonableness standard. *Criminology & Public Policy*, 8(1), 117–40.

Klostermann, K. C. and Fals-Stewart, W. (2006) Intimate partner violence and alcohol use: Exploring the role of drinking in partner violence and its implications for intervention. *Aggression and Violent Behavior*, 11(6), 587–97.

Knapp, M. L., Hall, J. A. and Horgan, T. G. (2014) The effects of the environment on human communication. In M. L. Knapp, J. A. Hall and T. G. Horgan, *Nonverbal Communication in Human Interaction* (8th edn, pp. 89–122). Wadsworth.

Knight, R. A. and Prentky, R. A. (1990) Classifying sexual offenders: The development and corroboration of taxonomic models. In W. L. Marshall, D. R. Laws and H. E. Barbaree (eds) *Handbook of Sexual Assault*. Plenum.

Knowles, G. J. (2016) Social psychological dynamics of hostage negotiation: forensic psychology, suicide intervention, police intelligence/counterintelligence, and tactical entry. *Journal of Criminal Psychology*, 6(1), 16–27.

Kocsis, R. N. (2003) An empirical assessment of content in criminal psychological profiles. *International Journal of Offender Therapy and Comparative Criminology*, 47(1), 37–46.

Kocsis, R. N. (2004) Profiling the criminal mind: Does it actually work? *Medicine, Crime and Punishment*, 364, 14–15.

Kocsis, R. N. (2010) Criminal profiling works and everyone agrees. *Journal of Forensic Psychology Practice*, 10(3), 224–37.

Kocsis, R. N. and Middledorp, J. (2004) Believing is seeing III: Perceptions of content in criminal psychological profiles. *International Journal of Offender Therapy and Comparative Criminology*, 48(4), 477–94.

Kocsis, R. N. and Palermo, G. B. (2005) Ten major problems with criminal profiling. *American Journal of Forensic Psychiatry*, 26(2), 1–26.

Kocsis, R. N. and Palermo, G. B. (2007) Contemporary problems in criminal profiling. In R. N. Kocsis (ed.) *Criminal Profiling: International Theory, Research, and Practice* (pp. 327–45). Humana Press.

Kocsis, R. N. and Palermo, G.B. (2013) Disentangling criminal profiling: Accuracy, homology and the myth of trait-based profiling. *International Journal of Offender Therapy and Comparative Criminology*, 59(3), 313–32.

Kocsis, R. N., Cooksey, R. W. and Irwin, H. J. (2002) Psychological profiling of offender characteristics from crime behaviors in serial rape offenses. *International Journal of Offender Therapy and Comparative Criminology*, 46(2), 144–69.

Kodellas, S., Giannakoulopoulos, A. and Floros, A. (2010) Cyberstalking victimisation: The role of online lifestyles and routine activities. In *The Proceedings of WebSci10: Extending the Frontiers of Society Online.* http://journal.web science .org/ 380/.

Koegel, R. L., Bradshaw, J. L., Ashbaugh, K. and Koegel, L. K. (2014) Improving question-asking initiations in young children with autism using pivotal response treatment. *Journal of Autism and Developmental Disorders*, 44(4), 816–27.

Koehler, J. J., Schweitzer, N. J., Saks, M. J. and McQuiston, D. E. (2016) Science, technology, or the expert witness: What influences jurors' judgments about forensic science testimony? *Psychology, Public Policy, and Law*, 22(4), 401–13.

Kogut, T. (2011) Someone to blame: When identifying a victim decreases helping. *Journal of Experimental Social Psychology*, 47, 748–55.

Kois, L. E., Chauhan, P. and Warren, J. I. (2019) Competence to stand trial and criminal responsibility. In N. Brewer and A. B. Douglass (eds) *Psychological Science and the Law* (pp. 293–317). Guilford Press.

Kolankiewicz, M. (2018) Closeness and distance in media reports on the Trollhättan attack. In M. Bhatia, S. Poynting and W. Tufail (eds) *Media, Crime and Racism* (pp. 235–53). Palgrave Macmillan.

Kolk, B. A. (2005) Developmental trauma disorder: Toward a rational diagnosis for children with complex trauma histories. *Psychiatric Annals*, 35(5), 401–8.

Kop, M., Read, P. and Walker, B. R. (2019) Pseudocommando mass murderers: A big five personality profile using psycholinguistics. *Current Psychology*, 1–9.

Korkmaz, B. (2011) Theory of mind and neurodevelopmental disorders of childhood. *Pediatric Research*, 69(5 Pt 2), 101–8.

Korkodeilou, J. (2020) Forget me not: Stalkers, modus operandi and perceived motivations. In J. Korkodeilou, *Victims of Stalking: Case Studies in Invisible Harms* (pp. 73–101). Palgrave Macmillan.

Korre, M., Farioli, A., Varvarigou, V., Sato, S. and Kales, S. N. (2014) A survey of stress levels and time spent across law enforcement duties: Police chief and officer agreement. *Policing: A Journal of Policy and Practice*, 8(2), 109–22.

Koubaridis, A. (2016) If an innocent person is locked up, there is a guilty person on the outside. News. com.au, 18 February. Available at www.news.com.au/ national/nsw-act/courts-law/if-an-innocent-person-is-locked-up-there-is-a-guilty-person-on-the-outside/news-story/7619f4d6a77d066f738475899 1fb4052.

Kovács, A., Kun, B., Griffiths, M. D. and Demetrovics, Z. (2019) A longitudinal study of adaption to prison after initial incarceration. *Psychiatry Research*, 273, 240–6.

Kovera, M. B. (2019) Racial disparities in the criminal justice system: Prevalence, causes, and a search for solutions. *Journal of Social Issues*, 75(4), 1139–64.

Kovera, M. B. and Austin, J. L. (2016) Identifying juror bias: Moving from assessment and prediction to a new generation of jury selection research. In C. Willis-Esqueda and B. H. Bornstein (eds) *The Witness Stand and Lawrence S. Wrightsman, Jr.* (pp. 75–94). Springer.

Kozel, F. A., Laken, S. J., Johnson, K. A., Boren, B., Mapes, K. S. et al. (2009) Replication of functional MRI detection of deception. *The Open Forensic Science Journal*, 2, 6–11.

Kozinski, W. (2018) The Reid interrogation technique and false confessions: A time for change. *Seattle Journal for Social Justice*, 16(2), 301–45.

Kraft, E. and Wang, J. (2010) An exploratory study of the cyberbullying and cyberstalking experiences and factors related to victimization of students at a public liberal arts college. *International Journal of Technoethics*, 1(4), 74–91.

Krajicek, D. J. (2008) The justice story: Murder in the onion field. *New York Daily News*, 25 March. Available at www.nydailynews.com/news/crime/justice-story-article-1.249124.

Kramers-Olen, A. (2019) The defense of sane automatism and non-pathological criminal incapacity in South Africa: An epistemological intersection between psychology and law. *South African Journal of Psychology*, 49(2), 188–98.

Krapohl, D. J., McCloughan, J. B. and Senter, S. M. (2009) How to use the concealed information test. *Polygraph*, 38(1), 34–49.

Kraus, L., Lauer, E., Coleman, R. and Houtenville, A. (2018) *2017 Disability Statistics Annual Report*. University of New Hampshire.

Krauss, U. R., Zeier, F., Wagner, W. W., Paelecke, M. and Hewig, J. (2017) Comparing the quality of memory reports in different initial eyewitness questioning approaches. *Cogent Psychology*, 4, 1–15.

Kruglanski, A. W. (1990) Lay epistemic theory in social-cognitive psychology. *Psychological Inquiry*, 1(3), 181–97.

Kruglanski, A. W., Atash, M. N., De Grada, E., Mannetti, L. and Pierro, A. (1997) Psychological theory testing versus psychometric nay saying: Need for closure scale and the Neuberg et al. critique. *Journal of Personality and Social Psychology*, 73, 1005–16.

Kruglanski, A. W., Chen, X., Dechesne, M., Fishman, S. and Orehek, E. (2009) Fully committed: Suicide bombers' motivation and the quest for personal significance. *Political Psychology*, 30(3), 331–57.

Kruglanski, A., Jasko, K., Webber, D., Chernikova, M. and Molinario, E. (2018) The making of violent extremists. *Review of General Psychology*, 22(1), 107–20.

Kudesia, R. S. (2019) Mindfulness as metacognitive practice. *Academy of Management Review*, 44(2), 405–23.

Kuhn, T. S. (1962) *The Structure of Scientific Revolutions*. Chicago University Press.

Kumar, R. and Nagpal, B. (2019) Analysis and prediction of crime patterns using big data. *International Journal of Information Technology*, 11(4), 799–805.

Kumar, V. D. (2019) Beyond Dunning–Kruger effect: Undermining the biases which would lead to flawed self-assessment among students. *Medical Science Educator*, 29(4), 1155–6.

Kunen, J. S. (2017) Opening minds behind bars. *Columbia Magazine*, Summer, 21–7.

Kupers, T. A. (2004) Malingering in correctional settings. *Correctional Mental Health Reports*, 5(6), 81–95.

Kurosawa, K. (1996) System variables in eyewitness identification: Control experiments and photospread evaluation. *Japanese Psychological Research*, 38(1), 25–38.

Kutin, J., Russell, R. and Reid, M. (2017) Economic abuse between intimate partners in Australia: prevalence, health status, disability and financial stress. *Australian and New Zealand Journal of Public Health*, 41(3), 269–74.

Kwong See, S. T., Hoffman, H. G. and Wood, T. L. (2001) Perceptions of an old female eyewitness: Is the older eyewitness believable? *Psychology and Aging*, 16(2), 346–50.

LaDuke, C., Locklair, B. and Heilbrun, K. (2018) Neuroscientific, neuropsychological, and psychological evidence comparably impact legal decision making: Implications for experts and legal practitioners. *Journal of Forensic Psychology Research and Practice*, 18(2), 114–42.

Lagdon, S., Armour, C. and Stringer, M. (2014) Adult experience of mental health outcomes as a result of intimate partner violence victimisation: A systematic review. *European Journal of Psychotraumatology*, 5(1), 1–12.

Lagorio, C. and Yanagita, B. (2015) Basic research informing the use of token economies in applied settings. In F. D. DiGennaro Reed and D. Reed (eds) *Autism Service Delivery* (pp. 209–56). Springer.

Lake, E. (2018) National outcry: What happened to Baby P and who are his killers, Tracey Connelly, Steven Barker and Jason Owen? *The Sun*, 30 December. Available at www.thesun.co.uk/news/4567187/baby-p-killers-tracey-connelly-steven-barker-jason-owen/.

Lam, C. (2017) Martin Tankleff documentary takes another look at 1988 case. Newsday, 19 April. Available at www.newsday.com/long-island/suffolk/new-show-takes-another-look-at-tankleff-case-1.13493667.

Lamb, K. (2015) Beyond solitary confinement: Lessons from European prison reform. *Brown Political Review*, 22 November. Available at http://brownpoliticalreview.org/2015/11/beyond-solitary-confinement-lessons-from-european-prison-reform/.

Lamb, M. E., Brown, D. A., Hershkowitz, I., Orbach, Y. and Esplin, P. W. (2018) *Tell Me What Happened: Questioning Children about Abuse*. John Wiley & Sons.

Lamb, M. E., Orbach, Y., Hershkowitz, I., Esplin, P. W. and Horowitz, D. (2007a) Structured forensic interview protocols improve the quality and informativeness of investigative interviews with children: A review of research using the NICHD Investigative Interview Protocol. *Child Abuse and Neglect*, 31(11/12), 1201–31.

Lamb, M. E., Orbach, Y., Hershkowitz, I., Horowitz, D. and Abbott, C. B. (2007b) Does the type of prompt affect the accuracy of information provided by alleged victims of abuse in forensic interviews? *Applied Cognitive Psychology*, 21(9), 1117–30.

Lamella, L. and Tincani, M. (2012) Brief wait time to increase response opportunity and correct responding of children with autism spectrum disorder who display challenging behavior. *Journal of Developmental and Physical Disabilities*, 24(6), 559–73.

LaMontagne, A. D., Milner, A. J., Allisey, A. F., Page, K. M., Reavley, N. J. et al. (2016) An integrated workplace mental health intervention in a policing context: Protocol for a cluster randomised control trial. *BMC Psychiatry*, 16(1), 49. doi: 10.1186/s12888-016-0741-9.

Lamparello, A. (2011) Using cognitive neuroscience to predict future dangerousness. *Columbia Human Rights Law Review*, 41(2), 1–59.

Lane, C. (2015) A secret theater: Inside Japan's capital punishment system. *Japan Society*. Available at www.japansociety.org/page/multimedia/articles/a_secret_theater.

Lane, K. A., Banaji, M. R., Nosek, B.A. and Greenwald, A. G. (2007) Understanding and using the Implicit Association Test: IV. What we know (so far) about the method. In B. Wittenbrink and N. Schwarz (eds) *Implicit Measures of Attitudes* (pp. 59–102). Guilford Press.

Laney, C. and Loftus, E. F. (2008) Emotional content of true and false memories. *Memory*, 16, 500–16.

Lang, P. J., Bradley, M. M. and Cuthbert, B. N. (1990) Emotion, attention, and the startle reflex. *Psychological Review*, 97(3), 377–95.

Langewiesche, W. (2019) What really happened to Malaysia's missing airplane. *The Atlantic*, July. Available at www.theatlantic.com/magazine/archive/2019/07/mh370-malaysia-airlines/590653/.

Langhoder, K. A. (2005) Unaccountable at the founding: The originalist case for anonymous juries. *Yale Law Journal*, 115, 1823. https://digitalcommons.law.yale.edu/ylj/vol115/iss7/8.

Langleben, D. D. (2010) Detection of deception with fMRI: Are we there yet? *Legal and Criminological Psychology*, 13(1), 1–9.

Langleben, D. D. and Moriarty, J. C. (2013) Using brain imaging for lie detection: Where science, law and research policy collide. *Psychology, Public Policy, and Law*, 19(2), 222–34.

Lanier, M. M. (2018) *Essential Criminology*. Routledge.

Lankford, A. (2016) Detecting mental health problems and suicidal motives among terrorists and mass shooters. *Criminal Behaviour and Mental Health*, 26(5), 315–21.

Lankford, A. and Madfis, E. (2018) Don't name them, don't show them, but report everything else: A pragmatic proposal for denying mass killers the attention they seek and deterring future offenders. *American Behavioral Scientist*, 62(2), 260–79.

Lankford, A., Adkins, K. G. and Madfis, E. (2019) Are the deadliest mass shootings preventable? An assessment of leakage information reported to law enforcement, and firearms acquisition prior to attacks in the United States. *Journal of Contemporary Criminal Justice*, 35(3), 315–41.

Larkin, H., Shields, J. J. and Anda, R. F. (2012) The health and social consequences of adverse childhood experiences (ACE) across the lifespan: An introduction to prevention and intervention in the community. *Journal of Prevention and Intervention in the Community*, 40(4), 263–70.

Larkin, M. (2009) *Vulnerable Groups in Health and Social Care*. Sage.

Larkin, R. W. (2009) The Columbine legacy: Rampage shootings as political acts. *American Behavioral Scientist*, 52(9), 1309–26.

Larney, S., Topp, L., Indig, D., O'Driscoll, C. and Greenberg, D. (2012) A cross-sectional survey of prevalence and correlates of suicidal ideation and suicide attempts among offenders in New South Wales, Australia. *BMC Public Health*, 12(1), 14–21.

La Rooy, D., Lamb, M. E. and Pipe, M. E. (2009) Repeated interviewing: A critical evaluation of the risks and potential benefits. In K. Kuehnle and M. Connell (eds) *The Evaluation of Child Sexual Abuse Allegations: A Comprehensive Guide to Assessment and Testimony* (pp. 327–61). John Wiley & Sons.

La Rooy, D., Heydon, G., Korkman, J. and Myklebust, T. (2016) Interviewing child witnesses. In G. Oxburgh, T. Myklebust, T. Grant and R. Milne (eds) *Communication in Investigative and Legal Contexts: Integrated Approaches from Forensic Psychology, Linguistics and Law Enforcement* (pp. 57–78). John Wiley & Sons.

La Rooy, D., Brubacher, S., Aromäki-Stratos, A., Cyr, M., Hershkowitz, I. et al. (2015) The NICHD protocol: A review of an internationally used evidence-based tool for training child forensic interviewers. *Journal of Criminological Research, Policy and Practice*, 1(2), 76–89.

Lassiter, G. D. and Geers, A. L. (2004) Bias and accuracy in the evaluation of confession evidence. In G. D. Lassiter (ed.) *Interrogations, Confessions, and Entrapment* (pp. 197–214). Kluwer Academic/Plenum.

Latané, B. and Darley, J. (1969) Bystander 'apathy', *American Scientist*, 57, 244–68.

Latessa, E. J. and Lowencamp, C. (2005) What are criminogenic needs and why are they important? Ohio Judiciary Conference, For the Record, 15–16.

Latshaw, B. A. (2015) Examining the impact of a domestic violence simulation on the development of empathy in sociology classes. *Teaching Sociology*, 43, 277–89.

Laub, C. E., Kimbrough, C. D. and Bornstein, B. H. (2016) Mock juror perceptions of eyewitnesses versus earwitnesses: Do safeguards help? *American Journal of Forensic Psychology*, 34(2), 33–56.

Laursen, J. and Henriksen, A. K. (2019) Altering violent repertoires: Perspectives on violence in the prison-based cognitive-behavioral program anger management. *Journal of Contemporary Ethnography*, 48(2), 261–86.

Lavergne, G. M. (1997) *A Sniper in the Tower: The Charles Whitman Murders*. University of North Texas Press.

Law Commission (2010) Unfitness to Plead, Consultation Paper No 197. Law Commission.

Layton, J. (2006) How police interrogation works. HowStuffWorks.com. Available at http://people.howstuffworks.com/police-interrogation.htm.

Leahy-Harland, S. and Bull, R. (2017) Police strategies and suspect responses in real-life serious crime interviews. *Journal of Police and Criminal Psychology*, 32(2), 138–51.

Lebel, C. and Beaulieu, C. (2011) Longitudinal development of human brain wiring continues from childhood into adulthood. *Journal of Neuroscience*, 31(30), 10937–47.

LeDuc, D. (1991) Marathon hoax: Track star, liar, ex-Princeton student in jail. *The Seattle Times*, 1 March. Available at http://community.seattletimes.nwsource.com/archive/?date=19910301&slug=1268952.

Lee, D. S. and McCrary, L. J. (2017) The deterrence effect of prison: Dynamic theory and evidence. *Regression Discontinuity Designs. Advances in Econometrics*, 38, 73–146.

Lee, H., Roh, S. and Kim, D. J. (2009) Alcohol-induced blackout. *International Journal of Environmental Research and Public Health*, 6(11), 2783–92.

Lee, K. H. (2009) Interpersonal violence and facial fractures. *Journal of Oral and Maxillofacial Surgery*, 67(9), 1878–83.

Leichtman, M. D. and Ceci, S. J. (1995) The effects of stereotypes and suggestions on preschoolers' reports. *Developmental Psychology*, 31(4), 563–78.

Leino, T. M., Selin, R., Summala, H., and Virtanen, M. (2011) Violence and psychological distress among police officers and security guards. *Occupational Medicine*, 61, 400–6.

Lenca, M. (2017) The right to cognitive liberty. *Scientific American*, 317(2), 10.

Leo, R. A. (2008) *Police Interrogation and American Justice*. Harvard University Press.

Leo, R. A. and Liu, B. (2009) What do potential jurors know about police interrogation techniques and false confessions? *Behavioral Sciences and the Law*, 27, 381–99.

Leo, R. A. and Ofshe, R. (1998) The consequences of false confessions: Deprivations of liberty and miscarriages of justice in the age of psychological interrogation. *Journal of Criminal Law & Criminology*, 88, 429–96.

Leonard, R. A., Ford, J. E. and Christensen, T. K. (2017) Forensic linguistics: Applying the science of linguistics to issues of the law. *Hofstra Law Review*, 45(3), 881–97.

L'Eplattenier, B. E. (2009) Opinion: An argument for archival research methods: Thinking beyond methodology. *College English*, 72(1), 67–79.

Lerner, M. J. (1980) The belief in a just world. In M. J. Lerner, *The Belief in a Just World: A Fundamental Delusion* (pp. 9–30). Springer.

Lerner, M. J. and Miller, D. T. (1978) Just world research and the attribution process: Looking back and ahead. *Psychological Bulletin*, 85(5), 1030–51.

Lerner, R. L. (2015) The collapse of civil jury trial and what to do about it. *The Jury Expert: The Art and Science of Litigation Advocacy*, 27(3), 1–8.

Leroy, M. and Haddad, D. (2018) *They Must Be Monsters: A Modern-Day Witch Hunt – The Untold Story of the McMartin Phenomenon: The Longest, Most Expensive Criminal Case in U.S. History*. The Manor Publishing House.

Levett, L. M. and Kovera, M. B. (2008) The effectiveness of opposing expert witnesses for educating jurors about unreliable expert evidence. *Law and Human Behavior*, 32(4), 363–74.

Levine, J. P. (1995) The impact of sequestration on juries. *Judicature*, 79(5), 266–72.

Levine, T. R. (2018) Ecological validity and deception detection research design. *Communication Methods and Measures*, 12(1), 45–54.

Levine, T. R. and McCornack, S. A. (2014) Theorizing about deception. *Journal of Language and Social Psychology*, 33(4), 431–40.

Levine, T. R., Asada, K. J. and Park, H. S. (2006) The lying chicken and the gaze avoidant egg: Eye contact, deception, and causal order. *Southern Communication Journal*, 71(4), 401–11.

Levine, T. R., Serota, K. B. and Shulman, H. C. (2010) The impact of *Lie to Me* on viewers' actual ability to detect deception. *Communication Research*, 37, 847–56.

Lewy, J., Cyr, M. and Dion, J. (2015) Impact of interviewers' supportive comments and children's reluctance to cooperate during sexual abuse disclosure. *Child Abuse Neglect*, 43, 112–22.

Li, D. K. (2019) Michelle Carter, convicted of urging boyfriend to take his own life, is denied parole. NBC News, 20 September. Available at www.nbcnews.com/news/us-news/michelle-carter-convicted-urging-boyfriend-take-his-own-life-denied-n1056876.

Liakopoulou, D., Tigani, X., Varvogli, L., Chrousos, G. P. and Darviri, C. (2020) Stress management and health promotion intervention program for police forces. *International Journal of Police Science & Management*, https://doi.org/10.1177/1461355719898202.

Lieber, A. L. and Agel, J. (1978) *The Lunar Effect: Biological Tides and Human Emotions*. Anchor Press.

Lieberman, J. D. and Krauss, D. A. (2009) *Jury Psychology: Social Aspects of the Trial Process*. Ashgate.

Lieberman, J. D. and Olson, J. (2009) The psychology of jury selection. In J. D. Lieberman and D. A. Krauss (eds) *Jury Psychology: Social Aspects of Trial Processes: Psychology in the Courtroom*, vol. 1 (pp. 97–128). Ashgate.

Liljegren, M., Waldö, M. L., Santillo, A. F., Ullén, S., Rydbeck, R. et al. (2019) Association of neuropathologically confirmed frontotemporal dementia and Alzheimer disease with criminal and socially inappropriate behavior in a Swedish cohort. *JAMA Network Open*, 2(3), e190261. doi: 10.1001/jamanetworkopen.2019.0261.

Lindgren, M. and Nikolic-Ristanovic, V. (2011) *Crime Victims: International and Serbian Perspective*. Organization for Security and Cooperation in Europe, Mission to Serbia, Law Enforcement Department.

Lindquist, K. A., Wager, T. D., Kober, H., Bliss-Moreau, E. and Barrett, L. F. (2012) The brain basis of emotion: A meta-analytic review. *Behavioral and Brain Sciences*, 35(3), 121–43.

Lindsay, R. C. and Wells, G. L. (1980) What price justice? Exploring the relationship between lineup fairness and identification accuracy. *Law and Human Behavior*, 4, 303–14.

Lindsay, R. C. and Wells, G. L. (1985) Improving eyewitness identifications from lineups: Simultaneous versus sequential lineup presentation. *Journal of Applied Psychology*, 70(3), 556–64.

Ling, S., Umbach, R. and Raine, A. (2019) Biological explanations of criminal behavior, *Psychology, Crime & Law*, 25(6), 626–40.

Link, N. W., Ward, J. T. and Stansfield, R. (2019) Consequences of mental and physical health for reentry and recidivism: Toward a health-based model of desistance. *Criminology*, 57(3), 544–73.

Linkins, J. R. (2007) Satisfy the demands of justice: Embrace electronic recording of custodial investigative interviews through legislation, agency policy, or court mandate. *American Criminal Law Review*, 44, 141–50.

Linnet, J. (2019) The anticipatory dopamine response in addiction: A common neurobiological underpinning of gambling disorder and substance use disorder? *Progress in Neuro-Psychopharmacology and Biological Psychiatry*, 98(8), https://doi.org/10.1016/j.pnpbp.2019.109802.

Liou, H. A. and Tran, J. (2019) Internet (re) search by judges, jurors, and lawyers. *IP Theory*, 9(1), 1–22.

Lippert, T., Cross, T. P. and Jones, L. and Walsh, W. (2009) Telling interviewers about sexual abuse: Predictors of child disclosure at forensic interviews. *Child Maltreatment*, 14(1), 100–13.

Lipsey, M. W. and Landenberger, N. A. (2006) Cognitive-behavioral interventions. In B. C. Welsh and D. P. Farrington (eds) *Preventing Crime: What Works for Children, Offenders, Victims, and Places* (pp. 57–71). Springer.

Liptak, A. (2002) Nameless juries are on the rise in crime cases. *The New York Times*, 18 November.

Lira, M. C., Xuan, Z., Coleman, S. M., Swahn, M. H., Heeren, T. C. and Naimi, T. S. (2019) Alcohol policies and alcohol involvement in intimate partner homicide in the US. *American Journal of Preventive Medicine*, 57(2), 172–9.

Lithwick, D. (2016) Still no answers. Jamycheal Mitchell's death in a Virginia jail cell still hasn't been explained. It should be a national scandal. *Slate*, 13 May. Available at https://slate.com/news-and-politics/2016/05/what-happened-to-jamycheal-mitchell.html.

Livneh, H. and Livneh, C. (1989) The five-factor model of personality: Is evidence of its cross-measure validity premature? *Personality and Individual Differences*, 10(1), 75–80.

Llewelyn, A. (2020) MH370 revelation: Real reason Malaysia Airlines plane was hijacked so quickly exposed. *Express*, 4 January Available at www.express.co.uk/news/weird/1223574/mh370-news-malaysia-airlines-missing-plane-hijack-boeing-777-spt.

Lofholm, N. ([2006]2017) The con artist next door. *The Denver Post*. Available at www.denverpost.com/2006/03/25/the-con-artist-next-door/.

Loftus, E. F. (1997) Creating false memories. *Scientific American*, 277(3), 70–5.

Loftus, E. F. (2003) Make-believe memories. *American Psychologist*, 58, 867–73.

Loftus, E. F. and Palmer, J. C. (1974) Reconstruction of automobile destruction: An example of the interaction between language and memory. *Journal of Verbal Learning and Verbal Behavior*, 13, 585–89.

Logan, C. (2018) Forensic clinical interviewing: Toward best practice. *International Journal of Forensic Mental Health*, 17(4), 297–309.

Logan, T. K. and Walker, R. (2004) Separation as a risk factor for victims of intimate partner violence: Beyond lethality and injury: A response to Campbell. *Journal of Interpersonal Violence*, 19(12), 1478–86.

Logan, T. K. and Walker, R. (2017) Stalking: A multidimensional framework for assessment and safety planning. *Trauma, Violence and Abuse*, 18(2), 200–22.

Loh, W. D. (1981) Perspectives on psychology and law. *Journal of Applied Social Psychology*, 11, 314–55.

Løkkegaard, S. S., Hansen, N. B., Wolf, N. M. and Elklit, A. (2019) When daddy stalks mommy: experiences of intimate partner stalking and involvement of social and legal authorities when stalker and victim have children together. *Violence against Women*, 25(14), 1759–77.

Longordo, F., Kopp, C. and Lüthi, A. (2009) Consequences of sleep deprivation on neurotransmitter receptor expression and function. *European Journal of Neuroscience*, 29(9), 1810–19.

López-Mosquera, N. (2016) Gender differences, theory of planned behaviour and willingness to pay. *Journal of Environmental Psychology*, 45, 165–75.

Lorek, J., Centifanti, L., Lyons, M. and Thorley, C. (2019) The impact of prior trial experience on mock jurors' note taking during trials and recall of trial evidence. *Frontiers in Psychology*, 10, 47. doi: 10.3389/fpsyg.2019.00047.

Lorettu, L., Nivoli, A. M., Milia, P. and Nivoli, G. (2020) Violence risk assessment in mental health. In B. Carpiniello, A. Vita and C. Mencacci (eds) *Violence and Mental Disorders* (pp. 231–52). Springer.

Lösel, F., Link, E., Schmucker, M., Bender, D., Breuer, M. et al. (2020) On the effectiveness of sexual offender treatment in prisons: A comparison of two different evaluation designs in routine practice. *Sexual Abuse*, 32(4), 452–75.

Loth, E., Garrido, L., Ahmad, J., Watson, E., Duff, A. and Duchaine, B. (2018) Facial expression recognition as a candidate marker for autism spectrum disorder: How frequent and severe are deficits? *Molecular Autism*, 9(7), 2–11.

Lovell, D., Johnson, L. C. and Cain, K. C. (2007) Recidivism of Supermax offenders in Washington State. *Crime and Delinquency*, 53(4), 633–56.

Lovell, M., Guthrie, J., Simpson, P. and Butler, T. (2018) Navigating the political landscape of Australian criminal justice reform: Senior policy-makers on alternatives to incarceration. *Current Issues in Criminal Justice*, 29(3), 227–41.

Lovell, R., Luminais, M., Flannery, D. J., Overman, L., Huang, D. et al. (2017) Offending patterns for serial sex offenders identified via the DNA testing of previously unsubmitted sexual assault kits. *Journal of Criminal Justice*, 52, 68–78.

Lowenkamp, C. T., Hubbard, D., Makarios, M. D. and Latessa, E. J. (2009) A quasi-experimental evaluation of thinking for a change: A 'real world' application. *Criminal Justice and Behavior*, 36(2), 137–46.

Lowry, R. (2017) *The Evolution of Psychological Theory: A Critical History of Concepts and Presuppositions.* Routledge.

Luke, T. J. and Alceste, F. (2019) The mechanisms of minimization: How interrogation tactics suggest lenient sentencing through pragmatic implication. *PsyArXiv*, https://doi.org/10.1037/lhb0000410.

Luke, T. J., Dawson, E., Hartwig, M. and Granhag, P. A. (2014) How awareness of possible evidence induces forthcoming counter-resistance strategies. *Applied Cognitive Psychology*, 28, 876–82.

Luke, T. J., Hartwig, M., Joseph, E., Brimbal, L. Chan, G. et al. (2016) Training in the strategic use of evidence technique: Improving deception detection accuracy of American law enforcement officers. *Journal of Police and Criminal Psychology*, 31(4), 270–8.

Lupariello, F., Curti, S., Duval, J., Abbattista, G. and Di Vella, G. (2018) Staged crime scene determination by handling physical and digital evidence: Reports and review of the literature. *Forensic Science International*, 288, 236–41.

Lurati, A. R. (2015) Identifying reverse malingering in the civilian occupational setting. *Workplace Health and Safety*, 64(7), 288–9.

Lussier, P., McCuish, E., Deslauriers-Varin, N. and Corrado, R. (2017) Crime specialization as a dynamic process?: Criminal careers, crime mix, and crime specialization in chronic, serious, and violent offenders. In A. Blokland and V. van der Geest (eds) *The Routledge International Handbook of Life-Course Criminology* (pp. 112–39). Routledge.

Luthra, R. and Gidycz, C. A. (2006) Dating violence among college men and women: Evaluation of a theoretical model. *Journal of Interpersonal Violence*, 21(6), 717–31.

Luxton, D. D. and Lexcen, F. J. (2018) Forensic competency evaluations via video conferencing: A feasibility review and best practice recommendations. *Professional Psychology: Research and Practice*, 49(2), 124–31.

Lydiah, M., Casper, M., Ngare, W. and Immaculate, M. (2019) Gender gaps in decision making power in households: Case of improved bee keeping among the Maasai community in Trans Mara, Narok county, Kenya. *International Journal of Gender Studies*, 4(1), 19–36.

Lykken, D. R. (1989) *A Tremor in the Blood: Uses and Abuses of the Lie Detector.* Plenum Trade.

Lynch, M. (2019) The narrative of the number: Quantification in criminal court. *Law & Social Inquiry*, 44(1), 31–57.

Lyon, A. D. (2018) The blame game: Public antipathy to mental health evidence in criminal trials. *New Criminal Law Review*, 21(2), 247–66.

Lyon, E. (2019) Imprisoning America's mentally ill. *Prison Legal News*, 4 February. Available at www. prisonlegalnews.org/news/2019/feb/4/imprisoning-americas-mentally-ill/.

Lyon, T. D. (2015) Twenty-five years of interviewing research and practice: Dolls, diagrams, and the dynamics of abuse disclosure, *APSAC Advisor*, 24, 14–19.

Lyon, T. D. and Evans, A. D. (2014) Young children's understanding that promising guarantees performance: the effects of age and maltreatment. *Law and Human Behavior*, 38(2), 162–70.

Lyon, T. D. and Saywitz, K. J. (1999) Young maltreated children's competence to take the oath. *Applied Developmental Science*, 3(1), 16–27.

McCarthy, T. W. (2018) The racial bias exception to the general rule that precludes jurors from offering testimony to impeach their own verdict. *American Journal of Trial Advocacy*, 42, 1–14.

McCauley, C. (2007) Toward a social psychology of professional military interrogation. *Peace and Conflict: Journal of Peace Psychology*, 13(4), 399–410.

McCorkel, J. and Defina, R. (2019) Beyond recidivism: Identifying the liberatory possibilities of prison higher education. *Critical Education*, 10(7), 1–17.

McCormick, C. T. (1972) *McCormick's Handbook of the Law of Evidence.* West Publishing.

McCreary, D. R., Fong, I. and Groll, D. L. (2017) Measuring policing stress meaningfully: Establishing norms and cut-off values for the operational and organizational police stress questionnaires. *Police Practice & Research: An International Journal*, 18(6), 612–23.

McDermott, B. E., Dualan, I. V. and Scott, C. L. (2013) Malingering in the correctional system: Does incentive affect prevalence? *International Journal of Law and Psychiatry*, 36, 287–92.

McDonald, J. D. (2008) Measuring personality constructs: The advantages and disadvantages of self-reports, informant reports and behavioural assessments. *Enquire*, 1(1), 1–19.

MacDonald, S., Snook, B. and Milne, R. (2017) Witness interview training: A field evaluation. *Journal of Police and Criminal Psychology*, 32(1), 77–84.

McDonald, S. E., Collins, E. A., Maternick, A., Nicotera, N., Graham-Bermann, S. et al. (2019) Intimate partner violence survivors' reports of their children's exposure to companion animal maltreatment: A qualitative study. *Journal of Interpersonal Violence*, 34(13), 2627–52.

McElvaney, R. (2015) Disclosure of child sexual abuse: Delays, non-disclosure and partial disclosure. What the research tells us and implications for practice. *Child Abuse Review*, 24(3), 159–69.

McEwan, T. E., Daffern, M., MacKenzie, R. D. and Ogloff, J. R. (2017) Risk factors for stalking violence, persistence, and recurrence. *Journal of Forensic Psychiatry & Psychology*, 28(1), 38–56.

McFadden, R. D. (1996) Prisoner of rage: A special report. From a child of promise to the Unabom suspect. *The New York Times*, 26 May.

MacFarlane, L. and Bocij, P. (2003) An exploration of predatory behaviour in cyberspace: Towards a typology of cyberstalkers. *First Monday*, 8(9). DOI: https://doi.org/10.5210/fm.v8i9.1076.

McGaughey, F., Tulich, T. and Blagg, H. (2017) UN decision on Marlon Noble case: Imprisonment of an Aboriginal man with intellectual disability found unfit to stand trial in Western Australia. *Alternative Law Journal*, 42(1), 67–70.

McGee, A. (2010) Juror misconduct in the twenty-first century: The prevalence of the internet and its effect on American courtrooms. *Loyola of Los Angeles Entertainment Law Review*, 30(2), 301–26.

McGillivray, L., Torok, M., Calear, A., Shand, F., Mackinnon, A. et al. (2020) Suicide prevention among young people: A study protocol for evaluating Youth Aware of Mental Health in Australian secondary schools. *Mental Health & Prevention*, 17, 200178. DOI: 10.1016/j.mhp.2019.200178.

McGilloway, A., Ghosh, P. and Bhui, K. (2015) A systematic review of pathways to and processes associated with radicalization and extremism amongst Muslims in Western societies. *International Review of Psychiatry*, 27(1), 39–50.

McGorrery, P. and McMahon, M. (2019) Prosecuting controlling or coercive behavior in England and Wales: Media reports of a novel offence. *Criminology & Criminal Justice*, 1–19.

McGrath, J. E. (1970) The ideas and influence of McCloy, Nash, and Williams. In J. E. McGrath (ed.) *Social and Psychological Factors in Stress* (pp. 1–13). Holt, Rinehart & Winston.

McGrath, M. G. (2000) Criminal profiling: Is there a role for the forensic psychiatrist? *Journal of the American Academy of Psychiatry and the Law*, 28(3), 315–24.

McGrath, R. J., Cumming, G. F., Burchard, B. L., Zeoli, S. and Ellerby, L. (2010) *Current Practices and Emerging Trends in Sexual Abuser Management: The Safer Society 2009 North American Survey*. Safer Society Press.

McGregor, H. A., Lieberman, J. D., Greenberg, J., Solomon, S., Arndt, J. et al. (1998) Terror management and aggression: Evidence that mortality salience motivates aggression against worldview-threatening others. *Journal of Personality and Social Psychology*, 74(3), 590–605.

Mackay, A. (2015) Overcrowding in Australian prisons: The human rights implications. *President*, 37(128), 37–41.

McKay, T. E., Lindquist, C. H., Landwehr, J., Ramirez, D. and Bir, A. (2018) Postprison relationship dissolution and intimate partner violence: Separation-instigated violence or violence-instigated separation? *Journal of Offender Rehabilitation*, 57(5), 294–310.

Mackmen, A., Clark, D. M. and McManus, F. (2000) Recurrent images and early memories in social phobia. *Behavior Research and Therapy*, 38(6), 601–10.

MacLean, M. J. and Chown, S. M. (1988) Just world beliefs and attitudes toward helping elderly people: A comparison of British and Canadian university students. *International Journal of Aging and Human Development*, 26(4), 249–60.

McLeod, M. S. (2016) Does the death penalty require death row: The harm of legislative silence. *Ohio State Law Journal*, 77(3), 525–92.

McMahon, M. and McGorrery, P. (2016) Criminalising controlling and coercive behaviour: The next step in the prosecution of family violence? *Alternative Law Journal*, 41(2), 98–101.

McMillen, N. R. (1990) *Dark Journey: Black Mississippians in the Age of Jim Crow, at 200*. University of Illinois Press.

Madeira, J. L. (2010) Why rebottle the genie: Capitalizing on closure in death penalty proceedings. *Indiana Law Journal*, 85(4), 1477–525.

Madfis, E. (2014) Averting school rampage: Student intervention amid a persistent code of silence. *Youth Violence and Juvenile Justice*, 12, 229–49.

Madfis, E. (2016) 'It's better to overreact': School officials' fear and perceived risk of rampage attacks and the criminalization of American public schools. *Critical Criminology*, 24(1), 39–55.

Madfis, E. (2018) Insight from averted mass shootings. In J. Schildkraut (ed.) *Mass Shootings in America: Understanding the Debates, Causes, and Responses* (pp. 79–84). Praeger.

Madhusoodanan, S., Ting, M. B., Farah, T. and Ugur, U. (2015) Psychiatric aspects of brain tumors: A review. *World Journal of Psychiatry*, 5(3), 273–85.

Madon, S., Guyll, M., Yang, Y., Smalarz, L., Marschall, J. and Lannin, D. G. (2017) A biphasic process of resistance among suspects: The mobilization and decline of self-regulatory resources. *Law and Human Behavior*, 41(2), 159–72.

Madsen, H. B. and Kim, J. H. (2016) Ontogeny of memory: An update on 40 years of work on infantile amnesia. *Behavioral Brain Research*, 298, 4–14.

Maeder, E. M., Yamamoto, S., McManus, L. A. and Capaldi, C. A. (2016) Race–crime congruency in the Canadian context. *Canadian Journal of Behavioural Science*, 48(2), 162–70.

Mafa, I., Kang'ethe, S. and Chikadzi, V. (2020) 'Revenge porn' and women empowerment issues: Implications for human rights and social work practice in Zimbabwe. *Journal of Human Rights and Social Work*, 1–11.

Magaldi, J. A., Sales, J. S. and Paul, J. (2020) Revenge porn: The name doesn't do nonconsensual pornography justice and the remedies don't offer the victims justice. *Oregon Law Review*, 98(1), 197.

Magen, A. (2018) Fighting terrorism: The democracy advantage. *Journal of Democracy*, 29(1), 111–25.

Main, D. (2019) 'I heard him die': The messages that convicted Michelle Carter. Boston 25 News, 11 February. Available at www.boston25news.com/news/i-heard-him-die-the-messages-that-convicted-michelle-carter/536320357/.

Makkar, S. (2019) Transgender woman who brutally hacked 7-Eleven customers with an axe begins 'de-transitioning' behind bars - because she says it's a 'reality' she'll never be accepted as a female. DailyMail.com, 4 August. Available at www.dailymail.co.uk/news/article-7319669/Evie-Amati-hacked-7-Eleven-customers-axe-begins-transitioning-process-bars.html.

Malle, B. F., Guglielmo, S. and Monroe, A. E. (2014) A theory of blame. *Psychological Inquiry*, 25(2), 147–86.

Malnic, E. (1994) Karl Hettinger: Survived 1963 'onion field' attack. *Los Angeles Times*, 5 May. Available at www.latimes.com/archives/la-xpm-1994-05-05-mn-53959-story.html.

Malpass, R. S. and Devine, P. G. (1981) Eyewitness identification: Lineup instructions and the absence of the offender. *Journal of Applied Psychology*, 66(4), 482–9.

Manley, N. R., Fabian, T. C., Sharpe, J., Magnotti, L. J. and Croce, M. A. (2017) Separating truth from alternative facts: Guns, murder, and patterns of violence over twenty years at a level I urban trauma center. *Journal of the American College of Surgeons*, 225, e114.

Manns, J. R., Hopkins, R. O., Reed, J. M., Kitchener, E. G. and Squire, L. R. (2003) Recognition memory and the human hippocampus. *Neuron*, 37(1), 171–80.

Mansour, J., Hamilton, C. and Gibson, M. (2018) Understanding the weapon focus effect: The role of threat, unusualness, exposure duration, and scene complexity. *Applied Cognitive Psychology*, 33(6), 991–1007.

Mansour, J., Beaudry, J., Bertrand, M., Kalmet, N., Melsom, E. and Lindsay, C. L. (2012) Impact of disguise on identification decisions and confidence with simultaneous and sequential lineups. *Law and Human Behavior*, 36(6), 513–26.

Maoz, U. and Yaffe, G. (2016) What does recent neuroscience tell us about criminal responsibility? *Journal of Law and the Biosciences*, 3(1), 120–39.

Maple, C., Short, E., Brown, A., Bryden, C. and Salter, M. (2012) Cyberstalking in the UK: Analysis and recommendations. *International Journal of Distributed Systems and Technologies (IJDST)*, 3(4), 34–51.

Maras, K., Mulcahy, S., Crane, L., Hawken, T. and Memon, A. (2018) Obtaining best evidence from the autistic interviewee: Police-reported challenges, legal requirements and psychological research-based recommendations. *Investigative Interviewing: Research and Practice (II-RP)*, 9(1), 52–60.

Marchand, A., Nadeau, C., Beaulieu-Prévost, D., Boyer, R. and Martin, M. (2015) Predictors of posttraumatic stress disorder among police officers: A prospective study. *Psychological Trauma: Theory, Research, Practice, and Policy*, 7(3), 212–21.

Marcopulos, B. A., Welner, M. and Campbell, K. T. (2019) Forensic challenges in medical settings for physicians and neuropsychologists. In K. Sanders (ed.) *Physician's Field Guide to Neuropsychology* (pp. 495–506). Springer.

Marcus, D. K., Lyons, P. M. and Guyton, M. R. (2000) Studying perceptions of juror influence in vivo: A social relations analysis. *Law and Human Behavior*, 24(2), 173–86.

Marder, N. S. (1986) Gender dynamics and jury deliberations. *Yale Law Journal*, 96(3), 593–612.

Marder, N. S. (2014) Jurors and social media: Is a fair trial still possible? *Southern Methodist University Law Review*, 67, 617–68.

Marder, N. S. (2015) Juror bias, voir dire, and the judge-jury relationship. *Chicago-Kent Law Review*, 90(3), 927–56.

Marder, N. S. (2017) Juries in film and television. In H. N. Pontell (ed.) *Oxford Research Encyclopedia of Criminology and Criminal Justice*. Oxford University Press.

Marin, M. F., Geoffrion, S., Juster, R. P., Giguère, C. E., Marchand, A. et al. (2019) High cortisol awakening response in the aftermath of workplace violence exposure moderates the association between acute stress disorder symptoms and PTSD symptoms. *Psychoneuroendocrinology*, 104, 238–42.

Marion, S., Kaplan, J. and Cutler, B. (2019) Expert testimony. In N. Brewer and A. B. Douglass (eds) *Psychological Science and the Law* (pp. 318–37). Guilford Press.

Martin, J. A. (2016) Applied human error theory: A police Taser-confusion shooting case study. *Proceedings of the Human Factors and Ergonomics Society Annual Meeting*, 60(1), 475–9.

Martin, L. (2013) Going Taser-happy in Canada? NCPR North Country Public Radio Blog, 7 September. Available at https://blogs.northcountrypublicradio.org/inbox/2013/09/07/going-taser-happy-in canada/.

Martin, M., Marchand, A., Boyer, R., and Martin, N. (2009) Predictors of the development of posttraumatic stress disorder among police officers. *Journal of Trauma & Dissociation*, 10(4), 451–68.

Martin, P. and Smyer, M. A. (1990) The experience of micro- and macroevents: A life span analysis. *Research on Aging*, 12(3), 294–310.

Martin, P. K., Schroeder, R. W., Olsen, D. H., Maloy, H., Boettcher, A. et al. (2019) A systematic review and meta-analysis of the Test of Memory Malingering in adults: Two decades of deception detection. *Clinical Neuropsychologist*, 8(2), 1–32.

Martinelli, R. (2010) Murder or stress-induced hypervigilance. *Peace Officers Research Association of California (PORAC) Law Enforcement News*, 47(12), 36–8.

Martschukat, J. (2005) Nineteenth-century executions as performances of law, death, and civilization. In A. Sarat and C. Boulanger (eds) *Cultural Lives of Capital Punishment: Comparative Perspectives* (pp. 49–68). Stanford University Press.

Maschi, T., Viola, D. and Koskinen, L. (2015) Trauma, stress, and coping among older adults in prison: Towards a human rights and intergenerational family justice action agenda. *Traumatology*, 21(3), 188–200.

Masson, J. M. (1984) Freud and the seduction theory. *The Atlantic Monthly*, 33–60.

Mastro, F. J. (2011) Preventing the 'Google mistrial': The challenge posed by jurors who use the internet and social media, *Litigation*, 37(2), 23–7.

Maswood, R., Rasmussen, A. S. and Rajaram, S. (2018) Collaborative remembering of emotional autobiographical memories: Implications for emotion regulation and collective memory. *Journal of Experimental Psychology: General*, 148(1), 65–79.

Math, S. B., Kumar, C. N. and Moirangthem, S. (2015) Insanity defense: Past, present, and future. *Indian Journal of Psychological Medicine*, 37(4), 381–7.

Mathes, E. W. and Kahn, A. (1975) Diffusion of responsibility and extreme behavior. *Journal of Personality and Social Psychology*, 31, 881–6.

Matsuda, I., Ogawa, T. and Tsuneoka, M. (2019) Broadening the use of concealed information test in the field. *Frontiers in Psychiatry*, 10(24), 1–10.

Matsumoto, D. and Hwang, H. (2018) Microexpressions differentiate truths from lies about future malicious intent. *Frontiers in Psychology*, available at www.frontiersin.org/articles/10.3389/fpsyg.2018.02545/full.

Matthews, S. (2004) Failed agency and the insanity defense. *International Journal of Law and Psychiatry*, 27, 413–24.

Mattison, M. A., Dando, C. and Ormerod, T. (2015) Sketching to remember: Episodic free recall task support for child witnesses and victims with autism spectrum disorder. *Journal of Autism and Developmental Disorders*, 45(6), 1751–65.

Max, D. T. (2007) *The Family that Couldn't Sleep: A Medical Mystery*. Random House.

Mayer, M. J. and Corey, D. M. (2017) Current issues in psychological fitness-for-duty evaluations of law enforcement officers: Legal and practice implications. In C. L. Mitchell and E. H. Dorian (eds) *Police Psychology and Its Growing Impact on Modern Law Enforcement* (pp. 93–117). IGI Global.

Meade, C. J. (1996) Reading death sentences: The narrative construction of capital punishment. *New York Law Review*, 71, 732–61.

Medrano, J. A., Ozkan, T. and Morris, R. (2017) Solitary confinement exposure and capital inmate misconduct. *American Journal of Criminal Justice*, 42(4), 863–82.

Meehl, P. E. (1954) *Clinical Versus Statistical Prediction: A Theoretical Analysis and a Review of the Evidence*. University of Minnesota Press.

Meenaghan, A., Nee, C., van Gelder, J. L., Vernham, Z., and Otte, M. (2020) Expertise, emotion and specialization in the development of persistent burglary. *British Journal of Criminology*, 60(3), 742–61.

Meichenbaum, D. (2017) Stress inoculation training: A preventative and treatment approach. In D. Meichenbaum (ed.) *The Evolution of Cognitive Behavior Therapy: A Personal and Professional Journey with Don Meichenbaum* (pp. 117–40). Routledge.

Meier, S. M., Petersen, L., Schendel, D. E., Mattheisen, M., Mortensen, P. B. and Mors, O. (2015) Obsessive-compulsive disorder and autism spectrum disorders: Longitudinal and offspring risk. *PloS One*, 10(11), e0141703. doi:10.1371/journal.pone.0141703.

Meijer, E. H. and van Koppen, P. J. (2017) Lie detectors and the law: The use of the polygraph in Europe. In D. Canter and R. Žukauskiene (eds) *Psychology and Law: Bridging the Gap* (pp. 45–64). Routledge.

Meijer, E. H. and Verschuere, B. (2010) The polygraph and the detection of deception. *Journal of Forensic Psychology Practice*, 10, 325–38.

Meijer, E. H., Verschuere, B., Gamer, M., Merckelbach, H. and Ben-Shakhar, G. (2016) Deception detection with behavioral, autonomic, and neural measures: Conceptual and methodological considerations that warrant modesty. *Psychophysiology*, 53, 593–604.

Meili, T. (2003) *I Am the Central Park Jogger: A Story of Hope and Possibility*. Scribner.

Meiser-Stedman, R., McKinnon, A., Dixon, C., Boyle, A., Smith, P. and Dalgleish, T. (2017) Acute stress disorder and the transition to posttraumatic stress disorder in children and adolescents: Prevalence, course, prognosis, diagnostic suitability, and risk markers. *Depression and Anxiety*, 34(4), 348–55.

Meissner, C. A., Surmon-Böhr, F., Oleszkiewicz, S. and Alison, L. J. (2017) Developing an evidence-based perspective on interrogation: A review of the U.S. government's high-value detainee interrogation group research program. *Psychology, Public Policy, and Law*, 23(4), 438–57.

Meloy, J. R. (1992) Revisiting the Rorschach of Sirhan Sirhan. *Journal of Personality Assessment*, 58(3), 548–70.

Meloy, J. R. (2006) Empirical basis and forensic application of affective and predatory violence. *Australian and New Zealand Journal of Psychiatry*, 40(6/7), 539–47.

Meloy, J. R. (2014) The seven myths of mass murder. *Violence and Gender*, 1(3), 102–4.

Meloy, J. R., Hoffmann, J., Guldimann, A. and James, D. (2012) The role of warning behaviors in threat assessment: An exploration and suggested typology. *Behavioral Sciences & the Law*, 30, 256–79.

Meloy, J. R., Hoffmann, J., Roshdi, K. and Guldimann, A. (2014) Some warning behaviors discriminate between school shooters and other students of concern. *Journal of Threat Assessment and Management*, 1(3), 203–11.

Meloy, J. R., Hempel, A. G., Mohandie, K., Shiva, A. A. and Gray, B. T. (2001) Offender and offense characteristics of a nonrandom sample of adolescent mass murderers. *Journal of the American Academy of Child and Adolescent Psychiatry*, 40, 719–28.

Melton, G. B., Petrila, J., Poythress, N. G. and Slobogin, C. (1997) *Psychological Evaluations for the Courts: A Handbook for Mental Health Professionals and Lawyers* (2nd edn). Guilford Press.

Memon, A. and Köhnken, G. (1992) Helping witnesses to remember more: The cognitive interview. *Expert Evidence*, 1(2), 39–48.

Memon, A. and Vartoukian, R. (1996) The effects of repeated questioning on young children's eyewitness testimony. *British Journal of Psychology*, 87(3), 403–15.

Memon, A., Meissner, C. A. and Fraser, J. (2010) The cognitive interview: A meta-analytic review and study space analysis of the past 25 years. *Psychology, Public Policy, & Law*, 16(4), 340–72.

Memon, A., Vrij, A. and Bull, R. (2003) *Psychology and Law: Truthfulness, Accuracy and Credibility* (2nd edn). John Wiley & Sons.

Memon, A., Wark, L., Holley, A., Koehnken, G. and Bull, R. (1997) Context effects and event memory: How powerful are the effects? In D. Payne and F. Conrad (eds) *Intersections in Basic and Applied Memory Research*. Lawrence Erlbaum.

Mendonça, R. D., Gouveia-Pereira, M. and Miranda, M. (2016) Belief in a just world and secondary victimization: The role of adolescent deviant behavior. *Personality and Individual Differences*, 97, 82–7.

Mendoza, M. (2013) The onion field kidnapping and killing—50 years later. *Los Angeles Daily News*, 9 March. Available at www.dailynews.com/2013/03/09/the-onion-field-kidnapping-and-killing-50-years-later/.

Mercer, J., Gibson, K. and Clayton, D. (2015) The therapeutic potential of a prison-based animal programme in the UK. *Journal of Forensic Practice*, 17(1), 43–54.

Merckelbach, H. and Merten, T. (2012) A note on cognitive dissonance and malingering. *Clinical Neuropsychologist*, 26(7), 1217–29.

Merrick, M. T. and Guinn, A. S. (2018) Child abuse and neglect: Breaking the intergenerational link. *American Journal of Public Health*, 108, 1117–18.

Mertes, M., Mazei, J. and Hüffmeier, J. (2020) 'We do not negotiate with terrorists!' But what if we did? *Peace and Conflict: Journal of Peace Psychology.* Advance online publication.

Metro News (2012) Alzheimer's sufferer Peter Russell shot repeatedly with a Taser. *Metro*, 10 May. Available at https://metro.co.uk/2012/05/10/alzheimers-sufferer-peter-russell-shot-repeatedly-with-a-taser-420961/.

Metzner, J. and Fellner, J. (2010) Solitary confinement and mental illness in U.S. prisons: A challenge for medical ethics. *Journal of the American Academy of Psychiatry and the Law*, 38(1), 104–8.

Mews, A., Di Bella, L. and Purver, M. (2017) *Impact Evaluation of the Prison-Based Core Sex Offender Treatment Programme.* London: Ministry of Justice.

Meyer, E. G. and Wynn, G. H. (2018) The importance of US military cultural competence. In L. W. Roberts and C. H. Warner (eds) *Military and Veteran Mental Health* (pp. 15–33). Springer.

Meynen, G. (2014) Neurolaw: Neuroscience, ethics, and law. Review essay. *Ethical Theory Moral Practice*, 17, 819–29.

Meynen, G. (2016) Arguments against the insanity defense and responses. In G. Meynen, *Legal Insanity: Explorations in Psychiatry, Law, and Ethics* (pp. 43–62). Springer.

Meynen, G. (2018) Forensic psychiatry and neurolaw: Description, developments, and debates. *International Journal of Law and Psychiatry*, 65, 1–6.

Michael, R. A. (2018) The American civil jury today. *University of Dayton Law Review*, 43, 247–59.

Miczek, K. A., DeBold, J. F., Gobrogge, K., Newman, E. L. and de Almeida, R. M. (2017) The role of neurotransmitters in violence and aggression. In P. Srurmey, *The Wiley Handbook of Violence and Aggression* (pp. 1–13). Wiley-Blackwell.

Milan, M. A., Throckmorton, W. R., McKee, J. M. and Wood, L. F. (1979) Contingency management in a cellblock token economy: Reducing rule violations and maximizing the effects of token reinforcement. *Criminal Justice and Behaviour*, 6(4), 307–25.

Miles, A. (2016) Responding to domestic violence and spiritual abuse. *Christian Reflection*, 71–4.

Milla, M. N., Putra, I. E. and Umam, A. N. (2019) Stories from jihadists: Significance, identity, and radicalization through the call for jihad. *Peace and Conflict: Journal of Peace Psychology*, 25(2), 111–21.

Miller, D. and Sabir, R. (2012) Counterterrorism as counterinsurgency in the UK 'war on terror'. In S. Poynting and D. Whyte (eds) *Counterterrorism and State Political Violence* (pp. 12–32). Routledge.

Miller, E. and McCaw, B. (2019) Intimate partner violence. *New England Journal of Medicine*, 380(9), 850–7.

Miller, H. A. (2001) *M-FAST: Miller Forensic Assessment of Symptoms Test Professional Manual.* Psychological Assessment Resources.

Miller, H. A. (2004) Examining the use of the M-FAST with criminal defendants incompetent to stand trial. *International Journal of Offender Therapy and Comparative Criminology*, 48(3), 268–80.

Miller, L. (2006) *Practical Police Psychology: Stress Management and Crisis Intervention for Law Enforcement.* Charles C. Thomas.

Miller, L. (2007) Negotiating with mentally disordered hostage takers: Guiding principles and practical strategies. *Journal of Police Crisis Negotiations*, 7(1), 63–83.

Miller, L. (2014) Serial killers: I. Subtypes, patterns, and motives. *Aggression and Violent Behavior*, 19(1), 1–11.

Miller, L. (2015) Flaw and order: The science and mythology of criminal profiling. *Skeptical Inquirer*, 39(1), 54–8.

Mills, J. F. (2017) Violence risk assessment: A brief review, current issues, and future directions. *Canadian Psychology/Psychologie Canadienne*, 58(1), 40–9.

Milroy, C. (2017) A brief history of the expert witness. *Academy of Forensic Pathology*, 7(4), 1–23, 516–26.

Minhas, H. M. (2017) Special topics in forensic psychiatry: The insanity defense and competence to stand trial. In T. Wasser (ed.) *Psychiatry and the Law* (pp. 173–82). Springer.

Ministry of Justice (2012) *The Registered Intermediary Procedural Guidance Manual.* London: Ministry of Justice.

Ministry of Justice (2019) *Proven Reoffending Statistics Quarterly Bulletin, January 2017 to March 2017.* Available at https://assets.publishing.service.gov.uk/government/uploads/system/uploads/attachment_data/file/775079/proven_reoffending_bulletin_January_to_March_17.pdf.

Mischel, W. (1973) Toward a cognitive social learning reconceptualization of personality. *Psychological Review*, 80, 252–83.

Mitchell, A.J., Beaumont, H., Ferguson, D., Yadegarfar, M. and Stubbs, B. (2014) Risk of dementia and mild cognitive impairment in older people with subjective memory complaints: meta-analysis. *Acta Psychiatrica Scandinavia*, 130(6), 439–51.

Mitchell, J. and Bray, G. (1990) *Emergency Services Stress.* Prentice-Hall.

Mjanes, K., Beauregard, E. and Martineau, M. (2017) Revisiting the organized/disorganized model of sexual homicide. *Criminal Justice and Behavior*, 44(12), 1604–19.

Mlinac, M. E. and Schwabenbauer, A. (2018) Psychological resilience. In B. Resnick, L. P. Gwyther and K. A. Roberto (eds) *Resilience in Aging: Concepts, Research, and Outcomes* (pp. 81–104). Springer.

Mobbs, D., Lau, H. C., Jones, O. D. and Frith, C. D. (2007) Law, responsibility, and the brain. *PLoS Biology*, 5(4), e103. https://doi.org/10.1371/journal.pbio.0050103.

Moghaddam, F. M. (2005) The staircase to terrorism: A psychological exploration. *American Psychologist*, 60(2), 161–9.

Moghaddam, F. M., Heckenlaible, V., Blackman, M., Fasano, S. and Dufour, D. J. (2016) Globalization and terrorism: The primacy of collective processes. In A. G. Miller (ed.) *Social Psychology of Good and Evil* (2nd edn, pp. 415–42). Guilford Press.

Mohandie, K., Meloy, J. R. and Collins, P. I. (2009) Suicide by cop among officer-involved shooting cases. *Journal of Forensic Sciences*, 54(2), 456–62.

Mokros, A. and Alison, L. (2002) Is offender profiling possible? Testing the predicted homology of crime scene actions and background characteristics in a sample of rapists. *Legal and Criminological Psychology*, 7(1), 25–43.

Molho, C., Tybur, J. M., Güler, E., Balliet, D. and Hofmann, W. (2017) Disgust and anger relate to different aggressive responses to moral violations. *Psychological Science*, 28(5), 609–19.

Monson, T. C., Hesley, J. W. and Chernick, L. (1982) Specifying when personality traits can and cannot predict behavior: An alternative to abandoning the attempt to predict single-act criteria. *Journal of Personality and Social Psychology*, 43(2), 385–99.

Moore, M. (2015) The quest for a responsible responsibility test: Norwegian insanity law after Breivik. *Criminal Law and Philosophy*, 9(4), 645–93.

Moore, T. (2015) Woman discovers her photos have been used to catfish others for years. Jezebell.com, 26 January. Available at https://jezebel.com/woman-discovers-her-photos-have-been-used-to-catfish-ot-1681189437.

Moran, R. (1977) Awaiting the Crown's pleasure: The case of Daniel M'Naughton. *Criminology*, 15(1), 7–26.

Moreland, M. B. and Clark, S. E. (2020) Absolute and relative decision processes in eyewitness identification. *Applied Cognitive Psychology*, 34(1), 142–56.

Morewitz, S. (2019) Partner abduction and hostage-taking. In S. Morewitz, *Kidnapping and Violence: New Research and Clinical Perspectives* (pp. 1–10). Springer.

Morgan, A. and Chadwick, H. (2009) Key issues in domestic violence. *Research in Practice*, 7. Australian Institute of Criminology, Canberra.

Moriarty, J. C. (2016) Seeing voices: Potential neuroscience contributions to a reconstruction of legal insanity, *Fordham Law Review*, 85, 599–618.

Moriarty, L. J. and Jerin, R. A. (eds) (1998) *Current Issues in Victimology Research*. Carolina Academic Press.

Morina, N., Wicherts, J. M., Lobbrecht, J. and Priebe, S. (2014) Remission from post-traumatic stress disorder in adults: A systematic review and meta-analysis of long-term outcome studies. *Clinical Psychology Review*, 34(3), 249–55.

Morris, R. G. (2015) Exploring the effect of exposure to short-term solitary confinement among violent prison inmates. *Journal of Quantitative Criminology*, 32(1), 1–22.

Morrison, C. M. and Conway, M. A. (2010) First words and first memories. *Cognition*, 116(1), 23–32.

Morse, S. J. (2004) New neuroscience, old problems: Legal implications of brain science. *Cerebrum*, 6(4), 81–90.

Morse, S. J. (2019) Neuroscience and criminal law: Perils and promises. In L. Alexander and K. K. Ferzan (eds) *The Palgrave Handbook of Applied Ethics and the Criminal Law* (pp. 471–96). Palgrave Macmillan.

Mortimer, C. (2017) Baby P's killer denied parole following sentence for campaign of abuse against little boy. *The Independent*, 2 August. Available at www.independent.co.uk/news/uk/crime/baby-p-stepfather-denied-parole-abuse-against-baby-boy-child-prison-sentence-release-a7872666.html.

Moskalenko, S. and McCauley, C. (2011) The psychology of lone-wolf terrorism. *Counselling Psychology Quarterly*, 24(2), 115–26.

Moss, J. and Samuels, D. (2003) *Con Man*. Film produced for HBO/Cinemax.

Moss, S. A., Lee, E., Berman, A. and Rung, D. (2019) When do people value rehabilitation and restorative justice over the punishment of offenders? *Victims & Offenders*, 14(1), 32–51.

Moston, S. (1990) How children interpret and respond to questions: Situational sources of suggestibility in eyewitness interviews. *Social Behaviour*, 5, 155–67.

Moston, S. and Stephenson, G. M. (1993) The changing face of police interrogation. *Journal of Community & Applied Social Psychology*, 3(2), 101–15.

Mothersill, O., Knee-Zaska, C. and Donohoe, G. (2016) Emotion and theory of mind in schizophrenia: Investigating the role of the cerebellum. *The Cerebellum*, 15(3), 357–68.

Motta, R. (2020) Secondary trauma in children and school personnel. In S. Taukeni (ed.) *Addressing Multicultural Needs in School Guidance and Counseling* (pp. 65–81). IGI Global.

Mowbray, A. (2016) European Court of Human Rights: May 2015 to April 2016. *European Public Law*, 22(4), 613–42.

Muftić, L. R. and Hunt, D. E. (2013) Victim precipitation: Further understanding the linkage between victimization and offending in homicide. *Homicide Studies*, 17(3), 239–54.

Mukundan, C. R., Sumit, S. and Chetan, S. M. (2017) Brain Electrical Oscillations Signature Profiling (BEOS) for measuring the process of remembrance. *EC Neurology*, 8(6), 217–30.

Muller, C. (2019) Ultra-right-wing white nationalism: Literature insights on Breivik and Tarrant, and the significance of the phenomenon in Australia. *Journal of the Australian Institute of Professional Intelligence Officers*, 27(2), 43.

Muller, D. A. (2000) Criminal profiling. *Homicide Studies*, 4(3), 234–64.

Mungan, M. C. (2019) Salience and the severity versus the certainty of punishment. *International Review of Law and Economics*, 57, 95–100.

Münsterberg, H. (1908) *On the Witness Stand: Essays on Psychology and Crime.* Doubleday, Page.

Muramatsu, K., Johnson, D. T. and Yano, K. (2018) The death penalty and homicide deterrence in Japan. *Punishment & Society*, 20(4), 432–57.

Murphy, G. and Greene, C. M. (2015) High perceptual load causes inattentional blindness and deafness in drivers. *Visual Cognition*, 23(7), 810–14.

Murray, S., Schallmo, M. P., Kolodny, T., Millin, R., Kale, A. et al. (2018) Sex differences in visual motion processing. *Current Biology*, 28(17), 2794–99.

Murrie, D. C., Warren, J. I., Kristiansson, M. and Dietz, P. E. (2002) Asperger's syndrome in forensic settings. *International Journal of Forensic Mental Health*, 1, 59–70.

Myles, B. S., Hagiwara, T., Dunn, W., Rinner, L., Reese, M. et al. (2004) Sensory issues in children with Asperger syndrome and autism. *Education and Training in Developmental Disabilities*, 39(4), 283–90.

Nagel, S. and Weitzman, L. (1972) Sex and the unbiased jury. *Judicature*, 56, 108–11.

Nagin, D. S. (2013) Deterrence in the twenty-first century: A review of the evidence. *Crime and Justice*, 42(1), 199–263.

Nahari, G., Ashkenazi, T., Fisher, R. P., Granhag, P. A., Hershkowita, I. et al. (2019) 'Language of lies': Urgent issues and prospects in verbal lie detection research. *Legal and Criminological Psychology*, 24(1), 1–23.

Najdowski, C. J. and Bonventre, C. L. (2014) Deception in the interrogation room. *American Psychological Association*, 45(5), 26–32.

Nakayma, M. (2002) Practical uses of the concealed information test for criminal investigation in Japan. In M. Kleiner (ed.) *Handbook of Polygraph Testing.* Academic Press.

Nathan, D. and Snedecker, M. (1995) *Satan's Silence: Ritual Abuse and the Making of a Modern American Witch Hunt.* Basic Books.

National Autism Resources (n.d.) Fidget Toys & Stress Balls. Available at www.nationalautismresources.com/autism-fidget-toys-stress-balls/.

National Institute on Aging (2019) Alzheimer's disease fact sheet. Available at www.nia.nih.gov/health/alzheimers-disease-fact-sheet.

National Research Council (2003) *The Polygraph and Lie Detection.* National Academies Press.

NCEA (National Center on Elder Abuse) (2019) Statistics and data. Available at https://ncea.acl.gov/What-We-Do/Research/Statistics-and-Data.aspx.

Neal, T. M. and Grisso, T. (2014) Assessment practices and expert judgement methods in forensic psychology and psychiatry: An international snapshot. *Criminal Justice and Behavior*, 41, 1406–21.

Neary, D., Snowden, J. and Mann, D. (2005) Frontotemporal dementia. *The Lancet: Neurology*, 4(11), 771–80.

Nestor, P. G. (2019) In defense of free will: Neuroscience and criminal responsibility. *International Journal of Law and Psychiatry*, 65, 101344. doi: 10.1016/j.ijlp.2018.04.004.

Neuberg, S. L., Judice, T. N. and West, S. G. (1997) What the Need for Closure Scale measures and what it does not: Toward differentiating among related epistemic motives. *Journal of Personality and Social Psychology*, 72(6), 1396–421.

Newlin, C., Steele, L. C., Chamberlin, A., Anderson, J., Kenniston, J. et al. (2015) *Child Forensic Interviewing: Best Practices.* US Department of Justice. Available at www.ojjdp.gov/pubs/248749.pdf.

Newlin, M., Webber, M., Morris, D. and Howarth, S. (2015) Social participation interventions for adults with mental health problems: A review and narrative synthesis. *Social Work Research*, 39(3), 167–80.

Newsome, J. and Cullen, F. T. (2017) The risk-need-responsivity model revisited: Using biosocial criminology to enhance offender rehabilitation. *Criminal Justice and Behaviour*, 44(8), 1030–49.

Newton, D., Day, A., Giles, M., Wodak, J., Graffam, J. and Baldry, E. (2016) The impact of vocational education and training programs on recidivism: A systematic review of current experimental evidence. *International Journal of Offender Therapy and Comparative Criminology*, 62(1), 187–207.

Newton, J. (2015) Man charged in murder of two Zion girls not expected to face trial this year. *Lake County News Sun*, 26 May. Available at www.chicagotribune.com/suburbs/lake-county-news-sun/ct-lns-torrez-trial-delay-st-0527-20150526-story.html.

Ngabonziza, O. and Singh, S. (2012) Offender reintegration programme and its role in reducing recidivism: Exploring perceptions of the effectiveness of tough enough programme. *Acta Criminologica: African Journal of Criminology & Victimology,* special edition 2, 87–102.

Nickerson, R. S. (1998) Confirmation bias: A ubiquitous phenomenon in many guises. *Review of General Psychology,* 2(2), 175–220.

Nieuwenhuys, A. and Oudejans, R. R. (2010) Effects of anxiety on handgun shooting behavior of police officers: A pilot study. *Anxiety, Stress and Coping,* 23(2), 225–33.

Nieuwenhuys, A. and Oudejans, R. R. (2017) Anxiety and performance: Perceptual-motor behavior in high-pressure contexts. *Current Opinion in Psychology,* 16, 28–33.

NIH (National Institute of Child Health and Human Development) (2019) Down syndrome: Research activities and scientific advances. Available at www.nichd.nih.gov/health/topics/down/researchinfo/activities.

Nirenberg, M. (2016) Meeting a forensic podiatry admissibility challenge: A Daubert case study. *Journal of Forensic Sciences,* 61(3), 833–41.

Nobles, M. R., Reyns, B. W., Fox, K. A. and Fisher, B. S. (2014) Protection against pursuit: A conceptual and empirical comparison of cyberstalking and stalking victimization among a national sample. *Justice Quarterly,* 31(6), 986–1014.

Nolan, H. (2013) George Zimmerman juror B37 hates media, called Trayvon 'Boy of Color'. Gawker.com, 15 July. Available at gawker.com/george-zimmerman-juror-b37-hates-media-called-trayvon-787873533.

North, M. A. and Smith, S. (2018) Victim precipitation: Let's not silence that voice. *Industrial and Organizational Psychology,* 11(1), 137–41.

Nosek, B. A. and Riskind, R. G. (2016) Policy implications of implicit social cognition. *Social Issues and Policy Review,* 6(1), 113–47.

Nosek, B. A., Hawkins, C. B. and Frazier, R. S. (2011) Implicit social cognition: From measures to mechanisms. *Trends in Cognitive Sciences,* 15(4), 152–9.

Novak, L. (2015) Domestic violence victim Zahra Abrahimzadeh's family establish foundation to help other women. *The Advertiser,* 20 March. Available at www.adelaidenow.com.au/news/south-australia/domestic-violence-victim-zahra-abrahimzadehs-family-establish-foundation-to-help-other-women/news-story/4e195638eb974b770ec2a61efc5a2ecb.

Novikova, I. A. and Vorobyeva, A. A. (2019) The five-factor model: Contemporary personality theory. In K. D. Keith (ed.) *Cross-Cultural Psychology: Contemporary Themes and Perspectives* (2nd edn, pp. 685–706). Wiley-Blackwell.

Nugent, W. R., Williams, M. and Umbreit, M. S. (2004) Participation in victim-offender mediation and the prevalence of subsequent delinquent behavior: A meta-analysis. *Research on Social Work Practice,* 14(6), 408–16.

Nuñez, N., Myers, B., Wilkowski, B. M. and Schweitzer, K. (2017) The impact of angry versus sad victim impact statements on mock jurors' sentencing decisions in a capital trial. *Criminal Justice and Behavior,* 44, 862–86.

Nuñez, N., Schweitzer, K., Chai, C. A. and Myers, B. (2015) Negative emotions felt during trial: The effect of fear, anger, and sadness on juror decision making. *Applied Cognitive Psychology,* 29(2), 200–9.

Obasogie, O. K. and Newman, Z. (2017) Police violence, use of force policies, and public health. *American Journal of Law & Medicine,* 43(2/3), 279–95.

Ochs, E. and Capps, L. (2009) *Living Narrative: Creating Lives in Everyday Storytelling.* Harvard University Press.

Ochs, H. A., Neuenschwander, M. C. and Dodson, T. B. (1996) Are head, neck and facial injuries markers of domestic violence? *Journal of the American Dental Association,* 127(6), 757–61.

O'Connor, A. M. and Evans, A. D. (2020) Perceptions of older adult jurors: The influence of aging stereotypes and jury laws. *Psychology, Crime & Law,* 1–19.

O'Connor, R. (2019) Banksy painting depicting MPs as chimpanzees sells for record £9.9m at auction. *Independent,* 4 October. Available at www.independent.co.uk/arts-entertainment/art/banksy-painting-mps-parliament-chimpanzees-monkeys-sale-auction-price-a9142486.html.

Odebade, A., Welsh, T., Mthunzi, S. and Benkhelifa, E. (2017) Mitigating anti-forensics in the cloud via resource-based privacy preserving activity attribution. In 2017 Fourth International Conference on Software Defined Systems (SDS) (pp. 143–9). IEEE.

Odgers, S. J. and Richardson, J. T. (1995) Keeping bad science out of the courtroom: Changes in American and Australian expert evidence law. *University of New South Wales Law Review,* 18, 108–29.

Ofori-Dua, K., Onzaberigu, N. J. and Nimako, R. K. (2019) Victims, the forgotten party in the criminal justices system: The perception and experiences of crime victims in Kumasi metropolis in Ghana. *Journal of Victimology and Victim Justice,* 2(2), 109–28.

Ogawa, T., Matsuda, I., Tsuneoka, M. and Verschuere, B. (2015) The Concealed Information Test in the laboratory versus Japanese field practice: Bridging the scientist-practitioner gap. *Archives of Forensic Psychology*, 1(2), 16–27.

Ogden, G. L. (2000) The role of demeanor evidence in determining credibility of witnesses in fact finding: Views of the ALJS. *Journal of the National Association of Administrative Law Judiciary*, 20(1), 1–95.

Oleszkiewicz, S. and Granhag, P. A. and Montecinos, C. S. (2014) The Scharff technique: Eliciting intelligence from human sources. *Law and Human Behavior*, 38(5), 478–89.

Oliver, M. (2002) John W. Powers, 90: Legendary officer in LAPD for 31 years. *Los Angeles Times*, 9 December. Available at www.latimes.com/archives/la-xpm-2002-dec-09-me-powers9-story.html.

Olsen, D. E., Harris, J. C., Capps, M. H., Ansley, N. (1997) Computerized polygraph scoring system. *Journal of Forensic Sciences*, 42(1), 61–71.

Olsen, E. A. and Charman, S. D. (2012) 'But can you prove it?' Examining the quality of innocent suspects' alibis. *Psychology, Crime & Law*, 18(5), 453–71.

Olsen, J. (1991) *Predator: Rape, Madness, and Injustice in Seattle*. Dell.

Olson, D. T. (1998) Improving deadly force decision making. *FBI Law Enforcement Bulletin*, 67(2), 1–9.

Olson, L. (2017) Assessing sexual orientation bias in witness credibility evaluations in a sample of student mock jurors. *Justice Policy Journal*, 14, 1–17.

Olver, M. E. and Wong, S. C. (2019) Offender risk and need assessment: Theory, research, and applications. In D. L. Polaschek, A. Day and C. R. Hollin (eds) *The Wiley International Handbook of Correctional Psychology* (pp. 461–75). Wiley-Blackwell.

Olver, M. E., Coupland, R. B. and Kurtenbach, T. J. (2018) Risk-need-responsivity applications of the MMPI-2 in sexual offender assessment. *Psychology, Crime & Law*, 24(8), 806–30.

O'Mahony, B. (2010) The emerging role of the registered intermediary with the vulnerable witness and offender: Facilitating communication with the police and members of the judiciary. *British Journal of Learning Disabilities*, 38(3), 232–7.

O'Malley, S. (2004) *Are You There Alone?: The Unspeakable Crime of Andrea Yates*. Simon and Schuster.

O'Malley, S. (2017) The autism community and police: A case study. Camh, 15 June. Available at www.camh.ca/en/camh-news-and-stories/the-autism-community-and-police-a-case-study.

O'Mara, S. (2009) Torturing the brain: On the folk psychology and folk neurobiology motivating enhanced and coercive interrogation techniques. *Trends in Cognitive Sciences*, 13(12), 497–500.

O'Mara, S. (2015) *Why Torture Doesn't Work: The Neuroscience of Interrogation*. Harvard University Press.

O'Mara, S. (2016) Human information gathering: How can we proceed? *Psychology Today Canada*, 11 April. Available at www.psychologytoday.com/us/blog/the-interrogated-brain/201604/human-information-gathering-how-can-we-proceed.

O'Mara, S. (2018) The captive brain: Torture and the neuroscience of humane interrogation. *QJM: An International Journal of Medicine*, 111(2), 73–8.

O'Neil, L. (2016) Sammy Yatim murder charge sparks strong reaction among Canadians: your community. CBC News. Available at www.cbc.ca/news/canada/toronto/sammy-yatim-s-family-relieved-officer-facing-murder-charge-1.1407462.

Onyishi, C. N., Ede, M. O., Ossai, O. V. and Ugwuanyi, C. S. (2020) Rational emotive occupational health coaching in the management of police subjective well-being and work ability: A case of repeated measures. *Journal of Police and Criminal Psychology*, 1–16.

Oorsouw, K. and Broers, N. J. and Sauerland, M. (2019) Alcohol intoxication impairs eyewitness memory and increases suggestibility: Two field studies. *Applied Cognitive Psychology*, 33(3), https://doi.org/10.1002/acp.3561.

Oostinga, M. and Willmott, D. (2017) Scientific jury selection. In B. Baker, R. Minhas and L. Wilson (eds) *Psychology & Law Factbook* (2nd edn, pp. 17–18). European Association of Psychology and Law.

Orbach, Y. and Pipe, M.-E. (2011) Investigating substantive issues. In M. E. Lamb, D. J. LaRooy, L. C. Malloy and C. Katz (eds) *Children's Testimony: A Handbook of Psychological Research and Forensic Practice* (pp. 147–63). Wiley.

Orbach, Y., Hershkowitz, I., Lamb, M. E., Sternberg, K. J., Esplin, P. W. and Horowitz, D. (2000) Assessing the value of structured protocols for forensic interviews of alleged child abuse victims. *Child Abuse & Neglect*, 24, 733–52.

Orman, T. F. (2016) 'Paradigm' as a central concept in Thomas Kuhn's thought. *International Journal of Humanities and Social Science*, 6(10), 47–52.

O'Rourke, T. E., Penrod, S. D., Cutler, B. L. and Stuve, T. (1989) The external validity of eyewitness identification research: Generalizing across subject populations. *Law & Human Behavior*, 13(4), 385–95.

Ortiz, J. M. and Jackey, H. (2019) The system is not broken, it is intentional: The offender reentry industry as deliberate structural violence. *The Prison Journal*, 99(4), 484–503.

Osberg, T. M. (1989) Self-report reconsidered: A further look at its advantages as an assessment technique. *Journal of Counseling & Development*, 68(1), 111–13.

Osborne, J. R. and Capellan, J. A. (2017) Examining active shooter events through the rational choice perspective and crime script analysis. *Security Journal*, 30(3), 880–902.

O'Shea, L. E., Picchioni, M. M. and Dickens, G. L. (2016) The predictive validity of the Short-Term Assessment of Risk and Treatability (START) for multiple adverse outcomes in a secure psychiatric inpatient setting. *Assessment*, 23(2), 150–62.

Otgaar, H., Howe, M. L., Merckelbach, H. and Muris, P. (2018) Who is the better eyewitness? Sometimes adults but at other times children. *Current Directions in Psychological Science*, 27(5), 378–85.

Otgaar, H., Howe, M. L., Muris, P. and Merckelbach, H. (2019) Dealing with false memories in children and adults: Recommendations for the legal arena. *Policy Insights from the Behavioral and Brain Sciences*, 6(1), 87–93.

Otgaar, H., Ruiter, C., Howe, M. L., Hoetmer, L. and Van-Reekum, P. (2017) A case concerning children's false memories of abuse: Recommendations regarding expert witness work. *Psychiatry, Psychology and Law*, 24(3), 365–378.

O'Toole, M. E. (2009) *The School Shooter: A Threat Assessment Perspective.* Diane Publishing.

Ott, T. and Nieder, A. (2019) Dopamine and cognitive control in the prefrontal cortex. *Trends in Cognitive Sciences*, 23(3), 213–34.

Pagliaro, J. (2015) Police college instructor says Const. James Forcillo out of options night he shot Sammy Yatim. *The Star*, 21 December. Available at www.thestar.com/news/gta/2015/12/21/police-college-instructor-says-const-james-forcillo-out-of-options-night-he-shot-sammy-yatim.html.

Pakkanen, T., Santtila, P. and Bosco, D. (2014) Crime linkage as expert evidence: Making a case for the Daubert standard. In J. Woodhams and C. Bennell (eds) *Crime Linkage: Theory, Research, and Practice* (pp. 225–50). CRC Press.

Palermo, G. (2018) Criminality and psychopathology: The profile of stalkers. *AGORA International Journal of Juridical Sciences*, 2, 76–84.

Palermo, G. B. and Kocsis, R. N. (2005) *Offender Profiling: An Introduction to the Sociopsychological Analysis of Violent Crime* (vol. 1107). Charles C. Thomas.

Palmer, M. A. and Brewer, N. (2012) Sequential lineup presentation promotes less-biased criterion setting but does not improve discriminability. *Law and Human Behavior*, 36(3), 247–55.

Palmer, S. J. (2019) The neuroscientific connections between the body and mind. *British Journal of Neuroscience Nursing*, 15(5), 246–8.

Paoline, E. A. III and Terrill, W. (2007) Police education, experience, and the use of force. *Criminal Justice and Behavior*, 34(2), 179–96.

Paoline, E. A. III and Terrill, W. (2011) Listen to me! Police officers' views of appropriate use of force. *Journal of Crime and Justice*, 34(3), 178–89.

Papp, J., Campbell, C. A. and Anderson, V. R. (2018) Assessing the incremental validity of Andrews and Bonta's 'moderate four' predictors of recidivism using a diverse sample of offending and truant youth. *International Journal of Offender Theory and Comparative Criminology*, 63(6), 854–73.

Papp, J., Wooldredge, J. and Pompoco, A. (2019) Timing of prison programs and the odds of returning to prison. *Corrections*, 1–26.

Park, H. S., Levine, T., McCornack, S., Morrison, K. and Ferrara, M. (2002) How people really detect lies. *Communication Monographs*, 69(2), 144–57.

Park, M. M. (2008) The strange case of Andrea Yates and Dr Park Dietz. *Victorian Bar News*, 143, 85.

Parr, H. and Stevenson, O. (2015) 'No news today': Talk of witnessing with families of missing people. *Cultural Geographies*, 22(2), 297–315.

Patel, S., Day, T. N., Jones, N. and Mazefsky, A. A. (2017) Association between anger rumination and autism symptom severity, depression symptoms, aggression, and general dysregulation in adolescents with autism spectrum disorder. *Autism*, 21(2), 181–9.

Patel-Carstairs, S. (2019) Islamic State brides: Where are the female jihadists now? Sky News, 14 February. Available at https://news.sky.com/story/islamic-state-brides-where-are-the-female-jihadists-now-11637068.

Paterline, A. and Orr, D. (2016) Adaptation to prison and inmate self-concept. *Journal of Psychology and Behavioral Science*, 4(2), 70–9.

Paton, D. (2006) Critical incident stress risk in police officers: Managing resilience and vulnerability. *Traumatology*, 12(3), 198–206.

Patton, C. L., Nobles, M. R. and Fox, K. A. (2010) Look who's stalking: Obsessive pursuit and attachment theory. *Journal of Criminal Justice*, 38(3), 282–90.

Paulhus, D. L. and Vazire, S. (2007) The self-report method. In R. Robins, R. Fraley and R. Krueger (eds) *Handbook of Research Methods in Personality Psychology* (pp. 224–39). Guilford Press.

Pauline, B. and Boss, P. (2009) *Ambiguous Loss: Learning to Live with Unresolved Grief.* Harvard University Press.

Paulo, R. M., Albuquerque, P. B., Vitorino, F. and Bull, R. (2017) Enhancing the cognitive interview with an alternative procedure to witness-compatible questioning: category clustering recall. *Psychology, Crime & Law*, 23(10), 967–82.

Paulsen, D. (2007) Improving geographic profiling through commuter/marauder prediction. *Police Practice and Research*, 8(4), 347–57.

Payne-James, J. J., Beynon, J. and Vieira, D. (2017) *Monitoring Detention, Custody, Torture and Ill-treatment: A Practical Approach to Prevention and Documentation.* CRC Press.

Payne-James, J. J., Stark, M. M., Nittis, M. and Sheasby, D. R. (2020) Injury assessment, documentation, and interpretation. In M. Stark (ed.) *Clinical Forensic Medicine* (pp. 143–94). Springer.

Pearlman, L. A. and Saakvitne, K. W. (1995) *Trauma and the Therapist: Countertransference and Vicarious Traumatization in Psychotherapy with Incest Survivors.* WW. Norton.

Pedahzur, A. (2005) *Suicide Terrorism.* Polity Press.

Pelfrey, W. V. Jr (2004) The relationship between malingerers' intelligence and MMPI-2 knowledge and their ability to avoid detection. *International Journal of Offender Therapy and Comparative Criminology*, 48(6), 649–63.

Pella, R. D., Hill, B. D., Singh, A. N., Hayes, J. S. and Gouvier, W. D. (2012) Noncredible performance in mild traumatic brain injury. In C. R. Reynolds and A. M. Horton (eds) *Detection of Malingering During Head Injury Litigation* (pp. 121–50). Springer.

Pennington, B., Rogers, S., Bennetto, L. et al. (1997) Validity test of the executive dysfunction hypothesis of autism. In J. Russell (ed.) *Executive Functioning and Autism* (pp. 143–78). Oxford University Press.

Pennington, N. and Hastie, R. (1992) Explaining the evidence: Tests of the story model for juror decision making. *Journal of Personality and Social Psychology*, 62(2), 189–206.

Penrod, S. and Bornstein, B. H. (2007) Generalizing eyewitness reliability research. In R. Lindsay, D. Ross, J. Read and M. Toglia (eds) *The Handbook of Eyewitness Psychology*, vol. II: *Memory for People* (pp. 529–56). Lawrence Erlbaum.

Penson, B. N., Ruchensky, J. R., Morey, L. C. and Edens, J. F. (2018) Using the personality assessment inventory antisocial and borderline features scales to predict behavior change: A multisite longitudinal study of youthful offenders. *Assessment*, 25(7), 858–66.

Perdilla-Delgado, E. and Payne, J. D. (2017) The Deese-Roediger-McDermott (DRM) task: A simple cognitive paradigm to investigate false memories in the laboratory. *Journal of Visualized Experiments*, 119, 1–10.

Pereboom, D. (2018) Incapacitation, reintegration, and limited general deterrence. *Neuroethics*, 1–11.

Perillo, J. T. and Kassin, S. M. (2011) Inside interrogation: The lie, the bluff, and false confessions. *Law and Human Behaviour*, 35(4), 327–37.

Perkins, J. E. and Bourgeois, M. J. (2006) Perceptions of police use of deadly force. *Journal of Applied Social Psychology*, 36(1), 161–77.

Perlin, M. L. (2017) The insanity defense: Nine myths that will not go away. In M. D. White (ed.) *The Insanity Defense: Multidisciplinary Views on its History, Trends, and Controversies* (pp. 3–22). Praeger/ABC-CLIO.

Perlman, M. (2018) How is skepticism different than cynicism? Find the answer in ancient Greece. *Columbia Journalism Review*, 15 October. Available at www.cjr.org/language_corner/skepticism-cynicism.php.

Perlmutter, M. and Myers, N. A. (1976) Recognition memory in preschool children. *Developmental Psychology*, 12(3), 271–2.

Perona, A. R., Bottoms, B. L. and Sorenson, E. (2005) Research-based guidelines for child forensic interviews. *Journal of Aggression, Maltreatment & Trauma*, 12(3/4), 81–130.

Perri, F. S. and Lichtenwald, T. G. (2009) When worlds collide: Criminal investigative analysis, forensic psychology, and the Timothy Masters case. *Forensic Examiner*, 18(2), 53–68.

Perron, B. E. and Hiltz, B. S. (2006) Burnout and secondary trauma among forensic interviewers of abused children. *Child and Adolescent Social Work Journal*, 23(2), 216–34.

Perske, R. (2008) False confessions from 53 persons with intellectual disabilities: The list keeps growing. *Intellectual and Developmental Disabilities*, 46(6), 468–79.

Perugini, M., Gallucci, M., Presaghi, F. and Ercolani, A. (2003) The personal norm of reciprocity. *European Journal of Personality*, 17(4), 251–83.

Peter-Hagene, L. C. and Ullman, S. E. (2018) Longitudinal effects of sexual assault victims' drinking and self-blame on posttraumatic stress disorder. *Journal of Interpersonal Violence*, 33(1), 83–93.

Peter-Hagene, L. C., Salerno, J. M. and Phalen, H. (2019) Jury decision making. In N. Brewer and A. B. Douglass, *Psychological Science and the Law* (pp. 338–66). Guilford Press.

Peters, B., Forlin, C., McInerney, D. and Maclean, R. (2013) Social interaction and cooperative activities: Drawing plans as a means of increasing engagement for children with ASD. *International Journal of Whole Schooling*, 9(2), 61–86.

Peterson, C. and Grant, M. (2001) Forced-choice: Are forensic interviewers asking the right questions?

Canadian Journal of Behavioural Science/Revue canadienne des sciences du comportement, 33(2), 118–27.

Peth, J., Vossel, G. and Gamer, M. (2012) Emotional arousal modulates the encoding of crime-related details and corresponding physiological responses in the Concealed Information Test. *Psychophysiology*, 49(3), 381–90.

Petherick, W. (2014) *Profiling and Serial Crime: Theoretical and Practical Issues* (3rd edn). Anderson.

Petherick, W. (2017) Victim precipitation: Why we need to expand upon the theory. *Forensic Research & Criminology International Journal*, 5(2), 00148. DOI: 10.15406/frcij.2017.05.00148.

Petherick, W. (2019) Forensic victimology assessments in child abuse and neglect cases. In I. Bryce, Y. Robinson and W. Petherick (eds) *Child Abuse and Neglect* (pp. 135–49). Academic Press.

Petherick, W. and Ferguson, C. (2012) Understanding victim behaviour through offender behaviour typologies. In G. Coventry and M. Shircore, *Proceedings of the 5th Annual Australian and New Zealand Critical Criminology Conference* (pp. 100–11). James Cook University.

Petherick, W. and Sinnamon, G. (eds) (2016) *The Psychology of Criminal and Antisocial Behavior: Victim and Offender Perspectives*. Academic Press.

Petry, N. M. (2011) Contingency management: what it is and why psychiatrists should want to use it. *Psychiatrist*, 35(5), 161–3.

Petsko, C. D. and Bodenhausen, G. V. (2019) Race-crime congruency effects revisited: Do we take defendants' sexual orientation into account? *Social Psychological and Personality Science*, 10(1), 73–81.

Pettigrew, M. (2019) The preference for strangulation in a sexually motivated serial killer. *International Journal of Offender Therapy and Comparative Criminology*, 63(5), 781–96.

Petty, R. E. and Cacioppo, J. T. (1986) *Communication and Persuasion: Central and Peripheral Routes to Attitude Change*. Springer.

Petty, R. E., Cacioppo, J. T. and Kasmer, J. A. (2015) The role of affect in the elaboration likelihood model of persuasion. In L. Donohew, H. E. Sypher and E. Tory Higgins (eds) *Communication, Social Cognition, and Affect (PLE: Emotion)* (pp. 133–62). Psychology Press.

Petty, R. E., Wegener, D. T., Leandre, R. and Fabrigar, L. R. (1997) Attitudes and attitude change. *Annual Review of Psychology*, 48, 609–47.

Pezdek, K. and Lam, S. (2007) What research paradigms have cognitive psychologists used to study 'false memory,' and what are the implications of these choices? *Consciousness and Cognition*, 16(1), 2–17.

Phalen, H., Nadler, J. and Salerno, J. M. (2019) Emotional evidence in court. *Northwestern Law & Economics Research Paper*, 19–02.

Pham, T., Habets, P., Saloppé, X., Ducro, C., Delaunoit, B. et al. (2019) Violence risk profile of medium-and high-security NGRI offenders in Belgium. *Journal of Forensic Psychiatry & Psychology*, 30(3), 530–50.

Phillips, J., Padfeld, N. and Gelsthorpe, L. (2018) Suicide and community justice. *Health Justice*, 6(1), 14.

Piaget, J. (1964) Part I: Cognitive development in children: Piaget development and learning. *Journal of Research in Science Teaching*, 2(3), 176–86.

Pica, E. and Pozzulo, J. (2018) Comparing younger and older adult eyewitnesses: Examining the simultaneous, elimination, and wildcard lineup procedures. *Psychiatry, Psychology and Law*, 25(1), 106–23.

Pickel, K. L., Ross, S. J. and Ruelove, R. S. (2006) Do weapons automatically capture attention? *Applied Cognitive Psychology*, 20, 871–93.

Pidd, H. (2017) Teenage killer of teacher Ann Maguire asked classmate to film attack. *The Guardian*, 13 November. Available at www.theguardian.com/uk-news/2017/nov/13/teenage-killer-of-teacher-ann-maguire-asked-classmate-to-film-attack.

Pierre, J. M. (2019) Assessing malingered auditory verbal hallucinations in forensic and clinical settings. *Journal of the American Academy of Psychiatry and the Law*, 47(4), 448–56.

Pike, G., Kemp, R., Brace, N., Allen, J. & Rowlands, G. (2000) The effectiveness of video identification parades. *Proceedings of the British Psychological Society*, 8(1), 44.

Pike, G., Brace, N. and Kynan, S. (2002) *The Visual Identification of Suspects: Procedures and Practice*. UK Home Office.

Pilkington, E. (2016) Albert Woodfox released from jail after 43 years in solitary confinement. *The Guardian*, 19 February. Available at www.theguardian.com/us-news/2016/feb/19/albert-woodfox-released-louisiana-jail-43-years-solitary-confinement.

Pinizzotto, A. J. and Finkel, N. J. (1990) Criminal personality profiling. *Law and Human Behavior*, 14(3), 215–33.

Pinker, S. (2011) Decline of violence: Taming the devil within us. *Nature*, 478(7369), 309–11.

Pinker, S. (2012) *The Better Angels of Our Nature: Why Violence Has Declined*. Penguin.

Pipe, M.-E., Lamb, M. E., Orbach, Y. and Cederborg, A.-C. (eds) (2007) *Child Sexual Abuse: Disclosure, Delay, and Denial*. Lawrence Erlbaum.

Piper, A. and Berle, D. (2019) The association between trauma experienced during incarceration and PTSD outcomes: A systematic review and meta-analysis. *Journal of Forensic Psychiatry & Psychology*, 30(5), 854–75.

Pirelli, G., Gottdiener, W. H. and Zapr, P. A. (2011) A meta-analytic review of competency to stand trial research. *Psychology Public Policy Law*, 17(1), 1–53.

Pitler, R. M. (1968) Fruit of the poisonous tree revisited and shepardized. *California Law Review*, 56(3), 579–650.

Piza, E. L., Welsh, B. C., Farrington, D. P. and Thomas, A. L. (2019) CCTV surveillance for crime prevention: A 40-year systematic review with meta-analysis. *Criminology & Public Policy*, 18(1), 135–59.

Place, C. J. and Meloy, J. R. (2018) Overcoming resistance in clinical and forensic interviews. *International Journal of Forensic Mental Health*, 17(4), 362–76.

Platania, J. and Crawford, J. (2012) Media exposure, juror decision-making, and the availability heuristic. *Jury Expert*, 24, 53.

Platt, A. M. and Diamond, B. L. (1965) The origins and development of the 'wild beast' concept of mental illness and its relation to theories of criminal responsibility. *Journal of the History of the Behavioral Sciences*, 1(4), 355–67.

Plotnikoff, J. and Woolfson, R. (2015) *Intermediaries in the Criminal Justice System: Improving Communication for Vulnerable Witnesses and Defendants*. Policy Press.

Plummer, D. L., Stone, R. T., Powell, L. and Allison, J. (2016) Patterns of adult cross-racial friendships: A context for understanding contemporary race relations. *Cultural Diversity and Ethnic Minority Psychology*, 22(4), 479–94.

Pokin, S. (2017) What happened to the Aurora man who was pardoned by Gov. Carnahan? *News-Leader*, 1 April. https://eu.news-leader.com/story/news/local/ozarks/2017/04/01/what-happened-aurora-man-who-pardoned-gov-carnahan/99862152/.

Ponder, J. (2018) From the Tower shootings in 1966 to Campus Carry in 2016: Collective trauma at the University of Texas at Austin. *International Journal of Applied Psychoanalytic Studies*, 15(4). https://doi.org/10.1002/aps.1558.

Pontillo, M., De Crescenzo, F., Vicari, S., Pucciarini, M. L., Averna, R. et al. (2016) Cognitive behavioural therapy for auditory hallucinations in schizophrenia: A review. *World Journal of Psychiatry*, 6(3), 372–80.

Pontis, S. (2018) *Making Sense of Field Research: A Practical Guide for Information Designers*. Taylor & Francis.

Poole, D. A. and Bruck, M. (2012) Divining testimony? The impact of interviewing props on children's reports of touching. *Developmental Review*, 32, 165–80.

Poole, D. A. and Dickinson, J. (2011) Evidence supporting restrictions on uses of body diagrams in forensic interviews. *Child Abuse & Neglect*, 35(9), 659–68.

Poole, D. A. and Lamb, M. (1998) *Investigative Interviews of Children: A Guide for Helping Professionals*. APA.

Popat, S. and Winslade, W. (2015) While you were sleepwalking: Science and neurobiology of sleep disorders and the enigma of legal responsibility of violence during parasomnia. *Neuroethics*, 8(2), 203–14.

Porter, S., Yuille, J. C. and Lehman, D. R. (1999) The nature of real, implanted, and fabricated memories for emotional childhood events: Implications for the recovered memory debate. *Law and Human Behavior*, 23(5), 517–37.

Ports, K., Holman, D., Guinn, A., Pampati, S., Dyer, K. et al. (2019) Adverse childhood experiences and the presence of cancer risk factors in adulthood: A scoping review of the literature from 2005 to 2015. *Journal of Pediatric Nursing*, 44, 81–96.

Postmus, J. L., Plummer, S. B. and Stylianou, A. M. (2016) Measuring economic abuse in the lives of survivors: Revising the Scale of Economic Abuse. *Violence against Women*, 22(6), 692–703.

Postmus, J. L., Hoge, G. L., Breckenridge, J., Sharp-Jeffs, N. and Chung, D. (2020) Economic abuse as an invisible form of domestic violence: A multicountry review. *Trauma, Violence, & Abuse*, 21(2), 261–83.

Powell, M. (2002) Specialist training in investigative and evidential interviewing: Is it having any effect on the behavior of professionals in the field? *Psychiatry, Psychology and Law*, 9, 44–55.

Powney, D. and Graham-Kevan, N. (2019) Male victims of intimate partner violence: A challenge to the gendered paradigm. In J. A. Barry et al. (eds) *The Palgrave Handbook of Male Psychology and Mental Health* (pp. 123–43). Palgrave Macmillan.

Poythress, N. G., Bonnie, R. J., Monahan, J., Otto, R. K. and Hoge, S. K. (2002) *Adjudicative Competence: The MacArthur Studies*. Kluwer Academic/Plenum.

Pratkanis, A. R. (2020) Why would anyone do or believe such a thing?: A social influence analysis. In R. J. Sternberg and D. F. Halpern (eds) *Critical Thinking in Psychology* (pp. 328–53). Cambridge University Press.

Pratt, J. and Eriksson, A. (2011) 'Mr. Larsson is walking out again.' The origins and development of Scandinavian prison systems. *Australian and New Zealand Journal of Criminology*, 44(1), 7–23.

Prendergast, C. (2009) The fighting style: Reading the Unabomber's Strunk and White. *College English*, 72(1), 10–28.

Price, H., Harvey, M., Anderson, S., Chadwick, L. and Fitzgerald, R. (2018) Evidence for the belief in live lineup superiority. *Journal of Police and Criminal Psychology*, https://doi.org/10.1007/s11896-018-9305-x.

Prins, S. J. (2014) Prevalence of mental illnesses in US state prisons: A systematic review. *Psychiatric Services*, 65(7), 862–72.

Pritchard, M. E. and Keenan, J. M. (2002) Does jury deliberation really improve jurors' memories? *Applied Cognitive Psychology: The Official Journal of the Society for Applied Research in Memory and Cognition*, 16(5), 589–601.

Pyo, J. (2018) The impact of jury experience on perception of the criminal justice system. *International Journal of Law, Crime and Justice*, 52, 176–84.

Pyszczynski, T., Motyl, M. and Abdollahi, A. (2009) Righteous violence: Killing for god, country, freedom, and justice. *Behavioral Sciences of Terrorism and Political Aggression*, 1, 12–39.

Qasir, S., Rodrigues, S., Wong, M., Weedon, A., Benson, A. and Hodes, D. (2018) Towards the barnahus (child house) multi-agency model of care for child sexual abuse: The value of a family therapist and a young person advocate. *Archives of Disease in Childhood*, 103, http://dx.doi.org/10.1136/archdischild-2018-rcpch.152.

Qazi, H. A., Philip, J., Manikandan, R. and Cornford, P. A. (2007) 'The Transylvania effect': Does the lunar cycle affect emergency urological admissions? *Current Urology*, 1(2), 100–2.

Qiu, C., von Strauss, E., Bäckman, L., Winblad, B. and Fratiglioni, L. (2013) Twenty-year changes in dementia occurrence suggest decreasing incidence in central Stockholm, Sweden. *Neurology*, 80(20), 1888–94.

Quincey, P. (1995) Why we are unmoved as oceans ebb and flow. *Skeptical Inquirer*, 18, 509–15.

Quinnell, F. A. and Bow, J. N. (2001) Psychological tests used in child custody evaluations. *Behavioural Sciences & the Law*, 19(4), 491–501.

Quinn-Evans, L., Keatley, D. A., Arntfield, M. and Sheridan, L. (2019) A behavior sequence analysis of victims' accounts of stalking behaviors. *Journal of Interpersonal Violence*, DOI: 10.1177/0886260519831389.

Rachul, C. and Zarzeczny, A. (2012) The rise of neuroskepticism. *International Journal of Law and Psychiatry*, 35(2), 77–81.

Radelet, M. L. (2015) The incremental retributive impact of a death sentence over life without parole. *University of Michigan Journal of Law Reform*, 49(4), 795–815.

Radelet, M. L., Bedau, H. A. and Putnam, C. E. (1994) *In Spite of Innocence: Erroneous Convictions in Capital Cases.* Northeastern Press.

Rafter, N. H. (2008) *The Criminal Brain: Understanding Biological Theories of Crime.* New York University Press.

Ralston, N. (2015) Martin Place siege victim Katrina Dawson struck by a police bullet, investigations show. *The Sydney Morning Herald*, 10 January. Available at www.smh.com.au/national/nsw/martin-place-siege-victim-katrina-dawson-struck-by-a-police-bullet-investigations-show-20150110-12lo8n.html.

Ramachandran, K., John Paul, F. U. and Mandal, M. K. (2019) Interpersonal relations among Indian Antarctic expedition members in isolated and confined environment. *Ministry of Earth Sciences, Technical publication*, 23, 259–76.

Ramos, R. A., Ferguson, C. J. and Frailing, K. (2016) Violent entertainment and cooperative behaviour: Examining media violence effects on cooperation in a primarily Hispanic sample. *Psychology of Popular Media Culture*, 5(2), 119–32.

Ramsland, K. (2013) The many sides of Ted Bundy. *Forensic Examiner*, 22(3), 18.

Ramya, S. and Roshanara, M. S. (2020) Changeover of a child into a serial killer: Victimization of the voiceless. *International Journal of English Literature and Social Sciences (IJELS)*, 5(1). https://dx.doi.org/10.22161/ijels.51.6.

Rashbaum, W. K. (2005) Gigante, Mafia boss, is mourned and buried with little fanfare. *New York Times*, 24 December. Available at www.nytimes.com/2005/12/24/nyregion/gigante-mafia-boss-is-mourned-and-buried-with-little-fanfare.html.

Rashed, M., Piorkowski, J. and McCulloh, I. (2019) Evaluation of extremist cohesion in a darknet forum using ERGM and LDA. In *Proceedings of the 2019 IEEE/ACM International Conference on Advances in Social Networks Analysis and Mining* (pp. 899–902).

Raskin, D. C. and Esplin, P. W. (1991) Statement validity assessment: Interview procedures and content analysis of children's statements of sexual abuse. *Behavioral Assessment*, 13(30), 265–91.

Rauch, A., Fink, M. and Hatak, I. (2018) Stress processes: An essential ingredient in the entrepreneurial process. *Academy of Management Perspectives*, 32(3), 340–57.

Raveh, D. and Lavie, N. (2015) Load-induced inattentional deafness. *Attention, Perception and Psychophysics*, 77(2), 483–92.

Rayner, R. (2003) *Drake's Fortune: The Fabulous True Story of the World's Greatest Confidence Artist.* Anchor.

Read, J. D., Connolly, D. A. and Welsh, A. (2006) An archival analysis of actual cases of historic child sexual abuse: A comparison of jury and bench trials. *Law and Human Behavior*, 30(3), 259–85.

Redding, R. (2006) The brain-disordered defendant: neuroscience and legal insanity in the twenty-first century. *American University Law Review*, 56(1), 51–127.

Redlich, A. D. and Meissner, C. A. (2009) *Techniques and Controversies in the Interrogation of Suspects: The Artful Practice versus the Scientific Study*. Guilford Press.

Redlich, A. D., Kelly, C. E. and Miller, J. C. (2014) The who, what, and why of human intelligence gathering: Self-reported measures of interrogation methods. *Applied Cognitive Psychology*, 28(6), 817–28.

Redondo, L., Fariña, F., Seijo, D., Novo, M. and Arce, R. (2018) A meta-analytical review of the responses in the MMPI-2/MMPI-2-RF clinical and restructured scales of parents in child custody dispute. *Annals of Psychology*, 35(1), 156–65.

Reed, M. D., Dabney, D. A., Tapp, S. N. and Ishoy, G. A. (2019) Tense relationships between homicide co-victims and detectives in the wake of murder. *Deviant Behavior*, 1–19.

Reeves, J. (2012) If you see something, say something: Lateral surveillance and the uses of responsibility. *Surveillance & Society*, 10(3/4), 235–48.

Reginelli, A., Russo, A., Micheletti, E., Picascia, R., Pinto, A. et al. (2020) Imaging techniques for forensic radiology in living individuals. In G. Lo Re, A. Argo, M. Midiri and C. Cattaneo (eds) *Radiology in Forensic Medicine: From Identification to Post-mortem Imaging* (pp. 19–27). Springer.

Reicher, S. D. and Haslam, S. A. (2016) Fueling extremes. *Scientific American Mind*, 27(3), 34–9.

Reid Meloy, J. and Yakeley, J. (2014) The violent true believer as a 'lone wolf': Psychoanalytic perspectives on terrorism. *Behavioral Sciences & the Law*, 32(3), 347–65.

Reimer, T. and Rieskamp, J. (2007) Fast and frugal heuristics. *Encyclopedia of Social Psychology*, 346–8.

Reiter, K. and Blair, T. (2015) Punishing mental illness: Trans-institutionalization and solitary confinement in the United States. In K. Reiter and A. Koenig (eds) *Extreme Punishment: Comparative Studies in Detention, Incarceration and Solitary Confinement* (pp. 177–96). Palgrave Macmillan.

Remmel, R. J., Glenn, A. L. and Cox, J. (2019) Biological evidence regarding psychopathy does not affect mock jury sentencing. *Journal of Personality Disorders*, 33(2), 164–84.

Renden, P. G., Savelsbergh, G. J. and Oudejans, R. R. (2017) Effects of reflex-based self-defence training on police performance in simulated high-pressure arrest situations. *Ergonomics*, 60(5), 669–79.

Resnick, J., VanCleave, A., Harrington, A. and Petchenik, M. (2019) Statement and Recommendations to the United States Commission on Civil Rights: Women in Prison: Seeking Justice Behind Bars. The Arthur Liman Center for Public Interest Law, Yale Law School.

Resnick, P. J. (1999) The detection of malingered psychosis. *Psychiatric Clinics of North America*, 22(1), 159–72.

Resnick, P. J. (2007) The Andrea Yates case: Insanity on trial. *Cleveland State Law Review*, 55, 147.

Resnick, P. J. and Knoll, J. (2005) Faking it: How to detect malingered psychosis. *Current Psychiatry*, 4(11), 12–25.

Ressler, R. K., Burgess, A. W., Douglas, J. E., Hartman, C. R. and D'Agostino, R. B. (1986) Sexual killers and their victims: Identifying patterns through crime scene analysis. *Journal of Interpersonal Violence*, 1(3), 288–308.

Reyns, B. W. (2019) Online pursuit in the twilight zone: Cyberstalking perpetration by college students. *Victims & Offenders*, 14(2), 183–98.

Reyns, B. W. and Fisher, B. S. (2018) The relationship between offline and online stalking victimization: A gender-specific analysis. *Violence and Victims*, 33(4), 769–86.

Reyns, B. W. and Fissel, E. R. (2020) Cyberstalking. In T. J. Holt and A. M. Bossler (eds) *The Palgrave Handbook of International Cybercrime and Cyberdeviance* (pp. 1283–306). Palgrave Macmillan.

Rezey, M. L. (2020) Separated women's risk for intimate partner violence: A multiyear analysis using the National Crime Victimization Survey. *Journal of Interpersonal Violence*, 35(5/6), 1055–80.

Rhodes, T. (2017) In South Sudan, girls are given away to settle family feuds. *Daily Beast*, 13 July. Available at www.thedailybeast.com/in-south-sudan-girls-are-given-away-to-settle-family-feuds.

Ricciardi, L. and Demos, M. (2015) *Making a Murderer*. A Netflix true crime documentary web TV series. Synthesis Films.

Rice, A., Phillips, P. J., Natu, V., An, X., O'Toole, A. J. (2013) Unaware person recognition from the body when face identification fails. *Psychological Science*, 24(11), 2235–43.

Riggins, T. and Rollins, L. (2015) Developmental differences in memory during early childhood: Insights from event-related potentials. *Child Development*, 86(3), 889–902.

Ritzheimer, K. L. (2016) *'Trash', Censorship, and National Identity in Early Twentieth Century Germany*. Cambridge University Press.

Rix, K. (2016) Towards a more just insanity defence: Recovering moral wrongfulness in the M'Naghten Rules. *British Journal of Psychiatric Advances*, 22(1), 44–52.

Robbennolt, J. K. (2005) Evaluating juries by comparison to judges: A benchmark for judging? *Florida State University Law Review*, 32(2), 469–509.

Roberts, B. W. and Mroczek, D. (2008) Personality trait change in adulthood. *Current Directions in Psychological Science*, 17, 31–5.

Roberts, B. W., Wood, D. and Smith, J. L. (2005) Evaluating five factor theory and social investment perspectives on personality trait development. *Journal of Research in Personality*, 39(1), 166–84.

Roberts, J. V. and Irwin-Rogers, K. (2015) Sentencing practices and trends, 1999–2013. In J. V. Roberts (ed.) *Exploring Sentencing Practice in England and Wales* (pp. 35–60). Palgrave Macmillan.

Roberts, S., Henry, J. D. and Molenberghs, P. (2018) Immoral behaviour following brain damage: A review. *Journal of Neuropsychology*, 13(3). https://doi.org/10.1111/jnp.12155.

Robinson, M. J., Fischer, A. M., Ahuja, A., Lesser, E. N. and Maniates, H. (2015) Roles of 'wanting' and 'liking' in motivating behavior: Gambling, food, and drug addictions. In E. Simpson and P. Balsam (eds) *Behavioral Neuroscience of Motivation* (pp. 105–36). Springer.

Rodes, M. (2018) Diagnostic and Statistical Manual of Mental Disorders and pain management. In H. T. Benzon et al. (eds) *Essentials of Pain Medicine* (4th edn, pp. 53–8). Elsevier.

Rodriguez, L., Agtarap, S., Boals, A., Kearns, N. T. and Bedford, L. (2019) Making a biased jury decision: Using the Steven Avery murder case to investigate potential influences in jury decision-making. *Psychology of Popular Media Culture*, 8(4), 429–36.

Roediger, H. L. and McDermott, K. B. (1995) Creating false memories: Remembering words not presented in lists. *Journal of Experimental Psychology: Learning, Memory, and Cognition*, 21(4), 803–14.

Roesch, R., Zapf, P. A. and Hart, S. D. (2010) *Forensic Psychology and Law*. John Wiley.

Rogers, C. (1975) Empathic: An unappreciated way of being. *The Counseling Psychologist*, 5(2), 2–10.

Rogers, C., Rushton, S. K. and Warren, P. A. (2017) Peripheral visual cues contribute to the perception of object movement during self-movement. *i-Perception*, 8(6), 2041669517736072.

Rogers, R. (1990) Development of a new classificatory model of malingering. *Bulletin of the American Academy of Psychiatry and Law*, 18, 323–33.

Rogers, R. (2008) *Clinical Assessment of Malingering and Deception*. Guilford Press.

Rogers, R. and Fiduccia, C. E. (2015) Forensic assessment instruments. In B. L. Cutler and P. A. Zapf (eds) *APA Handbook of Forensic Psychology*, vol. 1. *Individual and Situational Influences in Criminal and Civil Contexts* (pp. 19–34). APA.

Rogers, R., Seman, W. and Clark, C. R. (1986) Assessment of criminal responsibility: Internal validation of the R-CRAS with the M'Naghten and GBMI standards. *International Journal of Law and Psychology*, 9(1), 67–75.

Rogers, R., Sewell, K. W. and Gillard, N. D. (2010) *SIRS-2: Structured Interview of Reported Symptoms*. PAR.

Rogers, R., Tillbrook, C. E. and Sewell, K. W. (2004) *Evaluation of Competency to Stand Trial-Revised (ECST-R)*. PAR.

Rogers, R., Gillis, J. R., Bagba, M. and Monteiro, E. (1991) Detection of malingering on the Structured Interview of Reported Symptoms (SIRS): A study of coached and uncoached simulators. *Psychological Assessment*, 3(4), 673–77.

Rogers, R., Gillis, J. R., Dickens, S. E. and Bagby, R. M. (1991) Standardized assessment of malingering: Validation of the Structured Interview of Reported Symptoms. *Psychological Assessment: A Journal of Consulting and Clinical Psychology*, 3(1), 89–96.

Rogers, T. J. and Landers, D. M. (2005) Mediating effects of peripheral vision in the life event stress/athletic injury relationship. *Journal of Sport and Exercise Psychology*, 27(3), 271–88.

Roman, D. (2019) Prescription of the criminal responsibility of children. *Law, Society & Organizations*, 4(6), 21–6.

Rose, M. R. (2017) Can juries be lost in translation? *Law & Society Review*, 51(3), 500–9.

Rose, N. (2000) The biology of culpability: Pathological identity and crime control in biological culture. *Journal of Theoretical criminology*, 4(1), 5–34.

Rose, N. (2016) Neuroscience and the future for mental health? *Epidemiology and Psychiatric Sciences*, 25(2), 95–100.

Rose, T. and Unnithan, P. (2015) In or out of the group? Police subculture and occupational stress. *Policing: An International Journal of Police Strategies & Management*, 38(2), 279–94.

Rosenhan, D. (1973) On being sane in insane places. *Science*, 179(4070), 250–8.

Rosenthal, R. (1976) *Experimenter Effects in Behavioral Research*. Irvington.

Ross, D. L. and Murphy, R. L. (2017) Stress, perceptual distortions, and human performance. In D. L. Ross and G. M. Vilke, *Guidelines for Investigating Officer-Involved Shootings, Arrest-Related Deaths, and Deaths in Custody* (pp. 68–95). Routledge.

Ross, D. R., Ceci, S. J., Dunning, D. and Toglia, M. P. (1994) Unconscious transference and mistaken identity: When a witness misidentifies a familiar but innocent person. *Journal of Applied Psychology*, 79(6), 918–30.

Ross, G. M. (1996) Socrates versus Plato: The origins and development of Socratic thinking. *Thinking. The Journal of Philosophy for Children*, 12(4), 2–8.

Ross, L. D., Amabile, T. M. and Steinmetz, J. (1977) Social roles, social control and biases in social perception processes. *Journal of Personality and Social Psychology*, 35(7), 485–94.

Rossmo, D. K. (2000) *Geographic Profiling*. CRC Press.

Rossmo, D. K. (2006a) Criminal investigative failures: Avoiding the pitfalls. *FBI Law Enforcement Bulletin*, 75(9), 1–8.

Rossmo, D. K. (2006b) Geographic profiling in cold case investigations. In R. H. Walton (ed.) *Cold Case Homicides: Practical Investigative Techniques* (pp. 537–60). CRC Press.

Rossmo, K. (2016) Case rethinking: A protocol for reviewing criminal investigations. *Police Practice and Research*, 17(3), 212–28.

Rossner, M. (2019) Storytelling rituals in jury deliberations. *Oñati Socio-Legal Series*, 9(5), 747–70.

Roth, A. (2018) *Insane: America's Criminal Treatment of Mental Illness*. Hachette UK.

Rothman, D. J. (1971) *The Discovery of the Asylum: Social Order and Disorder in the New Republic*. Routledge.

Rotton, J. and Kelly, I. W. (1985) Much ado about the full moon: A meta-analysis of lunar-lunacy research. *Psychological Bulletin*, 97(2), 286–306.

Rouse, D. A. (1994) Patterns of stab wounds: A six-year study. *Medicine, Science and the Law*, 34(1), 67–71.

Rowan, J. (2007) Jury considering verdict in toddler murder case. *New Zealand Herald*, 16 November. Available at www.nzherald.co.nz/nz/news/article.cfm?c_id=1&objectid=10476404.

Rowe, B. I. and McCann, W. S. (2018) Runaway jury: An analysis of state laws concerning juror impeachment. *Criminal Justice Policy Review*, 31(3), 395–421.

Rumelhart, D. E. (1980) Schemata: The building blocks of cognition. In R. J. Spiro, B. C. Bruce and W. F. Brewer (eds) *Theoretical Issues in Reading Comprehension* (pp. 33–58). Erlbaum.

Runions, K. C., Bak, M. and Shaw, T. (2017) Disentangling functions of online aggression: The cyber-aggression typology questionnaire (CATQ). *Aggressive Behaviour*, 43(1), 74–84.

Russano, M. B., Meissner, C. A., Narchet, F. M. and Kassin, S. M. (2005) Investigating true and false confessions within a novel experimental paradigm. *Psychological Science*, 16(6), 481–6.

Russano, M. B., Narchet, F. M., Kleinman, S. M. and Meissner, C. A. (2014) Structured interviews of experienced HUMINT interrogators. *Applied Cognitive Psychology*, 28, 847–59.

Russell, A. (2006) Best practices in child forensic interviews: Interview instructions and truth-lie discussions. *Journal of Public Law & Policy*, 28(1), 99–130.

Russell, M., Schlesinger, L. B. and Leon, M. (2017) Undoing (or symbolic reversal) at homicide crime scenes. *Journal of Forensic Sciences*, 63(2), 478–83.

Russo, C., Aukhojee, P., Tuttle, B. M., Johnson, O., Davies, M. et al. (2020) *Compassion Fatigue and Burnout*. Academic Press.

Rusted, J. and Sheppard, L. (2002) Action-based memory in Alzheimer's disease: A longitudinal look at tea making. *Neurocase*, 8, 111–26.

Rutbeck-Goldman, A. (2017) An 'unfair and cruel weapon': Consequences of modern-day polygraph use in federal pre-employment screening. *UC Irvine Law Review*, 7, 715. Available at https://scholarship.law.uci.edu/ucilr/vol7/iss3/9.

Ruva, C. L. and Guenther, C. C. (2015) From the shadows into the light: How pretrial publicity and deliberation affect mock jurors' decisions, impressions, and memory. *Law and Human Behavior*, 39(3), 294–310.

Ryan, K. M. (2019) Rape mythology and victim blaming as a social construct. In W. T. O'Donohue and P. A. Schewe (eds) *Handbook of Sexual Assault and Sexual Assault Prevention* (pp. 151–74). Springer.

Sadozai, A. K., Kempen, K., Tredoux, C. and Robbins, R. A. (2019) Can we look past people's race? The effect of combining race and a non-racial group affiliation on holistic processing. *Quarterly Journal of Experimental Psychology*, 72(3), 557–69.

Sagan, C. (1986) *Broca's Brain: Reflections on the Romance of Science*. Ballantine Books.

Sageman, M. (2008) A strategy for fighting international Islamist terrorists. *Annals of the American Academy of Political and Social Science*, 618(1), 223–31.

Saikia, S., Fidalgo, E., Alegre, E. and Fernández-Robles, L. (2017) Object detection for crime scene evidence analysis using deep learning. In *International Conference on Image Analysis and Processing* (pp. 14–24). Springer.

Sakalli-Uğurlu, N., Yalçın, Z. S. and Glick, P. (2007) Ambivalent sexism, belief in a just world, and empathy as predictors of Turkish students' attitudes toward rape victims. *Sex Roles*, 57(11/12), 889–95.

Sakurai, R. (2019) Wildlife management in Japan. In *Human Dimensions of Wildlife Management in Japan* (pp. 13–23). Springer.

Salerno, J. M. (2017) Seeing red: Disgust reactions to gruesome photographs in color (but not in black and white) increase convictions. *Psychology, Public Policy, and Law*, 23(3), 336–50.

Salerno, J. M. and Bottoms, B. L. (2009) Emotional evidence and jurors' judgments: The promise of neuroscience for informing psychology and law. *Behavioral Sciences & the Law*, 27(2), 273–96.

Salerno, J. M. and Peter-Hagene, L. C. (2013) The interactive effect of anger and disgust on moral outrage and judgments. *Psychological Science*, 24(10), 2069–78.

Saletta, M., Kruger, A., Primoratz, T., Barnett, A., van Gelder, T. and Horn, R. E. (2020) The role of narrative in collaborative reasoning and intelligence analysis: A case study. *Plos One*, 15(1), e0226981.

Salfati, C. G. and Bateman, A. L. (2005) Serial homicide: An investigation of behavioral consistency. *Journal of Investigative Psychology and Offender Profiling*, 2(2), 121–44.

Salna, K. (2016) Sydney siege inquest hears Tori Johnson's execution was prompted by hostage escape. News.com.au, 16 June. Available at www.news.com.au/national/nsw-act/news/sydney-siege-inquest-hears-tori-johnsons-execution-was-prompted-by-hostage-escape/news-story/59af4115c56353e4c67c056bf0443bf9.

Saltman, E. M. and Smith, M. (2015) *'Till Martyrdom Do Us Part': Gender and the ISIS Phenomenon*. Institute for Strategic Dialogue.

Samson, F., Mottron, L., Soulières, I., Zeffiro, T. A. (2012) Enhanced visual functioning in autism: an ALE meta-analysis. *Human Brain Mapping*, 33(7), 1553–81.

Samuels, D. (2001) The runner. *The New Yorker Magazine*, 20 August. Available at www.newyorker.com/magazine/2001/09/03/the-runner.

Sandoval, V. A. (2003) Strategies to avoid interview contamination. FBI *Law Enforcement Bulletin*, 72(10). Available at www2.fbi.gov/publications/leb/2003/oct2003/oct03leb.htm#page_2.

Sands, A. (2005) Mountie sued by former suspect now heads Sherwood Park detachment, *Edmonton Sun*, 20 January. Available at www.injusticebusters.com/05/Steinke_Gary.shtml.

Sands, J. M. and Miller, L. E. (1991) Effects of moon phase and other temporal variables on absenteeism. *Psychological Reports*, 69(3), 959–62.

Santoyo, C. V. and Mendoza, B. G. (2018) Behavioural patterns of children involved in bullying episodes. *Frontiers in Psychology*, 9, 456. https://doi.org/10.3389/fpsyg.2018.00456.

Santtila, P., Fritzon, K. and Tamelander, A. L. (2004) Linking arson incidents on the basis of crime scene behavior. *Journal of Police and Criminal Psychology*, 19(1), 1–16.

Sapolsky, R. M. (2015) Stress and the brain: Individual variability and the inverted-U. *Nature Neuroscience*, 18(10), 1344–6.

Sargent, K. S., Krauss, A., Jouriles, E. N. and McDonald, R. (2016) Cyber victimization, psychological intimate partner violence, and problematic mental health outcomes among first-year college students. *Cyberpsychology, Behavior, and Social Networking*, 19(9), 545–50.

Sarrett, J. (2017) Interviews, disclosures, and misperceptions: Autistic adults' perspectives on employment related challenges. *Disabilities Studies Quarterly*, 37(2). Available at https://dsq-sds.org/article/view/5524/4652.

Satin, G. E. and Fisher, R. P. (2019) Investigative utility of the cognitive interview: Describing and finding perpetrators. *Law and Human Behavior*, 43(5), 491–506.

Sattler, J. M. (1998) *Clinical and Forensic Interviewing of Children and Families: Guidelines for the Mental Health, Education, Pediatric, and Child Maltreatment Fields*. Jerome M. Sattler.

Saults, J., Cowan, N., Sher, K. and Moreno, M. (2007) Differential effects of alcohol on working memory: Distinguishing multiple processes. *Experimental and Clinical Psychopharmacology*, 15(6), 576–87.

Savtchouk, I. and Liu, S. J. (2011) Remodeling of synaptic AMPA receptor subtype alters the probability and pattern of action potential firing. *Journal of Neuroscience*, 31(2), 501–11.

Saxe, L. (1991) Science and the CQT polygraph. A theoretical critique. *Integrative Physiological & Behavioral Science*, 26(3), 223–31.

Saywitz, K. J., Lyon, T. and Goodman, G. S. (2017) When interviewing children: A review and update. In J. Klika and J. Conte (eds) *The APSAC Handbook on Child Maltreatment* (4th edn, pp. 310–29). Sage.

Saywitz, K. J., Lyon, T.D. and Goodman, G.S. (2011) Interviewing children. In J. E. Myers (ed.) *The APSAC Handbook on Child Maltreatment* (3rd edn, pp. 337–60). Sage.

Schacter, D. L. (1999) The seven sins of memory: Insights from psychology and cognitive neuroscience. *American Psychologist*, 54, 182–203.

Schacter, D. L. (2012) Adaptive constructive processes and the future of memory. *American Psychologist*, 67(8), 603–13.

Schafer, S. (1977) *Victimology: The Victim and his Criminal*. Reston Publishing.

Schaller, G. B. (1972) *The Serengeti Lions: A Study of Predator–prey Relations*. University of Chicago Press.

Schank, R. C. and Abelson, R. P. (1977) *Scripts, Plans, Goals and Understanding: An Inquiry into Human Knowledge Structures*. Lawrence Erlbaum.

Schattauer, G. (2012) Millions for amok victims. *FOCUS Magazine*, 7 April. Available at https://web.

archive.org/web/20190804225903/https://www.focus.de/politik/deutschland/focussiert-millionen-fuer-amok-opfer_aid_733696.html.

Schenck, C. H. and Mahowald, M. W. (1995) A polysomnographically documented case of adult somnambulism with long-distance automobile driving and frequent nocturnal violence: Parasomnia with continuing danger as a noninsane automatism? *Sleep*, 18(9), 765–72.

Schildkraut, J., Naman, B. M. and Stafford, M. C. (2019) Advancing responses to mass shootings using a routine activity approach. *Crime Prevention and Community Safety*, 1–16.

Schlesinger, L., Kassen, M., Mesa, V. and Pinizzotto, A. (2010) Ritual and signature in serial sexual homicide. *Journal of the American Academy of Psychiatry and the Law*, 38(2), 239–46.

Schnepel, K. T. (2018) Good jobs and recidivism. *The Economic Journal*, 128(608), 447–69.

Schouten, R. (2012) The insanity defense: An intersection of morality, public policy and science. *Psychology Today*, 16 August. Available at www.psychologytoday.com/us/blog/almost-psychopath/201208/the-insanity-defense.

Schreiber, N. and Fisher, R. P. (2005) Police Interviewing Techniques: Types of Questions, Positive and Negative Techniques in a South Florida Sample. Paper presented at the American Psychology-Law Society, La Jolla.

Schreiber, N. and Parker, J. F. (2004) Inviting witnesses to speculate: Effects of age and interaction on children's recall. *Journal of Experimental Child Psychology*, 89(1), 31–52.

Schrenck-Notzing, A. (1897) About suggestion and falsification of memories in the Berchtold process. *Journal of Hypnotism*, 5, 128–79.

Schupf, N., Kapell, D., Nightingale, B., Rodriguez, A., Tycko, B. and Mayeux, R. (1998) Earlier onset of Alzheimer's disease in men with Down syndrome. *Neurology*, 50(4), 991–5.

Schwartz, J. (2009) As jurors turn to Google and Twitter, mistrials are popping up. *The New York Times*, 17 March. Available at www.nytimes.com/2009/03/18/us/18juries.html.

Schwarz, K. (2019) Presumption of innocence: Exclusive trial by media our true crime obsession. *LSJ: Law Society of NSW Journal*, 54, 40–3.

Scott, A. (2017) Crime prevention and offender rehabilitation in Australia: Lessons from Nordic nations. *Alternative Law Journal*, 42(2), 118–22.

Scrivner, E. M. (1994) *Controlling Police Use of Excessive Force: The Role of the Police Psychologist*. National Institute of Justice.

Seckiner, D., Mallett, X., Maynard, P., Meuwly, D. and Roux, C. (2019) Forensic gait analysis: Morphometric assessment from surveillance footage. *Forensic Science International*, 296, 57–66.

Seligman, M. (1972) Learned helplessness. *Annual Review of Medicine*, 23, 407–12.

Selke, W. L. (1983) Celerity: The ignored variable in deterrence research. *Journal of Police Science and Administration*, 11(1), 31–7.

Sellbom, M. (2019) The MMPI-2-Restructured Form (MMPI-2-RF): Assessment of personality and psychopathology in the twenty-first century. *Annual Review of Clinical Psychology*, 15(1), 149–77.

Semmler, C., Brewer, N. and Douglass, A. B. (2011) Jurors believe eyewitnesses. In B. L. Cutler (ed.) *Conviction of the Innocent: Lessons from Psychological Research* (pp. 185–209). APA Books.

Semmler, C., Brewer, N. and Wells, G. L. (2004) Effects of post-identification feedback on eyewitness identification and non-identification confidence. *Journal of Applied Psychology*, 89, 334–46.

Sentencing Advisory Council (2018) Released offenders returning to prison. Available at www.sentencingcouncil.vic.gov.au/statistics/sentencing-trends/released-offenders-returning-to-prison.

Setentia, W. (2004) Neuroethical considerations: Cognitive liberty and converging technologies for improving human cognition. In M. C. Roco and C. Montemagno (eds) *The Coevolution of Human Potential and Converging Technologies* (pp. 221–8). New York Academy of Sciences.

Shapira, A. A. and Pansky, A. (2019) Cognitive and metacognitive determinants of eyewitness memory accuracy over time. *Metacognition and Learning*, 14(3), 437–61.

Shapiro, P. N. and Penrod, S. D. (1986) Meta-analysis of racial identification studies. *Psychological Bulletin*, 100, 139–56.

Shaw, J. and Porter, S. (2015) Constructing rich false memories of committing crime. *Psychological Science*, 26(3), 291–301.

Shaw, J. S., Garvin, S. and Wood, J. M. (1997) Co-witness information can have immediate effects on eyewitness memory reports. *Law and Human Behavior*, 21, 503–23.

Shen, F. X., Hoffman, M. B., Jones, O. D., Greene, J. D. and Marois, R. (2011) Sorting guilty minds. *New York University Law Review*, 86, 1306–60.

Shenkin, S. D., Russ, T. C., Ryan, T. M. and MacLullich, A. M. (2013) Screening for dementia and other causes of cognitive impairment in general hospital in-patients. *Age and Ageing*, 43(2), 166–8.

Shepherd, E., Mortimer, A., Turner, V. and Watson, J. (1999) Spaced cognitive interviewing: Facilitating therapeutic and forensic narration of traumatic memories. *Psychology, Crime & Law*, 5(1/2), 117–43.

Shepherd, S. M. and Sullivan, D. (2017) Covert and implicit influences on the interpretation of violence risk instruments. *Psychiatry, Psychology, and Law*, 24(2), 292–301.

Sheridan, L. P. and Grant, T. (2007) Is cyberstalking different? *Psychology, Crime & Law*, 13(6), 627–40.

Shermer, M. (2008) How anecdotal evidence can undermine scientific results. *Scientific American Magazine*, 1 August. Available at www.scientificamerican.com/article/how-anecdotal-evidence-can-undermine-scientific-results/.

Shermer, M. (2017) *Ske?tic: Viewing the World with a Rational Eye*. St. Martin's Griffin.

Shifton, J. J. (2019) How confession characteristics impact juror perceptions of evidence in criminal trials. *Behavioral Sciences and the Law*, 37(1), 90–108.

Shimizu, A. (2013) Domestic violence in the digital age: Towards the creation of a comprehensive cyberstalking statute. *Berkeley Journal of Gender, Law & Justice*, 28, 116–37.

Shjarback, J. A. and Young, J. T. (2018) The 'tough on crime' competition: A network approach to understanding the social mechanisms leading to federal crime control legislation in the United States from 1973–2014. *American Journal of Crime Justice*, 43(2), 197–221.

Shlosberg, A., Ho, A. and Mandery, E. (2018) A descriptive examination of prisonization through the lens of post-exoneration offending. *Deviant Behavior*, 39(8), 1082–94.

Shoda, Y., Mischel, W. and Wright, J. C. (1994) Intraindividual stability in the organization and patterning of behavior: Incorporating psychological situations into the idiographic analysis of personality. *Journal of Personality and Social Psychology*, 67(4), 674–87.

Shore, S. and Rastelli, M. A. (2006) *Understanding Autism for Dummies*. For Dummies.

Shue, H. (1978) Torture. *Philosophy and Public Affairs*, 7(2), 124–43.

Siegal, M., Waters, L. J. and Dinwiddy, L. S. (1988) Misleading children: Causal attributions for inconsistency under repeated questioning. *Journal of Experimental Child Psychology*, 45, 438–56.

Siegman, A. and Reynolds, M. (1983) Effects of mutual invisibility and topical intimacy on verbal fluency in dyadic communication. *Journal of Psycholinguistic Research*, 12, 4443–55.

Sigurdsson, J. F. and Gudjonsson, G. H. (1996) The relationship between types of claimed false confession made and the reasons why suspects confess to the police according to the Gudjonsson Confession Questionnaire (GCQ). *Legal and Criminological Psychology*, 1(2), 259–69.

Silva, S. M. and Samimi, C. (2018) Social work and prison labor: A restorative model. *Social Work*, 63(2), 153–60.

Silver, E. (1995) Punishment or treatment? Comparing the lengths of confinement of successful and unsuccessful insanity defendants. *Law and Human Behavior*, 19, 375–88.

Silver, J., Horgan, J. and Gill, P. (2018) Foreshadowing targeted violence: Assessing leakage of intent by public mass murderers. *Aggression and Violent Behavior*, 38, 94–100.

Silver, J., Simons, A. and Craun, S. (2018) *A Study of the Pre-Attack Behaviors of Active Shooters in the United States between 2000 and 2013*. FBI.

Sim, J. J., Correll, J. and Sadler, M. S. (2013) Understanding police and expert performance: When training attenuates (vs. exacerbates) stereotypic bias in the decision to shoot. *Personality and Social Psychology Bulletin*, 39(3), 291–304.

Simon, R. J. (1980) The impact of pretrial publicity on the jury. In R. J. Simon (ed.) *The Jury: Its Role in American Society*. Lexington Books.

Simpson, J. R. (2008) Functional MRI lie detection: Too good to be true? *Journal of the American Academy of Psychiatry and Law*, 36, 491–8.

Sinclair, S., Raffin-Bouchal, S., Venturato, L., Mijovic-Kondejewski, J. and Smith-MacDonald, L. (2017) Compassion fatigue: A meta-narrative review of the healthcare literature. *International Journal of Nursing Studies*, 69, 9–24.

Singh, J. P., Fazel, S., Gueorguieva, R. and Buchanan, A. (2014) Rates of violence in patients classified as high risk by structured risk assessment instruments. *British Journal of Psychiatry*, 204(3), 180–7.

Singh, J., Avasthi, A. and Grover, S. (2007) Malingering of psychiatric disorders: A review. *German Journal of Psychiatry*, 10(4), 126–32.

Singh, K. D. and Maria, A. V. (2019) Bankruptcy fraud and victim redressal system: A time for change. *Journal of Victimology and Victim Justice*, 2(2), 184–201.

Sjöberg, M. (2015) The relationship between empathy and stringency of punishment in mock jurors. *Journal of European Psychology Students*, 6(1), 37–44.

Skinner, B. F. (1938) *The Behavior of Organisms: An Experimental Analysis*. Appleton-Century.

Skinner, B. F. (1953) *Science and Human Behavior*. Free Press.

Skinner, B. F. (1971) *Beyond Freedom and Dignity*. Hackett Publishing.

Skinner, B. F. (1986) Some thoughts about the future. *Journal of the Experimental Analysis of Behavior*, 45(2), 229–35.

Skolnick, J. H. and Fyfe, J. J. (1993) *Above the Law: Police and the Excessive Use of Force*. Free Press.

Slobogin, C. (2006) *Proving the Unprovable: The Role of Law, Science, and Speculation in Adjudicating*

Culpability and Dangerousness. Oxford University Press.

Slobogin, C. (2017) Neuroscience nuance: Dissecting the relevance of neuroscience in adjudicating criminal culpability. *Journal of Law and the Biosciences*, 4(3), 577–93.

Sloutsky, V. M. and Fisher, A. V. (2004) When development and learning decrease memory: Evidence against category-based induction in children. *Psychological Science*, 15(8), 553–8.

Slutkin, G. (2017) Reducing violence as the next great public health achievement. *Nature Human Behavior*, 1(25), DOI: 10.1038/s41562-016-0025.

Smith, A. C., Fritz, P. A. and Daskaluk, S. (2018) 'Drama' in interpersonal conflict and interactions among emerging adults: A qualitative focus group study. *Emerging Adulthood*, https://doi.org/10.1177/2167696818792989.

Smith, A. G. (2008) The implicit motives of terrorist groups: How the needs for affiliation and power translate into death and destruction. *Political Psychology*, 29(1), 55–75.

Smith, A. G. (2018) *How Radicalization to Terrorism Occurs in the United States: What Research Sponsored by the National Institute of Justice Tells Us.* National Institute of Justice. Available at www.ncjrs.gov/pdffiles1/nij/250171.pdf.

Smith, B. D., Rypma, C. B. and Wilson, R. J. (1981) Dishabituation and spontaneous recovery of the electrodermal orienting response: Effects of extraversion, impulsivity, sociability, and caffeine. *Journal of Research in Personality*, 15(2), 233–40.

Smith, G. (2012) Shoot-to-kill counter-suicide terrorism. In S. Poynting and D. Whyte (eds) *Counter-Terrorism and State Political Violence: War on Terror as Terror* (pp. 33–48). Routledge.

Smith, H. and Milne, E. (2009) Reduced change blindness suggests enhanced attention to detail in individuals with autism. *Journal of Child Psychology and Psychiatry*, 50(3), 300–6.

Smith, K. and Tilney, S. (2007) *Vulnerable Adult and Child Witnesses.* Oxford University Press.

Smith, P., Gendreau, P. and Swartz, K. (2009) Validating the principles of effective intervention: A systematic review of the contributions of meta-analysis in the field of corrections. *Victims and Offenders*, 4(2), 148–69.

Smith, P. S. (2006) The effects of solitary confinement on prison inmates: A brief history and review of the literature. *Crime and Justice*, 34(1), 441–528.

Smith, S. G., Fowler, K. A. and Niolon, P. H. (2014) Intimate partner homicide and corollary victims in 16 states: National Violent Death Reporting System, 2003–2009. *American Journal of Public Health*, 104(3), 461–6.

Smith, S. M., Stinson, V. and Patry, M. W. (2009) The Mr. Big technique: Successful innovation or dangerous development in the Canadian legal system? *Psychology, Public Policy, & Law*, 15, 168–93.

Smoker, M. and March, E. (2017) Predicting perpetration of intimate partner cyberstalking: Gender and the dark tetrad. *Computers in Human Behavior*, 72, 390–6.

Smukler, D. (2005) Unauthorized minds: How 'theory of mind' theory misrepresents autism. *Mental Retardation*, 43(1), 11–24.

Snook, B. and Keating, K. (2011) A field study of adult witness interviewing practices in a Canadian police organization. *Legal and Criminological Psychology*, 16(1), 160–72.

Snook, B., Luther, K. and Milne, R. (2012) Let 'em' talk! A field study of police questioning practices of suspects and accused persons. *Criminal Justice and Behavior*, 39(10), 1328–39.

Snook, B., Cullen, R. M., Mokros, A. and Harbort, S. (2005) Serial murderers' spatial decisions: Factors that influence crime location choice. *Journal of Investigative Psychology and Offender Profiling*, 2(3), 147–64.

Snook, B., Cullen, R. M., Bennell, C., Taylor, P. J. and Gendreau, P. (2008) The criminal profiling illusion: What's behind the smoke and mirrors? *Criminal Justice and Behavior*, 35(10), 1257–76.

Snook, B., Eastwood, J., Gendreau, P., Goggin, C. and Cullen, R. M. (2007) Taking stock of criminal profiling: A narrative review and meta-analysis. *Criminal Justice and Behavior*, 34(4), 437–53.

Snow, S. S., Alonzo, S. H., Servedio, M. R. and Prum, R. O. (2019) Female resistance to sexual coercion can evolve to preserve the indirect benefits of mate choice. *Journal of Evolutionary Biology*, 32(6), 545–58.

Søbjerg, L. M. and Thams, A. F. (2016) Adapting a model of response to child abuse to the conditions in the circumpolar north. *International Journal of Circumpolar Health*, 75(1), 10.3402/ijch.v75.32713.

Sokara, S., Bull, R., Vrij, A., Turner, M. and Cherryman, J. (2009) What really happens in police interviews of suspects? Tactics and confessions. *Psychology Crime and Law Crime & Law*, 6, 493–506.

Soliman, S. and Resnick, P. J. (2010) Feigning in adjudicative competence evaluations. *Behavioral Science and Law*, 28, 614–29.

Solomon, R. M. and Horn, J. M. (1986) Post-shooting traumatic reactions: A pilot study. In J. T. Reese and H. A. Goldstein (eds) *Psychological Services for Law*

Enforcement (pp. 383–93). US Government Printing Office.

Sommers, S. R. (2006) On racial diversity and group decision making: Identifying multiple effects of racial composition on jury deliberations. *Journal of Personality and Social Psychology*, 90(4), 597–612.

Sommers, S. R. (2009) On the obstacles to jury diversity. *Jury Expert*, 21, 1–10.

Soree, N. (2005) When the innocent speak: False confessions, constitutional safeguards, and the role of expert testimony. *American Journal of Criminal Law*, 32, 191–263.

Sorrentino, R. (2014) Performing capacity evaluations: What's expected from your consult. *Clinical Psychiatry News*, 13(1), 41–4.

Spagat, M. and van Weezel, S. (2020) The decline of war since 1950: New evidence. In N. Petter (ed.) *Lewis Fry Richardson: His Intellectual Legacy and Influence in the Social Sciences* (pp. 129–42). Springer.

Spalek, B. (2017) *Crime Victims: Theory, Policy and Practice* (2nd edn). Palgrave.

Spargo, C. (2019) 'Drink bleach. Hang yourself. Jump over a building, stab yourself, idk': How Michelle Carter listed ways boyfriend, 18, should kill himself and copied her texts from GLEE, but only saw him FIVE times before he killed himself. DailyMail. com, 9 July. Available at www.dailymail.co.uk/news/article-7230715/Michelle-Carter-listed-ways-boyfriend-kill-suicide-saw-FIVE-times.html.

Sparrow, M. (1991) The application of network analysis to criminal intelligence: An assessment of the prospects. *Social Networks*, 13, 251–74.

Speckhard, A. (2017) Seven promises of ISIS to its female recruits. International Center for the Study of Violent Extremism, 9 January.

Spencer, C. M. and Stith, S. M. (2020) Risk factors for male perpetration and female victimization of intimate partner homicide: A meta-analysis. *Trauma, Violence, & Abuse*, 21(3), 527–40.

Spencer, J. R. and Flin, R. H. (1990) *The Evidence of Children: The Law and the Psychology*. Blackstone Press.

Spierer, A. (2017) The right to remain a child: The impermissibility of the Reid technique in juvenile interrogations. *New York University Law Review*, 92, 1719–30.

Spillman, J. and Spillman, L. (1993) The rise and fall of Hugo Munsterberg. *Journal of the History of the Behavioral Sciences*, 29(4), 322–38.

Spino, J. and Cummins, D. (2014) The ticking time bomb: When the use of torture is and is not endorsed. *Review of Philosophy and Psychology*, 5, 543–63.

Spitzberg, B. H. and Cupach, W. R. (2003) What mad pursuit?: Obsessive relational intrusion and stalking related phenomena. *Aggression and Violent Phenomena*, 8(4), 345–75.

Spitzberg, B. H. and Hoobler, G. (2002) Cyberstalking and the technologies of interpersonal terrorism. *New Media & Society*, 4(1), 71–92.

Spitzberg, B. H., Cupach, W. R., Hannawa, A. F. and Crowley, J. P. (2014) A preliminary test of a relational goal pursuit theory of obsessive relational intrusion and stalking. *Studies in Communication Sciences*, 14(1), 29–36.

Spitzer, R. (1975) On pseudoscience in science, logic in remission, and psychiatric diagnosis: A critique of Rosenhan's 'On being sane in insane places'. *Journal of Abnormal Psychology*, 84(5), 442–52.

Sporer, S. L. (2016) Deception and cognitive load: Expanding our horizon with a working memory model. *Frontiers in Psychology*, 7, 420, https://doi.org/10.3389/fpsyg.2016.00420.

Spungen, D. (1998) *Homicide: The Hidden Victims: A Resource for Professionals* (vol. 20). Sage.

SSCI (Senate Select Committee on Intelligence) (2014) *Committee Study of the Central Intelligence Agency's Detention and Interrogation Program (Report)*. Senate Report 113–288. United States Senate.

Stack, L. (2016) Video released in Terence Crutcher's killing by Tulsa police. *New York Times*, 19 September. Available at https://web.archive.org/web/20160920021343/http://www.nytimes.com/2016/09/20/us/video-released-in-terence-crutchers-killing-by-tulsa-police.html.

Stamm, B. H. (2010) *The Concise ProQOL Manual* (2nd edn). ProQOL.org.

Stancel, K., Russo, C., Koskelainen, M., Papazoglou, K. and Tuttle, B. M. (2019) Police moral injury, compassion fatigue, and compassion satisfaction: A brief report. *Salus Journal*, 7(1), 42.

Stander, P. E. (1992) Cooperative hunting in lions: The role of the individual. *Behavioral Ecology and Sociobiology*, 29, 445–54.

Stannard, M. B. (2002) Documentary probes life of 'mystery boy'/filmmaker and ex-classmate analyzes drifter who duped Palo Alto High, Princeton. SFGATE, 18 March. Available at www.sfgate.com/bayarea/article/Documentary-probes-life-of-Mystery-Boy-2863784.php.

Stansfield, R., O'Connor, T. and Duncan, J. (2018) Religious identity and the long-term effects of religious involvement, orientation, and coping in prison. *Criminal Justice and Behavior*, 46(2), 337–54.

Stark, C. L., Okado, Y. and Loftus, E. F. (2010) Imaging the reconstruction of true and false memories using sensory reactivation and the misinformation paradigms. *Learning & Memory*, 17, 485–8.

Stearns, E. A., Swanson, R. and Etie, S. (2019) The walking dead? Assessing social death among long-term offenders, *Corrections*, 4(3), 153–68.

Steblay, N. K. (2018) All is not as it seems: Avoidable pitfalls in the interpretation of lineup field data. *Psychology, Public Policy, and Law*, 24(3), 292–306.

Steblay, N. K., Dysart, J., Fulero, S. and Lindsay, R. C. (2001) Eyewitness accuracy rates in sequential and simultaneous lineup presentations: A meta-analytic comparison. *Law and Human Behavior*, 25, 459–73.

Steblay, N. M. (1997) Social influence in eyewitness recall: A meta-analytic review of lineup instruction effects. *Law and Human Behavior*, 21, 293–7.

Steiker, C. S. and Steiker, J. M. (2020) The rise, fall, and afterlife of the death penalty in the United States. *Annual Review of Criminology*, 3, 299–315.

Steinberg, L. (2017) Adolescent brain science and juvenile justice policymaking. *Psychology, Public Policy, and Law*, 23(4), 410–20.

Stephens, L. and Sieckelinck, S. (2019) Radicalization and religion. *Religion and European Society: A Primer*, 159–70.

Stern, E., van der Heijden, I. and Dunkle, K. (2019) How people with disabilities experience programs to prevent intimate partner violence across four countries. *Evaluation and Program Planning*, 79, 101770. https://doi.org/10.1016/j.evalprogplan.2019.101770.

Stern, H. S., Cuellar, M. and Kaye, D. (2019) Reliability and validity of forensic science evidence. *Significance*, 16(2), 21–4.

Sternberg, K. J., Lamb, M. E. and Esplin, P. W. (2002) Using a structured interview to improve the quality of investigative interviews. In M. L. Eisen, J. A. Quas and G. S. Goodman (eds) *Memory and Suggestibility in the Forensic Interview* (pp. 409–27). Lawrence Erlbaum.

Sternberg, K. J., Lamb, M. E., Orbach, Y., Esplin, P. W. and Mitchell, S. (2001) Use of a structured investigative protocol enhances young children's responses to free-recall prompts in the course of forensic interviews. *Journal of Applied Psychology*, 86(5), 997–1005.

Stevenson, M. C., Lytle, B. L., Baumholser, B. J. and McCracken, E. W. (2017) Racially diverse juries promote self-monitoring efforts during jury deliberation. *Translational Issues in Psychological Science*, 3(2), 187–201.

Steyerl, H. (2016) A sea of data: Apophenia and pattern (mis-) recognition. *E-flux Journal*, 72, www.e-flux.com/journal/72/60480/a-sea-of-data-apophenia-and-pattern-mis-recognition/.

Stokoe, E. (2009) 'I've got a girlfriend': Police officers doing 'self-disclosure' in their interrogations of suspects. *Narrative Inquiry*, 19, 154–82.

Stolzenberg, S. N., McWilliams, K. and Lyon, T. D. (2017) Ask versus tell: Potential confusion when child witnesses are questioned about conversations. *Journal of Experimental Psychology – Applied*, 23, 447–59.

Stoughton, S. W., Noble, J. J. and Alpert, G. P. (2020) *Evaluating Police Uses of Force*. New York University Press.

Stoyanchev, S., Liu, A. and Hirschberg, J. (2012) Clarification questions with feedback. In *Interdisciplinary Workshop on Feedback Behaviors in Dialog*.

Strange, D., Sutherland, R. and Garry, M. (2006) Event plausibility does not affect children's false memories. *Memory*, 14(8), 937–51.

Strentz, T. (2017) The American Psychiatric Association (APA). In T. Strentz, *Psychological Aspects of Crisis Negotiation* (3rd edn, pp. 31–47). CRC Press.

Strier, F. (1999) Whither trial consulting? Issues and projections. *Law of Human Behavior*, 23(1), 93–115.

Stroessner, S. J. and Plaks, J. E. (2001) Illusory correlation and stereotype formation: Tracing the arc of research over a quarter century. In G. B. Moskowitz (ed.) *Cognitive Social Psychology: The Princeton Symposium on the Legacy and Future of Social Cognition* (pp. 247–59). Erlbaum.

Strömwall, L. A. and Granhag, P. A. (2003) How to detect deception? Arresting the beliefs of police officers, prosecutors and judges. *Psychology, Crime and Law*, 9(1), 19–36.

Strömwall, L. A., Alfredsson, H. and Landström, S. (2013) Rape victim and perpetrator blame and the just world hypothesis: The influence of victim gender and age. *Journal of Sexual Aggression*, 19(2), 207–17.

Strömwall, L. A., Granhag, P. A. and Hartwig, M. (2004) Practitioners' beliefs about deception. In L. A. Strömwall and P. A. Granhag (eds) *The Detection of Deception in Forensic Contexts*. Cambridge University Press.

Strömwall, L. A., Hartwig, M. and Granhag, P. A. (2006) To act truthfully: Nonverbal behavior and strategies during a police interrogation. *Psychology, Crime and Law*, 12, 207–19.

Stronge, A. M. (2009) Absolute truth of dues ex machine? The legal and philosophical ramifications of guilt assessment technology. *Journal of High Technology Law*, 10, 113–15.

Stuart, H. (2017) Mental illness stigma expressed by police to police. *Israel Journal of Psychiatry Related Science*, 54(1), 18–23.

Sturcke, J. (2009) Barry George cleared of Jill Dando murder after retrial. *The Guardian*, 9 August. Available at www.theguardian.com/uk/2008/aug/01/jilldando.ukcrime1.

Sturup, J. (2018) Comparing serial homicides to single homicides: A study of prevalence, offender, and offence characteristics in Sweden. *Journal of Investigative Psychology and Offender Profiling*, 15(2), 75–89.

Stylianou, A. M. (2018) Economic abuse experiences and depressive symptoms among victims of intimate partner violence. *Journal of Family Violence*, 33(6), 381–92.

Stylianou, A. M., Postmus, J. L. and McMahon, S. (2013) Measuring abusive behaviours: Is economic abuse a unique form of abuse? *Journal of Interpersonal Violence*, 28(16), 3186–204.

Sukumar, D., Wade, K. A. and Hodgson, J. (2018) Truth-tellers stand the test of time and contradict evidence less than liars, even months after a crime. *Law and Human Behavior*, 42(2), 145–55.

Sullivan, K. A., Lange, R. T. and Dawes, S. (2005) Methods of detecting malingering and estimated symptom exaggeration base rates in Australia. *Journal of Forensic Neuropsychology*, 4(4), 49–70.

Sullivan, T. P. (2005) Electronic recording of custodial interrogations: Everybody wins. *The Journal of Criminal Law and Criminology*, 95(3), 1127–44.

Sundt, J., Schwaeble, K. and Merritt, C. (2017) Good governance, political experiences, and public support for mandatory sentencing: Evidence from a progressive US state. *Punishment & Society*, 21(2), 141–61.

Sunstein, C. R. (2009) *Going to Extremes: How Like Minds Unite and Divide*. Oxford University Press.

Suonpää, K. and Savolainen, J. (2019) When a woman kills her man: Gender and victim precipitation in homicide. *Journal of Interpersonal Violence*, 34(11), 2398–413.

Supreme Court of Queensland (2016) *Equal Treatment Benchbook* (2nd edn). Brisbane, Supreme Court of Queensland Library.

Susser, M. (1986) The logic of Sir Karl Popper and the practice of epidemiology. *American Journal of Epidemiology*, 24(5), 869–74.

Sutherland, S. (2012) How chronic pain affects memory and mood. *Scientific American Magazine*, 23, 4–8.

Sutton, C. (2019) Evie Amati axe victim Ben Rimmer breaks silence: 'She nearly cut my head in half'. Nzherald.co.nz, 26 January. Available at www.nzherald.co.nz/world/news/article.cfm?c_id=2&objectid=12196662.

Sykes, R. E. and Brent, E. E. (1980) The regulation of interaction by police: A systems view of taking charge. *Criminology*, 18(2), 182–97.

Synnott, J., Dietzel, D. and Ioannou, M. (2015) A review of the polygraph: History, methodology and current status. *Crime Psychology Review*, 1(1), 59–83.

Szasz, T. S. (1986) What counts as disease? *Canadian Medical Association Journal*, 135(8), 859–60.

Szasz, T. S. (1997) *Insanity: The Idea and its Consequences*. Syracuse University Press.

Taddonio, P. (2015) How the CIA helped make *Zero Dark Thirty* – and shape the torture debate. *PRI's The World*, 19 May. Available at www.pri.org/stories/2015-05-19/how-cia-helped-make-zero-dark-thirty-and-legitimize-torture.

Tajfel, H. and Turner, J. C. (1979) An integrative theory of inter-group conflict. In W. G. Austin and S. Worchel (eds) *The Social Psychology of Inter-Group Relations* (pp. 33–47). Brooks/Cole.

Taleb, N. N. (2010) *The Black Swan: The Impact of the Highly Improbable* (2nd edn). Penguin.

Talwar, V., Gordon, H. M. and Kang, L. (2007) Lying in the elementary school years: Verbal deception and its relation to second-order belief understanding. *Developmental Psychology*, 43(3), 804–10.

Tandon, R., Gaebel, W., Barch, D. M., Bustillo, J., Gur, R. E. et al. (2013) Definition and description of schizophrenia in the DSM-5. *Schizophrenia Research*, 150(1), 3–10.

Tang, A. (2007) Afghan girls traded for debts, blood feuds. *USA Today*, 9 July.

Tang, T. L. and Hammontree, M. L. (1992) The effects of hardiness, police stress, and life stress on police officers' illness and absenteeism. *Public Personnel Management*, 21(4), 493–510.

Tavris, C. and Aronson, E. (2007) *Mistakes Were Made (but not by me): Why we Justify Foolish Beliefs, Bad Decisions, and Hurtful Acts*. Houghton Mifflin Harcourt.

Taxman, F. (2014) Second generation of RNR: The importance of systemic responsivity in expanding core principles of responsivity. *Federal Probation*, 78(2), 32–40.

Taylor, J. (2010) DNA retesting confirms murderer's guilt. ABC News, 29 July. Available at www.abc.net.au/news/2010-07-29/dna-retesting-confirms-murderers-guilt/925028.

Taylor, S. C. (2018) 'How to win my ex back?' A qualitative exploration of online forums of persistent unwanted pursuers of former romantic partners. Doctoral dissertation, Northcentral University.

Tcherni-Buzzeo, M. (2019) The 'great American crime decline': Possible explanations. In M. V. Krohn et al., *Handbook on Crime and Deviance* (2nd edn). Springer.

Teachman, G. and Gibson, B. E. (2018) Integrating visual methods with dialogical interviews in research with youth who use augmentative and alternative communication. *International Journal of Qualitative Methods*, 17(1), 1–12.

Technical Working Group on Eyewitness Evidence (2003) *Eyewitness Evidence: A Guide for Law Enforcement*. U.S. Department of Justice/National Institute of Justice, available at www.ncjrs.gov/pdffiles1/nij/178240.pdf.

Teigen, K. H. and Keren, G. (2020) Are random events perceived as rare? On the relationship between perceived randomness and outcome probability. *Memory & Cognition*, 1–15.

Temple-Raston, D. (2014) Report reveals deeply misguided interrogation tactics, Feinstein says. *NPR News*, 10 December. Available at www.wmot.org/post/report-reveals-deeply-misguided-interrogation-tactics-feinstein-says#stream/0.

Teoh, Y. S. and Lamb, M. (2001) Interviewer demeanor in forensic interviews of children. *Psychology, Crime and Law*, 19(2), 145–59.

Ternes, M. and Yuille, J. C. (2008) Eyewitness memory and eyewitness identification performance in adults with intellectual disabilities. *Journal of Applied Research in Intellectual Disabilities*, 21(6), 519–31.

Terrovitis, M., Mamoulis, N. and Kalnis, P. (2011) Local and global recoding methods for anonymizing set-valued data. *The VLDB Journal: The International Journal on Very Large Data Bases*, 20(1), 83–106.

Testa, M. and West, S. G. (2010) Civil commitment in the United States. *Psychiatry*, 7(10), 30–40.

Themeli, O. and Panagiotaki, M. (2014) Forensic interviews with children victims of sexual abuse: The role of the counselling psychologist. *European Journal of Counseling Psychology*, 3(1), 1–19.

Thomas, S. D., Purcell, R., Pathe, M. and Mullen, P. E. (2008) Harm associated with stalking victimization. *Australian & New Zealand Journal of Psychiatry*, 42(9), 800–6.

Thompson, A. G., Swain, D. P., Branch, J. D., Spina, R. J. and Grieco, C. R. (2015) Autonomic response to tactical pistol performance measured by heart rate variability. *The Journal of Strength & Conditioning Research*, 29(4), 926–33.

Thompson, D. A. and Adams, S. L. (1996) The full moon and ED patient volumes: Unearthing a myth. *American Journal of Emergency Medicine*, 14(2), 161–4.

Thompson, J. (2016) Crisis negotiation: How to talk to someone you're worried about. Available at https://afsp.org/crisis-negotiation-talk-someone-youre-worried-about.

Thompson, M. P. and Kingree, J. B. (2006) The roles of victim and perpetrator alcohol use in intimate partner violence outcomes. *Journal of Interpersonal Violence*, 21(2), 163–77.

Thompson-Cannino, J., Cotton, R. and Torneo, E. (2009) *Picking Cotton: Our Memoir of Injustice and Redemption*. St. Martin's.

Thorley, C. and Dewhurst, S. A. (2007) Collaborative false recall in the DRM procedure: Effects of group size and group pressure. *European Journal of Cognitive Psychology*, 19(6), 867–81.

Thorley, C., Dewhurst, S. A., Abel, J. W. and Knott, L. M. (2016) Eyewitness memory: The impact of a

negative mood during encoding and/or retrieval upon recall of a non-emotive event. *Memory*, 24, 838–52.

Thorpe, D. E. (2018) 'Nonsense rides piggyback on sensible things': The past, present, and future of graphology. In H. C. Tweed and D. G. Scott (eds) *Medical Paratexts from Medieval to Modern* (pp. 139–55). Palgrave Macmillan.

Tithecott, R. (1997) *Of Men and Monsters: Jeffrey Dahmer and the Construction of the Serial Killer*. University of Wisconsin Press.

Tjaden, P. G. and Thoennes, N. (2000) *Extent, Nature, and Consequences of Intimate Partner Violence*. National Institute of Justice.

Todd, C., Bryce, J. and Franqueira, V. N. (2020) Technology, cyberstalking and domestic homicide: Informing prevention and response strategies. *Policing and Society*, 1–18.

Tolisano, P., Sondik, T. M. and Dike, C. C. (2017) A positive behavioral approach for aggression in forensic settings. *Journal of the American Academy of Psychiatry and the Law*, 45(1), 31–9.

Toliver, R. F. (1997) *The Interrogator: The Story of Hanns Joachim Scharff, Master Interrogator of the Luftwaffe*. Schiffer Publishing.

Tomlinson, K. D. (2016) An examination of deterrence theory: Where do we stand? *Federal Probation*, 80(3), 33–8.

Tonellotto, M. (2020) Crime and victimization in cyberspace: A socio-criminological approach to cybercrime. In A. Balloni and R. Sette (eds) *Handbook of Research on Trends and Issues in Crime Prevention, Rehabilitation, and Victim Support* (pp. 248–64). IGI Global.

Tonkin, M. and Woodhams, J. (2017) The feasibility of using crime scene behaviour to detect versatile serial offenders: An empirical test of behavioural consistency, distinctiveness, and discrimination accuracy. *Legal and Criminological Psychology*, 22(1), 99–115.

Tonry, M. (2018) The President's commission and sentencing, then and now. *Criminology and Public Policy*, 17(2), 341–54.

Torres, A. N., Boccaccini, M. T. and Miller, H. A. (2006) Perceptions of the validity and utility of criminal profiling among forensic psychologists and psychiatrists. *Professional Psychology: Research and Practice*, 37(1), 51–8.

Tulving, E. (1982) Synergistic ecphory in recall and recognition. *Canadian Journal of Psychology*, 36(2), 130–47.

Tulving, E. (1983) *Elements of Episodic Memory*. Oxford University Press.

Tulving, E. (1984) Précis of elements of episodic memory. *Behavioral and Brain Sciences*, 7(2), 223–38.

Turgoose, D. and Maddox, L. (2017) Predictors of compassion fatigue in mental health professionals: A narrative review. *Traumatology*, 23(2), 172–85.

Turner, R. (1968) The origins of the medieval English jury: Frankish, English, or Scandinavian? *Journal of British Studies*, 7(2), 1–10.

Turvey, B. E. (1999) *Criminal Profiling: An Introduction to Behavioral Evidence Analysis*. Academic Press.

Turvey, B. E. (2012) *Criminal Profiling: An Introduction to Behavioral Analysis Evidence* (4th edn). Academic Press.

Turvey, B. E. (2013) Victimology: A brief history with an introduction to forensic victimology. In B. E. Turvey, *Forensic Victimology: Examining Violent Crime Victims in Investigative and Legal Contexts* (pp. 1–30). Academic Press.

Turvey, B. E. and Petherick, W. (2009) Forensic victimology. In B. E. Turvey (ed.) *Criminal Profiling: An Introduction to Behavioral Evidence Analysis* (pp. 163–86). Academic Press.

Tversky, B. (1973) Encoding processes in recognition and recall. *Cognitive Psychology*, 5(3), 275–87.

UNODC (UN Office on Drugs and Crime (2015) *The United Nations Standard Minimum Rules for the Treatment of Offenders (the Nelson Mandela Rules)*. United Nations. Available at www.unodc.org/documents/justice-and-prison-reform/GA-RESOLUTION/E_ebook.pdf.

Valerio, C. and Beck, C. J. (2017) Testing in child custody evaluations: An overview of issues and uses. *Journal of Child Custody*, 14(4), 260–80.

Vallano, J. P. and McQuiston, D. E. (2018) An exploration of psychological and physical injury schemas in civil cases. *Applied Cognitive Psychology*, 32(2), 241–52.

Vallano, J. P. and Winter, R. (2013) A look at expert testimony on false confessions. *Judicial Notebook: American Psychological Association Monitor*, 44(3), 25.

Van Abbema, D. and Bauer, P. (2005) Autobiographical memory in middle childhood: Recollections of the recent and distant past. *Memory*, 13(8), 829–45.

VanBenchoten, S., Bentley, J., Gregoire, N. B. and Lowencamp, C. T. (2016) The real-world application of the risk principle: Is it possible in the field of probation? *Federal Probation Journal*, 80(2), 3–9.

Van Boekel, M., Varma, K. and Varma, S. (2017) A retrieval-based approach to eliminating hindsight bias. *Memory*, 25(3), 377–90.

VanDercar, A. H. and Resnick, M. D. (2018) The insanity defense: Historical precedent and modern application. *Psychiatric Annals*, 48(2), 95–101.

Van Dijk, J., Tseloni, A. and Farrell, G. (eds) (2012) *The International Crime Drop: New Directions in Research*. Springer.

Van Hasselt, V. B., Baker, M. T., Romano, S. J., Schlessinger, K. M., Zucker, M. et al. (2006) Crisis (hostage) negotiation training: A preliminary evaluation of program efficacy. *Criminal Justice and Behavior*, 33(1), 56–69.

Van Kessel, C., den Heyer, K. and Schimel, J. (2020) Terror management theory and the educational situation. *Journal of Curriculum Studies*, 52(3), 428–42.

Van Nevel, J. and Bayless, C. (2016) The use of linkage analysis in the Jacob Wetterling cold case. *Journal of Cold Case Review*, 2(2), 5–10.

Vatnar, S. K., Friestad, C. and Bjørkly, S. (2019) The influence of substance use on intimate partner homicide: Evidence from a Norwegian national 22-year cohort. *International Journal of Forensic Mental Health*, 1–12.

Vecchi, G. M. (2009) Conflict and crisis communication: The behavioral influence stairway model and suicide intervention. *Annals of the American Psychotherapy Association*, 12(2), 32–40.

Vecchi, G. M., van Hasselt, V. B. and Romano, S. J. (2005) Crisis (hostage) negotiation: Current strategies and issues in high-risk conflict resolution. *Aggression and Violent Behavior*, 10(5), 533–51.

Vecchi, G. M., Wong, G. K., Wong, P. W. and Markey, M. A. (2019) Negotiating in the skies of Hong Kong: The efficacy of the Behavioral Influence Stairway Model (BISM) in suicidal crisis situations. *Aggression and Violent Behavior*, 48. DOI: 10.1016/j.avb.2019.08.002.

Velsor, S. and Rogers, R. (2018) Differentiating factitious psychological presentations from malingering: Implications for forensic practice. *Behavioral Science and Law*, 37, 1–15.

Ventresca, M. J. and Mohr, J. W. (2017) Archival research methods. In J. Baum (ed.) *The Blackwell Companion to Organizations* (pp. 805–28). Wiley-Blackwell.

Vera, L. M., Boccaccini, M. T., Laxton, K., Bryson, C., Pennington, C., Ridge, B. and Murrie, D. C. (2019) How does evaluator empathy impact a forensic interview? *Law and Human Behaviour*, 43(1), 56–68.

Verigin, B. L., Meijer, E. H., Bogaard, G. and Vrij, A. (2019) Lie prevalence, lie characteristics and strategies of self-reported good liars. *PLoS One*, 14(12), e0225566. doi: 10.1371/journal.pone.0225566.

Vickers, J. N. and Lewinski, W. (2012) Performing under pressure: Gaze control, decision making and shooting performance of elite and rookie police officers. *Human Movement Science*, 31, 101–17.

Viglione, J. (2018) The risk-need-responsivity model: How do probation officers implement the principles of effective intervention? *Criminal Justice and Behavior*, 46(5), 655–73.

Vignolo, L. A. (1964) Evolution of aphasia and language rehabilitation: A retrospective exploratory study. *Cortex*, 1(3), 344–67.

Vila, B. J. and Morrison, G. B. (1994) Biological limits to police combat handgun shooting accuracy. *American Journal of Police*, 13(1), 1–30.

Vincent, C., Gagnon, D. H., Dumont, F., Auger, E., Lavoie, V. et al. (2019) Service dog schools for PTSD as a tertiary prevention modality: Assessment based on assistance dogs international-criteria and theoretical domains framework. *Neurophysiology and Rehabilitation*, 2(1), 29–41.

Viner, J. (1949) Benthem and J. S. Mill: The utilitarian background. *American Economic Review*, 39(2), 360–82.

Vinokur, D. and Levine, S. Z. (2019) Non-suicidal self-harm in prison: A national population-based study. *Psychiatry Research*, 272, 216–21.

Violanti, J. M., Owens, S. L., McCanlies, E., Fekedulegn, D. and Andrew, M. E. (2019) Law enforcement suicide: A review. *Policing: An International Journal*, 42(2), 141–64.

Violanti, J. M., Charles, L. E., McCanlies, E., Hartley, T. A., Baughman, P. et al. (2017) Police stressors and health: A state-of-the-art review. *Policing: An International Journal of Police Strategies & Management*, 40(4), 642–56.

Violanti, J. M., Fekedulegn, D., Hartley, T. A., Charles, L. E., Andrew, M. E. et al. (2016) Highly rated and most frequent stressors among police officers: gender differences. *American Journal of Criminal Justice*, 41(4), 645–62.

Vitacco, M. J., Balduzzi, E., Rideout, K., Banfe, S. and Britton, J. (2018) Reconsidering risk assessment with insanity acquittees. *Law and Human Behavior*, 42(5), 403–12.

Vitacco, M. J., Gottfried, E. D. and Batastini, A. B. (2018) Using technology to improve the objectivity of criminal responsibility evaluations. *Journal of American Academy of Psychiatry and Law*, 46(1), 71–7.

Vitacco, M. J., Rogers, R., Babel, J. and Munizza, J. (2007) An evaluation of malingering screen with competency to stand trial patients: A known-groups comparison. *Law and Human Behavior*, 31, 249–60.

Vitopoulos, N. A., Peterson-Badali, M., Brown, S. and Skilling, T. A. (2019) The relationship between trauma, recidivism risk, and reoffending in male and female juvenile offenders. *Journal of Child Adolescent Trauma*, 12(3), 351–64.

Vitoria-Estruch, S., Romero-Martínez, A., Lila, M. and Moya-Albiol, L. (2018) Differential cognitive profiles of intimate partner violence perpetrators based on alcohol consumption. *Alcohol*, 70, 61–71.

Vollum, S., Longmire, D. R. and Buffington-Vollum, J. (2004) Confidence in the death penalty and support for its use: Exploring the value-expressive dimension of death penalty attitudes. *Justice Quarterly*, 21(3), 521–46.

Von Der Lühe, T., Manera, V., Barisic, I., Becchio, C., Vogeley, K. and Schilbach, L. (2016) Interpersonal predictive coding, not action perception, is impaired in autism. *Philosophical Transactions of the Royal Society B: Biological Sciences*, 371(1693), 20150373. doi: 10.1098/rstb.2015.0373.

Voogt, A., Klettke, B. and Crossman, A. (2016) Measurement of victim credibility in child sexual assault cases: A systematic review. *Trauma, Violence and Abuse*, 20(1), 51–66.

Vossekuil, B., Fein, R. A., Reddy, M., Borum, R. and Modzeleski, W. (2002) *The Final Report and Findings of the Safe School Initiative: Implications for the Prevention of School Attacks in the United States*. US Secret Service.

Vrij, A. (2000) *Detecting Lies and Deceit: The Psychology of Lying and its Implications for Professional Practice*. John Wiley & Sons.

Vrij, A. (2004) Why professionals fail to catch liars and how they can improve. *Legal and Criminological Psychology*, 9, 159–81.

Vrij, A. (2019) Deception and truth detection when analyzing nonverbal and verbal cues. *Applied Cognitive Psychology*, 33(2), 160–7.

Vrij, A. and Granhag, P. A. (2007) Interviewing to detect deception. In S. A. Christianson (ed.) *Offenders' Memories of Violent Crimes* (pp. 279–304). John Wiley & Sons.

Vrij, A. and Semin, G. R. (1996) Lie experts' beliefs about nonverbal indicators of deception. *Journal of Nonverbal Behavior*, 20(1), 65–80.

Vrij, A. and Turgeon, J. (2018) Evaluating credibility of witnesses: Are we instructing jurors on invalid factors? *Journal of Tort Law*, 11(2), 231–44.

Vrij, A., Fisher, R. P. and Blank, H. (2017) A cognitive approach to lie detection: A meta-analysis. *Legal and Criminological Psychology*, 22, 1–21.

Vrij, A., Granhag, P. A. and Mann, S. (2010) Good liars. *Journal of Psychiatry & Law*, 38(1/2), 77–98.

Vrij, A., Semin, G. R. and Bull, R. (1996) Insight into behavior displayed during deception. *Human Communication Research*, 22(4), 544–62.

Vrij, A., Fisher, R., Mann, S. and Leal, S. (2006) Detecting deception by manipulating cognitive load. *Trends in Cognitive Sciences*, 10, 141–2.

Vrij, A., Meissner, C. A., Fisher, R. P., Kassin, S. M., Morgan, C.A. and Kleinman, S. M. (2017)

Psychological perspectives on interrogation. *Perspectives on Psychological Science*, 12(6), 927–55.

Wachi, T., Watanabe, K., Yokota, K., Otsuka, Y. and Lamb, (2015) Japanese interrogation techniques from prisoners' perspectives. *Criminal Justice and Behavior*, 43(5), 617–34.

Walczyk, J. J., Sewell, N. and DiBenedetto, M. B. (2018) A review of approaches to detecting malingering in forensic contexts and promising cognitive load-inducing lie detection techniques. *Frontiers in Psychiatry*, 9, 700. DOI: 10.3389/fpsyt.2018.00700.

Walgrave, L., Ward, T. and Zinsstag, E. (2019) When restorative justice meets the Good Lives Model: Contributing to a criminology of trust. *European Journal of Criminology*, 3(2), 4–28.

Walker, L. E., Pann, J. M., Shapiro, D. L. and van Hasselt, V. B. (2016) A review of best practices for the treatment of persons with mental illness in jail. In L. E. Walker et al. (eds) *Best Practices for the Mentally Ill in the Criminal Justice System* (pp. 57–69). Springer.

Walker, N. (1985) The insanity defense before 1800. *Annals of the American Academy of Political and Social Science*, 477(1), 25–30.

Walker, N. (1991) *Why Punish?* Oxford University Press.

Walmsley, R. (2018) *World Prison Population List* (12th edn). Institute for Criminal Policy Research.

Walsh, D. W. and Milne, R. (2008) Keeping the PEACE? A study of investigative interviewing practices in the public sector. *Legal and Criminological Psychology*, 13(1), 39–57.

Walters, G. D. (2016) Decision to commit crime: Rational or nonrational. *Actual Problems of Economy & Law*, 10(3), 252–70.

Wang, Q., Peterson, C., Khuu, K., Reid, C. P., Maxwell, K. L. and Vincent, J. M. (2019) Looking at the past through a telescope: Adults postdated their earliest childhood memories. *Memory*, 27(1), 19–27.

Ward, K., Longaker, A. J., Williams, J., Naylor, A., Rose, C. A. and Simpson, C. G. (2013) Incarceration within American and Nordic prisons: Comparison of national and international policies. *International Journal of Research and Practice on Student Engagement*, 1(1), 36–47.

Ward, T. and Maruna, S. (2007) *Rehabilitation: Beyond the Risk Assessment Paradigm*. Routledge.

Warf, B. and Waddell, C. (2002) Heinous spaces, perfidious places: The sinister landscapes of serial killers. *Social & Cultural Geography*, 3(3), 323–45.

Waterhouse, G. F., Ridley, A. M., Bull, R., La Rooy, D. and Wilcock, R. (2016) Dynamics of repeated interviews with children. *Applied Cognitive Psychology*, 30(5), 713–21.

Waters, J. A. and Ussery, W. (2007) Police stress: History, contributing factors, symptoms, and interventions. *Policing: An International Journal of Police Strategies & Management*, 30(2), 169–88.

Watkins, L. E., Maldonado, R. C. and DiLillo, D. (2018) The Cyber Aggression in Relationships Scale: A new multidimensional measure of technology-based intimate partner aggression. *Assessment*, 25(5), 608–26.

Way, B. B., Miraglia, R., Sawyer, D. A., Beer, R. and Eddy, J. (2005) Factors related to suicide in New York state prisons. *International Journal of Law and Psychiatry*, 28(3), 207–21.

Webster, D. M. and Kruglanski, A. W. (1994) Individual differences in need for cognitive closure. *Journal of Personality and Social Psychology*, 67, 1049–62.

Webster, R. J. and Saucier, D. J. (2015) Demons are everywhere: The effects of belief in pure evil, demonization, and retribution on punishing criminal perpetrators. *Personality and Individual Differences*, 74, 72–7.

Weinberg, H. I., Wadsworth, J. and Baron, R. S. (1983) Demand and the impact of leading questions on eyewitness testimony. *Memory & Cognition*, 11(1), 101–4.

Weiner, I. B. and Hess, A. K. (eds) (2006) *The Handbook of Forensic Psychology*. John Wiley & Sons.

Weiser, B. (2016) Trial by jury, a hallowed American right, is vanishing. *The New York Times*, 8 August, A1. Available at www.nytimes.com/2016/08/08/nyregion/jury-trials-vanish-and-justice-is-served-behindclosed-doors.html.

Weiss, D. B., Santos, M. R., Testa, A. and Kumar, S. (2016) The 1990s homicide decline: A western world or international phenomenon? A research note. *Homicide Studies*, 20(4), 321–334.

Weiss, K. J. and van Dell, L. (2017) Liability for diagnosing malingering. *Journal American Academy of Psychiatry*, 45, 339–47.

Weiss, K. J., Friedman, S. H., Hatters, M. D. and Shand, J. P. (2019) Insanity: A legal diagnosis. *The Journal of Nervous and Mental Disease*, 207(9), 749–54.

Weissberger, G. H., Mosqueda, L., Nguyen, A. L., Samek, A., Boyle, P. A. et al. (2019) Physical and mental health correlates of perceived financial exploitation in older adults: Preliminary findings from the Finance, Cognition, and Health in Elders Study (FINCHES), *Aging & Mental Health*, 24(5), 740–6.

Weitzdörfer, J., Shiroshita, Y. and Padfield, N. (2018) Sentencing and punishment in Japan and England: A comparative discussion. In J. Liu and S. Miyazawa, *Crime and Justice in Contemporary Japan* (pp. 189–214). Springer.

Wells, G. L. (1978) Applied eyewitness-testimony research: System variables and estimator variables. *Journal of Personality and Social Psychology*, 36, 1546–57.

Wells, G. L. (1984) The psychology of lineup identifications 1. *Journal of Applied Social Psychology*, 14(2), 89–103.

Wells, G. L. and Bradfield, A. L. (1998) 'Good you identified the suspect': Feedback to eyewitnesses distort their reports of the witnessing experience. *Journal of Applied Psychology*, 66, 688–96.

Wells, G. L. and Luus, C. E. (1990) Police lineups as experiments: Social methodology as a framework for properly conducted lineups. *Personality and Social Psychology Bulletin*, 16(1), 106–17.

Wells, G. L. and Olson, E. (2003) Adult eyewitness testimony. *Annual Review of Psychology*, 54, 277–95.

Wells, G. L., Memon, A. and Penrod, S. D. (2006) Eyewitness evidence: Improving its probative value. *Psychological Science in the Public Interest*, 7(2), 45–75.

Wells, G. L., Steblay, N. K. and Dysart, J. E. (2015) Double-blind photo lineups using actual eyewitnesses: An experimental test of a sequential versus simultaneous lineup procedure. *Law and Human Behavior*, 39(1), 1–14.

Wells, G. L., Seelau, E., Rydell, S. and Luus, C. A. (1994) Recommendations for properly conducted lineup identification tasks. In D. F. Ross, J. D. Read and M. P. Toglia (eds) *Adult Eyewitness Testimony: Current Trends and Developments* (pp. 223–44). Cambridge University Press.

Wells, T. (2011) Baby P killer Jason Owen on the street: Brute mingles with shoppers. *The Sun*, 25 August. Available at www.thesun.co.uk/archives/news/739824/baby-p-killer-jason-owen-on-the-street/.

Wells, T. and Leo, R. A. (2008) *The Wrong Guys Murder, False Confessions, and the Norfolk Four*. New Press.

Welsh, A. and Lavoie, J. A. (2012) Risky ebusiness: An examination of risk-taking, online disclosiveness, and cyberstalking victimization. *Cyberpsychology: Journal of Psychosocial Research on Cyberspace*, 6(1), 1–12.

Wertheimer, M. (2012) *A Brief History of Psychology*. Psychology Press.

West, A. G. (2000) Clinical assessment of homicide offenders: The significance of crime scene in offense and offender analysis. *Homicide Studies*, 4, 219–33.

West, D. J. and Walk, A. (eds) (1977) *Daniel McNaughton: His Trial and the Aftermath*. Springer.

Westcott, H. L. (2006) Child witness testimony: What do we know and where are we going? *Child and Family Law Quarterly*, 18, 175–90.

Western District of Washington (2017) Criminal jury instructions: Unconscious bias. Available at wawd.

uscourts.gov/sites/wawd/files/CriminalJuryInstructions-ImplicitBias.pdf.

Westling, W. T. and Waye, V. (1998) Videotaping police interrogations: Lessons from Australia. *American Journal of Criminal Law*, 25, 493–500.

Wexler, D. B. (1973) Token and taboo: Behavior modification, token economies, and the law. *California Law Review*, 61(1), 81–109.

Wheeler, C., Fisher, A., Jamiel, A., Lynn, T. J. and Hill, W. T. (2018) Stigmatizing attitudes toward police officers seeking psychological services. *Journal of Police and Criminal Psychology*, 1–7.

Wheeler, R. and Gabbert, F. (2017) Using self-generated cues to facilitate recall: A narrative review. *Frontiers in Psychology*, 8(1830), 1–15.

Whitehead, J., Dawson, M. and Hotton, T. (2020) Same-sex intimate partner violence in Canada: Prevalence, characteristics, and types of incidents reported to police services. *Journal of Interpersonal Violence*, 26, 501–9.

Whitelock, A. (2009) Safeguarding in mental health: Towards a rights-based approach. *The Journal of Adult Protection*, 11(4), 30–42.

Whiting, J. B., Oka, M. and Fife, S. T. (2012) Appraisal distortions and intimate partner violence: Gender, power, and interaction. *Journal of Marital and Family Therapy*, 38(Suppl 1), 133–49.

Whittington, R., Hockenhull, J. C., McGuire, J., Leitner, M., Barr, W. et al. (2013) A systematic review of risk assessment strategies for populations at high risk of engaging in violent behavior: Update 2002–8. *Health Technology Assessment*, 17(50), 1–128.

WHO (World Health Organization) (2013) *Global and Regional Estimates of Violence against Women: Prevalence and Health Effects of Intimate Partner Violence and Non-Partner Sexual Violence*. WHO.

Wiener, R. L., Georges, L. C. and Cangas, J. (2014) Anticipated affect and sentencing decisions in capital murder. *Psychology, Public Policy, and Law*, 20(3), 263–80.

Wigmore, J. (1966) A treatise on the Anglo-American system of evidence. *Harvard Law Review*, 935, 954–9.

Wiley, T. R. and Bottoms, B. L. (2009) Effects of defendant sexual orientation on jurors' perceptions of child sexual assault. *Law and Human Behavior*, 33(1), 46–60.

Wilkinson, J. (2005) Evaluating evidence for the effectiveness of the reasoning and rehabilitation programme. *Howard Journal of Criminal Justice*, 44(1), 70–85.

Williams, D., Goldstein, G. and Minshew, N. (2006) The profile of memory function in children with autism. *Neuropsychology*, 20(1), 21–9.

Williams, V., Ciarrochi, J. and Deane, P. F. (2010) On being mindful, emotionally aware, and more resilient: Longitudinal pilot study of police recruits. *Australian Psychologist*, 45(4), 274–82.

Wilner, A. S. and Dubouloz, C. J. (2010) Homegrown terrorism and transformative learning: An interdisciplinary approach to understanding radicalization. *Global Change, Peace & Security*, 22(1), 33–51.

Wilpert, J., van Horn, J. and Boonmann, C. (2018) Comparing the central eight risk factors: Do they differ across age groups of sex offenders? *International Journal of Offender Therapy and Comparative Criminology*, 62(13), 4278–94.

Wilson, J., Hugenberg, K. and Bernstein, M. (2013) The cross-race effect and eyewitness identification: How to improve recognition and reduce decision errors in eyewitness situations. *Social Issues and Policy Review*, 7(1), 83–113.

Wilson, O., Lincon, R. and Kocsis, R. (1997) Validity, utility, and ethics of profiling for serial violent and sexual offenses. *Psychiatry, Psychology and Law*, 4, 1–11.

Wincup, E. (2019) Living 'good lives': Using mentoring to support desistance and recovery. *Addiction Research & Theory*, 27(1), 37–46.

Winerman, L. (2004) Forensic psychologists are working with law enforcement officials to integrate psychological science into criminal profiling. *Monitor on Psychology*, 35(7), 66–9.

WIN/Gallup International (2016) *People on War – 2016 Survey*. ICRC.

Winter, H. (2019) *The Economics of Crime: An Introduction to Rational Crime Analysis*. Routledge.

Winters, G. M. and Jeglic, E. L. (2016) I knew it all along: The sexual grooming behaviours of child molesters and the hindsight bias. *Journal of Child Sexual Abuse*, 25(1), 20–36.

Wise, R. A. and Safer, M. A. (2012) A method for analyzing the accuracy of eyewitness testimony in criminal cases. *Court Review: The Journal of the American Judges Association*, 48, 22–34.

Wise, R. A., Dauphinais, K. A. and Safer, M. A. (2007) A tripartite solution to eyewitness error. *Journal of Criminal Law and Criminology*, 97(3), 807–72.

Wixted, J. T. and Mickes, L. (2014) A signal-detection-based diagnostic-feature-detection model of eyewitness identification. *Psychological Review*, 121(2), 262–76.

Wixted, J. T., Mickes, L. and Fisher, R. P. (2018) Rethinking the reliability of eyewitness memory. *Perspectives on Psychological Science*, 13(3), 324–35.

Wixted, J., Mickes, L., Clark, S., Gronlund, S. and Roediger, H. (2015) Initial eyewitness confidence reliably predicts eyewitness identification accuracy. *American Psychologist*, 70, 515–26.

Wojcieszak, M., Winter, S. and Yu, X. (2020) Social norms and selectivity: Effects of norms of open-mindedness on content selection and affective polarization. *Mass Communication and Society*, https://doi.org/10.1080/15205436.2020.1714663.

Wolak, J., Finkelhor, D., Walsh, W. and Treitman, L. (2018) Sextortion of minors: Characteristics and dynamics. *Journal of Adolescent Health*, 62(1), 72–9.

Wolfman, M., Brown, D. and Jose, P. (2018) The use of visual aids in forensic interviews with children. *Journal of Applied Research in Memory and Cognition*, 7(4), 587–96.

Wondermagen, M. (2014) Depressed but not legally mentally impaired. *International Journal of Law and Psychiatry*, 37(2), 160–7.

Wood, J. M., Garth, D., Grounds, G., McKay, P. and Mulvahil, A. (2003) Pupil dilatation does affect some aspects of daytime driving performance. *British Journal of Ophthalmology*, 87(11), 1387–90.

Wood, M. E., Anderson, J. L. and Glassmire, D. M. (2017) The MacArthur Competence Assessment Tool—Criminal Adjudication: Factor structure, interrater reliability, and association with clinician opinion of competence in a forensic inpatient sample. *Psychological Assessment*, 29(6), 776–85.

Woodfox, A. (2019) *Solitary*. Grove Press.

Woodhams, J., Hollin, C. R. and Bull, R. (2007) The psychology of linking crimes: A review of the evidence. *Legal and Criminological Psychology*, 12(2), 233–49.

Woodhams, J., Tonkin, M., Burrell, A., Imre, H., Winter, J. M. et al. (2019) Linking serial sexual offences: Moving towards an ecologically valid test of the principles of crime linkage. *Legal and Criminological Psychology*, 24(1), 123–40.

Woodlock, D. (2017) The abuse of technology in domestic violence and stalking. *Violence against Women*, 23(5), 584–602.

Woods, B. and Pratt, R. (2005) Awareness in dementia: Ethical and legal issues in relation to people with dementia. *Aging & Mental Health*, 9(5), 423–9.

Woodworth, M. and Porter, S. (2002) In cold blood: Characteristics of criminal homicides as a function of psychopathy. *Journal of Abnormal Psychology*, 111(3), 436–45.

Woody, W. D. (2019) The history, present, and future of police deception during interrogation. In T. Docan-Morgan (ed.) *The Palgrave Handbook of Deceptive Communication*. Palgrave Macmillan.

Wrightsman, L. S. (2013) *Psychology and the Legal System* (8th edn). Cengage Learning.

Wu, C. C., Chu, C. L., Stewart, L., Chiang, C. H., Hou, Y. M. and Liu, J. H. (2020) The utility of the screening tool for autism in 2-year-olds in detecting autism in Taiwanese toddlers who are less than 24 months of age: A longitudinal study. *Journal of Autism and Developmental Disorders*, 1–10.

Wu, X. and Zhang, X. (2016) Automated inference on criminality using face images. *ArXiv, abs/1611.04135.*

Wuerch, M. A., Giesbrecht, C. J., Price, J. A., Knutson, T. and Wach, F. (2020) Examining the relationship between intimate partner violence and concern for animal care and safekeeping. *Journal of Interpersonal Violence*, 35(9/10), 1866–87.

Wyckoff, J. P., Buss, D. M. and Markman, A. B. (2019) Sex differences in victimization and consequences of cyber aggression: An evolutionary perspective. *Evolutionary Behavioural Sciences*, 13(3), 254.

Xue, G., Chen, C., Lu, Z. L. and Dong, Q. (2010) Brain imaging techniques and their applications in decision-making research. *Acta Psychologica Sinica*, 42(1), 120–37.

Yaffe, G. (2018) *The Age of Culpability*. Oxford University Press.

Yamamoto, S., Maeder, E. M. and Fenwick, K. L. (2017) Criminal responsibility in Canada: Mental disorder stigma education and the insanity defense. *International Journal of Forensic Mental Health*, 16(4), 313–35.

Yardi, S. and Boyd, D. (2010) Dynamic debates: An analysis of group polarization over time on Twitter. *Bulletin of Science, Technology & Society*, 30(5), 316–27.

Yarmey, A. D., Yarmey, M. J. and Yarmey, A. L. (1996) Accuracy of eyewitness identifications in showups and lineups. *Law and Human Behavior*, 20(4), 459–77.

Yarmey, D. A. (1984) Accuracy and credibility of the elderly witness. *Canadian Journal on Aging*, 3(2), 79–90.

Yee, J. W. (2019) Child custody decisions: Should the 'best interests of the child' standard be the primary determinant. *Wayne Law Review*, 65, 175–96.

Yokota, K., Watanabe, K., Wachi, T., Otsuka, Y., Hirama, K. and Fujita, G. (2017) Crime linkage of sex offences in Japan by multiple correspondence analysis. *Journal of Investigative Psychology and Offender Profiling*, 14(2), 109–19.

Young, A. (2019) Japanese atmospheres of criminal justice. *British Journal of Criminology*, 59(4), 765–79.

Young, G. (2014) *Malingering, Feigning, and Response Bias in Psychiatric/Psychological Injury: Implications for Practice and Court*. Springer.

Young, R. L. and Brewer, N. (2019) Brief report: Perspective taking deficits, autism spectrum disorder, and allaying police officers' suspicions about criminal involvement. *Journal of Autism and Developmental Disorders*, 50(6), 2234–9.

Young, T. J. (1992) Procedures and problems in conducting a psychological autopsy. *International Journal of Offender Therapy and Comparative Criminology*, 36(1), 43–52.

Youngs, D. (2017) *Applications of Geographic Offender Profiling*. Routledge.

Youstin, T. J. and Siddique, J. A. (2019) Psychological distress, formal help-seeking behaviour, and the role of victim services among violent crime victims. *Victims & Offenders*, 14(1), 52–74.

Yoxall, J., Bahr, M. and Barling, N. (2010) Australian psychologists' beliefs and practice in the detection of malingering. In R. E. Hicks (ed.) *Personality and Individual Differences: Current Directions* (pp. 315–26). Australian Academic Press.

Zacharski, M. (2018) Mens rea, the Achilles' heel of criminal law. *The European Legacy*, 23(1/2), 47–59.

Zadra, A., Desautels, A., Petit, D. and Montplaisir, J. (2013) Somnambulism: Clinical aspects and pathological hypotheses. *The Lancet*, 12, 285–94.

Zapf, P. A., Kukucka, J., Kassin, S. M. and Dror, I. E. (2018) Cognitive bias in forensic mental health assessment: Evaluator beliefs about its nature and scope. *Psychology, Public Policy, and Law*, 24(1), 1–10.

Ziemke, M. H. and Brodsky, S. L. (2015a) To flatter the jury: Ingratiation during closing arguments. *Psychiatry, Psychology and Law*, 22(5), 688–700.

Ziemke, M. H. and Brodsky, S. L. (2015b) Unloading the hired gun: Inoculation effects in expert witness testimony. *International Journal of Law and Psychiatry*, 42, 91–7.

Zimring, F. E. (2003) *The Contradictions of American Capital Punishment*. Oxford University Press.

INDEX

Page numbers in **bold** indicate tables and in *italic* indicate figures.

F

M

Q

R

S

V

W

Y

Z